The Yorkshire County Cricket Club Limited

Registered Number 28929R

YEARBOOK 2013

115th EDITION

Sponsors of

THE YORKSHIRE COUNTY CRICKET CLUB

Editor:

DAVID WARNER

Records and Statistics

Yorkshire First Eleven:

JOHN T POTTER

Yorkshire Second Eleven:

HOWARD CLAYTON

Production Editor:

JAMES M. GREENFIELD

Published by

THE YORKSHIRE COUNTY CRICKET CLUB LTD
HEADINGLEY CARNEGIE CRICKET GROUND
LEEDS LS6 3BU
Tel: 0871 971 1222 Fax: 0113 278 4099
Internet: http://www.yorkshireccc.com
e-mail: cricket@yorkshireccc.com

Solicitors: DLA PIPER UK LLP

Auditors: KPMG Audit plc

Medical Officer: Dr NIGEL MAYERS, MBChB, MRCGP
Burley Park Medical Centre, 273 Burley Road, Leeds LS4 2EL

The opinions expressed by contributors are not necessarily those of the Board.

TELEPHONE AND FAX NUMBERS

HEADINGLEY CRICKET GROUND	**Tel: 0871 971 1222** Fax: 0113 278 4099
NORTH MARINE ROAD, SCARBOROUGH	**Tel: 01723 365625** Fax: 01723 364287
BURNLEY ROAD, TODMORDEN	**Tel: 01706 813140**
SHIPTON ROAD, YORK	**Tel: 01904 623602**
BRADFORD & BINGLEY	**Tel: 01274 775441**
STAMFORD BRIDGE	**Tel: 01759 371545**

Produced by:

Great Northern Books
PO Box 213, Ilkley LS29 9WS
www.greatnorthernbooks.co.uk

ISBN: 978-0-9572951-8-6

CONTENTS

Officers for 2013

PATRONESS

THE DUCHESS OF KENT

PATRONS

PATRICIA,
COUNTESS OF HAREWOOD
The EARL OF MEXBOROUGH
DAVID LASCELLES, EARL OF HAREWOOD

HONORARY LIFE MEMBERS

Mr R APPLEYARD, MBE
Mr J G BINKS
Mr H D BIRD, OBE
Mr G BOYCOTT, OBE
Mr D BYAS
Sir LAWRENCE BYFORD, QPM, LLD, DL
Mr D B CLOSE, CBE
Mr J H HAMPSHIRE
Dr K HOWARD, OBE
Mr R ILLINGWORTH, CBE
Mr D S LEHMANN
Mr E I LESTER
Mr D E V PADGETT
Mr R K PLATT
Mr P J SHARPE
Mr M P VAUGHAN, OBE

PRESIDENT

Mr GEOFREY BOYCOTT OBE

VICE-PRESIDENTS

Mr P AKROYD
Mr B BOUTTELL,
Mr I M CHAPPELL
Mr G A COPE
Mr G D DRABBLE
Mr R L FEATHER
Mr C M FENTON, OBE, JP
Mr S FIELDEN
Mr D S HALL, CBE, TD
Mr R A HUTTON
Sir DAVID JONES
Mr K H MOSS MBE
Mr R A SMITH, TD, DL
Mr W B STOTT
Mr K TAYLOR
Mr P W TOWNEND
Mr A L VANN
Mr J D WELCH
Mr R D WILKINSON

THE BOARD

Mr C J GRAVES (Executive Chairman)
Mr R A SMITH TD, DL (Director)
Mr S DENISON (Director)
Mr M FARRINGTON (Leeds City Council)
MR G W DAVIES (Leeds Metropolitan University)

MEMBERS' COMMITTEE

Chairman: Mr S J MANN

ELECTED MEMBERS

Ms C EVERS
Mr R LEVIN
Mr S J MANN
Mr E STEPHENS

APPOINTED MEMBERS

Mr G A CLARK
Mr A KILBURN
Mr R W STOTT

MUSEUM DIRECTOR

Mr D S HALL CBE, TD

ARCHIVES COMMITTEE

Chairman: Mr J C D ALLAN

Mr J C D ALLAN
Mr H CLAYTON
Mr P E DYSON
Mr J M GREENFIELD
Mr M POPE
Mr B SANDERSON
Mr D O SMITH
Mr D WARNER
Mr R D WILKINSON

Changes announced after February 16 will be recorded in the 2014 edition of the Yorkshire County Cricket Club Yearbook

CRICKET ALWAYS MIRRORS THE TIMES WE LIVE IN

By Geoffrey Boycott OBE

What does Yorkshire cricket mean to each and every one of us who are passionate about the game and support the *White Rose* club?

All of us will have special memories about their introduction to the sport which they love the most. I grew up with my Uncle Algy, his friends and teammates always talking about how special Yorkshire cricket was. It really was everything to them.

It was just the same when I started playing league cricket as a boy, because my teammates talked of Yorkshire cricket as something very special. But what made it so special, and why did they all hold it in such high esteem? The players were revered and put on a pedestal. The county's performances were read and talked about, and opinions exchanged. Individual performances were discussed and dissected. Yorkshire was the only county where you had to be born in it to play for it.

That was "cool" — that was "special", and it is hardly surprising that their passion for the game rubbed off on me, too. I certainly felt this special thing from a very young age and when, age 13, I started playing for Ackworth Cricket Club they had a YCCC membership card which any member of the club could use to attend matches for free. It had an adult ticket and a ticket for anyone under 16 which brought entry to the members' pavilion. My best friend was George Hepworth, and in those early league days he was the first partner to run me out! I was able to forgive this heinous crime because twice he took me to watch Yorkshire. What a thrill and an adventure that was! We were to see our greatest batsman, Len Hutton, at Bradford and Sheffield. How I looked forward to it, but on both occasions it rained all day. I never saw the great man bat.

The young players coming up today perhaps don't have the same affinity to Yorkshire as we did, but times change and it is perfectly understandable. They want to play cricket, of course, but with so many overseas players coming into our team and with much greater movement of English-born players from county to county some of the "belonging" that we felt when we were all Yorkshire-born has gone. It had to be, and it is something which I accept, and so do the players and supporters.

If we didn't take on the occasional overseas player or from elsewhere in this country we simply could not compete. I am one of the last Yorkshire-born players from the 1960s when we won six Championship titles and two Gillette Cup Finals. We were able to compete and to win, but if you don't win there is huge criticism of the players and the Club. That is why we had to move forward. It was sad to have to change the policy, but it had to be done and there is no going back.

Yorkshire cricket is in my blood and always will be, but it has to be accepted that modern-day teams are ruled by the money. With agents behind them they will be interested in moving on if better contracts are offered elsewhere.

Cricket always mirrors the times we live in, and that is why they are doing it. Yorkshire playing with a full Yorkshire-born XI will never come back.

WIT AND CANDOUR: The President greets a question at the Sesquicentennial Soiree on January 8 with a straight bat and a dash of wit

I am extremely lucky to have been one of the last of an era who desperately wanted to play for Yorkshire above all else.

I am thrilled that Yorkshire achieved what I asked of them at the annual general meeting, and that was to get back into the First Division of the County Championship. This is still the competition which means most to the membership, and all of us are delighted that they are back in the top bracket as we celebrate the 150th anniversary of the Club's birth. The players worked hard for their success, and that is right because ambition is part and parcel of sport. Cricket is not a nine-to-five job; it is about scoring runs, taking wickets and winning matches. We all live and die by our performances, and if you play sport for a living you are always under pressure to succeed, both individually and collectively. If players cannot accept or handle that they need to find other employment.

Yorkshire cricket will always be more demanding than at any other county because of our tradition and past successes, and every player who turns out for the Club needs to embrace this truth. It is never possible to forecast entirely accurately what will happen in the world of sport, but I sincerely hope that Yorkshire will be a formidable force during 2013, and that what is to come in the future will be as big a source of pride as what our history has shown from the past.

Officials of the Yorkshire County Cricket Club

President

T R Barker 1863

M J Ellison 1864-97

Lord Hawke 1898-1938

Rt Hon Sir F S Jackson 1939-1947

T L Taylor 1948-1960

Sir W A Worsley Bart 1961-1973

Sir K Parkinson 1974-1981

N W D Yardley 1981-1983

The Viscount Mountgarret 1984-1989

Sir Leonard Hutton 1989-1990

Sir Lawrence Byford QPM, LLD, DL 1991-1999

R A Smith TD, LLB, DL 1999-2004

David Jones CBE 2004-6

Robert Appleyard 2006-8

Brian Close CBE 2008-10

Raymond Illingworth CBE 2010-12

Geoffrey Boycott OBE 2012-13

Treasurer

M J Ellison 1863-1893

M Ellison, jun 1894-1898

Chas Stokes 1899-1912

R T Heselton 1913-1931

A Wyndham Heselton 1932-1962

M G Crawford 1963-1979

J D Welch 1980-1984

P W Townend 1984-2002

Chairman

A H Connell, DL 1971-1979

M G Crawford 1980-1984

H R Kirk 1984-1985

B Walsh, QC 1986-1991

Sir Lawrence Byford CBE, QPM, LLD, DL 1991-1998

K H Moss MBE 1998-2002

GA Cope 2002

R A Smith TD, LLB, DL 2002-5

Colin J Graves 2005-

Captain

R Iddison 1863-1872

J Rowbotham 1873

L Greenwood 1874

J Rowbotham 1875

E Lockwood 1876-1877

T Emmett 1878-1882

Hon M B (Lord) Hawke 1883-1910

E J R H Radcliffe 1911

Sir A W White 1912-1918

D C F Burton 1919-1921

Geoff Wilson 1922-1924

A W Lupton 1925-1927

W A Worsley 1928-1929

A T Barber 1930

F E Greenwood 1931-1932

A B Sellers 1933-1947

N W D Yardley 1948-1955

W H H Sutcliffe 1956-1957

J R Burnet 1958-1959

J V Wilson 1960-1962

D B Close 1963-1970

G Boycott 1971-1978

J H Hampshire 1979-1980

C M Old 1981-1982

R Illingworth 1982-1983

Captain (Contd)

D L Bairstow 1984-1986

P Carrick 1987-1989

M D Moxon 1990-1995

D Byas 1996-2001

D S Lehmann 2002

A McGrath 2003

C White 2004-6

D Gough 2007-8

A McGrath 2009

A W Gale 2010-

Secretary

Geo Padley 1863

J B Wostinholm 1864-1902

F C (Sir Fredk.) Toone 1903-1930

J H Nash 1931-1971

J Lister 1972-1991

D M Ryder 1991-2002

Company Secretary

B Bouttell 2002-5

Charles Hartwell 2011-

Chief Executive

C D Hassell 1991-2002

Colin J Graves 2002-5

Stewart Regan 2006-10

Colin J Graves 2012-

COUNTY FIXTURES — 2013

LV COUNTY CHAMPIONSHIP — Division 1

(All four-day matches)

Date			*Opponents*	*Venue*
WED	**10-13**	**APRIL**	**SUSSEX**	**HEADINGLEY**
Wed	24-27	April	Durham	Riverside
MON	**29-2**	**APRIL/MAY**	**DERBYSHIRE**	**HEADINGLEY**
TUE	**7-10**	**MAY**	**SOMERSET**	**HEADINGLEY**
Wed	15-18	May	Warwickshire	Edgbaston
Tue	28-31	May	Somerset	Taunton
WED	**5-8**	**JUNE**	**NOTTINGHAMSHIRE**	**SCARBOROUGH**
Tue	11-14	June	Middlesex	Lord's
FRI	**21-24**	**JUNE**	**SURREY**	**HEADINGLEY**
Wed	17-20	July	Derbyshire	Chesterfield
FRI	**2-5**	**AUGUST**	**WARWICKSHIRE**	**HEADINGLEY**
Wed	21-24	August	Nottinghamshire	Trent Bridge
WED	**28-31**	**AUGUST**	**DURHAM**	**SCARBOROUGH**
Wed	11-14	September	Sussex	Hove
TUE	**17-20**	**SEPTEMBER**	**MIDDLESEX**	**HEADINGLEY**
Tue	24-27	September	Surrey	The Oval

YORKSHIRE BANK 40 LEAGUE

Sun	5	May	Glamorgan	Colwyn Bay
SAT	**11**	**MAY**	**SOMERSET**	**HEADINGLEY**
Sun	19	May	Unicorns	TBC
Mon	27	May	Middlesex	Radlett
SUN	**2**	**JUNE**	**GLOUCESTERSHIRE**	**HEADINGLEY**
SUN	**9**	**JUNE**	**LEICESTERSHIRE**	**SCARBOROUGH**
Sun	16	June	Gloucestershire	Bristol
THU	**20**	**JUNE**	**MIDDLESEX**	**HEADINGLEY**
Sun	11	August	Leicestershire	Leicester
TUE	**13**	August	**UNICORNS**	**HEADINGLEY**
Thu	15	August	Somerset	Bath
MON	**26**	**AUGUST**	**GLAMORGAN**	**HEADINGLEY**
Sat/Mon	7-9	September	Semi-Finals	TBC
Sat	21	September	Final	Lord's

FRIENDS PROVIDENT TWENTY20 CUP

FRI	**28**	**JUNE**	**DERBYSHIRE**	**HEADINGLEY**
SUN	**30**	**JUNE**	**DURHAM**	**SCARBOROUGH**
FRI	**5**	**JULY**	**LANCASHIRE**	**HEADINGLEY**
TUE	**9**	**JULY**	**LEICESTER**	**HEADINGLEY**
Fri	12	July	Durham	Riverside
Sun	14	July	Derbyshire	Chesterfield
SUN	**21**	**JULY**	**NOTTINGHAMSHIRE**	**HEADINGLEY**
Wed	24	July	Lancashire	Old Trafford
Fri	26	July	Nottinghamshire	Trent Bridge
Sun	28	July	Leicestershire	Leicester
Tue	6-8	August	Quarter-Finals	TBC
Sat	17	August	Semi-Finals and Final	Edgbaston

OTHER MATCHES

FRI	**5-7**	**APRIL**	**LEEDS/BRADFORD UCCE**	**HEADINGLEY**
WED	**26**	**JUNE**	**YCCC 150TH XI V MCC**	**HEADINGLEY**

INVESTEC TEST MATCHES

(All five-day matches)

ENGLAND V. NEW ZEALAND

Thu May 16 ....Lord's

FRI MAY 24 ....HEADINGLEY

ENGLAND v. AUSTRALIA

Wed July 10 ....Trent Bridge
Thu August 1 ....Old Trafford
Wed August 21 ....The Oval

Thu July 18 ....Lord's
Fri August 9 ....Emirates Durham ICG

NATWEST ONE-DAY INTERNATIONALS

Fri	31	May	England v. New Zealand ....Lord's
Sun	2	June	England v. New Zealand ....Ageas Bowl, Southampton
Wed	5	June	England v. New Zealand ....Trent Bridge (Day/Night)
FRI	**6**	**SEPTEMBER**	**ENGLAND V AUSTRALIA ....HEADINGLEY**
Sun	8	September	England v Australia ....Old Trafford
Wed	11	September	England v Australia ....Edgbaston (Day/Night)
Sat	14	September	England v Australia ....SWALEC Stadium, Cardiff
Mon	16	September	England v Australia ...Ageas Bowl, Southampton(Day/Night)

ICC CHAMPIONS TROPHY

6-17	June	Group Stages ....The Oval, Edgbaston and Cardiff
19-20	June	Semi-Finals ....The Oval and Cardiff
23	June	Final ....Edgbaston

NATWEST INTERNATIONAL TWENTY20

Tue	25	June	England v. New Zealand ....The Oval (Floodlit)
Thu	27	June	England v. New Zealand ....The Oval (Floodlit)
Thu	29	August	England v. Australia ...Ageas Bowl, Southampton (Floodlit)
Sat	31	August	England v. Australia ....Emirates Durham ICG

SECOND ELEVEN CHAMPIONSHIP

WED	**29-31**	**MAY**	**DERBYSHIRE ....HARROGATE**
Wed	5-7	June	Leicestershire ....TBC
TUES	**9-11**	**JULY**	**MCC YOUNG CRICKETERS .STAMFORD BRIDGE**
TUES	**16-18**	**JULY**	**GLAMORGAN ....HEADINGLEY**
Wed	31-2	July/August	Warwickshire ......Coventry and North Warwickshire CC
Tue	6-8	August	Worcestershire ....Barnt Green CC
Tue	13-15	August	Durham ....South North CC
WED	**21-23**	**AUGUST**	**LANCASHIRE ....TODMORDEN**
WED	**28-30**	**AUGUST**	**NOTTINGHAMSHIRE ....YORK**
Wed	11	September	Final ....TBC

SECOND ELEVEN TROPHY

TUE	**28**	**MAY**	**DERBYSHIRE ....HARROGATE**
Tue	4	June	Leicestershire ....Leicester
MON	**8**	**JULY**	**MCC YOUNG CRICKETERS .WEETWOOD, LEEDS**
FRI	**19**	**JULY**	**GLAMORGAN ....PUDSEY CONGS**
Tues	30	July	Warwickshire ....TBC
Mon	5	August	Worcestershire ....Barnt Green CC
Mon	12	August	Durham ....South North CC
Mon	19	August	Nottinghamshire ....Barnsley
TUE	**20**	**AUGUST**	**LANCASHIRE ....TODMORDEN**
Tue	27	August	Semi-Final

SECOND ELEVEN TWENTY20 (TWO MATCHES IN THE SAME DAY)

FRI	**14**	**JUNE**	**NOTTINGHAMSHIRE ....HEADINGLEY**
THUR	**20**	**JUNE**	**LANCASHIRE ....MARSKE**
Fri	21	June	England Under-19s ....Loughborough
Mon	24	June	Derbyshire ....Away TBC
Fri	12	July	Semi-Finals and Final ....TBC

SECOND ELEVEN FRIENDLIES

Tue	16-18	April	Durham	Hartlepool
TUE	**23-25**	**APRIL**	**LANCASHIRE**	**SCARBOROUGH**
Tue	30-2	April/May	Lancashire	Northop Hall
Tue	7-10	May	Kent/Surrey	Beckenham
Mon	13-16	May	Lancashire	Liverpool
WED	**12**	**JUNE**	**DURHAM**	**YORK (T20X2)**
Mon	9-11	September	Middlesex	Radlett CC
TUE	**17-19**	**SEPTEMBER**	**DURHAM**	**WEETWOOD**

YORKSHIRE ACADEMY IN THE YORKSHIRE LEAGUE

Sat	20	April	Castleford	Away
SAT	**27**	**APRIL**	**SHEFFIELD UNITED**	**WEETWOOD**
Sat	4	May	Rotherham	Away
SAT	**11**	**MAY**	**DRIFFIELD**	**WEETWOOD**
Sat	18	May	York	Away
SAT	**25**	**MAY**	**APPLEBY FRODINGHAM**	**WEETWOOD**
Mon	27	May	Cleethorpes	Away
SAT	**1**	**JUNE**	**HULL**	**WEETWOOD**
SAT	**8**	**JUNE**	**SCARBOROUGH**	**WEETWOOD**
SAT	**15**	**JUNE**	**BARNSLEY**	**WEETWOOD**
Sat	22	June	Doncaster	Away
Sat	29	June	Sheffield Collegiate	Away
Sun	30	June	Harrogate	Away
SAT	**6**	**JULY**	**CASTLEFORD**	**WEETWOOD**
Sat	13	July	Sheffield United	Away
SAT	**20**	**JULY**	**ROTHERHAM**	**WEETWOOD**
Sat	27	July	Driffield	Away
SAT	**3**	**AUGUST**	**YORK**	**WEETWOOD**
SUN	**4**	**AUGUST**	**HARROGATE**	**WEETWOOD**
Sat	10	August	Appleby Frodingham	Away
Sat	17	August	Hull	Away
Sat	24	August	Scarborough	Away
SAT	**31**	**AUGUST**	**SHEFFIELD COLLEGIATE**	**WEETWOOD**
SAT	**7**	**SEPTEMBER**	**DONCASTER**	**WEETWOOD**
SAT	**14**	**SEPTEMBER**	**CLEETHORPES**	**WEETWOOD**

YORKSHIRE ACADEMY IN THE YORKSHIRE LEAGUE CUP

Sun	19	May	Doncaster	Away

YORKSHIRE ACADEMY IN THE YORKSHIRE LEAGUE T20

Sun	9	June	Yorkshire League T20	TBC

YORKSHIRE ACADEMY FRIENDLIES

Sun	14	April	Barnard Castle	Barnard Castle School
TUE	**14**	**MAY**	**HYDERABAD UNDER-19S**	**TBC**
Mon	20	May	Derbyshire Academy	Staverley MW CC
WED	**29-30**	**MAY**	**DURHAM ACADEMY**	**SCARBOROUGH**
Mon	8	July	Gilespies Cricket Academy	TBC
WED	**10**	**JULY**	**T20s v. DURHAM & GCA**	**WEETWOOD**
Thu	8	August	Yorkshire Gents 150th	Escrick Park
TUE	**13-14**	**AUGUST**	**SCOTLAND UNDER-19S**	**WEETWOOD**
THU	**15**	**AUGUST**	**SCOTLAND UNDER-19S**	**WEETWOOD**

YORKSHIRE UNDER-17s in ONE-DAY AND TWO-DAY NATIONAL CHAMPIONSHIPs

TUE	**2**	**JULY**	**DURHAM**	**WEETWOOD**
Tue	16-17	July	Derbyshire	Away
Thu	18	July	Derbyshire	Away
TUE	**23-24**	**JULY**	**CHESHIRE**	**WEETWOOD**
THU	**25**	**JULY**	**CHESHIRE**	**WEETWOOD**
Tue	30-31	July	Lancashire	Away
Thu	1	August	Lancashire	Away
TUE	**6-7**	**AUGUST**	**DURHAM**	**WEETWOOD**
TUE	**20-21**	**AUGUST**	**SEMI-FINALS**	**WEETWOOD**
Thu	29-30	August	Two-Day Final	TBC
Sun	1	September	One-Day Final	TBC

150TH ANNIVERSARY GALA DINNER

THURSDAY 3RD OCTOBER 2013

THE CENTENARY PAVILION, ELLAND ROAD, LEEDS 6.30PM UNTIL 12.30AM

In 2013 we celebrate the 150th Anniversary of Yorkshire County Cricket Club. Since 1863 generations of Yorkshire talent have built our reputation as one of the most illustrious cricket clubs in the world. History and tradition are key elements, as we mark the milestone in a manner worthy of the Club's reputation.

MENU
Champagne Reception followed by a 4 course evening meal

HOST
BBC Cricket Correspondent Jonathan Agnew

GUEST SPEAKERS
Former and current Yorkshire County Cricket Club Players

INCLUDING A PERFORMANCE FROM THE ENCORE BAND!

TABLES OF 10 AVAILABLE FOR £800 + VAT
TABLES OF 8 PLUS A PLAYER AND THEIR GUEST AVAILABLE FOR £1,250 + VAT
INDIVIDUAL PLACES ALSO AVAILABLE AT £80 + VAT
DRESS CODE – BLACK TIE

Further sponsorship opportunities are also available for this event. For more information, or to book places, please contact Simon Pixsley on **0113 2033 667** or email **simon.pixsley@yorkshireccc.com**

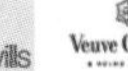

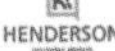

LET'S MAKE THIS EXTRA SPECIAL SEASON ONE TO REMEMBER

By David Warner

Heads can be held high in this momentous year in which Yorkshire County Cricket Club celebrates the 150th anniversary of its birth.

By the time this Yearbook reaches you the celebrations will already have been started at a sesquicentennial soiree in the Crucible Studio Theatre in Sheffield on January 8 — the very date on which the Club was formed in 1863 and on the very same site.

Yorkshire members and supporters always take a great pride in their Club, which they rightly maintain is second to none, and chests can be fully extended this summer as their team marks an historic milestone by competing in the First Division of the LV County Championship.

The Editor, who celebrates the 150th anniversary of the Yorkshire Club's founding with his 350-page volume, *The Sweetest Rose*

They can be proud, also, that Yorkshire begin the new season having made their mark on the international scene last October by competing honourably in the *Twenty20 Champions League* competition in South Africa, their presence being just reward for having contested the *Friends Life t20* final for the very first time in the August.

Yorkshire's return to Division One was particularly heart-warming for those who believe the Championship is the greatest of the domestic competitions, but it is just as satisfying that the younger fans now have a team who will not let them down in the rather more frenzied atmosphere of the flash, bang, wallop form of the game.

ANDREW GALE: Yorkshire skipper with team poised to achieve something worthy of a 150th birthday

It is not very often that a cricket season turns out exactly in the way that one has forecast that it will, and there is always the element of surprise that can make a mockery of predictions. Take, for example, Yorkshire's unexpected blossoming under new captain Andrew Gale in 2010. when they almost snatched the Championship, or their hard-to-explain demise the following season.

But it would be nice to hope that in this extra special year the team can at least achieve something that is way out of the ordinary and worthy of the Club's 150th birthday.

Last season's new-look coaching staff, headed by Director of Cricket Martyn Moxon and first-team coach Jason Gillespie, did all that could be expected of them — and more besides — in the rain-drenched apology of a summer, and they should be an even stronger force now that they know exactly how each of them works.

Yorkshire certainly entered 2013 with plenty to shout about, not the least of their splendid achievements being to have three members of the England squad who last December gained a memorable 2-1 series win over India — Tim Bresnan, Jonathan Bairstow and Joe Root.

It was a particularly memorable tour for Joe, who looked like being a passenger for most of the time until he made his debut in the fourth and final Test in Nagpur to put England back on an even keel with 73 before following up with an unbeaten 20 to draw the match and clinch the rubber. No one could have envisaged before the tour began that Root would make his debut at No. 6 rather than in his customary role as opener, but the Sheffield youngster quickly showed that he had the technique and the temperament to cope with any situation.

Ironically, Joe's debut possibly came at the expense of a place for Bairstow in that Test, but Jonny had already shown off his Test credentials with a sparkling performance when recalled for the Lord's Test against South Africa in the lengthening shadows of last summer.

Conditions in India made it a difficult tour for Bresnan, but Tim is among the most endurable of England's proven pace attack, and it will be a surprise if he does not feature prominently in the two Ashes series which will soon be upon us.

With these three Yorkshiremen already a part of the England set-up, the *White Rose* side may not feature them together as often as they would like in their 150th year, and who is to say that Adam Lyth, Gary Ballance and Azeem Rafiq will not gain recognition by their country before too long? And don't forget that Adil Rashid at 25 still has plenty of time to recover the sort of form that made him one of the nation's most exciting prospects.

But with England riding the crest of a wave and with plenty of talented players to choose from it is hard to imagine that Yorkshire will lose too many of their top performers all at the same time.

I believe that Yorkshire are well able to plug the gaps caused by Test match calls, particularly now that Liam Plunkett and Jack Brooks have been signed to add strength to the fast bowling.

It may be argued that Yorkshire could have got away with signing only one of this pair, but only time will tell. Certainly, the priority whenever possible must be to give every opportunity to the young players who come up through the Academy and the Second Eleven rather than seeking help from outside these ranks. Admittedly, some of the less experienced pacemen hardly advanced their claims last season, the weather doing little to assist those going through a thin patch to regain their form, but it would be comforting to feel that in future there will be sufficient home-grown reserves to step up to the plate.

For both Yorkshire and England, 2013 is going to be an action-packed season. Let us hope that Yorkshire will be able to add another distinguished chapter to their great and glorious history.

Exciting debutant for England

THE WORLD'S HIS STAGE NOW THAT JOE HAS TAKEN ROOT

By Graham Hardcastle

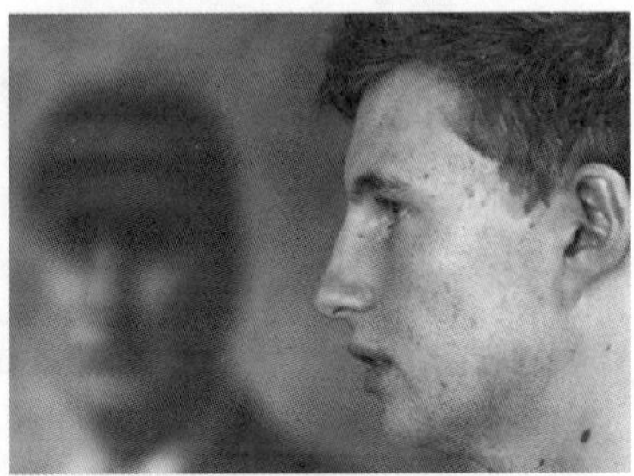

In the shadow of Lord Hawke

When Joe Root made 73 on Test debut for England against India at Nagpur last December it may have raised a few eyebrows around the cricket world.

To make your Test debut at the best of times is no menial task, so to do it with your team wobbling in a series-deciding match in a country that 99 per cent accept is the toughest to tour takes some doing. Yet those raised eyebrows would not have come from followers of Yorkshire cricket, county colleagues or coaches, for Root has impressed on countless occasions since first playing for Yorkshire Schools at the age of 11 and going on to score three LV County Championship hundreds in 2011 and 2012.

Root walked to the crease as a 21-year-old — he is now 22 — in the fourth and final Test with England leading the series 2-1 but, at 119-4 and having lost two quick wickets, in danger of letting India back into things. Kevin Pietersen followed shortly afterwards, but Root then forged partnerships of 103 for the sixth wicket with Matt Prior and 60 for the eighth with Graeme Swann during his 229-ball stay, including four boundaries. He became joint top-scorer alongside Pietersen.

He helped England to post a first-innings total of 330 before scoring a useful 20 not out in the second innings as the draw and series win were confirmed. In a flash Root seemed to be a fixture in the Test squad with back-to-back *Ashes* series on the horizon in 2013.

He grew up in Sheffield and played for the Collegiate club, so comparisons between his game and that of Michael Vaughan were always going to come. His elegant strokeplay is certainly one particular which

Master of all trades: Joe Root looks at home in all forms of the game, and here he powers one past Sussex wicket-keeper Ben Brown in the CB40

makes this not wide of the mark. The way things are going, there is every chance that young Yorkshire players of the future who will be compared to that fine batsman called Joe Root, holder of the Professional Cricketers' Association and Cricket Writers' Club Young Cricketer of the Year awards.

He still goes back to play for Collegiate when he gets a free weekend, which says a heck of a lot about his character and commitment to the game. From a cricketing family who have seen his father, Matt, become a successful league player and his younger brother, left-hander Billy, make it on to the MCC Young Cricketers' programme last year, Root has always enjoyed a debut.

He scored 57 on his Yorkshire Second Eleven debut in 2007 at his home ground in Sheffield before making 63 on his first-team bow in a 40-over game against Essex two summers later. The right-hander may have scored a duck and 21 not out on his Championship debut against Worcestershire at New Road in 2011, but he was back in the runs when he broke into the England Lions team later that summer, scoring 66 against the new ball in the second innings of a draw against Sri Lanka.

Root has been exceptional as an opener for Yorkshire, and in the long run he is expected to move up to that role in Tests alongside Alastair Cook. Those who were at the Rose Bowl last summer for his sublime 222 not out were treated to something special, an innings to savour and

remember. While his top-order teammates were struggling to come to terms with a bowler-friendly track, Root accrued 26 fours and three sixes in 270 balls and nearly six-and-a-half hours at the crease.

After his Test debut, Root was quickly drafted into England's *Twenty20* and one-day international plans for series in India either side of Christmas, performing so well that he was asked to tour with England in New Zealand rather than captaining England Lions in Australia.

Just take the Yorkshire President's word on Root. Geoffrey Boycott was full of praise at Yorkshire's Sesquicentennial Soiree in Sheffield in January for the player who was awarded his county and international caps less than four months apart:

"I think he'll be a terrific player like Jonny Bairstow will. I've got absolutely no doubt about that. He's got a lot to learn at that age, a lot of experiences to go through, but he'll get better in years to come."

Joe Root the bowler...and who knows where is off-spin will take him?

Sensation!

...nothing sold more newspapers than a Yorkshire cricket contents bill. From noon onwards the newsboys invented sensations daily. "YORKSHIRE — AMAZING COLLAPSE" or "SUTCLIFFE FAILS" if the idol of Pudsey was out for 49.

Gerald Pawle, 1978

NO SHRINKING VIOLETS AS GALE'S MEN BLOSSOM

By Graham Hardcastle

The main aim of 2012 was to make sure that Yorkshire's emerging squad had the chance to win the LV County Championship title in 2013, the Club's 150th anniversary year, and the pressure was on new first-team coach Jason Gillespie and his players after relegation from Division One amidst embarrassing performances and a famous, stinging broadside from Club Chairman Colin Graves.

In the immediate aftermath of relegation the hierarchy opted for wholesale changes to the coaching structure, which saw the return of former overseas player and ex-Australia Test and one-day international fast bowler Gillespie as first-team coach after cutting his teeth in Zimbabwe with MidWest Rhinos.

Paul Farbrace — a man with coaching experience at both county and international level — was brought in as second-team coach, while Richard Damms was appointed to the Club's development programme. Martyn Moxon would continue to oversee the whole shooting match as Director of Professional Cricket.

Farbrace was hailed as the man who made Yorkshire into such a formidable fielding side, especially in *Twenty20*, as well as recommending the loan signing of wicket-keeper Andrew Hodd from Sussex. Hodd played an important role with bat and gloves in the later stages of the Championship campaign, and he subsequently signed a contract with Yorkshire to take him to the end of the 2014 season.

The summer did not quite start as planned, but things kicked into gear pretty quickly in terms of performances, even though the weather proved to be the big winner. Captain Andrew Gale oversaw an unconvincing opening draw against Kent at Headingley, while Ajmal Shahzad failed to settle into the new regime. Shahzad was forced to accept a loan move across the Pennines to join arch-rivals and reigning county champions Lancashire, who ended up being relegated.

The summer will be remembered generally for the fact that it rained more than any of us would care to remember. Yorkshire had 13 days washed out in Championship cricket and many other days heavily affected, too — and that does not include the limited-over competitions.

Victory and promotion: high jinks at Cheltenham as the 239-run win over Essex sends Yorkshire back up

Ahead of the final month of the campaign it was starting to look as if the *White Rose* would miss promotion because of the weather...but three matches and three wins later the champagne was being sprayed across the outfield at Chelmsford after the last-day triumph against Essex.

One man who was there to enjoy the moment was Graves a year after telling the players to "take a long hard look at themselves".

He said amidst the celebrations: "I'm delighted for the guys. They've responded fantastically well since relegation, and to achieve what we have is great. We had a long way to climb, but we've done it. Last year I was so disappointed with where we ended up, and so were the players. I said what a lot of people were thinking, but it had to be said. If it gave them a spur, then I'm glad, because this just proves that we had the ability to do what we've done."

Gillespie's and Gale's side may have narrowly missed out on the Division Two title to Derbyshire, but gaining promotion was no mean feat, given circumstances above — quite literally — and beyond their control. No other county lost as many overs to the weather.

The Championship campaign saw players young and old shine. Jonny Bairstow made his Test debut for England, while Joe Root — who scored a sensational 222 not out on a sticky wicket against Hampshire at Southampton in July — earned a place on England's winter tour of India before Christmas alongside Bairstow and Tim Bresnan.

Gary Ballance, despite not piling on the runs, and Azeem Rafiq both enhanced their reputations and travelled to India over the winter with the England Performance Programme squad. Ballance can look back on the century he scored against Gloucestershire in the contrived run chase at Bristol as key to the outcome of the season.

Although not quite a young gun, Steven Patterson led the bowling attack expertly with 48 wickets at 20.81, while Moin Ashraf enjoyed success during the second half of the summer on the back of starring in the *Twenty20*.

Then there were the golden oldies: Phil Jaques returned after six years away to be the leading run-scorer with 792 from 15 matches, including two hundreds, and at the grand old age of 36 Anthony McGrath proved his doubters wrong with some valuable contributions, including two centuries, a 90 and a fantastic unbeaten 76 to help to clinch a vital, narrow win over Gloucestershire at Scarborough.

The Scarborough innings in particular was one to remember alongside the fantastic double-centuries from Root and Adam Lyth — who came into his own in the second half of the summer — Jaques's 160 against Gloucester at Bristol in May, and Ballance's unbeaten 121 in the same fixture as the county chased down 400 inside 108 overs. Jaques and Ballance shared a stand of 203 for the fourth wicket.

Ryan Sidebottom would have liked more wickets than the 24 he mustered, but injury played a large part in that. The left-arm swing bowler will definitely look back fondly on a fiery burst in Yorkshire's second qualifying match of the *Champions League t20* against Trinidad and Tobago at Centurion, South Africa, in October.

It may have been a disappointing *Clydesdale Bank* campaign, but Yorkshire fired on all *Twenty20* cylinders to reach Finals Day at Cardiff at the 10th time of asking and to qualify for South Africa. They played some exhilarating cricket, especially in the field, and were unfortunate to lose the domestic final against Hampshire, despite the best efforts of overseas signing David Miller, the South African left-hander.

Australian fast bowler Mitchell Starc appeared for Yorkshire in the Championship, but he only bowled 42.1 overs, mainly because of the weather. One of his fixtures was against Glamorgan at Colwyn Bay in June, when only 34 overs were possible in the game. The 22-year-old left-armer was sensational in *Twenty20*, with 21 wickets from 10 matches, more than anybody else in the competition. He could not play for Yorkshire in the Champions League due to his commitments to Sydney Sixers: he even shone in a group match against Yorkshire to secure a thumping eight-wicket win for the Sixers.

Injuries and unavailability hampered Yorkshire through their Group B odyssey, which consisted of three defeats and a washout against Sachin Tendulkar's Mumbai Indians at Newlands, but by reaching the competition's main stage the county had achieved something special.

Miller recovered from being hit on the nose by an Umar Gul bouncer — it turned out to be fractured — to help to secure a nailbiting opening qualifying win over Sri Lanka's star-studded UVA Next at Johannesburg, and T&T were sent packing as Sidebottom helped to reduce the West Indians, finalists in 2009, to 8-3 and a total of 148-9

First for Yorkshire: Gary Ballance and Adil Rashid seal qualification for the main stage of the *Champions' League t20* with an undefeated century partnership

with 3-13 from his four overs. It was down to Ballance — 64 not out off 37 balls — and Adil Rashid to seal qualification with an unbroken century stand for the fifth wicket after Yorkshire had been 51-4 in reply.

Considering what had been achieved through the summer, it was quite an admission from Gale that qualifying for the main stage of the *CLt20* had been the best moment of his career: "There was a heck of a lot of pressure on us during the season, and we stood up and did it. Promotion was the main thing, and it's going to be fantastic to play in Division One. There were no shrinking violets, and it bodes well for years to come."

Reflecting on the Champions League experience and the season as a whole, Director of Professional Cricket Martyn Moxon added: "We competed in three of our group games. The Sydney match was the only disappointing one. The rest of the time we were very competitive. There were definitely some 'what might have beens'. It was a great experience, and fantastic to be involved. Hopefully, the lads learned a lot.

"You look at the quality of the opposition players, and it was phenomenal. I think everybody played a part. For people like Iain Wardlaw and Oliver Hannon-Dalby to come in and return the figures they did was excellent when we had so many injuries.

"Dan Hodgson was superb behind the stumps during his first experience of first-team *Twenty20* cricket. It was a fantastic season for us. We always said that promotion in the Championship was the main priority, which we achieved. It's going to be an important season in 2013."

Dizzy's tactics bring change in perspective

CLAPPING AND SMILING ALL THE WAY TO FINALS DAY

By Dave Caldwell

One could be forgiven for thinking at the end of a narrow opening defeat against Durham in June, with grey clouds abounding and grumbles of "same old Yorkshire" and "this team will win nowt batting like that" that it would be yet another season of performances that flattered to deceive and ultimate disappointment in the shortest form of the game.

Yet I saw a change in attitude that evening, a change in perspective and, above all, a change of tactics. By the time of the second fixture two days later Yorkshire were up and running, and they never looked back, offering the sceptics several opportunities to review their concerns and to look forward with a new, young Yorkshire side.

From the onset of the *Twenty20* carnival 10 years ago the game had never really caught on in God's own country as a combination of traditionalists, myself being one, and those very much reticent to change picked holes in the format, swiftly brandishing it as nothing more than a slog. Slowly but surely, begrudgingly at first, I found myself completely embracing this new brand, as we witnessed some of the most innovative cricket ever seen — whether it be the "Dilshan scoop" or the reverse-sweep, the switch-hit or the slower-ball bouncer, not to mention fielding of the highest calibre.

The positive effect this has had on the longer forms of the game have not been acknowledged nearly enough, especially when we think of run-chases on the last day of a Championship match. The fixtures against Gloucestershire last summer, both rain-affected, proved that no one can be confident of defending 360 or even 400 anymore. Even to consider chasing these totals in days gone by would have been seen as foolhardy.

Admittedly, there were decent crowds for Yorkshire's first two seasons of *Twenty20*, but other than the hugely anticipated annual *Roses* fixture not many more than 3,000 would venture out to Headingley, while The Oval and Lord's were getting treble that figure. What would be the main reason for that? The team simply were not winning.

It is a simple calculation: your side win games and the people turn up in droves, with the feel-good factor often transferring itself to the other formats of the game.

Jewel in the crown: Coach Jason Gillespie looked towards Azeem Rafiq, 21, who took to the *t20* captaincy like a duck to water when Gale was away

So what did Yorkshire do so right last season that made them the formidable force they became? I would wager that the first name on everyone's lips would be David Miller, or maybe Mitchell Starc, but very few would mention Jason Gillespie. Yet that is where I start the plaudits: "Dizzy" had the changing-room right with him through being a good pro in the later days of his career at Headingley and his achievements in arguably the greatest Test team of all time.

What he brought to the *t20* campaign was simplicity...nothing more, nothing less. A desire to be professional, with everyone in it together, coupled with a simple approach to utilising their skills. Tactically, it was clear: go hard for the first six overs when batting, then consolidate until the 14-over mark, sometimes later. The key was to keep the middle-order in hand to go for it in the last phase, sometimes with devastating effect. Many a time 140 would appear to be a likely total after the half-way point, only for the likes of Ballance, Miller et al to start clearing the boundary and, before you knew where you were, Yorkshire had 170.

The promotion of Joe Root to No. 3 was inspired: a confident young man who was happy take chances early on to throw the bowlers off their line, often coming in with runs on the board and knowing that a heavy-weight middle-order was to follow. Conversely, the decision to resist the temptation to elevate Miller was also to be applauded.

The fielding was of as high a standard as I have ever seen in a Yorkshire or any other county side. Everyone knew their positions, and I would point to the fine victory at Grace Road where the catching, fielding and general outcricket was of the highest calibre. This was the standard that set the benchmark, and Yorkshire would never fall below it. Elements of Yorkshire's fielding bordered on the aggressive, but the action was speaking far louder than the words, and the opposition were left in no doubt that runs would have to be earned.

Now for the players not involved, with bold decisions to leave them out vindicated, it would seem. Yorkshire's leading *t20* run-scorer, Anthony McGrath, was omitted from the squad, the management possibly opting for a livelier figure in the field, but they had enough bowling options and the batting looked formidable. Steven Patterson, the leading four-day wicket-taker and in great form, was left out, but if you see Adil Rashid finding it hard to break into the side you can appreciate the strength in depth at Gillespie's disposal.

The bowlers kept things even more simplistic: full and straight as Starc, Ashraf and Sidebottom all utilised the nearly defunct yorker to its maximum potential, ensuring that only the best batsmen would manipulate such accurate pacemen. The desire to mix things up has often been Yorkshire's downfall, yet this new approach assisted not only the bowlers, but the skipper, who could set fields safe in the knowledge that he had the attack to carry out the plans to best effect.

The real jewel in the crown of Yorkshire's campaign was to give Azeem Rafiq, 21, the task of leading the side in the absence of Gale. The experts raised eyebrows and the members expressed their concerns, but there was no need for pessimism. The off-spinning all-rounder took to his role like a duck to water, often bowling himself at key moments, maintaining disciplined lines and seldom going for more than 30 in his spell. His fielding was livewire, and he had the unenviable task of operating at backward-point, a position Richard Pyrah had made his own. His decision-making at crucial times often spoke volumes about his own confidence and that of his team. It was *Roy of The Rovers* stuff.

Often, I watch the action from outside the Press Box, where I can enjoy the hubbub, the grumbling, the knowledge and the passion of the locals. Most tellingly in the Quarter-Final against Worcestershire one stalwart told me: "You can tell when they are playing well, as they are smiling and clapping out on the pitch. And you know what young man? I'm clapping and smiling with them."

RAIN STOPPED PLAY: John Potter and Howard Clayton, Yorkshire CCC's first and second team scorers, cast a watery eye back on the wettest summer on record

PROMOTION — DESPITE 8,590 MINUTES DOWN THE DRAIN

By John Potter

We Made It Through The Rain...This song title did apply to Yorkshire in 2012. I have been keeping records on weather stoppages since 1993, and this was the worst in those 20 seasons. Everything looked to be set fair, as March was very good weather-wise, but once the season started in earnest it all changed. The opening day on April 5 and the closing day on September 14 had no interruptions, but the period between brings another title to mind: *It Might As Well Rain Until September*.

I start with the Championship, where Yorkshire's main goal was to gain promotion. They had to wait until they played Glamorgan at Headingley on September 4-6, Match 15, to have a game without any weather interruption — and it brought victory in three days.

Yorkshire had 14 matches between April and August, losing 8,561 minutes. A total of 20,160 minutes — 56 days @ 360 minutes — could have been played, giving a percentage loss of 42.47. This dropped in the Championship to 37.28 per cent as only 29 minutes were blank in the eight days that could have been played in September. The grand total of 8,590 minutes equates to 2,291 overs lost. The number of full days lost was 13 — one at Headingley, two at Scarborough and 10 away.

The season was split into two halves: April 5 to June 9 and July 11 to September 14. The first half had five home matches, with 1,737 minutes lost, and three away matches, with 2,580 minutes void, a total of 4,317 minutes. The second half had three home games, with 1,111 minutes lost, and five away games, with 3,162 minutes lost, a total of 4,273 minutes. There was not much difference in the two halves, but there was a large difference in home and away — 33.15 per cent lost in Yorkshire compared with 66.85 per cent away.

The games at Colwyn Bay and Chesterfield had play only on the opening days, while at Southampton only 106 overs were bowled on days two and three with nothing on the other days. Those three fixtures lost 3,544 minutes out of a possible 4,320, a percentage loss of of 82.03.

Showpiece frustration: Headingley's one-day-international between England and West Indies on June 22 is called off just after 1pm without a ball bowled

Yet in spite of all these interruptions at 1.55pm on September 14 Yorkshire finished with a win and second place in Division Two, promotion having been guaranteed on the previous evening. The First Class three-day match against Leeds-Bradford MCCU lost 237 minutes.

Yorkshire's one-day campaign suffered two complete washouts — Northamptonshire at Headingley in the *CB40* and Lancashire at Old Trafford in the *FLt20. Clydesdale Bank 40* games lost 639 minutes to the weather and *Friends Life t20* 350 minutes. The forecast on *t20* Finals Day was hopelessly wrong, as there were no delays.

The one-day international between England and the West Indies at Headingley in June was washed out, as it was in 2009. This did have a silver lining, as I was freed from international duties to get to Chester-le-Street and see another win for Yorkshire in their *t20* campaign.

England's Test match against South Africa lost 539 minutes, with interruptions on all five days. The fifth day finished at 7.32pm, which I think must be the latest finish to a Test at Headingley.

A total of 10,775 minutes on 97 days of cricket were lost in all home and away matches involving Yorkshire, plus England in Test and one-day matches at Headingley. This easily beat 1997, the previous worst, which was 9,348 minutes wiped out over 116 days, 6,726 in the Championship. The average of minutes lost over the last 20 seasons is 5,721. The best year was 2010, with 3,449 minutes lost in 102 days of cricket, 2,413 in the Championship.

TWIDDLING OUR THUMBS FOR 47.77 PER CENT OF THE TIME

By Howard Clayton

The 2012 season was without doubt an unmitigated disaster from the point of view of the weather. The Second XI fixture list comprised nine Championship games, nine for the Trophy, eight *Twenty20* matches and six Friendlies. This should have added up to 62 days of cricket, but 36 were interrupted to some extent and 19 completely washed out.

That left only seven days without the young hopefuls being driven off at some stage or other: these were the four uninterrupted days at Northampton for the Championship and Trophy games and the whole of the match against Somerset at Taunton Vale. This comes to a staggering 2,366.2 overs lost to the elements — or 47.77 per cent of the available season. It all added up to a major frustration for players, coaches, scorers, umpires and the loyal band of spectators who delight in travelling to see the (hopefully) next generation of Yorkshire cricketers in action.

Those who suffered most undoubtedly were the young players who were wearing the *White Rose* for the first time: they have shown enough promise, usually in Academy games, and they are given the chance to show that they can make the next step up. They get a reasonable score or turn in a decent bowling performance, and they are told they have another Second Eleven game the following week. Then it rains again, and all momentum is lost. The team suffers similarly, and a good performance cannot be followed up by an even better one.

Hope springs eternal in the scorer's breast: a newspaper report stated that the wettest summers of the last three centuries had been in 1812, 1912 and now 2012. Each was followed by a good summer. We wait.

Ronald Stanyforth

It is regretted that an article by Martin Howe on Ronald Stanyforth, who captained England before he had played for Yorkshire, has had to be held over until the 2014 edition of the Yorkshire CCC *Yearbook* because of pressure on space. We would like to point out that Martin has written an absorbing 15,000-word monograph on Stanyforth, which can be obtained from him for £10, including postage. He can be contacted on martinhowe1@sky.com

YOUNG TALENT SHINES THROUGH THE GLOOM

By Howard Clayton

At about 5pm on February 7 last year the telephone rang in my flat: it was Ian Dews to inform me of the results of the interviews that had taken place that day for Mike Snook's replacement as Second Eleven scorer. I was offered it, and accepted immediately.

That answered a question that had been running through my head for several years: if a job such as this one suddenly fell into my lap, given that I had been involved with England Under-19s for 22 years, which would I choose? It took less time than it takes to blink to decide.

The season was marginally better than 2011 when we managed to get on the field, but only just. The first Championship victory for two years was gained at York against the MCC Universities. Two games were lost — to Durham heavily and to Northamptonshire disappointingly. The others were drawn, with vast chunks of play washed out. Matches at Harrogate v. Leicestershire and Denby v. Derbyshire were abandoned without a ball.

The Second Eleven Trophy brought two wins — against Unicorns A and Northamptonshire. Four games were lost — against Durham, Lancashire, Warwickshire and Worcestershire. The other three never started. We saw our first Trophy games at Weetwood (v Warwickshire), where Duckworth-Lewis called in to watch, and at the slightly more salubrious surroundings of Sheffield Collegiate (v Unicorns A) where the scoreboard operator was one Michael Snook.

Michael saw a strange game as the Unicorns succumbed for 52 — the lowest score ever recorded against Yorkshire in the competition — and Yorkshire had won just after 2pm. Lunch was served when play ended. Collegiate have had several senior figures on their books as juniors, and two of these luminaries, Michael Vaughan and Richard Kettleborough, joined us for lunch. Joe Root is following in their footsteps.

The result of the Unicorns match could not have contrasted more with the corresponding fixture in 2011 at Todmorden: there the opposition ran up a formidable 290-8 in their 40 overs and then dismissed Yorkshire for 121 in 29.1 to inflict on the home side their heaviest Trophy defeat.

Yorkshire's *T20* performances saw a very similar pattern to 2011. We have had 16 games over two seasons and still no win. Two matches are

Meteoric rise: wicket-keeper/batsman Dan Hodgson, who started to have some first-team one-day games

played on each date, one before lunch and one after. We lost both games to England Under-19s at Bradford & Bingley CC, and then both to Lancashire at Ormskirk CC where, once again, Duckworth-Lewis were employed, very much to the benefit of the *Red Rose*. Both fixtures against Derbyshire and Nottinghamshire sank without trace.

Not enough runs were scored in this format, the same problem as in Championship and Trophy cricket. Yorkshire's top *T20* score remains 142-1, set in 2011 against Nottinghamshire. The nearest we got in 2012 was one run less — for five wickets — against England Under-19s at Bradford & Bingley. This score, along with the Under-19s' reply of 145-5, created the highest match aggregate of 286 in the brief history of Yorkshire Second Eleven *T20* cricket.

Yorkshire appeared to have batted well enough in the Championship at Northampton, where Anthony McGrath's unbeaten double-hundred helped to set the hosts a target of 350 in a minimum of 74 overs on the last afternoon. Then the bowlers lost their radar en bloc, and Northamptonshire were home with four wickets and three overs to spare. This was Yorkshire's 100th Second Eleven Championship defeat.

The Seconds began their friendly programme at Marton CC in April, where the first two days went the way of much that was to follow. All wanted some cricket on the final day, so each team had a bat and a bowl. This was something of a sentimental journey for me as in 1965 I officiated in my first game as scorer — at Marton for the home side.

A four-day game against Lancashire at Stamford Bridge was cancelled on the Friday before the start four days later. Yorkshire instead played a one-dayer at Headingley (until 4.02 pm anyway) and moved on to St Anne's for a three-dayer, which the *Red Rose* won with one ball left. Alex Lees made a century. We went down to Beckenham for a ruined four-day match against combined Kent and Northamptonshire.

No more friendlies followed until late August, when Nottinghamshire came to Weetwood for three days, reduced to one by more rain. Yorkshire made 359, with five consecutive partnerships of 50 or more, and Dan Hodgson fell two short of a well-deserved century. Finally, it was down to Taunton Vale for four days, but a heavy innings defeat saw Yorkshire leave after two and a half. This match was memorable for the promising debut of slow left-armer Karl Carver.

McGrath`s double-century was the only triple-figure score in the Championship. Jack Leaning, Hodgson, Lees, Adil Rashid, Ryan Gibson and Ryan Sidebottom contributed 12 half-centuries between them — Sidebottom's first at this level. Hodgson's studious efforts contrast sharply with Gibson's swashbuckling at York against the Universities, but Gibson, along with Ben Coad, Will Rhodes, Jonathan Tattersall, Mosun Hussain, Lewis Stabler, Graeme Whiles, Carver and Josh Shaw all made their Second Eleven debuts, and all showed enough talent.

Hodgson began at Leeds University three years ago as second-choice wicket-keeper for the MCC University side, but soon became first choice and came to the attention of John Blain, who gave him Second Eleven games in 2011. Towards the end of 2012 he was first-team wicket-keeper in the *CB40*. He went to South Africa in the Champions League squad before going on to play first-class cricket in Zimbabwe.

Only Gurman Randhawa and Oliver Hannon-Dalby achieved the Club qualification for bowling averages. Randhawa had the best analysis of 5-42 against Worcestershire at Barnsley, and Hannon-Dalby took eight wickets against the MCC Universities, four in each innings. Only two half-centuries were scored in the Trophy games — both at Northampton, when Joe Sayers and Gerard Brophy added 126 for the third wicket. Sayers followed that with 5-27. Sayers, 162, and Lees, 141, were the only batsman to pass 100 runs for the season in this format. No bowler hit double-figures, six wickets for Alex Lilley being the best.

Only Lees made a *T20* half-century — at Ormskirk against Lancashire — and the best bowling return was 3-16 by Adil Rashid against England Under-19s at Bradford & Bingley.

Lees and McGrath set a team Championship record with their second-wicket stand against Northamptonshire of 253, and Lilley and Hannon-Dalby broke the 10th-wicket record against Durham with 72 in a lost cause at York. Sayers and Lees set a first-wicket Trophy record against Unicorns A, and Hodgson and Randhawa equalled the eighth-wicket record against Worcestershire. So did Randhawa and Ed Wilson for the eighth wicket against Northamptonshire.

TEST TRIO CELEBRATE: This happy photograph, provided exclusively for the *Yorkshire Yearbook*, shows the Yorkshire trio of Tim Bresnan, left, Joe Root and Jonny Bairstow making merry in Nagpur after their Test team had enjoyed a 2-1 series win over India. Joe's Test debut came in the final Test in Nagpur, and his sparkling 73, followed by an unbeaten 20, helped England to draw the match and clinch the series.

(Photo: Courtesy of Matt Root)

T20 FINALS DAY — PICTURE SPECIAL

FORWARD INTO BATTLE: Andrew Gale and Dimitri Mascarenhas lead out their teams in the Friends Life t20 final at the SWALEC stadium, Cardiff, on August 25, 2012. The umpires are Michael Gough, left, and Rob Bailey. BELOW: The tension is getting to Anthony McGrath.

T20 FINALS DAY — PICTURE SPECIAL

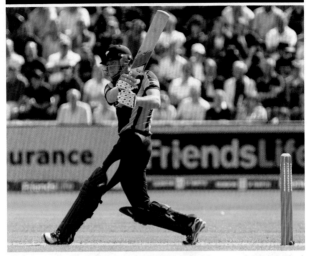

MAN OF THE MATCH: Jonathan Bairstow who won the Semi-Final award and the £1,000 cheque for his 68 not out to eliminate Sussex. BELOW: David Miller hits a valiant but vain 72 not out in the Final.

YORKSHIRE — 2012

APRIL LINE-UP: Front row, left to right: Richard Pyrah, Adil Rashid, Anthony McGrath, Joe Sayers, Jason Gillespie (First Team Coach), Andrew Gale (Captain), Martyn Moxon (Director of Cricket), Ryan Sidebottom, Gerard Brophy, Ajmal Shahzad and Jonathan Bairstow. Middle row: Scot McAllister (First Team Physiotherapist), Ian Dews (Director of Development), Iain Wardlaw, Azeem Rafiq, Adam Lyth, Steven Patterson, Oliver Hannon-Dalby, Joe Root, Gary Ballance, Moin Ashraf, Paul Farbrace (Second Team Coach), Tom Summers (Head of Strength and Conditioning) and James Clegg (Second Team Physiotherapist. Back row: Tony Pickersgill (Coach), Gurman Randhawa, Alex Lilley, Alex Lees, James Wainman, Callum Geldart, Dan Hodgson and Richard Damms (Youth Development Manager). *(Photo: VAUGHN RIDLEY)*

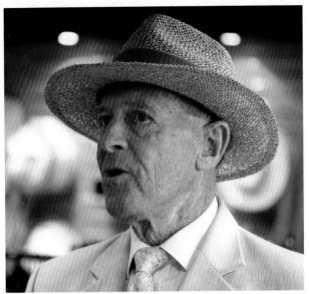

ALL IN A PRESIDENT'S DAY: Geoffrey Boycott OBE opens the new Yorkshire County Cricket Club shop behind the East Stand at Headingley on May 20, 2012.

GUARD OF HONOUR: The beefeaters were the first to congratulate Harold "Dickie" Bird when he collected his OBE at Buckingham Palace for services to cricket and charity. "Dickie" played for Yorkshire and Leicestershire before going on to umpire in 67 Test matches and 92 one-day internationals, world records at the time.

SCORER CALLS TIME: It was the end of an era when Michael Snook, right, left the scorebox for the last time after 15 years of service to Yorkshire Seconds. Chairman and Chief Executive Colin Graves presents Michael with a watch at the 2012 pre-season lunch.

BENDING HIS BACK: Tim Bresnan gives it his all in the hard-fought Second Test between England and South Africa at Headingley.

CAPPED AT SCARBOROUGH: It was the coldest match Yorkshire members could recall, with a bone-chilling east wind blowing off the sea, when the *White Rose* beat Leicestershire by an innings and 22 runs on May 5. *Yearbook* Correspondent NIGEL PULLAN wryly observed that the whole team had been awarded their county bobble hats. BELOW: It was somewhat warmer at North Marine Road on August 28 when skipper Andrew Gale, centre, awarded the genuine article to Gary Ballance, left, and Joe Root.

A LONG RAIN FOR THE TEAM — A SHORT REIGN FOR RAFIQ

By Harold D Galley

It was a foretaste of what was to come when on the first day of the season all Solly Adams Yorkshire ECB County Premier League fixtures were cancelled because the pitches were unfit.

Yorkshire Academy had 10 League matches seriously affected by the weather. We travelled to Doncaster for the second game, when not a ball was bowled, and the following week skipper Azeem Rafiq saw his batsmen score 246 in their allotted overs before he took 5-14 to ensure victory. First-team cricket then called for Rafiq.

JACK LEANING Skipper and leading batsman

Jack Leaning, the new captain, showed early form with the bat, as did Jonathan Tattersall and George Ross.

A cup win at Hull was followed by League defeats at Harrogate and York — the eventual table-toppers. Hopes of a cup run like 2011 were dashed at Driffield, and now the Colts had to concentrate on the League. They eventually finished fourth, and rarely looked like catching York or runners-up Barnsley.

Will Rhodes had an excellent season with the bat, averaging 73.56, and he took the most catches, 17. He scored an excellent century late in the season to ensure victory over Rotherham, while Jonathan Tattersall was the other century-maker with 114 v. Scarborough. Leaning was the leading run-scorer with 762, closely followed by Tattersall with 753.

Left-arm spinner Karl Carver took 22 wickets, opening bowler Ben Coad picking up 21. Mention must be made of Alex Leyshon's superb 8-56 v. Sheffield Collegiate, Jack Stabler's 6-10 v. Castleford and Coad's 6-16 v. Appleby Frodingham.

The batting was the strength of the team. As has happened to this young side in past years when faced with experienced opposition the bowlers rarely dominated matches. However, in 2012 it was the rain which influenced far too many fixtures.

YORKSHIRE COUNTY CRICKET CLUB 150 YEARS YOUNG AND BLOOMING

By David Hall

This year we celebrate the 150th anniversary of Yorkshire County Cricket Club. Since 1863 generations of Yorkshire talent has built our reputation as one of the most illustrious cricket clubs in the world. History and tradition are the key elements as we mark the milestone in a manner worthy of our great Club's reputation.

These celebrations began on the corresponding day and month the Club was formed at a meeting in the Adelphi Hotel, Sheffield, on January 8, 1863. That meeting was brief. The minutes recorded that the annual subscription would be not less than 10s.6d per member, and a sub-committee would be formed to carry out the approved resolution.

The Adelphi is no more, but is now the site of the famous Crucible Theatre, where the World Snooker Championships are held annually.

Our evening celebration on January 8, 2013, was dubbed a *Sesquicentennial Soiree* with the Master of Ceremonies, Harry Gration, taking us through an evening of readings, recollections and reminiscences. In conclusion a team of panellists comprised of Geoffrey Boycott, the Club President, Michael Vaughan, the former England captain, and Andrew Gale, the current Yorkshire captain, held a question-and-answer session.

On April 22, 1863, a further meeting took place at the Adelphi Hotel "of gentlemen in favour of the establishment of a County Cricket Club" at which officials and a committee were appointed to collect subscriptions, draw up rules and make all other preliminary arrangements. This date will be marked by the annual start-of-season lunch on Sunday, April 21, with John Barclay and Kevin Connelly as speakers. It is hoped that as many members as are able will attend this lunch to make it a really significant event in the year.

On Friday, June 14, at 2.30pm the focus of our celebrations will move to the Anniversary Commemorative Service in York Minster. The aim will be to involve the widest participation in the service. Lord Lieutenants, High Sheriffs and civic dignitaries, plus representatives from the ECB, MCC and YCB have been invited, and as many members as possible will be encouraged to join the congregation. The service will be led by the Dean of York Minster and Canon Max Wigley, the Club's Chaplain. It is the first time since the memorial service for Sir Leonard

Hutton that the Club has been involved in a service at the Minster.

Celebrations reach a climax on October 3 with a grand gala dinner at the Centenary Pavilion, Elland Road, Leeds, to mark the milestone in a style worthy of the Club's reputation. A champagne reception will be followed by a four-course meal. Jonathan Agnew, the BBC's cricket correspondent, will host the dinner, and the guest speakers will be Geoffrey Boycott, Michael Vaughan, Darren Gough and Jonathan Bairstow. The Encore Band will perform. This venue has been selected as the anticipated attendance will exceed the capacities available at Headingley.

Throughout the year the Museum and Long Room cabinets will feature special displays to highlight the many Championship and competition successes the Club has achieved in its 150-year history.

To mark the 150th anniversary David Warner has written a rich and detailed history of the Club in all its guts and glory entitled T*he Sweetest Rose*. The book will be on sale in the Club shop throughout the year. Ken Taylor, the former Yorkshire player and an artist of distinction, has created a wonderful picture which features our greatest players over the 150 years, as selected by the feature in the *Yorkshire Post*. It has been reproduced as a limited edition of prints for sale in the Club shop, and the original will hang in the Pavilion's Hawke Suite.

The shop has created a scintillating selection of special merchandise for the 150th. This includes two new tie designs, one silk edition and another available in polyester, both of which feature the 150th-anniversary logo, plus glassware, pottery, wristbands, caps, umbrellas and a ladies' silver rose pendant. A tea towel featuring all the players who have scored over 150 runs in an innings is a particularly novel item.

A special celebration match will take place between Yorkshire and the MCC on June 26 at Headingley, and the MCC team will include a number of international players.

This promises to be a very special year to mark a unique occasion.

Enjoy it!

David Hall CBE TD is Museum Director and a member of the 150th Committee

CORNERSTONE CALLS TIME ON ILLUSTRIOUS CAREER

By David Warner

The decision by Anthony McGrath to retire from first-class cricket meant that a cornerstone of the Yorkshire side from the mid-1990s had suddenly been removed and would take some replacing. Known to everyone as "Maggs", the 37-year-old Bradford-born batsman has deservedly earned a place in the list of Yorkshire's greatest run-scorers, and few since the 1939-45 war have bettered his achievements.

Anthony's final tally of first-class runs for his native county stands at 14,081, a figure topped by only 23 batsmen in the Club's history, and he would almost certainly have leapfrogged above a few others had he not decided to call it a day. He finished with 34 first-class centuries to his name, a figure exceeded by only two batsmen whose careers were played out exclusively after the last war. They are Geoffrey Boycott with 103 and Martyn Moxon with 41, so he is in exalted company indeed.

From his earliest days it was obvious to all who were responsible for his development that he was a player of outstanding ability, and some of his performances with the bat were at least the equal of other budding stars such as Marcus Trescothick and Yorkshire team-mate Michael Vaughan. Captaining Yorkshire Schoolboys from Under-13s through to Under-16s, Anthony then skippered England Under-17s, going on to open the batting with Trescothick for England Under-19s. He was a member of the England A teams which toured the West Indies in 1994-95 and Pakistan the following year, when he scored 290 runs at an average of 58 in the three unofficial Tests and 604 at 46.46 in all matches.

Anthony caught the eye with three centuries for Yorkshire Seconds in 1994, and he made his first-class debut against Glamorgan on his home ground at Bradford Park Avenue in May the following spring, opening with Vaughan. Like certain other illustrious players before him — including Len Hutton — he began with a duck. In September, however, he underlined his potential by striking 106 for Yorkshire against a strong West Indian side in a one-day encounter at the Scarborough Festival.

There were times when his progress seemed to stall while others of comparable ability moved forward, but his ability was never in doubt, and he became an even more important player when he turned from bowling occasional off-breaks into becoming a regular medium-pacer with a nagging length.

He will look back on 2003 as a red-letter year because he was first appointed Yorkshire captain and then, quite unexpectedly, summoned to the England ranks when Andrew Flintoff was injured.

Anthony responded with 69 on debut against Zimbabwe at Lord's, when he also returned figures of 3-16, and then in the Second Test at Chester-le-Street he top-scored with 81.

He did less well in two Tests which followed against South Africa, and he would probably have enjoyed more success in his 14 one-day internationals had he been given a settled spot rather than being held back to come in later, often with games well advanced.

Anthony willingly gave up the Yorkshire captaincy at the end of 2003 to concentrate more fully on his England career, but he faded at international level the following season, and may well have regretted his unselfish decision.

ANTHONY McGRATH: Vital key to Yorkshire promotion

There is no doubt, however, that playing for England gave Anthony that little extra self confidence to stamp his authority on the county circuit. and in 2005 he enjoyed his most prolific season for Yorkshire with 1,425 first-class runs, going on to top the 1,000 mark twice more.

He accepted the captaincy for a second time in 2009 but, again, graciously stood down at the end of the season because he felt that the extra responsibilities had adversely affected his batting form. His successor, Andrew Gale, was aided in no small degree by Anthony pledging his full support, and the result was that Yorkshire failed only narrowly to become County Champions in 2010.

Competition from younger players has put pressure on Anthony over the last two or three seasons, but he has shown that there is no substitute for class, and his contributions from the middle-order last season were a key feature of Yorkshire returning to Division One of the Championship.

Anthony can also look back with great pride on his one-day contributions to Yorkshire's cause. In 272 List A matches he accumulated 7,067 runs with six centuries for an average of 33.48 — only Boycott, Moxon, Richard Blakey and David Byas scored more — while in *Twenty20* cricket he played in 66 games, scoring 1,403 runs. His bowling record for the county is worthy of note: 121 wickets in first-class matches, 76 in List A games, and 23 in *Twenty20* contests.

Ajmal Shahzad, who left Yorkshire abruptly at the beginning of May and spent the remainder of the season with Lancashire, made history on May 23, 2004, when, just as unexpectedly, he became the first Yorkshire-born cricketer from an ethnic background to play for the *White Rose* county. Shahzad has now joined Nottinghamshire on a three-year contract, but his sudden departure from Yorkshire came as a big surprise to the fans, and it was unfortunate that he and the Club should reach an impasse on how it was felt he should bowl.

Now everyone will hope that he can rediscover the form that brought him a Test match appearance for England against Bangladesh at Old Trafford in 2010, plus 11 one-day international matches in which he collected 17 wickets. For a good number of years up to 2004 Yorkshire had been working hard to ensure that a homegrown player from an ethnic background would make it into the first team, but none could manage it until Shahzad came on the scene.

Born in Huddersfield, he developed his cricket with Bradford League club Windhill, and also at Woodhouse Grove School, where he was highly thought of by his cricket master, Graham Roope, the former Surrey and England all-rounder. He made splendid progress with both bat and ball at the Yorkshire Academy, and in 2003 he scored 383 runs and claimed 16 wickets in ECB County Premier League and Cup games.

Yet his first-team debut still came like a bolt from the blue that Sunday in May the following year when he was drafted into Yorkshire Phoenix's side at the last minute for their *totesport League* match against Worcestershire at Headingley. The 18-year-old was given his chance to boost an injury-hit attack after grabbing 5-20 in a league match the previous day, and although he did not take a wicket he showed signs of genuine quickness in six overs which cost him 35 runs.

I was the first cricket journalist to interview Shahzad before the match began, and he showed himself to be both articulate and diplomatic. "It is an awesome feeling to be the first ethnic cricketer born in Yorkshire to be chosen for the county," he said. "I hope I will be seen as a perfect role model from the Asian community, and I look upon this as the first stage in realising my ambition of playing regularly for Yorkshire."

Shahzad gained even more pace as time went on. He relished the tag of being Yorkshire's fastest bowler when he was really into his stride, but he suffered some setbacks with untimely injuries. His strength was his ability to swing the ball late, but he occasionally lacked consistency, and after a promising start he faded out of the picture with England.

In 45 first-class matches for Yorkshire between 2006-2012 he took 125 wickets at 33.56, three times enjoying five-wicket hauls with a career-best 5-51 against Durham at Chester-le-Street in 2010.

He scored 1,145 first-class runs at an average of 26.02, and hit three half-centuries — his best score being a splendid 88 against Sussex at Hove in 2009, when he put on 157 for the eighth wicket with David Wainwright, Yorkshire going on to win by 156 runs to avoid relegation.

In domestic List A cricket for Yorkshire, Shahzad captured 29 wickets in as many matches and scored 235 runs, while in Twenty20 matches he took 17 wickets from 22 matches and scored 129 runs.

AJMAL SHAHZAD
Bolt from the blue

Another sudden departure during the 2012 season was that of wicket-keeper/batsman Gerard Brophy, whose last match was a CB40 League fixture against Northamptonshire at Wantage Road on August 9, soon after which it was announced that his contract would not be renewed at the end of the summer.

He left with immediate effect, Director of Professional Cricket Martyn Moxon paying tribute to his service. Brophy was signed from Northamptonshire in the autumn of 2005 by Yorkshire's then Director of Cricket, David Byas, soon after the release of wicket-keeper/batsman Ismail Dawood. The hope was that the experienced 29-year-old would give added depth to the batting while possessing a safe pair of hands.

Ironically, while playing for Northamptonshire at Headingley the previous summer Brophy had broken a finger while standing up to the medium pace of Bilal Shafayat, and he was sidelined for three months. Born in South Africa of Irish parents, Brophy captained Free State before joining Northamptonshire, and with his Irish ancestry he was able to turn out for Ireland in 2000 in the NatWest Trophy.

Safe hands: Lancashire's Luke Sutton edges his shot and Brophy takes a good catch in the Cheltenham and Gloucester Trophy *Roses* clash on May 28, 2006

Six times Brophy held five catches or more in Championship matches, his best being seven against Warwickshire at Scarborough in 2007 when he took four in the first inning and three in the second. Against Durham at Chester-le-Street in 2009 Brophy held six catches in the first innings, only David Bairstow having managed more with seven.

He was a stroke-maker of the highest calibre, and had he shown his best form more often he could have been a top-order batsman. He hit three Championship centuries for Yorkshire, the highest an unbeaten 177 against Worcestershire at New Road in 2011, but his most astonishing innings came in a rain-wrecked Twenty20 encounter at Derby in 2006: he plundered 10 boundaries off his first 11 balls, all along the ground, and he rushed to his 50 off 14 legitimate deliveries. Trapped lbw for 57 by Steffan Jones, he had faced 19 balls and struck 13 boundaries.

Brophy hit 3,012 runs in 73 first-class games for Yorkshire at a respectable 30.12, placing 15 half-centuries alongside his three centuries. As wicket-keeper he held 176 catches and pulled off 15 stumpings. In all first-class matches he scored 5,520 runs with eight centuries and 27 half-centuries, and had 301 catches and 22 stumpings.

In domestic List A matches for Yorkshire he made 1,240 runs, top score 93 not out, held 67 catches and had 14 stumpings. In Twenty20 he scored 717 runs, with 25 catches and seven stumpings.

Fast bowler Oliver Hannon-Dalby moved to Warwickshire in February, and a full tribute will appear in our Farewells section in 2014.

ANTHONY McGRATH

FIRST-CLASS CRICKET FOR YORKSHIRE 1995 TO 2012

Right-hand batsman. Right-arm bowler

Born: Bradford October 6, 1975

Debut: Yorkshire v. Glamorgan at Bradford May 18, 1995

Last played: Yorkshire v. Essex at Chelmsford September 14, 2012

Capped: July 20, 1999

BATTING AND FIELDING

Season	*M*	*I*	*NO*	*Runs*	*HS*	*Avge*	*100s*	*50s*	*Ct*
1995	5	10	0	280	84	28.00	0	1	3
1995/96	2	3	0	110	48	36.66	0	0	2
1996	18	31	2	962	137	33.17	2	5	10
1997	14	23	1	724	141	32.90	2	2	4
1998	17	28	3	612	63*	24.48	0	3	5
1999	16	30	2	831	142*	29.67	1	6	15
2000	10	14	1	375	133	28.84	1	1	8
2001	9	15	2	417	116*	32.07	1	2	6
2002	14	26	1	803	165	32.12	1	3	7
2003	10	18	3	649	127*	43.26	1	5	5
2004	9	16	0	728	174	45.50	3	1	6
2005	16	28	4	1425	173*	59.37	5	5	20
2006	15	24	3	1293	140*	61.57	4	9	18
2007	14	22	2	931	188*	46.55	3	6	11
2008	14	21	0	728	144	34.66	2	3	11
2009	17	27	1	871	211	33.50	2	2	11
2010	16	29	1	1219	124*	43.53	3	9	9
2011	12	23	0	485	115	21.08	1	1	12
2012	14	17	3	648	106*	46.28	2	3	5
	242	405	29	14091	211	37.47	34	67	168

BOWLING

Season	*Matches*	*Overs*	*Mdns*	*Runs*	*Wkts*	*Avge*	*Best*	*5wI*
1995/96	2	3	0	9	0	—	0-9	0
1996	18	7	0	41	0	—	0-41	0
1997	14	8.5	0	44	1	44.00	1-19	0
1998	17	42	10	159	3	53.00	2-33	0
1999	16	86	26	204	9	22.66	3-18	0
2001	9	17	4	53	3	17.66	2-22	0
2002	14	174.3	38	498	18	27.66	4-49	0
2003	10	117.1	20	347	13	26.69	3-26	0
2004	9	102	21	280	8	35.00	5-39	1
2005	16	231	36	727	16	45.43	3-35	0
2006	15	216	28	734	18	40.77	4-62	0
2007	14	76	16	223	5	44.60	2-12	0
2008	14	100.1	16	282	9	31.33	2-27	0
2009	17	109	26	280	5	56.00	2- 1	0
2010	16	74	13	226	0	—	0- 2	0
2011	12	21	2	56	1	56.00	1-14	0
2012	14	196.1	59	489	19	25.73	4-21	0
	242	1580.5	315	4652	128	36.34	5-39	1

Centuries (34)

101	v. Kent at Canterbury, 1996
137	v. Hampshire at Harrogate, 1996
105*	v. Oxford University at Oxford, 1997
141	v. Worcestershire at Leeds, 1997
142*	v. Middlesex at Leeds, 1999
133	v. Kent at Canterbury, 2000
116*	v. Surrey at The Oval, 2001
165	v. Lancashire at Leeds, 2002
127*	v. Glamorgan at Colwyn Bay, 2003
126	v. Durham at Chester-le-Street, 2004
174	v. Derbyshire at Derby, 2004
109	v. Derbyshire at Leeds, 2004
165*	v. Leicestershire at Leicester, 2005
133*	v. Durham at Chester-le-Street, 2005
134	v. Derbyshire at Leeds, 2005
173*	v. Worcestershire at Leeds, 2005
158	v. Derbyshire at Derby, 2005
123*	v. Kent at Canterbury, 2006
127	v. Hampshire at Leeds, 2006
140*	v. Durham at Chester-le-Street, 2006
102	v. Lancashire at Manchester, 2006
100	v. Kent at Tunbridge Wells, 2007
188*	v. Warwickshire at Birmingham, 2007
120	v. Kent at Scarborough, 2007
144	v. Kent at Canterbury, 2008
128	v. Somerset at Scarborough, 2008
120	v. Worcestershire at Leeds, 2009
211	v. Warwickshire at Birmingham, 2009
105	v. Durham at Leeds, 2010
112	v. Essex at Scarborough, 2010
124*	v. Durham at Chester-le-Street, 2010
115	v. Hampshire at Southampton, 2011
106*	v. Hampshire at Leeds, 2012
104	v. Derbyshire at Leeds, 2012

Five wickets in an innings (1)

5-39	v. Derbyshire at Derby, 2004

TEST MATCHES

Debut: England v. Zimbabwe at Lord's	May 22, 2003
Last played: England v. South Africa at Lord's	July 31, 2003

Season	*M*	*I*	*NO*	*Runs*	*HS*	*Avge*	*100s*	*50s*	*Ct*
2003	4	5	0	201	81	40.20	0	2	3

Season	*Matches*	*Overs*	*Mdns*	*Runs*	*Wkts*	*Avge*	*Best*	*5wI*
2003	4	17	1	56	4	14.00	3-16	0

ALL FIRST-CLASS MATCHES

BATTING AND FIELDING

M	*I*	*NO*	*Runs*	*HS*	*Avge*	*100s*	*50s*	*Ct*
257	429	30	14698	211	36.83	35	70	181

BOWLING

Matches	*Overs*	*Mdns*	*Runs*	*Wkts*	*Avge*	*Best*	*5wI*
257	1623.1	319	4779	134	35.66	5-39	1

DOMESTIC LIST A CRICKET FOR YORKSHIRE 1995-2012

Debut: Benson & Hedges Cup v. Worcestershire at Leeds — May 30, 1995
Last played: Clydesdale Bank 40 v. Unicorns at Scarborough — May 27, 2012

BATTING AND FIELDING

Season	*M*	*I*	*NO*	*Runs*	*HS*	*Avge*	*100s*	*50s*	*Ct*
1995	3	2	0	74	72	37.00	0	1	2
1996	26	24	4	441	69	22.05	0	1	6
1997	22	20	4	539	109*	33.68	1	2	7
1998	22	20	1	458	55*	24.10	0	4	7
1999	22	20	2	695	84	38.61	0	6	7
2000	11	10	4	288	85*	48.00	0	2	6
2001	15	15	0	554	102	36.93	1	2	5
2002	25	22	4	619	85*	34.38	0	4	6
2003	10	10	1	168	56	18.66	0	1	4
2004	15	14	4	406	96*	40.60	0	3	5
2005	22	22	1	647	74	30.80	0	4	6
2006	13	12	1	308	148	28.00	1	1	5
2007	15	13	3	567	135*	56.70	2	3	5
2008	17	15	3	489	105*	40.75	1	3	7
2009	14	14	3	298	67	27.09	0	2	5
2010	12	11	3	414	77*	51.75	0	4	7
2011	5	5	1	76	63	19.00	0	1	0
2012	3	1	0	26	26	26.00	0	0	0
	272	250	39	7067	148	33.49	6	44	90

BOWLING

Season	*Matches*	*Overs*	*Mdns*	*Runs*	*Wkts*	*Avge*	*Best*	*4wI*
1996	26	2	0	10	2	5.00	2-10	0
1998	22	18	1	82	4	20.50	2-20	0
1999	22	30	3	119	3	39.66	1-16	0
2000	11	4	0	23	0	—	0-23	0
2001	15	0.3	0	1	1	1.00	1-1	0
2002	25	74	3	355	9	39.44	3-39	0
2003	10	52	1	259	9	28.77	4-41	1
2004	15	69	1	396	13	30.46	4-56	1
2005	22	91.5	4	450	11	40.90	3-64	0
2006	13	36	0	213	5	42.60	2-22	0
2007	15	29	1	156	4	39.00	2-19	0
2008	17	31.4	0	164	10	16.40	3-16	0
2009	14	11	0	44	0	—	0- 8	0
2010	12	22.5	0	137	5	27.40	2-24	0
2011	5	7	0	40	0	—	0-10	0
2012	3	16	0	65	3	21.66	2-24	0
		494.5	14	2514	79	31.82	4-41	2

Centuries (6)

109* v. Minor Counties at Leeds, 1997
102 v. Kent at Canterbury, 2001
148 v. Somerset at Taunton, 2006
135* v. Lancashire at Manchester, 2007
100 v. Durham at Leeds, 2007
105* v. Scotland at Leeds, 2008

Four wickets in an innings (2)

4-41 v. Surrey at Leeds, 2003
4-56 v. Devon at Exmouth, 2004

Man of the Match awards: Three

ONE-DAY INTERNATIONALS

Debut: England v. Pakistan at Manchester — June 17, 2003
Last played: England v India at Lord's — September 5, 2004

Season	*M*	*I*	*NO*	*Runs*	*HS*	*Avge*	*100s*	*50s*	*Ct*
2003	10	9	2	143	52	20.42	0	1	4
2004	4	3	0	23	12	7.66	0	0	0
	14	12	2	166	52	28.08	0	1	4

BOWLING

Season	*Matches*	*Overs*	*Mdns*	*Runs*	*Wkts*	*Avge*	*Best*	*4wI*
2003	10	26	1	126	2	63.00	1-15	0
2004	4	12	1	49	2	24.50	1-13	0
	14	38	2	175	4	43.75	1-13	0

ALL LIST A MATCHES

BATTING AND FIELDING

Matches	*Innings*	*Not Out*	*Runs*	*Highest Score*	*Avge*	*100s*	*50s*	*Ct*
296	272	41	7574	148	32.78	7	45	97

BOWLING

Overs	*Maidens*	*Runs*	*Wickets*	*Average*	*Best*	*4wI*
538.5	16	2715	83	32.71	4-41	2

DOMESTIC TWENTY20 CRICKET FOR YORKSHIRE 2004-2011

Debut: v. Nottinghamshire at Nottingham — July 7, 2004
Last played: v. Nottinghamshire at Leeds — July 3, 2011

BATTING AND FIELDING

Season	*M*	*I*	*NO*	*Runs*	*HS*	*Avge*	*100s*	*50s*	*Ct*
2004	4	3	0	47	37	15.66	0	0	1
2005	8	8	1	107	33*	15.28	0	0	3
2006	9	9	2	230	58*	32.85	0	2	2
2007	8	8	2	152	55	25.33	0	1	2
2008	9	9	2	392	72*	56.00	0	4	4
2009	7	7	1	132	34	22.00	0	0	5
2010	12	10	4	251	73*	41.83	0	1	7
2011	9	7	0	92	28	13.14	0	0	2
	66	61	12	1403	73*	28.63	0	8	26

BOWLING

Season	*M*	*Overs*	*Mdns*	*Runs*	*Wkts*	*Avge*	*Best*
2004	4	7.5	0	98	1	98.00	1-46
2005	8	16	0	139	7	19.85	3-27
2006	9	11	0	77	2	38.50	2-18
2007	8	12	0	104	2	52.00	1-18
2008	9	9.2	0	76	3	25.33	1-14
2009	7	9	0	70	2	35.00	1-17
2010	12	10	0	92	3	30.66	2-19
2011	9	4	0	42	3	14.00	3-17
		79.1	0	698	23	30.34	3-17

Man of the Match awards: Six

AJMAL SHAHZAD

FIRST-CLASS CRICKET FOR YORKSHIRE 2006-2012

Right-hand Batsman. Right-arm fast-medium bowler
Born: Huddersfield July 27, 1985
Debut: Yorkshire v. Middlesex at Scarborough August 30, 2006
Last played: Yorkshire v Kent at Canterbury April 26, 2012
Capped: April 8, 2010

BATTING AND FIELDING

Season	*M*	*I*	*NO*	*Runs*	*HS*	*Avge*	*100s*	*50s*	*Ct*
2006	1	1	0	2	2	2.00	0	0	0
2007	6	7	3	65	32*	16.25	0	0	0
2008	1	1	0	35	35	35.00	0	0	0
2009	14	18	6	451	88	37.58	0	2	4
2010	9	12	3	238	45	26.44	0	0	1
2011	11	16	2	320	70	22.85	0	1	0
2012	3	3	0	34	25	11.33	0	0	0
	45	58	14	1145	88	26.02	0	3	5

BOWLING

Season	*Matches*	*Overs*	*Mdns*	*Runs*	*Wkts*	*Avge*	*Best*	*5wI*
2006	1	12	1	45	0	—	0-45	0
2007	6	92.4	12	343	9	38.11	4-22	0
2008	1	24	7	64	3	21.33	2-43	0
2009	14	422.5	86	1405	41	34.26	4-72	0
2010	9	292.2	47	1013	34	29.79	5-51	1
2011	11	301.3	46	1116	30	37.20	5-61	2
2012	3	68.1	14	210	8	26.25	3-86	0
	45	1213.3	213	4196	125	33.56	5-51	3

Fifties (3)

78 v. Hampshire at Basingstoke, 2009
88 v. Sussex at Hove, 2009
70 v. Worcestershire at Scarborough, 2011

Five wickets in an innings (3)

5-51 v. Durham at Chester-le-Street, 2010
5-61 v. Durham MCCU at Durham, 2011
5-65 v. Hampshire at Leeds, 2011

TEST MATCH

England v. Bangladesh at Manchester June 4, 2010

Season	*Matches*	*Runs*	*HS*	*Avge*	*100*	*50*	*Ct*	*Wkts*	*BBI*	*Avge*
2010	1	5	5	5.00	0	0	2	4	3-45	15.75

ALL FIRST-CLASS MATCHES (up to September 7, 2012)

BATTING AND FIELDING

Matches	*Innings*	*Not Out*	*Runs*	*Highest Score*	*Average*	*50s*	*Catches*
59	77	21	1323	88	23.62	3	9

BOWLING

Overs	*Maidens*	*Runs*	*Wickets*	*Average*	*Best*	*5wI*	*10wM*
1537	281	5273	155	34.01	5-51	3	0

DOMESTIC LIST A CRICKET FOR YORKSHIRE 2004-2011

Debut: totesport League v. Worcestershire at Leeds	May 23, 2004
Last played: Clydesdale Bank 40 v. Worcestershire at Leeds	August 29, 2011

BATTING AND FIELDING

Season	*M*	*I*	*NO*	*Runs*	*HS*	*Avge*	*100s*	*50s*	*Ct*
2004	1	1	0	5	5	5.00	0	0	0
2006	3	3	1	13	11*	6.50	0	0	0
2007	2	1	0	1	1	1.00	0	0	0
2008	2	1	0	33	33	33.00	0	0	0
2009	6	5	1	66	43*	16.50	0	0	2
2010	6	2	2	12	9*	—	0	0	1
2011	9	8	2	105	59*	17.50	0	1	4
	29	21	6	235	59*	15.66	0	1	7

BOWLING

Season	*Matches*	*Overs*	*Mdns*	*Runs*	*Wkts*	*Avge*	*Best*	*4wI*
2004	1	6	0	35	0	—	0-35	0
2006	3	23	4	101	5	20.20	3-30	0
2007	2	13	0	92	1	92.00	1-63	0
2008	2	16	0	55	1	55.00	1-30	0
2009	6	45	3	184	6	30.66	2-19	0
2010	6	48	0	277	6	46.16	4-34	1
2011	9	63.4	2	387	10	38.70	2-22	0
	29	214.4	9	1131	29	39.00	4-34	1

Fifties (1)

59* v. Kent at Leeds, 2011

Four wickets in an innings (1)

4-34 v. Middlesex at Lord's, 2010

ONE-DAY INTERNATIONALS

Debut: Bangladesh v. England at Chittagong	March 5, 2010
Last played: Bangladesh v. England at Chittagong	March 11, 2011

Season	*M*	*I*	*NO*	*Runs*	*HS*	*Avge*	*100s*	*50s*	*Ct*
2010/11	11	8	2	39	9	6.50	0	0	4

Season	*M*	*Overs*	*Mdns*	*Runs*	*Wkts*	*Avge*	*Best*	*4wI*
2010/11	11	98	5	490	17	28.82	3-41	0

ALL LIST A MATCHES (up to September 1, 2012)

BATTING AND FIELDING

Matches	*Innings*	*Not Out*	*Runs*	*Highest Score*	*Average*	*50s*	*Catches*
57	37	10	356	59*	13.18	1	14

BOWLING

Overs	*Maidens*	*Runs*	*Wickets*	*Average*	*Best*	*4wI*
435.3	19	2296	79	29.06	5-51	3

DOMESTIC TWENTY20 CRICKET FOR YORKSHIRE 2006-2011

Debut: v. Essex at Chelmsford — July 24, 2006
Last played: v. Durham at Chester-le-Street — July 8, 2011

BATTING AND FIELDING

Season	*M*	*I*	*NO*	*Runs*	*HS*	*Avge*	*100s*	*50s*	*Ct*
2006	1	1	1	2	2*	—	0	0	0
2009	9	7	1	33	17*	5.50	0	0	3
2010	3	1	0	12	12	12.00	0	0	2
2011	9	7	2	82	20	16.40	0	0	0
	22	16	4	129	20	10.75	0	0	5

BOWLING

Season	*M*	*Overs*	*Mdns*	*Runs*	*Wkts*	*Avge*	*Best*
2006	1	3	0	22	2	11.00	2-22
2009	9	30	0	219	4	54.75	1-18
2010	3	12	0	93	2	46.50	1-21
2011	9	29	0	242	9	26.88	3-30
	22	74	0	576	17	33.88	3-30

T20Is INTERNATIONALS

Debut: England v Pakistan at Dubai (DSC) — February, 2010
Last played: Australia v. South England at Melbourne — January, 2011

BATTING AND FIELDING

Season	*M*	*I*	*NO*	*Runs*	*HS*	*Avge*	*100s*	*50s*	*Ct*
2010-11	3	1	1	0	0*	—	0	0	1

BOWLING

Season	*M*	*Overs*	*Mdns*	*Runs*	*Wkts*	*Avge*	*Best*
2010-11	3	11	0	97	3	32.33	2-38

ALL TWENTY20 MATCHES (up to July 8, 2012)

Matches	*Innings*	*Not Out*	*Runs*	*Highest Score*	*Average*	*50s*	*Catches*
27	18	5	133	20	10.23	0	6

Overs	*Maidens*	*Runs*	*Wickets*	*Average*	*Best*
90	0	709	21	33.76	3-30

GERARD LOUIS BROPHY

FIRST-CLASS CRICKET FOR YORKSHIRE 2006-2012

Right hand batsman — Right-arm bowler — Wicket-keeper
Born: Welkom, Orange Free State, South Africa — November 26, 1975
Debut: Yorkshire v. Derbyshire at Leeds — April 23, 2006
Last played: v. Glamorgan at Colwyn Bay — June 6, 2012
Capped: May 31, 2008

BATTING AND FIELDING

Season	*M*	*I*	*NO*	*Runs*	*HS*	*Avge*	*100s*	*50s*	*Ct/St*
2006	10	16	0	251	87	15.68	0	1	26/3
2007	13	19	1	593	100*	32.94	1	2	35/3
2008	16	24	1	546	70	23.73	0	4	43/6
2009	14	22	5	748	99	44.00	0	6	37/2
2010	9	17	1	472	103	29.50	1	1	20/0
2011	7	11	3	355	177*	44.37	1	1	7/1
2012	4	3	1	47	23	23.50	0	0	8/0
	73	112	12	3012	177*	30.12	3	15	176/15

Centuries (3)

100 *	v. Hampshire at West End, Southampton, 2007
103	v. Warwickshire at Leeds, 2010
177*	v. Worcestershire at Worcester, 2011

5 catches in a match (6)

6	(2 + 4)	v.	Durham at Chester-le-Street, 2006
7	(4 + 3)	v.	Warwickshire at Scarborough, 2007
6	(5 + 1)	v.	Hampshire at West End, Southampton, 2007
5	(3 + 2)	v.	Somerset at Scarborough, 2008
6	(6 + 0)	v.	Durham at Chester-le-Street, 2009
5	(2 + 3)	v.	Nottinghamshire at Nottingham, 2010

5 dismissals in a match (5)

5	(4ct, 1st)	v.	Hampshire at Leeds, 2006
7	(6ct, 1st)	v.	Surrey at The Oval, 2007
6	(5ct,1st)	v.	Surrey at The Oval, 2008
6	(5ct,1st)	v.	Kent at Canterbury, 2008
6	(5ct,1st)	v.	Hampshire at Basingstoke, 2009

3 catches in an innings (21)

4 v. Hampshire at Leeds, 2006
4 v. .Durham at Chester-le-Street, 2006
3 v. Nottinghamshire at Nottingham, 2006
5 v. Hampshire at West End, Southampton, 2007
5 v. Kent at Scarborough, 2007
4 v. Surrey at Leeds, 2007
4 v. Warwickshire at Scarborough (1st innings) 2007
3 v. Durham at Leeds, 2007
3 v. Warwickshire at Scarborough (2nd innings) 2007
3 v. Nottinghamshire at Leeds, 2008
3 v. Durham at Chester-le-Street, 2008
3 v. Somerset at Taunton, 2008
3 v. Durham at Leeds, 2008
3 v. Nottinghamshire at Nottingham, 2008
3 v. Somerset at Scarborough, 2008
6 v. Durham at Chester-le-Street, 2009
3 v. Somerset at Leeds, 2009
3 v. Sussex at Hove, 2009
3 v. Nottinghamshire at Nottingham, 2010
3 v. Kent at Leeds, 2010
3 v. Warwickshire at Leeds, 2011

3 dismissals in an innings (6)

5	(4ct,1st)	v.	Surrey at The Oval, 2007
4	(3ct,1st)	v.	Surrey at The Oval, 2008
4	(3ct.1st)	v.	Kent at Canterbury, 2008
3	(1ct,2st)	v.	Hampshire at West End, Southampton, 2008
4	(3ct,1st)	v.	Hampshire at Basingstoke, 2009
4	(3ct,1st)	v.	Warwickshire at Leeds, 2011

ALL FIRST-CLASS MATCHES (up to June 6, 2012)

BATTING AND FIELDING

Matches	*Innings*	*Not Out*	*Runs*	*Highest Score*	*Average*	*100s*	*50s*	*Ct/St*
126	198	26	5520	185	32.09	8	27	301/22

BOWLING: 4 overs, 1 maiden, 7 runs, 0 wickets

DOMESTIC LIST A CRICKET FOR YORKSHIRE 2006-2012

Debut: Cheltenham & Gloucester Trophy v. Derbyshire at Leeds	April 23, 2006
Last played: Clydesdale Bank 40 v. Northamptonshire at Northampton	August 9, 2012

BATTING AND FIELDING

Season	*M*	*I*	*NO*	*Runs*	*HS*	*Avge*	*100s*	*50s*	*Ct/St*
2006	12	8	1	112	32	16.00	0	0	7/2
2007	11	10	1	297	66	33.00	0	2	8/3
2008	17	15	5	238	61*	23.80	0	2	24/2
2009	6	5	2	201	68*	67.00	0	2	12/1
2010	11	10	2	315	93*	39.37	0	3	8/3
2011	6	6	1	53	28	10.60	0	0	5/2
2012	5	3	0	24	19	8.00	0	0	3/1
	68	57	12	1240	93*	27.55	0	9	67/14

3 catches in an innings (7)

3 v. Glamorgan at Cardiff, 2007
3 v. Durham at Leeds, 2008
3 v. Gloucestershire at Bristol, 2008
4 v. Kent at Scarborough, 2008
3 v. Durham at Chester-le-Street, 2009
4 v. Sussex at Leeds, 2009
3 v. Gloucestershire at Leeds, 2009

3 dismissals in an innings (3)

4 (3ct, 1st) v. Durham at Leeds, 2008
5 (4ct, 1st) v. Sussex at Leeds, 2009
3 (2ct, 1st) v. Kent at Canterbury, 2011

ALL LIST A MATCHES (up to August 9, 2012)

BATTING AND FIELDING

Matches	*Innings*	*Not Out*	*Runs*	*Highest Score*	*Average*	*100s*	*50s*	*Ct/St*
123	101	20	2069	93*	25.54	0	13	118/25

DOMESTIC TWENTY20 CRICKET FOR YORKSHIRE 2006-2012

Debut: v. Derbyshire at Leeds — June 27, 2006
Last played: v. Derbyshire at Leeds — July 8, 2012

BATTING AND FIELDING

Season	*M*	*I*	*NO*	*Runs*	*HS*	*Avge*	*100s*	*50s*	*Ct/St*
2006	9	7	2	152	57	30.40	0	1	2/0
2007	8	8	2	151	44	25.16	0	0	3/0
2008	9	9	1	177	57*	22.12	0	1	6/3
2009	4	3	1	42	26	21.00	0	0	0/1
2010	12	9	1	97	31*	12.12	0	0	7/2
2011	7	6	0	45	22	7.50	0	0	3/0
2012	5	4	2	53	32	26.50	0	0	4/1
	54	46	9	717	57*	19.37	0	2	25/7

3 catches in an innings (1)

4 v. Durham at Chester-le-Street, 2008

3 dismissals in an innings (1)

5 (4ct, 1st) v. Durham at Chester-le-Street, 2008

ALL TWENTY20 MATCHES (up July 8, 2012)

BATTING AND FIELDING

Matches	*Innings*	*Not Out*	*Runs*	*Highest Score*	*Average*	*100s*	*50s*	*Ct/St*
60	51	11	776	57*	19.40	0	2	28/8

CAUTIOUS YORKSHIRE PLAY SECOND FIDDLE TO KENT

By Derek Hodgson

SCHOFIELD HAIGH: Deadly cocktail mixed for last time
(Photo: www.adelphiarchive.co.uk)

If Kent had reason to feel robbed in the previous two years they won full compensation in 1913 when their 20 victories from 28 matches left Yorkshire trailing second with 16.

Neville Cardus was to write later that the utilitarian cricket of the 1920s was a reflection of society but, in fact, Yorkshire were already being criticised for "sitting on the splice" in the last two summers of the Golden Age of cavalier cricket.

Roy Webber, in his *County Championship* (1958) pointed out that the amateurs, prolific before 1914, had little to lose, while the professionals — and Yorkshire fielded few amateurs — had a living to earn and were, inevitably, the more cautious. Nevertheless, suggestions that Yorkshire were a dour batting side seem hardly credible of a team containing Denton, Booth and Hirst. Benny Wilson and Edgar Oldroyd took most of the fire, causing captain White to spring to their defence: "They were apt to be a little too deliberate in their methods, but this almost always happened after we had made a bad start."

He added that it had been Lord Hawke's dictum that if Yorkshire could not win they should make every effort not to lose.

The weather was fine, and because King George V was visiting Merseyside three *Roses* matches were played in 1913 — Yorkshire paying a first visit to Aigburth. Hirst and Haigh missed most of July through injury, otherwise Kent's margin might have been reduced. Lancashire

RUNNERS-UP 1913. Back row, left ro right: George Bayes, Benny Wilson, Percy Holmes, Major Booth, Tommy Birtles, Alonzo Drake and James Hoyland (scorer). Front row: Arthur Dolphin, Schofield Haigh, David Denton, Sir AW White (captain), George Hirst, Wilfred Rhodes and Roy Kilner.

(Photo: www.adelphiarchive.co.uk)

won two of those three *Roses* matches, dismissing Yorkshire for 74 and 53 at Old Trafford and also winning at Liverpool. Yorkshire got into their stride after the opening defeat in Manchester, winning 10 matches and no doubt persuading most that they would keep the Championship. Two games were lost by margins of two runs and 20, and the weather intervened three times. Three players — Booth, Drake and Hirst — performed the double of 100 wickets and 1,000 runs, and Rhodes was 14 wickets short. Seven players passed 1,000 runs.

An invaluable recruit in August was Winchester schoolmaster Rockley Wilson, leg-spinner, batsman and raconteur. He had played in 1899, and held a dual qualification for Hampshire. If his recall was to forestall his leaving his style of attack brought another string to the captain's bow, and his batting was useful late-order reinforcement.

Wilson's arrival may have had some connection with Haigh's retirement after 18 years to become coach at Winchester. *Yorkshire Post* Correspondent Old Ebor called him "the sunshine of the Yorkshire Eleven", and Altham and Swanton in *History* (1926) said that Haigh for 10 seasons led the bowling averages in a team containing Hirst and Rhodes. His combinations of fierce finger-spin, flight, variations of length with a devastating yorker and arm ball were deadly on the uncovered surfaces. He would not have been as effective today, but his batting and fielding would have ensured his ranking as a prodigious cricketer.

YORKSHIRE'S FIRST-CLASS HIGHLIGHTS OF 1913

Wins by an innings (5)

Somerset (90 and 67) lost to Yorkshire (289) by an innings and 132 runs at Bath
Yorkshire (300) beat Leicestershire (95 and 97) by an innings and 108 runs at Leeds
Yorkshire (512-9 dec) beat Essex (115 and 349) by an innings and 48 runs at Bradford
Somerset (149 and 124) lost to Yorkshire (298) by an innings and 25 runs at Bradford
Yorkshire (409-9 dec) beat Surrey (177 and 213) by an innings and 19 runs at The Oval

Totals of 400 and over (4)

512 for 9 wkts dec	v. Essex at Bradford
471	v. Nottinghamshire at Nottingham
409 for 9 wkts dec	v. Surrey at The Oval
405	v. Leicestershire at Leicester

Opponents dismissed for under 100 (6)

97	Leicestershire at Leicester (2nd innings)
95	Leicestershire at Leicester (1st innings)
92	Lancashire at Liverpool *
90	Somerset at Bath (1st innings)
68	Worcestershire at Huddersfield
67	Somerset at Bath (2nd innings)

* Non Championship

Century Partnerships (18)

For the 1st wicket (5)

197	W Rhodes and B B Wilson	v. Gloucestershire at Bristol
180	W Rhodes and B B Wilson	v. Leicestershire at Leicester
131	W Rhodes and B B Wilson	v. Sussex at Sheffield
109	W Rhodes and B B Wilson	v. Surrey at The Oval
108	W Rhodes and B B Wilson	v. Essex at Leyton

For the 2nd wicket (1)

115	W Rhodes and S Haigh	v. Warwickshire at Birmingham

For the 3rd wicket (5)

130	D Denton and R Kilner	v. England XI at Harrogate
117	D Denton and A Drake	v. Nottinghamshire at Nottingham
108	S Haigh and B B Wilson	v. Lancashire at Leeds
106	W Rhodes and R Kilner	v. Middlesex at Sheffield
105	B B Wilson and D Denton	v. Nottinghamshire at Dewsbury

For the 4th wicket (2)

212	B B Wilson and G H Hirst	v. Sussex at Hastings
148	R Kilner and G H Hirst	v. Essex at Bradford

For the 5th wicket (3)

175	A Drake and R Kilner	v. Cambridge University at Cambridge
121	A Drake and M W Booth	v. Hampshire at Harrogate
112	D Denton and R Kilner	v. Nottinghamshire at Nottingham

For the 6th wicket (1)

184	R Kilner and M W Booth	v. Leicestershire at Leeds

For the 8th wicket (1)

126	M W Booth and E R Wilson	v. Essex at Bradford

Centuries (15)

W Rhodes (4)

152 v. Leicestershire at Leicester
110 v. Gloucestershire at Bristol
110 v. Northamptonshire at Northampton
102 v. Cambridge University at Cambridge

G H Hirst (3)

166 * v. Sussex at Hastings
112 * v. Surrey at The Oval
102 * v. Kent at Bradford

D Denton (2)

148 v. Nottinghamshire at Nottingham
114 v. England XI at Harrogate

B B Wilson (2)

108 v. Sussex at Hastings
104 v. Gloucestershire at Bristol

M W Booth (1)

107 * v. Middlesex at Lord's

A Drake (1)

108 v. Cambridge University at Cambridge

R Kilner (1)

104 v. Leicestershire at Leeds

E R Wilson (1)

104 * v. Essex at Bradford

5 wickets in an innings (31)

M W Booth (16)

8 for 86 v. Middlesex at Sheffield
7 for 64 v. Northamptonshire at Leeds
7 for 65 v. Leicestershire at Leicester
7 for 77 v. Lancashire at Leeds
6 for 39 v. Somerset at Bath
6 for 49 v MCC at Scarborough
6 for 84 v Warwickshire at Sheffield
6 for 99 v. Nottinghamshire at Nottingham
6 for 108 v. Kent at Bradford (1st innings)
5 for 55 v. Gloucestershire at Sheffield
5 for 68 v. Worcestershire at Huddersfield
5 for 72 v. Middlesex at Lord's
5 for 77 v Sussex at Sheffield
5 for 80 v. Somerset at Bradford
5 for 94 v. Essex at Leyton
5 for 103 v. Kent at Bradford (2nd innings)

A Drake (6)

8 for 59 v Gloucestershire at Sheffield
7 for 69 v. Essex at Bradford
6 for 45 v. England XI at Harrogate
5 for 60 v. Surrey at The Oval
5 for 69 v. Northamptonshire at Northampton
5 for 71 v. Hampshire at Harrogate

W Rhodes (4)

7 for 45 v. Northamptonshire at Leeds
7 for 98 v. Cambridge University at Cambridge
5 for 35 v. Lancashire at Liverpool (Non Championship)
5 for 42 v. Kent at Tunbridge Wells

5 wickets in an innings *(Continued)*

G H Hirst (3)

7 for 33 v. Leicestershire at Leeds
6 for 70 v. Gloucestershire at Bristol
5 for 67 v. Warwickshire at Sheffield

S Haigh (1)

5 for 42 v. Lancashire at Manchester

E R Wilson (1)

6 for 89 v. Warwickshire at Birmingham

10 wickets in a match (5)

M W Booth (3)

11 for 158 (4 for 81 and 7 for 77) v. Lancashire at Leeds
11 for 164 (3 for 78 and 8 for 86) v. Middlesex at Sheffield
11 for 211 (6 for108 and 5 for 103) v. Kent at Bradford

G H Hirst (1)

10 for 48 (7 for 33 and 3 for 15) v. Leicestershire at Leeds

W Rhodes (1)

10 for 112 (7 for 98 and 3 for 14) v. Cambridge University at Cambridge

The Double (all First-Class matches) (3)

A Drake

1,029 runs @ 23.93 115 wickets @ 16.80

M W Booth

1,070 runs @ 26.09 167 wickets @ 18.52

G H Hirst

1,431 runs @ 36.69 100 wickets @ 19.59

3 catches in an innings (7)

A Dolphin (5)

4 v. Sussex at Sheffield
4 v. Nottinghamshire at Nottingham
4 v. Surrey at Hull
3 v. Kent at Bradford
3 v. Middlesex at Lord's

A Drake (1)

3 v. Hampshire at Bournemouth

R Kilner (1)

3 v. Somerset at Bradford

3 dismissals in an innings (4)

A Dolphin (4)

4 (3ct, 1st) v. Middlesex at Lord's
3 (1ct, 2st) v. Surrey at Hull
3 (2ct, 1st) v. Cambridge University at Cambridge
3 (2ct, 1st) v. Lancashire at Liverpool (Non Championship)

5 dismissals in a match (4)

A Dolphin (4)

7 (5ct, 2st) v. Surrey at Hull
6 (6ct) v. Sussex at Sheffield
6 (5ct, 1st) v. Middlesex at Lord's
5 (4ct, 1st) v. Kent at Bradford

Debuts (2)

In first-class cricket: T J D Birtles and P Holmes

100 YEARS AGO

YORKSHIRE AVERAGES 1913

ALL FIRST-CLASS MATCHES

Played 32 Won 16 Lost 5 Drawn 11

County Championship: Played 28 Won 16 Lost 4 Drawn 8

BATTING AND FIELDING *(Qualification 10 completed innings)*

Player	*M.*	*I.*	*N.O.*	*Runs*	*H.S.*	*Avge*	*100s*	*50s*	*ct/st*
G H Hirst	30	48	9	1431	166*	36.69	3	9	30
R Kilner	30	50	4	1586	104	34.47	1	12	23
W Rhodes	32	56	4	1805	152	34.71	4	9	28
B B Wilson	32	56	1	1533	108	27.87	2	9	10
D Denton	29	49	2	1264	148	26.89	2	8	22
M W Booth	31	48	7	1070	107*	26.09	1	5	23
A Drake	31	51	8	1029	108	23.93	1	3	17
T J D Birtles	12	18	5	294	47	22.61	0	0	11
S Haigh	24	33	1	710	92	22.18	0	5	14
Sir A W White	25	33	5	411	42	14.67	0	0	16
P Holmes	8	16	3	170	36	13.07	0	0	4
H C Stanley	7	11	0	138	42	12.54	0	0	5
A Dolphin	32	40	16	291	29	12.12	0	0	63/15
Also batted									
E R Wilson	7	9	3	192	104*	32.00	1	0	2
J Tasker	8	10	1	131	35	14.55	0	0	3
G W Bayes	4	5	1	39	13	9.75	0	0	1
J T Newstead	2	4	0	31	14	7.75	0	0	1
E Oldroyd	6	7	0	48	29	6.85	0	0	2
W E Bates	2	2	0	8	7	4.00	0	0	1

BOWLING *(Qualification 10 wickets)*

Player	*Overs*	*Mdns*	*Runs*	*Wkts*	*Avge*	*Best*	*5wI*	*10wM*
A Drake	804	223	1932	115	16.80	8-59	6	0
M W Booth	1072.5	172	3094	167	18.52	8-86	16	3
G H Hirst	810.3	225	1959	100	19.59	7-33	3	1
E R Wilson	176.5	64	354	18	19.66	6-89	1	0
S Haigh	362.4	98	791	38	20.81	5-42	1	0
W Rhodes	704.4	199	1818	81	22.44	7-45	4	1
R Kilner	204.4	53	454	18	25.22	3- 8	0	0
Also bowled								
G Bayes	101	18	351	8	43.87	4-36	0	0
J T Newstead	61.4	15	158	3	52.66	1-25	0	0
B B Wilson	4.4	0	22	1	22.00	1-22	0	0
D Denton	6	0	22	0	—	0-1	0	0
E Oldroyd	6	0	29	0	—	0-7	0	0

CLOSE CALL LEADS TO CENTENARY SUCCESS

By Anthony Bradbury

When Vic Wilson retired at the end of the 1962 season, some questioned the appointment of Brian Close as captain.

As it happened two teams excelled throughout 1963: the West Indies, led by Frank Worrell, who easily won the Test series, and then Yorkshire, led by Close, who by September were the clear winners of the Championship.

Close was chosen for England, captained Yorkshire, scored 1,529 runs in 50 innings, took 43 wickets and many brilliant catches, and became a *Wisden Cricketer of the Year* with four players from the Caribbean. Bill Bowes wrote:

FRED TRUEMAN
Highest number of Test wickets ever taken
(Photo: Ron Deaton Archive)

Because he was senior professional with the Club, and the job was his by right, Yorkshire offered the captaincy to Brian Close — left-handed batsman and right-arm utility bowler — who hitherto had never quite accomplished what was expected of him. It was a trial appointment. Nobody quite knew how it would work out.

The result was astonishing. Almost overnight it seemed that Brian Close matured. He showed knowledge of his own team and the play of opponents which immediately stamped him as a thinker and tactician. His field placings were as intelligent and antagonistic as any seen in the county for 25 years, and if a fielder was required in a "suicide position"

GEOFFREY BOYCOTT: Topped Yorkshire averages in his first full season and established himself as an opening batsman

(Photo: www.adelphiarchive.co.uk)

the captain himself was first for the job. Determination and purpose came into his own cricket. He regained his place in the England team, and won national approval for the unflinching way he played the West Indies fast bowlers Hall and Griffith.

To his own great delight he saw Yorkshire, in their centenary year, to their 28th outright Championship success.

Thus the legend of Brian Close was born, and in the 150th anniversary year of the Club his enthusiasm for Yorkshire CCC remains as great as ever. Close was fortunate to have in 1963 a wonderful group of players. The greatest of that year was Fred Trueman, who reached that summer the highest number of Test wickets ever taken, adding 76 for Yorkshire in the Championship, and he topped the national bowling averages with 129 wickets at 15.15 apiece. Trueman was at the height of his powers and Tony Nicholson, Ray Illingworth, Don Wilson and Mel Ryan between them took a further 288 wickets at a combined average of under 20. No one doubted that with that quintet Yorkshire could and would win matches.

Yet only Trueman of the bowlers was selected for the Tests.

At the start of the season there were potential places for new batsmen. Not only had Vic Wilson retired, but Brian Bolus also left the side. Bolus went to Trent Bridge, where in scoring over 2,000 runs and gaining an England place as an opening batsman he may have highlighted an error by his former club — though he had had a poor season in 1962.

Philip Sharpe — who played three Tests for England in 1963 at an average of over 50 — remained a very important player, and Ken Taylor, Bryan Stott and Doug Padgett gave batting support to the multi-talented Close. While they were not total newcomers two other batsmen cemented places. They were John Hampshire with 995 runs and, strikingly, Geoffrey Boycott, who in his first full season topped the Yorkshire averages and was second in the national averages to M J K Smith.

Boycott scored 1,446 runs for Yorkshire at an average of 46. In his first game against Cambridge University he batted at No. 6 immediately before Fred Trueman, who outscored him, but by the end of the season Boycott was established as an opening batsman, making 165 not out in his last Championship innings against Leicestershire when the title had already been won. Sharpe had been the *Cricket Writers' Young Cricketer of the Year* in 1962. Boycott took that award in 1963.

With Close and Illingworth as the all-rounders, and with the splendidly reliable wicket-keeper Jimmy Binks playing in every Championship game and completing 300 consecutive appearances for his county Yorkshire were always going to be the team to beat.

Because of the one uncertain one-day competition tentatively introduced in 1963 all the counties played 28 Championship matches rather than the 32 that some, including Yorkshire, had played in 1962. In what was a very wet summer Yorkshire drew 11 matches, with no decision in another. They lost three, but won the remaining 13. It must be remembered that these were three-day games, with few run chases set up on the last day. Ten points were awarded for a win and two bonus points for first-innings lead in a match drawn or lost. With 144 points at the season's end Yorkshire finished 20 ahead of a resurgent Glamorgan, having pulled well ahead of Sussex, who in mid-summer led the table.

There were some notable triumphs, of which perhaps the most satisfying was the crushing of Lancashire at Sheffield, when Yorkshire won by an innings and 110 runs having declared on 384-6 with Stott scoring 143 and Boycott - his first century — 145. Yorkshire scored 261 on a difficult wicket at Edgbaston, and yet won by an innings and 171 runs: Warwickshire were bowled out for 35 and then 55. Trueman took 10 match wickets for 36 runs, and Ryan 7-42. It was 55 years earlier, in 1908, that Yorkshire had bowled out a side twice more cheaply — Northamptonshire for 42 runs. Just to show the unpredictably of cricket Yorkshire bowled out Middlesex at Headingley for 47 to take a first innings lead of 100, but still lost the game, although they had declared in their second innings to try to force a win.

In late August the *White Rose* won two consecutive games against Leicestershire, and in the four innings Raymond Illingworth took 16 wickets for 87 runs. There were hard-fought matches against Surrey, both drawn, and in one of them Hampshire, as an opener, scored an outstanding first century. Yorkshire became the only county side to defeat the West Indian tourists — choosing nine players who were or became Test players, and in doing so they showed an attitude not prevalent in modern selections for such games.

The new unsponsored knockout competition, with three days allowed for each round in case of rain, provided for each side to bat for 65 overs

Championship No. 28: Leicestershire captain Maurice Hallam, extreme right, toasts Yorkshire on clinching the title on August 30, 1963, at Grace Road. Left to right: Don Wilson, Brian Close and Geoffrey Boycott, with umpire Syd Buller, centre, sneaking into the picture. Buller played a first-class match for Yorkshire in 1930

(Photo: Ron Deaton Archive)

and bowlers allowed up to 15 overs apiece. There were no power plays, and all the normal rules for First Class cricket applied. Yorkshire played their opening match against Nottinghamshire at Middlesbrough before a crowd of 3,000, and Nottinghamshire took the whole of their 65 overs to make 159 — Bolus 100 not out.Yorkshire took 55 overs to win by four wickets. It was a sedate start, but the next match at Hove revealed the future: 15,000 supporters packed the ground to see Sussex score 292 to beat Yorkshire by 22 runs in a game that finished at 7.45pm. Ground admission was 3s. Sussex went on to win the final, and in an air of wonderment the *Wisden* writer wrote "of the whole scene resembling an Association Football Cup Final more than the game of cricket...and ...there is no doubt that provided the competition is conducted wisely it will attract great support in the future and benefit the game accordingly". Fifty years on there is still debate.

The end of the season saw the retirement of Bryan Stott and Bob Platt. Both had had sterling success in the Yorkshire side, and both had been

CAPTAIN'S AWAY: Brian Close and Freddie Trueman were playing for England v. the West Indies at Headingley when Yorkshire travelled to New Road, Worcester, so Raymond Illingworth took charge. Back row, left to right: Geoffrey Boycott, Brian Bainbridge, Mel Ryan, Richard Hutton, John Hampshire, Tony Nicholson and Tony Clarkson. Front row: Doug Padgett, Jimmy Binks, Illingworth, Bryan Stott and Don Wilson. ***(Photo: Ron Deaton Archive)***

instrumental in the Championship success of 1959 which preceded the great years of the 1960s. Stott in 187 matches scored 9,168 runs with 17 centuries at 31.61. Platt in his 96 matches took 282 wickets at 22.65. Though his batting average was only 7.23 Platt proudly recalls his highest score of 57 not out. Both have remained active supporters of Yorkshire and are entitled to the continued gratitude of all members.

Yorkshire gave county caps during the close season to Nicholson, Hampshire and Boycott, and looked forward to more of distinction from these three cricketers. A grand dinner was held in the Cutlers Hall, Sheffield, to mark the centenary of the Club, and a special appeal raised over £15,000 to build new offices and dressing rooms at Headingley.

Lancashire gave Yorkshire a clock. Where is it now? So a hugely satisfying season ended. There were no clouds of substance on the horizon.

Will the 150th anniversary season be just as successful?

YORKSHIRE'S FIRST-CLASS HIGHLIGHTS OF 1963

Win by an innings (6)

Yorkshire (261) defeated Warwickshire (35 and 55) by an innings and 171 runs at Birmingham

Leicestershire (124 and 102) lost to Yorkshire (337-5 dec) by an innings and 111 runs at Scarborough

$ 1 Lancashire (151 and 123) lost to Yorkshire (384-6 dec) by an innings and 110 runs at Sheffield

Yorkshire (332-7dec) defeated Glamorgan (88 and 178) by an innings and 66 runs at Cardiff

$ 3 Derbyshire (238 and 110) lost to Yorkshire (404-4 dec) by an innings and 56 runs at Chesterfield

$ 2 Somerset (202 and 111) lost to Yorkshire (352) by an innings and 39 runs at Harrogate

$ Consecutive matches

Wins by 10 wickets (2)

Glamorgan (185 and 95) lost to Yorkshire (218 and 63-0) by 10 wickets at Sheffield
Sussex (103 and 112) lost to Yorkshire (188 and 28-0) by 10 wickets at Bradford

Win by over 250 runs (1)

Yorkshire (250 and 221-5 dec) defeated Leicestershire (133 and 69) by 269 runs at Leicester

Totals of 400 and over (2)

411 for 8 wkts	v. MCC at Lord's
404 for 4 wkts dec	v. Derbyshire at Chesterfield

Opponents dismissed for under 100 (10)

35	Warwickshire at Birmingham (1st innings)
47	Middlesex at Leeds
55	Warwickshire at Birmingham (2nd innings)
55	Nottinghamshire at Bradford
69	Leicestershire at Leicester
80	Gloucestershire at Bradford
83	Essex at Clacton
85	Derbyshire at Leeds
88	Glamorgan at Cardiff
95	Glamorgan at Sheffield

Century Partnerships (13)

For the 1st wicket (3)

105	G Boycott and K Taylor	v Leicestershire at Leicester (1st innings)
105	G Boycott and K Taylor	v Leicestershire at Leicester (2nd innings)
103	D E V Padgett and J H Hampshire	v Somerset at Harrogate

For the 2nd wicket (3)

190	G Boycott and P J Sharpe	v Lancashire at Manchester
178	D E V Padgett and P J Sharpe	v Derbyshire at Chesterfield
100	J H Hampshire and J G Binks	v MCC at Lord's

For the 3rd wicket (2)

124	J G Binks and P J Sharpe	v MCC at Lord's
100	D E V Padgett and D B Close	v Kent at Hull

For the 4th wicket (3)

249	W B Stott and G Boycott	v Lancashire at Sheffield
116	W B Stott and G Boycott	v Glamorgan at Cardiff
101	D B Close and R A Hutton	v Nottinghamshire at Bradford

Century Partnerships *(Continued)*

For the 6th wicket (2)

166	D B Close and F S Truman	v Northamptonshire at Northampton
114	D B Close and F S Truman	v Cambridge University at Cambridge

Centuries (12)

G Boycott (3)

165* v Leicestershire at Scarborough
145 v. Lancashire at Sheffield
113 v Lancashire at Manchester

D E V Padgett (2)

142 v Derbyshire at Chesterfield
101 v Kent at Hull

P J Sharpe (2)

138* v. Derbyshire at Chesterfield
106 v Lancashire at Manchester

D B Close (1)

161 v Northamptonshire at Northampton

J H Hampshire (1)

120 v Surrey at Sheffield

R Illingworth (1)

107* v Warwickshire at Birmingham

W B Stott (1)

143 v Lancashire at Sheffield

F S Trueman (1)

104 v Northamptonshire at Northampton

5 wickets in an innings (22)

F S Trueman (6)

8 for 45 v Gloucestershire at Bradford
6 for 18 v Warwickshire at Birmingham
6 for 51 v Nottinghamshire at Nottingham
5 for 38 v West Indies at Middlesbrough (1st innings)
5 for 43 v West Indies at Middlesbrough (2nd innings)
5 for 50 v Lancashire at Manchester

D Wilson (6)

7 for 92 v MCC at Scarborough
6 for 22 v Sussex at Bradford
6 for 47 v Cambridge University at Cambridge
5 for 33 v Glamorgan at Cardiff
5 for 44 v Leicestershire at Leicester
5 for 57 v Lancashire at Sheffield

A G Nicholson (4)

6 for 36 v Derbyshire at Chesterfield
5 for 7 v Middlesex at Leeds
5 for 26 v Sussex at Bradford
5 for 43 v Middlesex at Lord's

R Illingworth (3)

6 for 13 v Leicestershire at Leicester
5 for 13 v Leicestershire at Scarborough
5 for 35 v Warwickshire at Scarborough

5 wickets in an innings *(Continued)*

D B Close (1)

6 for 55 v Glamorgan at Sheffield

J H Hampshire (1)

7 for 52 v Glamorgan at Cardiff

J S Waring (1)

5 for 49 v Worcestershire at Bradford

10 wickets in a match (4)

F S Trueman (3)

10 for 36 (4 for-18 and 6 for 18) v Warwickshire at Birmingham
10 for 65 (8 for 45 and 2 for 20) v Gloucestershire at Bradford
10 for 81 (5 for 38 and 5 for 43) v West Indies at Middlesbrough

D B Close (1)

10 for 74 (6 for 55 and 4 for 19) v Glamorgan at Sheffield

3 catches in an innings (13)

J G Binks (9)

4 v Northamptonshire at Northampton
4 v Lancashire at Sheffield
4 v Somerset at Harrogate (1st inning)
4 v Lancashire at Manchester
4 v Leicestershire at Scarborough
3 v Warwickshire at Birmingham
3 v Somerset at Harrogate (2nd innings)
3 v Worcestershire at Bradford
3 v MCC at Scarborough

P J Sharpe (2)

3 v Lancashire at Sheffield
3 v Derbyshire at Chesterfield

D B Close (1)

3 v Gloucestershire at Bradford

M Ryan (1)

3 v Glamorgan at Sheffield

3 dismissals in an innings (3)

J G Binks (3)

3 (2ct, 1st) v Northamptonshire at Northampton
3 (2ct, 1st) v Derbyshire at Leeds
3 (2ct, 1st) v Leicestershire at Scarborough

5 catches in a match (2)

J G Binks (2)

7 (4 + 3) v Somerset at Harrogate
6 (4 + 2) v Northamptonshire at Northampton

5 dismissals in a match (3)

J G Binks (3)

7 (6ct, 1st) v Northamptonshire at Northampton
7 (6ct, 1st) v Leicestershire at Scarborough
5 (3ct, 2st) v Derbyshire at Leeds

Debuts (2)
In first-class cricket: A Clarkson and J S Waring

Capped (3)
G Boycott, J H Hampshire and A G Nicholson October 2, 1963

50 YEARS AGO

YORKSHIRE AVERAGES 1963

ALL FIRST-CLASS MATCHES

Played 33 Won 14 Lost 4 Drawn 15

County Championship: Played 28 Won 13 Lost 3 Drawn 12

BATTING AND FIELDING *(Qualification 10 completed innings)*

Player	*M.*	*I.*	*N.O.*	*Runs*	*H.S.*	*Avge*	*100s*	*50s*	*ct/st*
G Boycott	28	43	7	1628	165*	45.22	3	11	12
D B Close	24	36	3	1145	161	34.69	1	7	24
P J Sharpe	26	41	5	994	138*	27.61	2	6	37
K Taylor	10	17	2	413	85	27.53	0	2	7
W B Stott	20	30	2	758	143	27.07	1	4	10
R Illingworth	20	27	5	592	107*	26.90	1	0	14
J H Hampshire	32	50	4	1236	120	26.86	1	6	20
D E V Padgett	26	39	2	879	142	23.75	2	2	19
F S Trueman	20	27	3	515	104	21.45	1	1	10
R A Hutton	11	15	0	254	49	16.93	0	0	10
J G Binks	33	42	8	529	88	15.55	0	1	80/8
D Wilson	32	42	8	513	51	15.08	0	1	15
A G Nicholson	22	21	10	123	24*	11.18	0	0	10
M Ryan	32	33	11	217	26*	9.86	0	0	12
Also batted									
J C Baldertsone	9	10	1	125	44*	13.88	0	0	2
A Clarkson	6	8	1	80	30	11.42	0	0	5
A B Bainbridge	1	2	0	22	12	11.00	0	0	0
J S Waring	5	4	1	20	17*	6.66	0	0	5
R K Platt	4	1	0	0	0	0.00	0	0	0
J P G Chadwick	1	1	1	14	14*	—	0	0	2
M C Fearnley	1	1	1	0	0*	—	0	0	0

BOWLING *(Qualification 10 wickets)*

Player	*Overs*	*Mdns*	*Runs*	*Wkts*	*Avge*	*Best*	*5wI*	*10wM*
F S Trueman	558.5	146	1201	91	13.19	8-45	6	3
J S Waring	72.3	20	196	13	15.07	5-49	1	0
A G Nicholson	552.1	167	1114	66	16.87	6-36	4	0
R Illingworth	437.5	165	917	49	18.71	6-13	3	0
D Wilson	826.4	305	1911	99	19.30	7-92	6	0
M Ryan	704.2	194	1547	63	24.55	4-13	0	0
D B Close	388.2	127	1038	42	24.71	6-55	1	1
Also bowled								
D E V Padgett	0.5	0	4	1	4.00	1-4	0	0
A Clarkson	38	17	92	5	18.40	2-14	0	0
J H Hampshire	27	2	132	7	18.85	7-52	1	0
K Taylor	120	44	194	8	24.25	3-33	0	0
J P G Chadwick	21	6	58	2	29.00	2-58	0	0
R A Hutton	90.1	17	264	9	29.33	3-26	0	0
M C Fearnley	20	6	37	1	37.00	1-37	0	0
J C Balderstone	42.4	8	123	3	41.00	3-33	0	0
A B Bainbridge	31	13	70	1	70.00	1-70	0	0
R K Platt	44	15	108	1	108.00	1-37	0	0
P J Sharpe	5	1	17	0	—	0-17	0	0
G Boycott	2	0	20	0	—	0-20	0	0

50 YEARS AGO

YORKSHIRE AVERAGES 1963

LIST A KNOCKOUT COMPETITION

Played 2 Won 1 Lost 1

BATTING AND FIELDING

Player	*M.*	*I.*	*N.O.*	*Runs*	*H.S.*	*Avge*	*100s*	*50s*	*ct/st*
G Boycott	1	1	0	71	71	71.00	0	1	0
D B Close	2	2	1	58	29*	58.00	0	0	0
J C Balderstone	1	1	0	34	34	34.00	0	0	0
J H Hampshire	2	2	0	51	26	25.50	0	0	1
D E V Padgett	2	2	0	50	38	25.00	0	0	1
J G Binks	2	1	0	20	20	20.00	0	0	0/1
P J Sharpe	2	2	0	39	29	19.50	0	0	1
F S Trueman	2	2	0	39	21	19.50	0	0	1
W B Stott	2	2	0	30	30	15.00	0	0	0
K Taylor	1	1	0	4	4	4.00	0	0	1
A G Nicholson	1	1	0	3	3	3.00	0	0	0
R Illingworth	1	1	1	11	11*	—	0	0	1
M Ryan	2	1	1	6	6*	—	0	0	3
D Wilson	1	0	0	0	—	—	0	0	1

BOWLING

Player	*Overs*	*Mdns*	*Runs*	*Wkts*	*Avge*	*Best*	*4wI*	*RPO*
J C Balderstone	3	1	10	1	10.00	1-10	0	3.33
K Taylor	14	3	32	2	16.00	2-32	0	2.28
D B Close	30	3	102	6	17.00	4-60	1	3.40
F S Trueman	29	3	70	4	17.50	4-38	1	2.41
A G Nicholson	15	0	84	3	28.00	3-84	0	5.60
M Ryan	30	1	117	3	39.00	2-31	0	3.90
D Wilson	3	0	18	0	—	0-18	0	6.00
R Illingworth	2	0	3	0	—	0-3	0	1.50
J H Hampshire	2	0	4	0	—	0-4	0	2.00

1963 was the first year in which the first-class counties played one-day (List A) matches

THE NOBLE PATRONS OF YORKSHIRE CCC

By Anthony Bradbury

Lord Hawke had a great affection for the British nobility. During the 55 years in which he was Captain or President of Yorkshire County Cricket Club he became the friend or acquaintance of many peers of the realm. His autobiography, *Recollections and Reminiscences*, was published in 1924. Within its pages he wrote of those he had known. They included three monarchs, two future monarchs, five dukes, 39 other marquesses, earls, viscounts or barons, 31 baronets and knights, 11 honourables, with a variety of admirals and generals, a future Lord Chancellor, the President of South Africa, the Maharajah of Gwalior and the Jam Sahib of Nawanagar. Within that number were a select few who became patrons of Yorkshire County Cricket Club.

The Yorkshire Patrons are shown in every Yearbook as officers of the Club. They have included two specified patronesses, though the word "patron" does cover either sex. There has been nothing in the many variations of the Rules of the Club to provide for their nomination, selection or election. Their appointments were rarely formally noted in Committee minutes or at annual meetings of the Club, and they are never referred to in annual reports. The probability is that for over 80 per cent of the chosen few Lord Hawke was both nominator and electorate, and that the secretaries of the Club, of whom there were only three during Hawke's long years of dominance, accepted such appointments without demur. A similar practice may have followed with succeeding Presidents, though three of the last four Patrons did have their nomination considered by the Committee or Board. Up to 1971 the President chaired the General Committee, for there was until 1971 no Chairman of the Club. The President only thus lost executive powers in the 1970s, save when the same person then became both President and Chairman!

The 33 probable Patrons of Yorkshire County Cricket Club come from remarkably few families. Many of them have been related by marriage to other Patrons. The Zetland, Scarbrough, Grimthorpe and Savile peerages are all connected by past marriages, as was Lord Wenlock to the Earls of Harewood. A past family name of the Earls of Mexborough was also Savile. In some instances the son of a deceased Patron may have become Patron on hereditary principles rather than by appoint-

PATRONESS MEETS LEGEND: The Duchess of Kent with the late Fred Trueman. ***(Photo: Yorkshire Post)***

ment. Most of the dates and names of Patrons in this article arise from the simple fact of being so named in the annual *Yearbook* — which entries, however, do not specifically distinguish between past and present peers bearing the same name. Some entries may have arisen because the Editor had not detected the death of a previous title-holder.

The two earliest Patrons were the 15th Duke of Norfolk and the 1st Earl of Londesborough, in post before the first *Yearbook* of 1893 was published. Both were eminent within Yorkshire. The 15th Duke owned large estates in Sheffield, and his father had owned the land upon which Bramall Lane cricket ground was built. The 15th Duke, when he succeeded to his title in 1860, allowed his agent, Michael Ellison, the time and space to create the Yorkshire County Cricket Club, which in time became the most powerful county club in England. Ellison as President of Yorkshire from 1864 to 1897 would have been very glad to have his employer, the Duke, as Patron. The 15th Duke became the first Lord Mayor of Sheffield, and later Postmaster General. His son, Bernard Marmaduke, the 16th Duke, was President of MCC in 1957, and managed an MCC tour of Australia.

The 1st Earl of Londesborough was owner of 50,000 acres in and around Selby. He was a great breeder of cattle, and in his youth was an MP for Beverley and then Scarborough. He was active with the 2nd

Volunteer Battalion of the East Yorkshire Regiment, and his great affection for cricket led to him becoming President of Yorkshire United County Cricket Club from 1874 to 1877, and then a leading light in the formation of Scarborough Cricket Festival, into which he poured years of endeavour. He was President of MCC in 1876. Following his death in 1900 his son, the 2nd Earl of Londesborough, became a Yorkshire Patron. He, too, was an enthusiastic supporter of the Scarborough Festival, but he had much to manage elsewhere with his main home in Lincolnshire, two great houses in Yorkshire, one in Surrey and one in London's Mayfair. When he died in 1917 the Londesborough connection with Yorkshire cricket ceased, and in 1937 the Earldom became extinct. Today, Baron Londesborough lives in a Welsh cottage.

The other exceptionally well known Yorkshire families who each twice had a Yorkshire Patron among their numbers were the Scarbroughs and the Zetlands. The 10th Earl of Scarbrough — the spelling has sometimes been incorrect in the *Yearbook* — became the third Patron in 1894. His cricketing interest may have been limited, but he was Lord Lieutenant of West Yorkshire for over 20 years and Director-General of Britain's territorial forces in the First World War, holding the rank of Major-General. He was a man of distinction and influence, and after he died in 1939 — in the era when Sir Stanley Jackson held sway as President — his son, the 11th Earl, became a Patron. The 11th Earl had an astonishing public career, being an MP for East Hull and then York, Governor of Bombay, an acting Major-General, Under Secretary of State for India and Burma, Lord Lieutenant of the West Riding, High Steward of York Minster, Lord Chamberlain, and Chancellor of Durham University. He did fulfil some duties as a Yorkshire Patron at the Yorkshire v. Lancashire centenary dinner in 1949 and the centenary dinner of cricket at Bramall Lane in 1955.

The 10th Earl of Scarbrough had a brother-in-law, the 1st Marquess of Zetland, so it was perhaps natural that the 1st Marquess became a Patron in 1901. The Zetland family have always been active in North Yorkshire, and it was typical of the man that, having been Lord Lieutenant (Viceroy) of Ireland from 1889 to 1892, the Marquess chose to become an Alderman of the North Riding and Mayor of Richmond in 1895-96. The 1st Marquess died in 1929, but the name Marquess of Zetland appeared in the *Yearbook* until 1939, and those entries must relate to the 2nd Marquess. The present Marquess and his son, the Earl of Ronaldshay, actually have no knowledge that their predecessors were patrons, but the 2nd Marquess of Zetland was Secretary of State for India between1935 and 1940, and wrote biographies of Lords Curzon and Cromer. He was Lord Lieutenant of the North Riding from 1945 to 1951. The *Yearbook* was not published during the Second World War, and by 1946 the Marquess was no longer listed as a Patron, one of the few examples of apparent resignation from the position.

Patrons in the Club's 150th-anniversary year: Patricia, Countess of Harewood and the Earl of Mexborough

The Edwardian years were busy for the appointment of Patrons, especially in 1901, when in addition to the 1st Marquess of Zetland, the Earl of Dartmouth, the Earl of Mexborough and the Earl of Wharncliffe were announced in the *Yearbook* as patrons. William Heneage Legge, 6th Earl of Dartmouth, was a keen and good cricketer, and he is one of two Patrons to have played first-class cricket. Legge appeared for MCC v. Hampshire in 1877. Most of his landed estates were in the Midlands, and he was Lord Lieutenant of Staffordshire for 36 years. There was, too, an Earl of Dartmouth Estate at Morley in Yorkshire, where Dartmouth Park remains today. The Earl was President of MCC in 1893, and would have known Lord Hawke through Etonian and MCC connections. He seemingly resigned his patronage of Yorkshire in 1915.

The 5th Earl of Mexborough started his family connection of successive Patrons of Yorkshire in 1901, the year Queen Victoria died. The Mexboroughs, a notable Yorkshire family who lived at Methley Park, Leeds, and for three generations since at Arden Hall, North Yorkshire, have been enthusiastic and loyal members of the Yorkshire Club. The 5th Earl, like others since, had been a life member. He died in 1916, and his son, the 6th Earl, was appointed a Patron in 1926. The 7th Earl followed him and made his son, the 8th Earl of Mexborough, a life member as a 21st birthday present in 1951. The 7th Earl collected the autographs of all of the 1927 Yorkshire team in a lovely album recently given to the Club by the 8th Earl, who recalls walking out with the Yorkshire team between Hutton and Leyland in 1945 or 1946 at Headingley! The 8th Earl has been a Patron for more than 30 years, becoming one when his father died in 1980. The Mexboroughs have achieved their own century as Patrons, and the Club can be very grateful to them.

The 2nd Earl of Wharncliffe, like some other Patrons, was at Eton with Lord Hawke. He lived at Wortley Hall, near Barnsley, a Hall now used by the Trade Union movement as a training college, and he was a life member of Yorkshire CCC, which cost him 20 guineas 120 years ago. He died in 1926 and his son, the 3rd Earl, immediately took his father's place, remaining a Patron until his death in 1953. He, like the Earl of Scarbrough, was at the Yorkshire v. Lancashire centenary dinner of 1949. After the death of the 3rd Earl the Wharncliffe title moved to kinsmen, and the present Earl, a builder, lives in Maine, USA. There remains a Wharncliffe Estate at Wortley, Sheffield.

The Barons Hotham soon joined the growing list of Patrons. The 5th Baron, who was 64 when he became a Patron, had served in the Crimean War and been a member of Yorkshire CCC. He lived at Dalton Hall, Beverley, and was the owner of 15,000 acres of prime land. He died in 1907 but a cousin, the 6th Baron Hotham, had to wait until 1916 until his name appeared as a Patron in the *Yearbook*. His cousin, the 7th Baron, was a Patron from 1924 until his death in 1967. His son, the 8th Baron, in correspondence with the writer, said: "I have to confess that I was unaware that my father had been a Patron of the Yorkshire CCC, though three generations of us have been Presidents of the Great Yorkshire Show — which has gone from strength to strength. I hope that Yorkshire cricket will follow in their footsteps, and I do remember my father taking me to see Len Hutton play in Beverley at Hodgson's recreation ground." References to Len Hutton are a remarkable feature from recollections of current peers.

The first mention within the Yorkshire minute books of the 20th Century of the appointment of Patrons came on January 31,1911, when three nominees were approved. They were Baron Faber, Baron Wenlock and Earl Fitzwilliam. The Lord Faber — the only holder of that title — had been fagmaster to Lord Randolph Churchill at Eton, and was the first Patron to have made money through business. He was prominent in public life in Leeds, becoming senior partner of Beckett and Co, bankers, and a director of the LNWR with a steam locomotive named after him. He was chairman of the *Yorkshire Post*, and chairman of Harrogate Cricket Club. It was he who suggested in 1907 the subscription list for Lord Hawke to mark Hawke's 25 years as captain.

The 3rd Lord Wenlock's name appears only once in a *Yearbook*, for having been appointed in January 1911 he died in January 1912. Another Etonian, his enthusiasm for cricket was considerable, and he became President of MCC at the age of 36. No younger President was ever appointed, save for the Duke of Edinburgh in 1949. Wenlock's family home was at Escrick Park, south of York, and the lovely cricket ground

Patrons ancient and modern. Left to right: 15th Duke of Norfolk, 6th Baron Wenlock and 3rd Baron Savile

there is the one where the Yorkshire Gentlemen still play their matches.

The 7th Earl Fitzwilliam, who married a daughter of the Marquess of Zetland, had been MP for Wakefield before succeeding to his peerage in 1902. He was interested in mining engineering, and lived until 1943. If he had lived a few years longer he would have been horrified by the opencast mining on the compulsorily purchased land in front of his grand home at Wentworth Woodhouse authorised after the Second World War by the mining minister Emanuel Shinwell. When the Earl died the Fitzwilliam Patronage of Yorkshire ended until the 9th Earl Fitzwilliam, a distant relative of the 7th Earl and an MCC member, became a Patron from 1950 until his death in 1952.

To return to the Edwardian era, the next appointment after Faber, Wenlock and Fitzwilliam was Viscount Helmsley, MP for Thirsk and Malton, and Master of the Sinnington Hounds. He became a Patron in 1914, and succeeded his grandfather to become Lieutenant Colonel the 2nd Earl of Feversham in 1915. He commanded the Yorkshire Hussars at the start of the First World War, and he was commanding the 21st Battalion (Yeoman Rifles), Kings Royal Rifle Corps, when he was killed on the Somme in 1916 at the Battle of Flars. Sadly, the Yorkshire minutes make no mention of the death of one of their Patrons, though *Wisden* 1917 put Feversham's name in their Roll of Honour.

Wartime did not prevent the appointment of the 2nd Baron Derwent as Patron in 1916. Again an Etonian, he had been a Captain in the Life Guards, and as a landowner with 12,800 acres lived at Hackness Hall, Scarborough. His ancestor had been first President of the reconstituted Scarborough Cricket Club in 1863. Lord Derwent died in 1929 yet the *Yorkshire Yearbook* continued to show "The Lord Derwent" as a Patron until the 1932 issue. It is very unlikely that the 3rd Baron, a nephew of the 2nd Baron, was a Patron. He was a diplomat. and in 1930 was an attaché in Berne. He died in 1949. The present Lord Derwent doubted if his uncle, the 3rd Baron, had an interest in cricket as his interests lay more in artistic and literary fields.

The great industrialist Viscount Furness became a Patron in 1918. His father had created Furness, Withy and Co, ship owners, and the Viscount expanded the business into steel manufacturing and colliery ownership. One of the Viscount's three wives was Thelma Furness, a mistress of the Prince of Wales, later King Edward VIII. Furness lived and died at Grantley Hall, near Ripon. In 1940, when he died, the *Yearbook* was not being published, but after the war the name of Viscount Furness as a Patron continued up to 1949. This must have been a mistake. The 2nd Viscount was only 11 when his father died and, indeed, lived in America until his coming of age in 1950.

Twelve men had been appointed Patron between 1900 and 1920, but there was now a brief pause until April 1922, when the minutes record a resolution "to invite HRH Princess Mary and Viscount Lascelles to become Patroness and Patron of the Club, and also to receive Life Membership." HRH Princess Mary, later the Princess Royal and the only daughter of King George V, remained Patroness until her death in 1965. She married Viscount Lascelles, later the 6th Earl of Harewood, in 1922: he had won a DSO and Bar in the First World War, and became Lord Lieutenant of the West Riding from 1922 to 1947. He died in 1947, being succeeded by his son, the 7th Earl, who was a Yorkshire Patron from 1948 to 2011. The Harewood estates have no extant records relating to the Patronage of Yorkshire by these three members of the family.

The last of the inter-war Patrons to be chosen was the 3rd Baron Grimthorpe (1928-1963). He had been in the Yorkshire Hussars in the First World War, and later became a banking partner in Beckett and Co, the firm of which an earlier Patron, Lord Faber, had been a partner. Unlike nearly all other Patrons, Lord Grimthorpe became active in a practical way in Yorkshire CCC affairs. He became a Committee member for North Riding in 1953, and was active on the Finance Committee. He also became a President of Scarborough Cricket Club.

With the appointment of Lord Grimthorpe the heyday of Patrons coming from these major Yorkshire families was over. At one time the Secretary of the Club had sought to list them in the *Yearbook* in order of precedence, with a marquess first, followed by earls, viscounts and barons. All, though, were surmounted by the Royal Patroness. When after the Second World War Sir Stanley Jackson was President the numbers of Patrons started to diminish as death took its toll. Only a few further Patrons have been appointed in the last 65 years. The first of these was the 16th Viscount Mountgarret of Nidd Hall, Harrogate, who was trained as a Naval officer and owned 14,700 acres. Peers liked to put their ownership of land in *Who's Who*, and Lord Mountgarret was no exception. It was his son, the 17th Viscount, who became President of Yorkshire in turbulent times in the 1980s and received the support of many members.

Then, in the *Yearbook* of 1952 is noted the name of the 3rd Baron Savile a keen member of the Burma Star Association, whose seat and estate was at Gryce Hall, Shelley, near Huddersfield. He, like so many predecessors, was an Etonian, and he was a distant relative of the Scarbrough family. He was a Patron for over 50 years until his death in 2008.

The next male Patron, appointed in 1961, was the only one not to have inherited or been created into the peerage. He was Lieutenant Colonel R T Stanyforth CVO MC.

Churchill Link: Baron Faber as depicted in *Vanity Fair*

The Princess Royal died in 1965, leaving Yorkshire without a Royal Patroness, but Sir William Worsley's daughter, Katherine, had married the present Duke of Kent in 1961. With Worsley still President, the Duchess became an obvious choice for Patroness, and her acceptance was warmly received in 1966. She often attended the Kent v. Yorkshire games at Canterbury on Ladies' Day, and she was guest of honour at a Yorkshire dinner hosted by Lord Mountgarret in 1986.

Yorkshire created a new honour in the post-war years — that of Honorary Life Member. Many of the great Yorkshire and England players of the last 60 years, together with some others of merit, have been appointed to that position. Though different to the role of a Patron, and not directly concerned with status, influence, power or wealth, the Honorary Life Members have taken on some of the prestige of patronage. The President, once an executive position, has become an honorary one, and the Club has a new style of management. But the position of Patron remains, and the Board of Yorkshire CCC has recently reaffirmed that patronage by significant Yorkshire-connected persons remains of great value, since it sets the tone of the Club as an important Yorkshire institution. Following the death of the Earl of Harewood in 2011, the Board have been pleased to appoint the Earl's widow, Patricia, Countess of Harewood, and David Lascelles, the present Earl, as Patrons.

PATRONS and PATRONESSES OF YORKSHIRE with their titles upon appointment

1863-1913

15th Duke of Norfolk	1st Earl of Londesborough
10th Earl of Scarbrough	1st Marquess of Zetland
2nd Earl of Londesbrough	6th Earl of Dartmouth
5th Earl of Mexborough	2nd Earl of Wharncliffe
5th Baron Hotham	7th Earl Fitzwilliam
1st Baron Faber	3rd Baron Wenlock

1914-1963

Viscount Helmsley	3rd Baron Derwent
6th Baron Hotham	1st Viscount Furness
Viscount Lascelles	HRH Princess Mary, Viscountess Lascelles
7th Baron Hotham	6th Earl of Mexborough
3rd Earl of Wharncliffe	3rd Baron Grimthorpe
2nd Marquess of Zetland	11th Earl of Scarbrough
7th Earl of Mexborough	16th Viscount Mountgarret
7th Earl of Harewood	9th Earl Fitzwilliam
3rd Baron Saville	Lt Col RT Stanyforth

1964-2013

HRH the Duchess of Kent	8th Earl of Mexborough
Patricia, Countess of Harewood	
David Lascelles, the Earl of Harewood	

The writer is grateful for help received from Ian Goddard, the Earl of Mexborough, the late Michael Crawford, Sir Lawrence Byford, Robin Smith, West Yorkshire Archives, Martin Howe, David Hall and David Allan, together with the descendants and archivists of past patrons of Yorkshire CCC.

Yorkshire CCC's 150th anniversary

To mark this special birthday celebration we asked three *Yorkshire Yearbook* writers to each cover one of the 50-year periods in the Club's history and write about a favourite player from that era. Here are their choices:

FIRST EPOCH — 'NED' STEPHENSON

SAD LIFE OF 'KEEPER WHO SO OFTEN LED THE FIELD

By Mick Pope

G Anderson, G R Atkinson, J Berry, E Dawson, I Hodgson, R Iddison, J Rowbotham, W Slinn, E Stephenson, J Thewlis and Mr B W Waud — the names of the cricketers who made up the newly formed Yorkshire County Cricket Club's First Eleven for the inaugural "official" match against Surrey at the Kennington Oval on Thursday, June 4, 1863.

Yorkshire's ultimately rain-ruined maiden fixture got under way at 12.15pm in fine weather with a "large attendance" in the London ground despite the counter-attraction of Ascot Races. Surrey won the toss, batted and by close of play on that historic day had made 315. Thewlis and John Berry took the visitors to 12-0, and Yorkshire CCC had become an on-field reality.

The largely truncated game, badly affected through heavy rain, cold weather, and even lightning and thunder, was not particularly memorable, except for the performance of Edward Stephenson. To him fell the honour on the third morning of making Yorkshire's first half-century: 39 not out overnight on June 5 — Stephenson's 31st birthday — he extended his "finely played innings" to 67, a knock which included two fours and a six — a hit to square-leg out of the ground. He followed that with three fine stumpings and a catch when Surrey batted again.

"It was the great wicket-keeping of Edward Stephenson that was the feature of this day's play," wrote one Yorkshire newspaper reporter. In the tough years that lay ahead for 'Ned' Stephenson not many days would match that one at The Oval in June 1863.

Edwin Stephenson, although known as Edward, was born in Sheffield in June 1832, the son of George and Sarah. He was 17 when first engaged as a cricketer at Broomhead Hall, where he developed his all-round skills from 1849 to 1851. As a batsman he had a solid defence, aided by a long forward reach and, although not keen to give his wicket away, when he chose he could play in a more aggressive and forceful manner. He also bowled fast round-arm, but it was his skill as a wicket-keeper that won him lasting fame and brought him professional earnings. His grounding at Broomhead led to professional spells at Whitehaven in 1852, the following year Edge Hill, Liverpool, then St Helens, and in the mid-1850s Warminster, Wiltshire. Then for two seasons he acted as bowling professional to the MCC at Lord's.

His first-class debut was in July 1854 at Manchester for the Sheffield team. Opening the batting, he made 25, and his side won by an innings and 45 runs. He played for both the All England and United All England XIs in 1856. Batting for the North against Surrey in 1857, he made 49, but a year later in the same fixture at Kennington Oval he registered what would remain his highest first-class score of 76.

As well as serving the North over many years as a wicket-keeper/batsman he was Yorkshire's regular stumper from 1861 until the arrival of George Pinder. He scored the county's first 50 in 1863, and four years later made 54 in the first *Roses* match. Notable among Stephenson's list of firsts was being awarded a benefit match by Yorkshire: United North of England v. United South, was played at his "home" ground of Bramall Lane, Sheffield, in August 1870.

He did not play in the fixture, which lasted for only two days and yielded a relatively modest return. He played his final first-class match at the same venue in 1873, when alongside his old Sheffield colleague, Joe Rowbotham, he ended on the winning side as Yorkshire beat their Pennine rivals, Lancashire, by 64 runs. He scored 803 runs at 14.33 in his 36 matches for Yorkshire between 1861 and 1873, and claimed 30 catches and 27 stumpings.

Beyond question, Stephenson's greatest venture took place during the winter of 1861-62 as one of the pioneering 12 English professionals who journeyed to Australia on the SS Great Britain. He and fellow Yorkshireman Roger Iddison were the only players from outside of the South of England. Led by Surrey's HH Stephenson, known as "Surrey" Stephenson to distinguish him from his fellow wicket-keeper, they arrived on Christmas Eve 1861 to a huge welcome. They started their first match on New Year's Day 1862 at Melbourne Cricket Ground, and after Eighteen of Victoria had been bowled out for 118 Ned Stephenson and George Bennett walked out to open for the English XI: Bennett took strike, and played out a maiden before Stephenson, with a single off Cosstick's fast round-arm, scored England's first-ever run off Australian bowling — another historic first for the Sheffield player.

When the team left Australia behind after 93 days there in late March 1862 for the long voyage home they had played 15 matches in the major

First run: The English XI in Australia 1861-62. 'Ned' Stephenson is on the extreme left, next to Yorkshire's Roger Iddison. It fell to Yorkshire's stumper to score the first run off Australian bowling on that historic trip
(Photo: www.adelphiarchive.co.uk)

centres of Melbourne, Sydney and Hobart and other bush towns, and had laid the foundation stone for what would become Test cricket.

Stephenson played in 13 of the 15 matches, scoring 203 runs at 12.69. His best innings was at Hobart, where he compiled 60 opening the batting against 22 of Tasmania in February 1862. Surrey's William Caffyn captured several delightful memories of "Teddy", another of the names by which Stephenson was commonly known, in his book, *Seventy-One Not Out*, especially on the ship home. He recounted how Ned silenced the awful trombone playing of the ship's cook by stuffing a towel into it when an opportunity arose, and there was his innocent comment as the ship entered the Red Sea that "he could not see that the water was any redder here than in any other sea". All delivered with a straight face and a drier-than-dry manner that characterised his wit.

His associations with drink went back a long way. They were noted in Bell's Life in his early days as a cricketer: "...can be heard of at the Plough Inn, Hallam, any night..." No doubt entertaining the regulars with his comments while sharing a pint or two of the local brew. A drop or more of antique whisky taken at some noted wine cellars before a game at Wirksworth, Derbyshire, nearly ended his life. On reaching the ground Stephenson was completely overcome, and lay down in the empty tent which acted as the players' changing-room. He was discovered by the passing Sheffield scorecard-printer, Billy Whittam, choking and black in the face. Whittam had the presence of mind to whip out a knife and cut through Stephenson's neckerchief and shirt. A doctor was summoned, and Ned was finally brought round. To uncover how he had declined to the stage where he had fallen into very poor circumstances it is necessary to look deep into his tragic personal life.

In 1851 Stephenson was still living with his parents and his two brothers, George and Joseph, and his sister, Emma, in Broomhall Street, Sheffield. He was in his final year as a cricketer with JWR Wilson Esq. at Broomhead Hall. A year later he married Mary Jackson in Liverpool. Mary hailed from Sedbergh, then in Yorkshire but now in Cumbria. By 1861, just before his trip to Australia, Stephenson, Mary and their nine-month-old son, Edward, were living at 27 Cemetery Road, Ecclesall, Sheffield. He was listed as a "professional cricketer", but the trade directory of 1862 lists him as a tobacconist and dealer in cricket bats and balls at 17 Porter Street. His first venture as a publican is said to date from about 1860, when Scores and Biographies states that he was "mine host" of the Newcastle Arms in Portobello. The Stephensons suffered their first family tragedy in 1862 with the death of Edward, but happier times returned in 1863 when another son, Sydney, was born, and seven years later a daughter, Florence, arrived. It was about that time that Stephenson became landlord of the Cambridge Hotel in Sheffield. Wherever he lived, though, his troubles seemed able to seek him out.

The *Sheffield Times* of March 25, 1871, carried the following notice:

STEPHENSON — March 19. Mary, the beloved wife of
E Stephenson, Cambridge Hotel, Barker's pool.

At the time of the 1871 census Ned had found help in caring for his eight-year-old son and daughter of 10 months as well as run a business and play the odd game. His sister-in-law and niece were living with him at the Cambridge Hotel in what must have been difficult and dark days.

Agnes Jackson was two years younger than her sister, Mary. In 1871 she was working as a housemaid in the West Derby area of North Liverpool, but by late 1873 Ned's sister-in-law had become his second wife. Tragedy was soon back in the Stephenson home. Florence died at the age of four in late 1874. There would be no more children in Ned's life. He would have cherished even more the development of his remaining son, Sydney, who in 1881 was 18 and working as a chemist's apprentice in Sheffield, yet on April 1, 1883, Sydney died from a heart-valve problem and consumption at the age of 20.

Stephenson and Agnes were still living at the Cambridge Hotel in 1887, but by 1891 they had moved to 18 Chester Road, Tuebrook, Liverpool. Chester Road was a tight, packed area of back-to-back terraced housing typical of that part of West Derby. The couple were listed as "living on their own means" that year, which implies that some annuity or other funds were providing them with a regular income of sorts.

What became of Stephenson in the final few years of his life is uncertain from the sparse evidence. To what extent he was drinking is not known. The travesty of having lost his first wife and three children must have taken its toll on him mentally, and perhaps he blotted out the pain and grief. Some obituary notices state that he died at Tuebrook Asylum for Inebriates, but that was not the case. He died on July 5, 1898, at his home in Chester Road, with his wife close by. He was 66 and, clearly, life had been a real struggle from some years. Whether or not he was ever an inmate at the Tue Brook Villa Asylum for the insane in West Derby is impossible to confirm. Stephenson died from phthisis pulmonalis or consumption of the lungs, a condition he had been suffering from for at least 12 months. He left his "effects", £79 12s 9d, to his wife and a coal-merchant by the name of Henry Wainwright.

Stephenson was buried with his son, Sydney, in Anfield Cemetery on July 8. On the day their former wicket-keeper died Yorkshire were completing a seven-wicket victory over Sussex at Bradford. The *Roses* match got under way at Sheffield three days later with no mention of his passing. The cricket world, it seems, never even noticed.

No Sheffield newspaper carried any obituary details, and even AW Pullin had not tracked Stephenson down for his *Talks With Old Yorkshire Cricketers*. Best to remember Yorkshire's first gloveman from when he was able to laugh at himself and "put a roomful into a roar of laughter".

From the author's book, Headingley Ghosts: A Collection of Yorkshire Cricket Tragedies. Scratching Shed Publishing 2013. (www.scratchingshedpublishing.com)

EDWIN ('NED') STEPHENSON

Right-hand batsman	Wicket-keeper
Born: Sheffield	June 5, 1832
Died: Liverpool	July 5, 1898

Debut: Sheffield v. Manchester at The Botanical Gardens, Manchester	July 20, 1854
For "Yorkshire" v. Surrey at The Oval	May 23, 1861
For Yorkshire County Cricket Club v. Surrey at The Oval	June 4, 1863
Last match (last day) Yorkshire v. Lancashire at Sheffield	July 1, 1873

FIRST-CLASS MATCHES FOR YORKSHIRE (1863-1873)

Matches	*Innings*	*Not Out*	*Runs*	*Highest Score*	*Average*	*50s*	*Ct/St*
36	61	5	803	67	14.33	3	30/27

Highest Score 67 v. Surrey at The Oval, 1863 (on debut)

FIRST-CLASS MATCHES FOR "YORKSHIRE" (1861 and 1862)

Matches	*Innings*	*Not Out*	*Runs*	*Highest Score*	*Average*	*50s*	*Ct/St*
6	12	0	75	15	6.2	0	5/1

Highest Score 15 v. Kent at Sheffield, 1862

ALL FIRST-CLASS (OR GREAT) MATCHES (1854 to 1873)

Matches	*Innings*	*Not Out*	*Runs*	*Highest Score*	*Average*	*50s*	*Ct/St*
82	142	11	1940	76	14.80	7	56/48

Highest Score 76 for North v. Surrey at The Oval, 1858
He bowled 12 four-ball overs for 24 runs (3 maidens)

Roy D Wilkinson, October 2012

CORONATION ASHES WERE HIS CROWNING ACHIEVEMENT

By Martin Howe

What a challenge to write about my favourite Yorkshire cricketer of this particular period when so many of Yorkshire's most celebrated players graced the teams around that time. My favourite is Len Hutton.

During his career Len was Yorkshire and England's most prolific and reliable batsman. He scored 24,807 runs for his county with 85 centuries, and 6,971 runs in Test matches with 19 centuries. In all first-class games he scored 40,140 runs and made 129 centuries, 11 of them double-centuries or better. Over and above mere statistics, there were three defining events in Len Hutton's career that set him apart from his contemporaries.

These events were his record-breaking and monumental innings of 364 against Australia at The Oval in 1938; the war-time fracture to his left forearm, after which his left arm — the more important one to a right-hand batsman — was two inches shorter and weaker than the right, and his appointment as the first professional captain of England in 1952, in which role he was to wrest the Ashes from Australia in 1953 and retain them *Down Under* in 1954-55.

As a youngster growing up in Sheffield in the 1940s it was that innings of 364 that made him a hero to me and my pals. It was Len Hutton we would pretend to be when batting in our makeshift games in fields and parks. One day, we hoped, we would emulate him and play for Yorkshire. Then, on August 2, 1947, I attended my first first-class match, the *Roses* fixture at bomb-scarred Bramall Lane, and had the chance to see my hero in action. Norman Yardley won the toss, and Hutton came out to open the innings with W G Keighley. There was a buzz of anticipation in the crowd. I expected Hutton to score a faultless century. So did most of the spectators. It was an expectation that Hutton said proved a burden throughout his career: "I always felt I let the crowd down if I didn't get a big score," he said. He didn't get a big score. He was dismissed for 26. Instead, it was the young left-hander Gerald Smithson who held centre-stage with a sparkling 98 before lunch — and who was no doubt rebuked by Emmott Robinson for taking such liberties in a

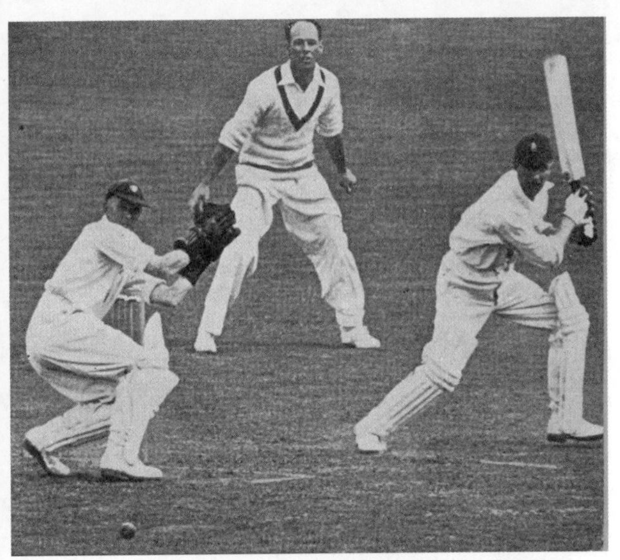

364 here I come: Hutton cuts at The Oval in 1938 as wicket-keeper Ben Barnett and Jack Fingleton look on
(Photo: Ron Deaton Archive)

Roses match. In the following seasons I documented Hutton's appearances for Yorkshire and England in a scrapbook of newspaper cuttings, but although I watched Yorkshire at Bramall Lane several times before I left Sheffield in the autumn of 1954 I never saw him make a big score. Nevertheless, even a modest Hutton innings was enough to demonstrate his consummate skill and his artistry.

Even if one had never seen Hutton in action there are images, books and tributes galore from which to distil the essence of his technique. Totally absorbed in the demands of batting, physical and mental, and whether against the fastest of bowlers or the shrewdest of spinners, his game was founded on concentration, watchful defence and judicious shot selection. Totally still, except for the continual tugging of the peak of his cap, and perfectly balanced at the crease, his movement into any stroke was unhurried, precise and economical. He had the quickness of eye and feet to make whatever adjustments might be required by the pitch and trajectory of a delivery. Hutton could play every stroke in the book, though with his injury-shortened left arm he rarely essayed the hook. His glorious cover-drives and delicate late-cuts were his eternal trademarks, but when the ball was turning or lifting disconcertingly — in his day wickets were uncovered — his defensive technique was beyond compare. Slight in stature, Hutton cut a rather frail figure at the crease, but he unflinchingly took on the Australians Lindwall and Miller at their fastest — and with none of the protective equipment of today.

Hutton was sometimes criticised for slow scoring. He could push it along as well as anyone if the needs dictated that, but otherwise he saw no benefit in undue haste. As an opener it was his job to build a score, and that would be done with care. Later batsmen would then be in a position to score more freely. Often the others would fail in their task. Then it fell upon Hutton to salvage the innings. It was Len Hutton who gave birth to the aphorism about Yorkshire cricketers: "We don't play for fun." Later he elaborated to his biographer: "Of course I enjoyed it, but at the level I played you had to be stern in your approach." Although he observed in another interview long after he had retired: "I would have enjoyed the one-day game," the remark does seem rather out of character, even tongue in cheek. Len Hutton was fashioned for the tough demands of Test and county cricket.

The sternness of Hutton's approach was fully revealed when he was appointed England's first professional captain in 1952. He said the appointment came as a surprise to him, but his knowledge of the game, the outstanding series he had had in Australia in 1950-51 and the absence of any better-qualified amateur made him an obvious choice, notwithstanding his lack of captaincy experience. Thereafter he had to shoulder the responsibilities both of the captaincy — with far less back room support than is available to present-day captains — and of England's leading and most dependable batsman.

His captaincy will be remembered for three series. In 1953, Coronation Year, the *Ashes* were regained with a convincing victory at The Oval after the first four Tests were drawn. In the West Indies that winter political and racial issues, fermented by the nationalism that was sweeping the Caribbean, presented as great a challenge to the captain as those he faced on the field. While never fully grasping the issues surrounding "the second most controversial tour in cricket history", he rose to the challenge. The first two Tests were lost, but the series was squared. Hutton was England's outstanding batsman, his innings of 205 at Kingston, Jamaica, in grilling heat was one of the finest of his career. In Australia in 1954-55, while his batting was less effective than on previous tours, his masterly direction of his fast-bowling attack, with some judicious slowing of the over rate, served to bring England a resounding victory by three Tests to one. This series was Hutton's crowning achievement, later to be recognised with a knighthood.

A reserved man by nature and upbringing, Hutton led by example and through the respect in which he was held rather than by exhortation. He

Len Hutton masterclass: ***(Photos: Ron Deaton Archive)***

was a man of few words, as cheekily recognised in the inscription on the silver salver presented to him by teammates on the West Indies tour of 1953-54: "Are you all right then?" There were no Henry V-type speeches or on-field huddles. No one thought more seriously about the game. During a match he could seem lost in a world of his own.

We have learned from memoirs and biographies that Hutton was not the easiest man to get on with — "one had to know him to know him" — and he could be insensitive to the feelings of colleagues. If he had a failing it was in what we now call man-management: examples include his handling of Fred Trueman on the West Indies tour and the hurtful way he allowed Alec Bedser to learn that he had been dropped after the disastrous First Test of 1954-55. This shortcoming aside, if shortcoming it is in captaincy at the highest level, Hutton was an outstanding captain on the field. He led England 23 times, with 11 matches won and four lost, a winning ratio that puts him at the forefront of England captains.

It is ironic that while MCC and the cricket establishment were prepared to make Hutton captain of England his county stuck to the tradition of appointing an amateur until Vic Wilson in 1961. The Yorkshire dressing-room in the 1950s, with Yardley captain and Hutton senior professional, was not the happiest of places with too many thrusting for the limelight. It is said that Yardley was "too nice a man" to curb these egos. Could Hutton have succeeded if the chalice had been passed to him? He would have had every player's respect, but he was, perhaps, too withdrawn a personality to accomplish the transformation that was to come when Ronnie Burnet took hold of the reins. Not that it was a real possibility while Hutton was captain of England after 1952. By the time he relinquished that position in 1955 and Yardley had announced his retirement Hutton was on the verge of calling it a day. He was admired throughout and beyond the world of cricket. He was revered by all lucky enough to know him. I met him only once: I sat next to him at a 1982 Scarborough Festival dinner with Don Mosey on Len's other side, but while the conversation between the two flowed easily I was too much in awe of my hero to make more than an occasional observation.

But I have dined in the company of my favourite Yorkshire cricketer of all time. More importantly, I had the privilege of seeing Yorkshire's master batsman in action. With Harold Pinter, I can say:

"I saw Len Hutton in his prime,
Another time another time"

Sir LEONARD BUTTON

Right-hand batsman   Leg-break bowler
Born: Fulneck,.Pudsey   June 23, 1916
Died: Kingston-upon-Thames   September 6, 1990
Debut: Yorkshire v. Cambridge University at Cambridge   May 2, 1934
Last match (last day): For Yorkshire   v. Hampshire at Bournemouth   June 30, 1955
Last match (last day): For MCC   v. Ireland at Dublin   September 6, 1960

Capped: July 11, 1936

Captain of England 1952 to 1954-55
Knighted in the Queen's Birthday Honours, June 1956

FIRST-CLASS MATCHES FOR YORKSHIRE

Matches	*Innings*	*Not Out*	*Runs*	*Highest Score*	*Average*	*100s*	*50s*	*Catches*
341	527	62	24807	280*	53.34	85	98	278

Highest Score 280* v. Hampshire at Sheffield, 1939

CENTURY IN EACH INNINGS

197 and 104	v. Essex at Southend-on-Sea, 1947
165 and 100	v. Sussex at Hove, 1949
103 and 137	v. MCC at Scarborough, 1952

*Balls**	*Maidens*	*Runs*	*Wickets*	*Average*	*Best*	*5wI*	*10wM*
8535	278	4221	154	27.40	6-76	4	1

* Hutton bowled both 6-ball and 8-ball overs

Best bowling in an innings 6-76 v. Leicestershire at Leicester (Aylestone Road), 1937
Best bowling in a match 10-101 (4-25 and 6-76) v. Leicestershire at Leicester (Aylestone Road), 1937

TEST MATCHES

Debut for England v. New Zealand at Lord's   June 26, 1937
Last Match (last day): England v. New Zealand at Auckland   March 28, 1955

Matches	*Innings*	*Not Out*	*Runs*	*Highest Score*	*Average*	*100s*	*50s*	*Catches*
79	138	15	6791	364	56.67	19	33	57

Highest Score 364 v. Australia at The Oval, 1938
Bowling: 3 wickets for 232 runs   Best 1-2 v. Australia at Sydney, 1954-55

ALL FIRST-CLASS MATCHES

Matches	*Innings*	*Not Out*	*Runs*	*Highest Score*	*Average*	*100s*	*50s*	*Catches*
513	814	91	40140	364	55.51	129	179	401

*Balls**	*Maidens*	*Runs*	*Wickets*	*Average*	*Best*	*5wI*	*10wM*
9740	293	5106	173	29.51	6-47	4	1

* Hutton bowled both 6-ball and 8-ball overs

Roy D Wilkinson, October 2012

HIS PRESENCE MADE EVEN A WEAK SIDE HARD TO BEAT

By Andrew Bosi

The final 50-year period coincides exactly with the introduction of one-day cricket: at first a single competition alongside a full programme of three-day first-class matches. A decline in the Championship in the 1970s was followed by a brief renaissance in the 1980s — back to 24 matches a season — and then the introduction of four-day matches, firstly playing each opponent home or away and then just under half of them both home and away.

One of the effects of limited-overs cricket has been to reduce the longevity of players. Whereas in the previous two eras scores of Yorkshire players appeared year in and year out, in this final period there are really only six players who can boast a sustained contribution: three batsmen, two wicket-keepers and an all-rounder. The lack of any pace bowlers in this list is a true reflection of the effect of one-day cricket, although Tony Nicholson runs them close with 861 wickets in the first 13 seasons under review.

When Yorkshire were winning championships in the 1960s, 100 wickets was not abnormal. In 2001 six pace bowlers made notable contributions, but no one had even 50 wickets at the end of the season. This is a great pity. That worthy representative of the Yorkshire Press, Peter Snape, always chose a bowler as his man-of-the-match, and he must be frowning from above that I have chosen a batsman!

The all-rounder was, of course, Phil Carrick, who played for 24 seasons and was within six runs of the career double of 10,000 runs and 1,000 wickets, which is otherwise only associated with the immortals: Hirst, Rhodes, Haigh, Illingworth and — until history was rewritten after his death — Ted Wainwright. Carrick made three centuries, but his most memorable innings was 73 at Lord's, when he shepherded a very young Kevin Sharp to his first three-figure score. His bowling career went through several phases, influenced again by one-day cricket, but his most memorable contribution was the polite appeal "How was that?" which, I believe, was once answered in the affirmative.

The gauntlets were taken — after Jimmy Binks, whose career crosses two quintenia — by David Bairstow and Richard Blakey. "'Bluey" signalled the end of the silent movie era: his verbal contributions were often worth hearing more than his wicket-keeping was worth watching.

He was a player of his time: the Trueman era would have lamented the untidiness behind the timbers, but the 1970s demanded the occasional match-turning batting performance, which we got, and proficiency standing back, which we also saw with a record haul of catches in a match against Derbyshire.

The man most worth seeing
(Photo: Ron Deaton Archive)

Blakey combined the quiet efficiency of Binks with an obvious batting ability, but the latter was never quite fulfilled. We saw early years of promise before he had the gloves, but we then had to wait until the last two seasons when his batting blossomed again, only for him to be discarded prematurely. Having only one 'keeper makes succession management much more difficult.

If you believe Kevin Pietersen — that people come to see the ball disappear from view — there is only one batsman to watch, and that would be Darren Lehmann. His skill at dissecting all but the very best bowlers, his consistency and his disdain for rigorous fitness regimes all added to the endearment. His unbeaten 130 against Sussex in 2006, while 27 were scored at the other end, must go down as one of the most brilliant innings in strike manipulation and shot selection.

Lehmann was only with us for seven seasons, but Martyn Moxon played for 17, and stands out because by that time it was no longer fashionable to put sound defence ahead of scoring runs. He was good to watch because one could see how, instead of quarrelling with Boycott, he had learned from him and his batting was the closest we could get to watching Geoffrey bat after his retirement. You could see Moxon in Michael Vaughan's batting, so the dynasty lived on.

All of which leaves the conclusion, disappointing for some modern commentators, that the player most worth seeing was Geoffrey Boycott. His presence in the side meant that even when it was a weak side it was

The big three: Brian Sellers, extreme left, who was Cricket Committee chairman when Geoffrey Boycott was appointed captain of Yorkshire in 1971, Club President Sir William Worsley, and Geoffrey
(Photo: Yorkshire Post)

hard to defeat. There were some stirring innings. I did not see, but heard the report on BBC Test Match Special of the unbeaten 220 at Bramall Lane in 1967. The message was: look what England are missing. They had dropped Geoffrey for slow-scoring after the Headingley Test against India when his first 106 had occupied a full day. No matter that he made 140 in the next two sessions...two years before they had dropped Ken Barrington for slow-scoring and had backed themselves into a corner.

What TMS failed to convey was the state of the Sheffield wicket. The 25 wickets that fell in the match could muster only twice as many runs in total as flowed from Boycott's bat. His best bad-wicket innings was also in Sheffield, but at Abbeydale Park. This innings stands out because the wicket was so treacherous that anyone could be out at any time. Boycott's response was to take calculated risks at the start of his innings — he might have been caught at third-man in the first over — and only once set was he able to revert to his risk-free style.

His career comprised three stages alongside the three ages of county cricket. The early learning years, the middle years when he dominated the scoring, and the latter years for which he is best remembered, not always with as much affection, for the elimination of all risk.

For me, two things stand out from that third era. Watching the overs keep pace with his score up to 50, followed by an exponential increase in the scoring rate, was a familiar pattern, but every now and again there would be a free-scoring session or innings. He once plundered 74 before lunch against Gloucestershire at Harrogate, but he was not in the same form after the break. When he was "up for it", which was most of the time, it was fascinating to see how he would ensure that he was at the business end for the first ball of each over. This may be one of the few cricket statistics that has not been analysed to death.

GEOFFREY BOYCOTT

Right-hand batsman   Right-arm medium bowler
Born: Fitzwilliam   October 21, 1940
Debut: Yorkshire v. Pakistanis at Bradford   June 16, 1962
Last match (last day): Yorkshire v. Northamptonshire at Scarborough   September 12, 1986
Capped: October 2, 1963

Captain of Yorkshire 1971 to 1978
Captain of England 1977-78

FIRST-CLASS MATCHES FOR YORKSHIRE

Matches	*Innings*	*Not Out*	*Runs*	*Highest Score*	*Average*	*100s*	*50s*	*Catches*
414	674	111	32570	260*	57.85	103	157	200

Highest Score 260* v. Essex at Colchester (Garrison Ground) 1970

CENTURY IN EACH INNINGS

103 and 105   v. Nottinghamshire at Sheffield, 1966
163 and 141*   v. Nottinghamshire at Bradford, 1983

Overs	*Maidens*	*Runs*	*Wickets*	*Average*	*Best*
321.2	106	665	28	23.57	4-14

Best Bowling 4-14 v. Lancashire at Leeds, 1979

TEST MATCHES

Debut for England v. Australia at Nottingham   June 4, 1964
Last Match (last day): England v. India at Calcutta   January 6, 1982

Matches	*Innings*	*Not Out*	*Runs*	*Highest Score*	*Average*	*100s*	*50s*	*Catches*
108	193	23	8114	246*	47.72	22	42	33

Highest Score 246* v. India at Leeds, 1967

Bowling: 7 wickets for 382 runs   Best 3-47 v. South Africa at Capetown, 1964-65

ALL FIRST-CLASS MATCHES

Matches	*Innings*	*Not Out*	*Runs*	*Highest Score*	*Average*	*100s*	*50s*	*Catches*
609	1014	162	48426	261*	56.83	151	238	264

Highest Score: 261*   For MCC v. President's XI at Bridgetown, 1973-74

*Balls**	*Maidens*	*Runs*	*Wickets*	*Average*	*Best*
3685	183	1459	45	32.42	4-14

* Boycott bowled both 6-ball and 8-ball overs

Roy D Wilkinson, October 2012

A CHANGE OF NAME, BUT THE OLD VALUES WILL CONTINUE

By David Allan

A busy and successful year for Yorkshire CCC Archives Committee drew to a close with it coming under the stewardship of the Yorkshire Cricket Foundation (YCF) from January 1, 2013, and being renamed the Yorkshire Cricket Archives Committee (YCAC).

The move was made on New Year's Day so that it would coincide with the 150th anniversary year of Yorkshire County Cricket Club. The work of the YCAC will feature on the new YCF website which was due to be launched in January, and on which there will be a clear click through from the Yorkshire CCC website.

Subject to budget, the YCAC will retain full responsibility for the acquisition of archives.

The Archives Committee met four times in 2012, and special thanks are due to Paul Dyson, who undertook to deal with all requests received by the Club concerning items for potential inclusion in the Archive or for research into existing items, together with many varied queries received by YCCC. At each meeting he was able to give a fascinating resume on the varied correspondence and the action taken.

At our February meeting, the minutes referred to the Capped Players' research — which is now complete so far as it is possible to establish unrecorded dates from many years ago — and to plaques from the old Press Box in the Grandstand that had been found a new home in the Long Room. A summary of the content of each of the 12 DVDs on notable Yorkshire players had been compiled by David Warner, and it was now to be found on the Yorkshire website.

I was able to report that a painting of Fred Trueman had indeed turned out, after professional inspection, to be an original, and the water colour is now hung in the museum. Items recently purchased mainly applied to Brian Close and e-bay sales. Brian Sanderson explained that the inventory now had some duplication of *Wisdens* — one of them from the Wilfred Rhodes Collection being leather-bound. The Rhodes set was now in our secure store.

The next Long Room display cabinets would feature ties, and also to be featured in 2012 were Raymond Illingworth, who would celebrate his 80th birthday, and Philip Sharpe, on the 50th anniversary of his catches record that might never be broken. There also was a cabinet display to commemorate the centenary of York and District Senior Cricket League. Work on our archive data base has come to a temporary halt, pending the completion of major fundraising by the Foundation.

A biography of the late Geoffrey Keighley, a gifted Yorkshire batsman of captaincy potential, had been produced in Australia, and a copy had been donated by his widow, Karin. The book on Geoffrey, who emigrated to Australia in 1951 to become a sheepfarmer, was handed to the committee by James Greenfield. Geoffrey died six years ago.

Other items either given or purchased during the year included:

* Second Eleven material, including photos and scorecards, from Mollie Staines
* Scorecard of a game in Omagh, Northern Ireland, involving the Green Howards with Hedley Verity and Norman Yardley
* A *Manchester Evening News* board covering the 1901 Roses match.
* A Lord Hawke testimonial card
* A scorebook containing Hedley Verity's last game
* A member's ticket from 1902
* *Vanity Fair* prints of Lord Hawke
* Chris Waters's book on Fred Trueman
* A Royal Doulton limited-edition Len Hutton character jug
* A commemorative scorecard of the Yorkshire v. Glamorgan match in Scarborough in 2001, which resulted in Yorkshire winning the County Championship title
* A copy of a limited edition of 20 concerning Yorkshire's 3,000th First Class match — a Roses fixture — given by Yorkshire County Cricket Supporters' Association
* Scorebook of Yorkshire's 1964 tour of America-Bermuda when Garry Sobers appeared as a guest player

Committee initiatives in 2012 including an open day during the Championship match with Glamorgan at Headingley when Yorkshire members and supporters were invited to bring their cricket memorabilia to be assessed. Brian Sanderson was on hand in the Long Room to offer advice, and similar events are being planned for 2013.

Archives Committee secretary Howard Clayton was appointed Second Eleven scorer ahead of the 2012 season, and his committee colleagues were delighted towards the end of the year when he received the Wombwell Cricket Lovers' Society's E H Umbers Award for Distinguished Services to Yorkshire cricket.

Howard, along with Paul Dyson and Brian Sanderson, agreed to compile a chronological list of all players who had turned out for Yorkshire Second Eleven, basing their researches on scorecards from the Minor

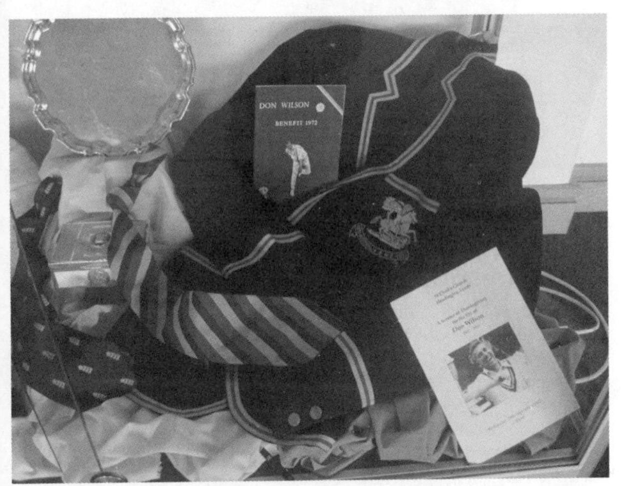

TRIBUTE TO DON WILSON: David Allan's shot of the glass case in Headingley Long Room highlights, top left, the silver plate presented to the late Yorkshire left-arm spin bowler by MCC Young Cricketers in appreciation of his work as Head Coach in 1979

Counties' Championship and the Second Eleven Championship.

Another committee representative, Mick Pope, jointly received the new Don Ambrose award from the Association of Cricket Statisticians to commemorate the best article in the association's Journal. The other recipient was Douglas Miller, a former chairman of the ACS.

The celebration of Yorkshire CCC's 150th anniversary in 2013 meant that a busy and exciting year lay ahead. Cabinets being prepared for display in the Long Room would contain interesting items from the Club's unparalleled history.

The Archives Committee throughout the year has consisted of J C David Allan (chairman), Howard Clayton (secretary), Paul E Dyson, James M Greenfield, Mick Pope, Brian Sanderson, Dennis Smith, David Warner and Roy D Wilkinson.

Towards the end of the year we were pleased to welcome Brian Warne, who joined us weekly as we attended to our collection at Morley.

I wish to thank the committee for their advice, endeavour and enthusiasm. They each through their individual interest and specialism bring depth to our discussions and decisions. I hope they have had fun.

CHARTING THE RISE AND RISE OF THE YORKSHIRE EMPIRE

By Duncan Hamilton

THE SWEETEST ROSE: 150 YEARS OF YORKSHIRE COUNTY CRICKET CLUB 1863-2013
David Warner (Great Northern Books, £17.99)

No one working in today's Press Box has seen more of Yorkshire than David Warner.

No one better understands the labyrinthine complexities that lie beneath its cricket; nor appreciates so acutely what cricket means to such a tribal county, where a sense of identity and status is drawn from it. No one, I think, is also more aware of the indissoluble chain connecting its past to its present.

Warner began watching Yorkshire when Churchill was Prime Minister, and began writing about them when evening newspapers, such as his own *Bradford Telegraph and Argus* were produced by hot metal and printed multiple daily editions, the tea score always appearing in the Stop Press. To the iPad and eBook generation this is will seem both ridiculously antiquated and about as distant as the repeal of the Corn Laws. But it establishes Warner's qualifications as an interpretative historian, because memory and experience are primary sources for him. He doesn't rely exclusively on other people's histories to produce his own.

The sort of book he has written to mark Yorkshire's sesquicentennial — *The Sweetest Rose* — reflects the sort of person he is: fair-minded, plainly spoken, scrupulously accurate in his reportage and exhaustively knowledgeable about his specialism. To read him is like having Mr Gibbon suddenly appear to talk you through the rise and fall of the Roman Empire. Warner has the advantage. Whereas Gibbon never got to meet Marcus Aurelius, Warner has spent almost as much time in

Geoffrey Boycott's company — as Mrs Boycott will testify. He was also, albeit briefly, a contemporary of J M Kilburn's; Gibbon, alas, didn't have the good fortune to drink tea with Tacitus.

What gusts off the 342 pages is Warner's integrity (this, coincidentally, is a word David Hopps uses about him, too, in his exemplary introduction) and his certitude. His mind is his own; and it is made up. Also communicated is the pride and pleasure he's taken from his job which, given Yorkshire's tendency to spontaneously combust on occasions, cannot be described as feather-bedded to say the least.

Without division and discord, Yorkshire would certainly be less interesting, and *The Sweetest Rose* picks its way well through each growl and grievance and plaint. The stupidity of some of these is stupefying. Whoever thought, for instance, that a 23-man committee was practicable — unless, of course, you actually wanted to ignite an oral riot? The feuding throughout the threadbare years, following the rampancy of the 1960s, is a suicide note written in instalments. The thought which occurs after Warner's assiduous documentation of it is unavoidable.

You think of lost Championships. What comes to mind for Warner as a rationalisation for this self-harm is the crooner Clarence "Frogman" Henry singing *You Always Hurt the One You Love.*

The lyrics include the lines:

You always take the sweetest rose
And crush it till the petals fall

Among the falling petals — which, at times, is like a snowstorm — Warner celebrates those who warrant it: Hawke and Hutton, Holmes and Sutcliffe, Jackson and Hirst, Trueman and Close and Illingworth and Boycott, et al. I didn't believe there was anything fresh to say about Boycott's hundredth hundred until I came across Warner's view of the boundary which, against Australia on that baking August afternoon in 1977, carried him from 96 into the record books: "It was as if Boycott wanted to see exactly 100. A scoreboard showing 101 or 102 would have spoiled the symmetry of it all." You nod your head after reading that line, and remark to yourself: "Of course."

Vignettes like this beautifully enliven *The Sweetest Rose.*

There's Ted Lester being upbraided at the fall of a wicket by Brian Sellers because his cap was askew. Lester was imitating a hero, Arthur "Ticker" Mitchell, who wore his cap pulled over one eye. Sellers went at him like a flame-thrower because of it. "The rollicking went on until the next man came in," said Lester.

There's the arm-wrestle for dressing room supremacy in 1930 between Alan Barber, a couple of weeks short of his 25th birthday, and Wilfred Rhodes, then approaching his 53rd. As captain Barber decided to bat on after lunch only to be told by another player: "Skipper, Mr Rhodes has declared." The tipping point occurred against Essex at Dewsbury, where Rhodes griped over-loudly that Barber hadn't made a specific bowling change. "Wilfred," said Barber, "I know you were playing cricket for England before I was even born — but I am the captain." Rhodes was instructed to pack his bags, and Barber telegrammed for a replacement for the next game. He called up a Championship debutant, a promising chap called Hedley Verity — he finished with match figures of 8-60. The injustice of his dismissal burnt on for Rhodes. Barber's nephew was introduced to the Great Man more than 30 years later. Asked if he remembered Barber, the response was curt: "Aye," said Rhodes, "'im that sent me 'ome".

Most wonderfully of all, there's Mark Johnson claiming Viv Richards's wicket at Abbeydale Park. Richards had made 153, and Somerset were on the brink of a declaration. "In the middle of an over," writes Warner, "the megastar approached Johnson, and asked where he would like him to give a catch. Richards said he had batted long enough, and would like to give the bowler his wicket because he was most impressed with the effort he had put into his work earlier on."

He duly did so.

The illustrations are particularly fine, too. Michael J Ellison, Yorkshire's first treasurer and first "proper" President, looks like Santa Claus after half of his milk-white beard has been singed away in a slide down a hot chimney. The team of 1875, including George Ulyett and Tom Emmett, resembles a group of press-ganged sailors who have just got back from the sea. They are a ragged assortment of stripes and whites, bowler hats and caps. The typed letter of rejection Warwickshire sent in 1897 represents one of the monumental blunders of cricket's Victorian era. "Dear Sir," it begins, "I am sorry my Committee are unable to offer you an engagement for next season."

The recipient was the aforementioned Rhodes.

It is impossible to quibble with Warner's conclusion that "cricket is imbued in the soul of all Yorkshiremen who play the game". The proof, after all, exists in *The Sweetest Rose*.

He also points out that: "Yorkshire like to mark significant dates in the calendar by finishing top of the Championship table." He cites those summers after each world war and at the beginning of the 20th Century and the Club's centenary season. Will we be similarly blessed during the sesquicentennial? Who can tell? I do know this, however. Whatever happens, David Warner will be here to tell us about it.

Be very thankful for that.

Duncan Hamilton is an author whose award-winning books include works on Harold Larwood and Brian Clough

WE'LL GET 'EM IN SEQUINS: Max Davidson (Bloomsbury, £18.99)

The author had the inspiration to record and interpret many of the changes in English social history through the lives of seven Yorkshire cricketers — Hirst, Sutcliffe, Verity, Trueman, Boycott, Gough and Vaughan — and how their careers altered our conception of masculinity. Max Davidson is not a Yorkshireman, but he does have a West Riding grandfather named Horsfall, who gives him a claim to greatness.

George Herbert (Hirst), one suspects, would have viewed Gough's cavortings on TV with a quizzical smile and an expression of mild incredulity. He would certainly have raised an eyebrow when an England captain — Vaughan — followed suit. Wilfred (Rhodes) would have been considerably more caustic, while Emmott's (Robinson) comments would have been unprintable.

Herbert (Sutcliffe) sensed significant changes were coming, and adapted. Hedley, as ever, would study technique. Fred would be amused by the description of Gough as "Trueman-lite", Geoffrey concluding that Goughie needed more practice. If George Herbert and the *Dazzler* had ever met the discussion would soon have got down to brass tacks — swing bowling.

Davidson's central theme is how the definition of an Englishman has changed — from the heroes of John Buchan and Rider Haggard, public-school empire builders, to the many faces and etiquettes of various James Bonds and entertainers of dual sexuality. Daniel Craig's character is almost as far from Ian Fleming's original as Hirst is from Vaughan.

The author is able to illustrate his thesis with many forgotten and half-forgotten tales, and as he is an erudite and witty writer the result is as entertaining and informative a book as cricket has known for a considerable time. One would have to go back to Derek Birley and John Ford to learn as much with so much enjoyment. While you may not agree with all the author's conclusions you will almost certainly feel you know more of the men, rather than the players, than you did from reading the biographies.

Hirst and Rhodes both denied saying: "We'll get 'em in singles", but Gough and Vaughan cannot disclaim the sequins of *Strictly Come Dancing*. What they could assert is that they are only turning the clock back. Those eminent Victorians, Billy Bates and David Hunter, were enthusiastic amateur song-and-dance men in the age of the music hall.

This is the second publication by *Wisden Sports Writing* whose aim is "to showcase and to produce books that are not just about sport. They are about life". It should be added that not since Old Ebor and Neville Cardus has anyone written so affectionately and engagingly about Yorkshire cricketers. Percy Horsfall would have been proud.

Derek Hodgson

DON WILSON

By David Warner

Yorkshire cricket lost one of its most devoted and popular former players on July 21, 2012, with the death in York Hospital of Don Wilson at the age of 74. Don was among the proudest of the Yorkshire team who famously regained the County Championship title in 1959 and went on to clinch it again six times over the next nine years.

The left-arm spinner and big-hitting batsman played in six Test matches for England between 1964 and 1971, and he went on to become a distinguished head coach at Lord's once his playing days were over.

But it was as a loyal Yorkshire cricketer and a tremendous teammate with an unflagging enthusiasm for the game for which he will always be remembered. The formation of the Yorkshire Players' Association in 2005 was warmly welcomed by Don, and he loved the reunions with all those who had represented the *White Rose*. He was moved almost to tears when he was elected President of the Association for 2008-2009, and he carried out his duties with dignity and charm.

Don managed to combine friendliness with greatness — and statistics show that he was among the elite of Yorkshire's bowlers.

Born and bred in Settle, he went on to play in 392 first-class matches for Yorkshire, taking 1,104 wickets at 20.49 runs apiece. Only 11 bowlers have claimed more Yorkshire wickets than that, and only three have done so since the 1939-45 war in Fred Trueman (1,745), Johnny Wardle, who was Don's left-arm predecessor in the side (1,539), and Raymond Illingworth (1,431).

In all first-class matches throughout his career he captured 1,189 wickets, each costing him exactly 21 runs. For Yorkshire his best figures were achieved against MCC at Scarborough in 1969, when he took 7-19. Ironically, his career-best batting and bowling figures were both for MCC: 8-36 against Ceylon, now Sri Lanka, at Colombo Oval in 1970 to give him a match return of 14-71, and 112 v. South Zone, Hyderabad, in 1964, when he added 102 for the fourth wicket with Ken Barrington.

Don was one of the greatest of fielders, stalking the mid-wicket area like few before him or since, and he held 250 catches, 235 for Yorkshire.

He was the old-fashioned sort of batsman the crowds loved to see, and he could hit the ball great distances, in 1967 receiving *The People's* silver trophy from Trueman for striking the most sixes. For Yorkshire, he made 5,788 runs at 13.88 with a top score of 83 against Surrey at

DON WILSON: Unflagging enthusiasm and a tremendous teammate
(Photo: Yorkshire Post)

Bramall Lane in 1960.

Don was appointed Yorkshire vice-captain when Geoff Boycott took over the reins from Brian Close in 1971, but it was an uneasy relationship, and with his form and confidence on the wane Don retired at the end of the 1974 season.

His great friend and colleague, Philip Sharpe, also left then for Derbyshire, and another close ally and teammate, Richard Hutton, did not have his contract renewed.

Richard's father, the incomparable Sir Leonard Hutton, was among those who strongly recommended Don to Yorkshire — and he had good cause to do so.

When Don was 15 Yorkshire took a star-studded side to play a benefit match at Settle and, to his amazement, he was included in the local team. In his autobiography, *Mad Jack*, written with cricket journalist, Stephen Thorpe, Don recalled: "The big day dawned, and farmers, sightseers and locals alike, including my mother and father, travelled from far and near for the auspicious occasion. It was not the first time my parents had seen me play, but it was certainly their first attendance together. Yorkshire batted, as is always the case in these affairs, and made a steady start before I was called on to bowl.

"The great Len Hutton was facing. I paced out my run, but counted the steps wrongly. I was so nervous. My palms were sweating so much that I could barely hold the ball. The first two deliveries were pushed quietly into the covers, and the third...went straight on, and he missed it. I'd bowled Len Hutton."

In 1965 Don accepted the position of coach during the winter months at a Catholic school in Johannesburg, and five years later he became coach to the Wanderers' Club in Johannesburg. In 1975 he was a member of the first mixed-race team ever to leave South Africa when the party went on a two-week tour of Rhodesia, the squad also including fellow left-armer Phil Carrick, who went on to captain Yorkshire.

Don played Minor Counties cricket for Lincolnshire after leaving Yorkshire, and he enjoyed spells with Holmfirth in the Huddersfield League and Manningham Mills in the Bradford League, where he teamed up with Philip Sharpe. While still playing for Manningham Mills he became head coach to MCC at Lord's towards the end of 1977, staying there until 1990, when he enjoyed the fresh challenge of coaching cricket at Ampleforth College in North Yorkshire.

Don Wilson **Born: August 7, 1937**
Died: July 21, 2012

DON WILSON

Left-hand batsman Slow left-arm bowler
Born: Settle August 7, 1937
Died: York July 21, 2012
Debut: Yorkshire v. Scotland at Paisley May 29, 1957
Last match (last day): Yorkshire v. Essex at Leyton August 9, 1974
Capped: September 29, 1960

FIRST-CLASS MATCHES FOR YORKSHIRE

Matches	*Innings*	*Not Out*	*Runs*	*Highest Score*	*Average*	*50s*	*Catches*
392	502	85	5788	83	13.88	10	235

Highest score: 83 v. Surrey at Sheffield, 1960

Overs	*Maidens*	*Runs*	*Wickets*	*Average*	*Best*	*5wI*	*10wM*
10613.5	4082	22626	1104	20.49	7-19	46	7

Best bowling in an innings 7-19 v. MCC at Scarborough, 1969
Best bowling in a match 13-52 (6-31 and 7-21) v. Warwickshire at Middlesbrough, 1967

Hat-tricks

v. Nottinghamshire at Middlesbrough, 1959
v. Nottinghamshire at Worksop, 1966
v. Kent at Harrogate, 1966

TEST MATCHES

Wilson played in six Test Matches — five v. India in 1963-1964, and one v. New Zealand in 1970-71. He scored 75 runs in seven innings, average 12.50, highest score 42 v. India at Madras in 1964. He took 11 wickets for 466 runs, average 42.36, best bowling 2-17 v. India at Kolkata in 1964.

Roy D Wilkinson, October 2012

RICHARD HUTTON'S MOVING TRIBUTE TO DON WILSON

A service of thanksgiving for the life of Don Wilson was held at St Chad's Church, Headingley, on September 19, attended by a wide range of friends, former colleagues and current members of the Yorkshire CCC playing staff.

Former Yorkshire and England captains Brian Close and Raymond Illingworth were among those present, along with current Yorkshire skipper Andrew Gale, and former captain Martyn Moxon, now Director of Professional Cricket, who attended with first-team coach Jason Gillespie, the former Australian Test bowler.

Two of Don Wilson's closest teammates and friends played a big part in the service, Richard Hutton paying the main tribute, which is produced below in full, and Philip Sharpe reciting a poem, The Pitch at Night by G D Martineau and reading tributes from former Australia captain Ian Chappell and former South Africa captain Dr Ali Bacher.

MCC was represented by its president, Philip Hodson, who said Don's retirement in 1974 had been Yorkshire's loss but MCC's gain because Don had become Head Coach at Lord's, a position absolutely made for him.

The text of Richard Hutton's address is:

Of all the many people who held great affection for Don Wilson, I am very flattered to be assigned this part in his memorial. I first came across Don in 1961 in a Yorkshire second-team match at Bridlington, when he was trying to regain his fitness and place in the first team after breaking a wrist in a County Championship match at Worcester, in which he had heroically won the game batting with one hand.

Don was approaching his mid-20s, and normally people would not have had much time for a nervous, callow schoolboy happening to find himself in an environment in which it was easy to feel lost. But Don's instant friendliness and cheerfulness were a reassurance and encouragement to any youngster. His great capacity for friendship gave him an affinity with all people, especially the young, and it was this quality that helped to make him such a fine coach after his own playing days were over. I feel privileged that he was a close colleague for 12 years and that he remained a friend for the rest of his life.

There is so much that can be said about Don Wilson, his life and his times, that it could be serialised, and knowing his passion for the theatrical it could even be put to music! Don was a remarkable character. He had a special magnetism, to which people were instinctively and instantly drawn. He was charismatic, jocular, humorous and comical. He had a great sense of theatre and showmanship, a tendency to the dramatic and a freedom with the actualitee. He was the centre of countless moments of hilarity, often at the deprecation of himself.

His most often told story against himself was the occasion in which he found himself as a mere lad at the Yorkshire pre-season practices, batting in a net against the county's three leading fast bowlers under the watchful eye of Coach Arthur Mitchell, who was usually concerned that those under his tutelage had a proper job. As ball after ball crashed into his wicket, Don spent most of the session retrieving stumps that had become entangled in the netting behind him and replacing them in their allotted holes. Mitchell decided that he should take no further punishment and, stopping the contest, beckoned Don towards him. They met halfway down the net where the following took place:

Mitchell: They tell me that tha's a joiner.

Wilson: Yes, Mr Mitchell. I'm an apprentice.

Mitchell: Is tha' cummin' to t'practices tomorrer?

Wilson: Yes, Mr Mitchell. I am.

Mitchell: I would like to gi' thi a bit of advice! When tha' cumms tomorrer bring thi' tools with thee and get that end boarded up!

Don had an even more unlikely start as a Yorkshire cricketer, coming from Settle. This faraway town, more Lancashire or Cumberland than Yorkshire, had never produced a Yorkshire cricketer, in contrast to, say, Pudsey where they were 10 a penny. However, his talent was undoubted from an early age, and he was already a local hero, although as a gangly youth his popularity was badly damaged when in a pre-season friendly against the full Yorkshire side visiting Settle for the first time — and probably the last — he happened to bowl out my father in single figures when he had been put on after only three overs so that the opening bowlers could change ends. Don's excitability was uncontained in contrast to the dismay surrounding him.

Early in his career he dismissed Cyril Washbrook in a *Roses* match at Old Trafford, causing Fred Trueman to shout out: "Better shut bloody gates afore he runs home to Settle to tell his dad!"

Don brought with him his own brand of the vernacular, in which he would insert additional vowels into words. It was assumed this was how people in Settle actually spoke. Making the most of any situation, he would refer to Settle as Seattle, as if he originated from the western seaboard of the United States. He didn't wear boots; he wore "booits". When he was hung over he was sick in the "heeard", and if he could be here now he would tell us that he is "deeard".

But Don was full of contradictions. The mockery he could make of life and the state of chaos in which he frequently seemed to live belied

Last bow: Richard Hutton and Don Wilson after a drizzly afternoon coaching at Malsis School in 1974. The picture was taken by a pupil on what may have been the pair's final appearance in Yorkshire colours

a commitment and discipline that made his life so successful. When he was serious he was fierce in his pride of what he was doing. He had high standards. He was intensely loyal, to Yorkshire and to the team. He was always well turned out, and expected it of others. He had a fetish for punctuality and hated being late, always allowing plenty of margin for error. He was even 45 minutes early for his own funeral, although there were extenuating circumstances!

Don's feats, achievements and statistics as a cricketer, for Yorkshire and England and so many other teams he was always keen and willing to play for, are in the record books and yearbooks for all to see. The quantity of his performances was huge, but was more than matched by its quality. He was always conscious that he was following a long line of distinguished Yorkshire left-arm spin bowlers, going back to Bobby Peel and, sequentially, Wilfred Rhodes, Hedley Verity and Johnny Wardle. He was under further pressure from the fact that his big chance came at the time of the acrimonious and controversial dismissal of Wardle, one of the county's greatest cricketers. As it turned out he was a worthy addendum to their list.

He bowled lengthy spells on unresponsive pitches, conceding very little. As a left-arm spinner he was a perfect foil for Ray Illingworth, and between them they engineered many a Yorkshire victory on rain-affected or worn third-day pitches. His act of delivery was a wonder to behold. Following the release of the ball, in anticipation or expectation of what might happen at the other end he went through a spring-heeled jig, involving a stamping of feet and a whirling of arms.

Don attracted soubriquets as a naked light bulb attracts flies, and these antics earned him several more. Having been christened the *Settle Express*, he was variously the *Settle Windmill*, *Zebedee* after the Jack-in-a-box in *Magic Roundabout*, and Mad Jack. How he came to be known as such, or even to adopt it as a title for his ghosted autobiography, remains a mystery. He was neither mad, although he could get cross, nor was he a Jack. He was one of the finest team men of all.

He was without equal as a mid-wicket fielder, where his left-handedness saved countless runs and brought many run-outs at the bowler's end. He was agile and a quick mover over short distances, which occasionally included getting from one end of the bar to the other! He was hugely entertaining with the bat, whether he was smashing sixes around the ground or failing to disguise his fear of fast bowlers trying to maim him. Idiosyncratically, he would scamper between the wickets with one gloved hand on the top of his head, but it was unclear whether this was to stop his cap falling off or to hold his head on.

The Yorkshire team of the 1960s contained some of the most talented cricketers in the country, and even the world. Despite the highly individual natures of some of the players the spirit of the team was its greatest strength, and Don Wilson provided much of the cement that kept it together. At times, with Don in full support of Fred Trueman, the team resembled a comedy road show as it toured the country in the quest of ever more County Championship titles.

Don was a born entertainer, on and off the field. He loved the bright lights, the smell of greasepaint, the roar of the crowd and the company of showbusiness people. Once he formed a friendship with the actor Peter O'Toole, and I remember seeing him giving private coaching sessions in the Indoor School at Lord's — a hopeless case if ever there was one! If the great thespian had brought a bucket of sand with him instead of his unorthodox array of togs Don would probably have sung him *The Desert Song*.

A favourite watering hole in London was the Victoria Palace Theatre, home of the *Black and White Minstrel Show*. Don and his great companion, Philip Sharpe, came to know every word of every line of every song in the repertoire, and they regaled all and sundry in hotels and bars wherever they happened to be. Don's intro of *Ring,*

ring the banjo; I like that good old song was the clarion call for the Yorkshire male voice choir, which included Tony Nicholson and John Hampshire. Don would have been deeply offended to know that the obituary of him in *The Times* contained the words: "Wilson was no singer". In fact, he was incredibly versatile. One of his party pieces was whistling through his teeth and fingers in accompaniment to Philip Sharpe's rendition of *She's only a bird in a gilded cage*.

The three of us saw Ken Dodd in his first show at the London Palladium. It was very funny and Don, who had an uproarious laugh, never stopped from start to finish. He was no ordinary stage-door Johnny, because he knew how to get into theatres, and somehow we went backstage after the show. Ken Dodd told Don that he would like to employ him to go on tour as his laughter-maker.

By then Don was an experienced tourist, and a fine one he was, too; a great ambassador wherever he went. He was probably at his best in 1963 in India, which was a dangerous place for him because as a child, riddled with asthma, epilepsy and other diseases, he was hardly expected to reach puberty. But he sailed through the subcontinent without so much as a sore throat, which is more than can be said for the rest of the party — many of whom spent much of the tour in hospital.

One such was the aforementioned Philip Sharpe, lying bedridden in a Bombay hospital, where he happened to be being visited by a fellow Bradfordian, a certain Miss Jill Roberts. Coincidentally, Don was also visiting his roommate of 11 years standing. From either side of the bed the patient was duly ignored as the two visitors, feasting their eyes on one another and their mouths on the patient's supply of fruit and other restorative palliatives, began a relationship that resulted in 20 years of marriage and the adoption and bringing up of Toby and Anna.

Later in that tour the team found itself in the city of Nagpur, which happens to be bang in the middle of the subcontinent. A sumptuous buffet supper of fish pie was served in the hotel, and Don, eyeing his first square meal for some time, filled his plate to overflowing. Before he had time to commit any of this to mouth fellow tourist Peter Parfitt tapped him on the shoulder to inform him that in whatever direction he might turn the sea was more than 1,000 miles away. Always concerned for his health, and as one that could be quite easily petrified as well as persuaded, Don returned the contents of his plate whence it had come.

Don's poor health latterly was a rotten reward for a man of such vitality with a boundless zest for life, whose life touched so many people. His enthusiasm and encouragement endeared him to people everywhere. His illness and his subsequent passing deprived us all of what we had once hoped would be years of fun to come.

To you, Don, we will never forget you. Rest in peace, my friend — you deserve to.

FURTHER TRIBUTES TO THE GREAT ENTERTAINER

The following tributes were also paid to Don Wilson by former colleagues following his death:

PHILIP SHARPE: The *Settle Gazelle, Settle Windmill, Zebedee* and *Mad Jack.* To whom could I possibly be referring? By now, those in the Yorkshire cricketing world will know perfectly well who I am talking about. To some these names may sound derogatory; to those who knew him they were terms of affection.

Don Wilson was an extraordinary man. Tall, gangly and amazingly agile, he was able to cover a lot of ground in next to no time, hence the *Gazelle* nickname. This was brought about by a natural ability and his great prowess early on in his career on the badminton court.

In the field he was dynamite, and before the opposition found him out he had several run-outs to his credit, particularly off the bowling of Raymond Illingworth, Brian Close and the like. He was a perfect foil for Raymond's off-spin at the other end.

He was known as *Zebedee* for a while because of his extraordinary leaps into the air, all of four feet, when he thought he had taken a wicket or a batsman had played and missed. He and Raymond worked so well in tandem. As for his batting, what can I say? This is where the *Windmill* gets a mention. He had a great eye for a ball, and was one of the best strikers ever. Because of his physique when he wound up to strike all the limbs went everywhere as the ball disappeared from sight. How far it would have gone with today's equipment is another story.

Two of the best moments in his batting career were his performances at Worcester and Hyderabad. Yorkshire looked like losing at Worcester and, to be fair, they had outplayed us. Wils had his right wrist in pot as he strode to the wicket at No. 11. Normally he would have batted at No. 8. He was greeted half way to the wicket by Bob Platt, who was endeavouring to save the game.

The conversation went something like this: Bob says, "Just take it easy, we have only a few overs to block it out." Wils was having none it. "No, we can win this," he said. "Don't be ridiculous," says Bob. Jack Flavell and Len Coldwell were bowling, two of the best in the land. For the next few overs Bob was playing for the draw while Don, who was not the greatest against the quicks, took it upon himself to smite the two England bowlers to all parts and, may I remind you, with one hand only. Yorkshire won the match! Talk about victory snatched from the jaws of defeat! The sight of the Worcester team returning up the steps to the pavilion was a sight we will never, ever forget.

He went in as nightwatchman in Hyderabad in 1964, when he was not out at the end of the day. Someone nicked his batting kit overnight, and the next morning was interesting. What did he do? He borrowed my bat with a short handle when he was used to a long-handled bat, pads and gloves. He smacked a century, didn't he? It was obviously my kit that helped. Another unforgettable moment.

Don was a one-off. He was my "roomie" for 11 years, and we covered a lot of ground together...not on the field, you understand, because I stood at slip, but along the highways and byways, as we used to say. Scarborough to Eastbourne, Bradford to Bournemouth. Motorways? What were they? A great pal and a lovely bloke.

Cheers, Mad Jack! Great to have known you, Wils!

RAYMOND ILLINGWORTH: Don was a member of my England squad when we regained the *Ashes* on the 1970-1971 tour of Australia and New Zealand, and although he did not play in any of the Test matches he was an extremely popular member of the party.

Nobody had a greater love of the game or was more enthusiastic, and you cannot say more than that. His enthusiasm was never greater than when he went to Lord's and was working with the kids. He got them really interested in what they were doing.

He became the latest in the long line of the county's great left-armers, and not many have achieved as much as that. He was a wonderful fielder at mid-wicket, and with his left arm stretched out was responsible for quite a few run-outs. He was not the best against the quicks, but he liked to give it a good whack and he scored a lot of useful runs.

Don had not been well for some time, but his passing is still very sad and he will be much missed.

GEOFF COPE: Don was a marvellous colleague and friend, and I always called him "Wilfred". His haul of 1,104 wickets at 20 runs apiece is testimony to what a splendid bowler he was.

He joked a lot about that famous occasion as a teenager when he bowled Len Hutton at Settle. He said he had bowled him through the gate, and if the gate had been closed he would have been bowling at him ever since! He said he got a lot of booing from his schoolmates who said they had come to see Hutton bat, not Wilson bowl.

I have never found anyone with so much enthusiasm for the game. The *White Rose* meant so much to him it was untrue.The work he did in South Africa was incredible. He got cricket going in the schools and is still very well thought of in that country. They thought the world of him at Lord's when he became Head Coach: he used to say he had a magnificent lawn which somebody came to cut every day.

When Raymond Illingworth left Yorkshire Don became the senior bowler, and he told me all about bowling in pairs and bowling for each other. It was always "we" and never "I". He was a great man.

MICHAEL CRAWFORD

By David Warner

Yorkshire lost one of the Club's leading figures over many years with the death in York District Hospital on Sunday, December 2, 2012, of Michael Crawford, right, at the age of 92.

Michael, who was born at Moortown Corner, Leeds, on July 30, 1920, lived at Kirk Deighton, near Wetherby, and was a former Chairman and Treasurer of Yorkshire County Cricket Club.

A well-organised batsman, he played for Yorkshire Second XI from 1947 to 1953, captained them in 1951 and was joint-captain with Ronnie Burnet in 1952.

One of his proudest moments was when he was called to captain Yorkshire for one Championship match in Norman Yardley's absence in 1951, scoring nine and 13 in a thrilling encounter with Worcestershire at Scarborough, which the visitors won by eight runs.

When I interviewed Michael a couple of years ago for my recently published book, *The Sweetest Rose*, he revealed that he had been invited to captain Yorkshire on a permanent basis in 1958, but turned down the job because of his business commitments. It was accepted by Burnet, and Yorkshire triumphed under his command the following season.

Michael captained Leeds CC for 14 seasons from 1949 to 1962, leading them to their first Yorkshire League title in 1958 and their third Yorkshire Council Championship the same year.

In 1963 he took over as Yorkshire Treasurer from A Wyndham-Heselton, who had held the post for 30 years. He gave continuous service until 1980, when he became Club Chairman for the next three years and Chairman of the Cricket Management Committee.

A member of Yorkshire's General Committee from 1954 to 1983, he was a trustee of the Club from 1963 to 1985, elected a Vice-President in 1979 and made an Honorary Life Member in 2003.

His reign as Club Chairman came to a sad end as a direct result of the Club's decision following the 1983 season to sack Geoffrey Boycott. The consequence of this action was the calling of a special general meeting of the Club in January 1984, at which a vote of no-confidence in the General Committee succeeded and Boycott was reinstated.

Michael decided in the circumstances to stand down as Chairman, and President Norman Yardley also declined to continue in his role.

Educated at Shrewsbury School and Magdalene College, Cambridge, Michael was also an outstanding amateur soccer player, obtaining a Blue and scoring a goal against Oxford University in 1946-1947, and playing in the same university side as Trevor Bailey and Doug Insole.

In 1939 he left Cambridge to spend the next five years in the Army, serving in the Middle East and Italy as a captain in the Royal Artillery and being Mentioned in Despatches. He returned to Cambridge in 1946, and scored all four goals in the university's 4-3 win over Tottenham Hotspur. His soccer career included spells with Cambridge Town, Corinthian Casuals and Old Salopians.

Another sport at which Michael excelled — and played until his illness — was golf. He was president of Alwoodley Golf Club, which was formed in 1907 by two great figures from Yorkshire's past, Lord Hawke and the Hon F S Jackson.

Michael was a chartered accountant, who retired at 60 and ran a property and investment company from 1980 to 1995.

Yorkshire CCC Board Director and former Club President and Chairman Robin Smith said: "I have known Michael Crawford for many years. He was a real gentleman, an urbane and friendly person of unquestioned integrity. He was a really decent man, and widely respected by everyone. All who came into contact with him would come away with a very warm impression of him. He was the sort of stalwart personality so many institutions need."

Michael's widow, Hazel, was formerly Miss Hazel Cameron, a cousin of former South Africa wicket-keeper Jock Cameron, who once hit Hedley Verity for so many runs in an over at Sheffield that wicket-keeper Arthur Wood shouted to Verity: "You've got him in two minds, Hedley — he doesn't know whether to hit you for four or six!"

Michael and Hazel had two sons, James and Neil. A thanksgiving service, attended by about 270 people, was held at All Saints' Church, Kirkdeighton, on January 7 this year.

Scarborough 1952: Fast bowler Eric Burgin flanked by Yorkshire captains of the future Brian Close, left, and Vic Wilson ***(Photo: Ron Deaton Archive)***

ERIC BURGIN

Sheffield-born Eric Burgin, who died on November 16 aged 88, was one of the proudest cricketers ever to play for Yorkshire — as well as one of several accomplished pacemen to share the new ball with the great Fred Trueman. Eric, a talented all-round sportsman who was also a former captain of York City AFC after turning out for Sheffield United Reserves, played in 12 first-class matches for Yorkshire in 1952 and 1953, capturing 31 wickets at a very respectable 25.64 runs apiece.

He enjoyed an outstanding *Roses* match at Old Trafford in the first of those two seasons when Lancashire clung on for a draw with their last pair at the crease. Yorkshire were sent back for 200, but Eric and Trueman decimated Lancashire with five wickets each to despatch them for 65 in 24 overs. Eric bowled unchanged, conceding only 20 runs, and Trueman claimed 5-26 in 10 overs. Yorkshire then declared at 163-8, but had insufficient time to bowl out their opponents, who closed on 166-9.

Later that season Eric returned his career-best of 6-43 as Surrey lost by nine wickets at Headingley. Centuries from Vic Wilson and Ted Lester enabled Yorkshire to declare on 423-5, and Surrey were put out for 192, Eric snatching the first three wickets with only seven scored. Surrey made a better fist of it second time, but Yorkshire romped home.

Eric maintained his allegiance to Yorkshire CCC for the rest of his life, and was on the General Committee as a Sheffield representative for four years from 1980, serving on the cricket, public relations, ground and fundraising subcommittees. He was a devoted founder member of Yorkshire Players' Association, regularly attending its social functions.

Eric was a leading fast bowler with Sheffield United, and played a prominent part in their switch from Bramall Lane to Bawtry Road in 1973. He leaves a widow, Betty, a son and a grandson.

David Warner

DOUGLAS VERITY

George Douglas Verity, right, whose father, the great Hedley, twice took 10 wickets in an innings for Yorkshire, died in August, 2012, at the age of 78.

Douglas was born in Rawdon, where Hedley first played cricket for Rawdon Cricket Club — as did both Brian Close and Bryan Stott.

No mean sportsman himself, Douglas — named after his father's two heroes, George Hirst and Douglas Jardine — lived for much of his life in North Wales, where he first worked as a professional at Bangor Golf Club, and then for almost 30 years up to his retirement in 1998 at Pwllheli, where he was given the rare accolade for a professional of being made club captain.

Douglas was a keen climber, and after moving from Yorkshire he became manager at Pen-y-Gwryd, the climbing club in North Wales, where he met Ann, whom he married in 1963.

He was always proud of his father's achievements, but as a young man playing league cricket he was dogged by suggestions that he was only there because of his father. It was one such incident which led him to realise that he must leave Yorkshire.

He was only 10 when his father, a captain in the 1st Battalion the Green Howards, died from wounds received while leading his men in Sicily in 1943. Hedley's wife, Kathleen, was left with two young boys to bring up on a widow's pension, and for some years life was a struggle. Eventually brother Wilfred opened a photographic shop in Otley, while Douglas, as he later put it, "scraped a living" as a groundsman and cricket professional in the Bradford League.

In 1975 Wilfred was killed by a runaway cattle trailer while walking with his young son, Hedley, near their Otley home. Hedley was seriously injured, but survived, and still lives in Yorkshire.

Douglas never forgot his roots or his father's achievements. Four years ago he returned to unveil a blue plaque erected by Leeds Civic Trust outside the house in Welton Grove, Burley, where Hedley was born, not far from Headingley Cricket Ground. He is survived by his wife Ann, sons Charles and James, and grandchildren India and Siena.

Felicity McCormick

DENNIS BOLTON

Dennis Bolton, right, Yorkshire CCC's longest-serving member, died on April 9, 2012, aged 89, after being closely associated with the club for 79 years.

His involvement began in 1933, when he was bought a junior membership ticket by his father, and he remained an avid follower of the team's fortunes right up to his death following a short illness.

Dennis was an equally loyal supporter of Leeds United. He was taken to see his first match at Elland Road in 1936, and he became a season-ticket holder in 1957, rarely missing a home fixture.

A journalist with the *Yorkshire Post* for 38 years, he reported on local government, covering the former West Riding County Council and then, as Municipal Correspondent, the affairs of Leeds City Council. Such was his love of cricket that in the post-war years, when his job was mainly lobbying council committees at Leeds Civic Hall, he would always make time to watch part of a day's play.

He would book a ticket for every day of a Headingley Test, and rely on being able to nip to the ground occasionally, having worked out how much time he could stay there before rushing back to Civic Hall by bus.

When Geoffrey Boycott scored his 100th hundred on August 11, 1977, he persuaded a colleague to stand in for him at Civic Hall, and he got to Headingley 10 minutes before Boycott made the vital hit. He shared in the celebrations, and immediately returned to work.

In Festival of Britain year, 1951, he was so moved by the atmosphere when Peter May scored 138 against South Africa on his Test debut that he wrote a colour piece for the *Yorkshire Post's* then whimsical Northerner column, earning a rare compliment from the editor, Sir Linton Andrews.

Dennis was born in Upper Armley, Leeds, into a family of staunch Methodists, and he was baptised at Armley Methodist Church. In 1950 he married his wife, Dorothy, at Headingley Methodist Church, and they moved to Burley-in-Wharfedale in 1990, celebrating their diamond wedding in 2010. They had three children, six grandchildren and a great granddaughter. A memorial service was held at Burley-in-Wharfedale Methodist Church, on Friday, May 11.

The Players

Andrew William GALE

Left-hand batsman

Born: Dewsbury, November 28, 1983

First-Class cricket:

Debut: v. Somerset at Scarborough, 2004

Highest score: 151* v. Nottinghamshire at Nottingham, 2010

Best bowling: 1-33 v. Loughborough UCCE at Leeds, 2007

CB 40:

Highest score: 125* v. Essex at Chelmsford, 2010

FP t20:

Highest score: 91 v. Nottinghamshire at Leeds, 2009

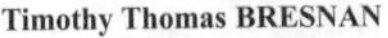

John Joseph SAYERS

Left-hand batsman, right-arm off-break bowler

Born: Leeds, November 5, 1983

First-Class cricket:

Debut: Oxford University v. Worcestershire at Oxford, 2002

Debut for Yorkshire: v. Leicestershire at Leicester, 2004

Highest score for Yorkshire: 187 v. Kent at Tunbridge Wells, 2007

Best bowling: 3-15 v. Durham MCCU at Durham, 2011

CB 40:

Highest score: 62 v. Gloucestershire at Leeds, 2005

Best bowling: 1-31 v. Warwickshire at Birmingham, 2005

FP t20:

Highest score: 44 v. Northamptonshire at Northampton, 2011

Timothy Thomas BRESNAN

Right-hand batsman, right-arm medium-fast bowler

Born: Pontefract, February 28, 1985

First-Class cricket:

Debut: v. Northamptonshire at Northampton, 2003

Highest score: 126* for England Lions v. Indians at Chelmsford, 2007

Highest for Yorkshire: 116 v. Surrey, at The Oval, 2007

Best bowling: 5-42 v. Worcestershire at Worcester, 2005

List A:

Highest score: 80 for England v. Australia at Centurion Park, 2009

CB 40:

Highest score: 61 v. Leicestershire at Leeds, 2003

Best bowling: 4-25 v. Somerset at Leeds, 2005

FP t20:

Highest score: 42 v. Leicestershire at Leeds, 2004

Best bowling: 3-10 England v. Pakistan at Cardiff, 2010

Best bowling for Yorkshire: 3-21 v. Durham at Chester-le-Street, 2006

Jonathan Marc BAIRSTOW

Right-hand batsman, wicket-keeper
Born: Bradford, September 26, 1989

First-Class Cricket:

Debut: v Somerset at Leeds, 2009
Highest score: 205 v. Nottinghamshire at Nottingham, 2011

CB 40:

Highest score: 114 v. Middlesex at Lord's, 2011

FP t20:

Highest score: 68* v. Sussex at Cardiff, 2012

Joe Edward ROOT

Right-hand batsman, right-arm off-spin bowler
Born: Sheffield, December 30, 1990

First-Class cricket:

Debut: v. Loughborough MCCU at Leeds, 2010
Highest score: 222* v. Hampshire at West End, Southampton, 2012
Best bowling: 3-33 v. Warwickshire at Birmingham, 2011

CB 40:

Highest score: 63 v Essex at Leeds, 2009
Best bowling: 2-14 v. Kent at Leeds, 2012

FP t20:

Highest score: 65 v. Worcestershire at Leeds, 2012
Best bowling: 1-12 v.Warwickshire at Leeds, 2011

Ryan Jay SIDEBOTTOM

Left-hand bat, left-arm fast-medium bowler
Born: Huddersfield, January 15, 1978

First-Class cricket:

Debut: v. Leicestershire at Leicester, 1997
Highest score: 61 v. Worcestershire at Worcester, 2011
Best bowling: 7-37 v. Somerset at Leeds 2011

CB 40:

Highest score: 32 for Nottinghamshire v. Middlesex at Nottingham, 2005
Highest score for Yorkshire: 30* v. Glamorgan at Leeds, 2002
Best bowling: 6-40 v. Glamorgan at Cardiff, 1998

FP t20:

Highest score for Yorkshire: 16* v. Worcestershire at Worcester, 2011
Best bowling: 4-25 v. Durham at Chester-le-Street, 2012

Philip Anthony JAQUES

Left-hand batsman, slow left-arm bowler
Born: Sydney, Australia, May 3, 1979

First-Class cricket:

Debut: New South Wales v Queensland at Brisbane, 2000-1
Debut for Yorkshire: v. Hampshire at Leeds, 2004
Highest score: 244 for Worcestershire v. Essex at Chelmsford, 2006
Highest score for Yorkshire: 243 v. Hampshire at Southampton, 2004

List A:

Highest score: 105 for Yorkshire v. Sussex at Leeds, 2004

FP t20:

Highest score: 92 v. Leicestershire at Leeds, 2004

Andrew John HODD

Right-hand batsman, wicket keeper
Born: Chichester, January 12, 1984

First-Class cricket:

Debut: Sussex v. Zimbabwe at Hove, 2003
Debut for Yorkshire: v. Derbyshire at Leeds, 2012
Highest score: 123 for Sussex v. Yorkshire at Hove, 2007
Highest score for Yorkshire: 58 v. Derbyshire at Leeds, 2012

List A:

Highest score: 91 for Sussex v. Lancashire at Hove, 2010
Awaiting Yorkshire debut

FP t20:

Highest score: 26 for Sussex v. Kent at Hove, 2010
Awaiting Yorkshire debut

Adam LYTH

Left-hand batsman, right-arm medium bowler
Born: Whitby, September 25, 1987

First-Class cricket:

Debut: v. Loughborough UCCE at Leeds, 2007
Highest score: 248* v. Leicestershire at Leicester, 2012
Best bowling: 1-12 v. Loughborough UCCE at Leeds, 2007

CB 40:

Highest score: 109* v. Sussex at Scarborough, 2009
Best bowling: 0-3 v. Essex at Chelmsford, 2009

t20:

Highest score: 78 v. Derbyshire at Leeds, 2012
Best bowling: 0-14 v. Mumbai at Capetown, 2012

Steven Andrew PATTERSON

Right-hand batsman, right-arm medium-fast bowler
Born: Beverley, October 3, 1983

First-Class cricket:

Debut: v. Bangladesh 'A' at Leeds, 2005
Highest score: 53 v. Sussex at Hove, 2011
Best bowling: 5-50 v. Essex at Scarborough, 2010

CB 40:

Highest score: 25* v. Worcestershire at Leeds, 2006
Best bowling: 6-32 v. Derbyshire at Leeds, 2010

FP t20:

Highest score: 3* v. Derbyshire at Leeds, 2010
Best bowling: 4-30 v. Lancashire at Leeds, 2010

Adil Usman RASHID

Right-hand batsman, leg-break bowler
Born: Bradford, February 17, 1988

First-Class cricket:

Debut: v. Warwickshire at Scarborough, 2006
Highest score: 157* v. Lancashire at Leeds, 2009
Best bowling: 7-107 v. Hampshire at Southampton, 2008

CB 40:

Highest score: 43 v. Netherlands at Amsterdam, 2011
Best bowling: 4-38 v. Northamptonshire at Northampton, 2012

FP t20:

Highest score: 34 v. Worcestershire at Worcester, 2010
Best bowling: 4-20 v. Leicestershire at Leeds, 2010

Richard Michael PYRAH

Right-hand batsman, right-arm medium bowler
Born: Dewsbury, November 1, 1982

First-Class cricket:

Debut: v. Glamorgan at Colwyn Bay, 2004
Highest score: 134* Loughborough v. MCCU at Leeds, 2010
Best bowling: 5-58 v. Nottinghamshire at Leeds, 2011

List A:

Best bowling: 5-50 for Yorkshire Cricket Board v. Somerset at Scarborough, 2002

CB 40:

Highest score: 69 v. Netherlands at Leeds, 2011
Best bowling: 4 for 24 v. Netherlands at Rotterdam, 2010

t20:

Highest score: 35 v. Leicestershire at Leicester, 2012
Best bowling: 5-16 v. Durham at Scarborough, 2011

Gary Simon BALLANCE

Left-hand batsman, leg-break bowler
Born: Harare, Zimbabwe, November 22, 1989

First-Class Cricket:
Debut: v Kent at Canterbury, 2008
Highest score: 210 for Mid-West Rhinos v. Southern Rocks at Masvingo, Zimbabwe, 2011-12
Highest score for Yorkshire: 121* Gloucestershire at Bristol, 2012

CB 40:
Highest score: 103* v. Unicorns at Scarborough, 2012

List A:
Highest score: 135* for Mid West Rhinos v Mashonaland Eagles 2010/11

t20:
Highest score: 64* v. Trinidad and Tobago at Centurion, 2012

Azeem RAFIQ

Right-hand batsman, off-break bowler
Born: Karachi, Pakistan, February 27, 1991

First-Class Cricket:
Debut: v Sussex at Leeds, 2009
Highest score: 100 v Worcestershire at Worcester, 2009
Best bowling: 5-50 Essex at Chelmsford, 2012

CB 40:
Highest score: 34* v. Unicorns at Leeds, 2012
Best bowling: 3-22 v. Kent at Leeds, 2012

t20:
Highest score: 11* v. Derbyshire at Leeds, 2009 and v. Lancashire at Manchester, 2011
Best bowling: 3-15 v. Lancashire at Manchester, 2011

Moin Aqeeb ASHRAF

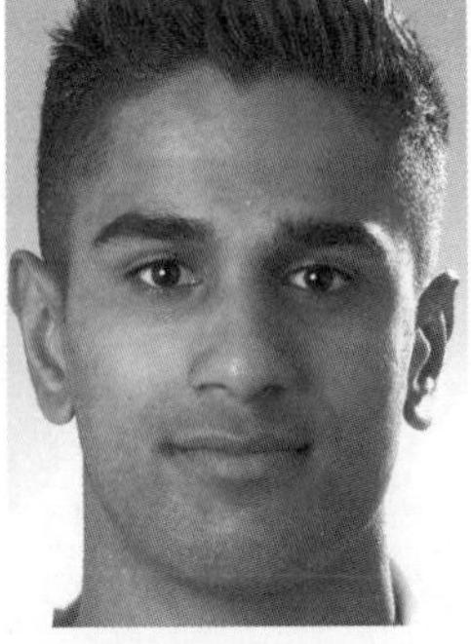

Left-hand batsman, right-arm fast-medium bowler
Born: Bradford, January 5, 1992

First-Class cricket:
Debut: v. Loughborough MCCU at Leeds, 2010
Highest score: 10 v. Kent at Leeds, 2010
Best bowling: 5-32 v. Kent at Leeds, 2010

CB 40:
Highest Score: 3* v. Kent at Leeds, 2012
Best bowling: 2-36 v. Kent at Canterbury, 2012

t20:
Has not batted
Best bowling: 4-18 v. Derbyshire at Derby, 2012

Daniel Mark HODGSON

Right-hand batsman, wicket-keeper
Born: Northallerton, February 22, 1990

First-Class cricket:
Debut: Leeds MCCU v. Surrey at The Oval, 2012
Awaiting Yorkshire debut
Highest score: 64 for Leeds MCCU v Surrey at The Oval, 2012

CB 40:
Highest score: 9 v. Warwickshire at Scarborough, 2012

t20:
Highest score: 18 v. Uva at Johannesburg, 2012

Liam Edward PLUNKETT

Right-hand batsman, right-arm fast-medium bowler
Born: Middlesbrough, April 6, 1985
Awaiting Yorkshire debut in all forms of the game

First-Class Cricket:
Debut: For Durham v. Durham UCCE at Durham, 2003
Highest score: 107* for Durham v. Durham MCCU at Durham, 2011
Best bowling: 6-63 for Durham v. Worcestershire at Chester-le-Street, 2009

List A:
Highest score: 72 for Durham v. Somerset at Chester-le-Street, 2008
Best bowling: 4-15 for Durham v. Essex at Chester-le-Street 2007

FP t20:
Highest score: 41 for Durham v. Lancashire at Manchester, 2011
Best bowling: 5-31 for Durham v. Lancashire at Chester-le-Street, 2011

Jack Alexander BROOKS

Right-hand batsman, right-arm medium-fast bowler
Born: Oxford, June 4, 1984
Awaiting Yorkshire debut in all forms of the game

First-Class Cricket:
Debut: For Northamptonshire v. Australia at Northampton, 2009
Highest score: 53 for Northamptonshire v. Gloucestershire at Bristol, 2010
Best bowling: 5-23 for Northamptonshire v. Leicestershire at Leicester, 2011

List A:
Highest score: 10 for Northamptonshire v. Middlesex at Uxbridge, 2009
Best bowling: 3-35 for England A v. Bangladesh A at Sylhet 2011-12

FP t20:
Highest score: 33* for Northamptonshire v. Warwickshire at Birmingham, 2011
Best bowling: 3-24 for Northamptonshire v. Yorkshire at Leeds, 2010

YORKSHIRE'S FIRST-CLASS HIGHLIGHTS OF 2012

Win by an innings (1)

Yorkshire (447) beat Leicestershire (116 and 309) by an innings and 22 runs at Scarborough

Totals of 400 and over (5)

486	v. Leicestershire at Leicester
447	v. Leicestershire at Scarborough
420	v. Derbyshire at Leeds
416	v. Northamptonshire at Leeds
402-6	v. Gloucestershire at Bristol (2nd innings)

Century Partnerships (15)

For the 1st wicket (2)

115	J E Root and J J Sayers	v. Kent at Leeds
106	J E Root and J J Sayers	v. Essex at Leeds

For the 3rd wicket (3)

120	A Lyth and A W Gale	v. Glamorgan at Leeds
116	A Lyth and G S Ballance	v. Derbyshire at Leeds
104	P A Jaques and A W Gale	v. Northamptonshire at Northampton

For the 4th wicket (5)

203	P A Jaques and G S Ballance	v. Gloucestershire at Bristol
197	A Lyth and J M Bairstow	v. Leicestershire at Leicester
160	A W Gale and J M Bairstow	v. Leicestershire at Scarborough
149	P A Jaques and G S Ballance	v. Hampshire at Leeds
147	J E Root and J M Bairstow	v. Northamptonshire at Leeds

For the 5th wicket (1)

115	J M Bairstow and G S Ballance	v. Kent at Leeds

For the 6th wicket (2)

159	J M Bairstow and A McGrath	v. Leicestershire at Scarborough
131	A McGrath and A J Hodd	v. Derbyshire at Leeds

For the 7th wicket (1)

110	A McGrath and Azeem Rafiq	v. Essex at Chelmsford

For the 8th wicket (1)

121	J E Root and S A Patterson	v. Hampshire at Southampton

Centuries (11)

J M Bairstow (3)

182 v. Leicestershire at Scarborough
118 v. Leicestershire at Leicester
107 v. Kent at Leeds

P A Jaques (2)

160 v. Gloucestershire at Bristol
126 v. Essex at Leeds

A McGrath (2)

106* v. Hampshire at Leeds
104 v. Derbyshire at Leeds

J E Root (2)

222* v. Hampshire at Southampton
125 v. Northamptonshire at Leeds

G S Ballance (1)

121* v. Gloucestershire at Bristol

A Lyth (1))

248* v. Leicestershire at Leicester

5 wickets in an innings (5)

Azeem Rafiq (1)

5 for 50 v. Essex at Chelmsford

T T Bresnan (1)

5 for 81 v. Gloucestershire at Bristol

S A Patterson (1)

5 for 77 v. Leicestershire at Scarborough

A U Rashid (1)

5 for 105 v. Northamptonshire at Northampton

R J Sidebottom (1)

5 for 30 v. Essex at Leeds

3 catches in an innings (5)

A J Hodd (3)

5 v. Derbyshire at Leeds
4 v. Glamorgan at Leeds (1st innings)
4 v. Glamorgan at Leeds (2nd innings)

J M Bairstow (1)

4 v. Leicestershire at Scarborough

A Lyth (1)

3 v. Essex at Chelmsford

5 catches in a match (2)

A J Hodd (2)

8 (4 + 4) v. Glamorgan at Leeds
6 (5 + 1) v. Derbyshire at Leeds

Debuts (3)

In first-class cricket for Yorkshire: A J Hodd, S J Harmison and M A Starc

Capped (3)

S A Patterson, G S Ballance and J E Root

LV CHAMPIONSHIP FACTFILE

Compiled by John T Potter

Versus KENT at Headingley

1. The earliest ever start to a First Class match at Headingley.
2. Kent's highest total against Yorkshire in Yorkshire.
3. R W T Key passed 16,000 First Class runs.
4. M T Coles scored his maiden First Class century.
5. Kent's ninth-wicket partnership of 153 in their one innings was the highest at Headingley by a visiting team.
6. J M Bairstow passed 3,000 First Class runs.

Versus LEEDS/BRADFORD MCCU at Headingley

1. This was the first First Class match between the sides.
2. A MacQueen made his First Class debut.

Versus ESSEX at Headingley

1. No play on the first day.
2. Essex last played a Championship match at Headingley in May 2005. Two players from each side in that match also played in 2012. They were P A Jaques and A McGrath for Yorkshire and R S Bopara and J S Foster for Essex.
3. P A Jaques's 126* came off 162 balls with one six and 21 fours.
4. R S Bopara's 117* came off 221 balls with 18 fours.

Versus KENT at St Lawrence Ground, Canterbury

1. R J Sidebottom passed 2,000 First Class career runs during Yorkshire's only innings.
2. B P Nash's 132* came off 214 balls with 14 fours.
3. There were 39 minutes play on the third day and none on the last.
4. A total of 1,765 minutes were lost to the weather in April — the most lost in April since I started keeping records in 1993.
5. This was Yorkshire's 200th Championship match against Kent.
6. Yorkshire played a Championship match with floodlights on for part of the time. This had happened once before in a match at Derby.

LV CHAMPIONSHIP FACTFILE *(Continued)*

Versus LEICESTERSHIRE at Scarborough

1. This was the earliest ever start to a First Class Match at Scarborough, and only the second First Class match to be played there in the month of May.
2. J M Bairstow's 182 came off 259 balls with four sixes and 19 fours.
3. S A Patterson took his 100th First Class wicket for Yorkshire when he dismissed R H Joseph in Leicestershire's first innings.
4. M A G Boyce's 122 came off 269 balls with 15 fours, a career best.
5. S A Patterson's match figures of 8-94 (5-77 and 3-17) were his best.
6. This was Leicestershire's 10th First Class match at Scarborough against Yorkshire — and they still have no wins.

Versus GLOUCESTERSHIRE at Bristol

1. Yorkshire had not played a Championship match at Bristol since 1996. A McGrath played in that match. R A Kettleborough played for Yorkshire in that match and umpired in this game.
2. No play on the first day.
3. Yorkshire's second-innings total of 402-6 was their second-highest successful fourth-innings total.
4. This fourth-inning's total was the highest winning score by a visiting team at Bristol.
5. G S Ballance's 124* was his highest score for Yorkshire.

Versus HAMPSHIRE at Headingley

1. M D Bates's 103 was his maiden First Class century.
2. Hampshire's first-innings sixth-wicket partnership of 170 between S M Katich and M D Bates equalled their best against Yorkshire — a record set by C P Mead and G C Harrison at Southampton in 1914.
3. R J Sidebottom took his 550th First Class wicket.
4. P A Jaques passed 14,000 First Class runs.

Versus NORTHAMPTONSHIRE at Headingley

1. O P Stone (Northamptonshire) made his First Class debut.
2. M A Starc made his First Class debut for Yorkshire.
3. A McGrath played his 250th First Class match.
4. J E Root's 125 came off 161 balls with 14 fours, and was Yorkshire's 700th Championship century scored in Yorkshire.

LV CHAMPIONSHIP FACTFILE *(Continued)*

Versus GLAMORGAN at Colwyn Bay

1. Only 127 minutes of play (34 overs) were possible. There was no play after 1.47pm on the first day, a total of 1,313 minutes lost.
2. Yorkshire last played at this venue on August 24-27, 2004, when there was a similar pattern — 51 overs were bowled on the third day, but none on the other days, a total of 1,340 minutes lost.
3. When Yorkshire played Middlesex at Headingley on June 26-28 and 30, 1997, only 41 overs were bowled with 1,377 minutes lost.

Versus HAMPSHIRE at The Rose Bowl, Southampton

1. No play on the first day — Yorkshire's fourth consecutive Championship day without play.
2. S J Harmison made his First Class debut for Yorkshire as the first player to be received on loan by the Club.
3. J E Root made his First Class career-best — 222* off 270 balls with three sixes and 26 fours.
4. 58* were added for the 10th wicket in 36 balls — Moin Ashraf contributed only four off nine balls with one four.
5. No play on the fourth day.
6. Only 106 overs bowled in total — the fewest in a Championship match at The Rose Bowl.

Versus DERBYSHIRE at Queen's Park, Chesterfield

1. Yorkshire's last First Class appearance match on this ground was on May 11-13, 1995, when J M Bairstow's brother, Andrew, made his First Class debut as wicket-keeper for Derbyshire.
2. P J Hartley, an umpire in the 2012 fixture, played in that 1995 match, taking 2-27 in the first innings and 9-41 in the second with four wickets in five balls, including a hat-trick.
3. Yorkshire's present-day Director of Professional Cricket Martyn Moxon contributed 2 retired hurt and 6 not out in 1995, vital runs as Yorkshire won by seven runs.
4. No play after the first day. Yorkshire had now lost 11 full days in the 2012 County Championship.

Versus LEICESTERSHIRE at Grace Road, Leicester

1. A Lyth achieved his highest First Class score, 228* off 395 balls with three sixes and 28 fours.
2. Lyth's innings was the 44th in which a Yorkshire player had carried his bat, and he was the first to do so with a double-century.
3. The fourth-wicket partnership of 197 by A Lyth and J M Bairstow was the second highest against Leicestershire by Yorkshire. The highest is 205* by G Boycott and P J Sharpe at Leicester in 1964.

LV CHAMPIONSHIP FACTFILE *(Continued)*

Versus NORTHAMPTONSHIRE at Northampton

1. Northamptonshire's 1,000th First Class match at Wantage Road.
2. D J Willey achieved his highest First Class score with 76.
3. J D Middlebrook took his 400th First Class wicket when he dismissed P A Jaques in Yorkshire's second innings.

Versus DERBYSHIRE at Headingley

1. Wicket-keeper/batsman A J Hodd made his First Class debut for Yorkshire — their second loan signing of the season. He scored 58, and took five catches in the first innings and one in the second.
2. W J Durston returned a career-best bowling analysis of 5-34.

Versus GLOUCESTERSHIRE at Scarborough

1. Yorkshire's 200th Championship match against Gloucestershire, who last played a First Class match at Scarborough in 1983.
3. There was no play on the second or third days. Yorkshire had now lost 13 full days lost in the 2012 County Championship.
4. 24 minutes (60 balls) of gentle bowling on the last morning saw Gloucestershire score 159 and leave a victory target of 314 runs.
5. A McGrath's 76* was his 100th First Class score for Yorkshire of 50 or over — 34 hundreds and 66 fifties.
6. Yorkshire did their first double over Gloucestershire since 1967

Versus GLAMORGAN at Headingley

1. D L Lloyd (Glamorgan) made his First Class debut with a pair.
2. This was Yorkshire's 15th Championship match of the season, and was the first to have no weather interruptions.

Versus ESSEX at The County Ground, Chelmsford

1. S A Patterson reached 50 First Class wickets for the season with his first wicket in Essex's second innings.
2. Azeem Rafiq's 5-50 in the second innings was his first five-wicket haul in an innings.
3. No batsman scored 1,000 runs in the season — 1999 was the last time this occurred.
4. Yorkshire recorded three wins in a row for the first time since 2005: Somerset at Headingley (April 20-23), Northamptonshire at Headingley (May 6-9) and Leicestershire at Leicester (May 11-14). Promotion was achieved that season as well.
5. The last time Yorkshire won their last three matches was in 1998.
6. Yorkshire went through the season without losing a First Class match for the first time since 1928.
7. This was the 333rd First Class match at this ground...not unlucky for Yorkshire.

LV Championship Division 2, 2012

Captain: A W Gale

*Captain

§ Wicket-Keeper

Figures in brackets ( ) indicate position in 2nd Innings batting order, where different from 1st Innings.

DETAILS OF PLAYERS WHO APPEARED FOR YORKSHIRE IN 2012 (ALL FIRST-CLASS MATCHES)

Player	Date of Birth	Birthplace	First-Class debut for Yorkshire	Date Capped
A W Gale	November 28, 1983	Dewsbury	July 21, 2004	Sept. 18, 2008
A McGrath	October 6, 1975	Bradford	May 18, 1995	July 20, 1999
R J Sidebottom	January 15, 1978	Huddersfield	July 2, 1997	July 23, 2000
P A Jaques	May 3, 1979	Wollongong, Aus	May 12, 2004	April 7, 2005
T T Bresnan	February 28, 1985	Pontefract	May 14, 2003	July 19, 2006
J J Sayers	November 5, 1983	Leeds	August 19, 2004	June 16, 2007
G L Brophy	November 26, 1975	Welkom, S A	April 19, 2006	May 31, 2008
A U Rashid	February 17, 1988	Bradford	July 19, 2006	Sept. 18, 2008
A Shahzad	July 27, 1985	Huddersfield	August 30, 2006	April 8, 2010
A Lyth	September 25, 1987	Whitby	May 16, 2007	Aug. 22, 2010
R M Pyrah	November 1, 1982	Dewsbury	August 24, 2004	Aug. 22, 2010
J M Bairstow	September 26, 1989	Bradford	June 11, 2009	Aug. 17, 2011
S A Patterson	October 3, 1983	Beverley	August 3, 2005	May 16, 2012
G S Ballance	November 22, 1989	Harare, Zim	July 11, 2008	Sept. 4, 2012
J E Root	December 30, 1990	Sheffield	May 10, 2010	Sept. 4, 2012
O J Hannon-Dalby	June 20, 1989	Halifax	May 21, 2008	—
Azeem Rafiq	February 27, 1991	Karachi, Pak	June 5, 2009	—
M A Ashraf	January 5, 1992	Bradford	May 10, 2010	—
I Wardlaw	June 29, 1985	Dewsbury	July 20, 2011	—
M A Starc	January 13, 1990	Sydney, Aus	May 30, 2012	—
S J Harmison	October 23, 1978	Ashington	July 11, 2012	—
A J Hodd	January 12, 1984	Chichester	August 15, 2012	—

Match-By-Match Reports **NIGEL PULLAN**
Scorecards **JOHN POTTER**
Pictures **SIMON WILKINSON**
VAUGHN RIDLEY
ALEX WHITEHEAD
SWpix.com

LV County Championship Division 2
Yorkshire v. Kent

Played at Headingley, Leeds, on April 5, 6, 7 and 8, 2012

Match drawn at 5pm on the Fourth Day

Toss won by Kent — Kent 10 points; Yorkshire 9 points

Close of play: First Day, Kent 345-5 (Stevens 22*, Riley 0*); Second Day, Yorkshire 32-0 (Root 13*, Sayers 19*); Third Day, Yorkshire 316-6 (Rashid 49*, Shahzad 17*)

KENT

S A Newman b Sidebottom	64
* R W T Key, run out (Gale)	97
B W Harmison, c Ballance b Rashid	45
B P Nash, c McGrath b Shahzad	67
M J Powell, lbw b Rashid	37
D I Stevens, c Sayers b Shahzad	29
A E N Riley, b Rashid	8
§ G O Jones, b Shahzad	2
M T Coles, not out	103
M Davies, c Ballance b McGrath	58
C E Shreck, not out	0
Extras b 8, lb 15, nb 4	27
Total (9 wkts dec)	537

Bonus points — Kent 4, Yorkshire 2 — Score at 110 overs: 371-7

FoW: 1-141 (Newman), 2-201 (Key), 3-239 (Harmison), 4-310 (Nash), 5-344 (Powell) 6-358(Stevens), 7-366(Jones), 8-374 (Riley), 9-527 (Davies)

	O	M	R	W
Sidebottom	28	6	74	1
Shahzad	31	7	86	3
Pyrah	19	4	81	0
Wardlaw	24	1	106	0
Rashid	40.3	7	141	3
McGrath	5	0	13	1
Root	1	0	13	0

YORKSHIRE

First Innings		Second Innings	
J E Root, c Jones b Coles	25	b Riley	76
J J Sayers, c Riley b Davies	24	lbw b Riley	43
A McGrath, lbw b Davies	0	not out	16
* A W Gale, lbw b Davies	44	c Jones b Shreck	0
§ J M Bairstow, c Jones b Stevens	107	c Newman b Shreck	8
G S Ballance, lbw b Riley	45	not out	0
A U Rashid, c Jones b Shreck	58		
A Shahzad, lbw b Shreck	25		
R J Sidebottom, c Harmison b Shreck	2		
I Wardlaw, not out	13		
R M Pyrah, b Shreck	0		
Extras b 3, lb 16, nb 2	21	Extras w 1, nb 2	3
Total	364	Total (4 wkts)	146

Bonus points — Yorkshire 4, Kent 3

FoW: 1st 1-37 (Sayers), 2-37 (McGrath), 3-79 (Root), 4-111 (Gale), 5-226 (Ballance) 6-290 (Bairstow), 7-347 (Shahzad), 8-351 (Sidebottom), 9-356 (Rashid), 10-364 (Pyrah)

2nd 1-115(Root), 2-124 (Sayers), 3-125 (Gale), 4-145 (Bairstow)

	O	M	R	W		O	M	R	W
Davies	23	7	48	3	Davies	7	1	13	0
Shreck	26.1	1	90	4	Shreck	10	4	22	2
Stevens	23	3	72	1	Stevens	7	0	32	0
Cole	11	0	49	1	Riley	16	6	43	2
Riley	12	2	68	1	Nash	1	0	1	0
Nash	6	0	18	0	Coles	12	3	35	0

Umpires: M A Eggleston and N A Mallender — Scorers: J T Potter and L A R Hart

Yorkshire v. Kent

Bairstow shows way to safety

JONATHAN BAIRSTOW
His first home century

The match began on Maundy Thursday as the Queen distributed money at York Minster, and it was played over Easter as the earliest Championship game on record.

Thursday was sunny, but it was cold and windy thereafter. Kent had six players with substantial first-class experience making their county debuts, and all did well.

Kent made a substantial but not incontestable total on the first day after Newman and Key had put on 141 for the first wicket. Key was run out in a moment of aberration by Gale for 97, and Nash played some graceful shots in an impressive 67.

Coles and Davies added 153 for the ninth wicket on the second day. Coles, a powerful young all-rounder from Maidstone, hit his first century off only 111 balls with three big sixes, the last a reverse-sweep into the East Stand to bring up his hundred. Leg-spinner Rashid's action appeared to have been modified, and he bowled with more flight and variety in unhelpful, cold conditions. Had he taken the last two wickets when he had 3-67 all would have looked well, but he suffered under the Coles/Davies onslaught.

Yorkshire had to bat just over two days to save the match. Davies, signed from Durham, bowled an excellent line and length with movement off the pitch, and Shreck was a formidable opening partner, but after three wickets had fallen Bairstow and Gale came together, and the middle batsmen provided more solidarity. Bairstow batted very well for his first home Championship hundred, and looked a high-class player. Gale, Ballance and Rashid all contributed, so it seemed that the follow-on might be averted until Shreck took the last four wickets, including Pyrah – who batted with a broken hand.

Yorkshire were 163 behind. The match was saved by some sound batting from Root and Sayers, bad light and rain, but at 146-4 Kent would have been optimistic, had the match run its full length. Jones's dropping of Root behind the stumps, which caused Davies some anguish, might have made a difference.

LV County Championship Division 2
Yorkshire v. Essex

Played at Headingley, Leeds, on April 19, 20, 21 and 22, 2012
Match drawn at 3.45pm on the Fourth Day

Toss won by Yorkshire — Yorkshire 7 points; Essex 6 points

Close of play: First Day, no play; Second Day, Essex 72-5 (Bopara 26*, Foster 9*); Third Day, Yorkshire 144-2 (Sayers 45*, Gale 6*)

First Innings	YORKSHIRE	Second Innings	
J E Root, c Godleman b Masters	2	c Foster b Smith	67
J J Sayers, c Foster b Mills	32	c Foster b Masters	45
P A Jaques, c Petersen b Chambers	126	lbw b Westley	18
* A W Gale, c Godleman b Westley	36	not out	48
§ J M Bairstow, c Petersen b Mills	4	c Wheater b Smith	24
G S Ballance, c sub (C M Willoughby) b Mills	20	not out	3
A McGrath, lbw b Mills	1		
A U Rashid, c sub (C M Willoughby) b Masters	0		
A Shahzad, c Foster b Masters	5		
R J Sidebottom, not out	4		
S A Patterson, lbw b Chambers	0		
Extras b 4, lb 7, nb 6	17	Extras b 2, lb 5, nb 2	9
Total	247	Total (4 wkts dec)	214

Bonus points — Yorkshire 1, Essex 3

FoW: 1st 1-2 (Root), 2-98 (Sayers), 3-184 (Gale), 4-203 (Bairstow), 5-225 (Ballance) 6-230 (McGrath), 7-231 (Rashid), 8-241 (Jaques), 9-241 (Shahzad), 10-246 (Patterson)
2nd: 1-106 (Root), 2-134 (Jaques), 3-144 (Sayers), 4-193 (Bairstow)

	O	M	R	W		O	M	R	W
Masters	25	10	65	3	Masters	20	5	45	1
Chambers	10.1	3	40	2	Chambers	7	0	37	0
Smith	10	2	50	0	Mills	8	1	15	0
Mills	13	3	62	4	Westley	13	2	79	1
Westley	6	0	18	1	Smith	9	2	31	2

First Innings	ESSEX	Second Innings	
B A Godleman, lbw b Sidebottom	9	lbw b Shahzad	2
A N Petersen, lbw b Patterson	16	lbw b Shahzad	3
T Westley, c Bairstow b Sidebottom	0	not out	12
R S Bopara, not out	117	not out	5
A J Wheater, c Bairstow b Patterson	0		
G M Smith, lbw b Patterson	0		
§ * J S Foster, c McGrath b Sidebottom	25		
D D Masters, b Shahzad	1		
T J Phillips, c Root b Sidebottom	7		
M A Chambers, lbw b Sidebottom	0		
T S Mills, run out (Patterson/Bairstow)	2		
Extras b 16, lb 4, nb 2	22	Extras lb 4	4
Total	199	Total (2 wkts)	26

Bonus points — Yorkshire 3

FoW: 1st 1-18 (Godleman), 2-24 (Westley), 3-42 (Petersen), 4-42 (Wheater), 5-42 (Smith) 6-107 (Foster), 7-119 (Masters), 8-149 (Phillips), 10-199 (Mills)
2nd: 1-4 (Petersen), 2-7 (Godleman)

	O	M	R	W		O	M	R	W
Sidebottom	24	10	30	5	Sidebottom	6	0	15	0
Shahzad	17	4	63	1	Shahzad	5.1	3	7	2
Patterson	20	8	54	3					
McGrath	9.5	2	22	0					
Rashid	7	3	8	0					
Root	2	0	2	0					

Umpires: R J Bailey and A G Wharf — Scorers: J T Potter and A E Choat

Yorkshire v. Essex

Comeback century for Jaques

The loss of the first day to rain and interruptions on the last day left the match drawn after a positive declaration by Gale.

It was a good, competitive game in which Yorkshire batted well and not so well but bowled throughout with exemplary determination. It was enhanced by two outstanding innings from Jaques and Bopara.

PHIL JAQUES: Solid but impossible to contain on his way to 126

Jaques and Sayers were in control up to lunch on Friday, but Sayers was caught down the leg side in the last over. Jaques was playing his first innings for some time and his first for Yorkshire since 2005. He provides solidity at the top of the order, but he also displayed a variety of adventurous shots and could never be contained for long. After Gale's dismissal all around him collapsed as seven wickets fell, including his own, for 42 runs and Yorkshire missed a second bowling point. Masters bowled very well from the start of the innings although he later suffered against Jaques, while the promising Dewsbury-born left-arm Mills's pace and enthusiasm earned him four wickets.

Yorkshire's bowling on Friday evening was outstanding, especially Patterson, who at one stage had an analysis of 3-3-0-3. Sidebottom was in good form and Shahzad unfortunate to have so little reward for his hostile bowling. Bopara was still in, and next morning he batted with great patience and concentration to build an invaluable innings for Essex: he played some delightful shots, remaining undefeated on 117.

Root batted well on Saturday evening, and next day Yorkshire hit out so that Gale could declare, leaving Essex to make 262 to win in a maximum of 74 overs. All was set for an exciting afternoon as Shahzad dismissed Godleman and Petersen, but the weather closed in. It was only April 22 and Yorkshire members, many of whom support the county and its players — not only in Championship and one-day games but also at Second Eleven, Academy and schools level — had already endured two cold and windy first-class matches under the fixture allocation.

LV County Championship Division 2
Kent v. Yorkshire

Played at the St Lawrence Ground, Canterbury, on April 26, 27, 28 and 29, 2012

Match drawn at 9.30am on the Fourth Day

Toss won by Kent — Kent 10 points; Yorkshire 7 points

Close of play: First Day, Kent 4-0 (Newman 2*, Northeast 1*); Second Day, Kent 316-6 (Nash 114*, Tredwell 28*); Third Day, Kent 350-9 (Nash 132*, Shreck 7*)

YORKSHIRE

J E Root, lbw b Stevens	21
J J Sayers, b Coles	12
P A Jaques, lbw b Stevens	30
* A W Gale, c Jones b Davies	22
§ J M Bairstow, c Northeast b Coles	32
G S Ballance, b Shreck	38
T T Bresnan, lbw b Tredwell	33
A U Rashid, c Jones b Shreck	27
A Shahzad, c Nash b Coles	4
R J Sidebottom, b Coles	17
S A Patterson, not out	3
Extras lb 5, w 1, nb 2	8
Total	247

Bonus points — Yorkshire 1, Kent 3

FoW: 1-23 (Sayers), 2-41 (Root), 3-70 (Gale), 4-102 (Jaques), 5-120 (Bairstow), 6-171 (Bresnan), 7-221 (Ballance), 8-226 (Rashid), 9-228 (Shahzad), 10-247 (Sidebottom)

	O	M	R	W
Davies	15	4	28	1
Shreck	27	8	65	2
Coles	23.3	4	70	4
Stevens	14	3	39	2
Tredwell	12	2	39	1
Nash	1	0	1	0

KENT

S A Newman, c Bairstow b Shahzad	31
S Northeast, lbw b Shahzad	26
B W Harmison, lbw b Patterson	43
B P Nash, not out	132
M J Powell, c Bresnan b Sidebottom	3
D I Stevens, lbw b Bresnan	8
§ * G O Jones, c Ballance b Sidebottom	47
J C Tredwell, c Jaques b Bresnan	37
M T Coles, c Bairstow b Bresnan	0
M Davies, b Rashid	0
C E Shreck, not out	7
Extras lb 11, w 1, nb 4	16
Total (9 wkts)	350

Bonus points — Kent 4, Yorkshire 3

FoW: 1-35 (Newman), 2-101 (Northeast), 3-125 (Harmison), 4-138 (Powell), 5-158 (Stevens) 6-235 (Jones), 7-333 (Tredwell), 8-333 (Coles), 9-334 (Davies)

	O	M	R	W
Bresnan	29.5	8	89	3
Sidebottom	21	2	86	2
Patterson	22	3	61	1
Shahzad	15	0	54	2
Rashid	15	0	44	1
Root	3	2	5	0

Umpires: T E Jesty and P Willey — Scorers: J T Potter and L A R Hart

Kent v. Yorkshire

Weather martyrs join Becket

GARY BALLANCE: Top-score 38

Heavy rain over the weekend reduced this to virtually a two-day contest, so no positive result was possible.

Kent put Yorkshire in on a damp wicket in bleak and windy conditions as the ball moved about disconcertingly.

It was to Yorkshire's credit that they batted through the day against the combined efforts of seamers Davies, Shreck, Coles and Stevens, but while almost everybody made runs nobody got beyond Ballance's 38.

Sayers and Root played sensibly in the morning until Sayers misjudged a ball from Coles, and Root fell lbw to Stevens. Bairstow appeared well set, hitting Coles for three successive boundaries before he was well caught by Northeast. Ballance and Bresnan, returning to the side from England duties, both did well, but Maidstone-born Coles, recruited into the England Lions side, finished off the innings just short of a second batting point. Davies bowled with characteristic skill and economy and Shreck, large and Cornish, should be an asset to his new county.

The accomplished batting of Nash was the crucial difference between the two sides. He was undefeated on 132, and gave Kent a lead of a little over a hundred. Newman, aggressive but profligate, and Northeast, dour and introspective, were a contrasting opening pair. Harmison batted well, but wickets fell around Nash until Jones and then Tredwell gave him resolute support. Nash added 77 with Jones, who was caught by Ballance at slip, and 97 with Tredwell, who eventually was dismissed by Bresnan on Saturday morning. There was much to admire in the tenacity of Tredwell, but the quality of Nash's strokeplay and judgment were the highlights of the second day and put Kent in a strong position.

A stormy weekend brought an early conclusion to proceedings, so there was either a visit to the shrine of Thomas a'Becket or an early train home for Yorkshire's weather martyrs.

LV County Championship Division 2
Yorkshire v. Leicestershire

Played at North Marine Road, Scarborough, on May 2, 3, 4 and 5, 2012

Yorkshire won by an innings and 22 runs at 3.43pm on the Fourth Day

Toss won by Leicestershire — Yorkshire 23 points, Leicestershire 1 point

Close of play: First Day, Yorkshire 329-5 (Bairstow 141*, McGrath 49*); Second Day, Leicestershire Second Innings, 3-1 (Boyce 0*); Third Day, Leicestershire 102-3 (Boyce 46*, Cobb 45*)

YORKSHIRE

J E Root, c Boyce b White	19
J J Sayers, lbw b Joseph	8
P A Jaques, lbw b Henderson	1
* A W Gale, c Eckersley b White	80
§ J M Bairstow, c du Toit b White	182
G S Ballance, c Boyce b Malik	10
A McGrath, c Eckersley b Henderson	90
T T Bresnan, run out (White)	1
A U Rashid, b White	4
R J Sidebottom, c Eckersley b White	20
S A Patterson, not out	8
Extras b 2, lb 11, w 3, nb 8	24
Total	447

Bonus points — Yorkshire 4, Leicestershire 1 — 110-over score: 375-5

FoW: 1-28 Sayers), 2-33 (Jaques), 3-33 (Root), 4-193 (Gale), 5-217 (Ballance), 6-376 (Bairstow), 7-390 (Bresnan), 8-407 (Rashid), 9-427 (McGrath), 10-447 (Sidebottom)

	O	M	R	W
Joseph	29	11	68	1
Wyatt	21	4	91	0
Henderson	36	5	94	2
White	27	4	90	5
Malik	20	2	91	1

LEICESTERSHIRE

First Innings		Second Innings	
G P Smith, c Bairstow b Patterson	12	lbw b Patterson	3
M A G Boyce, lbw b Sidebottom	0	b Sidebottom	122
J du Toit, c Bairstow b Sidebottom	0	c Sayers b Patterson	1
* R R Sarwan, lbw b McGrath	11	lbw b Patterson	5
J J Cobb, c Bairstow b McGrath	29	lbw b Patterson	69
§ E J H Eckersley, lbw b McGrath	4	b Bresnan	4
W A White, lbw b Patterson	6	c and b McGrath	67
C W Henderson, c Jaques b Bresnan	15	c Ballance b Patterson	17
R H Joseph, c Bairstow b Patterson	0	lbw b Sidebottom	0
M N Malik, not out	21	lbw b Rashid	1
A C F Wyatt, c Jaques b McGrath	8	not out	0
Extras b 1, lb 9	10	Extras b 11, lb 7, nb 2	20
Total	116	Total	309

Bonus points — Yorkshire 3

FoW: 1st — 1-12 (Boyce), 2-12 (du Toit), 3-12 (Smith), 4-33 (Sarwan), 5-43 (Eckersley), 6-64 (Cobb), 7-64 (White), 8-68 (Joseph), 9-104 (Henderson), 10-116 (Wyatt)

FoW: 2nd — 1-3 (Smith), 2-8 (du Toit), 3-14 (Sarwan), 4-142 (Cobb), 5-149 (Eckersley), 6-282 (White), 7-284 (Boyce), 8-284 (Joseph), 9-299 (Malik), 10-309 (Henderson)

	O	M	R	W
Bresnan	12	4	37	1
Sidebottom	13	6	31	2
Patterson	15	8	17	3
McGrath	12.2	4	21	4

	O	M	R	W
McGrath	21	7	33	1
Patterson	25.2	10	77	5
Sidebottom	19	2	52	2
Bresnan	15	1	57	1
Rashid	18	3	58	1
Root	5	2	14	0

Umpires: N A Mallender and M J Saggers — Scorers: J T Potter and P J Rogers

Yorkshire v. Leicestershire

Victory in the freezer

It was the coldest match any of us could recall with a bone-chilling east wind blowing off the sea.

All the Yorkshire players were awarded their county bobble hats in recognition of stoical endurance in temperatures said to be about average for Scarborough in mid-January.

Yorkshire lost three early wickets, but enjoyed a good opening day as Bairstow, Gale and McGrath batted well after Sarwan, deputising for the injured Hoggard, sent the hosts in.

The visitors did miss some catches — most crucially Bairstow on 19 — but that did not detract from a fine display by Gale and Bairstow, who was 140 not out by the close with 11 fours and four sixes, one of which landed in the Trafalgar Square stand.

Next morning Bairstow added 42, but missed a double-century when he was caught low in the covers by du Toit. It was an excellent exhibition of innate timing and elegant strokeplay.

STEVEN PATTERSON Eight wickets in the match...and soon it would be a proper cap

The value of McGrath, deputising for Shahzad as a bowler who could bat, is sometimes underestimated: he scored a solid 90, which made all the difference as others fell around him. Bresnan was run out when an overthrow was chased to the boundary and thrown back with unexpected alacrity.

Yorkshire had an impressive day in the field, as their attack was too strong for a relatively inexperienced Leicestershire side. Even Sarwan was unable to offer serious resistance. McGrath destroyed the middle batting with the wickets of Sarwan, Cobb and Eckersley. Rain disrupted Friday, but Leicestershire did better on Saturday.

Boyce made an excellent 122, showing patience and application that almost saved his side from defeat. Cobb contributed well, and White made 67 which added to his five wickets, constituted a sound, all-round performance. Yorkshire persisted, with Patterson taking 5-77 including four top-order batsmen, but it was the tireless Sidebottom who bowled Boyce to signal the end for gallant Leicestershire.

LV County Championship Division 2
Gloucestershire v. Yorkshire

Played at The County Ground, Bristol, on May 9, 10, 11 and 12, 2012

Yorkshire won by 4 wickets at 6pm on the Fourth Day

Toss won by Yorkshire — Yorkshire 19 points, Gloucestershire 4 points

Close of play: First Day, no play; Second Day, Gloucestershire 165-2 (Williamson 89*, A P R Gidman 6*); Third Day, Yorkshire 30-1 (Lyth 19*, Jaques 8*)

First Innings	GLOUCESTERSHIRE	Second Innings	
B A C Howell, c Jaques b Bresnan	4	not out	24
C D J Dent, lbw b Patterson	62	not out	24
K S Williamson, c Brophy b Bresnan	111		
* A P R Gidman, c Brophy b Bresnan	26		
H J H Marshall, b Bresnan	47		
I A Cockbain, c Jaques b Bresnan	38		
W R S Gidman, lbw b Patterson	1		
§ R G Coughtrie, c Ballance b Patterson	0		
E G C Young, c Bresnan b Patterson	0		
I D Saxelby, not out	27		
G J McCarter, not out	29		
Extras lb 5, w 1	6	Extras	0
Total (9 wkts dec)	351	Total (0 wkts dec)	48

Bonus points — Gloucestershire 4, Yorkshire 3

FoW: 1-9 (Howell), 2-155 (Dent), 3-203 (A P R Gidman), 4-216 (Williamson), 5-290 (Marshall), 6-293 (Cockbain), 7-294 (Coughtrie), 8-294 (Young), 9-299 (W R S Gidman)

	O	M	R	W
Sidebottom	26	8	75	0
Bresnan	32	10	81	5
McGrath	18	7	48	0
Patterson	20	3	77	4
Rashid	4	0	13	0
Lyth	2	0	26	0
Gale	1.1	0	26	0

	O	M	R	W
McGrath	6	2	12	0
Patterson	5	2	3	0
Rashid	8.1	4	9	0
Lyth	2	1	1	0
Ballance	6	1	23	0

First Innings	YORKSHIRE	Second Innings	
A Lyth,		lbw b Saxelby	36
J J Sayers		c Coughtrie b W R S Gidman	1
P A Jaques		b W R S Gidman	160
* A W Gale		c McCarter b Young	21
G S Ballance		not out	121
A McGrath	forfeited	c Dent b W R S Gidman	6
T T Bresnan		b Young	38
§ G L Brophy		not out	2
A U Rashid			
S A Patterson		Did not bat	
R J Sidebottom			
		Extras b 9, lb 7, w 1	17
		Total (6 wkts)	402

FoW: 1-14 (Sayers), 2-62 (Lyth), 3-117 (Gale), 4-320 (Jaques), 5-328 (McGrath)
2nd 6-383 (Bresnan)

	O	M	R	W
Saxelby	28	3	111	1
W R S Gidman	27	5	76	3
Young	24.4	5	99	2
McCarter	19	3	67	0
Howell	5	1	17	0
Williamson	4	0	16	0

Umpires: M J D Bodenham and R A Kettleborough — Scorers: J T Potter and A J Bull

Gloucestershire v. Yorkshire

Yorkshire beat the clock

PHIL JAQUES: Outstanding 160 backed by Ballance 121 not out

Yorkshire were set a target of 400 to win in a minimum of 110 overs, and an excellent final day ensued.

In my opinion it is legitimate for captains to agree to revive a match affected by weather with forfeitures and declarations provided that each side can win.

Gloucestershire had 110 overs in which to take 10 wickets, and at 117-3 this was a distinct possibility with some suspicion of uneven bounce.

A winning score of over 400 had been achieved only twice by Yorkshire and twice by opponents.

Yorkshire would need two major innings, but against an inexperienced attack on a generally placid wicket. Each side had to play well to win, and the alternative was a dreary compilation of bonus points.

The double contrivance to achieve this objective was long and complex. After Yorkshire took the ninth wicket at 299 Gloucestershire were given two more batting points and declared at 351-9. Then it became apparent that more overs needed to be bowled and more time expended, but only 48 runs had to be scored to set the 400 target. Howell and Dent made 48 in 27.1 innocuous overs.

Williamson, a young New Zealander, showed distinct promise in Gloucestershire's first innings while Bresnan and Patterson took wickets. Jaques played an outstanding innings of 160 on the last day to put Yorkshire in a strong position when he was dismissed at 340, but considerable credit should go to Ballance coming in at 117-3: if he had been out quickly a Yorkshire win would have been unlikely; he then batted with calm assurance, presenting a responsible defensive bat, scoring wherever possible and hitting brutally at the end of his best innings for Yorkshire. Bresnan batted with enterprise when Gloucestershire looked like gaining the initiative. Saxelby, whose figures did not do him justice, and Will Gidman bowled well, but in the end it was the quality of the batting and the enterprise of the captain that won this match.

LV County Championship Division 2
Yorkshire v. Hampshire

Played at Headingley, Leeds, on May 16, 17, 18 and 19, 2012

Match drawn at 4.50pm on the Fourth Day

Toss won by Hampshire — Hampshire 10 points; Yorkshire 9 points

Close of play: First Day, Hampshire 352-5 (Katich 180*, Bates 88*); Second Day, Yorkshire 100-3 (Jaques 59*, Ballance 26*); Third Day, Hampshire 21-1 (Adams 7*, Carberry 1*)

First Innings	HAMPSHIRE	Second Innings	
L A Dawson, c Brophy b Sidebottom	0	c Jaques b Rashid	8
* J H K Adams, lbw b Patterson	5	c Brophy b Wardlaw	49
M A Carberry, c Ballance b Wardlaw	15	not out	61
S M Katich, c Root b Rashid	196	not out	61
J M Vince, c Brophy b Patterson	11		
S M Ervine, c Patterson b Root	44		
§ M D Bates, run out (Gale/Brophy)	103		
C P Wood, c Root b Patterson	8		
Kabir Ali, c Wardlaw b Rashid	19		
J A Tomlinson, c McGrath b Rashid	11		
D J Balcombe, not out	2		
Extras b 4, lb 9	13	Extras b 1, lb 9, nb 2	12
Total	427	Total (2 wkts dec)	191

Bonus points — Hampshire 5, Yorkshire 2 — Score at 110 overs: 404-8

FoW: 1st — 1-2 (Dawson), 2-6 (Adams), 3-55 (Carberry), 4-83 (Vince), 5-207 (Ervine) 6-377 (Bates), 7-391 (Katich), 8-395 (Wood), 9-417 (Kabir Ali), 10-427 (Tomlinson)

2nd — 1-18 (Dawson), 2-88 (Adams)

	O	M	R	W		O	M	R	W
Sidebottom	24	5	78	1	Sidebottom	8	4	16	0
Patterson	27	3	87	3	Patterson	12	6	17	0
McGrath	7	0	42	0	Rashid	16	1	82	1
Wardlaw	21	0	82	1	Wardlaw	7	0	37	1
Rashid	24	1	86	3	McGrath	6	2	8	0
Root	16	4	39	1	Root	9	1	20	0
					Lyth	3	2	1	0

YORKSHIRE

A Lyth, lbw b Kabir Ali	4
J E Root, c Dawson b Balcombe	8
P A Jaques, c Balcombe b Dawson	93
* A W Gale, run out (Carberry)	0
G S Ballance, c Bates b Ervine	76
A McGrath, not out	106
§ G L Brophy, c Wood b Dawson	22
A U Rashid, b Balcombe	3
R J Sidebottom, c Bates b Kabir Ali	34
S A Patterson, c Katich b Dawson	12
I Wardlaw, not out	17
Extras b 8, lb 2, nb 14	24
Total (9 wkts dec)	399

Bonus points — Yorkshire 4, Hampshire 2 — 110-over score: 360-8

FoW: 1-4 (Lyth), 2-32 (Root), 3-32 (Gale), 4-181 (Jaques), 5-193 (Ballance) 6-232 (Brophy), 7-237 (Rashid), 8-321 (Sidebottom), 9-360 (Patterson)

	O	M	R	W
Kabir Ali	25	7	80	2
Tomlinson	19	4	57	0
Wood	22	5	72	0
Balcombe	24	3	81	2
Dawson	19	4	61	3
Ervine	11	1	38	1

Umpires: N L Bainton and S C Gale — Scorers: J T Potter and A E Weld

Yorkshire v. Hampshire

McGrath shows his worth

SKIPPER'S RUN-OUT: Gale throws and Brophy despatches Bates for 103 in Hampshire's first innings

This was already the seventh Championship match under the controversial fixture allocation. All have been played in predominantly cold, windy conditions, disrupted by bad light and rain. The players, especially spin bowlers, have found it difficult, and those who support first-class cricket have endured some bleak days. With time again lost neither side could be expected to break the deadlock on a tedious last day.

Hampshire elected to bat in the best weather on a good wicket. Yorkshire did well to take four wickets before lunch — including that of Carberry, who made 300 last year at the Rose Bowl. The wicket they did not take, despite a raucous appeal first ball, was that of Katich, who proceeded to dominate the innings with calm assurance and an impressive range of shots. Ervine joined him in a stand of 124 as Yorkshire's change bowlers proved not as effective as Patterson and Sidebottom. Young wicket-keeper Bates gave Hampshire added impetus with a praiseworthy maiden century until he was run out by an alert Gale. Katich was out sweeping on 196, but Hampshire had full batting points.

Yorkshire lost three wickets before play ended on the second day. They were 32-3 after Lyth was lbw playing no shot, Root caught at slip and Gale run out by a direct hit from Carberry after facing one ball. Yorkshire's priority was to avoid the follow-on, but Jaques and Ballance were dismissed before lunch, followed rapidly by Brophy and Rashid. McGrath was playing very well, and when he was joined by Sidebottom with his broad bat and stolidly orthodox methods the recovery was well under way. McGrath completed a century of considerable value as it brought Yorkshire almost to parity with Hampshire, but there were not enough overs left for any sort of contest to be arranged on the last day.

LV County Championship Division 2
Yorkshire v. Northamptonshire

Played at Headingley, Leeds, on May 30 and 31, June 1 and 2, 2012

Match drawn at 5.15pm on the Fourth Day

Toss won by Northamptonshire — Yorkshire 11 points; Northamptonshire 8 points

Close of play: First Day, Yorkshire 27-0 (Lyth 14*, Root 7*); Second Day, Yorkshire 190-3 (Root 98*, Bairstow 36*); Third Day, Northamptonshire 43-1 (Peters 20*, Coetzer 12*)

NORTHAMPTONSHIRE

First Innings		Second Innings	
S D Peters, c Jaques b Patterson	7	b Patterson	22
J D Middlebrook, lbw b Patterson	9	lbw b Starc	9
K J Coetzer, c Bairstow b Sidebottom	12	c Root b Azeem Rafiq	39
A G Wakely, b Starc	0	b Starc	66
R A White, lbw b Starc	12	b Patterson	42
* A J Hall, b Patterson	79	c Bairstow b Starc	7
§ D Murphy, c Bairstow b Sidebottom	40	not out	31
C D de Lange, lbw b McGrath	23	not out	20
D J Willey, lbw b Sidebottom	39		
O P Stone, b Azeem Rafiq	13		
L M Daggett, not out	4		
Extras b 4, lb 5, nb 6	15	Extras b 7, lb 5, nb 2	14
Total	253	Total (6 wkts)	250

Bonus points — Northamptonshire 2, Yorkshire 3

FoW: 1st: 1-11 (Peters), 2-20 (Middlebrook), 3-21 (Wakely), 4-39 (White), 5-45 (Coetzer) 6-121 (Murphy), 7-163 (de Lange), 8-232 (Hall), 9-232 (Willey), 10-253 (Stone)

FoW: 2nd: 1-15 (Middlebrook), 2-47 (Peters), 3-95 (Coetzer), 4-160 (White), 5-187 (Hall) 6-198 Wakely

	O	M	R	W		O	M	R	W
Sidebottom	18	4	37	3	Sidebottom	18	5	51	0
Patterson $	18.5	3	61	3	Patterson	24	11	46	2
Starc $	18.1	7	64	2	Azeem Rafiq	23	6	66	1
McGrath	11	4	30	1	Starc	16	4	50	3
Azeem Rafiq	18.4	5	41	1	McGrath	5	1	19	0
Root	4	2	11	0	Root	3	1	6	0

$ Patterson was unable to complete his 19th over. It was completed by Starc.

YORKSHIRE

A Lyth, c Murphy b Daggett	25
J E Root, c Murphy b Hall	125
P A Jaques, lbw b Daggett	3
* A W Gale, lbw b Stone	17
§ J M Bairstow, b Hall	68
G S Ballance, c Wakely b Middlebrook	24
A McGrath, lbw b Willey	47
Azeem Rafiq, c Murphy b Daggett	37
M A Starc, not out	28
R J Sidebottom, c Peters b Daggett	2
S A Patterson, b Middlebrook	10
Extras b 8, lb 7, w 1, nb 14	30
Total	416

Bonus points — Yorkshire 5, Northamptonshire 3

FoW: 1-42 (Lyth), 2-54 (Jaques), 3-96 (Gale), 4-243 (Root), 5-268 (Bairstow), 6-300 (Balance), 7-368 (Rafiq),8-370 (McGrath), 9-379 (Sidebottom), 10-416 (Patterson)

	O	M	R	W
Willey	31	6	111	1
Daggett $	30.5	5	109	4
Hall $	15.1	4	57	2
Stone	16	2	76	1
Middlebrook	11	1	41	2
de Lange	2	0	7	0

$ Hall was unable to complete his 16th over. It was completed by Daggett

Umpires: P J Hartley and M J Saggers — Scorers: J T Potter and A C Kingston

Yorkshire v. Northamptonshire

The bowlers could not do it

125 AND OUT: Joe Root is caught by wicket-keeper Murphy off Hall

Yorkshire played well in another match curtailed by rain, especially Root who made 125, but could not bowl the visitors out a second time on the last day.

Northamptonshire were reduced to 45-5 through Sidebottom, industrious, skilful and economical; Patterson, deservedly awarded his county cap in the morning, and Starc, the Australian debutant who was the fastest of the three and bowled Wakely with a very quick delivery.

Determined resistance led by Hall and supported all down the order enabled Northamptonshire to reach a respectable 253. David Willey, son of Peter the former Test cricketer and now a first-class umpire, made 39 and Murphy a useful 40.

A wet morning followed, but play was resumed unexpectedly in mid-afternoon sunshine. Root and Bairstow took full advantage after Daggett and debutant Stone, a young man from Norwich, had taken three early wickets. Root's fluency and correct technique were illustrated with impeccable cover-driving and straight hitting, but he did offer two chances before reaching 98 at the close. On Friday he made his second first-class century for Yorkshire before being caught by wicket-keeper Murphy off one that lifted disconcertingly. Bairstow was playing another good innings, but he would be disappointed to be bowled by Hall, the Northamptonshire captain who once made 99 not out for South Africa at Headingley. Rafiq's boldness, McGrath's solidity and Starc's hard hitting saw Yorkshire pass 400, and they took a wicket before play ended.

Success in first-class cricket usually depends on bowling a side out twice, and Yorkshire were able to take only five of the nine wickets they required to win on the final day. In particular they could not dislodge the obdurate Wakely, who made an invaluable dogged 66, nor part Murphy and de Lange as time and weather conspired to deny them a win which had seemed likely at the start of play on Saturday.

LV County Championship Division 2
Glamorgan v. Yorkshire

Played at Rhos-on-Sea Cricket Club, Colwyn Bay, on June 6, 7, 8 and 9, 2012

Match drawn at 9.30am on the Fourth Day

Toss won by Glamorgan — Yorkshire 4 points, Glamorgan 3 points

Close of play: First Day, Glamorgan 117-3 (Walters 37*, Wright 10*); Second Day, no play; Third Day, no play

GLAMORGAN

G P Rees, lbw b Starc	35
W D Bragg, c Brophy b Starc	20
S J Walters, not out	37
M J North, c and b Azeem Rafiq	14
B J Wright, not out	10
J Allenby	
* § M A Wallace	
W T Owen	
R D B Croft	
D A Cosker	
H T Waters	
Extra lb 1	1
Total (3 wkts)	117

Bonus point — Yorkshire 1

FoW: 1-55 (Bragg), 2-58 (Rees), 3- 79 (North)

	O	M	R	W
Sidebottom	7	2	21	0
Patterson	6	1	22	0
Azeem Rafiq	12	4	29	1
Starc	8	2	39	2
Rashid	1	0	5	0

YORKSHIRE

A Lyth
J E Root
P A Jaques
* A W Gale
G S Ballance
§ G L Brophy
A U Rashid
Azeem Rafiq
M A Starc
R J Sidebottom
S A Patterson

Umpires: P K Baldwin and M R Benson — Scorers: J T Potter and A K Hignell

Glamorgan v. Yorkshire

Rain and discrimination?

MITCHELL STARC: Two wickets at high pace before the deluge

There was play on the first morning up to lunch and two overs afterwards. Glamorgan 117-3 and that was all that was possible in the match.

It was a disappointment for both sides needing points in the Championship and for the numerous spectators, many of whom would have travelled from Yorkshire and might have been anticipating a holiday on the bracing North Wales coast.

It was Yorkshire's ninth first-class match, all of which have been rain-affected or played in cold, windy conditions, mostly both rain and cold.

It has been calculated that 1,159 overs have been lost — 37.47 per cent of the maximum possible. There were only 34 overs in this match, 54 when Yorkshire played here in 2004 and it got very cold in 2003. Colwyn Bay has been an unlucky ground for Yorkshire.

Perhaps the committee will put in a request to play at Llanfairpwllgwyngyllgogerychwyrndrobwllllantysiliogogogoch next year. No one can be responsible for bad weather in this exceptional year, but priority in the fixture allocation has been given to T20 and one-day cricket in June and July, so that most Championship matches have been arranged early in the season — which has been extended into early April — or in August, and then late in September.

Perhaps this can be justified on financial grounds, and this match was, after all, in June, but many members must feel that the cricket they most enjoy and regard as the most significant and demanding for first-class players has suffered undeserved discrimination. The last day of the Northamptonshire match at Headingley Carnegie was June 2, and the next home four-day Championship game starts on August 15 after five consecutive away games.

LV County Championship Division 2
Hampshire v. Yorkshire

Played at The Rose Bowl, West End, Southampton, on July 11, 12, 13 and 14, 2012

Match drawn at 1.40pm on the Fourth Day

Toss won by Hampshire — Yorkshire 7 points; Hampshire 6 points

Close of play: First Day, no play; Second Day, Yorkshire 83-3 (Root 46*, Ballance 17*); Third Day, Hampshire 39-0 (Adams 20*, McKenzie 14*)

YORKSHIRE

A Lyth, lbw b Tomlinson	2
J E Root, not out	222
* P A Jaques, c Bates b Kabir Ali	12
§ J M Bairstow, c Bates b Kabir Ali	0
G S Ballance, c Dawson b Tomlinson	19
A McGrath, c Bates b Mascarenhas	5
R M Pyrah, c and b Mascarenhas	0
Azeem Rafiq, b Kabir Ali	29
S A Patterson, c Bates b Tomlinson	37
S J Harmison, c Bates b Tomlinson	2
M A Ashraf, not out	4
Extras b 8, lb 9, w 1	18
Total (9 wkts dec)	350

Bonus points — Yorkshire 4, Hampshire 3

FoW: 1-9 (Lyth), 2-28 (Jaques), 3-28 (Bairstow), 4-95 (Ballance), 5-103 (McGrath) 6-108 (Pyrah), 7-161 (Rafiq),8-282 (Patterson), 9-292 (Harmison)

	O	M	R	W
Kabir Ali	24	6	88	3
Tomlinson	25	6	80	4
Balcombe	20	4	62	0
Mascarenhas	15	3	40	2
Ervine	1	0	13	0
Dawson	9	0	50	0

HAMPSHIRE

* J H K Adams, not out	20
N D McKenzie, not out	14
B M Shafayat	
S M Katich	
L A Dawson	
S M Ervine	
§ M D Bates	
A D Mascarenhas	
Kabir Ali	
D J Balcombe	
J A Tomlinson	
Extras lb 1, w 4	5
Total (0 wkts)	39

Bonus points — Yorkshire 0, Hampshire 0

	O	M	R	W
Harmison	5	1	25	0
Patterson	5	3	8	0
Azeem Rafiq	1	0	1	0
McGrath	1	0	4	0

Umpires: N G C Cowley and G Sharp — Scorers: J T Potter and A E Weld

Hampshire v. Yorkshire

Double-ton for ruthless Root

Root played an innings of the highest quality for 222 not out in a total of 350-9. The first and last days were completely washed out, and there were further interruptions.

Apart from Root the batsmen found it difficult against an attack in which Tomlinson and Kabir Ali were the most successful under heavy cloud. The second day, curtailed by rain, closed with Root 46 not out. Bairstow had suffered a first-ball duck.

On the only sunny day Root made an undefeated maiden double-century with 26 fours and three sixes. He resisted the experienced home attack in the early stages when conditions favoured swing and seam, and survival was imperative as Yorkshire fell to 108-6.

Rafiq stayed with him; then Patterson played an invaluable part in a stand of 121 for the eighth wicket, and Ashraf was four not out in an unbroken last-wicket stand of 58.

Root hit 21 from an over by Kabir Ali and 17 off a Tomlinson over. Root is tall and elegant, technically correct, strong on the off-side, and he has played some good innings this year, but here he showed a ruthlessness in dominating the bowling.

JOE ROOT
Warmed the hearts of damp travellers

He gave Yorkshire followers great pleasure on an otherwise damp and dismal excursion to Southampton. These supporters sitting in contemplative mood at the watery Rose or Aegas Bowl might have been thinking of days before Hampshire's fine Test ground was constructed at West End on the city outskirts. At one time Yorkshire usually came to Dean Park, Bournemouth, in late August. There were occasional visits to the United Services ground in Portsmouth and to the original county ground at Northlands Road, Southampton. Yorkshire twice visited May's Bounty at Basingstoke, but now Hampshire play all home matches here.

LV County Championship Division 2
Derbyshire v. Yorkshire

Played at Queen's Park, Chesterfield, on July 18, 19, 20 and 21, 2012

Match drawn at 1.55pm on the Fourth Day

Toss won by Yorkshire — Derbyshire 6 points; Yorkshire 6 points

Close of play: First Day, Derbyshire 135-7 (Johnson 15*, Palladino 21*); no further play

YORKSHIRE

A Lyth, c Johnson b Groenewald	19
J E Root, c Lineker b Groenewald	16
* P A Jaques, c Wainwright b Durston	61
§ J M Bairstow, b Palladino	27
G S Ballance, c Johnson b Turner	46
A McGrath, c Durston b Turner	0
R M Pyrah, lbw b Durston	9
Azeem Rafiq, c Turner b Durston	0
S A Patterson, c Durston b Groenewald	11
S J Harmison, c Madsen b Durston	23
M A Ashraf, not out	0
Extras lb 7	7
Total	219

Bonus points — Yorkshire 1, Derbyshire 3

FoW: 1-34 (Root), 2-43 (Lyth), 3-94 (Bairstow), 4-175 (Ballance), 5-175 (McGrath) 6-185 (Pyrah), 7-185 (Jaques), 8-185 (Rafiq), 9-219 (Patterson), 10-219 (Harmison)

	O	M	R	W
Palladino	11	0	62	1
Groenewald	13	3	38	3
Turner	15	4	53	3
Clare	5	0	27	0
Wainwright	3	1	9	0
Durston	9.1	3	23	3

DERBYSHIRE

* W L Madsen, c Rafiq b Patterson	15
M S Lineker, b Pyrah	33
U T Khawaja, b Ashraf	9
W J Durston, c Lyth b Harmison	16
D J Redfern, lbw b Ashraf	8
J L Clare, c Bairstow b Harmison	1
D J Wainwright, c Ashraf b Harmison	0
§ R M Johnson, not out	15
A P Palladino, not out	21
M L Turner	
T D Groenewald — Did not bat	
Extras lb 3, w 10, nb 4	17
Total (7 wkts)	135

Bonus points — Yorkshire 2

FoW: 1-43 (Madsen), 2-70 (Lineker), 3-70 (Khawaja), 4-80 (Redfern), 5-91 (Clare) 6-96 (Durston), 7-105 (Wainwright)

	O	M	R	W
Patterson	10	1	49	1
Harmison	9	2	49	3
Ashraf	8	2	13	2
Pyrah	6	2	9	1
McGrath	3	0	7	0
Azeem Rafiq	2	0	5	0

Umpires: P J Hartley and S Ravi — Scorers: J T Potter and J M Brown

Derbyshire v. Yorkshire

Setback for the outgrounds

MOIN ASHRAF
Two wickets and a catch

Everyone looked forward to Queen's Park, but play was possible only on the first day despite it having the worst forecast of the four.

Yorkshire were reasonably successful in the morning, having chosen to bat, as Jaques led the way, but Groenewald dismissed both Root and Lyth, and Palladino removed Bairstow just before lunch.

There followed a rain delay, after which Yorkshire's batting disintegrated: they lost five wickets for 10 runs, three of them to Turner. Harmison's 23 did at least provide one batting bonus point, but it was a disappointing display.

Batting proved no easier for Derbyshire. The three-man seam attack of Harmison, Patterson and Ashraf was soon among the wickets, although Harmison's opening spell conceded 27 in three overs, including four no-balls and nine wides. He then took three wickets as play extended into the evening, and only one over was lost. Palladino, who is having a good season, and Johnson, on loan from Warwickshire, made an unbeaten 30 for the eighth wicket in the last session.

Over many years it has been a pleasure as a Yorkshire member to visit many outgrounds to see cricket played on a variety of venues. Queen's Park is an attractive ground encircled with trees, enhanced by plants and shrubs, with the crooked spire of All Saints' Church in the distance. One thinks back to Castle Park at Colchester, The Mote at Maidstone, the ground at Bath by the Abbey and, perhaps the best of all, Arundel Castle, not forgetting our own Park Avenue, Abbeydale Park and Scarborough.

This unfortunate match may have set back the cause of the outgrounds, because Queen's Park was unable to deal with the consequences of the rainfall over the last three days when the ground became saturated at one end. The weather was awful, but more play may have been possible at Derby. I was not around in 1912, and cannot recall a season where the weather had such a devastating effect on cricket.

LV County Championship Division 2
Leicestershire v. Yorkshire

Played at Grace Road, Leicester, on July 27, 28, 29 and 30, 2012

Match drawn at 6.10pm on the Fourth Day

Toss won by Leicestershire — Yorkshire 11 points; Leicestershire 8 points

Close of play: First Day, Leicestershire 318-9 (Boyce 106*, Hoggard 1*); Second Day, Yorkshire 336-5 (Lyth 159*, McGrath 9*); Third Day, Leicestershire 57-2 (Eckersley 7*, Sarwan 2*)

First Innings	LEICESTERSHIRE	Second Innings	
G P Smith, lbw b Patterson	20	lbw b McGrath	26
M A Thornely, c Bairstow b Ashraf	31	b Harmison	17
E J H Eckersley, lbw b Patterson	4	c Root b Azeem Rafiq	26
R R Sarwan, b Harmison	8	b Harmison	6
M A G Boyce, c and b Azeem Rafiq	107	c Root b Harmison	4
S J Thakor, c Gale b Ashraf	35	lbw b Patterson	0
W A White, c Harmison b Azeem Rafiq	28	c Bairstow b Azeem Rafiq	44
§ P G Dixey, c Jaques b Harmison	6	not out	3
C W Henderson, c Root b Patterson	26	not out	8
N L Buck, c Ballance b McGrath	6		
* M J Hoggard, not out	2		
Extras b 5, lb 10, w 11, nb 21	47	Extras b 4, lb 7, w 1, nb 11	23
Total	320	Total (7 wkts)	157

Bonus points — Leicestershire 3, Yorkshire 3

FoW: 1st — 1-20 (Smith), 2-50 (Eckersley), 3-59 (Sarwan), 4-98 (Thornely), 5-166 (Thakor) 6-226 (White), 7-239 (Dixey), 8-289 (Henderson), 9-310 (Buck), 10-320 (Boyce)

FoW: 2nd — 1-43 (Smith), 2-49 (Thornely), 3-61 (Sarwan), 4-77 (Boyce), 5-78 (Thakor) 6-145 (White), 7-148 (Eckersley)

	O	M	R	W		O	M	R	W
Patterson	25	6	56	3	Patterson	20	6	38	1
Ashraf	17	4	71	2	Ashraf	12	3	25	0
Harmison	16	1	69	2	McGrath	8	3	13	1
McGrath	14	3	40	1	Harmison	12	0	52	3
Azeem Rafiq	23.3	7	64	2	Azeem Rafiq	7.4	2	18	2
Root	2	1	5	0					

YORKSHIRE

A Lyth, not out	248
J E Root, b Buck	0
P A Jaques, c Boyce b Buck	30
* A W Gale, c Sarwan b Henderson	11
§ J M Bairstow, c Smith b Buck	118
G S Balance, lbw b Hoggard	1
A McGrath, c Smith b Hoggard	8
Azeem Rafiq, c Dixey b White	23
S A Patterson, c Eckersley b Henderson	28
S J Harmison, lbw b Henderson	0
M A Ashraf, st Dixey b Henderson	0
Extras b 5, lb 6, w 2, nb 6	19
Total	486

Bonus points — Yorkshire 5, Leicestershire 2 — Score at 110 overs: 400-7

FoW: 1-6 (Root), 2-74 (Jaques), 3-112 (Gale), 4-309 (Bairstow), 5-310 (Ballance) 6-342 (McGrath), 7-387 (Rafiq), 8-460 (Patterson), 9-474 (Harmison), 10-486 (Ashraf)

	O	M	R	W
Hoggard	18	0	78	2
Buck	30	2	124	3
White	19	0	78	1
Henderson	47.1	11	126	4
Thornely	3	0	18	0
Sarwan	4	0	19	0
Thakor	6	1	32	0

Umpires: R J Bailey and I J Gould — Scorers: J T Potter and P J Rogers

Lyth 248* carries bat to record

Adam Lyth played an outstanding innings of 248 not out at Grace Road — the highest score by a Yorkshireman who carried his bat — and gave much pleasure to those who had faith in him after an indifferent 2011.

Leicestershire chose to bat first, and had a solid first day, closing at 318-9. Early wickets fell to Patterson, Ashraf and the erratic Harmison, who nevertheless yorked Sarwan twice in the match.

Boyce, a centurion at Scarborough, again proved resolute, receiving good support from the promising Thakor and White, and he reached his century just before the close.

ADAM LYTH: Added 197 with Bairstow, 118

The weekend belonged to Lyth, but there was also an excellent century from Bairstow on Saturday, he and Lyth adding 197 for the fourth wicket. Lyth began carefully, but he gradually gained assurance, eventually hitting 28 fours and three sixes, many boundaries through mid-off and extra-cover. He was 159 overnight, and made a further 89 on Sunday. Bairstow was under some pressure after his Test experiences against West Indies, but he responded with a fine innings, outscoring Lyth and looking the Test batsman we consider him to be. Full batting points came only in the 110th over as Patterson hit out. Henderson bowled a long spell of left-arm spin to earn his four wickets.

Once again weather intervened on Monday, probably preventing a Yorkshire win. Leicestershire ended on 157-7, still nine behind on a showery day when 60 overs were lost. The highlight was Harmison's dismissal of Sarwan and a defiant rearguard innings from White. It was good to see Leicestershire old players on this friendly informal ground. On Saturday evening I went down to Aylestone Road to see Electricity Sports playing on the ground where George Hirst made a record 341 for Yorkshire in 1905, still unsurpassed although Darren Lehmann made 339. They also have records of Don Bradman's 185 not out at Aylestone Road in May 1930, which was his second innings in England — his first had been 236 at Worcester.

LV County Championship Division 2
Northamptonshire v. Yorkshire

Played at The County Ground, Northampton, on August 1, 2, 3 and 4, 2012

Match drawn at 2.15pm on the Fourth Day

Toss won by Yorkshire — Northamptonshire 10 points, Yorkshire 7 points

Close of play: First Day, Yorkshire 249 all out; Second Day, Northamptonshire 175-3 (Peters 74*; Newton 40*); Third Day, Yorkshire 5-0 (Lyth 3*, Root 2*)

First Innings	YORKSHIRE	Second Innings	
A Lyth, c Middlebrook b Willey	6	c Coetzer b Stone	15
J E Root, c Murphy b Stone	25	c Peters b Willey	38
P A Jaques, run out (Daggett)	75	b Middlebrook	7
* A W Gale, c and b Daggett	38	not out	11
§ J M Bairstow, lbw b Daggett	17	not out	1
G S Ballance, c Stone b Middlebrook	24		
R M Pyrah, c Newton b Daggett	0		
A U Rashid, c Wakely b Middlebrook	15		
Azeem Rafiq, c Wakely b Willey	15		
S A Patterson, not out	25		
M A Ashraf, lbw b Hall	4		
Extras lb 3, nb 2	5	Extras lb 2	2
Total	249	Total (3 wkts)	74

Bonus points — Yorkshire 1, Northamptonshire 3

FoW: 1st 1-14 (Lyth), 2-44 (Root), 3-148 (Jaques), 4-148 (Gale), 5-175 (Bairstow) 6-185 (Pyrah), 7-201 (Ballance), 8-211 (Rashid), 9-223 (Rafiq), 10-249 (Ashraf)
2nd: 1-28 (Lyth), 2-55 (Jaques), 3-67 (Root)

	O	M	R	W		O	M	R	W
Willey	22	6	71	2	Willey	10	5	10	1
Daggett	24	8	64	3	Daggett	5	2	12	0
Stone	14	3	35	1	Middlebrook	14	6	29	1
Hall	14.3	3	33	1	Stone	5	2	6	1
Middlebrook	19	7	43	2	Hall	5	2	15	0

NORTHAMPTONSHIRE	
S D Peters, c Root b Rashid	107
K J Coetzer, c Jaques b Azeem Rafiq	31
D J G Sales, c Lyth b Pyrah	11
A G Wakely, c Jaques b Rashid	12
R I Newton, c Ballance b Ashraf	43
* A J Hall, lbw b Ashraf	0
J D Middlebrook, lbw b Rashid	10
§ D Murphy, lbw b Rashid	20
D J Willey, b Rashid	76
O P Stone, not out	26
L M Daggett, c Lyth b Azeem Rafiq	1
Extras b 6, lb 5, nb 4	15
Total	352

Bonus points — Northamptonshire 4, Yorkshire 3

FoW: 1-66 (Coetzer), 2-89 (Sales), 3-106 (Wakely), 4-191 (Newton), 5-191 (Hall), 6-212 (Middlebrook), 7-231 (Peters), 8-304 (Murphy), 9-347 (Willey), 10-352 (Daggett)

	O	M	R	W
Patterson	24	8	58	0
Ashraf	16	3	55	2
Pyrah	13	3	38	1
Azeem Rafiq	25.5	5	78	2
Rashid	31	2	105	5
Root	1	0	7	0

Umpires: J H Evans and N A Mallender

Scorers: J T Potter, A D Johnston and A C Kingston

Northamptonshire v. Yorkshire

The rain plays for Yorkshire

ADIL RASHID
Change for better

Once again rain disrupted a match, but on this occasion it may have saved Yorkshire as they finished still 30 behind with seven wickets remaining.

Apart from Jaques no Yorkshire batsman established himself, although most made a start, and then appeared to be guilty of poor shot selection. Some would argue there was irregular bounce. Northamptonshire bowled well, with Willey and Daggett a lively opening pair — and Middlebrook economical against his former county.

At one stage there was no score from 49 balls. Daggett ran Jaques out with a direct hit as the batsman answered his captain's call and caught Gale off his own bowling five balls later. Yorkshire gained one batting point, but missed a second by one run.

Northamptonshire batted well on a shortened second day, building their innings around Peters who went on to make his century on Friday. At the close on Thursday he and Newton had revived Northamptonshire with a partnership of 69. Peters played a responsible opener's innings, but when he was out for 107 Northamptonshire were struggling as Rashid and Ashraf took four wickets early on Friday morning.

Willey, an all-rounder who had been regarded as mainly an opening bowler, hit a rapid 76 when play resumed after a long break and he gave his side a lead of 103. Rashid would be encouraged by a return of 5-105, and he looked more confident with his arm higher. Ashraf took two wickets in succession, but Middlebrook saved the hat-trick. The final day frustrated Northamptonshire a further 61 overs were lost, giving a match total of 136.2. Heavy rain brought the match to a dismal conclusion just after lunch.

There are now four Championship matches left, and competition for promotion is intense between Yorkshire, Derbyshire, Kent and Hampshire. Let us hope that the rain relents to enable positive results to be achieved in the remaining matches.

LV County Championship Division 2
Yorkshire v. Derbyshire

Played at Headingley, Leeds, on August 15, 16, 17 and 18, 2012

Match drawn at 5.23pm on the Fourth Day

Toss won by Derbyshire — Yorkshire 11 points, Derbyshire 6 points

Close of play: First Day, Yorkshire 127-2 (Lyth 60*, Balance 11*); Second Day, Derbyshire 28-1 (Lineker 12*); Third Day, Derbyshire 233-8 (Wainwright 45*, Groenewald 0*)

YORKSHIRE

A Lyth, c Lineker b Whiteley	93
P A Jaques, b Groenewald	3
* A W Gale, c Turner b Whiteley	47
G S Ballance, c Poynton b Groenewald	79
A McGrath, c Wainwright b Durston	104
A U Rashid, b Durston	12
§ A J Hodd, c Lineker b Durston	58
T T Bresnan, c Khawaja b Wainwright	1
Azeem Rafiq, c Poynton b Durston	1
R J Sidebottom, c Whiteley b Durston	4
S A Patterson, not out	1
Extras lb 14, w 3	17
Total	420

Bonus points — Yorkshire 5, Derbyshire 1 — 110-over score: 406-5

M A Ashraf was in the Yorkshire Eleven until the afternoon of the Second Day, when he was replaced by T T Bresnan, who had returned from the England Test squad. Ashraf did not bat or bowl, but his participation is still classed as an appearance for Yorkshire

FoW: 1-8 Jaques), 2-95 (Gale), 3-211 (Lyth), 4-256 (Ballance), 5-280 (Rashid) 6-411 (McGrath), 7-412 (Hodd), 8-415 (Bresnan), 9-415 (Rafiq), 10-420 (Sidebottom)

	O	M	R	W
Palladino	27	8	82	0
Groenewald	27	5	93	2
Durston	8.4	0	34	5
Turner	15	0	83	0
Whiteley	10	2	40	2
Wainwright	26	3	74	1

DERBYSHIRE

First Innings		Second Innings	
* W L Madsen, lbw b Bresnan	14	c Azeem Rafiq b Bresnan	5
M S Lineker, c Hodd b Sidebottom	14	b Bresnan	8
U T Khawaja, c Hodd b Sidebottom	3	not out	110
W J Durston, b Azeem Rafiq	84	lbw b Patterson	39
D J Redfern, c Hodd b Sidebottom	3	c Hodd b Sidebottom	2
R A Whiteley, c Hodd b Patterson	35	c Gale b Azeem Rafiq	17
D J Wainwright, run out (Patterson/Hodd)	50	not out	1
§ T Poynton, lbw b Azeem Rafiq	25		
A P Palladino, lbw b Rashid	0		
T D Groenewald, c Hodd b Bresnan	21		
M L Turner, not out	8		
Extras lb 9, nb 2	11	Extras b 4, lb 3,w1	8
Total	268	Total (5 wkts)	190

Bonus points — Derbyshire 2, Yorkshire 3

FoW: 1st 1-28 (Madsen), 2-33 (Khawaja), 3-34 (Lineker), 4-42 (Redfern), 5-154 (Durston), 6-174 (Whiteley), 7-225 (Poynton), 8-226 (Palladino), 9-260 (Wainwright), 10-268 (Groenewald)
2nd 1-9 (Madsen), 2-18 (Lineker), 3-108 (Durston), 4-111 (Redfern), 5-177 (Whiteley)

	O	M	R	W		O	M	R	W
Bresnan	23.3	5	78	2	Bresnan	18	4	45	1
Sidebottom	14	3	38	3	Sidebottom	18	3	55	2
Patterson	11	2	50	1	Azeem Rafiq	9	4	15	1
McGrath	5	3	7	0	Patterson	12	7	24	1
Rashid	21	5	44	1	Rashid	11	0	39	0
Azeem Rafiq	16	6	42	2	McGrath	4	2	5	0

Umpires: S A Garratt and J W Lloyds — Scorers: J T Potter and J M Brown

Yorkshire v. Derbyshire

Cracking debut for Hodd

RUNS AND CATCHES: Hodd on his way to a half-century

Less play than usual this season was lost, so there was a competitive final day as Derbyshire saved the match — mainly because of a fine defensive innings from Khawaja — and attained their objective of ensuring that Yorkshire did not win this important promotion contest. Yorkshire gave an impressive batting display on a short first day and a full Thursday. McGrath scored his second century of the season; Lyth was unfortunate to fall at 93; Ballance was impressive, and so was Hodd — making his Yorkshire debut on loan from Sussex and adding 137 for the sixth wicket with McGrath. Palladino and Groenewald bowled well, yet Durston took 5-34 with apparently innocuous off-spin.

Durston was also Derbyshire's leading batsman as they performed with mixed fortune on a day that defied a gloomy forecast. Sidebottom claimed three top-order wickets for seven runs off 24 balls, but Durston and Whiteley added 112 to give Derbyshire hope of saving the follow-on. The last day began with them needing 38 with two wickets remaining. It seemed that this would be done as the spinners had no success until Wainwright was inexplicably run out and Derbyshire followed on.

It was now a matter of Yorkshire having to take 10 wickets to win, but they were frustrated by a Headingley wicket that offered virtually no assistance and the implacable resistance of Khawaja, embellished by 16 boundaries including two sixes. At first Yorkshire bowled very well, Sidebottom especially, with no luck. Bresnan removed Lineker and Madsen quickly, but Yorkshire resorted to more defensive fields and the impetus was lost. Hodd gave an excellent display of his wicket-keeping skills with six catches, some of high quality, and sound defensive batting in the first innings. A draw left Yorkshire 21 points adrift of Derbyshire and 10 behind Hampshire, who won their match in a run chase.

LV County Championship Division 2
Yorkshire v. Gloucestershire

Played at North Martine Road, Scarborough, on August 28, 29, 30 and 31, 2012

Yorkshire won by 2 wickets at 6.07pm on the Fourth Day

Toss won by Gloucestershire — Yorkshire 19 points, Gloucestershire 1 point

Close of play: First Day, Yorkshire 61-2 (Root 24*, Gale 23*); Second Day, no play; Third Day, no play

First Innings	GLOUCESTERSHIRE	Second Innings	
R J Nicol, c Hodd b Ashraf	4	not out	75
B A C Howell, b Patterson	0	not out	83
D M Housego, c Lyth b Patterson	0		
* H J H Marshall, lbw b Patterson	4		
I A Cockbain, c Jaques b Azeem Rafiq	30		
W R S Gidman, c Lyth b Ashraf	47		
§ J N Batty, b Ashraf	25		
J K Fuller, lbw b Azeem Rafiq	1		
J M R Taylor, c and b Azeem Rafiq	49		
A J Ireland, not out	25		
L C Norwell, c Hodd b Rashid	18		
Extras lb 4, nb 8	12	Extras w 1	1
Total	215	Total (0 wkts dec)	159

Bonus points — Gloucestershire 1, Yorkshire 3

FoW: 1-1 (Howell), 2-5 (Housego), 3-9 (Marshall), 4-9 (Nicol), 5-74 (Cockbain)
1st 6-102 (Gidman), 7-107 (Fuller), 8-179 (Batty), 10-215 (Norwell)

	O	M	R	W		O	M	R	W
Patterson	17	7	35	3	Gale	5	0	71	0
Ashraf	18	4	44	3	Lyth	5	0	88	0
McGrath	6	0	25	0					
Azeem Rafiq	28	6	85	3					
Rashid	6.1	0	22	1					
Root	1	1	0	0					

First Innings	YORKSHIRE	Second Innings	
A Lyth, c Batty b Gidman	0	c Norwell b Ireland	40
J E Root, not out	24	c Housego b Norwell	43
P A Jaques, c Batty b Gidman	9	c Cockbain b Fuller	79
* A W Gale, not out	23	c Marshall b Taylor	14
G S Ballance,)		c Cockbain b Taylor	5
A McGrath		not out	76
§ A J Hodd		lbw b Gidman	8
A U Rashid		c Batty b Gidman	10
Azeem Rafiq		c Fuller b Norwell	24
S A Patterson		not out	0
M A Ashraf Did not bat			
Extras lb 2, w 1, nb 2	5	Extras lb 5,w 2, nb 10	17
Total (2 wkts dec)	61	Total (8 wkts)	316

FoW: 1-0 (Lyth), 2-16 (Jaques)
2nd 1-72 (Lyth), 2-119 (Root), 3-159 (Gale), 4-183 (Ballance), 5-205 (Jaques) 6-245 (Hodd), 7-267 (Rashid), 8-312 (Rafiq)

	O	M	R	W		O	M	R	W
Gidman	6	2	12	2	Gidman	22	2	70	2
Norwell	6	1	15	0	Norwell	15.2	0	63	2
Ireland	4	0	28	0	Ireland	16	0	77	1
Taylor	1	0	4	0	Fuller	10	0	63	1
					Taylor	18	4	38	2

Umpires: D J Millns and S J O'Shaughnessy — Scorers: J T Potter and A J Bull

Yorkshire v. Gloucestershire

Mags trumps declaration deal

ANTHONY McGRATH: Old pro who did the business

The second and third days were a total washout, so there had to be improvisations on the last day very similar to Bristol in May.

Yorkshire declared on 61-2, 154 behind. Lyth and Gale bowled 10 overs to Nicol and Howell, who made 159 before what seemed a generous declaration, setting Yorkshire 314 to win off a minimum of 84 overs.

The deliberately innocuous bowling and inefficient fielding were embarrassing to watch, but they gave the match a purpose and both sides a chance of winning what otherwise would have been merely a contest for bonus points.

Yorkshire made a sound start, but when Jaques was dismissed by Fuller they stumbled, and the target looked formidable as wickets fell. Gidman, who had a good all-round match, bowled with energy and skill to remove Hodd and Rashid. McGrath stayed in, pacing himself sensibly, but when Rafiq arrived at 267-7 with 47 still needed the situation was precarious. Rafiq played well, with a mixture of adventure and resolve, and victory was almost achieved when he played an impetuous shot, hoping to win the match. McGrath was there at the end of a very good day's cricket.

There had been a dramatic start to the match on Tuesday morning when Gloucestershire found themselves 9-4 within the first hour as Patterson and Ashraf caused devastation. Credit is due to Gidman and Cockbain, who batted through to lunch at 70-4, but Cockbain went soon afterwards and Gidman was superbly caught at slip by Lyth. Taylor made a good 49, but Yorkshire bowled their opponents out for 215.

There was an eventful hour when Yorkshire batted: Lyth was out second ball, caught by Batty; next ball Jaques top-edged to Taylor who missed it; Batty then dropped Root off a straightforward chance, and Root was missed again off a more difficult slip catch. It should have been 0-3, but after losing Jaques the opener and Gale survived until the close...and for two more rainy days.

LV County Championship Division 2
Yorkshire v. Glamorgan

Played at Headingley, Leeds, on September 4, 5 and 6, 2012

Yorkshire won by 8 wickets at 4.45pm on the Third Day

Toss won by Yorkshire — Yorkshire 22 points, Glamorgan 5 points

Close of play: First Day, Yorkshire 20-0 (Lyth 5*, Root 9*); Second Day, Glamorgan 27-2 (Bragg 14*, Walters 5*)

First Innings	GLAMORGAN	Second Innings	
W D Bragg, c Hodd b Patterson	92	b Ashraf	25
N A James, c Hodd b Sidebottom	38	c Hodd b Patterson	4
SJ Walters, c Lyth b Azeem Rafiq	42	(4) c Hodd b Ashraf	9
D L Lloyd, c Hodd b Patterson	0	(5) c Hodd b Patterson	0
B J Wright, lbw b Sidebottom	24	(6) lbw b McGrath	21
J Allenby, c Lyth b McGrath	14	(7) b Ashraf	48
§ * M A Wallace, c Jaques b Azeem Rafiq	29	(8) lbw b Sidebottom	17
G G Wagg, b McGrath	0	(9) c Hodd b Azeem Rafiq	36
J G Glover, b Patterson	0	(3) c Lyth b Patterson	0
D A Cosker, c Hodd b Patterson	11	c Sidebottom b Patterson	2
H T Waters, not out	5	not out	11
Extras b 5, lb 10, nb 2	17	Extras lb 9	9
Total	272	Total	182

Bonus points — Glamorgan 2, Yorkshire 3

FoW: 1-124 (James), 2-140 (Bragg), 3-156 (Lloyd), 4-198 (Walters), 5-221 (Wright)
1st 6-223 (Allenby), 7-223 (Wagg), 8-236 (Glover), 9-257 (Wallace), 10-272 (Cosker)
FoW: 1-17 (James), 2-17 (Glover), 3-45 (Bragg), 4-46 (Walters), 5-46 (Lloyd)
2nd 6-101 (Wright), 7-125 (Allenby), 8-144 (Wallace), 9-149 (Cosker), 10-182 (Wagg)

	O	M	R	W		O	M	R	W
Sidebottom	19	5	66	2	Patterson	21	8	47	4
Patterson	19.2	6	49	4	Sidebottom	13	1	39	1
Ashraf	12	2	51	0	McGrath	6	1	28	1
Azeem Rafiq	18	6	57	2	Ashraf	12	4	42	3
McGrath	19	8	34	2	Azeem Rafiq	6.1	0	17	1

First Innings	YORKSHIRE	Second Innings	
A Lyth, lbw b Glover	95	lbw b Cosker	50
J E Root, lbw b Wagg	14	lbw b Glover	11
P A Jaques, lbw b Allenby	13	not out	28
* A W Gale, b Wagg	55	not out	19
G S Ballance, b Allenby	26		
A McGrath, lbw b Glover	39		
§ A J Hodd, c Walters b Allenby	2		
Azeem Rafiq, c Wallace b Glover	8		
R J Sidebottom, c Wallace b Wagg	35		
S A Patterson, b Allenby	22		
M A Ashraf, not out	0		
Extras b 4, lb 15, nb 16	35	Extras lb 2,w 1	3
Total	344	Total (2 wkts)	111

Bonus points — Yorkshire 3, Glamorgan 3

FoW: 1-39 (Root), 2-70 (Jaques), 3-190 (Lyth), 4-200 (Gale), 5-261 (Ballance)
1st 6-267 (Hodd), 7-283 (Rafiq), 8-286 (McGrath), 9-340 (Patterson), 10-344 (Sidebottom)
2nd 1-63 (Root), 2-63 (Lyth)

	O	M	R	W		O	M	R	W
Wagg	24.4	3	87	3	Allenby	7	2	20	0
Waters	9	1	34	0	Glover	8	1	35	1
Glover	22	4	78	3	Wagg	4	0	11	0
Allenby	18	2	61	4	Cosker	6	0	26	1
Cosker	14	0	63	0	Bragg	2.1	0	13	0
Bragg	1	0	2	0	James	1	0	4	0

Umpires: N L Bainton and T E Jesty — Scorers: J T Potter and A K Hignell

G D Lloyd replaced T E Jesty for the final session on the Second Day

Yorkshire v. Glamorgan

Running in for promotion

ON A ROLL: Yorkshire skipper Andrew Gale, top, and Glamorgan's John Glover

Yorkshire put Glamorgan in and may have regretted it as Bragg and James put on 124 for the first wicket.

But it was a 10.30 start on a wicket that looked helpful. Yorkshire would not have to bowl in two consecutive innings, so it was a justifiable decision. Wickets fell regularly after James was out to a Yorkshire attack well led by Patterson, who took 4- 49. Bragg made an estimable 92 and was unfortunate to miss his century. The crucial break-through was, perhaps, the wicket of Walters, twice missed but finally well caught by Lyth at slip. Yorkshire began well, but ultimately dropped two batting points as Allenby took four wickets. Lyth, playing gracefully on the off-side, was unfortunate to be adjudged lbw on 95. Despite Gale's 50 no other batsman was able to flourish, although Sidebottom and Patterson took the total well past 300. Allenby, Glover and left-armer Wagg all took wickets to restrict Yorkshire's lead to 72.

Patterson and Ashraf reduced Glamorgan to 46-5 on Wednesday evening and Thursday morning. Patterson added 4-47 to his 4-49, bowling with accuracy, a disconcerting bounce and movement off the seam to confirm his growing reputation as a new-ball bowler. Ashraf, bowling fast and straight and unlucky in the first innings, now took three wickets, bowling Bragg and Allenby. Hodd again impressed behind the stumps and was given a two-year contract to move north from Sussex. Lloyd from Flintshire, a young batsman on debut, failed to score in both innings. There was some resistance from Allenby and Wagg, but the visitors could muster only 182 and set Yorkshire 111 to make to win. The hosts had no problems despite losing Lyth to an injudicious shot and Root, but they were steered home by Jaques and Ballance.

Yorkshire go into the last match at Chelmsford one point behind Derbyshire and five ahead of Kent.

LV County Championship Division 2
Essex v. Yorkshire

Played at The County Ground, Chelmsford, on September 11, 12, 13 and 14, 2012

Yorkshire won by 239 runs at 1.55pm on the Fourth Day

Toss won by Yorkshire — Yorkshire 22 points, Essex 3 points

Close of play: First Day, Yorkshire 284-8 (Rafiq 49*); Second Day, Yorkshire 44-3 (Lyth 26*, Ballance 1*); Third Day, Essex 28-2 (Shah 4*, Craddock 4*)

First Innings	YORKSHIRE	Second Innings	
A Lyth, c Foster b Napier	67	c Mickleburgh b Westley	51
J E Root, lbw b Napier	0	c Pettini b Napier	2
P A Jaques, c Mills b Napier	38	c Shah b Napier	6
* A W Gale, c Mills b Westley	10	c Pettini b Napier	5
G S Ballance, c Mickleburgh b Topley	30	c Craddock b Westley	27
A McGrath, c Foster b Topley	18	c Wheater b Napier	68
§ A J Hodd, run out (ten Doeschate/Foster)	22	c Foster b Craddock	1
Azeem Rafiq, c Foster b Napier	53	not out	75
R J Sidebottom, c and b Craddock	37	(10) not out	9
S A Patterson, b Napier	17	(9) b Mills	0
M A Ashraf, not out	6		
Extras b 3, lb 6, nb 5	14	Extras lb 7, w 1	8
Total	312	Total (8 wkts dec)	252

Bonus points — Yorkshire 3, Essex 3

FoW: 1st 1-4 (Root), 2-86 (Lyth), 3-113 (Jaques), 4-134 (Gale), 5-165 (Ballance) 6-166 (McGrath) 7-224 (Hodd), 8-284 (Sidebottom), 9-299 (Rafiq), 10-312 (Patterson)

FoW: 2nd 1-14 (Root), 2-30 (Jaques), 3-36 (Gale), 4-95 (Lyth), 5-108 (Ballance) 6-111 (Hodd), 7-221 (McGrath), 8-222 (Patterson)

	O	M	R	W		O	M	R	W
Topley	25	6	85	2	Topley	18	4	41	0
Napier	27.2	3	65	5	Napier	21	6	54	4
Craddock	11	1	37	1	ten Doeschate	6	1	16	0
Mills	17	3	44	0	Mills	15	0	52	1
Westley	22	6	50	1	Westley	16	6	37	2
ten Doeschate	5	0	22	0	Craddock	21	6	45	1

First Innings	ESSEX	Second Innings	
T Westley, lbw b Azeem Rafiq	18	c Hodd b Patterson	18
J C Mickleburgh, b Patterson	4	c Jaques b Azeem Rafiq	2
O A Shah, c Lyth b Azeem Rafiq	6	not out	71
M L Pettini, lbw b Ashraf	1	(5) c Ballance b Azeem Rafiq	17
R N ten Doeschate, c Ballance b Patterson	62	(6) c Gale b Ashraf	1
§ * J S Foster, lbw b Patterson	16	(7) c Jaques b Azeem Rafiq	10
A J A Wheater, c Gale b Sidebottom	16	(8) c Hodd b Azeem Rafiq	19
G R Napier, c Lyth b Ashraf	20	(9) c Jaques b Azeem Rafiq	0
T R Craddock, c Lyth b Ashraf	8	(4) c Jaques b Patterson	5
R J W Topley, lbw b Ashraf	0	c Lyth b Patterson	0
T S Mills, not out	20	b Patterson	0
Extras b 2, nb 4	6	Extras lb 5	5
Total	177	Total	148

Bonus points — Yorkshire 3

FoW: 1st 1-10 (Mickleburgh), 2-25 (Westley), 3-26 (Pettini), 4-34 (Shah), 5-97 (Foster) 6-119 (Wheater), 7-147 (ten Doeschate), 8-148 (Napier), 9-148 (Topley), 10-177 (Craddock)

FoW: 2nd 1-8 (Mickleburgh), 2-22 (Westley), 3-34 (Craddock), 4-74 (Pettini), 5-75 (ten Doeschate) 6-109 (Foster), 7-135 (Wheater), 8-135 (Napier), 9-148 (Topley), 10-148 (Mills)

	O	M	R	W		O	M	R	W
Sidebottom	13	2	32	1	Patterson	14.5	2	34	4
Patterson	15	2	29	2	Sidebottom	8	3	12	0
Ashraf	11.5	3	36	4	Azeem Rafiq	17	3	50	5
Azeem Rafiq	15	4	65	3	Ashraf	11	2	39	1
McGrath	4	1	13	0	Root	1	0	8	0

Umpires: M J D Bodenham and P Willey — Scorers: J T Potter and A E Choat

Essex v. Yorkshire

Rafiq shines as Yorkshire go up

This was the last match with Derbyshire, Kent and Yorkshire in contention for two promotion places.

Yorkshire chose to bat first, and at the close were 284-8. Lyth batted well for 67, Rafiq made an important 50 and Sidebottom again made runs down the order.

Napier, who dismissed Root for a duck, had a good day as did the youthful Topley and off-spinner Westley.

AZEEM RAFIQ: Eight wickets and his best batting of the season

Huddersfield-born leg-spinner Craddock caught Sidebottom off his own bowling with the last ball of the day, and honours were even. Next morning Yorkshire reached 312 and three batting points.

All of Yorkshire's bowlers contributed to the dismissal of Essex for 177: Ashraf took four including two with successive balls; Rafiq removed Westley and Shah in the top order, and eventually won his battle with the assertive ten Doeschate, who had hit him for two mighty sixes. Patterson accounted for the adhesive Foster. Napier took three wickets to leave Yorkshire in some disarray, but well ahead. McGrath's calm, authoritative contribution in the middle of the order on Thursday was again important, and it enabled Rafiq to play his best innings of the summer. Rafiq and Patterson each took a wicket in the evening as Essex embarked on an impossible target of 388.

Meanwhile, Glamorgan needed only 61 to beat Kent at Cardiff. First news was that rain had ended the day with Glamorgan on 36-3, but further intelligence from the Principality revealed that the match had been resumed and Glamorgan had won, so Yorkshire would be promoted. Apart from an undefeated 71 from Shah the Essex batsmen did not trouble Yorkshire as Patterson took four wickets and Rafiq 5-50 to complete an excellent all-round match. There has been plenty of good batting and smart fielding, but let us end with a tribute to these bowlers: Patterson has been effective all season; Sidebottom has worked hard and never let the side down; Ashraf and Rafiq have advanced significantly and will look forward with optimism to next summer. Derbyshire did beat Kent so Yorkshire finished second on the number of matches won.

LV COUNTY CHAMPIONSHIP 2012

DIVISION 1

	P	W	L	D	Bonus Points BAT	Bonus Points BOWL	Pen.	Points
1 Warwickshire (Div 1, 2)	16	6	1	9	43	45	0.0	211
2 Somerset (Div 1, 4)	16	5	1	10	32	45	0.0	187
3 Middlesex (Div 2, 1)	16	5	4	7	33	38	0.0	172
4 Sussex (Div 1, 5)	16	5	5	6	28	41	0.0	167
5 Nottinghamshire (Div 1, 6)	16	4	2	10	26	43	0.0	163
6 Durham (Div 1, 3)	16	5	5	6	18	45	4.0	157
7 Surrey Div 2, 2)	16	3	4	9	26	40	2.0	139
8 Lancashire (Div 1, 1) *	16	1	5	10	25	35	0.0	106
9 Worcestershire (Div 1, 7) *	16	1	8	7	17	42	0.0	96

Pen. 1 point deducted for each over short in a match based on a rate of 16 overs per hour

* Relegated to Division 2 for 2013

DIVISION 2

	P	W	L	D	Bonus Points BAT	Bonus Points BOWL	Pen.	Points
1 Derbyshire (Div 2, 5) *	16	6	2	8	31	43	0.0	194
2 Yorkshire (Div 1, 8) *	**16**	**5**	**0**	**11**	**41**	**40**	**0.0**	**194**
3 Kent (Div 2, 8)	16	4	3	9	39	40	0.0	170
4 Hampshire (Div 1, 9)	16	4	5	7	28	40	0.0	153
5 Essex (Div 2, 7)	16	3	3	10	27	40	0.0	145
6 Glamorgan (Div 2, 6)	16	3	6	7	28	35	1.0	131
7 Leicestershire (Div 2, 9)	16	3	3	10	24	33	5.0	130
8 Northamptonshire (Div 2, 3)	16	2	5	9	37	34	0.0	130
9 Gloucestershire (Div 2, 4)	16	3	6	7	22	35	0.0	126

Pen. 1 point deducted for each over short in a match based on a rate of 16 overs per hour

* Promoted to Division 1 for 2013. Derbyshire were placed higher because of more wins.

(2011 positions in brackets)

YORKSHIRE AVERAGES 2012

LV COUNTY CHAMPIONSHIP

Played 16 Won 5 Lost 0 Drawn 11

BATTING AND FIELDING

(Qualification 10 completed innings)

Player	*M.*	*I.*	*N.O.*	*Runs*	*H.S.*	*Avge*	*100s*	*50s*	*ct/st*
A Lyth	12	15	1	751	248*	53.64	1	5	12
J M Bairstow	9	12	1	588	182	53.45	3	1	14/0
A McGrath	13	15	3	584	106*	48.66	2	3	4
P A Jaques	15	19	1	792	160	44.00	2	4	16
J E Root	14	19	2	738	222*	43.41	2	2	8
G S Ballance	16	19	4	613	121*	40.86	1	2	10
A W Gale	14	18	3	481	80	32.06	0	2	4
Also played									
Azeem Rafiq	10	10	1	265	75*	29.44	0	2	5
G L Brophy	3	2	1	24	22	24.00	0	0	6/0
J J Sayers	5	7	0	165	45	23.57	0	0	2
R J Sidebottom	11	10	2	164	37	20.50	0	0	1
S A Patterson	15	14	5	174	37	19.33	0	0	1
T T Bresnan	4	4	0	73	38	18.25	0	0	2
A J Hodd	4	5	0	91	58	18.20	0	1	18/0
A U Rashid	10	8	0	129	58	16.12	0	1	0
A Shahzad	3	3	0	34	25	11.33	0	0	0
S J Harmison	3	3	0	25	23	8.33	0	0	1
M A Ashraf	8	6	4	14	6*	7.00	0	0	1
R M Pyrah	4	4	0	9	9	2.25	0	0	0
I Wardlaw	2	2	2	30	17*	—	0	0	1
M A Starc	2	1	1	28	28*	—	0	0	0

BOWLING

(Qualification 10 wickets)

Player	*Overs*	*Mdns*	*Runs*	*Wkts*	*Avge*	*Best*	*5wI*	*10wM*
S A Patterson	389.2	116	999	48	20.81	5-77	1	0
M A Ashraf	117.5	27	376	17	22.11	4-36	0	0
Azeem Rafiq	222.5	58	633	26	24.34	5-50	1	0
T T Bresnan	130.2	31	397	14	28.35	5-81	1	0
R J Sidebottom	297	72	798	24	33.25	5-30	1	0
A McGrath	171.1	50	424	12	35.33	4-21	0	0
A U Rashid	202.5	26	656	16	41.00	5-105	1	0
Also bowled								
M A Starc	42.1	13	153	7	21.85	3-50	0	0
S J Harmison	42	4	195	8	24.37	3-49	0	0
A Shahzad	68.1	14	210	8	26.25	3-86	0	0
R M Pyrah	38	9	128	2	64.00	1-9	0	0
I Wardlaw	52	1	225	2	112.50	1-37	0	0
J E Root	48	14	130	1	130.00	1-39	0	0
A Lyth	12	3	116	0	—	0-1	0	0
A W Gale	6.1	1	0	97	—	0-26	0	0
G S Ballance	6	1	23	0	—	0-23	0	0

MCC University Match (First-Class)
Yorkshire v. Leeds/Bradford MCCU

Played at Headingley Carnegie, Leeds, on April 13, 14 and 15, 2012

Match drawn at 4.14pm on the Third Day

Toss won by Leeds/Bradford MCCU

Close of play: First Day, Yorkshire 80-6 (Azeem Rafiq 8*, Brophy 0*); Second Day, Leeds/Bradford MCCU 127-6 (Reece 58*, Hardman 28*)

First Innings	LEEDS/BRADFORD MCCU	Second innings	
B T Slater, run out (Lyth/Brophy)	14	lbw b McGrath	15
J P Webb, c McGrath b Patterson	5	lbw b Patterson	1
H Bush, c Ballance b Hannon-Dalby)	0	lbw b Patterson	7
J Leach, lbw b McGrath	11	c Hannon-Dalby b McGrath	5
L M Reece, c Sayers b Patterson	40	c Wardlaw b Azeem Rafiq	60
§ D M Hodgson, c Brophy b Wardlaw	0	lbw b McGrath	0
* R A L Moore, lbw b McGrath	29	lbw b McGrath	10
T Hardman, c Lyth b McGrath	0	lbw b Patterson	44
A MacQueen, c Rafiq b Hannon-Dalby	69	c Root b Azeem Rafiq	3
M Higginbottom, not out	31	not out	30
I A Thomas, c Rafiq b Hannon-Dalby	2	c Brophy b Hannon-Dalby	11
Extras b 1, lb 8, w 1	10	Extras lb 3	3
Total	211	Total	189

FoW: 1st 1-23 (Slater), 2-23 (Bush), 3-31 (Webb), 4-45 (Leach), 5-50 (Hodgson) 6-97 (Moore), 7-99 (Hardman), 8-114 (Reece), 9-209 (MacQueen), 10-211 (Thomas)

FoW: 2nd 1-1 (Webb), 2-9 (Bush), 3-24 (Leach), 4-38 (Slater), 5-38 (Hodgson) 6-56 (Moore), 7-129 (Reece), 8-133 (MacQueen), 9-159 (Hardman), 10-189 (Thomas)

	O	M	R	W		O	M	R	W
Patterson	15	4	45	2	Patterson	23	5	71	3
Hannon-Dalby	15	2	36	3	Hannon-Dalby	10.1	2	18	1
McGrath	12	5	28	3	McGrath	13	4	37	4
Wardlaw	8	1	45	1	Wardlaw	5	0	30	0
Azeem Rafiq	11	0	48	0	Azeem Rafiq	13	5	30	2

First Innings	YORKSHIRE	Second Innings	
J E Root, lbw b Thomas	8	lbw b Thomas	0
J J Sayers, c Webb b Thomas	35	not out	41
A McGrath, b Higginbottom	21	lbw b Leach	43
* A W Gale, b Higginbottom	2	not out	4
A Lyth, c Hodgson b Reece	0		
G S Ballance, lbw b Reece	4		
Azeem Rafiq, c Hodgson b Leach	28		
§ G L Brophy, c Moore b Thomas	23		
S A Patterson, lbw b Leach	6		
I Wardlaw, c Reece b Leach	1		
O J Hannon-Dalby, not out	5		
Extras nb 2	2	Extras w 1, nb 2	3
Total	135	Total (2 wkts)	91

FoW: 1st 1-18 (Root), 2-66 (McGrath), 3-66 (Sayers), 4-66 (Lyth), 5-72 (Gale) 6-80 (Ballance), 7-109 (Rafiq), 8-129 (Patterson), 9-129 (Brophy), 10-135 (Wardlaw)

2nd 1-0 (Root), 2-86 (McGrath)

	O	M	R	W		O	M	R	W
Thomas	14	5	24	2	Thomas	11	5	21	1
Hardman	6	0	25	0	Hardman	3	0	12	0
Reece	12	4	25	3	Reece	6	1	26	1
Higginbottom	12	4	46	2	Higginbottom	4	0	21	0
Leach	7.1	2	15	3	Leach	6.3	4	6	1
					MacQueen	1	0	5	0

Umpires: I Dawood and P J Hartley

Scorers: J T Potter and S N Churchman

Yorkshire v. Leeds/Bradford MCCU

Brought to book by students

JOE SAYERS: Too good starts

This was the first time that Leeds/Bradford University had played Yorkshire in a first-class match.

Until this year four MCCUs played first-class cricket and two did not — which was increasingly anomalous as Cardiff were the most successful side in 2011 and Leeds/Bradford had won three of the University Championship titles since 2005.

So both were granted first-class status. Each university's first two games are first class and the third is not, because counties have agreed to pick stronger sides early in the season.

Leeds/Bradford were the better side here. Reece arrested the decline with a good 40 after the loss of early wickets, and McQueen and Higginbottom added 95 for the ninth wicket. McQueen, 19, off-spinner from Surrey, made 69 and Higginbottom an unbeaten 31. The Yorkshire bowlers shared the wickets, but McGrath was the most successful with his medium pace. Sitting in late afternoon in frozen expectation of a large score we saw six Yorkshire batsmen removed for 80 by the close, Reece taking three wickets and Thomas looking a useful bowler. There was some recovery next morning, but Leach ensured that Yorkshire finished 76 behind.

In the Universities' second innings wickets fell to Patterson and McGrath until Reece, a left-hander who has done well in Lancashire's Second Eleven, and Hardman, who was to die tragically in November, enabled them to reach 189. McGrath took 4-37, match figures 7-65. Yorkshire needed 266, but time and climate allowed little progress. All of Leeds/Bradford's pace quintet had good games. Dan Hodgson, Yorkshire's third wicket-keeper, kept efficiently, but was excellently caught by Brophy, Yorkshire's second wicket-keeper, when he batted.

YORKSHIRE AVERAGES 2012

ALL FIRST-CLASS MATCHES

Played 17 Won 5 Lost 0 Drawn 12

BATTING AND FIELDING

(Qualification 10 completed innings)

Player	*M.*	*I.*	*N.O.*	*Runs*	*H.S.*	*Avge*	*100s*	*50s*	*ct/st*
J M Bairstow	9	12	1	588	182	53.45	3	1	14/0
A Lyth	13	16	1	751	248*	50.06	1	5	13
A McGrath	14	17	3	648	106*	46.28	2	3	5
P A Jaques	15	19	1	792	160	44.00	2	4	16
J E Root	15	21	2	746	222*	39.26	2	2	9
G S Ballance	17	20	4	617	121*	38.56	1	2	11
A W Gale	15	20	4	487	80	30.43	0	2	4
Azeem Rafiq	11	11	1	293	75*	29.30	0	2	7
S A Patterson	16	15	5	180	37	18.00	0	0	1
Also played									
J J Sayers	6	9	1	241	45	30.12	0	0	3
G L Brophy	4	3	1	47	23	23.50	0	0	8/0
R J Sidebottom	11	10	2	164	37	20.50	0	0	1
T T Bresnan	4	4	0	73	38	18.25	0	0	2
A J Hodd	4	5	0	91	58	18.20	0	1	18/0
A U Rashid	10	8	0	129	58	16.12	0	1	0
Ajmal Shahzad	3	3	0	34	25	11.33	0	0	0
S J Harmison	3	3	0	25	23	8.33	0	0	1
M A Ashraf	8	6	4	14	6*	7.00	0	0	1
R M Pyrah	4	4	0	9	9	2.25	0	0	0
M A Starc	2	1	1	28	28*	—	0	0	0
O J Hannon-Dalby	1	1	1	5	5*	—	0	0	1

BOWLING

(Qualification 10 wickets)

Player	*Overs*	*Mdns*	*Runs*	*Wkts*	*Avge*	*Best*	*5wI*	*10wM*
S A Patterson	427.2	125	1115	53	21.03	5-77	1	0
M A Ashraf	117.5	27	376	17	22.11	4-36	0	0
Azeem Rafiq	246.5	63	711	28	25.39	5-50	1	0
A McGrath	196.1	59	489	19	25.73	4-21	0	0
T T Bresnan	130.2	31	397	14	28.35	5-81	1	0
R J Sidebottom	297	72	798	24	33.25	5-30	1	0
A U Rashid	202.5	26	656	16	41.00	5-105	1	0
Also bowled								
O J Hannon-Dalby	25.1	4	54	4	13.50	3-36	0	0
M A Starc	42.1	13	153	7	21.85	3-50	0	0
S J Harmison	42	4	195	8	24.37	3-49	0	0
Ajmal Shahzad	68.1	14	210	8	26.25	3-86	0	0
R M Pyrah	38	9	128	2	64.00	1- 9	0	0
I Wardlaw	65	2	300	3	100.00	1-37	0	0
J E Root	48	14	130	1	130.00	1-39	0	0
A Lyth	12	3	116	0	—	0-1	0	0
A W Gale	6.1	0	97	0	—	0-26	0	0
G S Ballance	6	1	23	0	—	0-23	0	0

Second Investec Test Match
England v. South Africa

Played at Headingley Carnegie, Leeds, on August 2, 3, 4, 5 and 6, 2012

Match drawn at 7.32pm on the Fifth Day

Toss won by England

Close of play: First Day, South Africa 262-5 (Petersen 124*, Rudolph 1*); Second Day, England 48-0 (Strauss 19*, Cook 20*); Third Day, England 351-5 (Pietersen 149*, Prior 20*); Fourth Day, South Africa 39-0 (Rudolph 21*, Smith 17*)

First Innings	SOUTH AFRICA	Second innings	
A N Petersen, c Prior b Broad	182	(8) not out	16
* G C Smith, c Bell b Bresnan	52	c Taylor b Pietersen	52
H M Amla, run out (Bresnan/Prior)	9	c Cook b Pietersen	28
J H Kallis, c Cook b Anderson	19	(5) c Prior b Broad	27
§ A B de Villiers, b Broad	47	(4) lbw b Broad	44
D W Steyn, b Finn	0	(9) c and b Anderson	3
J A Rudolph, st Prior b Pietersen	19	(1) lbw b Pietersen	69
J P Duminy, not out	48	(6) lbw b Broad	0
V D Philander, c Bresnan b Finn	13	(7) lbw b Broad	6
M Morkel, c Cook b Broad	19	c Cook b Broad	10
Imran Tahir, c Cook b Anderson	0		
Extras b 5, lb 6	11	Extras lb 2, w 1	3
Total	419	Total (9 wkts dec)	258

FoW: 1st 1-120 (Smith), 2-132 (Amla), 3-157 (Kallis), 4-254 (de Villiers), 5-259 (Steyn) 6-318 (Rudolph), 7-353 (Petersen), 8-375 (Philander), 9-414 (Morke;). 10-419 (Tahir)

FoW: 2nd 1-120 (Rudolph), 2-129 (Smith), 3-182 (Amla), 4-209 (de Villiers), 5-209 (Duminy) 6-223 (Philander), 7-230 (Kallis), 8-247 (Steyn), 9-258 (Morkel)

	O	M	R	W		O	M	R	W
Anderson	33.2	10	61	2	Anderson	19	7	40	1
Broad	35	10	96	3	Broad	16.4	2	69	5
Finn	32	3	118	2	Finn	14	2	55	0
Bresnan	27	4	98	1	Bresnan	9	2	40	0
Trott	5	1	9	0	Pietersen	9	1	52	3
Pietersen	7	0	26	1					

First Innings	ENGLAND	Second innings	
* A J Strauss, c de Villiers b Steyn	37	(3) c and b Duminy	22
A N Cook, lbw b Philander	24	c Rudolph b Steyn	46
I J L Trott, c Smith b Steyn	35	(4) not out	30
K P Pietersen, lbw b Morkel	149	(1) c Imran Tahir b Philander	12
I R Bell, c Smith b Kallis	11	(6) not out	3
J W A Taylor, b Morkel	34		
§ M J Prior, c Steyn b Imran Tahir	68	(5) run out (Smith/de Villiers)	7
T T Bresnan, c Smith b Philander	9		
S C J Broad, c sub (F du Plessis) b Imran Tahir	1		
J M Anderson, b Imran Tahir	8		
S T Finn, not out	0		
Extras b 7, lb 17, w 14, nb 11	49	Extras lb 8, w 1, nb1	10
Total	425	Total (4 wkts)	130

FoW: 1st 1-65 (Cook), 2-85 (Strauss), 3-142 (Trott), 4-173 (Bell), 5-320 (Taylor) 6-351 (Pietersen), 7-396 (Bresnan), 8-407 (Broad), 9-420 (Prior), 10-425 (Anderson)

2nd 1-21 (Pietersen), 2-75 (Strauss), 3-90 (Cook), 4-106 (Prior)

	O	M	R	W		O	M	R	W
Morkel	32	9	96	2	Morkel	10	4	33	0
Philander	30	10	72	2	Philander	6	1	26	1
Steyn	28	8	102	2	Steyn	7	1	26	1
Kallis	12	3	34	1	Imran Tahir	4	0	20	0
Imran Tahir	23.4	0	92	3	Duminy	2	0	10	1
Duminy	1	0	5	0	Kallis	4	2	7	0

Man of the Match: K P Pietersen

Umpires: S J Davis and R J Tucker　　Scorers: J T Potter and H Clayton

Third Umpire: Asad Rauf　　Fourth Umpire: N G B Cook　　Referee: J J Crowe

CLYDESDALE BANK 40 HIGHLIGHTS OF 2012

Totals of 250 and over (1)

262-8 v. Northamptonshire at Northampton (won)

Match aggregates of 450 and over (4)

478 Yorkshire (238-9) lost to Sussex (240-6) by 4 wickets at Hove
477 Yorkshire (238-7) lost to Derbyshire (239-7) by 3 wickets at Chesterfield
455 Yorkshire (262-8) defeated Northamptonshire (193) by 69 run at Northampton
452 Yorkshire (213-8) lost to Warwickshire (239-7) by 3 wickets *D/L metho* at Birmingham

Century Partnerships (1)

For the 3rd wicket (1)

160* A Lyth and G S Ballance v. Unicorns at Scarborough

Centuries (1)

G S Ballance (1)

103* v. Unicorns at Scarborough

4 wickets in an innings (1)

A U Rashid (1)

4 for 38 v. Northamptonshire at Northampton

Debuts (4)

List A cricket: D M Hodgson and J A Leaning
For Yorkshire: D A Miller and M A Starc

Acker Taylor

Ken Taylor batted for Yorkshire, batted for England, played football for Huddersfield Town, could paint anything. Such talent! But not many people knew he could play the clarinet as well...*Stranger on the Shore*, the old Acker Bilk number.

Don Wilson, 2010

Clydesdale Bank 40 Matches Played by Yorkshire in 2012

*Captain
§Wicket Keeper

WINNERS

HAMPSHIRE, who beat Warwickshire by having lost fewer wickers with scores level

PREVIOUS WINNERS	*Yorkshire's Position*
2010 **Warwickshire**	1st Group B
2011 **Surrey**	6th Group A

NATIONAL LEAGUE

1999 **Lancashire**	5th Div 1
2000 **Gloucestershire**	2nd Div 1
2001 **Kent**	6th Div 1
2002 **Glamorgan**	4th Div 1
2003 **Surrey**	8th Div 1
2004 **Glamorgan**	4th Div 2
2005 **Essex**	8th Div 2
2006 **Essex**	9th Div 2
2007 **Worcestershire**	6th Div 2
2008 **Sussex**	2nd Div2
2009 **Sussex**	7th Div1

SUNDAY LEAGUE

PREVIOUS WINNERS	*Yorkshire's Position*	PREVIOUS WINNERS	*Yorkshire's Position*
1969 **Lancashire**	8th	1984 **Essex**	=13th
1970 **Lancashire**	14th	1985 **Essex**	6th
1971 **Worcestershire**	15th	1986 **Hampshire**	8th
1972 **Kent**	4th	1987 **Worcestershire**	=13th
1973 **Kent**	2nd	1988 **Worcestershire**	8th
1974 **Leicestershire**	=6th	1989 **Lancashire**	11th
1975 **Hampshire**	=5th	1990 **Derbyshire**	6th
1976 **Kent**	15th	1991 **Nottinghamshire**	7th
1977 **Leicestershire**	=13th	1992 **Middlesex**	15th
1978 **Hampshire**	7th	1993 **Glamorgan**	9th
1979 **Somerset**	=4th	1994 **Warwickshire**	5th
1980 **Warwickshire**	=14th	1995 **Kent**	12th
1981 **Essex**	=7th	1996 **Surrey**	3rd
1982 **Sussex**	16th	1997 **Warwickshire**	10th
1983 **Yorkshire**	1st	1998 **Lancashire**	9th

Match-By-Match Reports
Scorecards
Pictures

NIGEL PULLAN
JOHN POTTER
SIMON WILKINSON
VAUGHN RIDLEY
ALEX WHITEHEAD
SWpix.com

Clydesdale Bank 40 — Group C
Yorkshire v. Kent

Played at Headingley, Leeds, on May 6, 2012

Kent won by 4 wickets

Toss won by Yorkshire — Kent 2 points, Yorkshire 0 points

YORKSHIRE

* A W Gale, lbw b Stevens	44
J J Sayers, c Tredwell b Davies	1
P A Jaques, b Coles	0
§ J M Bairstow, c and b Coles	3
G S Ballance, lbw b Coles	0
J E Root, c Northeast b Ball	49
A U Rashid, c Stevens b Coles	32
Azeem Rafiq, c Stevens b Coles	11
S A Patterson, c Jones b Coles	14
M A Ashraf, not out	3
I Wardlaw, not out	6
Extras b 4, lb 4, w 4	12
Total (9 wkts, 40 overs)	175

FoW: 1-5 (Sayers), 2-10 (Jaques), 3-22 (Bairstow), 4-22 (Ballance), 5-92 (Gale) 6-113 (Root), 7-134 (Rafiq), 8-166 (Patterson), 9-166 (Rashid)

	O	M	R	W
Davies	8	3	17	1
Coles	8	0	32	6
Ball	8	1	42	1
Tredwell	8	0	35	0
Stevens	8	0	41	1

KENT

S W Billings, c Wardlaw b Azeem Rafiq	26
* R W T Key, c and b Azeem Rafiq	40
A J Blake, lbw b Azeem Rafiq	14
D I Stevens, c Ballance b Root	59
B P Nash, lbw b Root	24
S A Northeast, lbw b Ashraf	3
§ G O Jones, not out	8
J C Tredwell, not out	0
A J Ball M T Coles M Davies	Did not bat
Extras lb 1, w 1	2
Total (6 wkts, 39.2 overs)	176

FoW: 1-57 (Billings), 2-78 (Blake), 3-94 (Key), 4-159 (Stevens, 5-164 (Northeast) 6-175 (Nash)

	O	M	R	W
Ashraf	8	0	39	1
Patterson	8	0	39	0
Rashid	5	0	37	0
Rafiq	8	1	22	3
Wardlaw	7.2	1	24	0
Root	3	0	14	2

TV Man of the Match: M T Coles

Umpires: D J Millns and P Willey — Scorers: J T Potter and C A Booth

Third Umpire: M A Gough

Yorkshire v. Kent

Poor start to both halves

JOE ROOT: A reverse-sweep on the way to his side's top-score 49

TV cameras rolled into town for Yorkshire's first limited-overs fixture of the season and the rare chance of an uninterrupted day's play as the sun shone.

The hosts got off to a terrible start as wickets tumbled. Sayers drove to slip for one, Jaques inside-edged his first delivery on to his stumps off Coles for a duck, and Bairstow offered the same bowler a smart return catch. Next ball Ballance played across one from Coles and was lbw to make it 22-4. A fine rearguard action between Gale and Root produced 70 vital runs before Gale was adjudged lbw by umpire Millns to Stevens for 44 off as many balls, despite a feeling there had been an inside edge. Root's excellent innings ended tamely on 49 as he square-drove into the waiting hands of Northeast at point, and Yorkshire were teetering on the brink at 113-6.

Rafiq and Rashid then took the reins before Rafiq played a poor lofted drive and was caught by Stevens for 11. Yorkshire reached 175-9 after decent lower contributions, Coles taking career-best figures of 6-32 from his eight overs while his opening partner, Davies, bowled a miserly spell of 1-17 from his allocation.

What Yorkshire needed after the interval were quick wickets, but a wayward start from Patterson and Ashraf allowed Key and Billings to advance effortlessly to 54 before the introduction of Rafiq brought the first scalp: Billings, having played nicely for his 26, skied a simple chance to the gleeful Wardlaw in the deep. Rafiq followed this with the wicket of Blake lbw for 14 and then got the vital wicket of Spitfires talisman Key, caught and bowled for 40 as the off-spinner completed his spell to collect 3-22. The experienced Stevens, as is so often the case, was the thorn in Yorkshire's side as he and Nash added 66 in good time almost to see their side through. Stevens had made 59 when he was taken in the deep by Ballance off Root.

Clydesdale Bank 40 — Group C
Yorkshire v. Derbyshire

Played at Headingley, Leeds, on May 20, 2012

Yorkshire won by 7 wickets

Toss won by Yorkshire — Yorkshire 2 points, Derbyshire 0 points

DERBYSHIRE

C F Hughes, b Ashraf	50
M J Guptill, c Brophy b McGrath	89
W J Durston, c and b Azeem Rafiq	9
* W L Madson, lbw b McGrath	10
R A Whiteley, c Lyth b Starc	8
D J Redfern, c Brophy b Starc	13
G T Park, lbw b Wardlaw	2
D J Wainwright, not out	13
§ T Poynton, b Starc	7
A P Palladino, not out	9
T D Groenewald — Did not bat	
Extras lb 4, w 3, nb 2	9
Total (8 wkts, 40 overs)	219

FoW: 1-137 (Hughes), 2-154 (Durston), 3-160 (Guptill), 4-169 (Madsen), 5-182 (Whiteley), 6-186 (Park), 7-190 (Redfern), 8-208 (Poynton)

	O	M	R	W
Starc	8	1	28	3
Ashraf	7	0	34	1
Wardlaw	8	0	63	1
Root	3	0	22	0
McGrath	6	0	24	2
Rafiq	8	0	44	1

YORKSHIRE

* A W Gale, b Durstan	33
A Lyth, c Wainwright b Durston	31
P A Jaques, c Durston b Wainwright	47
G S Ballance, not out	77
J E Root, not out	28
A McGrath § G L Brophy Azeem Rafiq M A Starc I Wardlaw M A Ashraf — Did not bat	
Extras lb 6, w 1	7
Total (3 wkts, 37.4 overs)	223

FoW: 1-56 (Lyth), 2-84 (Gale), 3-153 (Jaques)

	O	M	R	W
Palladino	6	0	29	0
Groenewald	7	1	40	0
Durston	7	1	40	2
Park	6	0	48	0
Wainwright	8	0	35	1
Redfern	1	0	5	0
Hughes	2.4	0	20	0

Umpires: N L Bainton and S C Gale — Scorers: J T Potter and J M Brown

Savage Ballance calms nerves

MITCHELL STARC: Paceman the top wicket-taker on debut

Yorkshire collected their first victory in convincing fashion as Gary Ballance struck an exquisitely timed and unbeaten 77 from 60 deliveries to overtake Derbyshire's 219, a total that had threatened to be far more substantial

Choosing to field first, Carnegie were soon under pressure as Guptill and Hughes combined effortlessly at the top of the order to put the hosts on the back foot.

Left-arm fast debutant Mitchell Starc was keeping it relatively tight at one end while Ashraf and Wardlaw found the going a little tougher in their first spells.

Guptill raced to 50 from 53 deliveries, but Hughes took 72 to reach his half-century. Soon afterwards Hughes was yorked by Ashraf to end an opening partnership of 137 in 25 overs. Yorkshire clawed their way back. Durston went for nine to a fine return catch by Rafiq, and Guptill was caught at the wicket next over off McGrath for a sublime 89 in 83 balls. The veteran all-rounder struck again in his next over, trapping Falcons skipper Madsen in front. Derbyshire lost all impetus, Starc finishing with a fine debut analysis of 3-28.

Adam Lyth was put down by Guptill on 10, but Yorkshire got to grips with the chase in no uncertain terms — Gale and Lyth adding 56 before Lyth was caught for 31 by former teammate David Wainwright, who had received a warm reception on his return to Headingley. Gale, looking a little out of touch, was bowled by Durston for 33 to make it 84-2 nearing the 20th over. The match was pretty much won and lost in the next partership as Jaques and Ballance took it away from Falcons with 69 in just over 10 overs. Jaques was caught for 47 to give Wainwright a well-earned wicket, and 50 were needed in seven overs. Ballance calmed nerves with some savage strokeplay, and with Root completed the job in an unbeaten partnership of 70, with 14 deliveries remaining.

Clydesdale Bank 40 — Group C
Sussex v. Yorkshire

Played at The County Ground, Hove, on May 24, 2012

Sussex won by 4 wickets

Toss won by Yorkshire — Sussex 2 points, Yorkshire 0 points

YORKSHIRE

* A W Gale, b Nash	42
A Lyth, c Joyce b Nash	27
P A Jaques, c Gatting b Panesar	37
G S Ballance, c Joyce b Beer	40
J E Root, c Panesar b Amjad Khan	46
A McGrath, c Brown b Liddle	26
§ G L Brophy, b Liddle	5
Azeem Rafiq, c Brown b Amjad Khan	0
M A Starc, not out	4
R J Sidebottom, c and b Amjad Khan	2
M A Ashraf, not out	0
Extras b 1, lb 1, w 5, nb 2	9
Total (9 wkts, 40 overs)	238

FoW: 1-49 (Lyth), 2-97 (Gale), 3-135 (Jaques), 4-161 (Ballance), 5-226 (McGrath) 6-227 (Root), 7-228 (Rafiq), 8-234 (Brophy), 9-237 (Sidebottom)

	O	M	R	W
Liddle	7	0	42	2
Amjad Khan	8	0	51	3
Nash	8	1	34	2
Beer	7	0	55	1
Panesar	8	0	40	1
Wright	2	0	14	0

SUSSEX

C D Nash, run out (Starc)	44
* E C Joyce, c Root b Sidebottom	0
L J Wright, run out (Lyth)	103
M W Goodwin, c Ballance b Ashraf	1
J S Gatting, c sub (A U Rashid) b Root	45
M W Machin, c Ballance b Root	15
§ B C Brown, not out	11
W A T Beer, not out	1
Amjad Khan	
C J Liddle — Did not bat	
M S Panesar	
Extras b 4, lb 2, w 6, nb 8	20
Total (6 wkts, 33.5 overs)	240

FoW: 1-22 (Joyce), 2-71 (Nash), 3-87 (Goodwin), 4-177 (Gatting), 5-203 (Machin) 6-235 (Wright)

	O	M	R	W
Starc	8	0	71	0
Sidebottom	5	0	46	1
Ashraf	7	1	28	1
Root	4	0	21	2
Rafiq	5.5	0	47	0
McGrath	4	0	21	0

TV Man of the Match: L J Wright

Umpires: S J O'Shaughnessy and R T Robinson — Scorers: J T Potter and M J Charman

Third Umpire: N G C Cowley

Aussie eaten by the Sharks

Carnegie were very much second best spite posting a competitive total, and the Sharks' destructive batting put paid to any hopes of a second win.

Gale opted for first use, and in partnership with Lyth got his side off to a positive start. The left-handed pair put on 49 for the first wicket, but early in his innings Gale tried to pull a short one from Amjad Khan and was struck on the helmet.

There was a lengthy stoppage before Gale continued, clearly shaken and not feeling his best. He did not appear for Yorkshire in the field.

ANDREW GALE: Stricken but unbowed with 42

Lyth was going well on 29 from 19 balls when he drove straight into the hands of Joyce off Nash. Gale added 48 with Jaques for the second wicket before he was bowled for a gutsy 42 by Nash, the pick of the attack with 2-34. All of the middle order got themselves in, but none could pass 50, which is often the difference between a decent total and a very good one. Root top-scored with 46 from 36 deliveries, while Ballance, Jaques and McGrath all contributed without going on.

A total of 238 at Hove is certainly below par, and so it proved as Wright tucked into Yorkshire's attack with the gusto and undoubted quality the England selectors would have noted. Starc struggled in his second game for the Club, and his first over costing 20 runs very much set the tone. All of the *White Rose* bowlers struggled to bowl consistent lines, the notable exception being Ashraf whose 1-28 showed a glimpse of his capabilities with good control and attacking intent.

Sussex raced to 66 in the first six overs, and despite losing Joyce and Goodwin in single figures Wright and Nash took hold of the game in no uncertain terms before Nash, 44, was run out at the non-striker's end as Ashraf deflected a drive on to the stumps. Wright and Gatting added 46 for the fourth wicket, Wright's half-century coming at a run a ball. He dashed to his century off 91 deliveries by smashing Starc down the ground, as the Aussie was forced to lick his wounds with 0-71 from his eight overs. Sussex completed the task in the 34th over.

Clydesdale Bank 40 — Group C
Unicorns v. Yorkshire

Played at North Marine Road, Scarborough, on May 27, 2012
Yorkshire won by 8 wickets

Toss won by Yorkshire — Yorkshire 2 points, Unicorns 0 points

UNICORNS

J E Ord, b Sidebottom	0
M A Thorley, c Jaques b Sidebottom	20
§ T J New, not out	83
J R Levitt, lbw b McGrath	15
* K A Parsons, c Gale b Starc	19
L M Reece, lbw b Starc	4
B L Wadlan, b Starc	8
R G Querl, c Ballance b Rafiq	0
W W Lee, b Ashraf	5
L E Beaven, b Ashraf	10
S P Cheetham, b Sidebottom	0
Extras lb 7, w 9, nb 4	20
Total (all out, 40 overs)	184

FoW: 1-2 (Ord), 2-45 (Thornley), 3-80 (Levitt), 4-107 (Parsons), 5-125 (Reece) 6-149 (Wadlan), 7-150 (Querl), 8-171 (Lee), 9-183 (Beaven), 10-184 (Cheetham)

	O	M	R	W
Sidebottom	8	0	44	3
Starc	8	0	36	3
Ashraf	8	0	40	2
Root	2	1	5	0
Rafiq	8	1	32	1
McGrath	6	0	20	1

YORKSHIRE

* A W Gale, lbw b Lee	17
A Lyth, not out	60
P A Jaques, c New b Querl	3
G S Ballance, not out	103
J E Root	
A McGrath	
§ G L Brophy	
Azeem Rafiq — Did not bat	
M A Starc	
R J Sidebottom	
M A Ashraf	
Extras w 3	3
Total (2 wkts, 32.2 overs)	186

FoW: 1-23 (Gale), 2-26 (Jaques)

	O	M	R	W
Lee	6	0	53	1
Querl	7.2	2	33	1
Beaven	6	0	40	0
Cheetham	5	0	26	0
Reece	5	0	17	0
Wadlan	3	0	17	0

Umpires: S A Garratt and G Sharp — Scorers: J T Potter and K B O'Connell

Unicorns v. Yorkshire

Ballance century fireworks

GARY BALLANCE: Fourth List A 100 with eight fours and four sixes

Ballance spearheaded an excellent response after the heavy defeat in Hove with a fine, unbeaten century as Yorkshire passed the required 184 with 7.4 overs to be bowled.

A sparse crowd assembled to watch Unicorns bat first — and any late-comers would have missed seeing Ord's off-stump removed by Sidebottom in the first over for no score.

Thornely fell for 20, but Unicorns steadied the ship and moved to a creditable 80-2 in the 16th over. McGrath, as is so often the case, broke up the promising partnership of New and Levitt by trapping Levitt in front for 15. The seamers did the damage, chipping wickets away as only New provided an innings of substance. The batting powerplay arrived earlier than anticipated in the 31st over, and New tucked in, ending unbeaten on 83 from 92 balls. Starc finished with 3-36, Sidebottom 3-44 and Ashraf also impressed, especially in the later stages, by getting his full-length deliveries in with ease.

Yorkshire's reply faltered as skipper Andrew Gale played across the line to a straight delivery from Lee, and Jaques went cheaply when his attempted cut gave an under-edge to wicket-keeper New. At 26-2 in the sixth over there were a few nervous glances, but Lyth and Ballance provided the stability and the subsequent power to banish any notion of defeat. The 100 came up in the 20th over as Ballance took the lead, savaging anything loose, and Lyth completed the task with a boundary in the 33rd over to come in with 60 from 78 balls. The real fireworks came from Ballance, who ran up his fourth List A hundred in 91 balls with eight boundaries and four maximums.

Clydesdale Bank 40 — Group C

Yorkshire v. Northamptonshire

At Headingley, Leeds on June 3, 2012

Match abandoned without a ball bowled

Yorkshire 1 point, Northamptonshire 1 point

Umpires: P J Hartley and M J Saggers — Scorers: J T Potter and A C Kingston

Derbyshire v. Yorkshire

Played at Queen's Park, Chesterfield, on July 22, 2012

Derbyshire won by 3 wickets

Toss won by Derbyshire — Derbyshire 2 points, Yorkshire 0 points

YORKSHIRE

* A W Gale, hit wicket b Durston	51
P A Jaques, c Durston b Clare	25
J E Root, st Johnson b Durston	33
§ J M Bairstow, b Turner	25
G S Ballance, c Madsen b Groenewald	47
R M Pyrah, c Madsen b Groenewald	44
A U Rashid, c Khawaja b Clare	4
Azeem Rafiq, not out	3
M A Starc, not out	1
M A Ashraf	
I Wardlaw — Did not bat	
Extras b 1, lb 1, w 3	5
Total (7 wkts, 40 overs)	238

FoW: 1-54 (Jaques), 2-102 (Root), 3-115 (Gale), 4-152 (Bairstow), 5-208 (Ballance) 6-233 (Rashid), 7-236 (Pyrah

	O	M	R	W
Groenewald	8	0	39	2
Turner	8	0	59	1
Clare	6	0	51	2
Durston	8	0	32	2
Wainwright	8	0	39	0
C F Hughes	2	0	16	0

DERBYSHIRE

C F Hughes, b Starc	20
U T Khawaja, c Bairstow b Wardlaw	0
W J Durston, c Starc b Wardlaw	15
* W L Madsen, c and b Rashid	40
D J Redfern, b Starc	5
§ R M Johnson, c Pyrah b Wardlaw	79
J L Clare, c Jaques b Rashid	13
A L Hughes, not out	37
D J Wainwright, not out	8
M L Turner	
T D Groenewald — Did not bat	
Extras b 1, lb 4, w 9, nb 8	22
Total (7 wkts, 37.4 overs)	239

FoW: 1-1 (Khawaja), 2-37 (C F Hughes), 3-43 (Durston), 4-56 (Redfern), 5-123 (Madsen) 6-141 (Clare), 7-221 (Johnson)

	O	M	R	W
Wardlaw	8	0	60	3
Starc	7.4	0	46	2
Moin Ashraf	7	0	39	0
Azeem Rafiq	4	0	33	0
Rashid	8	0	36	2
Pyrah	3	0	20	0

Umpires: N G C Cowley and P J Hartley — Scorers: J T Potter and J M Brown

Derbyshire v. Yorkshire

Sloppy Carnegie lose chance

RICHARD PYRAH: Thrashed 44 with three sixes on the trot

A rare sun-kissed afternoon ended with a severe dent in *White Rose* hopes of a place in the semi-finals.

There was a sombre mood throughout as Yorkshire mourned the passing of left-arm spin legend Don Wilson.

Gale's men got off to a solid start with the skipper and Jaques adding 54 for the first wicket before Jaques miscued to Durston off the medium pace of Clare for 25.

Root joined his captain, and the pair looked comfortable, putting on 48 until Root was neatly stumped by the impressive Johnson for an excellent 33 in 25 balls. At 116 controversy struck. Gale had just reached his half-century on return from injury when he worked the ball to square-leg, only to see a bail dislodged, apparently with his foot. Gale was less than convinced, and the square-leg umpire did not at first give him out. After discussion with the wicket-keeper he was on his way.

Bairstow played as if it were the last over, with much swishing and aiming for maximums. He was bowled on 25 by Turner, who was showing serious pace, and again it was left to Ballance to propel Carnegie to a decent total with 47 in 42 balls, including six fours and a six. Pyrah helped himself to 44, with three successive sixes in the last-but-one over.

Yorkshire appeared in control: Khawaja edged Wardlaw to Bairstow in the first over; Starc castled Hughes, and Durston miscued Wardlaw to Starc. 43-3. It became 56-4 as Starc breached Redfern's defences, but Madsen and Johnson led the recovery with a stand of 67. The turning points came when Johnson was spilled at backward-point twice in single figures by the normally reliable Rafiq. These escapes spurred on the Falcons, and Yorkshire became sloppy with the ball. Wardlaw and Rafiq were expensive, and Johnson's dismissal for 79 was much too late as Derbyshire cruised home with 14 balls remaining.

Clydesdale Bank 40 — Group C
Warwickshire v. Yorkshire

Played at Edgbaston, Birmingham, on August 7, 2012

Warwickshire won by 3 wickets (D/L method)

Toss won by Warwickshire — Warwickshire 2 points, Yorkshire 0 points

YORKSHIRE

* A W Gale, st Ambrose b Best	76
P A Jaques, c Chopra b Best	37
A Lyth, c Chopra b Barker	69
D A Miller, lbw b Best	1
G S Ballance, c Patel b Barker	22
A U Rashid, c Ambrose b Wright	0
§ G L Brophy, c Ambrose b Wright	0
Azeem Rafiq, not out	2
I Wardlaw, run out (Ambrose/Barker)	0
S A Patterson, not out	0
M A Ashraf — Did not bat	
Extras b 1, lb 2, w 3	6
Total (8 wkts, 34 overs)	213

FoW: 1-86 (Jaques), 2-144 (Gale), 3-146 (Miller), 4-201 (Lyth), 5-203 (Rashid) 6-203 (Brophy), 7-210 (Balance), 8-212 (Wardlaw)

	O	M	R	W
Barker	6	0	36	2
Wright	6	1	51	2
Piolet	7	0	39	0
Patel	8	0	41	0
Best	7	0	43	3

WARWICKSHIRE

W T S Porterfield, c Miller b Patterson	19
V Chopra, c Brophy b Azeem Rafiq	34
* J O Troughton, b Azeem Rafiq	61
§ T R Ambrose, c Patterson b Ashraf	64
D L Maddy, run out (Miller/Brophy)	2
L J Evans, c Miller b Wardlaw	12
S A Piolet, not out	23
K H D Barker, run out (Miller/Brophy)	1
P M Best, not out	16
J S Patel	
C J C Wright — Did not bat	
Extras lb 2, w 5	7
Total (7 wkts, 33.2 overs)	239

D/L target to win: 238 runs off 34 overs

FoW:-1-27 (Porterfield), 2-80 (Chopra), 3-154 (Troughton), 4-160 (Maddy), 5-197 (Evans) 6-198 (Ambrose), 7-199 (Barker)

	O	M	R	W
Patterson	7	0	44	1
Wardlaw	6.2	0	45	1
Moin Ashraf	6	0	56	1
Azeem Rafiq	7	0	45	2
Rashid	7	0	47	0

TV Man of the Match: T R Ambrose

Umpires: M R Benson and S C Gale — Scorers: J T Potter and D E Wainwright

Third Umpire: N L Bainton

Warwickshire v. Yorkshire

Fine start washed off course

ADAM LYTH
Two huge sixes in 69

The Bears proved too strong in this rain-affected match, which ebbed and flowed, providing a meagre crowd with outstanding entertainment.

Yorkshire, asked to bat first, went about building an excellent opening partnership as Gale and Jaques took the score beyond 50 in 10 overs, Jaques in sublime form until he hit a full toss straight to Chopra at mid-wicket for 37 from 33 deliveries.

Lyth and Gale looked to have eyes on an imposing total. The score had raced to 144 in the 25th over when Gale was stumped off a leg-side wide for 76 in 83 balls with seven fours and a six. Lyth appeared unconcerned as he moved towards his half century, aided by two huge sixes off Piolet.

Lyth reached the milestone in 45 deliveries, but at 186-3 in the 31st over rain caused a half-hour stoppage, reducing Carnegie's allocation to 34 overs. Fireworks exploded on the resumption — mainly five wickets that went down for 27.

The recalculation meant that Warwickshire's target was 238 from 34 overs, and at 35-1 from six overs the visitors were in a strong position, Miller pulling off an outstanding running catch at deep square-leg to dismiss Porterfield. The rain returned, but no more overs were lost as the Bears resumed to take their total to a run a ball after 10 overs. Chopra fell for 34, neatly pouched by Brophy off Rafiq, but Warwickshire were very much in the game and Carnegie urgently needed wickets.

Rafiq provided the fillip needed as he bowled Troughton for 61, and Bears still required over eight runs an over with 10 still to be bowled. With Ambrose reaching his 50 from 38 balls Warwickshire looked home and dry until three wickets for two runs reduced them to 199-7. Less than four overs remained, but a fine stand of 40 between Best and Piolet hurried them home with four balls to spare to all but end Yorkshire's slim qualification hopes.

Clydesdale Bank 40 — Group C
Northamptonshire v. Yorkshire

Played at The County Ground, Northampton, on August 9, 2012

Yorkshire won by 69 runs

Toss won by Northamptonshire — Yorkshire 2 points, Northamptonshire 0 points

YORKSHIRE

* A W Gale, c Newton b Evans	16
P A Jaques, c Stone b Evans	87
A Lyth, c Murphy b Middlebrook	29
D A Miller, b Daggett	44
G S Ballance, c O'Brien b Daggett	15
A U Rashid, b Daggett	25
§ G L Brophy, st Murphy b Hall	19
Azeem Rafiq, c Wakely b Daggett	1
I Wardlaw, not out	3
S A Patterson, not out	3
M A Ashraf — Did not bat	
Extras b 4, lb 5, w 11	20
Total (8 wkts, 40 overs)	262

FoW: 1-42 (Gale), 2-99 (Lyth), 3-186 (Jaques), 4-191 (Miller), 5-229 (Rashid) 6-240 (Ballance), 7-245 (Rafiq), 8-257 (Brophy)

	O	M	R	W
Daggett	8	0	54	4
Stone	6	0	44	0
Evans	8	0	46	2
Middlebrook	5	0	35	1
Hall	5	0	27	1
Keogh	8	0	47	0

NORTHAMPTONSHIRE

R I Newton, c Ballance b Rashid	30
N J O'Brien, c Gale b Rashid	38
A G Wakely, st Brophy b Rashid	8
D J G Sales, run out (Miller/Wardlaw)	55
R I Keogh, lbw b Rashid	14
* A J Hall, c Miller b Patterson	28
§ D Murphy, run out (Miller)	6
J D Middlebrook, b Ashraf	2
O P Stone, not out	7
L M Daggett, b Wardlaw	0
L Evans, b Wardlaw	0
Extras lb 1, w 2, nb 2	5
Total (all out 40 overs)	193

FoW: 1-54 (Newton), 2-67 (Wakely), 3-97 (O'Brien), 4-129 (Keogh), 5-162 (Sales) 6-172 (Murphy), 7-179 (Middlebrook), 8-193 (Hall), 9-193 (Daggett), 10-193 (Evans)

	O	M	R	W
Patterson	8	0	35	1
Wardlaw	8	1	40	2
Ashraf	8	0	39	1
Rashid	8	0	38	4
Azeem Rafiq	8	0	40	0

TV Man of the Match: A U Rashid

Umpires: N G B Cook and R T Robinson — Scorers: J T Potter and A C Kingston

Third Umpire: G Sharp

Northamptonshire v. Yorkshire

Rashid back to all-round best

ADIL RASHID: A lovely knock followed by his top List A figures

Rashid starred with bat and ball as Yorkshire inflicted a crushing defeat under lights to hold a flimsy yet mathematical chance of being in the knockout stages.

Steelbacks showed no hesitation in sending Carnegie in to bat, a curious decision. Gale had 16 out of 42 when he slashed a catch straight to point, but at the other end Jaques was in sumptuous form.

Jaques lost Lyth for 29, but he and Miller contributed 87 before Jaques was caught in the deep on the leg-side for a swashbuckling 87 from 83 balls with nine boundaries.

Miller, who was starting to go through the gears, played into his stumps for 44 as wickets tumbled in the powerplay, but the last 10 overs saw 85 added for six out. Rashid's 25 not out was a lovely knock, full of timing and wristy strokeplay. Yorkshire's 262 was a formidable total.

Steelbacks had 54 up in the first 10 overs, both Newton and O'Brien playing some pleasing strokes, but the introduction of Rashid reaped instant rewards for Carnegie: Newton miscued to Ballance for 30, and Wakely was tempted down the track, only to find Brophy in sharp form to pull off the stumping. O'Brien was caught excellently by a full-length skipper Gale for 38, while Keogh was trapped in front for 14. Steelbacks had slipped to 129-4, all falling to Rashid. The leg-spinner closed his spell with 4-38, his best List A analysis and a real fillip. Two brilliant pieces of outfielding by Miller ran out Sales, 55, and Murphy. Middlebrook found Ashraf's full-length delivery too much, and the hosts needed 77 with three overs to go. Wardlaw despatched Daggett and Evans with two consecutive fast and straight full-length deliveries.

Clydesdale Bank 40 — Group C
Yorkshire v. Unicorns

Played at Headingley, Leeds, on August 12, 2012

Yorkshire won by 5 wickets (D/L method)

Toss won by Yorkshire — Yorkshire 2 points, Unicorns 0 points

UNICORNS

V Tripathi, b Rashid	19
B L Wadlan, b Sidebottom	0
§ T J New, c Hodgson b Sidebottom	13
J R Levitt, c and b Ashraf	10
J E Ord, lbw b Rashid	1
* K A Parsons, not out	48
L M Reece, b Rashid	25
R J Woolley, not out	28
R G Querl	
L E Beaven — Did not bat	
P R Hindmarsh	
Extras lb 3, w 3	6
Total (6 wkts, 37 overs)	150

FoW: 1-2 (Wadlan), 2-32 (New), 3-45 (Levitt), 4-47 (Tripathi), 5-48 (Ord) 6-94 (Reece)

	O	M	R	W
Sidebottom	7	1	28	2
Wardlaw	8	0	39	0
Ashraf	6	0	21	1
Rashid	8	0	24	3
Azeem Rafiq	8	0	35	0

YORKSHIRE

* A W Gale, b Woolley	14
P A Jaques, c Parsons b Woolley	19
A Lyth, c New b Querl	1
D A Miller, c New b Querl	0
G S Ballance, not out	69
A U Rashid, lbw b Hindmarsh	17
Azeem Rafiq, not out	34
§ D M Hodgson	
R J Sidebottom — Did not bat	
I Wardlaw	
M A Ashraf	
Extras w 6, nb 2	8
Total (5 wkts, 34 overs)	162

D/L Target to win: 162 runs off 37 overs

FoW: 1-34 (Gale), 2-39 (Lyth), 3-39 (Jaques), 4-41 (Miller), 5-71 (Rashid)

	O	M	R	W
Querl	8	3	34	2
Reece	2	0	18	0
Woolley	8	0	25	2
Hindmarsh	6	0	35	1
Beaven	6	0	34	0
Wadlan	4	1	16	0

Umpires: N G B Cook and M J Saggers — Scorers: J T Potter and K B O'Connell

Yorkshire v. Unicorns

Ballance and Rafiq to rescue

CRISIS POINT: Ballance and Rafiq talk the fight

A sixth-wicket stand of 91 between Ballance and Rafiq spared Yorkshire's blushes after they had slipped to a perilous 71-5 in pursuit of a modest total.

With Yorkshire reaching 34 without loss in five overs one could have been forgiven for thinking that Ballance would not be required to bat — never mind add a vital 69 not out to his ever growing reputation as one of the country's best one-day finishers.

Gale was bowled by a ball of full length for 14; Lyth edged behind off Querl for one; Jaques chased a wide one to be pouched at slip, and Miller also nicked a catch to the wicket, Querl and Woolley each claiming two.

Yorkshire were in the mire at 41-4, but Rashid played some extravagant shots before he was trapped in front for 17. Rafiq then joined Ballance: the pair batted with good discipline initially, and later with real power and precision. The 50 partnership came up in eight overs to keep Yorkshire's head above water, and when Ballance passed his 50 in 76 balls with a big six to the leg side the Unicorns were as good as beaten. Carnegie romped to victory with 18 balls remaining, Ballance, 69, and Rafiq, 34, having played a fine hand.

Earlier, rain had disrupted Unicorns' efforts with the bat, and we needed the Duckworth-Lewis method. Yorkshire bowled tightly, with Rashid again proving to be in fine form: his 3-24 from eight overs included two googlies to account for Tripathi and Ord. Dan Hodgson made his List A debut behind the timbers for Yorkshire, and he was soon celebrating his first scalp as Sidebottom induced a gloved chance from New. Sidebottom bowled beautifully in his first spell, but Unicorns had Parsons and Woolley to thank for an excellent seventh-wicket stand of 56 which ensured that they had a total of some substance to defend. Parsons finished unbeaten on 48 from 60 balls. The rain arrived with Unicorns on 141-6, thus reducing the match to 37 overs per side.

Clydesdale Bank 40 — Group C
Yorkshire v. Sussex

Played at Headingley, Leeds on August 19, 2012
Sussex won by 3 wickets (D/L method)

Toss won by Sussex — Sussex 2 points, Yorkshire 0 points

YORKSHIRE

* A W Gale, c Liddle b Wright	43
P A Jaques, b Liddle	18
J E Root, c and b Nash	41
A Lyth, c Liddle b Amjad Khan	19
G S Ballance, c Brown b Liddle	2
T T Bresnan, lbw b Yardy	27
R M Pyrah, c Gatting b Liddle	6
A U Rashid, c Brown b Amjad Khan	8
Azeem Rafiq, not out	13
§ D M Hodgson, not out	4
M A Ashraf — Did not bat	
Extras b 8, lb 1, w 10	19
Total (8 wkts, 28 overs)	200

FoW: 1-33 (Jaques), 2-108 (Gale), 3-124 (Root), 4-127 (Ballance), 5-156 (Lyth) 6-169 (Bresnan), 7-178 (Pyrah), 8-183 (Rashid)

	O	M	R	W
Yardy	4	1	24	1
Amjad Khan	6	0	34	2
Nash	5	0	28	1
Liddle	6	0	44	3
Panesar	2	0	19	0
Beer	3	0	20	0
Wright	2	0	22	1

SUSSEX

C D Nash, c Ballance b Rashid	53
L J Wright, c Jaques b Ashraf	6
* E C Joyce, c Pyrah b Azeem Rafiq	54
M W Goodwin, c Azeem Rafiq b Pyrah	0
M H Yardy, c Root b Azeem Rafiq	33
J S Gatting, b Azeem Rafiq	18
§ B C Brown, c Root b Bresnan	10
W A T Beer, not out	11
Amjad Khan, not out	16
M S Panesar	
C J Liddle — Did not bat	
Extras lb 3, w 3	6
Total (8 wkts, 28 overs)	207

D/L target to win: 207 runs off 28 overs

FoW: 1-15 (Wright), 2-104 (Nash), 3-110 (Goodwin), 4-127 (Joyce), 5-165 (Gatting) 6-172 (Yardy), 7-185 (Brown)

	O	M	R	W
Ashraf	4	0	30	1
Bresnan	5	0	46	1
Pyrah	6	0	31	1
Rashid	6	0	37	1
Root	1	0	14	0
Azeem Rafiq	6	0	46	3

Umpires: S A Garratt and J W Lloyds — Scorers: J T Potter and M J Charman

Yorkshire v. Sussex

Disaster at the death

AZEEM RAFIQ: Pulled the game back, only to see it edged away

The Sharks grabbed a thrilling win off the last ball in another rain-affected fixture.

The final over bowled by the seemingly nerveless Rafiq found Sussex needing 16 to win with three wickets in hand.

The first delivery to Amjad Khan was crashed for a glorious six, and the second went for four. Rafiq pulled it round with only four coming from his next three balls, leaving Khan on strike with two to win from the last ball.

This was achieved as Khan pushed a thick outside edge through backward point. The nail-biting defeat was hard on Rafiq, who with spin twin Rashid had bowled with guile to keep the Sharks in check. This game, reduced to 28 overs a side after early rain, was viewed almost as a dress rehearsal for the *T20* finals at the Swalec Stadium, so Yorkshire will not have been too disappointed about the way they set about their task.

Yorkshire reached 14 in the first four overs before the rain came, and Gale and Jaques then took the total to 33 before the Australian tried to make room and was bowled by Liddle. Root took up the gauntlet, striking his first four deliveries for three boundaries, and Gale set about Panesar with two lusty sixes. The innings was brought back into line when Gale was taken on the boundary for 43 from his 55 balls, and Root's enterprising 41 from 26 balls ended as Nash took a return catch. Yorkshire kept the late pressure on with Bresnan and Lyth making vital runs to take their side to a hard-earned but no less challenging 200.

The Sussex reply was well maintained by two excellent innings from Nash, 53, and Joyce, 54. Both scored half-centuries after the first wicket had fallen at 15. Rashid and Rafiq ended these splendid innings, and more wickets began to fall. Carnegie seemed in charge until Khan's last-over heroics inflicted another harsh *CB40* defeat.

Clydesdale Bank 40 — Group C
Kent v. Yorkshire

Played at St Lawrence Ground, Canterbury, on August 22, 2012

Kent won by 30 runs

Toss won by Yorkshire — Kent 2 points, Yorkshire 0 points

KENT

S W Billings, st Hodgson b Pyrah	15
* R W T Key, c Rashid b Ashraf	101
S A Northeast, c Gale b Rashid	26
D I Stevens, c and b Pyrah	43
A J Blake, b Ashraf	1
B P Nash, not out	18
§ G O Jones, not out	13
J C Tredwell M T Coles S J Cook — Did not bat M Davies	
Extras b 2, lb 1, w 6	9
Total (5 wkts, 40 overs)	226

FoW: 1-41 (Billings), 2-111 (Northeast), 3-182 (Key), 4-188 (Blake), 5-208 (Stevens)

	O	M	R	W
Sidebottom	8	0	56	0
Ashraf	8	1	36	2
Pyrah	8	0	55	2
Rashid	8	0	39	1
Azeem Rafiq	8	0	37	0

YORKSHIRE

* A W Gale, st Jones b Tredwell	57
P A Jaques, run out (Nash/Jones)	26
J E Root, c Blake b Davies	10
A Lyth, c Billings b Tredwell	24
A U Rashid, lbw b Tredwell	0
G S Ballance, c Jones b Stevens	26
R M Pyrah, c Blake b Cook	12
Azeem Rafiq, b Coles	17
§ D M Hodgson, c Davies b Coles	6
R J Sidebottom, c Northeast b Coles	0
M A Ashraf, not out	0
Extras b 1, lb 1, w 16	18
Total (all out, 38.2 overs)	196

FoW: 1-56 (Jaques), 2-67 (Root), 3-117 (Lyth), 4-118 (Rashid), 5-160 (Gale), 6-160 (Ballance), 7-186 (Pyrah), 8-191 (Rafiq), 9-196 (Hodgson), 10-196 (Sidebottom)

	O	M	R	W
Davies	8	0	50	1
Coles	4.2	0	25	3
Cook	6	0	32	1
Stevens	6	0	26	1
Tredwell	8	1	31	3
Nash	6	0	30	0

TV Man of the Match: R W T Key

Umpires: M J D Bodenham and R A Kettleborough — Scorers: J T Potter and L A R Hart

Third Umpire: S J O'Shaughnessy

Kent v. Yorkshire

Wheels fall off victory cart

ANDREW GALE: Charge too far

Yorkshire, chasing 227 to win, were found wanting after getting themselves into a strong position.

Kent showed why they are on course for a semi-final berth — squeezing the opposition with tight bowling and livewire fielding throughout.

The Spitfires started well with the bat, moving to 41 before Hodgson showed some sharp glove work to find Billings, 15, short of his crease off the bowling of Pyrah.

The experienced Key, along with Northeast, moved the score serenely to 111 before "Nelson" struck...or rather Rashid, Northeast providing a catch for skipper Gale. Key passed his 50 and was spilled by Jaques: Yorkshire were made to pay for this blemish, Key completing his century off 107 balls, only to fall one run later, a deserved wicket for Ashraf who impressed yet again. The explosive batting of Stevens once more proved a thorn in Yorkshire's side and took him to 43 until Pyrah held an outstanding return catch to halt his march at the death. The Spitfires added 40 in the last five overs to return to the runway on 226.

Gale and Jaques set about the chase with serious intent, the 50 opening partnership arriving in seven overs — only for Jaques to be sent back and run out some way short of his ground. It was not the first time these two had been in a mixup. Root arrived in confident manner, but on reaching double figures he fell to the metronomic skills of Davies. 67-2. Yorkshire were in need of a partnership, and Gale found his man in Lyth: the pair moved largely untroubled to 117 before Lyth holed out for 24. Rashid came and went, but again Yorkshire seemed to have it in the bag, Gale and Ballance, 26, taking Carnegie to 160 with ample time left. Gale passed his 50, but charged down the pitch to be stumped, and in the next over Ballance was caught behind. A total of 160-4 had slipped to 160-6, and from this point the wheels pretty much fell off. Despite a valiant attempt from Pyrah and Rafiq the run rate increased as wickets fell, the last going down with Yorkshire 30 short and 10 balls still to be bowled.

Clydesdale Bank 40 — Group C
Yorkshire v. Warwickshire

Played at North Marine Road, Scarborough, on August 27, 2012

Warwickshire won by 55 runs (D/L method)

Toss won by Yorkshire — Warwickshire 2 points, Yorkshire 0 points

WARWICKSHIRE

W T S Porterfield, c Hodgson b Rashid	43
V Chopra, c Hodgson b Patterson	15
* J O Troughton, c and b Root	1
§ T R Ambrose, not out	87
D L Maddy, c Root b Patterson	44
R Clarke, b Patterson	2
S A Piolet, b Wardlaw	7
I D Blackwell, not out	1
N M Carter	
P M Best — Did not bat	
C J C Wright	
Extras lb 5, w 4, nb 2	11
Total (6 wkts, 29 overs)	211

FoW: 1-37 (Chopra), 2-48 (Troughton), 3-83 (Porterfield), 4-172 (Maddy), 5-193 (Clarke) 6-210 (Piolet)

	O	M	R	W
Wardlaw	5	0	40	1
Patterson	6	0	25	3
Hannon-Dalby	6	0	58	0
Root	6	0	39	1
Rashid	6	0	44	1

YORKSHIRE

A Lyth, lbw b Carter	0
A Z Lees, c Troughton b Carter	23
J E Root, b Carter	1
* G S Ballance, c Clarke b Wright	68
J A Leaning, b Best	11
A U Rashid, lbw b Piolet	0
§ D M Hodgson, run out (Clarke/Piolet)	9
S A Patterson, c Clarke b Maddy	11
I Wardlaw, b Carter	1
O J Hannon-Dalby, not out	21
R M Pyrah, absent hurt	—
Extras b 5, lb 2, w 6	13
Total (all out, 25.1 overs)	158

D/L target to win: 214 runs off 29 overs

FoW: 1-0 (Lyth), 2-6 (Root), 3-43(Lees), 4-85 (Leaning). 5-86 (Rashid) 6-110 (Hodgson), 7-125 (Ballance), 8-158 (Wardlaw), 9-158 (Patterson)

	O	M	R	W
Carter	6	1	16	4
Wright	6	0	39	1
Blackwell	5	0	35	0
Piolet	6	0	38	1
Best	2	0	23	1
Maddy	0.1	0	0	1

Umpires: D J Millns and S J O'Shaughnessy — Scorers: J T Potter and D E Wainwright

Yorkshire v. Warwickshire

Bears picnic in the gloom

Under-strength Yorkshire were well beaten by strong Bears who marched into the semi-finals for the third successive year in another game shortened by the weather.

The rain arrived in the 11th over with Bears at 53-2: Patterson had Chopra caught behind down the leg side, and Root accepted a return catch from Troughton.

There was a lengthy stoppage before the game was resumed as 29 overs per side. Porterfield fell to Rashid for 43, while Ambrose reminded us of his past England credentials with an innings of real quality and no little power: the diminutive wicket-keeper finished unbeaten on 87 with nine fours and a six.

RICHARD PYRAH: Another hand injury ends his season

Medium-pacer Patterson impressed with a fine return of 3-25 as all around him found the going tough. Pyrah had to leave the field and not return after again damaging his previously injured left hand. A tough end to the season for the likeable Dewsbury all-rounder.

Warwickshire's 211 was upped by two, thanks to *Duckworth-Lewis*, a tricky proposition for a fairly inexperienced lineup. Lyth and Root, who were key to Yorkshire's chances, were back in the pavilion with only six runs scored. Lees, 23, showed the wrapped-up hardy souls that he was a man for the future before he skied an attempted drive to mid-off. Ballance lost debutant Jack Leaning for 11 and Rashid without scoring, and it all looked done and dusted. Ballance battled on, assisted by a confident Hodgson who played two pleasing strokes through the off side. The young wicket-keeper was run out by Clarke, but Ballance ran to 68 from 50 balls before he gave a catch on the mid-wicket boundary. The contest was as good as over. Conditions became so bad that it seemed barely feasible to continue. Patterson was caught by Clarke off Maddy.

Clydesdale Bank 40

FINAL TABLES 2012

GROUP A

		P	W	L	T	NR/A	PTS	NRR
1	Lancashire Lightning (C4) *	12	9	2	0	1	19	0.050
2	Middlesex Panthers (A2)	12	6	3	1	2	15	0.778
3	Gloucestershire Gladiators (C6)	12	5	5	0	2	12	0.995
4	Netherlands (A5)	12	5	6	0	1	11	-0.910
5	Essex Eagles (C3)	12	4	6	0	2	10	-0.185
6	Leicestershire Foxes (B6)	12	3	6	0	3	9	-0.732
7	Worcestershire Royals (A7)	12	3	7	1	1	8	-0.011

GROUP B

		P	W	L	T	NR/A	PTS	NRR
1	Hampshire Royals (B4) *	12	7	3	0	2	16	0.754
2	Surrey (A3)	12	6	3	0	3	15	0.466
3	Somerset (C1)	12	6	4	0	2	14	0.385
4	Nottinghamshire Outlaws (C2)	12	6	5	0	1	13	0.101
5	Durham Dynamos (B2)	12	5	5	0	2	12	0.262
6	Welsh Dragons (C5)	12	3	6	0	3	9	-0.971
7	Scottish Saltires (B7)	12	1	8	0	3	5	-1.359

GROUP C

		P	W	L	T	NR/A	PTS	NRR
1	Sussex Sharks (A1) *	12	7	1	0	4	18	1.012
2	Warwickshire Bears (B5) *	12	8	3	0	1	17	0.660
3	Kent Spitfires (A4)	12	7	2	0	3	17	0.870
4	Derbyshire Falcons (A3)	12	4	5	0	3	11	-0.438
5	**Yorkshire Carnegie (A6)**	**12**	**4**	**7**	**0**	**1**	**9**	**0.006**
6	Northamptonshire Steelbacks (B3)	12	1	6	0	5	7	-0.568
7	Unicorns (C7)	12	1	8	0	3	5	-1.545

* Qualified for Semi-Finals

(2011 positions in brackets)

YORKSHIRE AVERAGES 2012

CLYDESDALE BANK 40

Played 12 Won 4 Lost 7 Abandoned 1

BATTING AND FIELDING

(Qualification 4 completed innings)

Player	*M.*	*I.*	*N.O.*	*Runs*	*H.S.*	*Avge*	*100s*	*50s*	*ct/st*
G S Ballance	11	11	3	469	103*	58.62	1	3	6
A W Gale	10	10	0	393	76	39.30	0	3	3
J E Root	8	7	1	208	49	34.66	0	0	5
A Lyth	9	9	1	260	69	32.50	0	2	1
P A Jaques	10	10	0	299	87	29.90	0	1	3
Azeem Rafiq	10	8	4	81	34*	20.25	0	0	3
A U Rashid	8	8	0	86	32	10.75	0	0	2
Also played									
T T Bresnan	1	1	0	27	27	27.00	0	0	0
A McGrath	3	1	0	26	26	26.00	0	0	0
A Z Lees	1	1	0	23	23	23.00	0	0	0
R M Pyrah	4	3	0	62	44	20.66	0	0	3
D A Miller	3	3	0	45	44	15.00	0	0	3
S A Patterson	4	4	2	28	14	14.00	0	0	1
J M Bairstow	2	2	0	28	25	14.00	0	0	1/0
J A Leaning	1	1	0	11	11	11.00	0	0	0
D M Hodgson	4	3	1	19	9	9.50	0	0	3/1
G L Brophy	5	3	0	24	19	8.00	0	0	3/1
I Wardlaw	7	4	2	10	6*	5.00	0	0	1
R J Sidebottom	4	2	0	2	2	1.00	0	0	0
J J Sayers	1	1	0	1	1	1.00	0	0	0
O J Hannon-Dalby	1	1	1	21	21*	—	0	0	0
M A Starc	4	2	2	5	4*	—	0	0	1
M A Ashraf	10	3	3	3	3*	—	0	0	1

BOWLING

(Qualification 4 wickets)

Player	*Overs*	*Mdns*	*Runs*	*Wkts*	*Avge*	*Best*	*4wI*	*RPO*
M A Starc	31.4	1	181	8	22.62	3-28	0	5.71
J E Root	19	1	115	5	23.00	2-14	0	6.05
A U Rashid	56	0	302	12	25.16	4-38	1	5.39
S A Patterson	29	0	143	5	28.60	3-25	0	4.93
R J Sidebottom	28	1	174	6	29.00	3-44	0	6.21
M A Ashraf	69	2	362	11	32.90	2-36	0	5.24
Azeem Rafiq	70.5	2	381	10	38.10	3-22	0	5.37
I Wardlaw	50.4	2	311	8	38.87	3-60	0	6.13
Also bowled								
A McGrath	16	0	65	3	21.66	2-24	0	4.06
R M Pyrah	17	0	106	3	35.33	2-55	0	6.23
T T Bresnan	5	0	46	1	46.00	1-46	0	9.20
O J Hannon-Dalby	6	0	58	0	—	0-58	0	9.66

Third NatWest Series One-Day International
England v. West Indies

At Headingley Carnegie, Leeds, on June 22, 2012

Match abandoned without a ball bowled

Umpires: H D P K Dharmasena and R K Illingworth   Scorers: J T Potter and H Clayton
Third Umpire: A L Hill   Fourth Umpire: R J Bailey   Match Referee: J J Crowe

Southern Group

If you are a follower of Yorkshire cricket and live in the South, why not consider joining the Yorkshire CCC Southern Group? Formed in 1980 with Richard Hutton as Patron, the functions of the group are to promote and support the Club and provide financial or other assistance to young Yorkshire cricketers.

In the spring and autumn events are organised at London venues where the principal guest is usually a Yorkshire player, past or present, and sometimes another cricket personality. Andrew Gale, Martyn Moxon, Gerard Brophy, Matthew Hoggard and Ken Taylor are some of the recent guests. A number of visits to Yorkshire matches is arranged during the season, usually involving lunch and a private viewing area. Yorkshire cricketers who have benefited from YSG sponsorship in recent years include Joe Sayers and Jonathan Bairstow.

The annual subscription for all this, plus a quarterly newsletter, is a minimum of £7. More information can be found on the group's website at *www.ycccsg.cricketarchive.com* — or from David Wood. Tel. 01525-370204.

Books raise £6,167

The second-hand bookstall at Headingley Cricket Ground which is run by Geoff Holmes and Vivien Stone raised £6,167 in 2012 for the John Featherstone Foundation — a magnificent sum achieved despite the dreadful weather throughout last summer. About £1,700 of this resulted from the sale of books during the England v. South Africa Test match on the ground.

Level best

In our *50 Years Ago* feature in the 2012 Yearbook it was stated that Philip Sharpe in 1962 took 71 catches for Yorkshire to beat the record of 70 set by John Tunnicliffe in 1901. It has been pointed out that one of Sharpe's 71 catches was for the Players v. the Gentlemen in the last such fixture and that, in fact, he equalled Tunnicliffe's record for Yorkshire.

FRIENDS LIFE t20
HIGHLIGHTS OF 2012

Totals of 175 and over (3)

212-5	v. Worcestershire at Leeds (won)
180-5	v. Derbyshire at Leeds (won)
180-6	v. Lancashire at Leeds (won)

Match aggregates of 350 and over (1)

395 Yorkshire (212-5) defeated Worcestershire (183-6) by 29 runs at Leeds

Century Partnerships (2)

For the 1st wicket (2)

131	A Lyth and P A Jaques	v. Derbyshire at Leeds
116	A W Gale and P A Jaques	v. Leicestershire at Leeds

4 wickets in an innings (2)

M A Ashraf (1)

4 for 18 v. Derbyshire at Derby

R J Sidebottom (1)

4 for 25 v. Durham at Chester-le-Street

3 catches in an innings (3)

G S Ballance (3)

3	v. Leicestershire at Leeds
3	v. Worcestershire at Leeds
3	v. Sussex at Cardiff

Debuts (3)

t20 cricket: M A Ashraf

For Yorkshire: D A Miller and M A Starc

Friends Life t20 in 2012

WINNERS

Hampshire, who beat Yorkshire by 10 runs

PREVIOUS WINNERS

2003 **Surrey,** who beat Warwickshire by 9 wickets
2004 **Leicestershire,** who beat Surrey by 7 wickets
2005 **Somerset,** who beat Lancashire by 7 wickets
2006 **Leicestershire,** who beat Nottinghamshire by 4 runs
2007 **Kent,** who beat Gloucestershire by 4 wickets
2008 **Middlesex,** who beat Kent by 3 run
2009 **Sussex,** who beat Somerset by 64 runs
2010 **Hampshire**, who beat Somerset by losing fewer wickets with the scores level
2011 **Leicestershire**, who beat Somerset by 18 runs

NORTH GROUP

		P	W	L	T	NR/A	PTS	NRR
1	**Yorkshire Carnegie (N 6) ***	**10**	**7**	**1**	**0**	**2**	**16**	**0.863**
2	Nottinghamshire Outlaws(N 1) *	10	5	1	0	4	14	1.877
3	Durham Dynamos (N 4)	10	4	4	1	1	10	-0.251
4	Lancashire Lightning (N 3)	10	3	4	1	2	9	0.106
5	Derbyshire Falcons (N 7)	10	2	6	0	2	6	-0.561
6	Leicestershire Foxes (N 2)	10	2	7	0	1	5	-1.352

SOUTH GROUP

		P	W	L	T	NR/A	PTS	NRR
1	Sussex Sharks (S 6) *	10	6	1	0	3	15	1.389
2	Hampshire Royals (S 1) *	10	5	2	0	3	13	0.693
3	Essex Eagles (S 6) *	10	5	4	0	1	11	-0.032
4	Kent Spitfires (S 3)	10	4	5	0	1	9	-0.465
5	Middlesex Panthers (S 9)	10	3	7	0	0	6	-0.210
6	Surrey (S 5)	10	3	7	0	0	6	-0.700

MIDLAND/WALES and WEST GROUP

		P	W	L	T	NR/A	PTS	NRR
1	Somerset (S 4) *	10	5	2	0	3	13	0.275
2	Gloucestershire Gladiators (S 8) *	10	4	2	0	4	12	0.248
3	Worcestershire Royals (N 5) *	10	4	3	0	3	11	0.578
4	Warwickshire Bears (N 8)	10	4	3	0	3	11	-0.153
5	Welsh Dragons (S 7)	10	2	3	0	5	7	-0.525
6	Northamptonshire Steelbacks (N 9)	10	1	7	0	2	4	-0.611

* Qualified for the Quarter-Finals

(2011 divisional positions in brackets)

Match-By-Match Reports
Scorecards
Pictures

NIGEL PULLAN
JOHN POTTER
SIMON WILKINSON
VAUGHN RIDLEY
ALEX WHITEHEAD
SWpix.com

Friends Life t20 — North Group
Yorkshire v. Durham

Played at Headingley, Leeds, on June 15, 2012

Durham won by 2 runs

Toss won by Yorkshire — Durham 2 points, Yorkshire 0 points

DURHAM

H H Gibbs, c Ballance b Sidebottom	6
§ P Mustard, c Starc b Pyrah	19
B A Stokes, b Ashraf	36
J G Myburgh, lbw b Ashraf	10
* D M Benkenstein, c Ashraf b Starc	25
G J Muchall, not out	25
S G Borthwick, lbw b Starc	6
L E Plunkett, not out	9
M E Claydon, C Rushworth, G Onions	Did not bat
Extras lb 6	6
Total (6 wkts, 20 overs)	142

FoW: 1-9 (Gibbs), 2-50 (Mustard), 3-72 (Myburgh), 4-85 (Stokes), 5-122 (Benkenstein) 6-131 (Borthwick)

	O	M	R	W
Starc	4	0	21	2
Sidebottom	4	0	32	1
Ashraf	4	0	28	2
Root	1	0	8	0
Pyrah	4	0	25	1
Azeem Rafiq	3	0	22	0

YORKSHIRE

* A W Gale, c Muchall b Rushworth	0
P A Jaques, b Onions	8
D A Miller, c Muchall b Rushworth	4
G S Ballance, lbw b Claydon	6
J E Root, lbw b Onions	14
R M Pyrah, c Muchall b Plunkett	34
§ G L Brophy, b Borthwick	32
Azeem Rafiq, not out	21
M A Starc, b Borthwick	0
R J Sidebottom, not out	5
M A Ashraf	Did not bat
Extras b 1, lb 9, w 6	16
Total (8 wkts, 20 overs)	140

FoW: 1-4 (Gale), 2-11 (Miller), 3-23 (Ballance), 4-37 (Jaques), 5-42 (Root) 6-99 (Pyrah), 7-122 (Brophy), 8-122 (Starc)

	O	M	R	W
Rushworth	3	1	20	2
Onions	4	0	24	2
Claydon	3	0	22	1
Plunkett	4	0	24	1
Stokes	2	0	16	0
Borthwick	4	0	24	2

Man of the Match: G J Muchall

Umpires: D J Millns and P Willey — Scorers: J T Potter and B Hunt

Yorkshire v. Durham

Defeat without dishonour

DESPERATE DIVE: Yorkshire's Rafiq tries to run out Mustard at the non-striker's end. Pyrah is the bowler

Yorkshire slipped to a two-run defeat after failing to recover from a poor batting start in pursuit of a challenging yet achievable 142. They needed 14 runs off the last over when Rafiq smashed Borthwick for six first ball and the next through cover for what seemed a boundary, only for Stokes to claim innocence and only two were awarded. The next three balls yielded three runs, and again controversy followed as Rafiq shouldered arms to a delivery well outside off-stump only for Umpire Millns to remain unmoved. Rafiq needing a boundary from the last ball, but the gutsy off-spinner could manage only a single to finish unbeaten on 21.

Carnegie had slumped to a desperate 42-5 in the eighth over, with Gale, Jaques, Miller and Ballance all falling in single figures. A promising knock by Root was curtailed when Onions trapped him in front. Pyrah, returning from injury, was what was needed as with Brophy he added 57 in a fine counter-attack that put the visitors on the back foot. Pyrah's 34 was his *T20* best, including four fours and a six, ending at 99 when a full-blooded pull crashed into the hands of Muchall at deep square-leg. Brophy and Rafiq added 22, which left Yorkshire needing 22 from 18 balls, but Borthwick despatched Brophy, 32, and Starc first ball.

Yorkshire's relatively young attack will take heart from a combative display, Starc claiming 2-21, Ashraf 2-28 and Pyrah 1-25. Durham never quite got away. There were good knocks from Stokes, Benkenstein and Muchall, but none could go on to a big innings. The highlight was a fine one-handed catch by Ashraf at mid-off to send back Benkenstein.

Friends Life t20 — North Group
Yorkshire v. Leicestershire

Played at Headingley, Leeds on June 17, 2012

Yorkshire won by 22 runs

Toss won by Yorkshire — Yorkshire 2 points, Leicestershire 0 points

YORKSHIRE

* A W Gale, c Cobb b Hoggard	70
P A Jaques, c du Toit b Taylor	48
§ J M Bairstow, c Taylor b White	17
D A Miller, not out	30
G S Ballance, c Cobb b White	0
J E Root, not out	2
R M Pyrah	
Azeem Rafiq	
M A Starc — Did not bat	
R J Sidebottom	
M A Ashraf	
Extras lb 1, w 2	3
Total (4 wkts, 20 overs)	170

FoW: 1-116 (Jaques), 2-122 (Gale), 3-161 (Bairstow), 4-161 (Ballance)

	O	M	R	W
Hoggard	4	0	28	1
Abdul Razzaq	4	0	39	0
White	4	0	42	2
Taylor	4	0	28	1
Henderson	2	0	25	0
Cobb	2	0	7	0

LEICESTERSHIRE

J J Cobb, run out (Bairstow/Ashraf)	46
G P Smith, c Ballance b Pyrah	19
J du Toit, c and b Pyrah	1
R R Sarwan, c Ballance b Sidebottom	45
Abdul Razzaq, b Azeem Rafiq	3
M A G Boyce, c Bairstow b Azeem Rafiq	5
R M L Taylor, b Sidebottom	4
W A White, c Root b Starc	8
§ E J H Eckersley, c Ballance b Starc	6
C W Henderson, not out	0
* M J Hoggard, b Starc	0
Extras lb 3, w 8	11
Total (all out, 20 overs)	148

FoW: 1-37 (Smith), 2-48 (du Toit), 3-85 (Cobb), 4-92 (Razzaq), 5-107 (Boyce), 6-12 (Taylor), 7-137 (Sarwan), 8-146 (Eckersley), 9-148 (White), 10-148 (Hoggarc

	O	M	R	W
Starc	4	0	26	3
Sidebottom	4	0	25	2
Pyrah	3	0	24	2
Root	1	0	11	0
Azeem Rafiq	4	0	28	2
Ashraf	4	0	31	0

Man of the Match: A W Gale

Umpires: N G B Cook and R T Robinson — Scorers: J T Potter and P J Rogers

Yorkshire v. Leicestershire

Back to all-round excellence

RICHARD PYRAH: Stunning one-handed return catch off du Toit

An excellent all-round display brought Yorkshire a convincing victory against the title-holders.

They got off to an excellent start as skipper Gale and Jaques tucked into the Foxes with gusto. Gale was in particularly explosive form, striking the ball to both sides of the wicket and not allowing the bowlers to settle.

They raced to 50 in 35 balls, and soon it was 100 in 69. Jaques went for 48, caught on the deep mid-wicket boundary — but only after Yorkshire had reached their highest first-wicket partnership in this competition of 116, eclipsing the 104 set against the same opposition three years earlier.

Gale continued in tandem with Bairstow, and the total was moving towards heady heights when Bairstow was pouched expertly by Taylor on the long-off fence for 17. Gale was caught in the deep for a 42-ball 70 at 161, and Ballance followed next ball. Miller added a late flourish with an unbeaten 30, taking Yorkshire to a highly challenging 170.

Leicestershire made a decent start, Cobb providing some scintillating strokes as he and Smith advanced to 37. Pyrah had Smith easily taken by Ballance at mid-off — and then bagged du Toit with a stunning one-handed return catch to slam on the brakes. Cobb's was the key wicket, and his powerful innings of 46 ended when Bairstow and Ashraf got together with the opener short of his ground.

Still the Foxes were in the hunt with eight per over required at the halfway stage, but excellent straight and full bowling by every member of the attack kept runs to a premium. Sarwan offered hope but he, too, had the shackles wrapped round him as Sidebottom, Pyrah and Ashraf fired in yorker after yorker. The former West Indies Test star fell for 45 to an excellent catch by Ballance, and the chase lost its way. Wickets fell regularly, Starc finishing off the contest with three scalps in the last over to end Leicestershire's innings 22 runs short.

Friends Life t20 — North Group
Derbyshire v. Yorkshire

Played at The County Ground, Derby, on June 18, 2012

Yorkshire won by 41 runs

Toss won by Yorkshire — Yorkshire 2 points, Derbyshire 0 points

YORKSHIRE

* A W Gale, c Durston b Wainwright	39
P A Jaques, c Redfern b Durston	8
J E Root, c Poynton b Rana Naved-ul-Hasan	36
D A Miller, c Groenewald b Wainwright	0
G S Ballance, not out	47
R M Pyrah, b Turner	2
§ G L Brophy, not out	9
M A Ashraf	
Azeem Rafiq — Did not bat	
M A Starc	
R J Sidebottom	
Extras lb 3, w 4, nb 2	9
Total (5 wkts, 20 overs)	150

FoW: 1-36 (Jaques), 2-65 (Gale), 3-66 (Miller), 4-102 (Root), 5-107 (Pyrah)

	O	M	R	W
Turner	4	0	40	1
Groenewald	4	0	30	0
Durston	2	0	10	1
Hughes	2	0	19	0
Rana Naved-ul-Hasan	4	0	34	1
Wainwright	4	0	14	2

DERBYSHIRE

W J Durston, lbw b Ashraf	21
U T Khawaja, c Brophy b Starc	20
R A Whiteley, b Pyrah	8
* W L Madsen, b Ashraf	6
D J Redfern, run out (Azeem Rafiq)	2
C F Hughes, b Pyrah	11
Rana Naved-ul-Hasan, c Brophy b Ashraf	13
§ T Poynton, c Root b Pyrah	2
D J Wainwright, not out	15
T D Groenewald, b Ashraf	1
M L Turner, b Starc	3
Extras lb 2, w 5	7
Total (all out, 20 overs)	109

FoW: 1-43 (Khawaja), 2-46 (Durston), 3-56 (Madsen), 4-60 (Redfern), 5-63 (Whiteley), 6-78 (Hughes), 7-84 (Poynton), 8-101 (Rana), 9-103 (Groenewald), 10-109 (Turner)

	O	M	R	W
Sidebottom	4	0	23	0
Starc	3	0	16	2
Root	1	0	10	0
Pyrah	4	0	21	3
Ashraf	4	0	18	4
Azeem Rafiq	4	0	19	0

Man of the Match: G S Ballance

Umpires: T E Jesty and R A Kettleborough — Scorers: J T Potter and J M Brown

Third Umpire: J H Evans

Derbyshire v. Yorkshire

Ashraf the comfort zone

A finely timed unbeaten 47 from Ballance, backed by good old-fashioned full and straight pace bowling, proved the difference as Yorkshire ran out comfortable winners.

Again, Carnegie got away to a good start, spearheaded by the talismanic Gale who finished with an ebullient 39 after he and Jaques had put on 36 for the first wicket. Jaques departed for eight, caught in the deep off Durston, before Yorkshire's former left-arm spinner Wainwright began to weave his magic.

Wainwright induced a mistimed straight-drive from Gale, and two balls later he had Miller caught at first slip. Root and Ballance had the job of rebuilding, which they did to decent effect, although the run rate slipped, due in no small part to Wainwright's miserly 2-14.

Root hit 36 from 39 balls before he tried to reverse-sweep Naved-ul-Hasan and offered a catch to wicket-keeper Poynton, but the brakes had been applied and a total of 130 looked a long way off. Ballance had plenty up his sleeve: he launched into Turner, and then Naved, and 40 runs came in the last three overs to propel the *White Rose* to a respectable 150. Ballance smacked three fours and three sixes in an innings spanning 35 balls.

MOIN ASHRAF
Turned the game on its head

Durston and Khawaja put on 43 in under six overs, and Derbyshire looked in a strong position. It was the introduction of Ashraf and Pyrah that turned the game on its head: Pyrah claimed Khawaja as he lofted a simple chance to Brophy for 20, while Ashraf produced a wicked in-swinger to trap Durston in front for 21. From this point the innings subsided alarmingly, with once again Yorkshire's middle overs being of the highest calibre coupled with some outstanding outcricket. Rafiq again impressed with the ball, but it was Ashraf with 4-18 and Pyrah 3-21 who earned the most plaudits: Ashraf in particular really impressed with his accuracy and pace. As in the previous fixture a day earlier it was left to Starc to wrap things up with the last ball as he sent Turner's stumps cartwheeling. Yorkshire were home in emphatic style.

Friends Life t20 — North Group
Durham v. Yorkshire

Played at Durham ICG, Chester-le-Street on June 22, 2012

Yorkshire won by 12 runs

Toss won by Durham — Yorkshire 2 points, Durham 0 points

YORKSHIRE

A Lyth, c Mustard b Onions	30
P A Jaques, c Mustard b Claydon	2
J E Root, c Myburgh b Stokes	41
§ J M Bairstow, b Stokes	2
D A Miller, not out	74
G S Ballance, b Breese	10
R M Pyrah, c Gibbs b Borthwick	1
* Azeem Rafiq, not out	4
M A Starc	
R J Sidebottom — Did not bat	
M A Ashraf	
Extras b 1, lb 2, w 4	7
Total (6 wkts, 20 overs)	171

FoW: 1-15 (Jaques), 2-64 (Lyth), 3-71 (Bairstow), 4-85 (Root), 5-130 (Ballance), 6-137 (Pyrah)

	O	M	R	W
Plunkett	3	0	19	0
Onions	4	0	20	1
Claydon	2	0	25	1
Breese	4	0	30	1
Stokes	2	0	15	2
Benkenstein	1	0	13	0
Borthwick	4	0	46	1

DURHAM

§ P Mustard, c Root b Sidebottom	4
H H Gibbs, c Rafiq b Ashraf	76
B A Stokes, b Pyrah	12
J G Myburgh, c Ballance b Starc	14
* D M Benkenstein, c Miller b Azeem Rafiq	2
G J Muchall, not out	16
G R Breese, c Rafiq b Sidebottom	9
S G Borthwick, lbw b Sidebottom	0
L E Plunkett, b Sidebottom	15
M E Claydon, b Starc	0
G Onions, b Starc	0
Extras lb 7, w 2, nb 2	11
Total (all out, 19.5 overs)	159

FoW: 1-19 (Mustard), 2-68 (Stokes), 3-113 (Myburgh), 4-118 (Gibbs), 5-120 (Benkenstein), 6-137 (Breese), 7-138 (Borthwick), 8-156 (Plunkett), 9-159 (Claydon), 10-159 (Onions)

	O	M	R	W
Sidebottom	4	0	25	4
Starc	3.5	0	33	3
Pyrah	4	0	31	1
Ashraf	4	0	27	1
Azeem Rafiq	4	0	36	1

Man of the Match: D A Miller

Umpires: N G B Cook and M A Gough — Scorers: J T Potter and B Hunt

Durham v. Yorkshire

Rafiq sets captaincy records

DAVID MILLER: Battered 74 not out in only 35 balls

Azeem Rafiq showed maturity and a shrewd mind to lead Yorkshire to the summit of the *T20* North Division.

Deputising for the injured Gale, the 21-year-old became the youngest to captain Yorkshire in competition, as well as the first of Asian origin to do so.

Durham, chasing a testing 171, were in good shape at 113-2, needing a shade over a run a ball. Yet as the gloom descended Carnegie claimed eight wickets for 46 runs, including Herschelle Gibbs, 76, who had looked the man to take his side to a comfortable victory.

The key moments arrived after Myburgh's dismissal as the run rate plummeted and Carnegie turned the screw. Wickets fells as the pressure built, and despite a spirited partnership between Plunkett and Muchall the task became too much.

Starc completed proceedings with two-in-two to end his fine spell with 3-33, while Sidebottom contributed a career-best 4-25.

Yorkshire's innings featured strong contributions from Lyth and Root, but was then essentially about the power of Miller: his 74 not out from 35 deliveries took Carnegie from a conservative total to an excellent one, 31 coming in the last two overs. Lyth made 30 from 20 balls before being caught at the wicket off Onions, while Root cracked 41 in 32 balls. Onions was the pick of the Durham attack with a miserly 1-20 in his four overs.

Yorkshire showed excellence and aggression in the field, with tight, yet simple, bowling plans and a confidence in the middle-order batting which meant that wickets remained intact before the final onslaught. All of a sudden this *t20* looks an easier game.

Friends Life t20 — North Group
Yorkshire v. Nottinghamshire

Played at North Marine Road, Scarborough, on June 24, 2012

No result

Toss won by Yorkshire — Yorkshire 1 point, Nottinghamshire 1 point

NOTTINGHAMSHIRE

M J Lumb, b Sidebottom	2
M H Wessels, c Jaques b Starc	12
* A C Voges, c Root b Ashraf	29
J W A Taylor, not out	41
§ C M W Read, not out	15
S L Elstone	
S J Mullaney	
G G White — Did not bat	
D J Pattinson	
H F Gurney	
A Carter	
Extras lb 3, w 3	6
Total (3 wkts, 14 overs)	105

FoW: 1-2 (Lumb), 2-27 (Wessels), 3-72 (Voges)

	O	M	R	W
Sidebottom	2	0	24	1
Starc	2	0	10	1
Pyrah	3	0	19	0
Moin Ashraf	3	0	25	1
Azeem Rafiq	4	0	24	0

YORKSHIRE

A Lyth
P A Jaques
J E Root
D A Miller
G S Ballance
R M Pyrah
§ G L Brophy
* Azeem Rafiq
M A Starc
R J Sidebottom
M A Ashraf

Umpires: N G C Cowley and M A Gough — Scorers: J T Potter and I J Smith

Yorkshire v. Nottinghamshire

Neck and neck with Outlaws

Both sides remained at the summit of the *T20* North Division after only 14 overs were possible. Rain put paid to what promised to be a fantastic seaside match.

An expectant crowd had gathered as Yorkshire, keen to continue their excellent form, knew that a win would give them a clear advantage at the top of the table going into the last few fixtures.

With half an eye on the weather acting captain Azeem Rafiq opted to field first. It was clear that disruption was on the cards with inclement weather inevitable.

The Outlaws lost former Yorkshire left-hand batsman Michael Lumb to the third delivery of the innings for two, comprehensively bowled by Sidebottom, and Starc added the wicket of Wessels, nicely taken by Jaques close in on the leg side, in the fourth over.

Voges and Taylor had put on 45 for the third wicket when Voges was taken comfortably in the deep by Root off paceman Ashraf for 29 in a mere 30 balls. Rain arrived on a couple of occasions, and the umpires were given little option as the weather closed in permanently.

Nottinghamshire had reached 105 from 14 overs with Taylor well set on 41 and Read 15, and all the teams could do was go home with a no-result point each.

AZEEM RAFIQ: Acting skipper might well look frustrated

Friends Life t20 — North Group
Leicestershire v. Yorkshire

Played at Grace Road, Leicester, on June 27, 2012

Yorkshire won by 4 runs

Toss won by Leicestershire — Yorkshire 2 points, Leicestershire 0 points

YORKSHIRE

A Lyth, c Smith b Abdul Razzaq	1
P A Jaques, c White b Buck	20
J E Root, lbw b Buck	10
D A Miller, c Hoggard b Taylor	37
G S Ballance, c Sarwan b Hoggard	17
R M Pyrah, c Cobb c Abdul Razzaq	35
§ G L Brophy, c Taylor b Buck	12
A U Rashid, run out (Eckersley)	4
* Azeem Rafiq, c Eckersley b Abdul Razzaq	0
M A Starc, not out	0
M A Ashraf — Did not bat	
Extras lb 9, w 6	15
Total (9 wkts, 20 overs)	151

FoW:- 1-10(Lyth), 2-34 (Root), 3-35 (Jaques), 4-74 (Ballance), 5-119 (Miller) 6-135 (Brophy), 7-147 (Pyrah), 8-151 (Rashid), 9-151 (Rafiq)

	O	M	R	W
Buck	4	1	28	3
Abdul Razzaq	4	0	37	3
Taylor	4	0	23	1
Hoggard	4	0	24	1
Cobb	3	0	21	0
Henderson	1	0	9	0

LEICESTERSHIRE

Abdul Razzaq, run out (Miller/Starc/Brophy)	17
J J Cobb, run out (Pyrah/Brophy)	21
G P Smith, c and b Rashid	18
R R Sarwan, run out (Pyrah/Brophy)	39
M A G Boyce, c Brophy b Azeem Rafiq	12
W A White, b Starc	22
§ E J H Eckersley, b Ashraf	0
R M Taylor, run out (Root)	5
C W Henderson, not out	0
N L Buck, b Starc	0
* M J Hoggard — Did not bat	
Extras b 1, lb 7, w 1, nb 4	13
Total (9 wkts, 20 overs)	147

FoW: 1-38 (Razzaq), 2-54 (Cobb), 3-60 (Smith), 4-79 (Boyce), 5-135 (Sarwan) 6-136 (Eckersley), 7-145 (Taylor), 8-147 (White), 9-147 (Buck)

	O	M	R	W
Root	1	0	8	0
Starc	4	0	19	2
Ashraf	4	0	33	1
Pyrah	4	0	28	0
Rashid	3	0	30	1
Azeem Rafiq	4	0	21	1

Man of the Match: R M Pyrah

Umpires: N L Bainton and R K Illingworth — Scorers: J T Potter and P J Rogers

Third Umpire: S C Gale

Leicestershire v. Yorkshire

Yorkshire leave no doubt

RICHARD PYRAH: Two huge last-over sixes and two vital run-outs

Carnegie completed their fourth win in six matches after a nailbiting tussle on a rare evening of summer sun.

They made 151, and had to bowl with much skill and tenacity to keep at bay the Foxes, who will wonder how they missed the target.

Yorkshire were 34-3 after Lyth, Jaques and Root had all perished in the powerplay overs. Ballance and Miller added a circumspect 40, but Yorkshire exile Hoggard bagged the crucial wicket of Ballance for 17.

Miller rattled up 37 at a shade under a run a ball, while Pyrah batted with real purpose, the all-rounder striking two huge sixes over mid-wicket in the final over as he finished second-top scorer for Carnegie with 35.

The Foxes had reached 35 without loss in the fifth over when Razzaq was run out: Starc threw in from the deep, and Pyrah completed the job in combination with Brophy, whose wicket-keeping was in fine fettle. Smith fell to a smart return catch by Rashid, and Leicestershire had slumped to 60-3 in the ninth. Sarwan and White batted fluently to bring their side back into the reckoning, and with four overs still to be bowled the Foxes needed only 30 with Sarwan still at the crease.

Pyrah took the key wicket of Sarwan, diving full length to run out the West Indian off his own bowling for 39. Ashraf followed this three balls later with a full-length yorker to breach Eckersley's defences, and nine were needed from the last Starc over. Two singles came from the first two balls before Root added a fine run-out from mid-off to dismiss Taylor. Two runs ensued before Starc finished it with two wickets in two balls — castling both White and Buck to leave Foxes agonisingly short.

Yorkshire's outcricket was up there with the best, backing up some impressive bowling. There can be no doubt over this side's credentials.

Friends Life t20 — North Group
Yorkshire v. Lancashire

Played at Headingley, Leeds on June 29, 2012

Yorkshire won by 19 runs

Toss won by Lancashire — Yorkshire 2 points, Lancashire 0 points

YORKSHIRE

A Lyth, c Smith b Yasir Arafat	12
P A Jaques, run out (Croft/Smith)	40
J E Root, c Smith b Chapple	15
§ J M Bairstow, c Croft b Keedy	5
D A Miller, run out (Cross)	54
G S Ballance, c Horton b Newby)	42
R M Pyrah, not out	4
* Azeem Rafiq, not out	0
A U Rashid	
M A Starc — Did not bat	
M A Ashraf	
Extras lb 6, w 2	8
Total (6 wkts, 20 overs)	180

FoW: 1-18(Lyth), 2-39 (Root), 3-60 (Bairstow), 4-84 (Jaques), 5-175 (Ballance) 6-180 (Miller)

	O	M	R	W
Smith	3	0	21	0
Chapple	4	0	19	1
Yasir Arafat	4	0	55	1
Parry	3	0	25	0
Keedy	4	0	37	1
Newby	2	0	17	1

LANCASHIRE

S C Moore, b Starc	2
T C Smith, c Azeem Rafiq b Pyrah	33
S J Croft, c Ballance b Starc	56
K R Brown, c Root b Azeem Rafiq	46
P J Horton, b Ashraf	10
§ G D Cross, not out	6
Yasir Arafat, not out	1
* G Chapple	
O J Newby — Did not bat	
S D Parry	
G Keedy	
Extras lb 3, w 4	7
Total (5 wkts, 20 overs)	161

FoW: 1-7 (Moore), 2-45 (Smith), 3-127 (Brown), 4-153 (Horton), 5-155 (Croft)

	O	M	R	W
Root	3	0	33	0
Starc	4	0	21	2
Pyrah	3	0	28	1
Rashid	2	0	23	0
Azeem Rafiq	4	0	22	1
Ashraf	4	0	31	1

Man of the Match: D A Miller

Umpires: J H Evans and R T Robinson — Scorers: J T Potter and A West

Yorkshire v. Lancashire

The *Red Rose* blown away

DESTROYER SUNK: Cross throw ends Miller carnage

A 10,000-plus crowd saw a resurgent *White Rose* add two points to their claim for a Quarter-Final place against a shell-shocked Lancashire blown away by the destructive clean hitting of Miller and Ballance.

Lancashire chose to field, and looked to be in a decent position after Lyth had picked out Smith at deep mid-on for 12 and Root and Bairstow added little weight to the proceedings. Yorkshire 60-3 in the 10th over. Jaques was run out after splendid work by Croft for a workmanlike 40 from 28 balls, and Carnegie were 80-4 with less than seven overs remaining. Left-handers Miller and Ballance combined excellent running with fine strokeplay and no little destruction to put on 91 in six overs: Arafat took the brunt of this punishment, his four overs costing 55 runs — a *T20* record for a Lancashire bowler.

Miller cleared the rope three times and hit four other boundaries in his 54 from only 30 balls before he was run out in the final over attempting a second. Ballance was taken in the deep in the last over for a 23-ball 42, and of Yorkshire's 180 the last 50 had come in three overs.

Starc bowled Moore for two in Lancashire's second over, but Smith began to strike the ball cleanly — three maximums disappearing over wide mid-wicket — and with Croft keeping him company Yorkshire had a problem: it was solved in Pyrah's second over as Smith cut hard to backward-point where Rafiq held a stinging catch. The run rate needed acceleration, but an excellent spell from Rafiq made that difficult. Desperation set in. The *Red Rose* needed big overs, but Brown was taken in the deep by Root for 46 in the 19th, and when Croft was caught by Ballance for 56 in the last over the rate had become unmanageable.

Friends Life t20 — North Group
Nottinghamshire v. Yorkshire

Played at Trent Bridge, Nottingham, on July 5, 2012

Yorkshire won by 6 wickets

Toss won by Nottinghamshire — Yorkshire 2 points, Nottinghamshire 0 points

NOTTINGHAMSHIRE

M H Wessels, c Pyrah b Root	0
M J Lumb, c Jaques b Pyrah	20
* A C Voges, b Starc	70
S R Patel, c Lyth b Azeem Rafiq	5
J W A Taylor, b Ashraf	15
§ C M W Read, c Miller b Azeem Rafiq	14
S J Mullaney, not out	12
G G White, not out	4
D J Pattinson	
H F Gurney — Did not bat	
A Carter	
Extras b 1, lb 2, w 3, nb 2	8
Total (6 wkts, 20 overs)	148

FoW: 1-0 (Wessels), 2-38 (Lumb), 3-56 (Patel), 4-87 (Taylor), 5-115 (Read) 6-136 (Voges)

	O	M	R	W
Root	2	0	16	1
Starc	4	0	21	1
Wardlaw	2	0	22	0
Pyrah	4	0	20	1
Ashraf	4	0	33	1
Azeem Rafiq	4	0	33	2

YORKSHIRE

A Lyth, c Patel b Mullaney	33
P A Jaques, not out	58
J E Root, c Voges b Patel	27
§ J M Bairstow, st Read b White	1
D A Miller, c Wessels b Voges	3
G S Ballance, not out	26
R M Pyrah	
* Azeem Rafiq	
I Wardlaw — Did not bat	
M A Starc	
M A Ashraf	
Extras lb 1, w 1	2
Total (4 wkts, 17.4 overs)	150

FoW: 1-48 (Lyth), 2-99 (Root), 3-102 (Bairstow), 4-107 (Miller)

	O	M	R	W
White	3.4	0	39	1
Gurney	2	0	10	0
Pattinson	3	0	28	0
Patel	4	0	30	1
Mullaney	3	0	20	1
Carter	1	0	19	0
Voges	1	0	3	1

Man of the Match: P A Jaques

Umpires: M J D Bodenham and S J O'Shaughnessy — Scorers: J T Potter and R Marshall

Nottinghamshire v. Yorkshire

Quarter-Finals here we come

JOE ROOT: Off-spinning opening bowler who struck first ball

Yet another fine all-round display ensured Carnegie's first victory against a strong Nottinghamshire under the lights and booked a Quarter-Finals place for only the third time in their history.

The Outlaws opted to bat — this pointed to a home win as the record books show that nine times out of 10 the side batting first at Trent Bridge go on to win.

Off-spinner Root, as is often the way in this competition, opened the attack, and this time he had a wicket with his first ball as Wessels crashed a short delivery straight to Pyrah at mid-wicket.

The hosts were still 2-1 after two overs. Lumb was 20 when he fell victim to Pyrah the bowler, and Nottinghamshire were under 40 at the end of the powerplays. Despite an excellent innings from Voges, who advanced to 70, Carnegie had the lid on the Outlaws, and good spells from Pyrah, Starc and Rafiq held them down.

Yorkshire's reply got off to a flier, Lyth flashing three boundaries in the first over. The *White Rose* never looked back. Lyth's form was returning in spades, and it was a surprise when he fell to Mullaney, having struck 33 from 21 balls in a stand of 48 with Jaques. The Aussie left-hander then combined effortlessly with Root in an excellent second-wicket partnership of 51 before Root, 27, was pouched by Voges off the wily slow left arm of Patel.

A mini-collapse followed as Bairstow and Miller came and went, yet the early impetus of Yorkshire's innings had left ample time to rebuild. Jaques completed his half-century and finished unbeaten on 58 from 47 deliveries, while Ballance rounded of the proceedings with two straight sixes off White, taking Carnegie over the line with 14 balls to be bowled.

Friends Life t20 — North Group

Lancashire v. Yorkshire

At Old Trafford, Manchester, on July 6, 2012

Match abandoned without a ball bowled

Lancashire 1 point, Yorkshire 1 point

Umpires: S A Garratt and S J O'Shaughnessy Scorers: J T Potter and A West

Third Umpire: J H Evans

Yorkshire v. Derbyshire

Played at Headingley, Leeds, on July 8, 2012

Yorkshire won by 21 runs

Toss won by Derbyshire Yorkshire 2 points, Derbyshire 0 points

YORKSHIRE

A Lyth, c Khawaja b C F Hughes	78
P A Jaques, c A L Hughes b Knight	64
D A Miller, c Khawaja b Groenewald	19
G S Ballance, c and b Rana Naved-ul-Hasan	1
J E Root, not out	13
R M Pyrah, c Durston b Rana Naved-ul-Hasan	4
§ G L Brophy, not out	0
* Azeem Rafiq M A Starc A U Rashid M A Ashraf	Did not bat
Extras lb 1	1
Total (5 wkts, 20 overs)	180

FoW: 1-131 (Lyth), 2-150 (Jaques), 3-154 (Ballance), 4-163 (Miller), 5-167 (Pyrah)

	O	M	R	W
Durston	4	0	21	0
Groenewald	4	0	36	1
Clare	1	0	18	0
C F Hughes	3	0	20	1
Rana Naved-ul-Hasan	4	0	38	2
A L Hughes	2	0	23	0
Knight	2	0	23	1

DERBYSHIRE

U T Khawaja, c Brophy b Pyrah	6
W J Durston, b Starc	11
C F Hughes, run out (Pyrah/Brophy)	30
* W L Madsen, c and b Azeem Rafiq	21
G T Park, c Lyth b Ashraf	25
J L Clare, st Brophy b Rashid	14
A L Hughes, lbw b Ashraf	2
Rana Naved-ul-Hasan, not out	40
T D Groenewald, b Ashraf	0
§ C M Durham, c Miller b Starc	0
T C Knight, not out	1
Extras b 1, lb 3, w 3, nb 2	9
Total (9 wkts, 20 overs)	159

FoW: 1-13 (Khawaja), 2-19 (Durston), 3-74 (Madsen), 4-77 (C F Hughes), 5-96 (Clare) 6-99 (A L Hughes), 7-154 (Park), 8-155 (Groenewald), 9-156 (Durham)

	O	M	R	W
Root	1	0	6	0
Starc	4	0	27	2
Pyrah	4	0	43	1
Moin Ashraf	4	0	24	3
Azeem Rafiq	3	0	36	1
Rashid	4	0	19	1

Man of the Match: A Lyth

Umpires: G D Lloyd and N A Mallender Scorers: J T Potter and J M Brown

Yorkshire v. Derbyshire

Group No. 1 and home draw

Yorkshire ended their North Group fixtures with yet another win, so clinching top spot and a home draw in the Quarter-Finals.

The Falcons pounced to put Carnegie in to bat, but the hosts were soon piling on the runs as Jaques and Lyth continued their good form — racing to 50 in 32 balls with Lyth in particular striking the ball impressively both sides of the wicket.

The left-handed pair continued to force the pace as Lyth reached his half-century from 34 deliveries and Yorkshire's second century opening partnership of the competition arrived in 70.

Yorkshire's record opening stand arrived as Jaques also completed his 50, again off 34 balls, with a particular fondness for the "Dilshan scoop" which brought him three boundaries.

PILING ON THE AGONY: Lyth and Jaques in their 131 stand

Carnegie's record partnership for any wicket of 136 was in danger until Lyth, on a career-best 78, offered Durston a simple catch on the mid-wicket boundary at 131. Yorkshire will probably feel that their total fell 20 short of what had seemed achievable: a late flurry of wickets stemmed the flow, but they closed on an impressive 180.

Derbyshire's reply ran into trouble from the start as Khawaja edged Pyrah behind to Brophy, and Starc bowled Durston leg stump with only 19 on the board. A recovery of sorts was mounted by Hughes and Madsen, not without luck as they added 55 for the third wicket before Madsen gave Rafiq a simple return catch after inflicting some harsh treatment. Hughes followed almost immediately, run out after great work from Pyrah, and two more wickets went down, including a welcome success for Rashid. Rana Naved despatched Pyrah for 24 with three sixes in one over, but good bowling at the death by Starc, 2-27, and Ashraf, 3-24, ensured that the last three overs yielded only four runs.

Friends Life t20 — Quarter-Final
Yorkshire v. Worcestershire

Played at Headingley, Leeds, on July 25, 2012

Yorkshire won by 29 runs

Toss won by Yorkshire

YORKSHIRE

* A W Gale, c and b Mitchell	30
P A Jaques, run out (Scott/Shantry)	2
J E Root, c and b Kapil	65
§ J M Bairstow, c Ali b Mitchell	2
D A Miller, c D'Oliveira b Lucas	50
G S Ballance, not out	46
R M Pyrah, not out	10
Azeem Rafiq	
A U Rashid — Did not bat	
M A Starc	
M A Ashraf	
Extras b 2, lb 1, w 4	7
Total (5 wkts, 20 overs)	212

FoW: 1-5 (Jaques), 2-64 (Gale), 3-74 (Bairstow), 4-126 (Root), 5-173 (Miller)

	O	M	R	W
Shantry	3	0	46	0
Lucas	4	0	48	1
Andrew	3	0	34	0
Ali	4	0	29	0
Mitchell	4	0	23	2
D'Oliveira	1	0	11	0
Kapil	1	0	18	1

WORCESTERSHIRE

M M Ali, c Ballance b Pyrah	17
V S Solanki, lbw b Starc	1
P J Hughes, not out	80
J G Cameron, c Miller b Pyrah	29
G M Andrew, c Ballance b Azeem Rafiq	27
* D K H Mitchell, c Ballance b Starc	11
A Kapil, b Starc	4
§ B J M Scott, not out	3
B L D'Oliveira	
D S Lucas — Did not bat	
J D Shantry	
Extras lb 6, w 3, nb 2	11
Total (6 wkts, 20 overs)	183

FoW: 1-16 (Solanki), 2-20 (Ali), 3-95 (Cameron), 4-143 (Andrew), 5-165 (Mitchell) 6-180 (Kapil)

	O	M	R	W
Root	1	0	10	0
Starc	4	0	24	3
Pyrah	4	0	53	2
Ashraf	4	0	35	0
Rashid	3	0	29	0
Azeem Rafiq	4	0	26	1

Man of the Match: J E Root

Umpires: R J Bailey and J H Evans — Scorers: J T Potter and D E Pugh

Third Umpire: N A Mallender

Quarter-Final: Yorkshire v. Worcestershire

Triumphant festival of hitting

JOE ROOT: Shot selection way beyond his years

Carnegie stormed into their first *T20* Finals Day after an explosive display of batting — Root, Miller and Ballance providing some of the cleanest hitting this historic ground has seen for many a year.

Yorkshire chose to bat first, but things did not go to plan immediately, with Jaques left stranded well short of his ground with five on the board.

Skipper Gale shouldered the responsibility in a stand of 59 with Root, who was rolling out shot selection way beyond his years with reverse-sweeps and expansive cover-drives on the up as his highlights.

Gale, on 30 from 23 deliveries, was just going through the gears when he checked his shot and Mitchell took a return catch. A third wicket followed as an out-of-sorts Bairstow holed out in the deep.

Root took centre stage in his partnership with Miller, passing his first Yorkshire 50 in *T20* cricket: he struck Kapil for 18 in his first five balls before the seamer hit back with a spiralling catch. Root's 65 took only 40 balls in a stand of 52 with Miller, who was starting to open his own shoulders: the South African bullied his way to another half-century, using only 25 deliveries before he was taken in the deep. What happened in the last over took the game away from Royals: Ballance started it on 18 — and six balls later he had added 26, with four sixes, two of them were struck with a ferocity seldom seen. Yorkshire closed one short of their *T20* record — against Royals two years earlier.

Hughes offered a superb 80 not out from 53 balls in reply, but Yorkshire were just able to keep a lid on the left-handed Australian. Starc again provided outstanding control for his 3-24, while Ballance pouched three catches in the deep. The final overs were played out in celebratory fashion by Yorkshire fans and their heroes alike.

Friends Life t20 — Semi-Final
Sussex v. Yorkshire

Played at Swalec Stadium, Cardiff, on August 25, 2012

Yorkshire won by 36 runs

Toss won by Yorkshire

YORKSHIRE

* A W Gale, c Nash b Styris	11
P A Jaques, b Styris	2
J E Root, lbw b Styris	11
§ J M Bairstow, not out	68
D A Miller, c Gatting b Nash	47
G S Ballance, c Yardy b Liddle	7
T T Bresnan, c Nash b Liddle	6
R M Pyrah, not out	3
Azeem Rafiq	
R J Sidebottom — Did not bat	
M A Ashraf	
Extras lb 15, nb 2	17
Total (6 wkts, 20 overs)	172

FoW:- 1-13 (Gale), 2-19 (Jaques), 3-36 (Root), 4-118 (Miller), 5-147 (Ballance) 6-153 (Bresnan)

	O	M	R	W
Yardy	4	0	23	0
Styris	4	1	22	3
Liddle	3	0	26	2
Beer	3	0	30	0
Amjad Khan	3	0	24	0
Nash	2	0	20	1
Wright	1	0	12	0

SUSSEX

C D Nash, not out	80
L J Wright, b Sidebottom	3
§ M J Prior, c Ballance b Bresnan	2
M W Goodwin, c Ballance b Pyrah	15
J S Gatting, b Pyrah	3
S B Styris, c Ballance b Azeem Rafiq	8
M W Machin, c Bairstow b Bresnan	7
* M H Yardy, run out (Root/Bairstow)	2
W A Beer, run out (Sidebottom)	3
Amjad Khan, not out	5
C J Liddle — Did not bat	
Extras b 1, w 7	8
Total (8 wkts, 20 overs)	136

FoW: 1-12 (Wright), 2-15(Prior), 3-55 (Goodwin), 4-62 (Gatting), 5-81 (Styris) 6-93 (Machin), 7-101 (Yardy), 8-123 (Beer)

	O	M	R	W
Root	1	0	3	0
Sidebottom	3	0	28	1
Bresnan	4	0	22	2
Pyrah	4	0	30	2
Ashraf	4	0	31	0
Azeem Rafiq	4	0	21	1

Man of the Match: J M Bairstow

Umpires: M A Gough and J W Lloyds — Scorers: J T Potter and M J Charman

Third Umpire: R J Bailey — Fourth Umpire: N G B Cook

Semi-Final: Sussex v. Yorkshire

Bairstow blasts way to Final

Bresnan was welcomed back into the fold from his England duties, the unfortunate Rashid making way as the sun shone on a packed stadium.

Carnegie were further boosted by the return of Miller, Root and Bairstow from various international commitments.

Yorkshire opted to bat first, and were soon a wicket down — after a couple of lusty boundaries skipper Gale lobbed a straightforward catch to Nash at mid-on off Styris.

A strange passage of play followed as Carnegie made frantic attempts to score and the Sharks started to turn the screw. Jaques struggled to get one away from the first three balls of the third over before aiming a scoop over the wicket-keeper and finding his stumps rearranged. Styris completed what was remarkably only the fourth maiden in a decade of *T20* finals days.

JONATHAN BAIRSTOW: Three sixes in his undefeated 68

Root got his account under way with two sweeps to fine-leg, and Bairstow added a six over square-leg, only for Styris to claim his third wicket in the sixth over — Root lbw reverse-sweeping a full straight ball. Yorkshire were in the mire at 36-3, and a period of consolidation was required. Miller and Bairstow did just that, opting to see out Styris and Yardy, 3-22 and 3-23, before starting to increase the pace from the 10th over. Miller struck an enormous straight six off Liddle, and then climbed into a full toss from Beer that just evaded the fielder on the leg side, landing one bounce for four.

The 50 partnership came in 44 deliveries, and it was vital that this pair should drive on as Carnegie now eyed a total in excess of 150. Miller added another lusty boundary and a straight six off Beer as 16 came

HAT-TRICK CATCHER: Gary Ballance holds Matt Prior, one of three victims for the dashing batsman with one of the best pairs of hands on the circuit

from the 14th over. Nash was introduced to the attack, and this move paid instant dividends as the prized Miller holed out to Gatting on the long-off fence.

The explosive South African had struck 47 from 35 balls in a partnership of 82. Bairstow now took the lead, bringing up his 50 in 39 balls with a huge six over wide long-on as Nash's second over yielding 14 runs and Yorkshire were 147 after 18.

Ballance fell to the first ball of the 19th over, miscuing to Yardy at extra-cover. The 150 came up soon afterwards, the last 50 coming in 28 balls. Bresnan departed third ball for six, cutting to Goodwin at backward-point as an action-packed last-but-one over produced two wickets and 11 runs.

Yorkshire closed on 172, with much scampering of ones, two and threes. Bairstow returned to the pavilion on an unbeaten 68 from 45 deliveries with two fours and three sixes. The innings had been rescued by the superbly timed partnership of Miller and Bairstow, initially working the ball into the gaps before unleashing a fine selection of attacking strokes against what can only be described as a very good Sharks attack.

Root's first over in the Sussex reply yielded a mere three runs, Sidebottom then taking the vital wicket of Wright, who played on to his stumps attempting to cut. Things improved even further for Carnegie in the next over as Bresnan induced a false shot from Prior, who could only guide the ball to the waiting Ballance at wide mid-on. 15-2. Nash raced to 30 in no time before the Yorkshire bowlers, backed up by some livewire fielding, began to enforce some serious pressure. The Sussex 50 came in 51 balls. Just as the rain started to fall Yorkshire claimed anoth-

DOWN...AND NOT OUT: Bowler Rafiq falls to make a smart stop and tries to catch the batsman napping

er wicket — Goodwin lofting to the ever dependable Ballance on the long-off fence. 55-3 after nine overs. The rain abated; the sun took over, and Pyrah bagged his second victim as Gatting heaved across the line and lost his middle stump. Styris, mysteriously coming in at No. 6, partnered Nash in a desperate attempt to get the innings back on track. Nash reached his 50 from 40 deliveries before the excellent Rafiq drew Styris down the pitch and the big-hitting Kiwi could only pick out that man again, Ballance, on the boundary. Yorkshire were in the ascendency.

Rafiq completed his four overs, claiming 1-21, before Bresnan took his second wicket: Machan got a faint edge to be caught behind, and Sussex were teetering on the brink at 93-6. The boundaries dried up as Bresnan and Ashraf turned the screw. Ashraf bowled an excellent 16th over, conceding only three as he fired yorker after yorker into the despairing Yardy, who was on his way when a dreadful mix-up saw him run out.

Bresnan's last over yielded only four as he finished with 2-22. Nash was still there, but the asking rate was getting out of hand. Ashraf proved expensive in the 18th, as 16 runs flowed, but the target was now beyond the Sharks. Sidebottom deflected a rasping drive from Nash on to the stumps to run out the unfortunate Beer, but Nash batted through, unbeaten on 80. Sussex closed on 136-8 as Yorkshire strode into the final.

Bairstow accolade

Friends Life t20 — Final
Hampshire v. Yorkshire

Played at Swalec Stadium, Cardiff, on August 25, 2012
Hampshire won by 10 runs
Toss won by Hampshire

HAMPSHIRE

M A Carberry, b Sidebottom	8
J H K Adams, c Balance b Pyrah	43
J M Vince, b Ashraf	36
N D McKenzie, lbw b Azeem Rafiq	4
S M Ervine, c Root b Sidebottom	21
S M Katich, run out (Rafiq/Bairstow)	25
L A Dawson, not out	8
* A D Mascarenhas	
§ M D Bates — Did not bat	
C P Wood	
D R Briggs	
Extras lb 1, w 4	5
Total (6 wkts, 20 overs)	150

FoW: 1-23 (Carberry), 2-70 (Adams), 3-76 (McKenzie), 4-113 (Vince), 5-131 (Ervine) 6-150 (Katich)

	O	M	R	W
Root	1	0	9	0
Sidebottom	4	0	20	2
Bresnan	3	0	18	0
Pyrah	4	0	37	1
Ashraf	4	0	43	1
Azeem Rafiq	4	0	22	1

YORKSHIRE

* A W Gale, b Mascarenhas	15
P A Jaques, b Dawson	11
J E Root, b Mascarenhas	7
§ J M Bairstow, c Bates b Briggs	3
D A Miller, not out	72
G S Ballance, c Briggs b Ervine	7
T T Bresnan, c Ervine b Wood	18
R M Pyrah, b Wood	1
Azeem Rafiq, c Ervine b Wood	0
R J Sidebottom	
M A Ashraf — Did not bat	
Extras b 1, lb 3, w 2	6
Total (8 wkts, 20 overs)	140

FoW: 1-24 (Gale), 2-34 (Root), 3-38 (Jaques), 4-47 (Bairstow), 5-87 (Ballance) 6-137 (Bresnan), 7-140 (Pyrah), 8-140 (Rafiq)

	O	M	R	W
Dawson	4	0	21	1
Mascarenhas	4	0	20	2
Wood	4	0	26	3
Briggs	4	0	27	1
Ervine	4	0	42	1

Man of the Match: D A Miller

Umpires: R J Bailey and M A Gough
Third Umpire: N G B Cook

Scorers: J T Potter and K R Baker
Fourth Umpire: J W Lloyds

Final: Hampshire v. Yorkshire

Out, but certainly not down

This was the first meeting of these two sides in the shortest format.

Hampshire went against their standard philosophy by choosing to bat first. The toss looked vital, the pitch now getting slower and lower, and likely to suit the Royals' attack.

Carnegie's bowling was steady if not spectacular, and Hampshire had reached 23 in the fourth over when Sidebottom bowled Carberry for eight, the left-hander aiming at something fairly substantial.

The next two overs delivered by Sidebottom and Bresnan yielded only four runs as Yorkshire aimed to get through the powerplay overs relatively unscathed.

Two boundaries followed in Pyrah's first over — one of which narrowly evaded the diving Root — and Hampshire were on 36 by the end of the fielding restrictions. The 50 arrived in a shade over a run a ball as Yorkshire's disciplined attack stuck to the fundamental values followed throughout the 2012 competition. Just as the Royals were starting to increase the pace Pyrah struck, Adams on 43 lofting high and into Ballance's waiting hands at 70 in the 11th over. Next over, Rafiq showed excellent control in flighting one up to trap McKenzie lbw. The 100 arrived in the 15th over as Vince in particular looked menacing, especially through the off side: this much respected middle-order batsmen thumped 10 from Ashraf's first three deliveries before the bowler got his

DAVID MILLER: Became the country's leading six-hitter

RYAN SIDEBOTTOM: Pick of the attack with a fine, tight 2-20

revenge on his man for 36. Sidebottom sent down a fine last-but-one over, conceding only six and having Ervine caught in the deep by Root.

The final over was bowled by Ashraf — a big call from skipper Gale, as Bresnan still had an over up his sleeve: it gave away 14 runs, with only a run-out from the last ball.

Hampshire posted a challenging total of 150, a stiff target under lights and on a slow, low pitch. Sidebottom was the pick of Yorkshire's attack with 2-20.

Carnegie got off to a comfortable start, with 24 runs on the board in three overs before Gale was bowled playing across the line by the metronomic Mascarenhas. Root departed the same way, and the *White Rose* were in a spot of bother. It would have been even worse two balls later had Jaques not been dropped in the deep by Vince, an extremely difficult chance. This did not prove a costly miss, as Jaques got one from Dawson that kept low and took his off stump.

The real turning point came with the wicket of Bairstow, caught behind off Briggs for three after a spell of four overs that conceded a mere eight runs. Miller appeared to be caught by Mackenzie at short-mid-wicket on seven, but the batsman stood his ground and the TV cameras were inconclusive, as is often the case in these decisions. This incident clearly provoked a reaction from Miller: the 12th over, bowled by Ervine, proved to be the catalyst for a Yorkshire comeback as Miller went after him with three huge sixes, the third of which is probably still airborne. Ballance at the other end was finding it hard to get going, and he was to hole out in the 15th over to wide third-man for seven to end a stand of 40 for the fifth wicket.

The acceleration continued as Yorkshire's 100 arrived with a blistering straight-drive for four by Miller, the second 50 coming in only 34 deliveries. A further six concluded Wood's over, and with four overs left Yorkshire required 45. This became 36 from three overs.

The 18th over brought Yorkshire 15 runs as Bresnan and Miller cracked some timely boundaries. The 19th over brought seven runs and a near run-out for Miller.

The first ball of the last over from Wood saw the end of Bresnan. Having added 50 with Miller, the England all-rounder skied a catch to the on-rushing Ervine at cover.

TIM BRESNAN: Stand with Miller kept target in sight

The second ball brought only a single, putting Pyrah on strike. A single was followed by another single for Miller, and the game appeared up for a valiant Carnegie who wanted 11 from two balls. Pyrah was bowled by Wood, and Rafiq was caught in desperate fashion off the final ball. Miller finished unbeaten on 72 from 46 balls, and became the country's leading six-hitter. Defeated Yorkshire were able to hold their heads high after an outstanding *T20* campaign — and the promise of Champions League cricket to come.

TURNING POINT: Grim faces in the Yorkshire dugout

YORKSHIRE AVERAGES 2012

FRIENDS LIFE t20

Played 13 Won 9 Lost 2 No Result 1 Abandoned 1

BATTING AND FIELDING

(Qualification 4 completed innings)

Player	*M.*	*I.*	*N.O.*	*Runs*	*H.S.*	*Avge*	*100s*	*50s*	*ct/st*
D A Miller	12	11	3	390	74*	48.75	0	4	4
A Lyth	6	5	0	154	78	30.80	0	1	2
A W Gale	6	6	0	165	70	27.50	0	1	0
J E Root	12	11	2	241	65	26.77	0	1	6
P A Jaques	12	11	1	263	64	26.30	0	2	2
G S Ballance	12	11	3	209	47*	26.12	0	0	13
J M Bairstow	7	7	1	98	68*	16.33	0	1	2/0
R M Pyrah	12	9	3	94	35	15.66	0	0	2
Also played									
G L Brophy	5	4	2	53	32	26.50	0	0	4/1
Azeem Rafiq	12	5	3	25	21*	12.50	0	0	4
T T Bresnan	2	2	0	24	18	12.00	0	0	0
A U Rashid	4	1	0	4	4	4.00	0	0	1
M A Starc	10	2	1	0	0*	0.00	0	0	1
R J Sidebottom	7	1	1	5	5*	—	0	0	0
M A Ashraf	12	0	0	0	—	—	0	0	1
I Wardlaw	1	0	0	0	—	—	0	0	0

BOWLING

(Qualification 4 wickets)

Player	*Overs*	*Mdns*	*Runs*	*Wkts*	*Avge*	*Best*	*4wI*	*RPO*
M A Starc	36.5	0	218	21	10.38	3-24	0	5.91
R J Sidebottom	25	0	177	11	16.09	4-25	1	7.08
M A Ashraf	47	0	359	15	23.93	4-18	1	7.63
R M Pyrah	45	0	359	15	23.93	3-21	0	7.97
Azeem Rafiq	46	0	310	11	28.18	2-28	0	6.73
Also bowled								
T T Bresnan	7	0	40	2	20.00	2-22	0	5.71
A U Rashid	12	0	101	2	50.50	1-19	0	8.41
J E Root	13	0	114	1	114.00	1-16	0	8.76
I Wardlaw	2	0	22	0	—	0-22	0	11.00

Karbonn Smart Champions League 2012

WINNERS

Sydney Sixers, who beat Highveld by 10 wickets

QUALIFIERS — POOL ONE

		P	W	L	NR/A	PTS	NRR
1	Auckland (Q)	2	2	0	0	8	1.904
2	Sialkot	2	1	1	0	4	-0.511
3	Hampshire	2	0	2	0	0	-1.331

QUALIFIERS — POOL TWO

		P	W	L	NR/A	PTS	NRR
1	**Yorkshire (Q)**	**2**	**2**	**0**	**0**	**8**	**0.507**
2	UVA	2	0	1	1	2	-0.244
3	Trinidad & Tobago	2	0	1	1	2	-0.777

Q — qualified for main competition

GROUP A

		P	W	L	NR/A	PTS	NRR
1	Delhi (QS)	4	2	0	2	12	1.440
2	Titans (QS)	4	2	1	1	10	-0.017
3	Kolkata	4	1	2	1	6	0.488
4	Perth	4	1	2	1	6	-0.474
5	Auckland	4	1	2	1	6	-0.963

GROUP B

		P	W	L	NR/A	PTS	NRR
1	Sydney Sixers (QS)	4	4	0	0	16	1.656
2	Highveld (QS)	4	3	1	0	12	0.140
3	Chennai	4	2	2	0	8	-0.049
4	Mumbai	4	0	3	1	2	-0.471
5	**Yorkshire**	**4**	**0**	**3**	**1**	**2**	**-1.791**

QS — qualified for semi-finals

Statistics and scorecards **JOHN POTTER**

Karbonn Smart Champions League Twenty 20 — Qualifier Pool B
Uva v. Yorkshire

Played at Wanderers Stadium, Johannesburg, on October 9, 2012
Yorkshire won by 5 wickets

Toss won by Yorkshire Yorkshire 4 points, Uva 0 points

UVA

E M D Y Munaweera, c Miller b Ashraf	22
P B B Rajapaksa, b Rashid	24
S Chanderpaul, c Hodgson b Patterson	27
A B McDonald, c Ballance b Azeem Rafiq	17
* S H T Kandamby, not out	29
J D P Oram, c Ballance b Patterson	8
C U Jayasinghe, c Miller b Ashraf	3
S M S M Senanayake, b Sidebottom	9
Umar Gul, not out	2
W M C Jayampathi	
§ R S S S de Zoysa Did not bat	
Extras lb 2, w7	9
Total (7 wkts, 20 overs)	150

FoW: 1-42 (Munaweera), 2-56 (Rajapaksa), 3-94 (McDonald), 4-100 (Chanderpaul), 5-116 (Oram), 6-121 (Jayasinghe), 7-145 (Senanayake)

	O	M	R	W
Root	1	0	6	0
Sidebottom	4	0	33	1
Patterson	4	0	30	2
Ashraf	4	0	29	2
Azeem Rafiq	4	0	25	1
Rashid	3	0	25	1

YORKSHIRE

* A W Gale, st de Zoysa b Senanayake	13
P A Jaques, c and b Munaweera	32
J E Root, c McDonald b Jayampathi	11
D A Miller, not out	39
G S Ballance, b Munaweera	0
A U Rashid, not out	36
§ D M Hodgson, st de Zoysa b Munaweera	18
Azeem Rafiq	
R J Sidebottom Did not bat	
S A Patterson	
M A Ashraf	
Extras w 2	2
Total (5 wkts, 19.3 overs)	151

FoW: 1-15 (Gale), 2-47 (Root), 3-66 (Jaques), 4-66 (Ballance), (5)-91 (Miller 22* rh) 5-133 (Hodgson)

D A Miller retired when struck in the face by a bouncer, but returned at fall of fifth wicket

	O	M	R	W
Oram	4	0	42	0
Senanayake	3	0	19	1
Umar Gul	3.3	0	24	0
Jayampathi	1	0	11	1
McDonald	4	0	23	0
Munaweera	4	0	32	3

Man of the Match: A U Rashid

Umpires: Asad Rauf and M Erasmus Match Referee: D C Boon
Third Umpire: H D P K Dharmasena Fourth Umpire: J D Cloete

Karbonn Smart Champions League Twenty20 — Qualifier Pool B
Trinidad and Tobago v. Yorkshire

Played at Centurion Park, Centurion, on October 10, 2012

Yorkshire won by 6 wickets

Toss won by Trinidad and Tobago Yorkshire 4 points, Trinidad and Tobago 0 points

TRINIDAD AND TOBAGO

L M P Simmons, c Hodgson b Sidebottom	7
W K D Perkins, c Ballance b Root	0
A B Barath, b Patterson	0
D M Bravo, c Ballance b Rashid	45
* § D Ramdin, run out (Root/Rashid)	59
J N Mohammed, run out (Gale/Rashid)	0
K Cooper, c Lyth b Sidebottom	15
R Rampaul, b Sidebottom	6
K Y G Ottley, run out (Lyth/Hodgson)	5
R R Emrit, not out	3
S Badree Did not bat	
Extras lb 3, w 5	8
Total (9 wkts, 20 overs)	148

FoW: 1-7 (Perkins), 2-8 (Simmons), 3-8 (Barath), 4-101 (Bravo), 5-102 (Mohammed) 6-122 (Ramdin), 7-140 (Cooper), 8-140 (Rampaul), 9-148 (Ottley)

	O	M	R	W
Root	2	0	15	1
Sidebottom	4	0	13	3
Patterson	4	1	32	1
Azeem Rafiq	4	0	32	0
Ashraf	3	0	28	0
Rashid	3	0	25	1

YORKSHIRE

* A W Gale, b Badree	2
P A Jaques, lbw b Rampaul	6
J E Root, c and b Ottley	16
A Lyth, b Emrit	18
G S Ballance, not out	64
A U Rashid, not out	33
§ D M Hodgson	
Azeem Rafiq	
R J Sidebottom Did not bat	
S A Patterson	
M A Ashraf	
Extras b 4, lb 2, nb 1, w 8	15
Total (4 wkts, 18.5 overs)	154

FoW: 1-12 (Jaques), 2-16 (Gale), 3-44 (Lyth), 4-51 (Root)

	O	M	R	W
Badree	4	0	22	1
Rampaul	4	0	22	1
Emrit	3	0	29	1
Ottley	2	0	16	1
Mohammed	1	0	11	0
Cooper	2.5	0	28	0
Simmons	2	0	20	0

Man of the Match: G S Ballance

Umpires: Asad Rauf and M Erasmus Match Referee: D C Boon
Third Umpire: H D P K Dharmasena Fourth Umpire: S George

Karbonn Smart Champions League Twenty20 — Group B
Sydney Sixers v. Yorkshire

Played at Newlands, Capetown, on October 16, 2012

Sydney Sixers won by 8 wickets

Toss won by Yorkshire — Sydney Sixers 4 points, Yorkshire 0 points

YORKSHIRE

* A W Gale, b Hazlewood	8
P A Jaques, c Thornely b Starc	21
J E Root, b Henriques	25
A Lyth, c Rohrer b Watson	18
G S Ballance, c Haddin b Cummins	8
A U Rashid, c Haddin b Cummins	1
§ D M Hodgson, c Smith b Watson	7
Azeem Rafiq, c Hazlewood b Starc	0
R J Sidebottom, not out	3
S A Patterson, b Starc	2
M A Ashraf — Did not bat	
Extras lb 1, w 2	3
Total (9 wkts, 20 overs)	96

FoW: 1-30 (Gale), 2-30 (Jaques), 3-62 (Root), 4-78 (Lyth), 5-79 (Rashid) 6-88 (Hodgson), 7-90 (Ballance), 8-92 (Rafiq), 9-96 (Patterson)

	O	M	R	W
O'Keefe	2	0	14	0
Starc	4	1	22	3
Cummins	4	0	13	2
Hazlewood	4	0	9	1
Watson	4	0	27	2
Henriques	2	0	10	1

SYDNEY SIXERS

S R Watson, c Root b Sidebottom	11
M J Lumb, not out	43
* § B H Haddin, c Lyth b Azeem Rafiq	41
D J Thornely, not out	1
S P D Smith	
M C Henriques	
B J Rohrer	
P J Cummins — Did not bat	
M A Starc	
J R Hazlewood	
S N J O'Keefe	
Extras lb 1, w 1	2
Total (2 wkts, 8.5 overs)	98

FoW: 1-11 (Watson), 2-89 (Haddin)

	O	M	R	W
Root	1	0	11	0
Sidebottom	2	0	28	1
Patterson	2	0	15	0
Moin Ashraf	1	0	14	0
Azeem Rafiq	1.5	0	21	1
Rashid	1	0	8	0

Man of the Match: B J Haddin

Umpires: Aleem Dar and R J Tucker — Match Referee: R S Madugalle

Third Umpire: H D P K Dharmasena — Fourth Umpire: S George

Karbonn Smart Champions League Twenty20 — Group B
Mumbai v. Yorkshire

Played at Newlands, Capetown, on October 18, 2012

No result

Toss won by Yorkshire — Mumbai 2 points, Yorkshire 2 points

MUMBAI

D R Smith, c Patterson b Root	37
S R Tendulkar, run out (Balance/Hodgson)	7
R G Sharma, b Azeem Rafiq	25
§ K D Karthik, c Azeem Rafiq b Rashid	12
A T Rayudu, c Gale b Azeem Rafiq	15
K A Pollard, not out	37
* Harbhajan Singh, c Azeem Rafiq b Rashid	12
M G Johnson, not out	5
D S Kulkarni	
S L Malinga — Did not bat	
P P Ojha	
Extras lb 5, w 1	6
Total (6 wkts, 17.5 overs)	156

FoW: 1-23 (Tendulkar), 2-59 (Smith), 3-86 (Sharma), 4-86 (Karthik), 5-109 (Rayudu) 6-136 (Harbhajan)

	O	M	R	W
Root	2	0	26	1
Sidebottom	3	0	17	0
Patterson	3	0	12	0
Ashraf	0.3	0	4	0
Lyth	1.3	0	14	0
Azeem Rafiq	4	0	36	2
Rashid	3.5	0	42	2

M A Ashraf broke down after three balls, and his over was completed by A Lyth
Rashid's fourth over was incomplete when bad weather ended the match

YORKSHIRE

* A W Gale
P A Jaques
J E Root
A Lyth
G S Ballance
A U Rashid — Unable to bat
§ D M Hodgson
Azeem Rafiq
R J Sidebottom
S A Patterson
M A Ashraf

Umpires: Aleem Dar and R J Tucker — Match Referee: R S Madugalle
Third Umpire: H D P K Dharmasena — Fourth Umpire: S George

Karbonn Smart Champions League Twenty20 — Group B
Highveld v. Yorkshire

Played at Wanderers Stadium, Johannesburg, on October 20, 2012
Highveld won by 5 wickets

Toss won by Highveld — Highveld 4 points, Yorkshire 0 points

YORKSHIRE

* A W Gale, c Tsolekile b Pretorius	21
P A Jaques, b Petersen	31
J E Root, c Sohail Tanvir b Phangiso	5
A Lyth, c Nannes b Morris	21
G S Ballance, c Nannes b Phangiso	17
A U Rashid, lbw b Sohail Tanvir	8
§ D M Hodgson, not out	10
Azeem Rafiq, c Phangiso b Sohail Tanvir	4
S A Patterson, I Wardlaw, O J Hannon-Dalby — Did not bat	
Extras lb 4, w 9, nb 1	14
Total (7 wkts, 20 overs)	131

FoW: 1-54 (Gale), 2-60 (Root), 3-67 (Jaques), 4-100 (Ballance), 5-111 (Lyth), 6-118 (Rashid), 7-131 (Rafiq)

	O	M	R	W
Sohail Tanvir	4	1	25	2
Nannes	4	0	30	0
Morris	4	0	25	1
Phangiso	4	0	23	2
Petersen	2	0	11	1
Pretorius	2	0	13	1

HIGHVELD

* A N Petersen, c Hodgson b Hannon-Dalby	19
G H Bodi, lbw b Patterson	8
Q de Kock, c Hodgson b Wardlaw	32
N D McKenzie, lbw b Azeem Rafiq	13
D Pretorius, c sub (E Wilson) b Patterson	25
J Symes, not out	27
§ T L Tsolekile, not out	4
C H Morris, Sohail Tanvir, D P Nannes, A M Phangiso — Did not bat	
Extras lb 1, w 5	6
Total (5 wickets, 19.2 overs)	134

FoW: 1-27 (Petersen), 2-31 (Bodi), 3-69 (McKenzie), 4-89 (de Kock), 5-107 (Pretorius)

	O	M	R	W
Wardlaw	4	1	23	1
Patterson	3.2	0	21	2
Hannon-Dalby	4	0	35	1
Root	1	0	4	0
Azeem Rafiq	4	0	14	1
Rashid	3	0	36	0

Man of the Match: J Symes

Umpires: Aleem Dar and H D P K Dharmasena — Match Referee: D C Boon
Third Umpire: R J Tucker — Fourth Umpire: S George

Karbonn Smart Champions League Twenty20 — Group B
Chennai v. Yorkshire

Played at Kingsmead, Durban, on October 22, 2012
Chennai won by 4 wickets

Toss won by Chennai — Chennai 4 points, Yorkshire 0 points

YORKSHIRE

* A W Gale, c Bollinger b Morkel	23
A Lyth, c Vijay b Hilfenhaus	11
J E Root, c Saha b Morkel	6
D A Miller, c Ashwin b Bollinger	28
G S Ballance, run out (Saha)	58
A U Rashid, not out	4
§ D M Hodgson, c du Plessis b Bollinger	1
Azeem Rafiq, I Wardlaw, S A Patterson, O J Hannon-Dalby — Did not bat	
Extras b 1, lb 2, w 6	9
Total (6 wkts, 20 overs)	140

FoW: 1-35 (Gale), 2-36 (Lyth), 3-43 (Root), 4-121 (Miller), 5-137 (Ballance) 6-140 (Hodgson)

	O	M	R	W
Ashwin	4	0	25	0
Bollinger	4	0	16	2
Hilfenhaus	4	0	32	1
Morkel	4	0	12	2
Raina	1	0	12	0
Jadeja	1	0	15	0
Dhoni	2	0	25	0

CHENNAI

F du Plessis, c Azeem Rafiq b Patterson	1
M Vijay, c Lyth b Hannon-Dalby	13
* S K Raina, c Miller b Hannon-Dalby	31
S Badrinath, b Wardlaw	47
M S Dhoni, b Wardlaw	31
R A Jadeja, c Ballance b Patterson	5
J A Morkel, not out	4
§ W P Saha, not out	1
R Ashwin, D E Bollinger, B W Hilfenhaus — Did not bat	
Extras lb 7, w 1	8
Total (6 wkts, 19 overs)	141

FoW: 1-3 (du Plessis), 2-26 (Vijay), 3-74 (Raina), 4-117 (Badrinath), 5-132 (Jadeja) 6-140 (Dhoni)

	O	M	R	W
Wardlaw	4	0	23	3
Patterson	3	0	22	2
Hannon-Dalby	4	0	23	2
Root	1	0	8	0
Azeem Rafiq	3	0	26	0
Rashid	4	0	32	0

Man of the Match: S Badrinath

Umpires: Aleem Dar and R J Tucker — Match Referee: D C Boon
Third Umpire: S Ravi — Fourth Umpire: S George

YORKSHIRE AVERAGES 2012

KARBONN SMART CHAMPIONS LEAGUE TWENTY20

Played 6 Won 2 Lost 3 No Result 1

BATTING AND FIELDING

Player	*M.*	*I.*	*N.O.*	*Runs*	*H.S.*	*Avge*	*100s*	*50s*	*ct/st*
D A Miller	2	2	1	67	39*	67.00	0	0	3
A U Rashid	6	5	3	82	36*	41.00	0	0	0
G S Ballance	6	5	1	147	64*	36.75	0	2	5
P A Jaques	5	4	0	90	32	22.50	0	0	0
A Lyth	5	4	0	68	21	17.00	0	0	3
A W Gale	6	5	0	67	23	13.40	0	0	1
J E Root	6	5	0	63	25	12.60	0	0	1
D M Hodgson	6	4	1	36	18	12.00	0	0	4
Azeem Rafiq	6	2	0	4	4	2.00	0	0	3
S A Patterson	6	1	0	2	2	2.00	0	0	1
R J Sidebottom	4	1	1	3	3*	—	0	0	0
M A Ashraf	4	0	0	0	—	—	0	0	0
O J Hannon-Dalby	2	0	0	0	—	—	0	0	0
I Wardlaw	2	0	0	0	—	—	0	0	0

BOWLING

Player	*Overs*	*Mdns*	*Runs*	*Wkts*	*Avge*	*Best*	*4wI*	*RPO*
I Wardlaw	8	1	46	3	15.33	2-23	0	5.75
R J Sidebottom	13	0	91	5	18.20	3-13	0	7.00
S A Patterson	19.2	1	132	7	18.85	2-21	0	6.82
O J Hannon-Dalby	8	0	58	3	19.33	2-23	0	7.25
Azeem Rafiq	20.5	0	154	5	30.80	2-36	0	7.39
J E Root	8	0	70	2	35.00	1-15	0	8.75
M A Ashraf	8.3	0	75	2	37.50	2-29	0	8.82
A U Rashid	17.5	0	168	4	42.00	2-42	0	9.42
A Lyth	1.3	0	14	0	—	0-14	0	9.33

Second Eleven 2012

PLAYERS WHO APPEARED FOR YORKSHIRE SECOND ELEVEN IN 2012
(excluding First Eleven capped players)

Player	Date of Birth	Birthplace	Type
O J Hannon-Dalby *	June 20, 1989	Halifax	LHB/RFM
Azeem Rafiq *	February 27, 1991	Karachi, Pakistan	RHB/OB
M A Ashraf *	January 5, 1992	Bradford	RHB/RF
G S Randhawa*	January 25, 1992	Huddersfield	LHB/SLA
A Z Lees*	April 14, 1993	Halifax	LHB/LB
I Wardlaw *	June 29, 1985	Dewsbury	RHB/RMF
C J Geldart	December 17, 1991	Huddersfield	LHB/RM
W T Root	August 5, 1992	Sheffield	LHB/OB
A E Lilley	April 17, 1992	Halifax	RHB/LM
E Wilson	July 7, 1994	Huddersfield	LHB/WK
G S Ross	October 29, 1993	Leeds	LHB/OB
J A Leaning	October 18, 1993	Bristol	RHB/RMF
D M Hodgson	February 26, 1990	Northallerton	RHB/WK
D F Girling	September 26, 1992	Edgware	RHB/RMF
J A Tattersall	December 15, 1994	Knaresborough	RHB/LB
W M H Rhodes	March 2, 1995	Nottingham	LHB/RM
R Gibson	January 22, 1996	Middlesbrough	RHB/RM
M Hussain	March 27, 1997	Leeds	RHB/RM
B O Coad	January 10, 1994	Harrogate	RHB/RM
D Evans	July 24, 1987	Hartlepool	RHB/RFM
G P Whiles	October 14, 1993	Harrogate	LHB/RMF
J Shaw	January 3, 1996	Wakefield	RHB/RMF
S P Cheetham	September 5, 1987	Oldham	RHB/RFM
L R Stabler	September 18, 1994	Darlington	RHB/LMF

* Second Eleven cap

SECOND ELEVEN HIGHLIGHTS OF 2012

CHAMPIONSHIP

Century partnerships (3)

For the 2nd wicket (1)

253 A Z Lees and A McGrath v Northamptonshire at Northampton

For the 5th wicket (1)

125 J A Leaning and D M Hodgson v Northamptonshire at Northampton

For the 8th wicket (1)

138 R Gibson and R J Sidebottom v MCC Universities at York

Centuries (1)

A McGrath (1)

200 * v Northamptonshire at Northampton

Four wickets in an innings (3)

O J Hannon-Dalby (2)

4 for 21 v MCC Universities at York (1st innings)
4 for 43 v MCC Universities at York (2nd innings)

G S Randhawa (1)

5 for 42 v Worcestershire at Barnsley

Four victims in an innings (1)

D M Hodgson (1)

4 (4ct) v. MCC Universities at York

TROPHY

Century Partnerships (1)

For the 3rd wicket (1)

126 J J Sayers and G L Brophy v Northamptonshire at Northampton

No centuries were scored for Yorkshire in the One-Day Trophy in 2012

4 wickets in an innings (2)

J J Sayers (1)

5 for 27 v Northamptonshire at Northampton

O J Hannon-Dalby (1)

4 for 10 v Unicorns A at Sheffield Collegiate

No Yorkshire fielder effected four dismissals in an innings in 2012. The nearest was J J Sayers, who took three catches v. Unicorns A at Sheffield Collegiate

T20 COMPETITION

No century partnerships were compiled for Yorkshire in 2012. The highest was R M Pyrah and A U Rashid's 55 for the third wicket v. England Under-19s at Bradford and Bingley (second match). There were no individual centuries for Yorkshire in the T20 Competition — the highest score (50) made by A Z Lees v. Lancashire at Ormskirk (second match). There were no instances of four wickets in an innings — the best performance was the 3-16 by A U Rashid v. England Under-19s at Bradford and Bingley (second match). There were no instances of four victims in an innings — the best performance was three victims (two caught and one stumped) by Ed Wilson v. Lancashire at Ormskirk (first match).

DEBUTS (5)

R Gibson, M Hussain, J Shaw, L R Stabler, G P Whiles.

Second Eleven Championship
Yorkshire v. Leicestershire

At St George's Road, Harrogate, on April 25, 26 and 27, 2012

Match abandoned at 9.30am on the Second Day without a ball bowled

No toss made — Yorkshire 3 points, Leicestershire 3 points

Umpires: N J Long and B J Debenham — Scorers: H Clayton and P N Johnson

Yorkshire v. Durham

Played at Clifton Park, York, on May 22, 23 and 24, 2012

Durham won by an innings and 69 runs at 6.05 pm on the Second Day

Toss won by Yorkshire — Yorkshire 2 points, Durham 24 points

Close of play: First Day, Yorkshire 39-2 first innings (Sayers 19 *, Randhawa 4 *)

DURHAM

B A Raine, lbw b Pyrah	9
K K Jennings, not out	207
* G J Muchall, c Ross b Randhawa	63
§ M J Richardson, c Hodgson b Randhawa	2
H Bush, lbw b Randhawa	17
R Singh, c Lees b Lilley	37
G Clark, c Hodgson b Hannon-Dalby	5
M A Wood, not out	73
P Coughlin	
P R Hindmarch — Did not bat	
R M R Brathwaite	
M G Morley	
Extras b 1, lb 3, w 1, nb 6)	11
Total (6 wickets dec, 89 overs)	424

FoW: 1-29 (Raine); 2-174 (Muchall); 3-186 (Richardson); 4-272 (Bush); 5-281 (Singh) 6-296 (Clark)

	O	M	R	W
Hannon-Dalby	16	1	98	1
Pyrah	19	4	53	1
Whiles	7	1	36	0
Lilley	9	1	45	1
Randhawa	26	1	116	3
Ross	12	0	72	0

YORKSHIRE

First Innings		Second Innings	
A Z Lees, lbw b Brathwaite	0	c Bush b Coughlin	6
*J J Sayers, c Bush b Coughlin,	25	c Muchall b Coughlin	0
J A Leaning, c Richardson b Raine	7	c Clark b Brathwaite	10
G S Randhawa, c Muchall b Coughlin	8	(9) b Morley	34
R M Pyrah, lbw b Brathwaite	7	(4) c Bush b Raine	31
E Wilson, c Muchall b Hindmarch	23	(8) c Jennings b Coughlin	2
G S Ross, c Richardson b Brathwaite	0	(6) c Bush b Coughlin	34
M Hussain, b Brathwaite	0	(7) c Clark b Hindmarch	41
§ D M Hodgson, not out	27	(5) c Richardson b Raine	0
A E Lilley, b Hindmarch	1	run out	40
O J Hannon-Dalby, c Richardson b Bush	4	not out	19
Extras b 1, lb 9, w 2, nb 4	16	Extras b 1, lb 3, w 10, nb 6	20
Total (42.2 overs)	118	Total (59.2 overs)	237

FoW: 1st 1-6 (Lees), 2-35 (Leaning), 3-43 (Randhawa), 4-60 (Pyrah), 5-60 (Sayers) 6-75 (Ross), 7-75 (Hussain), 8-96 (Wilson), 9-108 (Lilley), 10-118 (Hannon-Dalby)

FoW: 1-0 (Sayers), 2-15 (Lees), 3-44(Leaning), 4-48 (Pyrah), 5-63 (Hodgson) 6-104 (Ross), 7-106 (Wilson), 8-163 (Randhawa), 9-165 (Hussain), 10-237 (Lilley)

	O	M	R	W		O	M	R	W
Brathwaite	14	6	23	4	Brathwaite	13	6	37	1
Hindmarch	11	2	40	2	Hindmarch	13	3	68	1
Raine	7	2	17	1	Raine	6	1	14	2
Coughlin	5	1	11	2	Coughlin	14	4	50	4
Jennings	5	2	13	0	Bush	5	0	20	0
Bush	0.2	0	4	1	Morley	8	1	44	1

Umpires: M Burns and R J.Newham — Scorers: H Clayton and R V Hilton

Second Eleven Championship
Yorkshire v Worcestershire

Played at Shaw Lane, Barnsley, on June 26, 27 and 28, 2012

Match drawn. Rain prevented any play on the last day

Toss won by Yorkshire — Yorkshire 9 points, Worcestershire 10 points

Close of play: First Day, Worcestershire 109-7 (Pardoe 72 *); Second Day, Yorkshire 139-6 (W H N Rhodes 30 *, A E Lilley 8 *)

YORKSHIRE

First Innings		Second Innings	
*A Z Lees, lbw b Harrison	24	c Kervezee b Harrison	18
J J Sayers, lbw b Russell	22	c Cox b Richardson	6
§ D M Hodgson, c Manuel b Russell	10	b Choudhry	34
A U Rashid, b Jones	53		
J A Leaning, c Harrison b Choudhry	71	(4) b Choudhry	20
E Wilson, lbw b Russell	21	(5) c Kervezee b Choudhry	14
W M H Rhodes, run out	4	(6) not out	30
G S Randhawa, c Manuel b Russell	0	(7) c Kervezee b Choudhry	0
S A Patterson, c Cox b Russell	4		
A E Lilley, b Russell	3	(8) not out	8
B O Coad, not out	1		
G P Whiles — Did not bat			
Extras b 5, lb 5, w 1	11	Extras lb 9	9
Total (67.4 overs)	224	Total (6 wickets, 62 overs)	139

FoW: 1st — 1-51 (Sayers), 2-55 (Lees), 3-79 (Hodgson), 4-125 (Rashid), 5-179 (Wilson), 6-198 (Rhodes); 7-198 (Randhawa); 8-206 (Patterson); 9-210 (Lilley); 10-224 (Leaning),

FoW: 2nd — 1-11 (Sayers), 2-34 (Lees), 3-73 (Leaning), 4-94 (Hodgson), 5-99 (Wilson), 6-107 (Randhawa)

	O	M	R	W
Jones	15	4	50	1
Richardson	13	4	34	0
Harrison	7	2	15	1
Russell	19	2	75	6
Choudhry	13.4	1	40	1

	O	M	R	W
Richardson	13	8	7	1
Jones	10	1	38	0
Russell	7	0	23	0
Harrison	7	2	15	1
Choudhry	19	5	29	4
Pinner	5	1	18	0
Pardoe	1	1	0	0

WORCESTERSHIRE

M G Pardoe, not out	156
J K Manuel, b Patterson	6
A N Kervezee, lbw b Patterson	2
*N D Pinner, lbw b Rashid	16
J Leach, c Hodgson b Randhawa	2
S H Choudhry, lbw b Rashid	0
N L Harrison, b Randhawa	7
C J Russell, lbw b Rashid	0
§ O B Cox, c Hodgson b Randhawa	36
G H Rhodes, b Randhawa	7
R A Jones, lbw b Randhawa	17
A J Richardson — Did not bat	
Extras b 3, lb 7, w 1	11
Total (82.4 overs)	260

FoW: 1-17 (Manuel), 2-27 (Kervezee), 3-77 (Pinner), 4-80 (Leach), 5-89 (Choudhry), 6-108 (Harrison), 7-109 (Russell), 8-190 (Cox), 9-236 (G H Rhodes), 10-260 (Jones)

	O	M	R	W
S A Patterson	14	4	26	2
A E Lilley	7	1	30	0
B O Coad	5	0	28	0
G P Whiles	9	2	33	0
A U Rashid	22	1	77	3
G P Randhawa	21.4	6	42	5
W M H Rhodes	4	0	14	0

Umpires: P K Baldwin and N Bagh — Scorers: H Clayton and P M Mellish

NOTE: Rashid and Patterson were summoned to first-team t20 duty at Leicester at lunchtime on the Second Day, leaving Yorkshire with 10 men, only nine of whom could have batted on the Third Day if Rashid and Patterson had not returned. Rain solved the problem.

Second Eleven Championship
Derbyshire v. Yorkshire

At the Grange, Ticknall on July 3, 4 and 5, 2012

Match abandoned at 9.30am on the First Day

No toss made — Derbyshire 3 points, Yorkshire 3 points

Umpires: B J Debenham and N R Roper — Scorers: T M Cottam and H Clayton

NOTE: The venue for the previous day's Trophy game, Denby, was unfit for that game. Ticknall CC were available to stage the Championship fixture, but on the first morning the ground was under water.

Nottinghamshire v. Yorkshire

Played at Nottinghamshire Sports Ground, West Bridgford, on July 17, 18 and 19, 2012

Match drawn at 6.52pm on the Third Day

Toss won by Nottinghamshire — Nottinghamshire 9 points, Yorkshire 7 points

Close of play: First Day, Yorkshire first innings 30-0 (Lees 8 *, Sayers 1 *); Second Day, Nottinghamshire 36-0 (Turner 16 *, Edwards 20 *)

First Innings	NOTTINGHAMSHIRE	Second Innings	
K Turner, c Brophy b Evans	22	not out	105
N J Edwards, c Wardlaw b Rashid	138	c Brophy b Wardlaw	33
S Kelsall, c Wardlaw b Rashid	50	c Lilley b Evans	5
S L Elstone, not out	79	not out	30
T C Rowe, lbw b Randhawa	23		
* P J Franks, b Rashid	2		
§ M H Cross, lbw b Randhawa	4		
A D Tilcock, not out	24		
G G White			
L J Fletcher — Did not bat			
G P W Bacon			
L Wood			
Extras b 2, lb 4, nb 4	10	Extras b2	2
Total (6 wkts dec, 93 overs)	352	Total (2 wkts dec, 34 overs)	175

NOTE: Dan Hodgson kept wicket in Nottinghamshire's second innings

FoW: 1st 1-60 (Turner), 2-185 (Kelsall), 3-218 (Edwards), 4-278 (Rowe), 5-285 (Franks), 6-290 (Cross)

2nd 1-63 (Edwards), 2-75 (Kelsall

	O	M	R	W		O	M	R	W
Hannon-Dalby	15	0	71	0	Hannon-Dalby	9	1	45	0
Wardlaw	14	5	42	0	Lilley	8	0	44	0
Lilley	5	1	24	0	Wardlaw	5	0	14	1
Evans	13	2	53	1	Evans	5	1	21	1
Rashid	29	6	84	3	Randhawa	4	0	9	0
Randhawa	17	0	72	2	Rashid	3	0	40	0

First Innings	YORKSHIRE	Second Innings	
* A Z Lees, c Kelsall b Fletcher	15	not out	1
J J Sayers, run out	46	c Edwards b Bacon	0
§ G L Brophy, c Edwards b Fletcher	0	not out	0
D M Hodgson, lbw b Fletcher	0		
J A Leaning, lbw b White	34		
A U Rashid, not out	69		
E Wilson, run out	17		
G S Randhawa, not out	8		
A E Lilley			
O J Hannon-Dalby — Did not bat			
I Wardlaw			
D Evans			
Extras b 5, lb 7, nb 12	24	Extras 1 lb	1
Total (6 wkts dec, 53.1 overs)	213	Total (1 wkt, 5 overs)	2

FoW: 1st 1-40 (Lees), 2-40 (Brophy), 3-40 (Hodgson), 4-110 (Sayers), 5-132 (Leaning), 6-180 (Wilson)

2nd 1-0 (Sayers)

	O	M	R	W		O	M	R	W
Fletcher	14	5	27	3	Fletcher	3	2	1	0
Bacon	14	2	72	0	Bacon	2	2	0	1
Wood	7	0	27	0					
Franks	8	1	37	0					
White	8	1	38	1					

Umpires: R J Evans and T Riley — Scorers: Mrs A Cusworth and H Clayton

Second Eleven Championship
Nothamptonshire v. Yorkshire

Played at the County Ground, Northampton, on July 24, 25 and 26, 2012

Northamptonshire won by 4 wickets at 6.03pm on the Third Day

Toss won by Yorkshire — Northamptonshire 21 points, Yorkshire 6 points

Close of play: First Day, Northamptonshire 12-1 (Howgego 2 *, Keogh 9 *); Second Day, Yorkshire 168-1 (Lees 75 *, McGrath 85 *)

First Innings	YORKSHIRE	Second Innings	
A Z Lees, c O`Brien b Daggett	77	c Peters b Keogh	85
* J J Sayers, c O'Brien b Keogh	47	c Duckett b Daggett	6
A McGrath, b Evans	0	not out	200
§ G L Brophy, c Peters b Daggett	38	not out	6
J A Leaning, not out	68		
D M Hodgson, c Daggett b de Lange	61		
E Wilson, c O'Brien b Daggett	11		
G S Randhawa			
D Evans			
O J Hannon-Dalby — Did not bat			
S P Cheetham			
G P Whiles			
Extras b 5, lb 13	18	Extras b 1, lb 1, w 1	3
Total (6 wkts dec, 94.4 overs)	311	Total (2 wkts dec, 64 overs)	300

FoW: 1st 1-98 (Sayers), 2-99 (McGrath), 3-169 (Brophy), 4-184 (Lees), 5-309 (Hodgson) 6-311 (Wilson)

2nd 1-11 (Sayers); 2-264 (Lees)

	O	M	R	W		O	M	R	W
Daggett	18.4	5	51	3	Daggett	14	4	46	1
Burton	14	5	41	0	L Evans	10	3	44	0
L Evans	16	3	70	1	Burton	11	1	49	0
Stone	19	5	26	0	Stone	6	1	19	0
Keogh	19	0	57	1	Keogh	12	0	79	1
de Lange	14	3	48	1	de Lange	10	1	50	0
					O'Brien	1	0	11	0

First Innings	NORTHAMPTONSHIRE	Second Innings	
S D Peters, b Cheetham	1	lbw b Cheetham	21
B H N Howgego, c Whiles b McGrath	44	c Hannon-Dalby b Randhawa	71
R I Keogh, c Brophy b Evans	83	c Lees b Randhawa	73
* § N J O'Brien, c Brophy b Evans	17	b Evans	26
B M Duckett, c Brophy b Evans	22	c Brophy b Leaning	50
J M Kettleborough, c McGrath b Hannon-Dalby	36	not out	45
C A L Davis, not out	50	c Leaning b Whiles	33
C D W de Lange, not out	1	not out	18
L M Daggett			
D A Burton — Did not bat			
O P Stone			
L Evans			
Extras b 3, lb 1, nb 2	6	Extras b 6, lb 8, w 1, nb 2	17
Total (6 wkts dec, 68 overs)	260	Total (6 wkts, 71 overs)	354

FoW: 1st 1-1 (Peters), 2-98 (Howgego), 3-148 (O'Brien), 4-149 (Keogh), 5-176 (Duckett), 6-247 (Kettleborough)

FoW: 2nd 1-37 (Peters), 2-168 (Keogh), 3-181 (Howgego), 4-249 (Duckett), 5-261 (O'Brien), 6-317 (Davis)

	O	M	R	W		O	M	R	W
Hannon-Dalby	16	4	49	1	Hannon-Dalby	11	0	59	0
Cheetham	12	2	50	1	Cheetham	8	0	53	1
D Evans	12	1	63	3	Whiles	8	0	52	1
Whiles	8	0	44	0	D Evans	12	3	48	1
McGrath	8	4	12	1	Randhawa	17	1	82	2
Randhawa	12	2	40	0	McGrath	8	2	16	0
					Leaning	7	1	30	1

Umpires: B V Taylor and P W Joy — Scorers: M E Woolley and H Clayton

Second Eleven Championship
Yorkshire v. MCC Universities

Played at Clifton Park, York, on August 7, 8 and 9, 2012

Yorkshire won by 181 runs at 5.05 pm on the Third Day

Toss won by Yorkshire — Yorkshire 24 points, MCC Universities 3 points

Close of play: First Day, MCC Universities 8-2 (Patel 0 *); Second Day, Yorkshire 208-7 (Randhawa 9 *, Sidebottom 24 *)

First Innings	YORKSHIRE	Second Innings	
A Z Lees, lbw b Bush	50	b Morris	6
* J J Sayers, b Lester	0	c Bell b Lester	15
A McGrath, c Salisbury b Morris	12	c Johnson b MacQueen	78
§ D M Hodgson, c Bell b Salisbury	60	lbw b MacQueen	13
E Wilson, b MacQueen	23	lbw b Lester	12
G S Ross, run out	4	b MacQueen	12
R Gibson, c Blackaby b MacQueen	88	c Johnson b MacQueen	18
G S Randhawa, lbw b MacQueen	0	not out	9
R J Sidebottom, not out	55	not out	24
S P Cheetham, not out	1		
O J Hannon-Dalby			
B O Coad — Did not bat			
Extras b 5, lb 2, w 2, nb 2	11	Extras b 2, nb 2	4
Total (8 wkts dec, 82 overs)	304	Total (7 wkts dec, 60 overs)	208

FoW: 1st — 1-2 (Sayers), 2-19 (McGrath), 3-116 (Lees), 4-137 (Hodgson), 5-145 (Ross), 6-152 (Wilson), 7-154 (Randhawa), 8-292 (Gibson)

FoW: 2nd — 1-14 (Lees), 2-26 (Sayers), 3-81 (Hodgson), 4-108 (Wilson), 5-144 (McGrath), 6-171 (Gibson), 7-175 (Ross)

	O	M	R	W		O	M	R	W
Morris	7	1	21	1	Morris	11	4	15	1
Lester	11	2	33	1	Lester	13	4	36	2
Salisbury	14	2	49	1	MacQueen	23	2	101	4
Harris	6	2	23	0	Salisbury	5	4	4	0
MacQueen	26	4	79	3	Bush	3	0	34	0
Bush	11	2	45	1	Harris	5	0	16	0
Endersby	4	0	22	0					
Ackland	3	0	25	0					

First Innings	MCC UNIVERSITIES	Second Innings	
B J Ackland, c Hodgson b Hannon-Dalby	1	c Hodgson b Hannon-Dalby	49
N Patel, lbw b Hannon-Dalby	5	lbw b Hannon-Dalby	48
P Harris, b Cheetham	5	(8) b Randhawa	29
J A M Johnson, c Hodgson b Hannon-Dalby	1	(3) lbw b Cheetham	13
D M Endersby, lbw b McGrath	25	(4) lbw b Hannon-Dalby	4
H Bush, c Gibson b Cheetham	38	(5) b Hannon-Dalby	1
* L A Blackaby, c McGrath b Coad	0	(6) c Lees b Cheetham	10
§ D W Bell, c Hodgson b Hannon-Dalby	19	(7) b McGrath	15
A MacQueen, c Hodgson b McGrath	0	c Randhawa b McGrath	9
M E T Salisbury, c Ross b Cheetham	20	lbw b McGrath	4
C A J Morris, not out	5	not out	2
T Lester — Did not bat			
Extras b 4, lb 4, w 2	10	Extras b 13, lb 2, w 1, nb 2	18
Total (47.3 overs)	129	Total (77.2 overs)	202

FoW: 1st — 1-3 (Ackland), 2-8 (Harris), 3-14 (Johnson), 4-17 (Patel), 5-74 (Bush), 6-75 (Blackaby), 7-84 (Endersby), 8-84 (MacQueen), 9-103 (Bell), 10-129 (Salisbury)

FoW: 2nd — 1-90 (Ackland), 2-101 (Patel), 3-109 (Endersby), 4-111 (Bush), 5-139 (Johnson), 6-140 (Blackaby), 7-186 (Bell), 8-196 (MacQueen), 9-198 (Harris), 10-202 (Salisbury)

	O	M	R	W		O	M	R	W
Hannon-Dalby	14	10	21	4	Sidebottom	12	4	17	0
Cheetham	10.3	1	37	3	Hannon-Dalby	14	3	43	4
Sidebottom	9	0	36	0	Coad	7	1	24	0
Coad	6	2	13	1	Cheetham	14	2	34	2
McGrath	4	2	10	2	McGrath	11.2	3	25	3
Randhawa	4	1	4	0	Gibson	8	1	24	0
					Randhawa	11	6	20	1

Umpires: M A Eggleston and I Dixon — Scorers: K Hutchinson and H Clayton

Second Eleven Championship
Lancashire v. Yorkshire

Played at Centre Vale, Todmorden, on August 15, 16 and 17, 2012

Match drawn at 1.15pm on the First Day. There was no further play in the match

Toss won by Lancashire — Lancashire 3 points, Yorkshire 4 points

LANCASHIRE

S C Moore, b Cheetham	13
Usman Tariq, b Hannon-Dalby	9
L M Reece, not out	43
L N Bentley, c Hodgson b Shaw	19
J Clark, not out	26
* S D Parry	
O J Newby	
A M Lilley	
§ A Gowers — Did not bat	
N S Tahir	
G T Griffiths	
T E Bailey	
Extras lb 1	1
Total (3 wickets, 34 overs)	111

FoW: 1-17 (Usman Tariq); 2-23 (Moore); 3-80 (Bentley)

	O	M	R	W
Hannon-Dalby	6	3	11	1
Cheetham	7	2	19	1
Wardlaw	5	1	21	0
Lilley	5	1	20	0
Shaw	5	1	23	1
Randhawa	6	1	16	0

YORKSHIRE

A Z Lees
* J J Sayers
§ D M Hodgson
J A Leaning
G S Randhawa
W M H Rhodes
R Gibson
A E Lilley
I Wardlaw
J Shaw
S P Cheetham
O J Hannon-Dalby

Umpires: B V Taylor and K Fergusson — Scorers: D M White and H Clayton

Second Eleven Championship
Yorkshire v. Warwickshire

Played at Low Catton Road, Stamford Bridge, on August 22, 23 and 24, 2012

Match drawn at 2.27pm on the Second Day. There was no play on the Third Day

Toss won by Yorkshire — Yorkshire 8 points, Warwickshire 9 points

Close of play: First Day, Warwickshire 62-4 (Evans 42 *)

YORKSHIRE

A Z Lees, c Cornick b Miller	4
* J J Sayers, c P M Best b Miller	11
A McGrath, c Evans b Javid	83
J A Leaning, lbw b Allin	53
J A Tattersall, b Grundy	23
§ E Wilson, lbw b Gleeson	32
W H M Rhodes, not out	19
R Gibson, lbw b Gleeson	0
G S Randhawa, lbw b Javid	0
A E Lilley, c Cornick b Milnes	9
O J Hannon-Dalby, b Javid	2
S P Cheetham — Did not bat	
Extras b 9, lb 5, w 2, nb 12	28
Total (78.2 overs)	264

NOTE: Anthony McGrath retired injured on 24, with the score at 42-2 after 14.2 overs. He resumed his innings on the fall of Tattersall's wicket at 107-3.

FoW: 1-5 (Lees), 2-32 (Sayers), 3-107 (Tattersall), 4-159 (Leaning), 5-216 (Wilson), 6-230 (McGrath), 7-231 (Gibson), 8-236 (Randhawa), 9-256 (Lilley); 10-264 (Hannon-Dalby)

	O	M	R	W
Milnes	18	4	55	1
Miller	9	3	25	2
Gleeson	13	1	36	2
Allin	10	2	36	1
Grundy	9	4	18	1
P M Best	7	0	35	0
Javid	12.2	0	45	3

WARWICKSHIRE

J P Webb, lbw b Cheetham	8
L J Evans, not out	114
T R H Burton, c Lees b Lilley	1
T W Allin, c Sayers b Lilley	0
§ J P P Cornick, lbw b Lilley	3
* A Javid, c Tattersall b Randhawa	25
T P Milnes, lbw b Randhawa	10
P M Best, not out	39
M T Best	
A S Miller — Did not bat	
J O Grundy	
R J Gleeson	
Extras lb 11, w 1, nb 4	16
Total (6 wkts, 66 overs)	216

FoW: 1-17 (Webb), 2-32 (Burton), 3-32 (Allin), 4-62 (Cornick), 5-118 (Javid), 6-146 (Milnes)

	O	M	R	W
Hannon-Dalby	15	8	35	0
Cheetham	16	4	42	1
Lilley	10	2	39	3
Gibson	8	4	26	0
Randhawa	8	1	39	2
McGrath	7	2	20	0
Rhodes	2	1	4	0

Umpires: I Dawood and D Koch — Scorers: H Clayton and S Smith

SECOND ELEVEN CHAMPIONSHIP 2012

FINAL

Kent (355 and 225-9) beat Leicestershire (360 and 219) by one wicket

NORTHERN GROUP FINAL TABLE

		P	W	L	D	Tied	Aban.	Bonus Points Bat	Bonus Points Bowl	Pen.	Points
1	Leicestershire (2)	9	3	0	5	0	1	16	27	0	109
2	Durham (4)	9	2	0	7	0	0	19	24	0	96
3	Lancashire (3)	9	2	1	6	0	0	19	24	0	93
4	Northamptonshire (8)	9	1	0	7	0	1	20	22	0	82
5	Worcestershire (6)	9	1	1	5	0	2	16	23	0	76
6	MCC Universities (9)	9	1	4	4	0	0	17	30	0	75
7	Derbyshire (7)	9	1	2	5	0	1	14	22	-1	69
8	Warwickshire (1)	9	0	1	8	0	0	17	26	0	67
9	**Yorkshire (10)**	**9**	**1**	**2**	**4**	**0**	**2**	**15**	**17**	**0**	**66**
10	Nottinghamshire (5)	9	0	1	7	0	1	16	20	0	60

SOUTHERN GROUP FINAL TABLE

		P	W	L	D	Tied	Aban.	Bonus Points Bat	Bonus Points Bowl	Pen.	Points
1	Kent (9)	9	3	2	3	0	1	18	28	-1.5	104.5
2	Surrey (7)	9	3	2	3	0	1	17	28	-2	103
3	Glamorgan (1)	9	3	0	3	0	3	20	15	0	101
4	Middlesex (2)	9	3	2	3	0	1	14	25	0	99
5	Hampshire (4)	9	3	4	1	0	1	19	25	0	98
6	Essex (3)	9	2	0	5	0	2	19	20	0	92
7	Sussex (6)	9	2	2	3	0	2	17	21	-2	83
8	MCC YC (8)	9	1	2	3	0	3	18	14	-2.5	63.5
9	Somerset (5)	9	0	3	5	0	1	9	26	0	53
10	Gloucestershire (10)	9	0	3	3	0	3	15	17	0	50

(2011 group positions in brackets)

SECOND ELEVEN CHAMPIONS

(In the seasons in which Yorkshire have competed. The Championship has been split into two groups since 2009, the group winners playing off for the Championship. These groups were deemed North and South for the 2012 season.)

Season	*Champions*	*Yorkshire's Position*
1959	Gloucestershire	7th
1960	Northamptonshire	14th
1961	Kent	11th
1975	Surrey	4th
1976	Kent	5th
1977	**Yorkshire**	**1st**
1978	Sussex	5th
1979	Warwickshire	3rd
1980	Glamorgan	5th
1981	Hampshire	11th
1982	Worcestershire	14th
1983	Leicestershire	2nd
1984	**Yorkshire**	**1st**
1985	Nottinghamshire	12th
1986	Lancashire	5th
1987	**Yorkshire** and Kent	**1st**
1988	Surrey	9th
1989	Middlesex	9th
1990	Sussex	17th
1991	**Yorkshire**	**1st**
1992	Surrey	5th
1993	Middlesex	3rd
1994	Somerset	2nd
1995	Hampshire	5th
1996	Warwickshire	4th
1997	Lancashire	2nd
1998	Northamptonshire	9th
1999	Middlesex	14th
2000	Middlesex	5th
2001	Hampshire	2nd
2002	Kent	3rd
2003	**Yorkshire**	**1st**
2004	Somerset	8th
2005	Kent	10th
2006	Kent	3rd
2007	Sussex	10th
2008	Durham	5th
2009	Surrey	A 2nd
2010	Surrey	A 8th
2011	Warwickshire	A 10th
2012	Kent	North 9th

SECOND ELEVEN CHAMPIONSHIP
AVERAGES 2012

Played 9 Won 1 Lost 2 Drawn 4 Abandoned 2

BATTING AND FIELDING

(Qualification 5 innings)

Player	*M.*	*I.*	*N.O.*	*Runs*	*H.S.*	*Avge*	*100s*	*50s*	*ct/st*
A McGrath	4	5	1	373	200*	93.25	1	1	2
J A Leaning	8	7	1	263	71	43.33	0	3	1
D M Hodgson	8	8	1	206	61	29.28	0	2	10/0
A Z Lees	9	11	1	286	85	28.60	0	3	4
J J Sayers	9	11	0	178	47	18.18	0	0	1
E Wilson	8	9	0	146	32	16.22	0	0	0
A E Lilley	6	5	1	61	40	15.25	0	0	1
G S Randhawa	9	8	2	59	34	9.83	0	0	1
Also played									
A U Rashid	2	2	1	122	69*	122.00	0	2	0
W M H Rhodes	3	3	2	53	30*	53.00	0	0	0
R Gibson	3	3	0	106	88	35.33	0	1	1
J A Tattersall	1	1	0	23	23	23.00	0	0	1
G L Brophy	2	4	2	44	38	22.00	0	0	6/0
M Hussain	2	2	0	41	41	20.50	0	0	0
R M Pyrah	2	2	0	38	31	19.00	0	0	0
G S Ross	3	4	0	67	34	16.75	0	0	2
O J Hannon-Dalby	8	3	1	25	19*	12.50	0	0	1
S A Patterson	2	1	0	4	4	4.00	0	0	0
R J Sidebottom	1	2	2	79	55*	—	0	0	0
S P Cheetham	5	1	1	1	1*	—	0	0	0
B O Coad	2	1	1	1	1*	—	0	0	0
W T Root	1	0	0	0	0	—	0	0	0
D Evans	2	0	0	0	0	—	0	0	0
G P Whiles	3	0	0	0	0	—	0	0	1
I Wardlaw	3	0	0	0	0	—	0	0	2
J Shaw	1	0	0	0	0	—	0	0	0

BOWLING

(Qualification 10 wickets)

Player	*Overs*	*Mdns*	*Runs*	*Wkts*	*Avge*	*Best*	*5wI*	*10wM*
G S Randhawa	126.4	19	440	15	29.33	5-42	1	0
O J Hannon-Dalby	116	20	432	11	39.27	4-21	0	0
Also bowled								
S A Patterson	14	4	26	2	13.00	2-26	0	0
A McGrath	38.2	13	83	6	13.83	3-25	0	0
J Shaw	5	1	23	1	23.00	1-23	0	0
S P Cheetham	64.3	11	235	9	26.11	3-37	0	0
J A Leaning	7	1	30	1	30.00	1-30	0	0
D Evans	42	7	183	6	30.50	3-61	0	0
A U Rashid	54	7	201	6	33.50	3-77	0	0
A E Lilley	44	6	202	4	50.50	3-39	0	0
R M Pyrah	19	4	53	1	53.00	1-53	0	0
B O Coad	18	3	65	1	65.00	1-13	0	0
I Wardlaw	24	6	77	1	77.00	1-14	0	0
G P Whiles	32	3	165	1	165.00	1-52	0	0
W M H Rhodes	6	1	18	0	—	—	0	0
R Gibson	16	5	50	0	—	—	0	0
R J Sidebottom	21	4	53	0	—	—	0	0
G S Ross	12	0	72	0	—	—	0	0

Second Eleven Trophy
Yorkshire v. Leicestershire

At St George's Road, Harrogate, on April 24, 2012

Match abandoned without a ball bowled at 10am

No toss made — Yorkshire 1 point, Leicestershire 1 point

Umpires: N J Llong and D Koch — Scorers: H Clayton and P N Johnson

Yorkshire v. Durham

Played at Windy Hill Lane, Marske-by-the-Sea, on May 21, 2012

Durham won by 21 runs at 5.35pm

Toss won by Yorkshire — Durham 2 points; Yorkshire 0 points

DURHAM

B A Raine, c Lees b Hannon-Dalby	6
K K Jennings, c Hannon-Dalby b Pyrah	85
* G J Muchall, c and b Ashraf	1
§ M J Richardson, not out	109
R D Pringle, not out	43
G Clark	
R Singh	
M E Claydon — Did not bat	
P Coughlin	
M A Wood	
R M R Brathwaite	
Extras b 1, lb 3, w 2, nb 2)	8
Total (3 wkts, 40 overs)	252

FoW: 1-16 (Raine), 2-17 (Muchall), 3-166 (Jennings)

	O	M	R	W
Hannon-Dalby	8	2	26	1
Ashraf	7	0	51	1
Pyrah	8	1	43	1
Lilley	4	0	30	0
Rashid	7	0	38	0
Randhawa	6	0	60	0

YORKSHIRE

A Z Lees, lbw b Coughlin	20
* J J Sayers, lbw b Coughlin	26
E Wilson, c and b Jennings	33
A U Rashid, c Muchall b Claydon	45
R M Pyrah, c Claydon b Jennings	24
J A Leaning, b Claydon	26
§ D M Hodgson, c Muchall b Jennings	9
G S Randhawa, b Jennings	2
A E Lilley, b Claydon	4
M A Ashraf, b Raine	25
O J Hannon-Dalby, not out	4
Extras lb 3, w 10	13
Total (39.1 overs)	231

FoW: 1-43 (Lees), 2-57 (Sayers), 3-110 (Wilson), 4-146 (Pyrah), 5-166 (Rashid), 6-194 (Leaning), 7-196 (Hodgson), 8-196 (Randhawa), 9-204 (Lilley), 10-231 (Ashraf)

	O	M	R	W
Claydon	8	2	28	3
Brathwaite	8	0	62	0
Coughlin	8	2	41	2
Raine	8	0	47	1
Jennings	8	0	50	4

Umpires: R M Kettleborough and I A Ward — Scorers: H Clayton and R V Hilton

Second Eleven Trophy
Yorkshire v. Worcestershire

Played at Pudsey Congs CC on June 25, 2012

Worcestershire won by 33 runs at 5.24 pm. Match reduced to 34 overs per side

Toss won by Yorkshire — Worcestershire 2 points, Yorkshire 0 points

WORCESTERSHIRE

A N Kervezee, c Hodgson b Wardlaw	0
§ O B Cox, b Lilley	41
J K Manuel, b Paterson	5
* N D Pinner, run out	50
M G Pardoe, c Lees b Wardlaw	68
A Kapil, c Lees b Wardlaw	38
B L d'Oliveira not out	6
S H Choudhry, run out	2
R A Jones, not out	0
C J Russell	
N L Harrison Did not bat	
Extras b 5, lb 3, w 6	14
Total (7 wkts, 34 overs)	224

FoW: 1-0 (Kervezee), 2-17 (Manuel), 3-74 (Cox), 4-101 (Pinner), 5-207 (Kapil) 6-212 (Pardoe), 7-215 (Choudhry)

	O	M	R	W
Wardlaw	7	1	50	3
Patterson	7	2	27	1
Rashid	7	0	45	0
Lilley	7	0	36	1
Randhawa	2	0	28	0
Leaning	4	1	30	0

YORKSHIRE

A Lyth, c Kervezee b Russell	20
J J Sayers, st Cox b Pinner	49
* A Z Lees, st Cox b Choudhry	46
A U Rashid, run out	0
A E Lilley, c Cox b d'Oliveira	12
J A Leaning, c Harrison b Jones	20
E Wilson, c Kapil b Russell	0
§ D M Hodgson, not out	13
G S Randhawa, b Jones	14
I Wardlaw, b Russell	0
S A Patterson, not out	5
Extras b 2, lb 4, w 2, nb 4	12
Total (9 wkts, 34 overs)	191

FoW: 1-46 (Lyth), 2-95 (Sayers), 3-96 (Rashid), 4-111 (Lilley), 5-146 (Leaning) 6-146 (Wilson), 7-153 (Lees), 8-177 (Randhawa), 9-178 (Wardlaw)

	O	M	R	W
Harrison	4	1	16	0
Jones	7	0	36	2
Russell	7	0	44	3
Kapil	3	1	17	0
Pinner	4	0	28	1
d'Oliveira	6	0	30	1
S A Choudhry	3	0	14	1

Umpires: P K Baldwin and N Bagh — Scorers: H Clayton and P M Mellish

Second Eleven Trophy

Derbyshire v. Yorkshire

At Denby CC on July 2, 2012

Match abandoned without a ball bowled at 11.30am

No toss made — Derbyshire 1 point, Yorkshire 1 point

Umpires: M A Eggleston and A Payne — Scorers: T M Cottam and H Clayton

Nottinghamshire v. Yorkshire

At Worksop College on July 17, 2012

Match abandoned without a ball bowled at 11.55am

No toss made — Nottinghamshire 1 point, Yorkshire 1 point

Umpire: R J Evans and R J Warren — Scorers: Mrs A Cusworth and H Clayton

Northamptonshire v. Yorkshire

Played at Northampton on July 27, 2012

Yorkshire won by 108 runs at 5.13pm

Toss won by Yorkshire — Yorkshire 2 points, Northamptonshire 0 points

YORKSHIRE

A Z Lees, c Burton b Evans	24
* J J Sayers, run out	55
R Gibson, b Keogh	7
§ G L Brophy, c and b Beaven	69
J A Leaning, c Keogh b Beaven	2
D M Hodgson, lbw b Sohal	2
I Wardlaw, b Beaven	2
E Wilson, c O'Brien b Sweeney	16
G S Randhawa, c Howgego b Burton	22
A E Lilley, not out	8
O J Hannon-Dalby, not out	0
Extras b 4, lb 10, w 8, nb 4	26
Total (9 wkts, 40 overs)	233

FoW: 1-28 (Lees), 2-41 (Gibson), 3-167 (Brophy), 4-171 (Leaning), 5-177 (Hodgson) 6-179 (Sayers), 7-179 (Wardlaw), 8-218 (Randhawa), 9-231 (Wilson)

	O	M	R	W
Evans	4	0	27	1
Keogh	8	0	30	1
Sweeney	8	0	52	1
Sohal	7	0	40	1
Beaven	8	0	37	3
Burton	5	0	33	1

NORTHAMPTONSHIRE

B H N Howgego, b Lilley	17
R I Newton, c Leaning b Lilley	15
R I Keogh, b Sayers	27
* § N J O'Brien b Sayers	12
A Patel, c Lees b Sayers	2
J M Kettleborough, lbw b Sayers	1
V V S Sohal, run out	1
L C Beaven, lbw b Wardlaw	18
S A Sweeney, st Brophy b Sayers	0
D A Burton, not out	10
L Evans, c Randhawa b Gibson	2
Extras lb 5, w 11; nb 4	20
Total (34.2 overs)	125

FoW: 1-31 (Newton), 2-37 (Howgego), 3-66 (O'Brien), 4-74 (Patel), 5-78 (Kettleborough) 6-82 (Sohal), 7-92 (Keogh), 8-94 (Sweeney), 9-109 (Beaven), 10-125 (Evans)

	O	M	R	W
Wardlaw	6	1	34	1
Hannon-Dalby	6	1	14	0
Lilley	5	0	20	2
Sayers	7	0	27	5
Randhawa	8	1	20	0
Gibson	2.2	0	5	1

Umpires: B V Taylor and C Jones — Scorers: M E Woolley and H Clayton

Second Eleven Trophy
Yorkshire v. Unicorns A

Played at Sheffield Collegiate on August 10, 2012

Yorkshire won by nine wickets at 2.31pm

Toss won by Unicorns A — Yorkshire 2 points, Unicorns A 0 points

UNICORNS A

V Tripathi, c Hodgson b Cheetham	1
B L Wadlan, b Hannon-Dalby	0
A S T West, c Sayers b Hannon-Dalby	13
J E Ord, c Sayers b Hannon-Dalby	2
J R Levitt, c Hodgson b Hannon-Dalby	0
* S M Park, c and b Randhawa	10
A Reynoldson, c Randhawa b Lilley	0
§ M W Thompson, c Cheetham b Gibson	14
D T Reed, c Wilson b Gibson	5
C Brown, c Sayers b Randhawa	0
A J Syddall, not out	0
Extras lb 1, w 6	7
Total (24.4 overs)	52

FoW: 1-1 (Wadlan), 2-1 (Tripathi), 3-18 (Ord), 4-18 (Levitt), 5-28 (West) 6-30 (Reynoldson), 7-34 (Park), 8-51 (Reed), 9-52 (Thompson), 10-52 (Brown)

	O	M	R	W
Hannon-Dalby	6	0	10	4
Cheetham	5	1	19	1
Lilley	4.3	1	8	1
Randhawa	6.4	0	11	2
Sayers	0.3	0	3	0
Gibson	2	2	0	2

YORKSHIRE

A Z Lees, c Park b Wadlan	27
* J J Sayers, not out	13
E Wilson, not out	8
§ D M Hodgson	
J A Leaning	
R Gibson	
G S Ross — Did not bat	
G S Randhawa	
A E Lilley	
S P Cheetham	
O J Hannon-Dalby	
Extras lb 3, w 2	5
Total (1 wkt, 11.4 overs)	53

FoW: 1-39 (Lees)

	O	M	R	W
Syddall	3	1	13	0
Reed	3	0	16	0
Brown	3	1	8	0
Wadlan	2	0	12	1
Ord	0.2	0	1	0

Umpires: G D Lloyd and I Dixon — Scorers: H Clayton and K O'Donnell

Second Eleven Trophy
Lancashire v. Yorkshire

Played at Centre Vale, Todmorden, on August 14, 2012

Lancashire won by 5 wickets at 4.25pm

Toss won by Lancashire — Lancashire 2 points, Yorkshire 0 points

YORKSHIRE

A Z Lees, c Clark b Griffiths	17
* J J Sayers, c Gowers b Griffiths	8
§ D M Hodgson, b Mahmood	15
J A Leaning, b Parry	7
G S Randhawa, run out	1
W M H Rhodes, c Reece b Proctor	39
R Gibson, b Mahmood	2
A E Lilley, run out	19
I Wardlaw, not out	7
S P Cheetham, c Reece b Newby	3
O J Hannon-Dalby run out	0
Extras b 2, lb 1, w 12, nb 8	23
Total (37.3 overs)	141

FoW: 1-25 (Lees), 2-42 (Sayers), 3-46 (Hodgson), 4-49 (Randhawa), 5-64 (Leaning), 6-71 (Gibson), 7-128 (Lilley), 8-132 (Rhodes), 9-138 (Cheetham), 10-141 (Hannon-Dalby)

	O	M	R	W
Newby	7	0	29	1
Griffiths	6	2	17	2
Parry	8	1	22	1
Mahmood	6.3	2	13	2
Proctor	6	0	32	1
Lilley	4	0	25	0

LANCASHIRE

L N Bentley, c Gibson b Wardlaw	50
L A Proctor, c Wardlaw b Lilley	42
L M Reece, lbw b Lilley	11
J Clark, not out	13
* S D Parry, st Hodgson b Randhawa	5
L S livingstone, lbw b Randhawa	4
O J Newby, not out	10
A M Lilley	
S A Mahmood — Did not bat	
§ A Gowers	
G T Griffiths	
Extras lb 1, w 5, nb 2	8
Total (5 wkts, 23.2 overs)	143

FoW: 1-84 (Bentley), 2-107 (Reece), 3-110 (Proctor), 4-122 (Parry), 5-126 (Livingstone)

	O	M	R	W
Hannon-Dalby	5	0	32	0
Cheetham	3	0	17	0
Wardlaw	3	0	37	1
Randhawa	7	0	39	2
Lilley	5.2	0	17	2

Umpires: B V Taylor and D Warburton — Scorers: D M White and H Clayton

Second Eleven Trophy
Yorkshire v. Warwickshire

Played at Weetwood, Leeds, on August 21, 2012

Warwichsire won by 56 runs (D/L Method) at 4.05 pm

Toss won by Warwickshire — Warwickshire 2 points, Yorkshire 0 points

YORKSHIRE

A Z Lees, c McKay b Grundy	7
* J J Sayers, c Evans b Burton	11
R Gibson, lbw b Grundy	0
J A Leaning, lbw b Grundy	6
§ E Wilson, c Burton b Grundy	6
W M H Rhodes, lbw b Grundy	11
G S Randhawa, not out	30
A E Lilley, b P M Best	0
J Shaw, b P M Best	7
S P Cheetham, run out	4
O J Hannon-Dalby, not out	15
Extras lb 4, w 12, nb 6)	22
Total (9 wkts, 40 overs)	125

FoW: 1-27 (Lees), 2-27 (Gibson), 3- 33 (Sayers), 4-33 (Leaning), 5-56 (Wilson), 6-65 (Rhodes), 7-74 (Lilley), 8-78 (Shaw), 9-85 (Cheetham)

	O	M	R	W
Miller	6	2	13	0
Allin	7	0	25	0
Grundy	8	2	17	5
Burton	5	1	21	1
Javid	8	2	21	0
P M Best	6	1	24	2

WARWICKSHIRE

J P Webb, c Gibson b Shaw	52
L J Evans, not out	37
J P P Cornick, not out	0
T R H Burton	
* A Javid	
M T Best	
P M Best	Did not bat
§ P J McKay	
A S Miller	
J O Grundy	
T W Allin	
Extras	0
Total (1 wkt, 14.3 overs)	89

FoW: 1-85 (Webb)

	O	M	R	W
Hannon-Dalby	6	0	35	0
Cheetham	3	0	24	0
Lilley	2	0	18	0
Shaw	2	1	4	1
Gibson	1.3	0	8	0

Umpires: I Dawood and D Koch — Scorers: H Clayton and S Smith

SECOND ELEVEN TROPHY 2012

NORTHERN GROUP – FINAL TABLE *(2011 in brackets)*

		P	W	L	Tie	No result	Aban.	Net run rate	Points
1	Durham (3)	9	6	2	0	0	1	0.840	13
2	Lancashire (2)	9	5	1	0	0	3	0.876	13
3	Worcestershire (5)	9	4	2	0	0	3	0.205	11
4	Warwickshire (8)	9	4	3	0	1	1	0.326	10
5	Leicestershire (4)	9	3	2	0	1	3	0.196	10
6	Yorkshire (6)	9	2	4	0	0	3	0.291	7
7	Nottinghamshire (1)	9	1	3	0	1	4	1.680	7
8	Derbyshire (9)	9	1	3	0	0	5	-0.153	7
9	Northamptonshire (10)	9	1	3	0	1	4	-1.792	7
10	Unicorns A (7)	9	2	6	0	0	1	-1.942	5

SOUTHERN GROUP – FINAL TABLE *(2011 in brackets)*

		P	W	L	Tie	No result	Aban.	Net run rate	Points
1	Middlesex (4)	9	6	0	0	0	3	1.222	15
2	Sussex (5)	9	4	2	0	1	2	1.096	11
3	Essex (9)	9	4	2	0	2	1	-0.210	11
4	Surrey (7)	9	3	2	0	0	4	0.270	10
5	Glamorgan (2)	9	3	3	0	1	2	0.423	9
6	Gloucestershire (10)	9	2	3	0	2	2	0.711	8
7	Somerset (1)	9	2	3	0	1	3	-1.673	8
8	Kent (3)	9	3	5	0	0	1	-0.854	7
9	MCC YC (8)	9	1	4	0	0	4	0.098	6
10	Hampshire (6)	9	1	5	0	1	2	-0.704	5

SEMI-FINALS

Durham (125-6) beat Sussex (122) by 4 wickets.
Lancashire (206-7) beat Middlesex (192) by 14 runs

FINAL

Lancashire (190) beat Durham (114) by 76 runs

PREVIOUS WINNERS

1986 **Northamptonshire**, who beat Essex by 14 runs
1987 **Derbyshire**, who beat Hampshire by 7 wickets
1988 **Yorkshire**, who beat Kent by 7 wickets
1989 **Middlesex**, who beat Kent by 6 wickets
1990 **Lancashire**, who beat Somerset by 8 wickets
1991 **Nottinghamshire**, who beat Surrey by 8 wickets
1992 **Surrey**, who beat Northamptonshire by 8 wickets
1993 **Leicestershire**, who beat Sussex by 142 runs
1994 **Yorkshire**, who beat Leicestershire by 6 wickets
1995 **Leicestershire**, who beat Gloucestershire by 3 runs
1996 **Leicestershire**, who beat Durham by 46 runs
1997 **Surrey**, who beat Gloucestershire by 3 wickets
1998 **Northamptonshire**, who beat Derbyshire by 5 wickets
1999 **Kent**, who beat Hampshire by 106 runs.
2000 **Leicestershire,** who beat Hampshire by 25 runs.
2001 **Surrey**, who beat Somerset by 6 wickets
2002 **Kent**, who beat Hampshire by 5 wickets
2003 **Hampshire**, who beat Warwickshire by 8 wickets
2004 **Worcestershire**, who beat Essex by 8 wickets
2005 **Sussex**, who beat Nottinghamshire by 6 wickets
2006 **Warwickshire**, who beat Yorkshire by 93 runs
2007 **Middlesex**, who beat Somerset by 1 run
2008 **Hampshire**, who beat Essex by 7 runs
2009 **Yorkshire,** who beat Lancashire by 2 wickets
2010 **Essex**, who beat Lancashire by 14 runs
2011 **Nottinghamshire**, who beat Lancashire by 4 wickets

SECOND ELEVEN TROPHY AVERAGES 2012

Played 9 Won 2 Lost 4 Abandoned 3

BATTING AND FIELDING

(Qualification 3 innings)

Player	*M.*	*I.*	*N.O.*	*Runs*	*H.S.*	*Avge*	*100s*	*50s*	*ct/st*
J J Sayers	9	6	1	162	55	32.40	0	1	3
A Z Lees	9	6	0	141	46	23.50	0	0	4
O J Hannon-Dalby	8	4	3	19	15*	19.00	0	0	1
G S Randhawa	9	5	1	69	30*	17.25	0	0	4
E Wilson	8	5	1	63	33	15.75	0	0	1
D M Hodgson	8	4	1	39	15	13.00	0	0	3/1
A E Lilley	8	5	1	50	19	12.50	0	0	0
J A Leaning	9	5	0	61	26	12.20	0	0	1
I Wardlaw	5	3	1	9	7*	4.50	0	0	0
R Gibson	4	3	0	9	7	3.00	0	0	1
Also played									
G L Brophy	2	1	0	69	69	69.00	0	1	0/1
W M H Rhodes	3	2	0	50	39	25.00	0	0	0
M A Ashraf	1	1	0	25	25	25.00	0	0	1
R M Pyrah	2	1	0	24	24	24.00	0	0	0
A U Rashid	3	2	0	45	45	22.50	0	0	0
A Lyth	1	1	0	20	20	20.00	0	0	0
S P Cheetham	3	2	0	9	6	4.50	0	0	1
J Shaw	1	1	0	4	4	4.00	0	0	0
S A Patterson	2	1	1	5	5*	—	0	0	0
A McGrath	1	0	0	0	0	—	0	0	0
W T Root	1	0	0	0	0	—	0	0	0
D Evans	1	0	0	0	0	—	0	0	0
G S Ross	2	0	0	0	0	—	0	0	0
M Hussain	1	0	0	0	0	—	0	0	0

BOWLING

(Qualification 5 wickets)

Player	*Overs*	*Mdns*	*Runs*	*Wkts*	*Avge*	*Best*	*4wI*
J J Sayers	7.3	0	30	5	6.00	5-27	1
A E Lilley	28.2	1	129	6	21.50	2-17	0
O J Hannon-Dalby	31	3	117	5	23.40	4-10	1
I Wardlaw	16	2	121	5	24.20	3-50	0
Also bowled							
J Shaw	2	1	4	1	4.00	1-4	0
R Gibson	5.5	2	13	3	4.33	2-0	0
S A Patterson	7	2	27	1	27.00	2-11	0
G S Randhawa	29.4	1	158	4	39.50	1-27	0
R M Pyrah	8	1	43	1	43.00	1-43	0
M A Ashraf	7	0	51	1	51.00	1-51	0
S P Cheetham	11	1	60	1	60.00	1-19	0
A U Rashid	14	0	83	0	—	—	0
J A Leaning	4	1	30	0	—	—	0

Second Eleven Twenty20
Yorkshire v. England Under-19s

Played at Bradford and Bingley CC on Tuesday, May 29, 2012

England Under-19s won by 7 wickets at 1.45pm

Toss won by England Under-19s — England Under-19s 2 points, Yorkshire 0 points

YORKSHIRE

A Z Lees, c Davies b Griffiths	23
J J Sayers, c Collins b Knight	2
E Wilson, b Knight	2
* A U Rashid, c Abid b Hutton	21
G S Ross, c Davies b Griffiths	3
§ D M Hodgson, run out	4
G S Randhawa, c and b Hutton	4
A E Lilley, not out	31
L R Stabler, st Davies b Hutton	5
O J Hannon-Dalby, not out	1
B O Coad — Did not bat	
Extras lb 4, w 3	7
Total (8 wkts, 20 overs)	103

FoW: 1-3 (Sayers), 2-12 (Wilson), 3-43 (Lees), 4-51 (Ross), 5-58 (Hodgson), 6-61 (Rashid), 7-71 (Randhawa), 8-92 (Stabler)

	O	M	R	W
Knight	4	1	12	2
Helm	3	0	19	0
Griffiths	3	1	18	2
Collins	4	0	20	0
Hutton	4	0	22	3
Abid	2	0	8	0

ENGLAND UNDER-19s

T C Rowe, c Sayers b Lilley	11
§ A L Davies, not out	38
J A Leaning, c Hodgson b Lilley	2
R Singh, c Hodgson b Hannon-Dalby	18
S K W Wood, not out	29
* B A Hutton	
T C Knight	
G T Griffiths — Did not bat	
T G Helm	
B F Collins	
Mohamed Abid	
Extras lb 6, w 2	8
Total (3 wkts, 14 overs)	106

FoW: 1-17 (Rowe), 2-19 (Leaning), 3-44 (Singh)

	O	M	R	W
Hannon-Dalby	3	0	26	1
Lilley	2	0	22	2
Ross	2	0	10	0
Randhawa	4	0	25	0
Rashid	3	0	17	0

Umpires: S C Gale and D Koch — Scorers: H Clayton and H D Galley

Second Eleven Twenty20
Yorkshire v. England Under-19s

Played at Bradford and Bingley CC on Tuesday, May 29, 2012

England Under-19s won by 5 wickets at 5.43pm

Toss won by Yorkshire — England Under-19s 2 points, Yorkshire 0 points

YORKSHIRE

A Z Lees, c Collins b Griffiths	10
J J Sayers, b Abid	21
R M Pyrah, c Helm b Abid	21
A U Rashid, c Rowe b Griffiths	49
§ E Wilson, lbw b Knight	5
D M Hodgson, run out	7
A E Lilley, not out	14
* G S Randhawa, c Wood b Helm	8
M A Ashraf, run out	4
L R Stabler, not out	1
O J Hannon-Dalby — Did not bat	
Extras w 1	1
Total (8 wkts, 20 overs)	141

FoW: 1-28 (Lees), 2-31 (Sayers), 3-86 (Pyrah), 4-107 (Wilson), 5-113 (Rashid), 6-115 (Hodgson), 7-131 (Randhawa), 8-138 (Ashraf)

	O	M	R	W
Abid	4	0	24	2
Helm	3	0	25	1
Griffiths	4	0	24	2
Hutton	2	0	13	0
Knight	4	0	32	1
Collins	3	0	23	0

ENGLAND UNDER-19s

T C Rowe, lbw b Rashid	32
§ A L Davies, b Randhawa	54
J A Leaning, b Rashid	1
R Singh, c Ashraf b Rashid	2
S K W Wood, b Ashraf	25
* B A Hutton, not out	19
T G Helm, not out	0
T C Knight G T Griffiths B F Collins Mohamnmed Abid — Did not bat	
Extras lb 4, w 6, nb 2	12
Total (5 wkts, 19 overs)	145

FoW: 1-93 (Rowe), 2-95 (Davies), 3-97 (Leaning), 4-104 (Singh), 5-135 (Wood)

	O	M	R	W
Hannon-Dalby	2	0	23	0
Ashraf	3	0	18	1
Pyrah	3	0	30	0
Lilley	2	0	30	0
Randhawa	4	0	15	1
Rashid	4	0	16	3
Stabler	1	0	9	0

Umpires: S C Gale and D Koch — Scorers: H Clayton and H D Galley

Second Eleven Twenty20

Yorkshire v. Derbyshire

At Bradford and Bingley CC on Thursday, May 31, 2012

Matches 1 and 2 abandoned witout a ball bowled at 10.30am and 2.05pm

No toss made — Yorkshire 1 point, Derbyshire 1 point for each fixture

Umpires: M Burns and G Baxter — Scorers: H Clayton and T M Cottam

Lancashire v. Yorkshire

Played at Ormskirk CC on June 6, 2012

Lancashire won by 45 runs at 2.04 pm

Toss won by Yorkshire — Lancashire 2 points, Yorkshire 0 points

LANCASHIRE

* A P Agathangelou, c Hussain b Shaw	25
T C Smith, c Wilson b Lilley	35
N L Bentley, c Wilson b Pyrah	1
J Clark, c Hannon-Dalby b Lilley	10
§ A L Davies, lbw b Randhawa	17
O J Newby, st Wilson b Randhawa	6
S D Parry, not out	23
L S Livingstone, b Pyrah	1
A R Lilley, c Lees b Hannon-Dalby	4
N A Tahir, run out	0
G T Griffiths, not out	7
Extras w 3, nb 2	5
Total (9 wkts, 20 overs)	134

FoW: 1-34 (Agathangelou), 2-36 (Bentley), 3-75 (Smith), 4-77 (Clark), 5-99 (Newby), 6-102 (Davies), 7-103 (Livingstone), 8-112 (Lilley), 9-113 (Tahir)

	O	M	R	W
Hannon-Dalby	4	0	22	1
Wardlaw	4	0	39	0
Shaw	3	0	14	1
Pyrah	4	1	26	2
Randhawa	3	0	15	2
Lilley	2	0	18	2

YORKSHIRE

A Z Lees, c Davies b Tahir	1
J J Sayers, c Bentley b Newby	0
R M Pyrah, c Parry b Newby	7
G S Randhawa, c Clark b Tahir	5
J A Leaning, c Newby b Griffiths	9
I Wardlaw, c Lilley b Griffiths	28
§ E Wilson, c Lilley b Griffiths	10
M Hussain, st Davies b Parry	14
* A E Lilley, lbw b Parry	0
J Shaw, not out	8
O J Hannon-Dalby, lbw b Lilley	2
Extras b1, lb 1, w 1, nb 2	5
Total (15.4 overs)	89

FoW: 1-3 (Sayers), 2-4 (Lees), 3-14 (Pyrah), 4-20 (Randhawa), 5-24 (Leaning), 6-40(Wilson), 7-65 (Hussain), 8-65 (Lilley), 9-83 (Wardlaw), 10-89 (Hannon-Dalby)

	O	M	R	W
Newby	2	0	15	2
Tahir	3	1	8	2
Griffiths	4	0	34	3
Parry	4	0	21	2
Lilley	2	0	8	1

Umpires: A G Wharf and G Baxter — Scorers: C Rimmer and H Clayton

Second Eleven Twenty20

Lancashire v. Yorkshire

Played at Ormskirk CC on June 6, 2012

Lancashire won by 6 wickets (D/L Method) at 4.41pm. D/L target was 73 off eight overs

Toss won by Yorkshire — Lancashire 2 points, Yorkshire 0 points

YORKSHIRE

A Z Lees, lbw b Lilley	50
A E Lilley, c Davies b Tahir	20
R M Pyrah, run out	9
G S Randhawa, b Parry	4
J A Leaning, c Parry b Newby	25
I Wardlaw, run out	1
§ E Wilson not out	0
M Hussain	
M A Ashraf — Did not bat	
J Shaw	
* O J Hannon-Dalby	
Extras b 4, lb 1, w 11	16
Total (6 wkts, 17 overs)	125

FoW: 1-46 (Lilley), 2-63 (Pyrah), 3-70 (Randhawa), 4-109 (Lees), 5-116 (Wardlaw), 6-125 (Leaning)

	O	M	R	W
Newby	3	0	21	1
Tahir	3	0	24	1
Griffiths	4	0	30	0
Parry	4	0	24	1
Lilley	3	0	21	1

LANCASHIRE

A P Agathangelou, c Wilson b Hannon-Dalby	0
T C Smith, c Lees b Pyrah	13
J Clark, c Leaning b Wardlaw	18
L N Bentley, c and b Pyrah	4
§ A L Davies, not out	24
* O J Newby, not out	15
S D Parry	
L S Livingstone	
A R Lilley — Did not bat	
N A Tahir	
G T Griffiths	
Extras b1, lb 1, w 1	3
Total (4 wkts, 7.2 overs)	77

FoW: 1-0 (Agathangelou), 2-20 (Clark), 3-38 (Smith), 4-38 (Bentley)

	O	M	R	W
Hannon-Dalby	1	0	10	1
Wardlaw	1.2	0	22	1
Ashraf	2	0	19	0
Pyrah	2	0	16	2
Lilley	1	0	8	0

Umpires: A G Wharf and G Baxter — Scorers: C Rimmer and H Clayton

Nottinghamshire v. Yorkshire

At Nottinghamshire Sports Ground, West Bridgford, on June 8, 2012

Matches 1 and 2 abandoned without a ball bowled at 10.30am

No toss made — Nottinghamshire 1 point, Yorkshire 1 point for each fixture

Umpires: G Sharp and W B Jones — Scorers: Mrs A Cusworth and H Clayton

SECOND ELEVEN TWENTY20 2012

(Two matches played against the same opponents at the same venue on the same day)

GROUP A – FINAL TABLE

		P	W	L	Tie	No result	Aban.	Net run rate	Points
1	England Under-19 (—)	8	6	2	0	0	0	0.564	12
2	Lancashire (3)	8	4	3	1	0	0	-0.019	9
3	Durham (1)	8	4	4	0	0	0	0.470	8
4	Derbyshire (2)	8	3	3	0	0	2	-0.121	8
5	Nottinghamshire (4)	8	2	3	1	0	2	-0.234	7
6	**Yorkshire (5)**	**8**	**0**	**4**	**0**	**0**	**4**	**-1.702**	**4**

GROUP B – FINAL TABLE

		P	W	L	Tie	No result	Aban.	Net run rate	Points
1	Worcestershire (3)	8	3	2	0	0	3	0.674	9
2	Somerset (4)	8	4	4	0	0	0	1.016	8
3	Glamorgan (2)	8	3	3	0	0	2	-0.407	8
4	Gloucestershire (1)	8	3	3	0	0	2	-0.546	8
5	Warwickshire (5)	8	2	3	0	0	3	-1.205	7

GROUP C – FINAL TABLE

		P	W	L	Tie	No result	Aban.	Net run rate	Points
1	Essex (5)	8	4	0	1	0	4	2.924	12
2	Middlesex (2)	8	3	1	0	0	4	0.949	10
3	Unicorns A (4)	8	3	3	0	0	2	-0.612	8
4	Northamptonshire (3)	8	3	5	0	0	0	-0.569	6
5	Leicestershire (1)	8	1	5	0	0	2	-1.040	4

GROUP D – FINAL TABLE

		P	W	L	Tie	No result	Aban.	Net run rate	Points
1	Sussex (1)	8	6	0	0	0	2	1.904	14
2	Kent (3)	8	3	3	0	0	2	0.193	8
3	Surrey (5)	8	3	3	0	0	2	-0.927	8
4	Hampshire (2)	8	3	5	0	0	0	0.333	6
5	MCC YC (4)	8	1	5	0	0	2	-1.644	4

(2011 positions in brackets)

SEMI-FINALS

England Under-19s (123-6) beat Worcestershire (122-8) by 4 wickets

Sussex (166-6) beat Essex (107-8) by 59 runs.

FINAL

England Under-19s (159-2) beat Sussex (156-6) by 8 wickets

PREVIOUS WINNERS

2011 **Sussex**, who beat Durham by 24 runs

SECOND ELEVEN TWENTY20 AVERAGES 2012

Played 8 Won 0 Lost 4 Abandoned 4

BATTING AND FIELDING

(Qualification 3 innings)

Player	*M.*	*I.*	*N.O.*	*Runs*	*H.S.*	*Avge*	*100s*	*50s*	*ct/st*
A E Lilley	8	4	2	65	31*	32.50	0	0	0
A Z Lees	8	4	0	84	50	21.00	0	1	2
R M Pyrah	7	3	0	37	21	12.33	0	0	1
J J Sayers	5	3	0	23	21	7.00	0	0	1
E Wilson	8	4	1	17	10	5.66	0	0	3/1
G S Randhawa	8	4	0	21	8	5.25	0	0	0
Also played									
A U Rashid	4	2	0	70	49	35.00	0	0	0
J A Leaning	4	2	0	34	25	17.00	0	0	0
I Wardlaw	4	2	0	29	28	14.50	0	0	0
M Hussain	2	1	0	14	14	14.00	0	0	0
L R Stabler	2	2	1	6	5	6.00	0	0	0
D M Hodgson	6	2	0	11	7	5.50	0	0	0
M A Ashraf	6	1	0	4	4	4.00	0	0	0
O J Hannon-Dalby	8	2	1	3	2	3.00	0	0	0
G S Ross	3	1	0	3	3	3.00	0	0	0
J Shaw	6	1	1	8	8*	—	0	0	0
G L Brophy	2	0	0	0	0	—	0	0	0
B O Coad	1	0	0	0	0	—	0	0	0

BOWLING

(Qualification 5 wickets)

There were no qualifiers in 2012

Player	*Overs*	*Mdns*	*Runs*	*Wkts*	*Avge*	*Best*	*4wI*
A U Rashid	7	0	33	3	11.00	3-16	0
J Shaw	3	0	14	1	14.00	1-14	0
R M Pyrah	9	1	72	4	18.00	2-16	0
G S Randhawa	11	0	55	3	18.33	2-15	0
A E Lilley	7	0	78	4	19.50	2-18	0
O J Hannon-Dalby	10	0	81	3	27.00	1-10	0
M A Ashraf	5	0	37	1	37.00	1-18	0
I Wardlaw	5.2	0	61	1	61.00	1-22	0
G S Ross	2	0	10	0	—	—	0
L R Stabler	1	0	9	0	—	—	0

Other Second Eleven Match
Yorkshire v. Durham

Played at Marton Cricket Club, Middlesbrough, on April 11,12 and 13, 2012

Match drawn at 6pm on the Third Day

Toss won by Durham

Close of play: First Day, no play; Second Day, no play

YORKSHIRE

*A Z Lees, c Richardson b Plunkett	15
C J Geldart, c Richardson b Rushworth	9
J A Tattersall, c Raine b Rushworth	5
G S Ross, c Coughlin b Plunkett	5
D L Girling, c Richardson b Harrison	27
§ E Wilson, b Harrison	21
A E Lilley, lbw b Arshad	1
W I Rhodes, not out	9
G S Randhawa, b Coughlin	6
M A Ashraf, c Rushworth b Coughlin	0
B O Coad, not out	0
Extras (nb 10, w 6, lb 4)	20
Total (9 wkts dec, 52 overs)	118

FoW: 1-25 (Geldart), 2-38 (Tattersall), 3-40 (Lees), 4-53 (Ross), 5-97 (Wilson), 6-98 (Girling), 7-98 (Lilley), 8-117 (Randhawa), 9-118 (Ashraf)

	O	M	R	W
Rushworth	12	3	37	2
Plunkett	11	4	31	2
Harmison	6	2	11	0
Harrison	10	0	22	2
Arshad	7	4	8	1
Coughlin	5	4	4	2
Raine	1	0	1	0

DURHAM

B A Raine, c Tattersall b Geldart	31
K K Jennings, not out	43
G Clark, not out	40
P Coughlin	
§ M J Richardson	
U Arshad	
L E Plunkett Did not bat	
* C Rushworth	
R B Buckley	
J Harrison	
S J Harmison	
Extras (nb 6, lb 2)	8
Total (1 wkt, 35 overs)	122

Twelfth man: R D Pringle

FoW: 1-59 (Raine)

	O	M	R	W
Ashraf	9	2	37	0
Lilley	4	1	12	0
Rhodes	5	2	6	0
Girling	4	1	19	0
Coad	5	2	13	0
Geldart	2	0	6	1
Randhawa	6	0	27	0

Umpires: P.R.Pollard and P.Brown   Scorers: R.V.Hilton and H.Clayton

Other Second Eleven Match
Yorkshire v. Lancashire

Played at Headingley Carnegie, Leeds, on May 2, 2012

Match abandoned at 4.02 pm

Toss won by Yorkshire

LANCASHIRE

§ A.L.Davies, c Brophy b Ashraf	11
L.N.Bentley, c McGrath b Hannon-Dalby	3
A.P.Agathangelou, run out	39
J.Clark, b McGrath	16
*S.D.Parry, run out	1
L.S.Livingstone, not out	6
A.R.Lilley, not out	0
N.S.Tahir	
R.G.Querl — Did not bat	
C.Connolly	
G.A.Griffiths	
Extras (lb 4, w 5)	9
Total (5 wkts, 23 overs)	85

Twelfth man: H.Thompson

FoW: 1-7 (Bentley), 2-19 (Davies), 3-67 (Clark), 4-74 (Parry), 5-74 (Agathangelou)

	O	M	R	W
Hannon-Dalby	4	0	21	1
Ashraf	4	0	13	1
McGrath	8	2	23	1
Wardlaw	5	1	20	0
Azeem Rafiq	2	0	4	0

YORKSHIRE

A Z Lees
A Lyth
A McGrath
C J Geldart
§ G L Brophy
*Azeem Rafiq — Did not bat
G S Randhawa
I Wardlaw
O J Hannon-Dalby
M A Ashraf
A E Lilley

Twelfth man: J A Leaning

Umpires: A G Wharf and H Evans — Scorers: H Clayton and D M White

Other Second Eleven Match
Lancashire v. Yorkshire

Played at St Anne's CC on May 2, 3 and 4, May 2012

Lancashire won by 3 wkts at 6.21pm on the Third Day

Toss won by Lancashire

Close of play: First Day, Lancashire 32-0 (Agathangelou 20*, Thompson 12*); Second Day, Yorkshire Second Innings 169-2 (Lyth 80*, Rafiq 54*)

YORKSHIRE First Innings		Second Innings	
A Lyth, c Livingstone b Tahir	0	c Davies b Tahir	80
A Z Lees, st Davies b Parry	100	b Querl	0
C.J.Geldart, c Parry b Lilley	15	c Davies b Tahir	21
*Azeem Rafiq, c.Agathangelou b Querl	35	lbw b Querl	85
J.A.Leaning, c Livingstone b Tahir	4	c Davies b Querl	20
§ E.Wilson, lbw b Querl	25	b Agathangelou	14
A.E.Lilley, c Davies b Tahir	30	c Davies b Clark	50
G.S.Randhawa, not out	32	not out	7
M.A.Ashraf, not out	18		
O J Hannon-Dalby			
I.Wardlaw Did not bat			
Extras (b 8, lb 6, w 2, nb 2)	18	Extras (b 5, lb 6, w 5, nb 6)	22
Total (7 wkts dec, 90 overs)	277	Total (7 wkts dec, 70 overs)	299

FoW: 1st 1-0 (Lyth), 2-37 (Geldart), 3-86 (Rafiq), 4-99 (Leaning), 5-177 (Wilson), 6-216 (Lees), 7-234 (Lilley)

FoW: 2nd 1-2 (Lees), 2-43 (Geldart), 3-172 (Lyth), 4-220 (Leaning), 5-223 (Rafiq), 6-261 (Wilson), 7-299 (Lilley)

	O	M	R	W		O	M	R	W
Tahir	20	9	40	3	Tahir	16	2	57	2
Querl	20	9	56	2	Querl	14	5	42	3
Lilley	16	1	61	1	Lilley	4	1	8	0
Connolly	10	0	43	0	Connolly	3	0	27	0
Parry	20	3	53	1	Parry	21	3	59	0
Clark	4	0	10	0	Clark	3	0	32	1
					Newby	4	1	32	0
					Agathangelou	5	0	31	1

LANCASHIRE First Innings		Second Innings	
A P Agathangelou, c Lilley b Ashraf	51	lbw b Randhawa	35
H Thompson, lbw b Lilley	34	lbw b Hannon-Dalby	0
L N Bentley, b Hannon-Dalby	47	lbw b Randhawa	37
J Clark, c Wilson b Lilley	0	c Ashraf b Randhawa	27
* S D Parry, b Randhawa	32	c Randhawa b Wardlaw	81
O J Newby, c Leaning b Ashraf	8		
L S Livingstone, c. Lyth b Randhawa	4	(7) run out	44
§ A.L.Davies, not out	64	(6) b Randhawa	4
A.R.Lilley, lbw b Randhawa	5	(8) not out	35
N S Tahir, lbw b Hannon-Dalby	5	(9) not out	11
R G Querl, not out	37		
Extras (b 8, lb 6)	14	Extras (lb 2, nb 2)	4
Total (9 wkts dec, 75.5 overs)	301	Total (7 wkts, 44.5 overs)	278

FoW: 1st 1-94 (Agathangelou), 2-94 (Thompson), 3-94 (Clark), 4-154 (Parry), 5-177 (Newby) 6-189 (Livingstone), 7-189 (Bentley), 8-194 (Lilley), 9-201 (Tahir)

FoW: 2nd 1-5 (Thompson), 2-45 (Agathangelou), 3-101 (Clark), 4-101 (Bentley), 5-113 (Davies) 6-209 (Livingstone), 7-249 (Parry)

	O	M	R	W		O	M	R	W
Hannon-Dalby	17	3	58	2	Hannon-Dalby	7	0	57	1
Ashraf	14	4	41	2	Ashraf	9.5	2	52	0
Wardlaw	12	4	50	0	Wardlaw	12	1	63	1
Rafiq	7	3	29	0	Rafiq	5	0	45	0
Lilley	9	3	35	2					
Randhawa	17	7	74	3	Randhawa	11	1	59	4

Umpires: A G Wharf and H Evans

Scorers: D.M.White and H Clayton

YOUNG MAN IN A HURRY: Joe Root smacks a quick 43 to send Yorkshire off on their desperate run chase against Gloucestershire at Scarborough. Yorkshire won by two wickets at 6.07pm. on the last day.

THE TWO FIRSTS: Former Yorkshire captain and president Brian Close meets wicket-keeper/batsman Barney Gibson, who became the youngest English-born first-class cricketer upon his Yorkshire debut against Durham MCCU at The Racecourse on April 27, 2011, at the age of 15 years and 27 days. Brian, now 82, remains the youngest player to represent England when he made his debut against New Zealand at Old Trafford in 1949 at 18 years and 149 days. RIGHT: "Dickie" Bird arrives on the third day of the Headingley Test against South Africa to bend the ears of Brian and Yorkshire's immediate past-president, Raymond Illingworth.

CHART-TOPPER: The finger goes up, and Steven Patterson has trapped Leicestershire's Joshua Cobb in front on the last day of the LV County Championship match at Scarborough. Paceman Steven led Yorkshire's Championship bowling with 48 dismissals — almost twice as many as his nearest rival, Azeem Rafiq, who had 26.

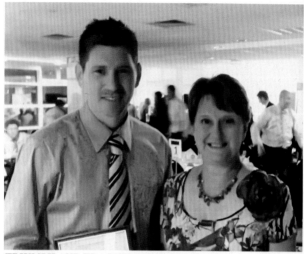

TRIUMPH AND TRAGEDY: Yorkshire Supporters' Chairwoman Charlotte Evers presents Richard Pyrah with a limited-edition signed scorecard from Yorkshire's 3,000th Championship match v. Lancashire in 2011. Richard, going in at No. 9 when Yorkshire were up against it, struck 117 in one of the best innings seen for the county, and with Ryan Sidebottom added a record 154 for the ninth wicket at Headingley.

RIGHT: Pyrah is bowled by Charlie Shreck for a duck after breaking his left hand while fielding in the opening encounter of 2012 v. Kent at Headingley. Richard missed 12 Championship, eight Clydesdale Bank 40 and six Champions' League matches last year through illness and injury.

LYTH SPIRIT: As well as heading Yorkshire's LV County Championship batting averages Adam Lyth, with an unbeaten 248 against Leicestershire at Grace Road, became the only *White Rose* batsman ever to carry his bat through a first-class innings with a double century.

DIAMOND JUBILEE: It was the weekend the nation were celebrating the 60th anniversary of the Accession to the Throne of Her Majesty Queen Elizabeth II that Yorkshire Supporters marked the golden anniversary of Philip Sharpe's 70 first-class catches for Yorkshire in 1962 to equal the Club record set by John Tunnicliffe in 1901. Presenting a framed statistical table to Philip at Headingley are, left to right, Alan Kaye, Joan Fort, Eric Stephens (also of the Yorkshire County Cricket Club Members' Committee) and John Briggs.

LONG ROOM TRIBUTE: Part of the glass case which has been on display in the East Stand Long Room at Headingley to mark the passing of Yorkshire and England left-arm spinner Don Wilson. The silver tray was presented to Don by MCC Young Cricketers at Lord's with thanks for his work as Head Coach. See *Obituaries.*

KEY TO THE SEASON: Gary Ballance, above, cracked a 23-ball 42 to help Yorkshire to a 19-run *Roses T20* victory at Headingley, but he can look back on his century against Gloucestershire in the run chase at Bristol as key to the outcome of Yorkshire's Championship season. Gary and Azeem Rafiq travelled to India over the winter with the England Performance Programme squad.

ACADEMY LINE-UP: Yorkshire Colts, who battled their way through the rain-ravaged 2012. Back row, left to right: Matthew Fisher, Ben Coad, Ryan Gibson, William Rhodes, Edward Wilson (wicket-keeper), Mosun Hussain and Sam Davies. Front row: George Ross, Jonathan Tattersall, Jack Leaning (captain), Karl Carver and Alex Leyshon.

STING IN THE TAIL: Ryan Sidebottom often scores valuable lower-order runs for Yorkshire, and here he is in aggressive mode on his way to a valuable 35 against Glamorgan at Headingley, his team going on to win by eight wickets. It was the last-but-one Championship game of the season — and the first without any weather delays.

Other Second Eleven Match

A Kent-Northamptonshire XII v. Yorkshire

Played at Worsley Bridge Road, Beckenham, on May 8, 9, 10 and 11, 2012

Match drawn at 5pm on the Fourth Day

Toss won by Yorkshire

Close of play: First Day, Yorkshire 232-8 (Randhawa 25*, Ashraf 3*); Second Day, Kent-Northamptonshire 104-1 (Northeast 55*, Bell-Drummond 16*); Third Day, Kent-Northamptonshire 267-6 (Murphy 7*, Piesely 0*)

First Innings	YORKSHIRE	Second Innings	
A Z Lees, run out	7	c Davis b Kemp	15
C J Geldart, c Murphy b Burton	5	c Northeast b Cook	4
* A Rafiq, c and b Kemp	50	c Davis b Burton	24
J A Leaning, c Kemp b Burton	12	c Davis b Blake	42
G S Ross, c White b Kemp	51	not out	32
§ E Wilson, c and b Blake	33	not out	17
A E Lilley, c Davis b Kemp	14		
D F Girling, c Murphy b Burton	13		
G S Randhawa, not out	50		
M A Ashraf, lbw b Cook	11		
I Wardlaw, lbw b Cook	0		
Extras (lb 5, w 1, nb 14)	20	Extras ((lb 1, nb 4)	5
Total (111.3 overs)	266	Total (4 wkts, 50 overs)	139

Twelfth man: O J Hannon-Dalby

FoW: 1st 1-11 (Geldart), 2-27 (Lees), 3-61 (Leaning), 4-89 (Rafiq), 5-152 (Wilson) 6-186 (Ross), 7-199 (Lilley), 8-219 (Girling), 9-254 (Ashraf)
2nd: 1-6 (Geldart), 2-39 (Rafiq), 3-57 (Lees), 4-113 (Leaning)

	O	M	R	W		O	M	R	W
Burton	31	8	76	3	Burton	11	1	40	1
Cook	26.3	8	38	2	Cook	10	4	19	1
Davis	15	1	49	0	Davis	6	0	23	0
Kemp	19	5	58	3	Kemp	5	3	7	1
de Lange	16	4	35	0	de Lange	10	1	24	0
Piesley	2	0	3	0	Piesley	4	1	14	0
Blake	2	1	2	1	Blake	4	1	11	1

KENT-NORTHAMPTONSHIRE	
*S A Northeast, c Leaning b Wardlaw	72
B H N Howgego, c Wilson b Wardlaw	24
D J Bell-Drummond, c Geldart b Rafiq	31
R A White, c Randhawa b Wardlaw	36
A J Blake, c Lilley b Randhawa	63
C D W de Lange, c Hannon-Dalby b Lilley	22
D Murphy, c Girling b Hannon-Dalby	24
C D Piesley, Run Out	6
C A L Davis, not out	39
J Cook, c Geldart b Lilley	14
D A Burton, run out	6
Extras (b 4, lb 4, nb 10)	18
Total (103.5 overs)	355

Twelfth man: B W Kemp

FoW: 1-67 (Howgego), 2-126 (Bell-Drummond), 3-171 (White), 4-180 (Northeast), 5-216 (de Lange) 6-266 (Blake), 7-274 (Piesley), 8-309 (Murphy), 9-339 (Cook)

	O	M	R	W
Hannon-Dalby	20	4	52	1
Ashraf	6	2	9	0
Lilley	18	6	49	2
Girling	4	1	19	0
Wardlaw	19	3	75	3
Rafiq	25.5	2	89	1
Randhawa	11	2	54	1

Umpires: N Duguid and R L Collins — Scorers: C A Booth and H Clayton

Other Second Eleven Match
Yorkshire v. Durham

Played at Weetwood, Leeds, on July 10, 2012

Match abandoned as a draw

Toss won by Yorkshire

DURHAM

B A Raine, c Hodgson b Wardlaw	12
K K Jennings, retired out	40
R Singh, retired out	58
* I D Blackwell, c Wilson b Coad	8
G R Breese, not out	4
R D Pringle, not out	19
R M R Brathwaite	
R S Buckley	
G Clark — Did not bat	
P Coughlin	
§ C J Pearce	
M A Wood	
Extras b 1, lb 1, w 5, nb 2	9
Total (4 wkts, 40 overs)	150

FoW: 1-29 (Raine), 2-82 (Jennings), 3-116 (Singh), 4-119 (Blackwell)

	O	M	R	W
Hannon-Dalby	10	2	26	0
Wardlaw	11	4	30	1
Lilley	5	1	16	0
Whiles	4	2	17	0
Coad	5	0	28	1
Rhodes	5	0	31	0

YORKSHIRE

A Z Lees
G S Randhawa
§ D M Hodgson
W M H Rhodes
J A Leaning
E Wilson
G S Ross
A E Lilley
* O J Hannon-Dalby
I Wardlaw
B O Coad
G P Whiles

Umpires: I J Dixon and R Smith — Scorers: C N Rawson and R V Hilton

Other Second Eleven Match
Yorkshire v. Nottinghamshire

Played at Weetwood on August 28, 29 and 30, 2012

Match abandoned as a draw. No play on the second or third days

Toss won by Nottinghamshire

YORKSHIRE

A Z Lees, lbw b Bacon	5
G S Randhawa, c Mullaney b Tillcock	74
§ D M Hodgson, c Edwards b Elstone	98
J A Leaning, c Lanford b Bacon	32
J A Tattersall, c Edwards b Pringle	16
* E Wilson, b Gurney	39
W M H Rhodes, lbw b Tillcock	11
L R Stabler, c Gurney b Ball	24
J Shaw, b Tillcock	12
I Wardlaw, c Ball b Tillcock	12
O J Hannon-Dalby, not out	0
Extras b 10, lb 12, nb 14)	36
Total (89.5 overs)	359

FoW: 1-19 (Lees), 2-102 (Randhawa), 3-162 (Leaning), 4-213 (Tattersalll), 5-270 (Hodgson), 6-297(Rhodes), 7-327 (Wilson), 8-333 (Stabler), 9-359 (Wardlaw), 10-359 (Shaw)

	O	M	R	W
Ball	19	3	63	1
Bacon	13	3	58	2
Mullaney	12	3	47	0
Pringle	15	3	44	1
Tillcock	15.5	1	62	4
Elstone	5	1	14	1
Gurney	10	0	49	1

NOTTINGHAMSHIRE

K Turner, not out	13
N J Edwards, not out	18
§ S Kelsall	
* S L Elstone	
S J Mullaney	
N G Lanford	
T C Rowe	Did not bat
A D Tillcock	
G P W Bacon	
J T Ball	
O M Pringle	
H F Gurney	
Extras	0
Total (0 wkts, 6 overs)	31

	O	M	R	W
Hannon-Dalby	3	1	6	0
Wardlaw	3	0	25	0

Umpires: I Dawood and D Koch   Scorers: H Clayton and Mrs A Cusworth

Other Second Eleven Match
Somerset v. Yorkshire

Played at Taunton Vale Sports Club, Taunton, on September 4, 5 and 6, 2012
Somerset won by an innings and 171 runs at 1.32pm on the Third Day
Toss won by Yorkshire

Close of play: First Day, Somerset 133-2 (Jenkins 67 *, Lawrence 39 *); Second Day, Yorkshire Second Innings 16-3 (Compton 3)

First Innings	YORKSHIRE	Second Innings	
A Z Lees, c J Overton b C Overton	31	b J Overton	8
N R D Compton		(2) retired out	39
G S Randhawa, c Gregory b Hussain	10	(5) c Regan b C Overton	9
D M Hodgson, c J Overton b C Overton	24	(6) c C Overton b Waller	8
J A Leaning, lbw b Rouse	2	(7) c Regan b C Overton	2
§ * E Wilson, c J Overton b Sutton	2	(8) c Lawrence b Gregory	26
G S Ross, c Waller b J Overton	14	(9) c Regan b Gregory	5
W H M Rhodes, c Regan b J Overton	6	(10) not out	10
J Shaw, c C Overton b Hussain	8	(4) b J Overton	0
I Wardlaw, c J Overton b C Overton	13	(11) b Gregory	0
O J Hannon-Dalby, c Rouse b Waller	15	(3) lbw b J Overton	0
G P Whiles, not out	0		
K Carver Did not bat			
Extras b 1, lb 6, w 1, nb 20	28	Extras b 5, lb 8, nb 4	17
Total (48.5 overs)	153	Total (45.5 overs)	124

NOTE: N R D Compton batted for Yorkshire in their second innings by mutual agreement to test his recovery after a back problem in the run-up to England's winter tour of India

FoW: 1st 1-15 (Randhawa), 2-73 (Lees), 3-78 (Leaning), 4-80 (Hodgson), 5-80 (Wilson), 6-105 (Rhodes), 7-114 (Shaw), 8-114 (Ross), 9-137 (Wardlaw), 10-153 (Hannon-Dalby)

FoW: 2nd 1-16 (Lees), 2-16 (Hannon-Dalby), 3-16 (Shaw), 4-54 (Randhawa), 5-66 (Compton), 6-69 (Leaning), 7-80 (Hodgson), 8-85 (Ross), 9-124 (Wilson), 10-124 (Wardlaw)

	O	M	R	W
Hussain	13	3	51	2
J Overton	10	2	33	2
C Overton	13	6	22	3
Gregory	7	0	27	0
Rouse	2	0	6	1
Sutton	2	1	4	1
Waller	1.5	0	3	1

	O	M	R	W
J Overton	10	4	28	3
Hussain	15	5	26	0
C Overton	8	2	13	2
Gregory	7.5	2	24	3
Waller	5	0	20	1

SOMERSET	
T B Abell, c Lees b Hannon-Dalby	7
W H Jenkins, c Lees b Hannon-Dalby	72
* L Gregory, c Lees b Wardlaw	5
J M Lawrence, lbw b Randhawa	104
C Overton, c Lees b Wardlaw	90
§ J A Regan, b Carver	0
M T C Waller, lbw b Randhawa	3
H P Rouse, not out	63
J Overton, c Hannon-Dalby b Wardlaw	24
S A Mount, c Ross b Hanon-Dalby	0
G M Hussain, c Hannon-Dalby b Carver	54
A P Sutton Did not bat	
Extras b 5, lb 7, w 2, nb 12	26
Total (136.4 overs)	448

FoW: 1-14 (Abell), 2-27 (Gregory), 3-150 (Jenkins), 4-265 (Lawrence), 5-266 (Regan), 6-281 (Waller), 7-308 (C Overton), 8-342 (J Overton), 9-342 (Mount), 10-448 (Hussain)

	O	M	R	W
Hannon-Dalby	24	9	54	3
Wardlaw	23	6	74	3
Whiles	13	0	60	0
Shaw	11	0	56	0
Randhawa	36	5	106	2
Carver	29.4	5	86	2

Umpires: P R Pollard and R W Tolchard   Scorers: Mrs L M Rhodes and H Clayton

YORKSHIRE ECB COUNTY PREMIER LEAGUE 2012

*	P	CW	IW1	IW2	IW3	IL1	IL2	IL3	CL	T	C/A	Points
York	26	15	1	2	1	0	0	1	1	0	5	159
Harrogate	26	11	0	2	2	0	0	0	2	0	9	139
Barnsley	26	8	2	2	3	1	0	0	2	0	8	132
Yorkshire Academy	**26**	**7**	**1**	**1**	**3**	**0**	**1**	**1**	**2**	**0**	**10**	**117**
Rotherham Town	26	6	3	1	3	0	1	1	4	0	7	112
Driffield Town	26	6	2	2	3	0	1	2	7	0	3	100
Scarborough	26	6	0	0	3	2	0	2	5	0	8	94
Cleethorpes	26	7	0	0	2	2	0	5	4	0	6	90
Hull	26	3	0	1	1	1	1	1	9	0	9	66
Sheffield United	26	4	0	0	0	2	3	2	7	0	8	63
Doncaster Town	26	3	0	1	0	1	2	2	8	0	9	61
Castleford	26	4	0	1	0	1	0	2	12	0	6	58
Appleby Frodingham	26	2	2	0	0	1	2	2	10	0	7	53
Sheffield Collegiate	26	1	0	0	1	0	2	1	10	0	11	49

* P = Played; CW = Complete win (8 points); IW1 = Incomplete win (6 points); IW2 = Incomplete win (6 points); IW3 = Incomplete win (6 points); IL1 = Incomplete loss (2 points); IL2 = Incomplete loss 1 (1 point); IL3 = Incomplete loss (0 points); CL = Complete loss (0 points); T = Tied (4 points); C/A = Cancelled or Abandoned (3 points).

Yorkshire League Cup: Winners: **Driffield Town.** Runners-up:Barnsley

YORKSHIRE ACADEMY BATTING IN ECB LEAGUE AND CUP

Player	*M.*	*I.*	*N.O.*	*Runs*	*H.S.*	*Avge*	*100s*	*50s*	*4s*	*6s*	*ct/st*
W Rhodes	22	18	8	630	131	63.00	1	3	55	0	16
J Leaning	22	21	2	762	92	40.11	0	9	70	3	7
J Tattersall	20	19	0	753	114	39.63	1	5	65	0	6
R Gibson	16	13	3	299	79	29.90	0	2	35	3	5
G Ross	21	20	2	515	108	28.61	1	1	35	11	6
E Wilson	23	19	1	403	83	22.39	0	2	35	4	13/4
G Ross	21	20	2	515	108	28.61	1	1	35	11	6
M Hussain	15	14	5	178	38	19.78	0	0	18	1	3
E Callis	13	12	0	232	82	19.33	0	1	20	1	5
M Fisher	10	5	3	25	15	12.50	0	0	1	1	1
L Stabler	13	6	1	53	16*	10.60	0	0	4	1	3
A Rafiq	3	3	0	31	14	10.33	0	0	4	0	0
B Coad	22	5	1	41	16*	10.25	0	0	2	0	5
A Rashid	1	1	0	10	10	10.00	0	0	2	0	0
J McNichol	8	7	3	29	9*	7.25	0	0	2	0	2
J Shaw	18	8	3	33	9*	6.60	0	0	0	0	1
A Robinson	3	0	0	0	—	—	0	0	0	0	1
K Carver	18	5	5	25	17*	—	0	0	1	1	2
A Leyshon	5	1	1	4	4*	—	0	0	1	0	0

YORKSHIRE ACADEMY BOWLING IN ECB LEAGUE AND CUP

Player	*M*	*Overs*	*Mdns*	*Runs*	*Wkts*	*Avge*	*Econ.*	*5wh*	*Best*
A Rashid	1	7	4	9	2	4.50	1.29	0	2-9
A Leyshon	5	25.5	7	75	10	7.50	2.90	1	8-56
M Fisher	14	61.5	9	206	15	13.73	3.33	1	5-13
A Rafiq	3	27.2	6	113	8	14.13	4.13	1	5-14
L Stabler	21	75	11	278	19	14.63	3.71	2	6-10
B Coad	29	149	39	395	21	18.81	2.65	1	6-16
K Carver	24	137.3	18	515	22	23.41	3.75	0	3-29
J Tattersall	25	36.5	1	194	8	24.25	5.27	0	3-47
A Robinson	6	8	1	26	1	26.00	3.25	0	1-16
W Rhodes	28	85	6	371	13	28.54	4.36	0	3-27
Leaning	24	56	8	201	7	28.71	3.59	0	2-30
Shaw	21	98.2	11	377	10	37.70	3.83	0	2-13
G Ross	25	38	1	195	5	39.00	5.13	0	4-30
R Gibson	20	49.3	6	236	6	39.33	4.77	0	2-27
McNichol	13	3	0	24	0	—	8.00	0	0-24

RECORDS SECTION

(All records in this section relate to First-Class Yorkshire matches only — except where otherwise stated)

HONOURS

County Champions (32)

1867, 1870, 1893, 1896, 1898, 1900, 1901, 1902, 1905, 1908, 1912, 1919, 1922, 1923, 1924, 1925, 1931, 1932, 1933, 1935, 1937, 1938, 1939, 1946, 1959, 1960, 1962, 1963, 1966, 1967, 1968, 2001.

Joint Champions (2)

1869, 1949

Promoted to Division 1

2005

Gillette Cup Winners (2)

1965, 1969

Cheltenham & Gloucester Trophy (1)

2002

Benson & Hedges Cup Winners (1)

1987

John Player Special League Winners (1)

1983

Fenner Trophy Winners (3)

1972, 1974, 1981

Asda Challenge Winners (1)

1987

Ward Knockout Cup (1)

1989

Joshua Tetley Festival Trophy (7)

1991, 1992 (Joint), 1993, 1994, 1996, 1997 and 1998

Tilcon Trophy Winners (2)

1978 and 1988

Pro-Arch Trophy (1)

2007-08

Second Eleven Champions (4)

1977, 1984, 1991, 2003

Joint Champions (1)

1987

Minor Counties Champions (5)

1947, 1957, 1958, 1968, 1971

Under-25 Competition Winners (3)

1976, 1978, 1987

Bain Clarkson Trophy Winners (2)

1988 and 1994

Second Eleven Trophy (1)

2009

YORKSHIRE'S CHAMPIONSHIP CAPTAINS

1867 to 2001

R Iddison (2)	1867, 1870
Lord Hawke (8)	1893, 1896, 1898, 1900, 1901, 1902, 1905, 1908
Sir Archibald White (1)	1912
D C F Burton (1)	1919
G Wilson (3)	1922, 1923, 1924
A W Lupton (1)	1925
F E Greenwood (2)	1931, 1932
A B Sellers (6)	1933, 1935, 1937, 1938, 1939, 1946
J R Burnet (1)	1959
J V Wilson (2)	1960, 1962
D B Close (4)	1963, 1966, 1967, 1968
D Byas (1)	2001

Joint Champions

R Iddison (1)	1869
N W D Yardley (1)	1949

RECORDS SECTION INDEX

CHAMPION COUNTIES SINCE 1873

The County Championship

The County Championship was officially constituted in 1890, and before that Yorkshire were generally considered Champions by the Press in 1867 and 1870, and equal top in 1869. From 1873 the list was generally accepted in the form as it is today.

Year	Champion	Yorkshire's Position
1873	Gloucestershire / Nottinghamshire	7th
1874	Gloucestershire	4th
1875	Nottinghamshire	4th
1876	Gloucestershire	3rd
1877	Gloucestershire	7th
1878	Middlesex	6th
1879	Nottinghamshire/Lancashire	6th
1880	Nottinghamshire	5th
1881	Lancashire	3rd
1882	Nottinghamshire/Lancashire	3rd
1883	Nottinghamshire	2nd
1884	Nottinghamshire	3rd
1885	Nottinghamshire	2nd
1886	Nottinghamshire	4th
1887	Surrey	3rd
1888	Surrey	2nd
1889	Surrey/Lancashire / Nottinghamshire	7th
1890	Surrey	3rd
1891	Surrey	8th
1892	Surrey	6th
1893	**Yorkshire**	**1st**
1894	Surrey	2nd
1895	Surrey	3rd
1896	**Yorkshire**	**1st**
1897	Lancashire	4th
1898	**Yorkshire**	**1st**
1899	Surrey	3rd
1900	**Yorkshire**	**1st**
1901	**Yorkshire**	**1st**
1902	**Yorkshire**	**1st**
1903	Middlesex	3rd
1904	Lancashire	2nd
1905	**Yorkshire**	**1st**
1906	Kent	2nd
1907	Nottinghamshire	2nd
1908	**Yorkshire**	**1st**
1909	Kent	3rd
1910	Kent	8th
1911	Warwickshire	7th
1912	**Yorkshire**	**1st**
1913	Kent	2nd
1914	Surrey	4th
1919	**Yorkshire**	**1st**
1920	Middlesex	4th
1921	Middlesex	3rd
1922	**Yorkshire**	**1st**
1923	**Yorkshire**	**1st**
1924	**Yorkshire**	**1st**
1925	**Yorkshire**	**1st**
1926	Lancashire	2nd
1927	Lancashire	3rd
1928	Lancashire	4th
1929	Nottinghamshire	2nd
1930	Lancashire	3rd
1931	**Yorkshire**	**1st**
1932	**Yorkshire**	**1st**
1933	**Yorkshire**	**1st**
1934	Lancashire	5th
1935	**Yorkshire**	**1st**
1936	Derbyshire	3rd
1937	**Yorkshire**	**1st**
1938	**Yorkshire**	**1st**
1939	**Yorkshire**	**1st**
1946	**Yorkshire**	**1st**
1947	Middlesex	7th
1948	Glamorgan	4th
1949	**Yorkshire**/Middlesex	**1st**
1950	Lancashire/Surrey	3rd
1951	Warwickshire	2nd
1952	Surrey	2nd
1953	Surrey	12th
1954	Surrey	2nd
1955	Surrey	2nd
1956	Surrey	7th
1957	Surrey	3rd

CHAMPION COUNTIES SINCE 1873 *(Continued)*

Year	County	Yorkshire's Position
1958	Surrey	11th
1959	**Yorkshire**	**1st**
1960	**Yorkshire**	**1st**
1961	Hampshire	2nd
1962	**Yorkshire**	**1st**
1963	**Yorkshire**	**1st**
1964	Worcestershire	5th
1965	Worcestershire	4th
1966	**Yorkshire**	**1st**
1967	**Yorkshire**	**1st**
1968	**Yorkshire**	**1st**
1969	Glamorgan	13th
1970	Kent	4th
1971	Surrey	13th
1972	Warwickshire	10th
1973	Hampshire	14th
1974	Worcestershire	11th
1975	Leicestershire	2nd
1976	Middlesex	8th
1977	Kent/Middlesex	12th
1978	Kent	4th
1979	Essex	7th
1980	Middlesex	6th
1981	Nottinghamshire	10th
1982	Middlesex	10th
1983	Essex	17th
1984	Essex	14th
1985	Middlesex	11th
1986	Essex	10th
1987	Nottinghamshire	8th
1988	Worcestershire	13th
1989	Worcestershire	16th
1990	Middlesex	10th
1991	Essex	14th
1992	Essex	16th
1993	Middlesex	12th
1994	Warwickshire	13th
1995	Warwickshire	8th
1996	Leicestershire	6th
1997	Glamorgan	6th
1998	Leicestershire	3rd
1999	Surrey	6th
2000	Surrey	3rd
2001	**Yorkshire**	**1st**
2002	Surrey	9th
2003	Sussex	Div 2, 4th
2004	Warwickshire	Div 2, 7th
2005	Nottinghamshire	Div 2, 3rd
2006	Sussex	Div 1, 6th
2007	Sussex	Div 1, 6th
2008	Durham	Div 1, 7th
2009	Durham	Div 1, 7th
2010	Nottinghamshire	Div 1, 3rd
2011	Lancashire	Div 1, 8th
2012	Warwickshire	Div 2, 2nd

Prediction

First-class cricket can preserve its future only by being a form of the game more desirable than any other to players and spectators. Without this assurance there would be no purpose in maintaining first-class cricket in its county organisation. The Sunday League, and its equivalents, would have proved not a help but become an executioner.

J M Kilburn, 1968

SEASON-BY-SEASON RECORD OF ALL FIRST-CLASS MATCHES PLAYED BY YORKSHIRE 1863-2012

Season	*Played*	*Won*	*Lost*	*Drawn*	*Abd§*
1863	4	2	1	1	
1864	7	2	4	1	
1865	9	—	7	2	
1866	3	—	2	1	
1867	7	7	—	—	
1868	7	4	3	—	
1869	5	4	1	—	
1870	7	6	—	1	
1871	7	3	3	1	
1872	10	2	7	1	
1873	13	7	5	1	
1874	14	10	3	1	
1875	12	6	4	2	
1876	12	5	3	4	
1877	14	2	7	5	
1878	20	10	7	3	
1879	17	7	5	5	
1880	20	6	8	6	
1881	20	11	6	3	
1882	24	11	9	4	
1883	19	10	2	7	
1884	20	10	6	4	
1885	21	8	3	10	
1886	21	5	8	8	
1887	20	6	5	9	
1888	20	7	7	6	
1889	16	3	11	2	1
1890	20	10	4	6	
1891	17	5	11	1	2
1892	19	6	6	7	
1893	23	15	5	3	
1894	28	18	6	4	1
1895	31	15	10	6	
1896	32	17	6	9	
1897	30	14	7	9	
1898	30	18	3	9	
1899	34	17	4	13	
1900	32	19	1	12	
1901	35	23	2	10	1
1902	31	15	3	13	1
1903	31	16	5	10	
1904	32	10	2	20	1
1905	33	21	4	8	
1906	33	19	6	8	
1907	31	14	5	12	2
1908	33	19	—	14	
1909	30	12	5	13	
1910	31	11	8	12	
1911	32	16	9	7	
1912	35	14	3	18	1
1913	32	16	5	11	
1914	31	16	4	11	2
1919	31	12	5	14	
1920	30	17	6	7	
1921	30	17	5	8	
1922	33	20	2	11	
1923	35	26	1	8	
1924	35	18	4	13	
1925	36	22	—	14	
1926	35	14	—	21	1
1927	34	11	3	20	1
1928	32	9	—	23	
1929	35	11	2	22	
1930	34	13	3	18	2
1931	33	17	1	15	1
1932	32	21	2	9	2
1933	36	21	5	10	
1934	35	14	7	14	
1935	36	24	2	10	
1935-6	3	1	—	2	
1936	35	14	2	19	
1937	34	22	3	9	1
1938	36	22	2	12	
1939	34	23	4	7	1
1945	2	—	—	2	
1946	31	20	1	10	
1947	32	10	9	13	
1948	31	11	6	14	
1949	33	16	3	14	
1950	34	16	6	12	1
1951	35	14	3	18	
1952	34	17	3	14	
1953	35	7	7	21	
1954	35	16	3	16*	
1955	33	23	6	4	
1956	35	11	7	17	
1957	34	16	5	13	1
1958	33	10	8	15	2
1959	35	18	8	9	
1960	38	19	7	12	
1961	39	19	5	15	
1962	37	16	5	16	
1963	33	14	4	15	
1964	33	12	4	17	
1965	33	12	4	17	
1966	32	16	6	10	1
1967	31	16	5	10	2
1968	32	13	4	15	
1969	29	4	7	18	
1970	26	10	5	11	
1971	27	5	8	14	
1972	21	4	5	12	1
1973	22	3	5	14*	
1974	22	6	7	9	1
1975	21	11	1	9	
1976	22	7	7	8	
1977	23	7	5	11	1
1978	24	10	3	11	1

SEASON-BY-SEASON RECORD OF ALL FIRST-CLASS MATCHES PLAYED BY YORKSHIRE 1863-2012 *(Contd.)*

Season	*Played*	*Won*	*Lost*	*Drawn*	*Abd§*
1979	22	6	3	13	1
1980	24	5	4	15	
1981	24	5	9	10	
1982	22	5	1	16	1
1983	23	1	5	17	1
1984	24	5	4	15	
1985	25	3	4	18	1
1986	25	4	6	15	
1986-7	1	—	—	1	
1987	24	7	4	13	1
1988	24	5	6	13	
1989	22	3	9	10	
1990	24	5	9	10	
1991	24	4	6	14	
1991-2	1	—	1	—	
1992	22	4	6	12	1
1992-3	1	—	—	1	
1993	19	6	4	9	
1994	20	7	6	7	
1995	20	8	8	4	
1995-6	2	2	—	—	
1996	19	8	5	6	
1997	20	7	4	9	
1998	19	9	3	7	
1999	17	8	6	3	
2000	18	7	4	7	
2001	16	9	3	4	
2002	16	2	8	6	
2003	17	4	5	8	
2004	16	3	4	9	
2005	17	6	1	10	
2006	16	3	6	7	
2007	17	5	4	8	
2008	16	2	5	9	
2009	17	2	2	13	
2010	18	6	2	10	
2011	17	4	6	7	
2012	17	5	0	12	
	3532	1483	645	1404	38

*Includes one tie in each season.

§ All these matches were abandoned without a ball being bowled, except Yorkshire v Kent at Harrogate, 1904, which was abandoned under Law 9. The two in 1914 and the one in 1939 were abandoned because of war. All these matches are excluded from the total played.

Of the 1,483 matches won, 507 have been by an innings margin, 82 by 200 runs or more, and 130 by 10 wickets. Of the 645 matches lost, 108 have been by an innings margin, 12 by 200 runs or more and 34 by 10 wickets.

ANALYSIS OF RESULTS VERSUS ALL FIRST-CLASS TEAMS 1863-2012

COUNTY CHAMPIONSHIP

Opponents	*Played*	*Won*	*Lost*	*Drawn*	*Tied*
Derbyshire	203	101	19	83	—
Durham	28	12	7	9	—
Essex	160	84	25	51	—
Glamorgan	111	53	13	45	—
Gloucestershire	200	102	43	55	—
Hampshire	165	72	19	74	—
Kent	200	84	39	77	—
Lancashire	253	74	52	127	—
Leicestershire	166	84	15	66	1
Middlesex	225	78	54	92	1
Northamptonshire	140	65	26	49	—
Nottinghamshire	246	87	47	112	—
Somerset	165	89	22	54	—
Surrey	238	85	67	86	—
Sussex	193	83	32	78	—
Warwickshire	182	80	31	71	—
Worcestershire	138	68	21	49	—
Cambridgeshire	8	3	4	1	—
Total	3021	1304	536	1179	2

ANALYSIS OF RESULTS VERSUS ALL FIRST-CLASS TEAMS 1863-2012 *(continued.)*

OTHER FIRST-CLASS MATCHES

Opponents	*Played*	*Won*	*Lost*	*Drawn*	*Tied*
Derbyshire	2	1	1	0	—
Essex	2	2	0	0	—
Hampshire	1	0	0	1	—
Lancashire	12	5	3	4	—
Leicestershire	2	1	1	0	—
Middlesex	1	1	0	0	—
Nottinghamshire	2	1	1	0	—
Surrey	1	0	0	1	—
Sussex	2	0	0	2	—
Warwickshire	2	0	0	2	—
Totals	27	11	6	10	—
Australians	55	6	19	30	—
Indians	14	5	1	8	—
New Zealanders	10	2	0	8	—
Pakistanis	4	1	0	3	—
South Africans	17	1	3	13	—
Sri Lankans	3	0	0	3	—
West Indians	17	3	7	7	—
Zimbabweans	2	0	1	1	—
Bangladesh A	1	1	0	0	—
India A	2	0	0	2	—
Pakistan A	1	1	0	0	—
South Africa A	1	0	0	1	—
Totals	127	20	31	76	—
Cambridge University/U C C E	88	42	17	29	—
Canadians	1	1	0	0	—
Combined Services	1	0	0	1	—
Durham MCCU	1	1	0	0	—
England XI's	6	1	2	3	—
Hon. M.B. Hawke's XI	1	0	1	0	—
International XI	1	1	0	0	—
Ireland	3	3	0	0	—
Jamaica	3	1	0	2	—
Leeds/Bradford MCCU	1	0	0	1	—
Liverpool and District*	3	2	1	0	—
Loughborough UCCE	2	1	0	1	—
MCC	153	54	39	60	—
Mashonaland	1	1	0	0	—
Matebeleland	1	1	0	0	—
Minor Counties	1	1	0	0	—
Oxford University	44	21	3	20	—
Philadelphians	1	0	0	1	—
Rest of England	16	4	5	7	—
Royal Air Force	1	0	0	1	—
Scotland**	11	7	0	4	—
South of England	2	1	0	1	—
C. I. Thornton's XI	5	2	0	3	—
United South of England	1	1	0	0	—
Western Province	2	0	1	1	—
Windward Islands	1	0	0	1	—
I Zingari	6	2	3	1	—
Totals	357	148	72	137	0
Grand Totals	3532	1483	645	1402	2

*Matches played in 1889, 1891, 1892 and 1893 are excluded. **Match played in 1878 is included

ABANDONED MATCHES (38)

1889 v. MCC at Lord's
1891 (2) v. MCC at Lord's
v. MCC at Scarborough
1894 v. Kent at Bradford
1901 v. Surrey at The Oval
1902 v. Leicestershire at Leicester (AR)
1904 v. Kent at Harrogate (Law 9 — now Law 10)
1907 (2) v. Derbyshire at Sheffield
v. Nottinghamshire at Huddersfield
1912 v. Surrey at Sheffield
1914 (2) v. England at Harrogate (due to war)
v. MCC at Scarborough (due to war)
1926 v. Nottinghamshire at Leeds
1927 v. Kent at Bradford
1930 (2) v. Derbyshire at Chesterfield*
v. Northampstonshire at Harrogate*
1931 v. Sussex at Hull
1932 (2) v. Derbyshire at Chesterfield
v. Kent at Sheffield
1937 v. Cambridge University at Bradford
1939 v. MCC at Scarborough (due to war)
1950 v. Cambridge University at Cambridge
1957 v. West Indians at Bradford
1958 (2) v. Nottinghamshire at Hull
v. Worcestershire at Bradford
1966 v. Oxford University at Oxford
1967 (2) v. Leicestershire at Leeds
v. Lancashire at Manchester
1972 v. Australians at Bradford
1974 v. Hampshire at Bournemouth
1977 v. Gloucestershire at Bristol
1978 v. Pakistan at Bradford
1979 v. Nottinghamshire at Sheffield (AP)
1982 v. Nottinghamshire at Harrogate
1983 v. Middlesex at Lord's
1985 v. Essex at Sheffield (AP)
1987 v. Sussex at Hastings
1992 v. Oxford University at Oxford

*Consecutive matches

ANALYSIS OF RESULTS ON GROUNDS IN YORKSHIRE USED IN 2012

FIRST-CLASS MATCHES

Ground	*Played*	*Won*	*Lost*	*Drawn*	*Tied*
Leeds					
Headingley 1891-2012	424	158 (37.26%)	77 (18.16%)	189 (44.58%)	0 (0.0%)
Scarborough					
North Marine Road 1874-2012	245	98 (40.00%)	34 (13.88%)	113 (46.12%)	0 (0.0%)

HIGHEST MATCH AGGREGATES – OVER 1350 RUNS

Runs	*Wkts*	
1665	33	Yorkshire (351 and 481) lost to Warwickshire (601:9 dec and 232:4) by 6 wkts at Birmingham, 2002
1606	31	Yorkshire (438 and 363:5 dec) lost to Somerset (326 and 479:6) by 4 wkts at Taunton, 2009
1479	28	Yorkshire (405 and 333:4 dec) lost to Somerset (377 and 364:4) by 6 wkts at Taunton , 2010
1473	17	Yorkshire (600:4 dec. and 231:3 dec.) drew with Worcestershire (453:5 dec. and 189:5) at Scarborough, 1995.
1442	29	Yorkshire (501:6 dec. and 244:6 dec.) beat Lancashire (403:7 dec. and 294) by 48 runs at Scarborough, 1991.
1439	32	Yorkshire (536:8 dec. and 205:7 dec.) beat Glamorgan (482: 7 dec. and 216) by 43 runs at Cardiff, 1996.
1431	32	Yorkshire (388 and 312:6) drew with Sussex (398 and 333:6 dec) at Scarborough, 2011
1417	33	Yorkshire (422 and 193:7) drew with Glamorgan (466 and 336:6 dec) at Colwyn Bay, 2003
1406	37	Yorkshire (354 and 341:8) drew with Derbyshire (406 and 305:9 dec) at Derby, 2004
1400	32	Yorkshire (299 and 439: 4 dec.) drew with Hampshire (296 and 366:8) at Southampton, 2007
1393	35	Yorkshire (331 and 278) lost to Kent (377 and 407:5 dec) by 175 runs at Maidstone, 1994.
1390	34	Yorkshire (431:8 dec and 265:7) beat Hampshire (429 and 265) by 3 wkts at Southampton, 1995.
1376	33	Yorkshire (531 and 158:3) beat Lancashire (373 and 314) by 7 wkts at Leeds, 2001
1376	20	Yorkshire (677: 7 dec.) drew with Durham (518 and 181:3 dec.) at Leeds, 2006
1374	36	Yorkshire (594: 9 dec. and 266:7 dec.) beat Surrey (344 and 170) by 346 runs at The Oval, 2007
1373	36	Yorkshire (520 and 114:6) drew with Derbyshire (216 and 523) at Derby, 2005
1364	35	Yorkshire (216 and 433) lost to Warwickshire (316 and 399:5 dec.) by 66 runs at Birmingham, 2006
1359	25	Yorkshire (561 and 138:3 dec.) drew with Derbyshire (412:4 dec. and 248:8) at Sheffield, 1996.
1359	30	Yorkshire (358 and 321) lost to Somerset (452 and 228:0) by 10 wickets at Taunton, 2011
1353	18	Yorkshire (377:2 dec. and 300:6) beat Derbyshire (475:7 dec. and 201:3 dec.) by 4 wkts at Scarborough, 1990.

LOWEST MATCH AGGREGATES – UNDER 225 RUNS IN A COMPLETED MATCH

Runs	*Wkts*	
165	30	Yorkshire (46 and 37:0) beat Nottinghamshire (24 and 58 by 10 wkts at Sheffield, 1888.
175	29	Yorkshire (104) beat Essex (30 and 41) by an innings and 33 runs at Leyton, 1901.
182	15	Yorkshire (4:0 dec. and 88.5) beat Northamptonshire (4:0 dec. and 86) by 5 wkts at Bradford, 1931.
193	29	Yorkshire (99) beat Worcestershire (43 and 51) by an innings and 5 runs at Bradford, 1900.
219	30	Yorkshire (113) beat Nottinghamshire (71 and 35) by an innings and 7 runs at Nottingham, 1881.
222	32	Yorkshire (98 and 14:2) beat Gloucestershire (68 and 42) by 8 wkts at Gloucester, 1924.
223	40	Yorkshire (58 and 51) lost to Lancashire (64 and 50) by 5 runs at Manchester, 1893.

LOWEST MATCH AGGREGATES – UNDER 325 RUNS IN A MATCH IN WHICH ALL 40 WICKETS FELL

Runs	*Wkts*	
223	40	Yorkshire (58 and 51) lost to Lancashire (64 and 50) by 5 runs at Manchester, 1893.
288	40	Yorkshire (55 and 68) lost to Lancashire (89 and 76) by 42 runs at Sheffield, 1872.
295	40	Yorkshire (71 and 63) lost to Surrey (56 and 105) by 27 runs at The Oval, 1886.
303	40	Yorkshire (109 and 77) beat Middlesex (63 and 54) by 69 runs at Lord's, 1891.
318	40	Yorkshire (96 and 96) beat Lancashire (39 and 87) by 66 runs at Manchester, 1874.
318	40	Yorkshire (94 and 104) beat Northamptonshire (61 and 59) by 78 runs at Bradford, 1955.
319	40	Yorkshire (84 and 72) lost to Derbyshire (106 and 57) by 7 runs at Derby, 1878.
320	40	Yorkshire (98 and 91) beat Surrey (72 and 59) by 58 runs at Sheffield, 1893.
321	40	Yorkshire (88 and 37) lost to I Zingari (103 and 93) by 71 runs at Scarborough, 1877.
321	40	Yorkshire (80 and 67) lost to Derbyshire (129 and 45) by 27 runs at Sheffield, 1879.

LARGE MARGINS OF VICTORY – BY AN INNINGS AND OVER 250 RUNS

Inns and 397 runs	Yorkshire (548:4 dec.) beat Northamptonshire (58 and 93) at Harrogate, 1921
Inns and 387 runs	Yorkshire (662) beat Derbyshire (118 and 157) at Chesterfield, 1898.
Inns and 343 runs	Yorkshire (673:8 dec) beat Northamptonshire (184 and 146) at Leeds, 2003
Inns and 321 runs	Yorkshire (437) beat Leicestershire (58 and 58) at Leicester, 1908.
Inns and 314 runs	Yorkshire (356:8 dec) beat Northamptonshire (27 and 15) at Northampton, 1908. (Yorkshire's first match v. Northamptonshire).
Inns and 313 runs	Yorkshire (555:1 dec) beat Essex (78 and 164) at Leyton, 1932.
Inns and 307 runs	Yorkshire (681:5 dec.) beat Sussex (164 and 210) at Sheffield, 1897.
Inns and 302 runs	Yorkshire (660) beat Leicestershire (165 and 193) at Leicester, 1896.
Inns and 301 runs	Yorkshire (499) beat Somerset (125 and 73) at Bath, 1899.
Inns and 294 runs	Yorkshire (425:7 dec.) beat Gloucestershire (47 and 84) at Bristol, 1964.

LARGE MARGINS OF VICTORY – BY AN INNINGS AND OVER 250 RUNS *(Continued)*

Inns and 284 runs	Yorkshire (467:7 dec) beat Leicestershire (111 and 72) at Bradford, 1932.
Inns and 282 runs	Yorkshire (481:8 dec) beat Derbyshire (106 and 93) at Huddersfield, 1901.
Inns and 280 runs	Yorkshire (562) beat Leicestershire (164 and 118) at Dewsbury, 1903.
Inns and 271 runs	Yorkshire (460) beat Hampshire (128 and 61) at Hull, 1900.
Inns and 271 runs	Yorkshire (495:5 dec) beat Warwickshire (99 and 125) at Huddersfield, 1922.
Inns and 266 runs	Yorkshire (352) beat Cambridgeshire (40 and 46) at Hunslet, 1869.
Inns and 260 runs	Yorkshire (521: 7dec.) beat Worcestershire (129 and 132) at Leeds, 2007.
Inns and 258 runs	Yorkshire (404:2 dec) beat Glamorgan (78 and 68) at Cardiff, 1922. (Yorkshire's first match v. Glamorgan).
Inns and 256 runs	Yorkshire (486) beat Leicestershire (137 and 93) at Sheffield, 1895.
Inns and 251 runs	Yorkshire (550) beat Leicestershire (154 and 145) at Leicester, 1933.

LARGE MARGINS OF VICTORY – BY OVER 300 RUNS

389 runs	Yorkshire (368 and 280:1 dec) beat Somerset (125 and 134) at Bath, 1906.
370 runs	Yorkshire (194 and 274) beat Hampshire (62 and 36) at Leeds, 1904.
351 runs	Yorkshire (280 and 331) beat Northamptonshire (146 and 114) at Northampton, 1947.
346 runs	Yorkshire (594: 9 dec. and 266: 7 dec.) beat Surrey (344 and 179) at The Oval, 2007.
328 runs	Yorkshire (186 and 318:1 dec) beat Somerset (43 and 133) at Bradford, 1930.
328 runs	Yorkshire (280 and 277:7 dec) beat Glamorgan (104 and 105) at Swansea, 2001
320 runs	Yorkshire (331 and 353:9 dec) beat Durham (150 and 214) at Chester-le-Street, 2004
308 runs	Yorkshire (89 and 420) beat Warwickshire (72 and 129) at Birmingham, 1921.

LARGE MARGINS OF VICTORY – BY 10 WICKETS (WITH OVER 100 RUNS SCORED IN THE 4th INNINGS)

4th Innings	
167:0 wkt	Yorkshire (247 and 167:0) beat Northamptonshire 233 and 180) at Huddersfield, 1948.
147:0 wkt	Yorkshire (381 and 147:0) beat Middlesex (384 and 142) at Lord's, 1896.
142:0 wkt	Yorkshire (304 and 142:0) beat Sussex (254 and 188) at Bradford, 1887.
139:0 wkt	Yorkshire (163:9 dec and 139:0) beat Nottinghamshire (234 and 67) at Leeds, 1932.
138:0 wkt	Yorkshire (293 and 138:0) beat Hampshire (251 and 179) at Southampton, 1897.
132:0 wkt	Yorkshire (328 and 132:0) beat Northamptonshire (281 and 175) at Leeds, 2005
129:0 wkt	Yorkshire (355 and 129:0) beat Durham MCCU (196 and 287) at Durham, 2011
127:0 wkt	Yorkshire (258 and 127:0) beat Cambridge University (127 and 257) at Cambridge, 1930.
119:0 wkt	Yorkshire (109 and 119:0) beat Essex (108 and 119) at Leeds, 1931.
118:0 wkt	Yorkshire (121 and 118:0) beat MCC (125 and 113) at Lord's, 1883.
116:0 wkt	Yorkshire (147 and 116:0) beat Hampshire (141 and 120) at Bournemouth, 1930.
114:0 wkt	Yorkshire (135 and 114:0) beat Hampshire (71 and 176) at Bournemouth, 1948.

HEAVY DEFEATS – BY AN INNINGS AND OVER 250 RUNS

Inns and 272 runs	Yorkshire (78 and 186) lost to Surrey (536) at The Oval, 1898.
Inns and 261 runs	Yorkshire (247 and 89) lost to Sussex (597: 8 dec.) at Hove, 2007.
Inns and 255 runs	Yorkshire (125 and 144) lost to All England XI (524) at Sheffield, 1865.

HEAVY DEFEATS – BY OVER 300 RUNS

324 runs	Yorkshire (247 and 204) lost to Gloucestershire (291 and 484) at Cheltenham, 1994.
305 runs	Yorkshire (119 and 51) lost to Cambridge University (312 and 163) at Cambridge, 1906.

HEAVY DEFEATS – BY 10 WICKETS (WITH OVER 100 RUNS SCORED IN THE 4th INNINGS)

4th Innings

228:0 wkt — Yorkshire (358 and 321) lost to Somerset (452 and 228:0) at Taunton, 2011

148:0 wkt — Yorkshire (83 and 216) lost to Lancashire (154 and 148:0) at Manchester, 1875.

119:0 wkt — Yorkshire (92 and 109) lost to Nottinghamshire (86 and 119:0 wkt) at Leeds, 1989.

108:0 wkt — Yorkshire (236 and 107) lost to Hampshire (236 and 108:0 wkt) at Southampton, 2008

100:0 wkt — Yorkshire (95 and 91) lost to Gloucestershire (88 and 100:0) at Bristol, 1956.

NARROW VICTORIES – BY 1 WICKET

Yorkshire (70 and 91:9) beat Cambridgeshire (86 and 74) at Wisbech, 1867.
Yorkshire (91 and 145:9) beat MCC (73 and 161) at Lord's, 1870.
Yorkshire (265 and 154:9) beat Derbyshire (234 and 184) at Derby, 1897.
Yorkshire (177 and 197:9) beat MCC (188 and 185) at Lord's, 1899.
Yorkshire (391 and 241:9) beat Somerset (349 and 281) at Taunton, 1901.
Yorkshire (239 and 168:9) beat MCC (179 and 226) at Scarborough, 1935.
Yorkshire (152 and 90:9) beat Worcestershire (119 and 121) at Leeds, 1946.
Yorkshire (229 and 175:9) beat Glamorgan (194 and 207) at Bradford, 1960.
Yorkshire (265.9 dec and 191:9) beat Worcestershire (227 and 227) at Worcester, 1961.
Yorkshire (329:6 dec and 167:9) beat Essex (339.9 dec and 154) at Scarborough, 1979.
Yorkshire (Innings forfeited and 251:9 beat Sussex (195 and 55.1 dec) at Leeds, 1986.
Yorkshire (314 and 150:9) beat Essex (200 and 261) at Scarborough, 1998.

NARROW VICTORIES – BY 5 RUNS OR LESS

By 1 run — Yorkshire (228 and 214) beat Middlesex (206 and 235) at Bradford, 1976.

By 1 run — Yorkshire (383 and inns forfeited) beat Loughborough UCCE (93: 3 dec. and 289) at Leeds, 2007.

By 2 runs — Yorkshire (108 and 122) beat Nottinghamshire (56 and 172) at Nottingham, 1870.

By 2 runs — Yorkshire (304:9 dec and 135) beat Middlesex (225:2 dec and 212) at Leeds, 1985.

By 3 runs — Yorkshire (446:9 dec and 172:4 dec) beat Essex (300:3 dec and 315) at Colchester, 1991.

By 5 runs — Yorkshire (271 and 147:6 dec) beat Surrey (198 and 215) at Sheffield, 1950.

By 5 runs — Yorkshire (151 and 176) beat Hampshire (165 and 157) at Bradford, 1962.

By 5 runs — Yorkshire (376:4 and 106) beat Middlesex (325:8 and 152) at Lord's, 1975

By 5 runs — Yorkshire (323:5 dec and inns forfeited) beat Somerset (inns forfeited and 318) at Taunton, 1986.

NARROW DEFEATS – BY 1 WICKET

Yorkshire (224 and 210) lost to Australian Imperial Forces XI (265 and 170:9) at Leeds, 1985.

Yorkshire (101 and 159) lost to Warwickshire (45 and 216:9) at Scarborough, 1934.

Yorkshire (239 and 184:9 dec.) lost to Warwickshire (125 and 302:9) at Birmingham, 1983.

Yorkshire (289 and 153) lost to Surrey (250:2 dec and 193:9) at Guildford, 1991.

Yorkshire (341 and Inns forfeited) lost to Surrey (39:1 dec and 306:9) at Bradford, 1992.

NARROW DEFEATS – BY 5 RUNS OR LESS

By 1 run	Yorkshire (135 and 297) lost to Essex (139 and 294) at Huddersfield, 1897.
By 1 run	Yorkshire (159 and 232) lost to Gloucestershire (164 and 228) at Bristol, 1906.
By 1 run	Yorkshire (126 and 137) lost to Worcestershire (101 and 163) at Worcester, 1968.
By 1 run	Yorkshire (366 and 217) lost to Surrey (409 and 175) at The Oval, 1995.
By 2 runs	Yorkshire (172 and 107) lost to Gloucestershire (157 and 124) at Sheffield, 1913.
By 2 runs	Yorkshire (179:9 dec and 144) lost to MCC (109 and 216) at Lord's, 1957.
By 3 runs	Yorkshire (126 and 181) lost to Sussex (182 and 128) at Sheffield, 1883.
By 3 runs	Yorkshire (160 and 71) lost to Lancashire (81 and 153) at Huddersfield, 1889.
By 3 runs	Yorkshire (134 and 158) lost to Nottinghamshire (200 and 95) at Leeds, 1923.
By 4 runs	Yorkshire (169 and 193) lost to Middlesex (105 and 261) at Bradford, 1920.
By 5 runs	Yorkshire (58 and 51) lost to Lancashire (64 and 50) at Manchester, 1893.
By 5 runs	Yorkshire (119 and 115) lost to Warwickshire (167 and 72) at Bradford, 1969.

HIGH FOURTH INNINGS SCORES – 300 AND OVER

By Yorkshire		
To Win:	406:4	beat Leicestershire by 6 wkts at Leicester, 2005
	402:6	beat Gloucestershire by 4 wkts at Bristol, 2012
	400:4	beat Leicestershire by 6 wkts at Scarborough, 2005
	331:8	beat Middlesex by 2 wkts at Lord's, 1910.
	327:6	beat Nottinghamshire by 4 wkts at Nottingham, 1990.*
	323:5	beat Nottinghamshire by 5 wkts at Nottingham, 1977.
	318:3	beat Glamorgan by 7 wkts at Middlesbrough, 1976.
	316:8	beat Gloucestershire by 2 wkts at Scarborough, 2012
	309:7	beat Somerset by 3 wkts at Taunton, 1984.
	305:8	beat Nottinghamshire by 2 wkts at Worksop, 1982.
	305:3	beat Lancashire by 7 wickets at Manchester, 1994.
	304:4	beat Derbyshire by 6 wkts at Chesterfield, 1959.
	300:4	beat Derbyshire by 6 wkts at Chesterfield, 1981.
	300:6	beat Derbyshire by 4 wkts at Scarborough, 1990.*
To Draw:	341:8	(set 358) drew with Derbyshire at Derby, 2004.
	333:7	(set 369) drew with Essex at Chelmsford, 2010
	316:6	(set 326) drew with Oxford University at Oxford, 1948.
	312:6	(set 344) drew with Sussex at Scarborough 2011
	316:7	(set 320) drew with Somerset at Scarborough, 1990.
	300:5	(set 392) drew with Kent at Canterbury, 2010
To Lose:	433	(set 500) lost to Warwickshire by 66 runs at Birmingham, 2006
	380	(set 406) lost to MCC. by 25 runs at Lord's, 1937.
	343	(set 490) lost to Durham by 146 runs at Leeds 2011
	324	(set 485) lost to Northamptonshire by 160 runs at Luton, 1994.
	322	(set 344) lost to Middlesex by 21 runs at Lord's, 1996.
	309	(set 400) lost to Middlesex by 90 runs at Lord's 1878.

*Consecutive matches

By Opponents:		
To Win:	479:6	Somerset won by 4 wkts at Taunton, 2009
	404:5	Hampshire won by 5 wkts at Leeds, 2006
	392:4	Gloucestershire won by 6 wkts at Bristol, 1948.
	364:4	Somerset won by 6 wickets at Taunton, 2010
	354:5	Nottinghamshire won by 5 wkts at Scarborough, 1990.
	337:4	Worcestershire won by 6 wkts at Kidderminster, 2007.
	334:6	Glamorgan won by 4 wkts at Harrogate, 1955.
	329:5	Worcestershire won by 5 wkts at Worcester, 1979.
	306:9	Surrey won by 1 wkt at Bradford, 1992.
	305:7	Lancashire won by 3 wkts at Manchester, 1980.
	302:9	Warwickshire won by 1 wkt at Birmingham, 1983.

HIGH FOURTH INNINGS SCORES – 300 AND OVER *(Continued)*

By Opponents:

To Draw:	366:8	(set 443) Hampshire drew at Southampton, 2007.
	334:7	(set 339) MCC. drew at Scarborough, 1911.
	322:9	(set 334) Middlesex drew at Leeds, 1988.
	317:6	(set 355) Nottinghamshire drew at Nottingham, 1910.
	300:9	(set 314) Northamptonshire drew at Northampton, 1990.
To Lose:	370	(set 539) Leicestershire lost by 168 runs at Leicester, 2001
	319	(set 364) Gloucestershire lost by 44 runs at Leeds, 1987.
	318	(set 324) Somerset lost by 5 runs at Taunton, 1986.
	315	(set 319) Essex lost by 3 runs at Colchester, 1991.
	314	(set 334) Lancashire lost by 19 runs at Manchester, 1993.
	310	(set 417) Warwickshire lost by 106 runs at Scarborough, 1939.
	306	(set 413) Kent lost by 106 runs at Leeds, 1952.
	300	(set 330) Middlesex lost by 29 runs at Sheffield, 1930.

TIE MATCHES

Yorkshire (351:4 dec and 113) tied with Leicestershire (328 and 136) at Huddersfield, 1954.
Yorkshire (106:9 dec and 207) tied with Middlesex (102 and 211) at Bradford, 1973.

HIGHEST SCORES BY AND AGAINST YORKSHIRE

Yorkshire versus: —

Derbyshire:	**By Yorkshire:**	**Against Yorkshire:**
In Yorkshire:	570 at Leeds, 2005	491 at Bradford, 1949
Away:	662 at Chesterfield, 1898	523 at Derby, 2005
Durham:		
In Yorkshire:	677:7 dec. at Leeds, 2006	518 at Leeds, 2006
Away:	448 at Chester-le-Street, 2003	481 at Chester-le-Street, 2007
Essex:		
In Yorkshire:	516 at Scarborough, 2010	622:8 dec. at Leeds, 2005
Away:	555:1 dec. at Leyton, 1932	521 at Leyton, 1905
Glamorgan:		
In Yorkshire:	580:9 dec at Scarborough, 2001	498 at Leeds, 1999
Away:	536:8 dec. at Cardiff, 1996	482:7 dec. at Cardiff, 1996
Gloucestershire:		
In Yorkshire:	504:7 dec. at Bradford, 1905	411 at Leeds, 1992
Away:	494 at Bristol, 1897	574 at Cheltenham, 1990
Hampshire:		
In Yorkshire:	493:1 dec. at Sheffield, 1939	498:6 dec at Scarborough, 2010
Away	585:3 dec at Portsmouth 1920	599:3 at Southampton, 2011
Kent:		
In Yorkshire	550:9 at Scarborough, 1995	537:9 dec at Leeds, 2012
Away:	559 at Canterbury, 1887	580: 9 dec. at Maidstone, 1998
Lancashire:		
In Yorkshire:	590 at Bradford, 1887	517 at Leeds, 2007.
Away:	528:8 dec. at Manchester, 1939	537 at Manchester, 2005
Leicestershire:		
In Yorkshire	562 { at Scarborough, 1901 at Dewsbury, 1903	681:7 dec. at Bradford, 1996
Away:	660 at Leicester, 1896	425 at Leicester, 1906

HIGHEST SCORES BY AND AGAINST YORKSHIRE *(Continued)*

Yorkshire versus: —

Middlesex:	**By Yorkshire:**	**Against Yorkshire:**
In Yorkshire:	575:7 dec. at Bradford, 1899	527 at Huddersfield, 1887
Away:	538:6 dec. at Lord's, 1925	488 at Lord's, 1899
Northamptonshire:		
In Yorkshire:	673:8 dec. at Leeds, 2003	517:7 dec. at Scarborough, 1999
Away:	523:8 dec. at Wellingborough, 1949	531:4 at Northampton, 1996
Nottinghamshire:		
In Yorkshire:	562 at Bradford, 1899	545:7 dec at Leeds, 2010
Away	534:9 dec at Nottingham, 2011	490 at Nottingham, 1897
Somerset:		
In Yorkshire:	525:4 dec. at Leeds, 1953	630 at Leeds, 1901
Away:	589:5 dec at Bath, 2001	592 at Taunton, 1892
Surrey:		
In Yorkshire:	582:7 dec. at Sheffield, 1935	510 at Leeds, 2002
Away:	704 at The Oval, 1899	560:6 dec. at The Oval, 1933
Sussex:		
In Yorkshire:	681:5 dec. at Sheffield, 1897	566 at Sheffield, 1937
Away:	522:7 dec. at Hastings, 1911	597:8 dec. at Hove, 2007
Warwickshire:		
In Yorkshire	561:7 dec at Scarborough 2007	482 at Leeds, 2011
Away:	887 at Birmingham, 1896 (Highest score by a First-Class county)	601:9 dec. at Birmingham, 2002
Worcestershire:		
In Yorkshire:	600: 4 dec. at Scarborough, 1995	453:5 dec. at Scarborough, 1995
Away:	560:6 dec. at Worcester, 1928	456:8 at Worcester, 1904
Australians:		
In Yorkshire:	377 at Sheffield, 1953	470 at Bradford, 1893
Indians:		
In Yorkshire:	385 at Hull, 1911	490:5 dec. at Sheffield, 1946
New Zealanders:		
In Yorkshire:	419 at Bradford, 1965	370:7 dec. at Bradford, 1949
Pakistanis:		
In Yorkshire:	433:9 dec. at Sheffield, 1954	356 at Sheffield, 1954
South Africans:		
In Yorkshire:	579 at Sheffield, 1951	454:8 dec at Sheffield, 1951
Sri Lankans:		
In Yorkshire:	314:8 dec. at Leeds, 1991	422:8 dec. at Leeds, 1991
West Indians:		
In Yorkshire:	312:5 dec. at Scarborough, 1973	426 at Scarborough, 1995
Zimbabweans:		
In Yorkshire:	298:9 dec at Leeds, 1990	235 at Leeds, 2000
Cambridge University:		
In Yorkshire:	359 at Scarborough, 1967	366 at Leeds, 1998
Away:	540 at Cambridge, 1938	425:7 at Cambridge, 1929
Durham MCCU:		
Away:	355 at Durham, 2011	287 at Durham, 2011
Leeds/Bradford MCCU:		
In Yorkshire	135 at Leeds, 2012	211 at Leeds, 2012
Loughborough MCCU:		
In Yorkshire:	383:6 dec at Leeds, 2007	289 at Leeds, 2007

HIGHEST SCORES BY AND AGAINST YORKSHIRE *(Continued)*

Yorkshire versus: —

MCC:	**By Yorkshire:**	**Against Yorkshire:**
In Yorkshire:	557:8 dec. at Scarborough, 1933	478:8 at Scarborough, 1904
Away:	528:8 dec. at Lord's, 1919	488 at Lord's, 1919
Oxford University:		
In Yorkshire:	173 at Harrogate, 1972	190:6 dec at Harrogate, 1972
Away:	468:6 dec. at Oxford, 1978	422:9 dec. at Oxford, 1953

LOWEST SCORES BY AND AGAINST YORKSHIRE

Yorkshire versus:

Derbyshire:	**By Yorkshire:**	**Against Yorkshire:**
In Yorkshire:	50 at Sheffield, 1894	20 at Sheffield, 1939
Away:	44 at Chesterfield, 1948	26 at Derby, 1880
Durham:		
In Yorkshire:	93 at Leeds, 2003	125 at Harrogate, 1995
Away:	108 at Durham, 1992	74 at Chester-le-Street, 1998
Essex:		
In Yorkshire:	31 at Huddersfield, 1935	52 at Harrogate, 1900
Away:	98 at Leyton, 1905	30 at Leyton, 1901
Glamorgan:		
In Yorkshire:	83 at Sheffield, 1946	52 at Hull, 1926
Away:	92 at Swansea, 1956	48 at Cardiff, 1924
Gloucestershire:		
In Yorkshire:	61 at Leeds, 1894	36 at Sheffield, 1903
Away:	35 at Bristol, 1959	42 at Gloucester, 1924
Hampshire:		
In Yorkshire:	23 at Middlesbrough, 1965	36 at Leeds, 1904
Away:	96 at Bournemouth, 1971	36 at Southampton, 1898
Kent:		
In Yorkshire:	30 at Sheffield, 1865	39 { at Sheffield, 1882 at Sheffield, 1936
Away:	62 at Maidstone, 1889	63 at Canterbury, 1901
Lancashire:		
In Yorkshire:	33 at Leeds, 1924	30 at Holbeck, 1868
Away:	51 { at Manchester, 1888 at Manchester, 1893	39 at Manchester, 1874
Leicestershire:	By Yorkshire:	Against Yorkshire:
In Yorkshire:	93 at Leeds, 1935	34 at Leeds, 1906
Away:	47 at Leicester, 1911	57 at Leicester, 1898
Middlesex:		
In Yorkshire:	45 at Leeds, 1898	45 at Huddersfield, 1879
Away:	43 at Lord's, 1888	49 at Lord's in 1890
Northamptonshire:		
In Yorkshire:	85 at Sheffield, 1919	51 at Bradford, 1920
Away	64 at Northampton, 1959	15 at Northampton, 1908 (and 27 in first innings)
Nottinghamshire:		
In Yorkshire:	32 at Sheffield, 1876	24 at Sheffield, 1888
Away:	43 at Nottingham, 1869	13 at Nottingham, 1901 (second smallest total by a First-Class county)

LOWEST SCORES BY AND AGAINST YORKSHIRE *(continued)*

Yorkshire versus:		
Somerset:	**By Yorkshire:**	**Against Yorkshire:**
In Yorkshire:	73 at Leeds, 1895	43 at Bradford, 1930
Away:	83 at Wells, 1949	35 at Bath, 1898
Surrey:		
In Yorkshire:	54 at Sheffield, 1873	31 at Holbeck, 1883
Away:	26 at The Oval, 1909	44 at The Oval, 1935
Sussex:		
In Yorkshire:	61 at Dewsbury, 1891	20 at Hull, 1922
Away:	42 at Hove, 1922	24 at Hove, 1878
Warwickshire:		
In Yorkshire:	49 at Huddersfield, 1951	35 at Sheffield, 1979
Away:	54 at Birmingham, 1964	35 at Birmingham, 1963
Worcestershire:		
In Yorkshire:	62 at Bradford, 1907	24 at Huddersfield, 1903
Away:	72 at Worcester, 1977	65 at Worcester, 1925
Australians:		
In Yorkshire:	48 at Leeds, 1893	23 at Leeds, 1902
Indians:		
In Yorkshire:	146 at Bradford, 1959	66 at Harrogate, 1932
New Zealanders:		
In Yorkshire:	189 at Harrogate, 1931	134 at Bradford, 1965
Pakistanis:		
In Yorkshire:	137 at Bradford, 1962	150 at Leeds, 1967
South Africans:		
In Yorkshire:	113 at Bradford, 1907	76 at Bradford, 1951
Sri Lankans:		
In Yorkshire:	Have not been dismissed. Lowest is 184:1 dec at Leeds, 1991	287:5 dec at Leeds, 1988
West Indians:		
In Yorkshire:	50 at Harrogate, 1906	58 at Leeds, 1928
Zimbabweans:		
In Yorkshire:	124 at Leeds, 2000	68 at Leeds, 2000
Cambridge University:		
In Yorkshire:	110 at Sheffield, 1903	39 at Sheffield, 1903
Away:	51 at Cambridge, 1906	30 at Cambridge, 1928
Durham MCCU:		
Away	355 at Durham, 2011	196 at Durham, 2011
Loughborough MCCU:		
In Yorkshire	348:5 dec at Leeds, 2010	289 at Leeds, 2007
MCC:		
In Yorkshire:	46 { at Scarborough, 1876 at Scarborough, 1877	31 at Scarborough, 1877
Away:	44 at Lord's, 1880	27 at Lord's, 1902
Oxford University:		
In Yorkshire:	Have not been dismissed. Lowest is 115:8 at Harrogate, 1972	133 at Harrogate, 1972
Away:	141 at Oxford, 1949	46 at Oxford, 1956

INDIVIDUAL INNINGS OF 150 AND OVER

A complete list of all First-class Centuries up to and including 2007 is to be found in the 2008 edition

J M BAIRSTOW (2)

205	v Nottinghamshire	Nottingham	2011
182	v Leicestershire	Scarborough	2012

W BARBER (7)

162	v Middlesex	Sheffield	1932
168	v MCC	Lord's	1934
248	v Kent	Leeds	1934
191	v Sussex	Leeds	1935
255	v Surrey	Sheffield	1935
158	v Kent	Sheffield	1936
157	v Surrey	Sheffield	1938

M G BEVAN (2)

153*	v Surrey	The Oval	1995
160*	v Surrey	Middlesbrough	1996

H D BIRD (1)

181*	v Glamorgan	Bradford	1959

R J BLAKEY (3)

204*	v Gloucestershire	Leeds	1987
196	v Oxford University	Oxford	1991
223*	v Northamptonshire	Leeds	2003

G BLEWETT (1)

190	v Northamptonshire	Scarborough	1999

M W BOOTH (1)

210	v Worcestershire	Worcester	1911

G BOYCOTT (32)

165*	v Leicestershire	Scarborough	1963
151	v Middlesex	Leeds	1964
151*	v Leicestershire	Leicester	1964
177	v Gloucestershire	Bristol	1964
164	v Sussex	Hove	1966
220*	v Northamptonshire	Sheffield	1967
180*	v Warwickshire	Middlesbrough	1968
260*	v Essex	Colchester (Garrison Ground)	1970
169	v Nottinghamshire	Leeds	1971
233	v Essex	Colchester (Garrison Ground)	1971
182*	v Middlesex	Lord's	1971
169	v Lancashire	Sheffield	1971
151	v Leicestershire	Bradford	1971
204*	v Leicestershire	Leicester	1972
152*	v Worcestershire	Worcester	1975
175*	v Middlesex	Scarborough	1975
201*	v Middlesex	Lord's	1975
161*	v Gloucestershire	Leeds	1976
207*	v Cambridge University	Cambridge	1976
156*	v Glamorgan	Middlesbrough	1976

INDIVIDUAL INNINGS OF 150 AND OVER *(Continued)*

G BOYCOTT (Continued)

154	v Nottinghamshire	Nottingham	1977
151*	v Derbyshire	Leeds	1979
167	v Derbyshire	Chesterfield	1979
175*	v Nottinghamshire	Worksop	1979
154*	v Derbyshire	Scarborough	1980
159	v Worcestershire	Sheffield (Abbeydale Park)	1982
152*	v Warwickshire	Leeds	1982
214*	v Nottinghamshire	Worksop	1983
163	v Nottinghamshire	Bradford	1983
169*	v Derbyshire	Chesterfield	1983
153*	v Derbyshire	Harrogate	1984
184	v Worcestershire	Worcester	1985

G L BROPHY (1)

177*	v Worcestershire	Worcester	2011

J T BROWN (8)

168*	v Sussex	Huddersfield	1895
203	v Middlesex	Lord's	1896
311	v Sussex	Sheffield	1897
300	v Derbyshire	Chesterfield	1898
150	v Sussex	Hove	1898
168	v Cambridge University	Cambridge	1899
167	v Australians	Bradford	1899
192	v Derbyshire	Derby	1899

D BYAS (5)

153	v Nottinghamshire	Worksop	1991
156	v Essex	Chelmsford	1993
181	v Cambridge University	Cambridge	1995
193	v Lancashire	Leeds	1995
213	v Worcestershire	Scarborough	1995

D B CLOSE (5)

164	v Combined Services	Harrogate	1954
154	v Nottinghamshire	Nottingham	1959
198	v Surrey	The Oval	1960
184	v Nottinghamshire	Scarborough	1960
161	v Northamptonshire	Northampton	1963

D DENTON (11)

153*	v Australians	Bradford	1905
165	v Hampshire	Bournemouth	1905
172	v Gloucestershire	Bradford	1905
184	v Nottinghamshire	Nottingham	1909
182	v Derbyshire	Chesterfield	1910
200*	v Warwickshire	Birmingham	1912
182	v Gloucestershire	Bristol	1912
221	v Kent	Tunbridge Wells	1912
191	v Hampshire	Southampton	1912
168*	v Hampshire	Southampton	1914
209*	v Worcestershire	Worcester	1920

INDIVIDUAL INNINGS OF 150 AND OVER *(Continued)*

A W GALE (2)

150	v Surrey	The Oval	2008
151*	v Nottinghamshire	Nottingham	2010

P A GIBB (1)

157*	v Nottinghamshire	Sheffield	1935

S HAIGH (1)

159	v Nottinghamshire	Sheffield	1901

L HALL (1)

160	v Lancashire	Bradford	1887

J H HAMPSHIRE (5)

150	v Leicestershire	Bradford	1964
183*	v Sussex	Hove	1971
157*	v Nottinghamshire	Worksop	1974
158	v Gloucestershire	Harrogate	1974
155*	v Gloucestershire	Leeds	1976

I J HARVEY (1)

209*	v Somerset	Leeds	2005

LORD HAWKE (1)

166	v Warwickshire	Birmingham	1896

G H HIRST (15)

186	v Surrey	The Oval	1899
155	v Nottinghamshire	Scarborough	1900
214	v Worcestershire	Worcester	1901
153	v Leicestershire	Dewsbury	1903
153	v Oxford University	Oxford	1904
152	v Hampshire	Portsmouth	1904
157	v Kent	Tunbridge Wells	1904
341	v Leicestershire	Leicester (Aylestone Road)	1905
232*	v Surrey	The Oval	1905
169	v Oxford University	Oxford	1906
158	v Cambridge University	Cambridge	1910
156	v Lancashire	Manchester	1911
218	v Sussex	Hastings	1911
166*	v Sussex	Hastings	1913
180*	v MCC	Lord's	1919

P HOLMES (16)

302*	v Hampshire	Portsmouth	1920
150	v Derbyshire	Chesterfield	1921
277*	v Northamptonshire	Harrogate	1921
209	v Warwickshire	Birmingham	1922
220*	v Warwickshire	Huddersfield	1922
199	v Somerset	Hull	1923
315*	v Middlesex	Lord's	1925
194	v Leicestershire	Hull	1925
159	v Hampshire	Southampton	1925
180	v Gloucestershire	Gloucester	1927
175*	v New Zealanders	Bradford	1927
179*	v Middlesex	Leeds	1928

INDIVIDUAL INNINGS OF 150 AND OVER *(Continued)*

P HOLMES (Continued)

275	v Warwickshire	Bradford	1928
285	v Nottinghamshire	Nottingham	1929
250	v Warwickshire	Birmingham	1931
224*	v Essex	Leyton	1932

L HUTTON (31)

196	v Worcestershire	Worcester	1934
163	v Surrey	Leeds	1936
161	v MCC	Lord's	1937
271*	v Derbyshire	Sheffield	1937
153	v Leicestershire	Hull	1937
180	v Cambridge University	Cambridge	1938
158	v Warwickshire	Birmingham	1939
280*	v Hampshire	Sheffield	1939
151	v Surrey	Leeds	1939
177	v Sussex	Scarborough	1939
183*	v Indians	Bradford	1946
171*	v Northamptonshire	Hull	1946
197	v Glamorgan	Swansea	1947
197	v Essex	Southend-on-Sea	1947
270*	v Hampshire	Bournemouth	1947
176*	v Sussex	Sheffield	1948
155	v Sussex	Hove	1948
167	v New Zealanders	Bradford	1949
201	v Lancashire	Manchester	1949
165	v Sussex	Hove	1949
269*	v Northamptonshire	Wellingborough	1949
156	v Essex	Colchester (Castle Park)	1950
153	v Nottinghamshire	Nottingham	1950
156	v South Africans	Sheffield	1951
151	v Surrey	The Oval	1951
194*	v Nottinghamshire	Nottingham	1951
152	v Lancashire	Leeds	1952
189	v Kent	Leeds	1952
178	v Somerset	Leeds	1953
163	v Combined Services	Harrogate	1954
194	v Nottinghamshire	Nottingham	1955

R A HUTTON (1)

189	v Pakistanis	Bradford	1971

R ILLINGWORTH (2)

150	v Essex	Colchester (Castle Park)	1959
162	v Indians	Sheffield	1959

Hon F S JACKSON (3)

160	v Gloucestershire	Sheffield	1898
155	v Middlesex	Bradford	1899
158	v Surrey	Bradford	1904

P A JAQUES (6)

243	v Hampshire	Southampton (Rose Bowl)	2004
173	v Glamorgan	Leeds	2004
176	v Northamptonshire	Leeds	2005
219	v Derbyshire	Leeds	2005
172	v Durham	Scarborough	2005
160	v Gloucestershire	Bristol	2012

INDIVIDUAL INNINGS OF 150 AND OVER *(Continued)*

R KILNER (5)

169	v Gloucestershire	Bristol	1914
206*	v Derbyshire	Sheffield	1920
166	v Northamptonshire	Northampton	1921
150	v Northamptonshire	Harrogate	1921
150	v Middlesex	Lord's	1926

F LEE (1)

165	v Lancashire	Bradford	1887

D S LEHMANN (13)

177	v Somerset	Taunton	1997
163*	v Leicestershire	Leicester	1997
182	v Hampshire	Portsmouth	1997
200	v Worcestershire	Worcester	1998
187*	v Somerset	Bath	2001
252	v Lancashire	Leeds	2001
193	v Leicestershire	Leicester	2001
216	v Sussex	Arundel	2002
187	v Lancashire	Leeds	2002
150	v Warwickshire	Birmingham	2006
193	v Kent	Canterbury	2006
172	v Kent	Leeds	2006
339	v Durham	Leeds	2006

E I LESTER (5)

186	v Warwickshire	Scarborough	1949
178	v Nottinghamshire	Nottingham	1952
157	v Cambridge University	Hull	1953
150	v Oxford University	Oxford	1954
163	v Essex	Romford	1954

M LEYLAND (17)

191	v Glamorgan	Swansea	1926
204*	v Middlesex	Sheffield	1927
247	v Worcestershire	Worcester	1928
189*	v Glamorgan	Huddersfield	1928
211*	v Lancashire	Leeds	1930
172	v Middlesex	Sheffield	1930
186	v Derbyshire	Leeds	1930
189	v Middlesex	Sheffield	1932
153	v Leicestershire	Leicester (Aylestone Road)	1932
166	v Leicestershire	Bradford	1932
153*	v Hampshire	Bournemouth	1932
192	v Northamptonshire	Leeds	1933
210*	v Kent	Dover	1933
263	v Essex	Hull	1936
163*	v Surrey	Leeds	1936
167	v Worcestershire	Stourbridge	1937
180*	v Middlesex	Lord's	1939

E LOCKWOOD (1)

208	v Kent	Gravesend	1883

J D LOVE (4)

163	v Nottinghamshire	Bradford	1976
170*	v Worcestershire	Worcester	1979
161	v Warwickshire	Birmingham	1981
154	v Lancashire	Manchester	1981

F A LOWSON (10)

155	v Kent	Maidstone	1951
155	v Worcestershire	Bradford	1952
166	v Scotland	Glasgow	1953
259*	v Worcestershire	Worcester	1953
165	v Sussex	Hove	1954
164	v Essex	Scarborough	1954
150*	v Kent	Dover	1954
183*	v Oxford University	Oxford	1956
154	v Somerset	Taunton	1956
154	v Cambridge University	Cambridge	1957

R G LUMB (2)

159	v Somerset	Harrogate	1979
165*	v Gloucestershire	Bradford	1984

A LYTH (1)

248 *	v Leicestershire	Leicester	2012

A McGRATH (7)

165	v Lancashire	Leeds	2002
174	v Derbyshire	Derby	2004
165*	v Leicestershire	Leicester	2005
173*	v Worcestershire	Leeds	2005
158	v Derbyshire	Derby	2005
188*	v Warwickshire	Birmingham	2007
211	v Warwickshire	Birmingham	2009

D R MARTYN (1)

238	v Gloucestershire	Leeds	2003

A A METCALFE (7)

151	v Northamptonshire	Luton	1986
151	v Lancashire	Manchester	1986
152	v MCC	Scarborough	1987
216*	v Middlesex	Leeds	1988
162	v Gloucestershire	Cheltenham	1990
150*	v Derbyshire	Scarborough	1990
194*	v Nottinghamshire	Nottingham	1990

A MITCHELL (7)

189	v Northamptonshire	Northampton	1926
176	v Nottinghamshire	Bradford	1930
177*	v Gloucestershire	Bradford	1932
150*	v Worcestershire	Worcester	1933
158	v MCC	Scarborough	1933
152	v Hampshire	Bradford	1934
181	v Surrey	Bradford	1934

F MITCHELL (2)

194	v Leicestershire	Leicester	1899
162*	v Warwickshire	Birmingham	1901

INDIVIDUAL INNINGS OF 150 AND OVER *(Continued)*

M D MOXON (14)

153	v Lancashire	Leeds	1983
153	v Somerset	Leeds	1985
168	v Worcestershire	Worcester	1985
191	v Northamptonshire	Scarborough	1989
162*	v Surrey	The Oval	1989
218*	v Sussex	Eastbourne	1990
200	v Essex	Colchester (Castle Park)	1991
183	v Gloucestershire	Cheltenham	1992
171*	v Kent	Leeds	1993
161*	v Lancashire	Manchester	1994
274*	v Worcestershire	Worcester	1994
203*	v Kent	Leeds	1995
213	v Glamorgan	Cardiff (Sophia Gardens)	1996
155	v Pakistan 'A'	Leeds	1997

E OLDROYD (5)

151*	v Glamorgan	Cardiff	1922
194	v Worcestershire	Worcester	1923
162*	v Glamorgan	Swansea	1928
168	v Glamorgan	Hull	1929
164*	v Somerset	Bath	1930

D E V PADGETT (1)

161*	v Oxford University	Oxford	1959

R PEEL (2)

158	v Middlesex	Lord's	1889
210*	v Warwickshire	Birmingham	1896

A U RASHID (1)

157*	v Lancashire	Leeds	2009

W RHODES (8)

196	v Worcestershire	Worcester	1904
201	v Somerset	Taunton	1905
199	v Sussex	Hove	1909
176	v Nottinghamshire	Harrogate	1912
152	v Leicestershire	Leicester (Aylestone Road)	1913
167*	v Nottinghamshire	Leeds	1920
267*	v Leicestershire	Leeds	1921
157	v Derbyshire	Leeds	1925

P E ROBINSON (2)

150*	v Derbyshire	Scarborough	1990
189	v Lancashire	Scarborough	1991

J E ROOT (2)

160	v Sussex	Scarborough	2011
222 *	v Hampshire	Southampton (West End)	2012

J W ROTHERY (1)

161	v Kent	Dover	1908

J A RUDOLPH (5)

220	v Warwickshire	Scarborough	2007
155	v Somerset	Taunton	2008
198	v Worcestershire	Leeds	2009
191	v Somerset	Taunton	2009
228*	v Durham	Leeds	2010

INDIVIDUAL INNINGS OF 150 AND OVER *(Continued)*

H RUDSTON (1)

164	v Leicestershire	Leicester (Aylestone Rd)	1904

J J SAYERS (3)

187	v Kent	Tunbridge Wells	2007
173	v Warwickshire	Birmingham	2009
152	v Somerset	Taunton	2009

A B SELLERS (1)

204	v Cambridge University	Cambridge	1936

K SHARP (2)

173	v Derbyshire	Chesterfield	1984
181	v Gloucestershire	Harrogate	1986

P J SHARPE (4)

203*	v Cambridge University	Cambridge	1960
152	v Kent	Sheffield	1960
197	v Pakistanis	Leeds	1967
172*	v Glamorgan	Swansea	1971

G A SMITHSON (1)

169	v Leicestershire	Leicester	1947

W B STOTT (2)

181	v Essex	Sheffield	1957
186	v Warwickshire	Birmingham	1960

H SUTCLIFFE (39)

174	v Kent	Dover	1919
232	v Surrey	The Oval	1922
213	v Somerset	Dewsbury	1924
160	v Sussex	Sheffield	1924
255*	v Essex	Southend-on-Sea	1924
235	v Middlesex	Leeds	1925
206	v Warwickshire	Dewsbury	1925
171	v MCC	Scarborough	1925
200	v Leicestershire	Leicester (Aylestone Road)	1926
176	v Surrey	Leeds	1927
169	v Nottinghamshire	Bradford	1927
228	v Sussex	Eastbourne	1928
150	v Northamptonshire	Northampton	1929
150*	v Essex	Dewsbury	1930
173	v Sussex	Hove	1930
173*	v Cambridge University	Cambridge	1931
230	v Kent	Folkestone	1931
183	v Somerset	Dewsbury	1931
195	v Lancashire	Sheffield	1931
187	v Leicestershire	Leicester (Aylestone Road)	1931
153*	v Warwickshire	Hull	1932
313	v Essex	Leyton	1932
270	v Sussex	Leeds	1932
182	v Derbyshire	Leeds	1932
194	v Essex	Scarborough	1932
205	v Warwickshire	Birmingham	1933
177	v Middlesex	Bradford	1933

INDIVIDUAL INNINGS OF 150 AND OVER *(Continued)*

H SUTCLIFFE (Continued)

174	v Leicestershire	Leicester (Aylestone Road)	1933
152	v Cambridge University	Cambridge	1934
166	v Essex	Hull	1934
203	v Surrey	The Oval	1934
187*	v Worcestershire	Bradford	1934
200*	v Worcestershire	Sheffield	1935
212	v Leicestershire	Leicester (Aylestone Road)	1935
202	v Middlesex	Scarborough	1936
189	v Leicestershire	Hull	1937
165	v Lancashire	Manchester	1939
234*	v Leicestershire	Hull	1939
175	v Middlesex	Lord's	1939

W H H SUTCLIFFE (3)

171*	v Worcestershire	Worcester	1952
181	v Kent	Canterbury	1952
161*	v Glamorgan	Harrogate	1955

K TAYLOR (8)

168*	v Nottinghamshire	Nottingham	1956
159	v Leicestershire	Sheffield	1961
203*	v Warwickshire	Birmingham	1961
178*	v Oxford University	Oxford	1962
163	v Nottinghamshire	Leeds	1962
153	v Lancashire	Manchester	1964
160	v Australians	Sheffield	1964
162	v Worcestershire	Kidderminster	1967

T L TAYLOR (1)

156	v Hampshire	Harrogate	1901

J TUNNICLIFFE (2)

243	v Derbyshire	Chesterfield	1898
158	v Worcestershire	Worcester	1900

G ULYETT (1)

199*	v Derbyshire	Sheffield	1887

M P VAUGHAN (7)

183	v Glamorgan	Cardiff (Sophia Gardens)	1996
183	v Northamptonshire	Northampton	1996
161	v Essex	Ilford	1997
177	v Durham	Chester-le-Street	1998
151	v Essex	Chelmsford	1999
153	v Kent	Scarborough	1999
155*	v Derbyshire	Leeds	2000

E WAINWRIGHT (3)

171	v Middlesex	Lord's	1897
153	v Leicestershire	Leicester	1899
228	v Surrey	The Oval	1899

INDIVIDUAL INNINGS OF 150 AND OVER *(Continued)*

W WATSON (7)

153*	v Surrey	The Oval	1947
172	v Derbyshire	Scarborough	1948
162*	v Somerset	Leeds	1953
163	v Sussex	Sheffield	1955
174	v Lancashire	Sheffield	1955
214*	v Worcestershire	Worcester	1955
162	v Northamptonshire	Harrogate	1957

C WHITE (6)

181	v Lancashire	Leeds	1996
172*	v Worcestershire	Leeds	1997
186	v Lancashire	Manchester	2001
183	v Glamorgan	Scarborough	2001
161	v Leicestershire	Scarborough	2002
173*	v Derbyshire	Derby	2003

B B WILSON (2)

150	v Warwickshire	Birmingham	1912
208	v Sussex	Bradford	1914

J V WILSON (7)

157*	v Sussex	Leeds	1949
157	v Essex	Sheffield	1950
166*	v Sussex	Hull	1951
223*	v Scotland	Scarborough	1951
154	v Oxford University	Oxford	1952
230	v Derbyshire	Sheffield	1952
165	v Oxford University	Oxford	1956

M J WOOD (5)

200*	v Warwickshire	Leeds	1998
157	v Northamptonshire	Leeds	2003
207	v Somerset	Taunton	2003
155	v Hampshire	Scarborough	2003
202*	v Bangladesh 'A'	Leeds	2005

N W D YARDLEY (2)

177	v Derbyshire	Scarborough	1947
183*	v Hampshire	Leeds	1951

YOUNUS KHAN (2)

202*	v Hampshire	Southampton (Rose Bowl)	2007
217*	v Kent	Scarborough	2007

CENTURIES BY CURRENT PLAYERS

A complete list of all First-class Centuries up to and including 2007 is to be found in the 2008 edition

AZEEM RAFIQ (1)

100	v Worcestershire	Worcester	2009

J M BAIRSTOW (5)

205	v. Nottinghamshire	Nottingham	2011
136	v. Somerset	Taunton	2011
182	v. Leicestershire	Scarborough	2012
118	v. Leicestershire	Leicester	2012
107	v. Kent	Leeds	2012

G S BALLANCE (2)

111	v Warwickshire	Birmingham	2011
121*	v.Gloucestershire	Bristol	2012

T T BRESNAN (2)

116	v Surrey	The Oval	2007
101*	v Warwickshire	Scarborough	2007

A W GALE (11)

149	v Warwickshire	Scarborough	2006
138	v Hampshire	Leeds	2008
150	v Surrey	The Oval	2008
136	v Lancashire	Manchester	2008
101	v Worcestershire	Worcester	2009
121	v Lancashire	Manchester	2009
101	v Somerset	Leeds	2010
135	v Essex	Scarborough	2010
151*	v Nottinghamshire	Nottingham	2010
145*	v Nottinghamshire	Leeds	2011
101*	v Durham	Chester-le-Street	2011

P A JAQUES (9)

115	v. Essex	Chelmsford	2004
243	v. Hampshire	Southampton (Rose Bowl)	2004
173	v. Glamorgan	Leeds	2004
176	v. Northamptonshire	Leeds	2005
219	v. Derbyshire	Leeds	2005
106	v. Somerset	Taunton	2005
172	v. Durham	Scarborough	2005
126	v. Essex	Leeds	2012
160	v. Gloucestershire	Bristol	2012

A LYTH (5)

132	v Nottinghamshire	Nottingham	2008
142	v Somerset	Taunton	2010
133	v Hampshire	Southampton	2010
100	v Lancashire	Manchester	2010
248*	v. Leicestershire	Leicester	2012

R M PYRAH (3)

106	v Loughborough UCCE	Leeds	2007
134*	v Loughborough MCCU	Leeds	2010
117	v Lancashire	Leeds	

CENTURIES BY CURRENT PLAYERS *(Continued)*

A U RASHID (4)

108	v Worcestershire	Kidderminster	2007
111	v Sussex	Hove	2008
117*	v Hampshire	Basingstoke	2009
157*	v Lancashire	Leeds	2009

J E ROOT (3)

160	v Sussex	Scarborough	2011
222 *	v Hampshire	Southampton (West End)	2012
125	v Northamptonshire	Leeds	2012

J J SAYERS (9)

104	v Leicestershire	Scarborough	2005
115	v Bangladesh 'A'	Leeds	2005
122*	v Middlesex	Scarborough	2006
149*	v Durham	Leeds	2007
123	v Worcestershire	Leeds	2007
187	v Kent	Tunbridge Wells	2007
173	v Warwickshire	Birmingham	2009
152	v Somerset	Taunton	2009
139	v Durham MCCU	Durham	2011

CENTURIES

(Including highest score)

112	H Sutcliffe	313	v Essex	at Leyton	1932
103	G Boycott	260*	v Essex	at Colchester (Garrison Gd)	1970
85	L Hutton	280*	v Hampshire	at Sheffield	1939
62	M Leyland	263	v Essex	at Hull	1936
61	D Denton	221	v Kent	at Tunbridge Wells	1912
60	P Holmes	315*	v Middlesex	at Lord's	1925
56	G H Hirst	341	v Leicestershire	at Leicester (Aylestone Rd)	1905
46	W Rhodes	267*	v Leicestershire	at Leeds	1921
41	M D Moxon	274*	v Worcestershire	at Worcester	1994
39	A Mitchell	189	v Northamptonshire	at Northampton	1926
37	E Oldroyd	194	v Worcestershire	at Worcester	1923
34	J H Hampshire	183*	v Sussex	at Hove	1971
34	A McGrath	211	v Warwickshire	at Birmingham	2009
33	D B Close	198	v Surrey	at The Oval	1960
30	F A Lowson	259*	v Worcestershire	at Worcester	1953
29	D E V Padgett	161*	v Oxford University	at Oxford	1959
29	J V Wilson	230	v Derbyshire	at Sheffield	1952
28	D Byas	213	v Worcestershire	at Scarborough	1995
27	W Barber	255	v Surrey	at Sheffield	1935
26	D S Lehmann	339	v Durham	at Leeds	2006
26	W Watson	214*	v Worcestershire	at Worcester	1955
25	A A Metcalfe	216*	v Middlesex	at Leeds	1988
24	E I Lester	186	v Warwickshire	at Scarborough	1949
23	J T Brown	311	v Sussex	at Sheffield	1897
23	P J Sharpe	203*	v Cambridge University	at Cambridge	1960
22	R G Lumb	165*	v Gloucestershire	at Bradford	1984
22	J Tunnicliffe	243	v Derbyshire	at Chesterfield	1898
21	Hon F S Jackson	160	v Gloucestershire	at Sheffield	1898
20	M P Vaughan	183	v Glamorgan	at Cardiff (Sophia Gardens)	1996
	and	183	v Northamptonshire	at Northampton	1996
19	C White	186	v Lancashire	at Manchester	2001
18	J A Rudolph	228*	v Durham	at Leeds	2010

CENTURIES (Including highest score) *(Continued)*

18	E Wainwright	228	v Surrey	at The Oval	1899
17	W B Stott	186	v Warwickshire	at Birmingham	1960
17	N W D Yardley	183*	v Hampshire	at Leeds	1951
16	K Taylor	203*	v Warwickshire	at Birmingham	1961
16	M J Wood	207	v Somerset	at Taunton	2003
15	R Kilner	206*	v Derbyshire	at Sheffield	1920
15	G Ulyett	199*	v Derbyshire	at Sheffield	1887
15	B B Wilson	208	v Sussex	at Bradford	1914
14	R Illingworth	162	v Indians	at Sheffield	1959
13	J D Love	170*	v Worcestershire	at Worcester	1979
12	R J Blakey	223*	v Northamptonshire	at Leeds	2003
12	H Halliday	144	v Derbyshire	at Chesterfield	1950
11	A W Gale	151*	v Nottinghamshire	at Nottingham	2010
11	K Sharp	181	v Gloucestershire	at Harrogate	1986
10	C W J Athey	134	v Derbyshire	at Derby	1982
10	Lord Hawke	166	v Warwickshire	at Birmingham	1896
10	F Mitchell	194	v Leicestershire	at Leicester	1899
9	D L Bairstow	145	v Middlesex	at Scarborough	1980
9	M G Bevan	160*	v Surrey	at Middlesbrough	1996
9	P A Jaques	243	v Hampshire	at Southampton (Rose Bowl)	2004
9	L Hall	160	v Lancashire	at Bradford	1887
9	J J Sayers	187	v Kent	at Tunbridge Wells	2007
8	W Bates	136	v Sussex	at Hove	1886
8	M J Lumb	144	v Middlesex	at Southgate	2006
8	T L Taylor	156	v Hampshire	at Harrogate	1901
7	J B Bolus	146*	v Hampshire	at Portsmouth	1960
7	E Robinson	135*	v Leicestershire	at Leicester (Aylestone Rd)	1921
7	P E Robinson	189	v Lancashire	at Scarborough	1991
6	E Lockwood	208	v Kent	at Gravesend	1883
6	R Peel	210*	v Warwickshire	at Birmingham	1896
6	W H H Sutcliffe	181	v Kent	at Canterbury	1952
5	J M Bairstow	205	v Nottinghamshire	at Nottingham	2011
5	A Lyth	248 *	v Leicestershire	at Leicester	2012
5	C M Old	116	v Indians	at Bradford	1974
4	I Grimshaw	129*	v Cambridge University	at Sheffield	1885
4	S Haigh	159	v Nottinghamshire	at Sheffield	1901
4	S N Hartley	114	v Gloucestershire	at Bradford	1982
4	R A Hutton	189	v Pakistanis	at Bradford	1971
4	A U Rashid	157*	v Lancashire	at Leeds	2009
4	A B Sellers	204	v Cambridge University	at Cambridge	1936
3	G L Brophy	177*	v Worcestershire	at Worcester	2011
3	P Carrick	131*	v Northamptonshire	at Northampton	1980
3	A J Dalton	128	v Middlesex	at Leeds	1972
3	A Drake	147*	v Derbyshire	at Chesterfield	1911
3	F Lee	165	v Lancashire	at Bradford	1887
3	G G Macaulay	125*	v Nottinghamshire	at Nottingham	1921
3	R Moorhouse	113	v Somerset	at Taunton	1896
3	R M Pyrah	134*	v Loughborough MCCU	at Leeds	2010
3	J E Root	222 *	v Hampshire	at Southampton (West End)	2012
3	J W Rothery	161	v Kent	at Dover	1908
3	J Rowbotham	113	v Surrey	at The Oval	1873
3	T F Smailes	117	v Glamorgan	at Cardiff	1938
3	Younus Khan	217*	v Kent	at Scarborough	2007
2	G S Ballance	121 *	v Gloucestershire	at Bristol	2012
2	M W Booth	210	v Worcestershire	at Worcester	1911
2	T T Bresnan	116	v Surrey	at The Oval	2007

CENTURIES (Including highest score) *(Continued)*

2	D C F Burton	142*	v Hampshire	at Dewsbury	1919
2	K R Davidson	128	v Kent	at Maidstone	1934
2	P A Gibb	157*	v Nottinghamshire	at Sheffield	1935
2	P J Hartley	127*	v Lancashire	at Manchester	1988
2	I J Harvey	209*	v Somerset	at Leeds	2005
2	C Johnson	107	v Somerset	at Sheffield	1973
2	S A Kellett	125*	v Derbyshire	at Chesterfield	1991
2	N Kilner	112	v Leicestershire	at Leeds	1921
2	B Parker	138*	v Oxford University	at Oxford	1997
2	A Sellers	105	v Middlesex	at Lord's	1893
2	E Smith (Morley)	129	v Hampshire	at Bradford	1899
2	G A Smithson	169	v Leicestershire	at Leicester	1947
2	G B Stevenson	115*	v Warwickshire	at Birmingham	1982
2	F S Trueman	104	v Northamptonshire	at Northampton	1963
2	C Turner	130	v Somerset	at Sheffield	1936
2	D J Wainwright	104*	v Sussex	at Hove	2008
2	T A Wardall	106	v Gloucestershire	at Gloucester (Spa Ground)	1892
1	Azeem Rafiq	100	v Worcestershire	at Worcester	2009
1	A T Barber	100	v England XI	at Sheffield	1929
1	H D Bird	181*	v Glamorgan	at Bradford	1959
1	T J D Birtles	104	v Lancashire	at Sheffield	1914
1	G S Blewett	190	v Northamptonshire	at Scarborough	1999
1	M T G Elliott	127	v Warwickshire	at Birmingham	2002
1	T Emmett	104	v Gloucestershire	at Clifton	1873
1	G M Fellows	109	v Lancashire	at Manchester	2002
1	J N Gillespie	123*	v Surrey	at The Oval	2007
1	D Gough	121	v Warwickshire	at Leeds	1996
1	A K D Gray	104	v Somerset	at Taunton	2003
1	A P Grayson	100	v Worcestershire	at Worcester	1994
1	F E Greenwood	104*	v Glamorgan	at Hull	1929
1	G M Hamilton	125	v Hampshire	at Leeds	2000
1	W E Harbord	109	v Oxford University	at Oxford	1930
1	R Iddison	112	v Cambridgeshire	at Hunslet	1869
1	W G Keighley	110	v Surrey	at Leeds	1951
1	R A Kettleborough	108	v Essex	at Leeds	1996
1	B Leadbeater	140*	v Hampshire	at Portsmouth	1976
1	D R Martyn	238	v Gloucestershire	at Leeds	2003
1	J T Newstead	100*	v Nottinghamshire	at Nottingham	1908
1	R B Richardson	112	v Warwickshire	at Birmingham	1993
1	H Rudston	164	v Leicestershire	at Leicester (Aylestone Road)	1904
1	A Sidebottom	124	v Glamorgan	at Cardiff (Sophia Gardens)	1977
1	I G Swallow	114	v MCC	at Scarborough	1987
1	S R Tendulkar	100	v Durham	at Durham	1992
1	J Thewlis	108	v Surrey	at The Oval	1868
1	C T Tyson	100*	v Hampshire	at Southampton	1921
1	H Verity	101	v Jamaica	at Kingston (Sabina Park)	1935/36
1	A Waddington	114	v Worcestershire	at Leeds	1927
1	W A I Washington	100*	v Surrey	at Leeds	1902
1	H Wilkinson	113	v MCC	at Scarborough	1904
1	W H Wilkinson	103	v Sussex	at Sheffield	1909
1	E R Wilson	104*	v Essex	at Bradford	1913
1	A Wood	123*	v Worcestershire	at Sheffield	1935
1	J D Woodford	101	v Warwickshire	at Middlesbrough	1971

SUMMARY OF CENTURIES
FOR AND AGAINST YORKSHIRE 1863-2012

FOR YORKSHIRE				AGAINST YORKSHIRE		
Total	**In Yorkshire**	**Away**		**Total**	**In Yorkshire**	**Away**
106	63	43	**Derbyshire**	**55**	26	29
20	9	11	**Durham**	**16**	10	6
75	34	41	**Essex**	**46**	21	25
68	38	30	**Glamorgan**	**23**	13	10
87	41	46	**Gloucestershire**	**53**	27	26
88	36	52	**Hampshire**	**56**	25	31
81	37	44	**Kent**	**60**	29	31
109	56	53	**Lancashire**	**112**	58	54
97	52	45	**Leicestershire**	**46**	23	23
89	45	44	**Middlesex**	**84**	36	48
78	34	44	**Northamptonshire**	**53**	25	28
118	55	63	**Nottinghamshire**	**81**	32	49
93	47	46	**Somerset**	**56**	20	36
111	47	64	**Surrey**	**104**	37	67
87	41	46	**Sussex**	**70**	31	39
101	35	66	**Warwickshire**	**71**	27	44
72	30	42	**Worcestershire**	**40**	14	26
1	1	—	**Cambridgeshire**	—	—	—
1481	701	780	**Totals**	**1026**	454	572
9	9	—	**Australians**	**16**	16	—
9	9	—	**Indians**	**7**	7	—
8	8	—	**New Zealanders**	**3**	3	—
5	5	—	**Pakistanis**	**1**	1	—
9	9	—	**South Africans**	**7**	7	—
5	5	—	**Sri Lankans**	**1**	1	—
5	5	—	**West Indians**	**6**	6	—
1	1	—	**Zimbabweans**	—	—	—
3	3	—	**Bangladesh 'A'**	**1**	1	—
—	—	—	**India 'A'**	**1**	1	—
1	1	—	**Pakistan 'A'**	**1**	1	—
45	1	44	**Cambridge University**	**20**	2	18
2	2	—	**Combined Services**	—	—	—
1	—	1	**Durham MCCU**	1	—	1
4	3	1	**England XI's**	**3**	2	1
—	—	—	**International XI**	**1**	1	—
1	—	1	**Ireland**	—	—	—
3	—	3	**Jamaica**	**3**	—	3
1	—	1	**Liverpool & District**	—	—	—
2	2	—	**Loughborough MCCU**	**1**	1	—
1	—	1	**Mashonaland**	—	—	—
2	—	2	**Matebeleland**	**1**	—	1
52	38	14	**MCC**	**52**	34	18
39	—	39	**Oxford University**	**11**	—	11
6	—	6	**Rest of England**	**15**	—	15
9	5	4	**Scotland**	**1**	—	1
3	3	—	**C I Thornton's XI**	**4**	4	—
—	—	—	**Western Province**	**1**	—	1
1	1	—	**I Zingari**	**1**	1	—
227	110	117	**Totals**	**161**	91	70
1708	811	897	**Grand Totals**	**1187**	545	642

FOUR CENTURIES IN ONE INNINGS

1896	v.	Warwickshire at Birmingham	F S Jackson	117
			E Wainwright	126
			Lord Hawke	166
			R Peel	*210

(First instance in First-Class cricket)

THREE CENTURIES IN ONE INNINGS

1884	v.	Cambridge University at Cambridge	L Hall	116
			W Bates	133
			I Grimshaw	115
1887	v.	Kent at Canterbury	G Ulyett	124
			L Hall	110
			F Lee	119
1897	v.	Sussex at Sheffield	J T Brown	311
			J Tunnicliffe	147
			E Wainwright	*104
1899	v.	Middlesex at Bradford	F S Jackson	155
			D Denton	113
			F Mitchell	121
1904	v.	Surrey at The Oval	D Denton	105
			G H Hirst	104
			J Tunnicliffe	*139
1919	v.	Gloucestershire at Leeds	H Sutcliffe	118
			D Denton	122
			R Kilner	*115
1925	v.	Glamorgan at Huddersfield	P Holmes	130
			H Sutcliffe	121
			E Robinson	*108
1928	v.	Middlesex at Lord's	P Holmes	105
			E Oldroyd	108
			A Mitchell	105
1928	v.	Essex at Leyton	H Sutcliffe	129
			P Holmes	136
			M Leyland	*133
1929	v.	Glamorgan at Hull	E Oldroyd	168
			W Barber	114
			F E Greenwood	*104
1933	v.	MCC at Scarborough	H Sutcliffe	107
			A Mitchell	158
			M Leyland	133
1936	v.	Surrey at Leeds	H Sutcliffe	129
			L Hutton	163
			M Leyland	*163
1937	v.	Leicestershire at Hull	H Sutcliffe	189
			L Hutton	153
			M Leyland	*118
1947	v.	Leicestershire at Leicester	L Hutton	137
			N W D Yardley	100
			G.A Smithson	169
1971	v.	Oxford University at Oxford	J H Hampshire	*116
			R A Hutton	101
			A J Dalton	111

THREE CENTURIES IN ONE INNINGS *(Continued)*

1975 v. Gloucestershire at Bristol	G Boycott	141
	R G Lumb	101
	J H Hampshire	*106
1995 v. Cambridge University at Cambridge	M D Moxon	130
	D Byas	181
	M G Bevan	*113
2001 v. Leicestershire at Leeds	M J Wood	102
	M J Lumb	122
	D S Lehmann	104
2001 v. Glamorgan at Scarborough	C White	183
	M J Wood	124
	D Byas	104
2007 v. Surrey at The Oval	J A Rudolph	122
	T T Bresnan	116
	J N Gillespie	*123

CENTURY IN EACH INNINGS

D Denton	107 and 109*	v. Nottinghamshire at Nottingham, 1906
G H Hirst	111 and 117*	v. Somerset at Bath, 1906
D Denton	133 and 121	v. MCC at Scarborough, 1908
W Rhodes	128 and 115	v. MCC at Scarborough, 1911
P Holmes	126 and 111*	v. Lancashire at Manchester, 1920
H Sutcliffe	107 and109*	v. MCC at Scarborough, 1926
H Sutcliffe	111 and 100*	v. Nottinghamshire at Nottingham, 1928
E I Lester	126 and 142	v. Northamptonshire at Northampton, 1947
L Hutton	197 and 104	v. Essex at Southend, 1947
E I Lester	125* and 132	v. Lancashire at Manchester, 1948
L Hutton	165 and 100	v. Sussex at Hove, 1949
L Hutton	103 and 137	v. MCC at Scarborough, 1952
G Boycott	103 and 105	v. Nottinghamshire at Sheffield, 1966
G Boycott	163 and 141*	v. Nottinghamshire at Bradford, 1983
M D Moxon	123 and 112*	v. Indians at Scarborough, 1986
A A Metcalfe	194* and 107	v. Nottinghamshire at Nottingham, 1990
M P Vaughan	100 and 151	v. Essex at Chelmsford, 1999
Younus Khan	106 and 202*	v. Hampshire at Southampton, 2007

HIGHEST INDIVIDUAL SCORES FOR AND AGAINST YORKSHIRE

Highest For Yorkshire:

341 G H Hirst v. Leicestershire at Leicester, 1905

Highest Against Yorkshire:

318* W G Grace for Gloucestershire at Cheltenham, 1876

Yorkshire versus:

Derbyshire	*For Yorkshire:*	300 — J T Brown at Chesterfield, 1898
	Against:	219 — J D Eggar at Bradford, 1949
Most Centuries	*For Yorkshire:*	G Boycott 9
	Against:	K J Barnett and W Storer 4 each
Durham	*For Yorkshire:*	339 — D S Lehmann at Leeds, 2006
	Against:	184 — M J di Venuto at Chester-le-Street, 2008
Most Centuries	*For Yorkshire:*	A McGrath 5
	Against:	M J Di Venuto 4
Essex	*For Yorkshire:*	313 — H Sutcliffe at Leyton, 1932
	Against:	219* — D J Insole at Colchester, 1949
Most Centuries	*For Yorkshire:*	H Sutcliffe 9
	Against:	F L Fane, K W R Fletcher, G A Gooch and D J Insole 3 each

HIGHEST INDIVIDUAL SCORES FOR AND AGAINST YORKSHIRE *(continued)*

Yorkshire versus

Glamorgan	*For Yorkshire:*	213 –- M D Moxon at Cardiff, 1996
	Against:	202* — H Morris at Cardiff, 1996
Most Centuries	*For Yorkshire:*	G Boycott, P Holmes and H Sutcliffe 5 each
	Against:	H Morris 5
Gloucestershire	*For Yorkshire:*	238 — D R Martyn at Leeds, 2003
	Against:	318*— W G Grace at Cheltenham, 1876
Most Centuries	*For Yorkshire:*	G Boycott 6
	Against:	W G Grace 9
Hampshire	*For Yorkshire:*	302* — P Holmes at Portsmouth, 1920
	Against:	300* — M A Carberry at Southampton, 2011
Most Centuries	*For Yorkshire:*	H Sutcliffe 6
	Against:	C P Mead 10
Kent	*For Yorkshire:*	248 — W Barber at Leeds, 1934.
	Against:	207 — D P Fulton at Maidstone, 1998
Most Centuries	*For Yorkshire:*	A McGrath 6
	Against:	F E Woolley 5
Lancashire	*For Yorkshire:*	252 — D S Lehmann at Leeds, 2001
	Against:	225 — G D Lloyd at Leeds, 1997 (Non-Championship)
		206 — S G Law at Leeds, 2007
Most Centuries	*For Yorkshire:*	G Boycott and H Sutcliffe 9 each
	Against:	M A Atherton and C H Lloyd 6 each.
Leicestershire	*For Yorkshire:*	341— G H Hirst at Leicester, 1905
	Against:	218— J J Whitaker at Bradford, 1996
Most Centuries	*For Yorkshire:*	H Sutcliffe 10
	Against:	J J Whitaker and C J B Wood 5 each
Middlesex	*For Yorkshire:*	315*— P Holmes at Lord's, 1925
	Against:	243*— A J Webbe at Huddersfield, 1887
Most Centuries	*For Yorkshire:*	P Holmes and H Sutcliffe 7 each
	Against:	M W Gatting 8
Northamptonshire	*For Yorkshire:*	277* — P Holmes at Harrogate, 1921
	Against:	235 — A J Lamb at Leeds, 1990
Most Centuries	*For Yorkshire:*	H Sutcliffe 5
	Against:	W Larkins 5
Nottinghamshire	*For Yorkshire:*	285 — P Holmes at Nottingham, 1929
	Against:	251* — D J Hussey at Leeds, 2010
Most Centuries	*For Yorkshire:*	G Boycott 15
	Against:	R T Robinson 6
Somerset	*For Yorkshire:*	213 — H Sutcliffe at Dewsbury, 1924
	Against:	297 — M J Wood at Taunton, 2005
Most Centuries	*For Yorkshire:*	G Boycott 6
	Against:	L C H Palairet, IVA. Richards, M E Trescothick 5 each
Surrey	*For Yorkshire:*	255 — W Barber at Sheffield, 1935
	Against:	273 — T W Hayward at The Oval, 1899
Most Centuries	*For Yorkshire:*	H Sutcliffe 9
	Against:	J B Hobbs 8

HIGHEST INDIVIDUAL SCORES FOR AND AGAINST YORKSHIRE *(continued)*

Yorkshire versus

Sussex	*For Yorkshire:*	311 — J T Brown at Sheffield, 1897
	Against:	274* — M W Goodwin at Hove, 2011
Most Centuries	*For Yorkshire:*	L Hutton 8
	Against:	C B Fry 7
Warwickshire	*For Yorkshire:*	275 — P Holmes at Bradford, 1928
	Against:	225 — D P Ostler at Birmingham, 2002
Most Centuries	*For Yorkshire:*	G Boycott and H Sutcliffe 8 each
	Against:	D L Amiss, H E Dollery, R B Khanhai and W G Quaife 4 each.
Worcestershire	*For Yorkshire:*	274* — M D Moxon at Worcester, 1994
	Against:	259 — D Kenyon at Kidderminster, 1956
Most Centuries	*For Yorkshire:*	M Leyland 6
	Against:	D Kenyon and G M Turner 5 each
Australians	*For Yorkshire:*	167 — J T Brown at Bradford, 1899
	Against:	193* — B C Booth at Bradford, 1964
Most Centuries	*For Yorkshire:*	G Boycott and D Denton 2 each
	Against:	N C O'Neill 2
Indians	*For Yorkshire:*	183* — L Hutton at Bradford, 1946
	Against:	244* — V S Hazare at Sheffield, 1946
Most Centuries	*For Yorkshire:*	M D Moxon 2
	Against:	V S Hazare, VMankad, PR Umrigar D K Gaekwad, G A Parkar and R Lamba 1 each
New Zealanders	*For Yorkshire:*	175 — P Holmes at Bradford, 1927
	Against:	126 — W M Wallace at Bradford, 1949
Most Centuries	*For Yorkshire:*	L Hutton and DB Close 2 each
	Against:	H G Vivian, WM Wallace and J G Wright 1 each
Pakistanis	*For Yorkshire:*	197 — P J Sharpe at Leeds, 1967
	Against:	139 — A H Kardar at Sheffield, 1954
Most Centuries	*For Yorkshire:*	P J Sharpe 2
	Against:	A H Kardar 1
South Africans	*For Yorkshire:*	156 — L Hutton at Sheffield, 1951
	Against:	168 — I J Seidle at Sheffield, 1929
Most Centuries	*For Yorkshire:*	L Hutton 2
	Against:	H B Cameron, J D Lindsay, B Mitchell, D P B Morkel, I J Seidle, L J Tancred, C B van Ryneveld 1 each
Sri Lankans	*For Yorkshire:*	132 — M D Moxon at Leeds, 1988
	Against:	112 — S A R Silva at Leeds, 1988
Most Centuries	*For Yorkshire:*	K Sharp 2
	Against:	S A R Silva 1
West Indians	*For Yorkshire:*	112* — D Denton at Harrogate, 1906
	Against:	164 — S F A Bacchus at Leeds, 1980
Most Centuries	*For Yorkshire:*	M G Bevan, D Denton, L Hutton, R G Lumb and A A Metcalfe 1 each
	Against:	S F A Bacchus, C O Browne, S Chanderpaul P A Goodman, C L Hooper and G St A Sobers 1 each

HIGHEST INDIVIDUAL SCORES FOR AND AGAINST YORKSHIRE *(continued)*

Yorkshire versus

Zimbabweans	*For Yorkshire:*	113 — M D Moxon at Leeds, 1990
	Against:	89 — G J Whittall at Leeds, 2000
Most Centuries	*For Yorkshire:*	M D Moxon 1
	Against:	None
Cambridge University	*For Yorkshire:*	207* — G Boycott at Cambridge, 1976
	Against:	171* — G L Jessop at Cambridge, 1899
		171 — P B H May at Cambridge, 1952
Most Centuries	*For Yorkshire:*	H Sutcliffe 4
	Against:	G M Kemp 2
Durham MCCU	*For Yorkshire:*	139 — J J Sayers at Durham, 2011
	Against:	127 — T Westley at Durham, 2011
Most Centuries	*For Yorkshire:*	J J Sayers 1
	Against:	T Westley 1
Leeds Bradford MCCU	*For Yorkshire:*	43 — A McGrath at Leeds, 2012
	Against:	69 — A MacQueen at Leeds, 2012
Loughborough MCCU	*For Yorkshire:*	134* — R M Pyrah at Leeds, 2010
	Against:	107 — C P Murtagh at Leeds, 2007
Most Centuries	*For Yorkshire:*	R M Pyrah 2
	Against:	C P Murtagh 1
MCC	*For Yorkshire:*	180* — G H Hirst at Lord's, 1919
	Against:	214 — E H Hendren at Lord's, 1919
Most Centuries	*For Yorkshire:*	L Hutton 8
	Against:	R E S Wyatt 5
Oxford University	*For Yorkshire:*	196 — R J Blakey at Oxford, 1991
	Against:	201— J E Raphael at Oxford, 1904
Most Centuries	*For Yorkshire:*	M Leyland 4
	Against:	A A Baig and Nawab of Pataudi (Jun.) 2 each

J B Hobbs scored 11 centuries against Yorkshire – the highest by any individual (8 for Surrey and 3 for the Rest of England).

Three players have scored 10 centuries against Yorkshire – W G Grace (9 for Gloucestershire and 1 for MCC). E H Hendren (6 for Middlesex, 3 for MCC and 1 for the Rest of England) and C P Mead (all 10 for Hampshire).

CARRYING BAT THROUGH A COMPLETED INNINGS

Batsman	*Score*	*Total*	*Against*	*Season*
G R Atkinson	30*	73	Nottinghamshire at Bradford	1865
L Hall	31*	94	Sussex at Hove	1878
L Hall	124*	331	Sussex at Hove	1883
L Hall	128*	285	Sussex at Huddersfield	1884
L Hall	32*	81	Kent at Sheffield	1885
L Hall	79*	285	Surrey at Sheffield	1885
L Hall	37*	96	Derbyshire at Derby	1885
L Hall	50*	173	Sussex at Huddersfield	1886
L Hall	74*	172	Kent at Canterbury	1886
G Ulyett	199*	399	Derbyshire at Sheffield	1887
L Hall	119*	334	Gloucestershire at Dewsbury	1887
L Hall	82*	218	Sussex at Hove	1887
L Hall	34*	104	Surrey at The Oval	1888
L Hall	129*	461	Gloucestershire at Clifton	1888
L Hall	85*	259	Middlesex at Lord's	1889
L Hall	41*	106	Nottinghamshire at Sheffield	1891
W Rhodes	98*	184	MCC at Lord's	1903
W Rhodes	85*	152	Essex at Leyton	1910
P Holmes	145*	270	Northamptonshire at Northampton	1920
H Sutcliffe	125*	307	Essex at Southend	1920
P Holmes	175*	377	New Zealanders at Bradford	1927
P Holmes	110*	219	Northamptonshire at Bradford	1929
H Sutcliffe	104*	170	Hampshire at Leeds	1932
H Sutcliffe	114*	202	Rest of England at The Oval	1933
H Sutcliffe	187*	401	Worcestershire at Bradford	1934
H Sutcliffe	135*	262	Glamorgan at Neath	1935
H Sutcliffe	125*	322	Oxford University at Oxford	1939
L Hutton	99*	200	Leicestershire at Sheffield	1948
L Hutton	78*	153	Worcestershire at Sheffield	1949
F A Lowson	76*	218	MCC at Lord's	1951
W B Stott	144*	262	Worcestershire at Worcester	1959
D E V Padgett	115*	230	Gloucestershire at Bristol	1962
G Boycott	114*	297	Leicestershire at Sheffield	1968
G Boycott	53*	119	Warwickshire at Bradford	1969
G Boycott	182*	320	Middlesex at Lord's	1971
G Boycott	138*	232	Warwickshire at Birmingham	1971
G Boycott	175*	360	Nottinghamshire at Worksop	1979
G Boycott	112*	233	Derbyshire at Sheffield	1983
G Boycott	55*	183	Warwickshire at Leeds	1984
G Boycott	55*	131	Surrey at Sheffield	1985
M J Wood	60*	160	Somerset at Scarborough	2004
J J Sayers	122*	326	Middlesex at Scarborough	2006
J J Sayers	149*	414	Durham at Leeds	2007
A Lyth	248*	486	Leicestershire at Leicester	2012

44 instances, of which L Hall (14 times), G Boycott (8) and H Sutcliffe (6) account for 28 between them.

The highest percentage of an innings total is 61.17 by H. Sutcliffe (104* v. Hampshire at Leeds in 1932) but P Holmes was absent ill, so only nine wickets fell.

Other contributions exceeding 55% are:

59.48%	G Boycott	(138*	v. Warwickshire at Birmingham, 1971)
56.87%	G Boycott	(182*	v. Middlesex at Lord's, 1971)
56.43%	H Sutcliffe	(114*	v. Rest of England at The Oval, 1933)
55.92%	W Rhodes	(85*	v. Essex at Leyton, 1910)

2,000 RUNS IN A SEASON

Batsman	*Season*	*M*	*I*	*NO*	*Runs*	*HS*	*Avge*	*100s*
G H Hirst	1904	32	44	3	2257	157	55.04	8
D Denton	1905	33	52	2	2258	172	45.16	8
G H Hirst	1906	32	53	6	2164	169	46.04	6
D Denton	1911	32	55	4	2161	137*	42.37	6
D Denton	1912	36	51	4	2088	221	44.23	6
P Holmes	1920	30	45	6	2144	302*	54.97	7
P Holmes	1925	35	49	9	2351	315*	58.77	6
H Sutcliffe	1925	34	48	8	2236	235	55.90	7
H Sutcliffe	1928	27	35	5	2418	228	80.60	11
P Holmes	1928	31	40	4	2093	275	58.13	6
H Sutcliffe	1931	28	33	8	2351	230	94.04	9
H Sutcliffe	1932	29	41	5	2883	313	80.08	12
M Leyland	1933	31	44	4	2196	210*	54.90	7
A Mitchell	1933	34	49	10	2100	158	53.84	6
H Sutcliffe	1935	32	47	3	2183	212	49.61	8
L Hutton	1937	28	45	6	2448	271*	62.76	8
H Sutcliffe	1937	32	52	5	2054	189	43.70	4
L Hutton	1939	29	44	5	2316	280*	59.38	10
L Hutton	1947	19	31	2	2068	270*	71.31	10
L Hutton	1949	26	44	6	2640	269*	69.47	9
F A Lowson	1950	31	54	5	2067	141*	42.18	5
D E V Padgett	1959	35	60	8	2158	161*	41.50	4
W B Stott	1959	32	56	2	2034	144*	37.66	3
P J Sharpe	1962	36	62	8	2201	138	40.75	7
G Boycott	1971	18	25	4	2221	233	105.76	11
A A Metcalfe	1990	23	44	4	2047	194*	51.17	6

1,000 RUNS IN A SEASON

Batsman		*Runs scored*	*Runs scored*	*Runs scored*
C W J Athey	(2)	1113 in 1980	1339 in 1982	—
D L Bairstow	(3)	1083 in 1981	1102 in 1983	1163 in 1985
J M Bairstow	(1)	1015 in 2011	—	—
W Barber	(8)	1000 in 1932	1595 in 1933	1930 in 1934
. . . .		1958 in 1935	1466 in 1937	1455 in 1938
. . . .		1501 in 1939	1170 in 1946	—
M G Bevan	(2)	1598 in 1995	1225 in 1996	—
R J Blakey	(5)	1361 in 1987	1159 in 1989	1065 in 1992
. . . .		1236 in 1994	1041 in 2002	
J B Bolus	(2)	1245 in 1960	1970 in 1961	—
M W Booth	(2)	1189 in 1911	1076 in 1913	—
G Boycott	(19)	1628 in 1963	1639 in 1964	1215 in 1965
		1388 in 1966	1530 in 1967	1004 in 1968
		1558 in 1970	2221 in 1971	1156 in 1972
		1478 in 1974	1915 in 1975	1288 in 1976
		1259 in 1977	1074 in 1978	1160 in 1979
		1913 in 1982	1941 in 1983	1567 in 1984
		1657 in 1985	—	—
J T Brown	(9)	1196 in 1894	1260 in 1895	1755 in 1896
		1634 in 1897	1641 in 1898	1375 in 1899
		1181 in 1900	1627 in 1901	1291 in 1903
D Byas	(5)	1557 in 1991	1073 in 1993	1297 in 1994
		1913 in 1995	1319 in 1997	—
D B Close	(13)	1192 in 1952	1287 in 1954	1131 in 1955
		1315 in 1957	1335 in 1958	1740 in 1959
		1699 in 1960	1821 in 1961	1438 in 1962
		1145 in 1963	1281 in 1964	1127 in 1965
		1259 in 1966	—	—

1,000 RUNS IN A SEASON *(Continued)*

Batsman		*Runs scored*	*Runs scored*	*Runs scored*
K R Davidson	(1)	1241 in 1934	—	—
D Denton	(20)	1028 in 1896	1357 in 1897	1595 in 1899
		1378 in 1900	1400 in 1901	1191 in 1902
		1562 in 1903	1919 in 1904	2258 in 1905
		1905 in 1906	1128 in 1907	1852 in 1908
		1765 in 1909	1106 in 1910	2161 in 1911
		2088 in 1912	1364 in 1913	1799 in 1914
		1213 in 1919	1324 in 1920	—
A Drake	(2)	1487 in 1911	1029 in 1913	—
A P Grayson	(1)	1046 in 1994	—	—
S Haigh	(1)	1031 in 1904	—	—
L Hall	(1)	1120 in 1887	—	—
H Halliday	(4)	1357 in 1948	1484 in 1950	1351 in 1952
		1461 in 1953	—	—
J H Hampshire	(12)	1236 in 1963	1280 in 1964	1424 in 1965
		1105 in 1966	1244 in 1967	1133 in 1968
		1079 in 1970	1259 in 1971	1124 in 1975
		1303 in 1976	1596 in 1978	1425 in 1981
Lord Hawke	(1)	1005 in 1895	—	—
G H Hirst	(19)	1110 in 1896	1248 in 1897	1546 in 1899
		1752 in 1900	1669 in 1901	1113 in 1902
		1535 in 1903	2257 in 1904	1972 in 1905
		2164 in 1906	1167 in 1907	1513 in 1908
		1151 in 1909	1679 in 1910	1639 in 1911
		1119 in 1912	1431 in 1913	1655 in 1914
		1312 in 1919	—	—
P Holmes	(14)	1876 in 1919	2144 in 1920	1458 in 1921
		1614 in 1922	1884 in 1923	1610 in 1924
		2351 in 1925	1792 in 1926	1774 in 1927
		2093 in 1928	1724 in 1929	1957 in 1930
		1431 in 1931	1191 in 1932	—
L Hutton	(12)	1282 in 1936	2448 in 1937	1171 in 1938
		2316 in 1939	1322 in 1946	2068 in 1947
		1792 in 1948	2640 in 1949	1581 in 1950
		1554 in 1951	1956 in 1952	1532 in 1953
R Illingworth	(5)	1193 in 1957	1490 in 1959	1029 in 1961
		1610 in 1962	1301 in 1964	—
F S Jackson	(4)	1211 in 1896	1300 in 1897	1442 in 1898
		1468 in 1899	—	—
P A Jaques	(2)	1118 in 2004	1359 in 2005	—
S A Kellett	(2)	1266 in 1991	1326 in 1992	—
R Kilner	(10)	1586 in 1913	1329 in 1914	1135 in 1919
		1240 in 1920	1137 in 1921	1132 in 1922
		1265 in 1923	1002 in 1925	1021 in 1926
		1004 in 1927	—	—
D S Lehmann	(5)	1575 in 1997	1477 in 2000	1416 in 2001
		1136 in 2002	1706 in 2006	
E I Lester	(6)	1256 in 1948	1774 in 1949	1015 in 1950
		1786 in 1952	1380 in 1953	1330 in 1954
M Leyland	(17)	1088 in 1923	1203 in 1924	1560 in 1925
		1561 in 1926	1478 in 1927	1554 in 1928
		1407 in 1929	1814 in 1930	1127 in 1931
		1821 in 1932	2196 in 1933	1228 in 1934
		1366 in 1935	1621 in 1936	1120 in 1937
		1640 in 1938	1238 in 1939	—

1,000 RUNS IN A SEASON *(Continued)*

Batsman		*Runs scored*	*Runs scored*	*Runs scored*
J D Love	(2)	1161 in 1981	1020 in 1983	—
F A Lowson	(8)	1678 in 1949	2067 in 1950	1607 in 1951
		1562 in 1952	1586 in 1953	1719 in 1954
		1082 in 1955	1428 in 1956	—
M J Lumb	(1)	1038 in 2003	—	—
R G Lumb	(5)	1002 in 1973	1437 in 1975	1070 in 1978
		1465 in 1979	1223 in 1980	—
A Lyth	(1)	1509 in 2010	—	—
A McGrath	(3)	1425 in 2005	1293 in 2006	1219 in 2010
A A Metcalfe	(6)	1674 in 1986	1162 in 1987	1320 in 1988
		1230 in 1989	2047 in 1990	1210 in 1991
A Mitchell	(10)	1320 in 1928	1633 in 1930	1351 in 1932
		2100 in 1933	1854 in 1934	1530 in 1935
		1095 in 1936	1602 in 1937	1305 in 1938
		1219 in 1939	—	—
F Mitchell	(2)	1678 in 1899	1801 in 1901	—
R Moorhouse	(1)	1096 in 1895	—	—
M D Moxon	(11)	1016 in 1984	1256 in 1985	1298 in 1987
		1430 in 1988	1156 in 1989	1621 in 1990
		1669 in 1991	1314 in 1992	1251 in 1993
		1458 in 1994	1145 in 1995	—
E Oldroyd	(10)	1473 in 1921	1690 in 1922	1349 in 1923
		1607 in 1924	1262 in 1925	1197 in 1926
		1390 in 1927	1304 in 1928	1474 in 1929
		1285 in 1930	—	—
D E V Padgett	(12)	1046 in 1956	2158 in 1959	1574 in 1960
		1856 in 1961	1750 in 1962	1380 in 1964
		1220 in 1965	1194 in 1966	1284 in 1967
		1163 in 1968	1078 in 1969	1042 in 1970
R Peel	(1)	1193 in 1896	—	—
W Rhodes	(17)	1251 in 1904	1353 in 1905	1618 in 1906
		1574 in 1908	1663 in 1909	1355 in 1910
		1961 in 1911	1030 in 1912	1805 in 1913
		1325 in 1914	1138 in 1919	1329 in 1921
		1368 in 1922	1168 in 1923	1030 in 1924
		1256 in 1925	1071 in 1926	—
E Robinson	(2)	1104 in 1921	1097 in 1929	—
P E Robinson	(3)	1173 in 1988	1402 in 1990	1293 in 1991
J A Rudolph	(4)	1078 in 2007	1292 in 2008	1366 in 2009
		1375 in 2010	—	—
J J Sayers	(1)	1150 in 2009	—	—
A B Sellers	(1)	1109 in 1938	—	—
K Sharp	(1)	1445 in 1984	—	—
P J Sharpe	(10)	1039 in 1960	1240 in 1961	2201 in 1962
		1273 in 1964	1091 in 1965	1352 in 1967
		1256 in 1968	1012 in 1969	1149 in 1970
		1320 in 1973	—	—
W B Stott	(5)	1362 in 1957	1036 in 1958	2034 in 1959
		1790 in 1960	1409 in 1961	—

1,000 RUNS IN A SEASON *(Continued)*

Batsman		*Runs scored*	*Runs scored*	*Runs scored*
H Sutcliffe	(21)	†1839 in 1919	1393 in 1920	1235 in 1921
		1909 in 1922	1773 in 1923	1720 in 1924
		2236 in 1925	1672 in 1926	1814 in 1927
		2418 in 1928	1485 in 1929	1636 in 1930
		2351 in 1931	2883 in 1932	1986 in 1933
		1511 in 1934	2183 in 1935	1295 in 1936
		2054 in 1937	1660 in 1938	1416 in 1939

† First season in First-Class cricket – The record for a debut season.

Batsman		*Runs scored*	*Runs scored*	*Runs scored*
W H H Sutcliffe	(1)	1193 in 1955	—	—
K Taylor	(6)	1306 in 1959	1107 in 1960	1494 in 1961
		1372 in 1962	1149 in 1964	1044 in 1966
T L Taylor	(2)	1236 in 1901	1373 in 1902	—
S R Tendulkar	(1)	1070 in 1992	—	—
J Tunnicliffe	(12)	1333 in 1895	1368 in 1896	1208 in 1897
		1713 in 1898	1434 in 1899	1496 in 1900
		1295 in 1901	1274 in 1902	1650 in 1904
		1096 in 1905	1232 in 1906	1195 in 1907
C Turner	(1)	1153 in 1934	—	—
G Ulyett	(4)	1083 in 1878	1158 in 1882	1024 in 1885
		1285 in 1887	—	—
M P Vaughan	(4)	1066 in 1994	1235 in 1995	1161 in 1996
		1161 in 1998	—	—
E Wainwright	(3)	1492 in 1897	1479 in 1899	1044 in 1901
W A I Washington	(1)	1022 in 1902	—	—
W Watson	(8)	1331 in 1947	1352 in 1948	1586 in 1952
		1350 in 1953	1347 in 1954	1564 in 1955
		1378 in 1956	1455 in 1957	—
W H Wilkinson	(1)	1282 in 1908	—	—
B B Wilson	(5)	1054 in 1909	1455 in 1911	1453 in 1912
		1533 in 1913	1632 in 1914	—
B B Wilson	(5)	1054 in 1909	1455 in 1911	1453 in 1912
J V Wilson	(12)	1460 in 1949	1548 in 1950	1985 in 1951
		1349 in 1952	1531 in 1953	1713 in 1954
		1799 in 1955	1602 in 1956	1287 in 1957
		1064 in 1960	1018 in 1961	1226 in 1962
A Wood	(1)	1237 in 1935	—	—
M J Wood	(4)	1080 in 1998	1060 in 2001	1432 in 2003
		1005 in 2005		
N W D Yardley	(4)	1028 in 1939	1299 in 1947	1413 in 1949
		1031 in 1950	—	—

PLAYERS WHO HAVE SCORED CENTURIES FOR AND AGAINST YORKSHIRE

Player		For	Venue	Season
C W J Athey (5)	114*	Gloucestershire	Bradford	1984
(10 for Yorkshire)	101	Gloucestershire	Gloucester	1985
	101*	Gloucestershire	Leeds	1987
	112	Sussex	Scarborough	1993
	100	Sussex	Eastbourne	1996
M G Bevan (1)	142	Leicestershire	Leicester	2002
(9 for Yorkshire)				
J B Bolus (2)	114	Nottinghamshire	Bradford	1963
(7 for Yorkshire)	138	Derbyshire	Sheffield	1973
D B Close (1)	102	Somerset	Taunton	1971
(33 for Yorkshire)				
M T G Elliott (1)	125	Glamorgan	Leeds	2004
(1 for Yorkshire)				
P A Gibb (1)	107	Essex	Brentwood	1951
(2 for Yorkshire)				
P A Jaques (1)	222	Northamptonshire	Northampton	2003
(7 for Yorkshire)				
N Kilner (2)	119	Warwickshire	Hull	1932
(2 for Yorkshire)	197	Warwickshire	Birmingham	1933
P J Sharpe (1)	126	Derbyshire	Chesterfield	1976
(23 for Yorkshire)				

BATSMEN WHO HAVE SCORED OVER 10,000 RUNS

Player	*M*	*I*	*NO*	*Runs*	*HS*	*Av'ge*	*100s*
H Sutcliffe	602	864	96	38558	313	50.20	112
D Denton	676	1058	61	33282	221	33.38	61
G Boycott	414	674	111	32570	260*	57.85	103
G H Hirst	717	1050	128	32024	341	34.73	56
W Rhodes	883	1195	162	31075	267*	30.08	46
P Holmes	485	699	74	26220	315*	41.95	60
M Leyland	548	720	82	26180	263	41.03	62
L Hutton	341	527	62	24807	280*	53.34	85
D B Close	536	811	102	22650	198	31.94	33
J H Hampshire	456	724	89	21979	183*	34.61	34
J V Wilson	477	724	75	20548	230	31.66	29
D E V Padgett	487	774	63	20306	161*	28.55	29
J Tunnicliffe	472	768	57	19435	243	27.33	22
M D Moxon	277	476	42	18973	274*	43.71	41
A Mitchell	401	550	69	18189	189	37.81	39
P J Sharpe	411	666	71	17685	203*	29.72	23
E Oldroyd	383	509	58	15891	194	35.23	37
J T Brown	345	567	41	15694	311	29.83	23
W Barber	354	495	48	15315	255	34.26	27
R Illingworth	496	668	131	14986	162	27.90	14
D Byas	268	449	42	14398	213	35.37	28
G Ulyett	355	618	31	14157	199*	24.11	15
R J Blakey	339	541	84	14150	223*	30.96	12
A McGrath	242	405	29	14091	211	37.47	34
W Watson	283	430	65	13953	214*	38.22	26
F A Lowson	252	404	31	13897	259*	37.25	30
Lord Hawke	510	739	91	13133	166	20.26	10
R Kilner	365	478	46	13018	206*	30.13	15
D L Bairstow	429	601	113	12985	145	26.60	9
K Taylor	303	505	35	12864	203*	27.37	16
N W D Yardley	302	420	56	11632	183*	31.95	17
R G Lumb	239	395	30	11525	165*	31.57	22
E Wainwright	352	545	30	11092	228	21.53	18
S Haigh	513	687	110	10993	159	19.05	4
E I Lester	228	339	27	10616	186	34.02	24
A A Metcalfe	184	317	19	10465	216*	35.11	25
C White	221	350	45	10376	186	34.01	19
Hon F S Jackson	207	328	22	10371	160	33.89	21
J D Love	247	388	58	10263	170*	31.10	13

RECORD PARTNERSHIPS FOR YORKSHIRE

1st wkt	555	P Holmes (224*) and H Sutcliffe (313) v. Essex at Leyton, 1932
2nd wkt	346	W Barber (162) and M Leyland (189) v. Middlesex at Sheffield, 1932
3rd wkt	346	J J Sayers (173) and A McGrath (211) v. Warwickshire at Birmingham, 2009
4th wkt	358	D S Lehmann (339) and M J Lumb (98) v. Durham at Leeds, 2006
5th wkt	340	E Wainwright (228) and G H Hirst (186) v. Surrey at The Oval, 1899
6th wkt	276	M Leyland (191) and E Robinson (124*) v. Glamorgan at Swansea, 1926
7th wkt	254	W Rhodes (135) and D C F Burton (142*) v. Hampshire at Dewsbury, 1919
8th wkt	292	R Peel (210*) and Lord Hawke (166) v. Warwickshire at Birmingham, 1896
9th wkt	246	T T Bresnan (116) and J N Gillespie (123*) v. Surrey at The Oval, 2007
10th wkt	149	G Boycott (79) and G B Stevenson (115*) v. Warwickshire at Birmingham, 1982

RECORD PARTNERSHIPS AGAINST YORKSHIRE

1st wkt	372	R R Montgomerie (127) and M B Loye (205) for Northamptonshire at Northampton, 1996
2nd wkt	417	K J Barnett (210*) and TA Tweats (189) for Derbyshire at Derby, 1997
3rd wkt	523	M A Carberry (300*) and N D McKenzie (237) for Hampshire at Southampton, 2011
4th wkt	447	R Abel (193) and T Hayward (273) for Surrey at The Oval, 1899
5th wkt	261	W G Grace (318*) and W O Moberley (103) for Gloucestershire at Cheltenham, 1876
6th wkt	294	D R Jardine (157) and P G H Fender (177) for Surrey at Bradford, 1928
7th wkt	315	D M Benkenstein (151) and O D Gibson (155) for Durham at Leeds, 2006
8th wkt	178	A P Wells (253*) and B T P Donelan (59) for Sussex at Middlesbrough, 1991
9th wkt	233	I J L Trott (161*) and J S Patel (120) for Warwickshire at Birmingham, 2009
10th wkt	132	A Hill (172*) and M Jean-Jacques (73) for Derbyshire at Sheffield, 1986

CENTURY PARTNERSHIPS FOR THE FIRST WICKET IN BOTH INNINGS

128	108	G Ulyett (82 and 91) and L Hall (87 and 37) v. Sussex at Hove, 1885 (First instance in First-Class cricket)
138	147*	J T Brown (203 and 81*) and J Tunnicliffe (62 and 63*) v. Middlesex at Lord's, 1896 (Second instance in First-Class cricket)
105	265*	P Holmes (51 and 127*) and H Sutcliffe (71 and 131*) v. Surrey at The Oval, 1926
184	210*	P Holmes (83 and 101*) and H Sutcliffe (111 and 100*) v. Nottinghamshire at Nottingham, 1928
110	117	L Hutton (95 and 86) and W Watson (34 and 57) v. Lancashire at Manchester, 1947
122	230	W B Stott (50 and 114) and K Taylor (79 and 140) v. Nottinghamshire at Nottingham, 1957
136	138	J B Bolus (108 and 71) and K Taylor (89 and 75) v. Cambridge University at Cambridge, 1962
105	105	G Boycott (38 and 64) and K Taylor (85 and 49) v. Leicestershire at Leicester, 1963
116	112*	K Taylor (45 and 68) and J H Hampshire (68 and 67*) v. Oxford University at Oxford, 1964
104	104	G Boycott (117 and 49*) and R G Lumb (47 and 57) v. Sussex at Leeds, 1974
134	185*	M D Moxon (57 and 89*) and A A Metcalfe (216* and 78*) v. Middlesex at Leeds, 1988
118	129*	G S Ballance (72 and 73*) and J J Sayers (139 and 53*) v. Durham MCCU at Durham, 2011

CENTURY PARTNERSHIPS FOR THE FIRST WICKET IN BOTH INNINGS BUT WITH CHANGE OF PARTNER

109		W H H Sutcliffe (82) and F A Lowson (46)
	143	W H H Sutcliffe (88) and W Watson (52) v. Canadians at Scarborough, 1954
109		G Boycott (70) and R G Lumb (44)
	135	G Boycott (74) and JH Hampshire (58) v. Northamptonshire at Bradford, 1977

CENTURY PARTNERSHIPS

FIRST WICKET (Qualification 200 runs)

555	P Holmes (224*) and H Sutcliffe (313) v. Essex at Leyton, 1932
554	J T Brown (300) and J Tunnicliffe (243) v. Derbyshire at Chesterfield, 1898
378	J T Brown (311) and J Tunnicliffe (147) v. Sussex at Sheffield, 1897
362	M D Moxon (213) and M P Vaughan (183) v. Glamorgan at Cardiff, 1996
351	G Boycott (184) and M D Moxon (168) v. Worcestershire at Worcester, 1985
347	P Holmes (302*) and H Sutcliffe (131) v. Hampshire at Portsmouth, 1920
323	P Holmes (125) and H Sutcliffe (195) v. Lancashire at Sheffield, 1931
315	H Sutcliffe (189) and L Hutton (153) v. Leicestershire at Hull, 1937
315	H Sutcliffe (116) and L Hutton (280*) v. Hampshire at Sheffield, 1939
309	P Holmes (250) and H Sutcliffe (129) v. Warwickshire at Birmingham, 1931
309	C White (186) and M J Wood (115) v. Lancashire at Manchester, 2001
290	P Holmes (179*) and H Sutcliffe (104) v. Middlesex at Leeds, 1928
288	G Boycott (130*) and R G Lumb (159) v. Somerset at Harrogate, 1979
286	L Hutton (156) and F A Lowson (115) v. South Africans at Sheffield, 1951
282	M D Moxon (147) and A A Metcalfe (151) v. Lancashire at Manchester, 1986
281*	W B Stott (138*) and K Taylor (130*) v. Sussex at Hove, 1960
279	P Holmes (133) and H Sutcliffe (145) v. Northamptonshire at Northampton, 1919
274	P.Holmes (199) and H Sutcliffe (139) v. Somerset at Hull, 1923
274	P Holmes (180) and H Sutcliffe (134) v. Gloucestershire at Gloucester, 1927
272	P Holmes (194) and H Sutcliffe (129) v. Leicestershire at Hull, 1925
272	M J Wood (202*) and J J Sayers (115) v. Bangladesh 'A' at Leeds, 2005
268	P Holmes (136) and H Sutcliffe (129) v. Essex at Leyton, 1928
267	W Barber (248) and L Hutton (70) v. Kent at Leeds, 1934
265*	P Holmes (127*) and H Sutcliffe (131*) v. Surrey at The Oval, 1926
264	G Boycott (161*) and R G Lumb (132) v. Gloucestershire at Leeds, 1976
253	P Holmes (123) and H Sutcliffe (132) v. Lancashire at Sheffield, 1919
248	G Boycott (163) and A A Metcalfe (122) v. Nottinghamshire at Bradford, 1983
245	L Hutton (152) and F A Lowson (120) v. Lancashire at Leeds, 1952
244	J A Rudolph (149) and J J Sayers (86) v Nottinghamshire at Nottingham, 2009
241	P Holmes (142) and H Sutcliffe (123*) v. Surrey at The Oval, 1929
240	G Boycott (233) and P J Sharpe (92) v. Essex at Colchester, 1971
238*	P Holmes (126*) and H Sutcliffe (105*) v. Cambridge University at Cambridge, 1923
236	G Boycott (131) and K Taylor (153) v. Lancashire at Manchester, 1964
235	P Holmes (130) and H Sutcliffe (132*) v. Glamorgan at Sheffield, 1930
233	G Boycott (141*) and R G Lumb (90) v. Cambridge University at Cambridge, 1973
233	H Halliday (116) and W Watson (108) v. Northamptonshire at Northampton, 1948
231	M P Vaughan (151) and D Byas (90) v. Essex at Chelmsford, 1999
230	H Sutcliffe (129) and L Hutton (163) v. Surrey at Leeds, 1936
230	W B Stott (114) and K Taylor (140*) v. Nottinghamshire at Nottingham, 1957
228	H Halliday (90) and J V Wilson (223*) v. Scotland at Scarborough, 1951
228	G Boycott (141) and R G Lumb (101) v. Gloucestershire at Bristol, 1975
227	P Holmes (110) and H Sutcliffe (119) v. Leicestershire at Leicester, 1928
225	R G Lumb (101) and C W J Athey (125*) v. Gloucestershire at Sheffield, 1980
224	C W J Athey (114) and J D Love (104) v. Warwickshire at Birmingham, 1980

222 W B Stott (141) and K Taylor (90) v. Sussex at Bradford, 1958
221 P Holmes (130) and H Sutcliffe (121) v. Glamorgan at Huddersfield, 1925
221 M D Moxon (141) and A A Metcalfe (73) v. Surrey at The Oval, 1992
219 P Holmes (102) and A Mitchell (130*) v. Somerset at Bradford, 1930
218 M Leyland (110) and H Sutcliffe (235) v. Middlesex at Leeds, 1925
218 R G Lumb (145) and M D Moxon (111) v. Derbyshire at Sheffield, 1981
210* P Holmes (101*) and H Sutcliffe (100*) v. Nottinghamshire at Nottingham, 1928
210 G Boycott (128) and P J Sharpe (197) v. Pakistanis at Leeds, 1967
209 F A Lowson (115) and D E V Padgett (107) v. Scotland at Hull, 1956
208 A Mitchell (85) and E Oldroyd (111) v. Cambridge University at Cambridge, 1929
207 A Mitchell (90) and W Barber (107) v. Middlesex at Lord's, 1935
206 G Boycott (118) and R G Lumb (87) v. Glamorgan at Sheffield, 1978
204 M D Moxon (66) and A A Metcalfe (162) v. Gloucestershire at Cheltenham, 1990
203 L Hutton (119) and F A Lowson (83) v. Somerset at Huddersfield, 1952
203 M D Moxon (117) and S A Kellett (87) v. Somerset at Middlesbrough, 1992
203 M D Moxon (134) and M P Vaughan (106) v. Matebeleland at Bulawayo, 1996
200* P Holmes (107*) and H Sutcliffe (80*) v. Oxford University at Oxford, 1930

Note: P Holmes and H Sutcliffe shared 69 century opening partnerships for Yorkshire; G Boycott and R G Lumb 29; L Hutton and F A Lowson 22; M D Moxon and A A Metcalfe 21; J T Brown and J Tunnicliffe 19; H Sutcliffe and L Hutton 15, and L Hall and G Ulyett 12.

SECOND WICKET (Qualification 200 runs)

346 W Barber (162) and M Leyland (189) v. Middlesex at Sheffield, 1932
343 F A Lowson (183*) and J V Wilson (165) v. Oxford University at Oxford, 1956
333 P Holmes (209) and E Oldroyd (138*) v. Warwickshire at Birmingham, 1922
314 H Sutcliffe (255*) and E Oldroyd (138) v. Essex at Southend-on-Sea, 1924
305 J W.Rothery (134) and D Denton (182) v. Derbyshire at Chesterfield, 1910
302 W Watson (172) and J V Wilson (140) v. Derbyshire at Scarborough, 1948
301 P J Sharpe (172*) and D E V Padgett (133) v. Glamorgan at Swansea, 1971
288 H Sutcliffe (165) and A Mitchell (136) v. Lancashire at Manchester, 1939
280 L Hall (160) and F Lee (165) v. Lancashire at Bradford, 1887
266* K Taylor (178*) and D E V Padgett (107*) v. Oxford University at Oxford, 1962
261* L Hutton (146*) and J V Wilson (110*) v. Scotland at Hull, 1949
260 R G Lumb (144) and K Sharp (132) v. Glamorgan at Cardiff, 1984
258 H Sutcliffe (230) and E Oldroyd (93) v. Kent at Folkestone, 1931
253 B B Wilson (150) and D Denton (200*) v. Warwickshire at Birmingham, 1912
248 H Sutcliffe (200) and M. Leyland (116) v. Leicestershire at Leicester, 1926
244 P. Holmes (138) and E Oldroyd (151*) v. Glamorgan at Cardiff, 1922
243 G Boycott (141) and J D Love (163) v. Nottinghamshire at Bradford, 1976
243 C White (183) and M J Wood (124) v. Glamorgan at Scarborough, 2001
237 H Sutcliffe (118) and D Denton (122) v. Gloucestershire at Leeds, 1919
237 M D Moxon (132) and K Sharp (128) v. Sri Lankans at Leeds, 1988
236 F A Lowson (112) and J V Wilson (157) v. Essex at Leeds, 1950
235 M D Moxon (130) and D Byas (181) v. Cambridge University at Cambridge, 1995
230 L Hutton (180) and A Mitchell (100) v. Cambridge University at Cambridge, 1938
230 M P Vaughan (109) and B Parker (138*) v. Oxford University at Oxford, 1997.
227 M J Wood (102) and M J Lumb (122) v. Leicestershire at Leeds, 2001
225 H Sutcliffe (138) and E Oldroyd (97) v. Derbyshire at Dewsbury, 1928
223 M D Moxon (153) and R J Blakey (90) v. Somerset at Leeds, 1985
222 H Sutcliffe (174) and D Denton (114) v. Kent at Dover, 1919
219 F S Jackson (155) and D Denton (113) v. Middlesex at Bradford, 1899
217 R G Lumb (107) and J D Love (107) v. Oxford University at Oxford, 1978
216 M P Vaughan (105) and D Byas (102) v. Somerset at Bradford, 1994

CENTURY PARTNERSHIPS *(Continued)*

215 A W Gale (136) and A McGrath (99) v. Lancashire at Manchester, 2008
211 J A Rudolph (141) and A McGrath (80) v Nottinghamshire at Leeds, 2010
207 P A Jaques (115) and A McGrath (93) v. Essex at Chelmsford, 2004
206 J Tunnicliffe (102) and F S Jackson (134*) v. Lancashire at Sheffield, 1898
206 H Sutcliffe (187) and M Leyland (90) v. Leicestershire at Leicester, 1931
205 H Sutcliffe (174) and A Mitchell (95) v. Leicestershire at Leicester, 1933
205 G Boycott (148) and P J Sharpe (108) v. Kent at Sheffield, 1970
203 A T Barber (100) and E Oldroyd (143) v. An England XI at Sheffield, 1929
203 J J Sayers (187) and A McGrath (100) v. Kent at Tunbridge Wells, 2007
202* W Rhodes (115*) and G H Hirst (117*) v. Somerset at Bath, 1906
202 G Boycott (113) and C W J Athey (114) v. Northamptonshire at Northampton, 1978

THIRD WICKET (Qualification 200 runs)

346 J J Sayers (173) and A McGrath (211) v. Warwickshire at Birmingham, 2009
323* H Sutcliffe (147*) and M Leyland (189*) v. Glamorgan at Huddersfield, 1928
317 A McGrath (165) and D S Lehmann (187) v. Lancashire at Leeds, 2002
310 A McGrath (134) and P A Jaques (219) v. Derbyshire at Leeds, 2005
301 H Sutcliffe (175) and M Leyland (180*) v. Middlesex at Lord's, 1939
293* A A Metcalfe (150*) and P E Robinson (150*) v. Derbyshire at Scarborough, 1990
269 D Byas (101) and R J Blakey (196) v. Oxford University at Oxford, 1991
258* J T Brown (134*) and F Mitchell (116*) v. Warwickshire at Bradford, 1901
252 D E V Padgett (139*) and D B Close (154) v. Nottinghamshire at Nottingham, 1959
249 D E V Padgett (95) and D B Close (184) v. Nottinghamshire at Scarborough, 1960
248 C Johnson (102) and J H Hampshire (155*) v. Gloucestershire at Leeds, 1976
247 P Holmes (175*) and M Leyland (118) v. New Zealanders at Bradford, 1927
244 D E V Padgett (161*) and D B Close (144) v. Oxford University at Oxford, 1959
240 L Hutton (151) and M Leyland (95) v. Surrey at Leeds, 1939
237 J A Rudolph (198) and A McGrath (120) v. Worcestershire at Leeds, 2009
236 H Sutcliffe (107) and R Kilner (137) v. Nottinghamshire at Nottingham, 1920
236 M J Wood (94) and D S Lehmann (200) v. Worcestershire at Worcester, 1998
234* D Byas (126*) and A McGrath (105*) v. Oxford University at Oxford, 1997.
233 L Hutton (101) and M Leyland (167) v. Worcestershire at Stourbridge, 1937
230 D Byas (103) and M J Wood (103) v. Derbyshire at Leeds, 1998
229 L Hall (86) and R Peel (158) v. Middlesex at Lord's, 1889
228 A Mitchell (142) and M Leyland (133) v. Worcestershire at Sheffield, 1933
228 W Barber (141) and M Leyland (114) v. Surrey at The Oval, 1939
228 J V Wilson (132*) and D E V Padgett (115) v. Warwickshire at Birmingham, 1955
226 D E V Padgett (117) and D B Close (198) v. Surrey at The Oval, 1960
224 J V Wilson (110) and D B Close (114) v. Cambridge University at Cambridge, 1955
224 G Boycott (140*) and K Sharp (121) v. Gloucestershire at Cheltenham, 1983
221 A Mitchell (138) and M Leyland (134) v. Nottinghamshire at Bradford, 1933
219 L Hall (116) and W Bates (133) v. Cambridge University at Cambridge, 1884
218 J A Rudolph (127) and A W Gale (121) v. Lancashire at Manchester, 2009
217 A McGrath (144) and J A Rudolph (129) v. Kent at Canterbury, 2008
216 R G Lumb (118) and J H Hampshire (127) v. Surrey at The Oval, 1975
215 A Mitchell (73) and M Leyland (139) v. Surrey at Bradford, 1928
213 E Oldroyd (168) and W Barber (114) v. Glamorgan at Hull, 1929
208 J V Wilson (157*) and E I Lester (112) v. Sussex at Leeds, 1949
206 A McGrath (105) and J A Rudolph (228*) v Durham at Leeds, 2010
205* E Oldroyd (122*) and M Leyland (100*) v. Hampshire at Harrogate, 1924
205 F S Jackson (124) and D Denton (112) v. Somerset at Taunton, 1897
205 D E V Padgett (83) and D B Close (128) v. Somerset at Bath, 1959
204 M P Vaughan (113) and A McGrath (70) v. Essex at Scarborough, 2001
203 D Denton (132) and J Tunnicliffe (102) v. Warwickshire at Birmingham, 1905
203 A A Metcalfe (216*) and P E Robinson (88) v. Middlesex at Leeds, 1988
201 J Tunnicliffe (101) and T L Taylor (147) v. Surrey at The Oval, 1900

CENTURY PARTNERSHIPS *(Continued)*

THIRD WICKET (Qualification 200 runs) *(Continued)*

201	H Sutcliffe (87) and W Barber (130) v. Leicestershire at Leicester, 1938
200	M D Moxon (274*) and A P Grayson (100) v. Worcestershire at Worcester, 1994

FOURTH WICKET (Qualification 175 runs)

358	D S Lehmann (339) and M J Lumb (98) v. Durham at Leeds, 2006
330	M J Wood (116) and D R Martyn (238) v. Gloucestershire at Leeds, 2003
312	D Denton (168*) and G H Hirst (146) v. Hampshire at Southampton, 1914
299	P Holmes (277*) and R Kilner (150) v. Northamptonshire at Harrogate, 1921
272	D Byas (138) and A McGrath (137) v. Hampshire at Harrogate, 1996
271	B B Wilson (208) and W Rhodes (113) v. Sussex at Bradford, 1914
259	A Drake (115) and G H Hirst (218) v. Sussex at Hastings, 1911
258	J Tunnicliffe (128) and G H Hirst (152) v. Hampshire at Portsmouth, 1904
258	P E Robinson (147) and D Byas (117) v. Kent at Scarborough, 1989
249	W B Stott (143) and G Boycott (145) v. Lancashire at Sheffield, 1963
247*	R G Lumb (165*) and S N Hartley (104*) v. Gloucestershire at Bradford, 1984
247	M Leyland (263) and L Hutton (83) v. Essex at Hull, 1936
238	D S Lehmann (216) and M J Lumb (92) v. Susex at Arundel, 2002
233	D Byas (120) and P E Robinson (189) v. Lancashire at Scarborough, 1991.
226	W H Wilkinson (89) and G H Hirst (140) v. Northamptonshire at Hull, 1909
225	C H Grimshaw (85) and G H Hirst (169) v. Oxford University at Oxford, 1906
212	B B Wilson (108) and G H Hirst (166*) v. Sussex at Hastings, 1913
212	G Boycott (260*) and J H Hampshire (80) v. Essex at Colchester, 1970
211	J V Wilson (120) and W Watson (108) v. Derbyshire at Harrogate, 1951
210*	A Mitchell (150*) and M Leyland (117*) v. Worcestershire at Worcester, 1933
210	E I. Lester (178) and W Watson (97) v. Nottinghamshire at Nottingham, 1952
207	D Byas (213) and C White (107*) v. Worcestershire at Scarborough, 1995
206	J A Rudolph (121) and A W Gale (150) v. Surrey at The Oval, 2008
205*	G Boycott (151*) and P J Sharpe (79*) v. Leicestershire at Leicester, 1964
205	E Oldroyd (121) and R Kilner (117) v. Worcestershire at Dudley, 1922
205	W Watson (162*) and E I Lester (98) v. Somerset at Leeds, 1953
201*	J H Hampshire (105*) and D B Close (101*) v. Surrey at Bradford, 1965
203	P A Jaques (160) and G S Ballance (121*) v. Gloucestershire at Bristol, 2012
201	W H H Sutcliffe (181) and L Hutton (120) v. Kent at Canterbury, 1952
200	J V Wilson (92) and W Watson (122) v. Somerset at Taunton, 1950
198	A A Metcalfe (138) and D Byas (95) v. Warwickshire at Leeds, 1989
197	N W D Yardley (177) and A Coxon (58) v. Derbyshire at Scarborough, 1947
197	A Lyth (248*) and J M Bairstow (118) v. Leicestershire at Leicester, 2012
196	M D Moxon (130) and D L Bairstow (104) v. Derbyshire at Harrogate, 1987
193	A Drake (85) and G H Hirst (156) v. Lancashire at Manchester, 1911
192	J V Wilson (132) and W Watson (105) v. Essex at Bradford, 1955
191	M Leyland (114) and C Turner (63) v. Essex at Ilford, 1938
188	H Myers (60) and G H Hirst (158) v. Cambridge University at Cambridge, 1910
187	E Oldroyd (168) and F E Greenwood (104*) v. Glamorgan at Hull, 1929
187	K Taylor (203*) and W B Stott (57) v. Warwickshire at Birmingham, 1961
186	D S Lehmann (193) and D Byas (100) v. Leicestershire at Leicester, 2001
184	J H Hampshire (96) and R Illingworth (100*) v. Leicestershire at Sheffield, 1968
182*	E I Lester (101*) and W Watson (103*) v. Nottinghamshire at Bradford, 1952
180*	G Boycott (207*) and B Leadbeater (50*) v. Cambridge University at Cambridge, 1976
180	J Tunnicliffe (139*) and G H Hirst (108) v. Surrey at The Oval, 1904
179	J H Hampshire (179) and S N Hartley (63) v. Surrey at Harrogate, 1981
179	M D Moxon (171*) and R J Blakey (71) v. Kent at Leeds, 1993
178	E I Lester (186) and J V Wilson (71) v. Warwickshiire at Scarborough, 1949
177	J D Love (105*) and J H Hampshire (89) v. Lancashire at Manchester, 1980
175	L Hutton (177) and W Barber (84) v. Sussex at Scarborough, 1939
175	A McGrath (188*) and J A Rudolph (82) v. Warwickshire at Birmingham, 2007

CENTURY PARTNERSHIPS *(Continued)*

FIFTH WICKET (Qualification 150 runs)

340	E Wainwright (228) and G H Hirst (186) v. Surrey at The Oval, 1899
329	F Mitchell (194) and E Wainwright (153) v. Leicestershire at Leicester, 1899
276	W Rhodes (104*) and R Kilner (166) v. Northamptonshire at Northampton, 1921
273	L Hutton (270*) and N W D Yardley (136) v. Hampshire at Bournemouth, 1947
245*	H Sutcliffe (107*) and W Barber (128*) v. Northamptonshire at Northampton, 1939
229	D S Lehmann (193) and C White (79) v. Kent at Canterbury, 2006
217	D B Close (140*) and R Illingworth (107) v. Warwickshire at Sheffield, 1962
198	E Wainwright (145) and R Peel (111) v. Sussex at Bradford, 1896
198	W Barber (168) and K R Davidson (101*) v. MCC at Lord's, 1934
196*	R Kilner (115*) and G H Hirst (82*) v. Gloucestershire at Leeds, 1919
195	M J Lumb (93) and C White (173*) v. Derbyshire at Derby, 2003
194*	Younus Khan (202*) and G L Brophy (100*) v. Hampshire at Southampton, 2007
193	A Mitchell (189) and W Rhodes (88) v. Northamptonshire at Northampton, 1926
193	J D Love (106) and S N Hartley (108) v. Oxford University at Oxford, 1985
192	C W J Athey (114*) and J D Love (123) v. Surrey at The Oval, 1982
191*	L Hutton (271*) and C Turner (81*) v. Derbyshire at Sheffield, 1937
191	M G Bevan (105) and A A Metcalfe (100) v. West Indians at Scarborough, 1995
190*	R J Blakey (204*) and J D Love (79*) v. Gloucestershire at Leeds, 1987
189	J E Root (160) and G S Ballance (87) v. Sussex at Scarborough 2011
188	D E V Padgett (146) and J V Wilson (72) v. Sussex at Middlesbrough, 1960
187	J V Wilson (230) and H Halliday (74) v. Derbyshire at Sheffield, 1952
185	G Boycott (104*) and K Sharp (99) v. Kent at Tunbridge Wells, 1984
182	E Lockwood (208) and E Lumb (40) v. Kent at Gravesend, 1882
182	B B Wilson (109) and W Rhodes (111) v. Sussex at Hove, 1910
182	D B Close (164) and J V Wilson (55) v. Combined Services at Harrogate, 1954
181	A A Metcalfe (149) and J D Love (88) v. Glamorgan at Leeds, 1986
177	Hon F S Jackson (87) and G H Hirst (232*) v. Surrey at The Oval, 1905
176	L Hutton (176*) and A Coxon (72) v. Sussex at Sheffield, 1948
175	A Drake (108) and R Kilner (77) v. Cambridge University at Cambridge, 1913
173	H Sutcliffe (206) and R Kilner (124) v. Warwickshire at Dewsbury, 1925
170	W Rhodes (157) and R Kilner (87) v. Derbyshire at Leeds, 1925
170	J V Wilson (130*) and N W D Yardley (67) v. Lancashire at Manchester, 1954
169	W Watson (147) and A B Sellers (92) v. Worcestershire at Worcester, 1947
168	A T Barber (63) and A Mitchell (122*) v. Worcestershire at Worcester, 1929
167	J M Bairstow (136) and G S Ballance (61) v. Somerset at Taunton 2011
165	E Oldroyd (143) and W Rhodes (110) v. Glamorgan at Leeds, 1922
165	K Sharp (100*) and P Carrick (73) v. Middlesex at Lord's, 1980
164	A A Metcalfe (151) and D L Bairstow (88) v. Northamptonshire at Luton, 1986
159*	J D Love (170*) and D L Bairstow (52*) v. Worcestershire at Worcester, 1979
159	D B Close (128) and R Illingworth (74) v. Lancashire at Sheffield, 1959
159	J H Hampshire (183*) and C Johnson (53) v. Sussex at Hove, 1971
158*	G Boycott (153*) and P E Robinson (74*) v. Derbyshire at Harrogate, 1984
157	T L Taylor (135*) and G H Hirst (72) v. An England XI at Hastings, 1901
157	G H Hirst (142) and F Smith (51) v. Somerset at Bradford, 1903
157	W Barber (87) and N W D Yardley (101) v. Surrey at The Oval, 1937
156	A McGrath (158) and I J Harvey (103) v. Derbyshire at Derby, 2005
153	S N Hartley (87) and M D Moxon (112*) v. Indians at Scarborough, 1986
152	J H Hampshire (83) and S N Hartley (106) v. Nottinghamshire at Nottingham, 1981
151*	G H Hirst (102*) and R Kilner (50*) v. Kent at Bradford, 1913
151	G H Hirst (120) and F Smith (55) v. Kent at Leeds, 1903
151	W Rhodes (57) and R Kilner (90) v. Nottinghamshire at Nottingham, 1925

CENTURY PARTNERSHIPS *(Continued)*

SIXTH WICKET (Qualification 150 runs)

276 M Leyland (191) and E Robinson (124*) v. Glamorgan at Swansea, 1926
252 C White (181) and R J Blakey (109*) v. Lancashire at Leeds, 1996
233 M W Booth (210) and G H Hirst (100) v. Worcestershire at Worcester, 1911
229 W Rhodes (267*) and N Kilner (112) v. Leicestershire at Leeds, 1921
225 E Wainwright (91) and Lord Hawke (127) v. Hampshire at Southampton, 1899
217* H Sutcliffe (200*) and A Wood (123*) v. Worcestershire at Sheffield, 1935
214 W Watson (214*) and N W D Yardley (76) v. Worcestershire at Worcester, 1955
205 G H Hirst (125) and S Haigh (159) v. Nottinghamshire at Sheffield, 1901
200 D Denton (127) and G H Hirst (134) v. Essex at Bradford, 1902
198 M Leyland (247) and W Rhodes (100*) v. Worcestershire at Worcester, 1928
190 W Rhodes (126) and M Leyland (79) v. Middlesex at Bradford, 1923
190 J A Rudolph (122) and A U Rashid (86) v. Surrey at The Oval, 2007
188 W Watson (174) and R Illingworth (53) v. Lancashire at Sheffield, 1955
188 M P Vaughan (161) and R J Blakey (92) v. Essex at Ilford, 1997.
188 G S Ballance (111) and A U Rashid (82) v. Warwickshire at Birmingham 2011
184 R Kilner (104) and M W Booth (79) v. Leicestershire at Leeds, 1913
183 G H Hirst (131) and E Smith (129) v. Hampshire at Bradford, 1899
183 W Watson (139*) and R Illingworth (78) v. Somerset at Harrogate, 1956
178* D Denton (108*) and G H Hirst (112*) v. Lancashire at Manchester, 1902
178* N W D Yardley (100*) and R Illingworth (71*) v. Gloucestershire at Bristol, 1955
178 E Robinson (100) and D C F Burton (83) v. Derbyshire at Hull, 1921
178 H Sutcliffe (135) and P A Gibb (157*) v. Nottinghamshire at Sheffield, 1935
175 G M Fellows (88) and R J Blakey (103) v. Warwickshire at Birmingham, 2002
174 D S Lehmann (136) and G M Hamilton (73) v. Kent at Maidstone, 1998
172 A J Dalton (119*) and D L Bairstow (62) v. Worcestershire at Dudley, 1971
170 A W Gale (101) and T T Bresnan (97) v. Worcestershire at Worcester, 2009
169 W Barber (124) and H Verity (78*) v. Warwickshire at Birmingham, 1933
169 R Illingworth (162) and J Birkenshaw (37) v. Indians at Sheffield, 1959
166 E Wainwright (116) and E Smith (61) v. Kent at Catford, 1900
166 D B Close (161) and F S Trueman (104) v. Northamptonshire at Northampton, 1963
162* G Boycott (220*) and J G Binks (70*) v. Northamptonshire at Sheffield, 1967
161* D L Bairstow (100*) and P Carrick (59*) v. Middlesex at Leeds, 1983
159* D S Lehmann (187*) and R J Blakey (78*) v. Somerset at Bath, 2001
159 J M Bairstow (182) and A McGrath (90) v. Leicestershire at Scarborough, 2012
156 W Rhodes (82*) and E Robinson (94) v. Derbyshire at Chesterfield, 1919
154 C Turner (84) and A Wood (79) v. Glamorgan at Swansea, 1936
153* J A Rudolph (92*) and A U Rashid (73*) v. Worcestershire at Kidderminster, 2007
153 J A Rudolph (69*) and J M Bairstow (81) v. Warwickshire at Birmingham, 2010
151 D Denton (91) and W Rhodes (76) v. Middlesex at Sheffield, 1904
151 G Boycott (152*) and P Carrick (75) v. Warwickshire at Leeds, 1982
150 G Ulyett (199*) and J M Preston (93) v. Derbyshire at Sheffield, 1887

SEVENTH WICKET (Qualification 125 runs)

254 W Rhodes (135) and D C F Burton (142*) v. Hampshire at Dewsbury, 1919
247 P Holmes (285) and W Rhodes (79) v. Nottinghamshire at Nottingham, 1929
215 E Robinson (135*) and D C F Burton (110) v. Leicestershire at Leicester, 1921
185 E Wainwright (100) and G H Hirst (134) v. Gloucestershire at Bristol, 1897
183 G H Hirst (341) and H Myers (57) v. Leicestershire at Leicester, 1905
183 J A Rudolph (220) and T T Bresnan (101*) v. Warwickshire at Scarborough, 2007
180 C Turner (130) and A Wood (97) v. Somerset at Sheffield, 1936
168 G L Brophy (99) and A U Rashid (157*) v. Lancashire at Leeds, 2009
170 G S Blewett (190) and G M Hamilton (84*) v. Northamptonshire at Scarborough, 1999
166 R Peel (55) and I Grimshaw (122*) v. Derbyshire at Holbeck, 1886
162 E Wainwright (109) and S Haigh (73) v. Somerset at Taunton, 1900
162 R J Blakey (90) and R K J Dawson (87) v. Kent at Canterbury, 2002
162 A W Gale (149) and G L Brophy (97) v. Warwickshire at Scarborough, 2006

161	R G Lumb (118) and C M Old (89) v. Worcestershire at Bradford, 1980
160	J Tunnicliffe (158) and D Hunter (58*) v. Worcestershire at Worcester, 1900
157*	F A Lowson (259*) and R Booth (53*) v. Worcestershire at Worcester, 1953
155	D Byas (122*) and P Carrick (61) v. Leicestershire at Leicester.1991.
154*	G H Hirst (76*) and J T Newstead (100*) v. Nottinghamshire at Nottingham, 1908
148	J Rowbotham (113) and J Thewlis (50) v. Surrey at The Oval, 1873
147	E Wainwright (78) and G Ulyett (73) v. Somerset at Taunton, 1893
147	M P Vaughan (153) and R J Harden (64) v. Kent at Scarborough, 1999
143	C White (135*) and A K D Gray (60) v. Durham at Chester-le-Street, 2003
141	G H Hirst (108*) and S Haigh (48) v. Worcestershire at Worcester, 1905
141	J H Hampshire (149*) and J G Binks (72) v. MCC at Scarborough, 1965
140	E Wainwright (117) and S Haigh (54) v. CI Thornton's XI at Scarborough, 1900
140	D Byas (67) and P J Hartley (75) v. Derbyshire at Chesterfield, 1990
138	D Denton (78) and G H Hirst (103*) v. Sussex at Leeds, 1905
136	GH Hirst (93) and S Haigh (138) v. Warwickshire at Birmingham, 1904
136	E Robinson (77*) and A Wood (65) v. Glamorgan at Scarborough, 1931
133*	W Rhodes (267*) and M Leyland (52*) v. Leicestershire at Leeds, 1921
133*	E I Lester (86*) and A B Sellers (73*) v. Northamptonshire at Northampton, 1948
133	D Byas (100) and P W Jarvis (80) v. Northamptonshire at Scarborough, 1992
132	W Rhodes (196) and S Haigh (59*) v. Worcestershire at Worcester, 1904
131*	D L Bairstow (79*) and A Sidebottom (52*) v. Oxford University at Oxford, 1981
130	P J Sharpe (64) and J V Wilson (134) v. Warwickshire at Birmingham, 1962
128	W Barber (66) and T F Smailes (86) v. Cambridge University at Cambridge, 1938
128	D B Close (88*) and A Coxon (59) v. Essex at Leeds, 1949
126	E Wainwright (171) and R Peel (46) v. Middlesex at Lord's, 1897
126	W Rhodes (91) and G G Macaulay (63) v. Hampshire at Hull, 1925
126	J C Balderstone (58) and J G Binks (95) v. Middlesex at Lord's, 1964
126	J M Bairstow (70) and A U Rashid (59) v. Kent at Canterbury, 2010
125	A B Sellers (109) and T F Smailes (65) v. Kent at Bradford, 1937

EIGHTH WICKET (Qualification 125 runs)

292	R Peel (210*) and Lord Hawke (166) v. Warwickshire at Birmingham, 1896
238	I J Harvey (209*) and T T Bresnan (74) v. Somerset at Leeds, 2005
192*	W Rhodes (108*) and G G Macaulay (101*) v. Essex at Harrogate, 1922
192	A U Rashid (117*) and A Shahzad (78) v. Hampshire at Basingstoke, 2009
180	W Barber (191) and T F Smailes (89) v. Sussex at Leeds, 1935
165	S Haigh (62) and Lord Hawke (126) v. Surrey at The Oval, 1902
163	G G Macaulay (67) and A Waddington (114) v. Worcestershire at Leeds, 1927
159	E Smith (95) and W Rhodes (105) v. MCC at Scarborough, 1901
157	A Shahzad (88) and D J Wainwright (85*) v. Sussex at Hove, 2009
152	W Rhodes (98) and J W Rothery (70) v. Hampshire at Portsmouth, 1904
151	W Rhodes (201) and Lord Hawke (51) v. Somerset at Taunton, 1905
151	R J Blakey (80*) and P J Hartley (89) v. Sussex at Eastbourne, 1996
149	G L Brophy (177*) and R J Sidebottom (61) v. Worcestershire at Worcester 2011
147	J P G Chadwick (59) and F S Trueman (101) v. Middlesex at Scarborough, 1965
146	S Haigh (159) and Lord Hawke (89) v. Nottinghamshire at Sheffield, 1901
144	G L Brophy (85) and D J Wainwright (102*) v. Warwickshire at Scarborough, 2009
138	E Wainwright (100) and Lord Hawke (81) v. Kent at Tonbridge, 1899
137	E Wainwright (171) and Lord Hawke (75) v. Middlesex at Lord's, 1897
135	P W Jarvis (55) and P J Hartley (69) v. Nottinghamshire at Scarborough, 1992
133	R Illingworth (61) and F S Trueman (74) v. Leicestershire at Leicester, 1955
132	G H Hirst (103) and E Smith (59) v. Middlesex at Sheffield, 1904
132	W Watson (119) and J H Wardle (65) v. Leicestershire at Leicester, 1949
131	P E Robinson (85) and P Carrick (64) v. Surrey at Harrogate, 1990
130	E Smith (98) and Lord Hawke (54) v. Lancashire at Leeds, 1904
128	H Verity (96*) and T F Smailes (77) v. Indians at Bradford, 1936
128	D L Bairstow (145) and G B Stevenson (11) v. Middlesex at Scarborough, 1980

CENTURY PARTNERSHIPS *(Continued)*

127	E Robinson (70*) and A Wood (62) v. Middlesex at Leeds, 1928
126	R Peel (74) and E Peate (61) v. Gloucestershire at Bradford, 1883
126	M W Booth (56) and E R Wilson (104*) v. Essex at Bradford, 1913
126	J D Middlebrook (84) and C E W Silverwood (70) v. Essex at Chelmsford, 2001
126	M J Lumb (115*) and D Gough (72) v. Hampshire at Southampton, 2003

NINTH WICKET (Qualification 100 runs)

246	T T Bresnan (116) and J N Gillespie (123*) v. Surrey at The Oval, 2007
192	G H Hirst (130*) and S Haigh (85) v. Surrey at Bradford, 1898
179	R A Hutton (189) and G A Cope (30*) v. Pakistanis at Bradford, 1971
176*	R Moorhouse (59*) and G H Hirst (115*) v. Gloucestershire at Bristol, 1894
173	S Haigh (85) and W Rhodes (92*) v. Sussex at Hove, 1902
167	H Verity (89) and T F Smailes (80) v. Somerset at Bath, 1936
162	W Rhodes (94*) and S Haigh (84) v. Lancashire at Manchester, 1904
161	E Smith (116*) and W Rhodes (79) v. Sussex at Sheffield, 1900
154	R M Pyrah (117) and R J Sidebottom (52) v.Lancashire at Leeds 2011
151	J M Bairstow (205) and R J Sidebottom (45*) v. Nottinghamshire at Nottingham 2011
150	Azeem Rafiq (100) and M J Hoggard (56*) v. Worcestershire at Worcester, 2009
149*	R J Blakey (63*) and A K D Gray (74*) v. Leicestershire at Scarborough, 2002
149	G H Hirst (232*) and D Hunter (40) v. Surrey at The Oval, 1905
146	G H Hirst (214) and W Rhodes (53) v. Worcestershire at Worcester, 1901
144	T T Bresnan (91) and J N Gillespie (44) v. Hampshire at Leeds, 2006
140	A U Rashid (111) and D J Wainwright (104) v. Sussex at Hove, 2008
136	R Peel (210*) and G H Hirst (85) v. Warwickshire at Birmingham, 1896
125*	L Hutton (269*) and A Coxon (65*) v. Northamptonshire at Wellingborough, 1949
124	P J Hartley (87*) and P W Jarvis (47) v. Essex at Chelmsford, 1986
120	G H Hirst (138) and W Rhodes (38) v. Nottinghamshire at Nottingham, 1899
119	A B Sellers (80*) and E P Robinson (66) v. Warwickshire at Birmingham, 1938
118	S Haigh (96) and W Rhodes (44) v. Somerset at Leeds, 1901
114	E Oldroyd (194) and A Dolphin (47) v. Worcestershire at Worcester, 1923
114	N Kilner (102*) and G G Macaulay (60) v. Gloucestershire at Bristol, 1923
113	G G Macaulay (125*) and A Waddington (44) v. Nottinghamshire at Nottingham, 1921
113	A Wood (69) and H.Verity (45*) v. MCC at Lord's, 1938
112	G H Hirst (78) and Lord Hawke (61*) v. Essex at Leyton, 1907
109	Lees Whitehead (60) and W Rhodes (81*) v. Sussex at Harrogate, 1899
108	A McGrath (133*) and C E W Silverwood (80) v. Durham at Chester-le-Street, 2005
105	J V Wilson (134) and A G Nicholson (20*) v. Nottinghamshire at Leeds, 1962
105	C M Old (100*) and H P Cooper (30) v. Lancashire at Manchester, 1978
105	C White (74*) and J D Batty (50) v. Gloucestershire at Sheffield, 1993
104	L Hall (129*) and R Moorhouse (86) v. Gloucestershire at Clifton, 1888
100	G Pollitt (51) and Lees Whitehead (54) v. Hampshire at Bradford, 1899

TENTH WICKET (Qualification 100 runs)

149	G Boycott (79) and G B Stevenson (115*) v. Warwickshire at Birmingham, 1982
148	Lord Hawke (107*) and D Hunter (47) v. Kent at Sheffield, 1898
144	A Sidebottom (124) and A L Robinson (30*) v. Glamorgan at Cardiff, 1977
121	J T Brown (141) and D Hunter (25*) v. Liverpool & District at Liverpool, 1894
118	Lord Hawke (110*) and D Hunter (41) v. Kent at Leeds, 1896
113	P J Hartley (88*) and R D Stemp (22) v. Middlesex at Lord's, 1996
110	C E W. Silverwood (45*) and R D Stemp (65) v. Durham at Chester-le-Street, 1996
109	A Shahzad (70) and R J Sidebottom (28*) v. Worcestershire at Scarborough, 2011
108	Lord Hawke (79) and Lees Whitehead (45*) v. Lancashire at Manchester, 1903
108	G Boycott (129) and M K Bore (37*) v. Nottinghamshire at Bradford, 1973
106	A B Sellers (79) and D V Brennan (30) v. Worcestershire at Worcester, 1948
103	A Dolphin (62*) and E Smith (49) v. Essex at Leyton, 1919
102	D Denton (77*) and D Hunter (45) v. Cambridge University at Cambridge, 1895

FIFTEEN WICKETS OR MORE IN A MATCH

A complete list of 12, 13 and 14 wickets in a match up to and including 2007 is to be found in the 2008 edition

W E BOWES (1)

16 for 35 (8 for 18 and 8 for 17) v. Northamptonshire at Kettering, 1935

A DRAKE (1)

15 for 51 (5 for 16 and 10 for 35) v. Somerset at Weston-super-Mare, 1914

T EMMETT (1)

16 for 38 (7 for 15 and 9 for 23) v. Cambridgeshire at Hunslet, 1869

G H HIRST (1)

15 for 63 (8 for 25 and 7 for 38) v. Leicestershire at Hull, 1907

R ILLINGWORTH (1)

15 for 123 (8 for 70 and 7 for 53) v. Glamorgan at Swansea, 1960

R PEEL (1)

15 for 50 (9 for 22 and 6 for 28) v. Somerset at Leeds, 1895

W RHODES (1)

15 for 56 (9 for 28 and 6 for 28) v. Essex at Leyton, 1899

H VERITY (4)

17 for 91 (8 for 47 and 9 for 44) v. Essex at Leyton, 1933
15 for 129 (8 for 56 and 7 for 73) v. Oxford University at Oxford, 1936
15 for 38 (6 for 26 and 9 for 12) v. Kent at Sheffield, 1936
15 for 100 (6 for 52 and 9 for 48) v. Essex at Westcliffe-on-Sea, 1936

J H WARDLE (1)

16 for 112 (9 for 48 and 7 for 64) v. Sussex at Hull, 1954

TEN WICKETS IN A MATCH

(including best analysis)

61	W Rhodes	15 for	56	v Essex	at Leyton	1899
48	H Verity	17 for	91	v Essex	at Leyton	1933
40	G H Hirst	15 for	63	v Leicestershire	at Hull	1907
31	G G Macaulay	14 for	92	v Gloucestershire	at Bristol	1926
28	S Haigh	14 for	43	v Hampshire	at Southampton	1898
27	R Peel	14 for	33	v Nottinghamshire	at Sheffield	1888
25	W E Bowes	16 for	35	v Northamptonshire	at Kettering	1935
25	J H Wardle	16 for	112	v Sussex	at Hull	1954
22	E Peate	14 for	77	v Surrey	at Huddersfield	1881
20	F S Trueman	14 for	123	v Surrey	at The Oval	1960
19	T Emmett	16 for	38	v Cambridgeshire	at Hunslet	1869
17	R Appleyard	12 for	43	v Essex	at Bradford	1951
15	E Wainwright	14 for	77	v Essex	at Bradford	1896
11	R Illingworth	15 for	123	v Glamorgan	at Swansea	1960
10	A Waddington	13 for	48	v Northamptonshire	at Northampton	1920
9	M W Booth	14 for	160	v Essex	at Leyton	1914
9	R Kilner	12 for	55	v Sussex	at Hove	1924
8	W Bates	11 for	47	v Nottinghamshire	at Nottingham	1881
8	G Freeman	13 for	60	v Surrey	at Sheffield	1869
7	E P Robinson	13 for	115	v Lancashire	at Leeds	1939
7	D Wilson	13 for	52	v Warwickshire	at Middlesbrough	1967

TEN WICKETS IN A MATCH (Including best analysis) *(Continued)*

6 G A Cope	12 for 116	v Glamorgan	at Cardiff (Sophia Gardens)	1968
6 A Hill	12 for 59	v Surrey	at The Oval	1871
6 T F Smailes	14 for 58	v Derbyshire	at Sheffield	1939
5 P Carrick	12 for 89	v Derbyshire	at Sheffield (Abbeydale Pk)	1983
5 J M Preston	13 for 63	v MCC	at Scarborough	1888
5 E Robinson	12 for 95	v Northamptonshire	at Huddersfield	1927
4 J T Newstead	11 for 72	v Worcestershire	at Bradford	1907
3 T W Foster	11 for 93	v Liverpool & District	at Liverpool	1894
3 G P Harrison	11 for 76	v Kent	at Dewsbury	1883
3 F S Jackson	12 for 80	v Hampshire	at Southampton	1897
3 P W Jarvis	11 for 92	v Middlesex	at Lord's	1986
3 S P Kirby	13 for 154	v Somerset	at Taunton	2003
3 A G Nicholson	12 for 73	v Glamorgan	at Leeds	1964
3 R K Platt	10 for 87	v Surrey	at The Oval	1959
3 A Sidebottom	11 for 64	v Kent	at Sheffield (Abbeydale Pk)	1980
3 G Ulyett	12 for 102	v Lancashire	at Huddersfield	1889
2 T Armitage	13 for 46	v Surrey	at Sheffield	1876
2 R Aspinall	14 for 65	v Northamptonshire	at Northampton	1947
2 J T Brown (Darfield)	12 for 109	v Gloucestershire	at Huddersfield	1899
2 R O Clayton	12 for 104	v Lancashire	at Manchester	1877
2 D B Close	11 for 116	v Kent	at Gillingham	1965
2 M J Cowan	12 for 87	v Warwickshire	at Birmingham	1960
2 A Coxon	10 for 57	v Derbyshire	at Chesterfield	1949
2 D Gough	10 for 80	v Lancashire	at Leeds	1995
2 G M Hamilton	11 for 72	v Surrey	at Leeds	1998
2 P J Hartley	11 for 68	v Derbyshire	at Chesterfield	1995
2 R A Hutton	11 for 62	v Lancashire	at Manchester	1971
2 E Leadbeater	11 for 162	v Nottinghamshire	at Nottingham	1950
2 M A Robinson	12 for 124	v Northamptonshire	at Harrogate	1993
2 M Ryan	10 for 77	v Leicestershire	at Bradford	1962
2 E Smith (Morley)	10 for 97	v MCC	at Scarborough	1893
2 R J Sidebottom	11 for 43	v Kent	at Leeds	2000
2 G B Stevenson	11 for 74	v Nottinghamshire	at Nottingham	1980
2 S Wade	11 for 56	v Gloucestershire	at Cheltenham	1886
2 E R Wilson	11 for 109	v Sussex	at Hove	1921
1 A B Bainbridge	12 for 111	v Essex	at Harrogate	1961
1 J Birkenshaw	11 for 134	v Middlesex	at Leeds	1960
1 A Booth	10 for 91	v Indians	at Bradford	1946
1 H P Cooper	11 for 96	v Northamptonshire	at Northampton	1976
1 A Drake	15 for 51	v Somerset	at Weston-Super-Mare	1914
1 L Greenwood	11 for 71	v Surrey	at The Oval	1867
1 P M Hutchison	11 for 102	v Pakistan 'A'	at Leeds	1997
1 L Hutton	10 for 101	v Leicestershire	at Leicester (Aylestone Rd)	1937
1 R Iddison	10 for 68	v Surrey	at Sheffield	1864
1 M Leyland	10 for 94	v Leicestershire	at Leicester (Aylestone Rd)	1933
1 J D Middlebrook	10 for 170	v Hampshire	at Southampton	2000
1 F W Milligan	12 for 110	v Sussex	at Sheffield	1897
1 H Myers	12 for 192	v Gloucestershire	at Dewsbury	1904
1 C M Old	11 for 46	v Gloucestershire	at Middlesbrough	1969
1 D Pickles	12 for 133	v Somerset	at Taunton	1957
1 A U Rashid	11 for 114	v Worcestershire	at Worcester	2011
1 W Ringrose	11 for 135	v Australians	at Bradford	1905
1 C E W Silverwood	12 for 148	v Kent	at Leeds	1997
1 W Slinn	12 for 53	v Nottinghamshire	at Nottingham	1864
1 J Waring	10 for 63	v Lancashire	at Leeds	1966
1 F Wilkinson	10 for 129	v Hampshire	at Bournemouth	1938
1 A C Williams	10 for 66	v Hampshire	at Dewsbury	1919

TEN WICKETS IN AN INNINGS

Bowler				*Year*
A Drake	10 for 35	v.	Somerset at Weston-super-Mare	1914
H Verity	10 for 36	v.	Warwickshire at Leeds	1931
*H Verity	10 for 10	v.	Nottinghamshire at Leeds	1932
T F Smailes	10 for 47	v.	Derbyshire at Sheffield	1939

*Includes the hat trick.

EIGHT WICKETS OR MORE IN AN INNINGS

(Ten wickets in an innings also listed above)

A complete list of seven wickets in an innings up to and including 2007 is to be found in the 2008 edition

R APPLEYARD (1)

8 for 76 v. MCC at Scarborough, 1951

R ASPINALL (1)

8 for 42 v. Northamptonshire at Northampton, 1947

W BATES (2)

8 for 45 v. Lancashire at Huddersfield, 1878
8 for 21 v. Surrey at The Oval, 1879

M W BOOTH (4)

8 for 52 v. Leicestershire at Sheffield, 1912
8 for 47 v. Middlesex at Leeds, 1912
8 for 86 v. Middlesex at Sheffield, 1913
8 for 64 v. Essex at Leyton, 1914

W E BOWES (9)

8 for 77 v. Leicestershire at Dewsbury, 1929
8 for 69 v. Middlesex at Bradford, 1930
9 for 121 v. Essex at Scarborough, 1932
8 for 62 v. Sussex at Hove, 1932
8 for 69 v. Gloucestershire at Gloucester, 1933
8 for 40 v.Worcestershire at Sheffield, 1935
8 for 18 v. Northamptonshire at Kettering, 1935
8 for 17 v. Northamptonshire at Kettering, 1935
8 for 56 v. Leicestershire at Scarborough, 1936

J T BROWN (Darfield) (1)

8 for 40 v. Gloucestershire at Huddersfield, 1899

P CARRICK (2)

8 for 33 v. Cambridge University at Cambridge, 1973
8 for 72 v. Derbyshire at Scarborough, 1975

R O CLAYTON (1)

8 for 66 v. Lancashire at Manchester, 1877

D B CLOSE (2)

8 for 41 v. Kent at Leeds, 1959
8 for 43 v. Essex at Leeds, 1960

H P COOPER (1)

8 for 62 v. Glamorgan at Cardiff, 1975

EIGHT WICKETS OR MORE IN AN INNINGS *(Continued)*

G A COPE (1)

8 for 73 v. Gloucestershire at Bristol, 1975

M J COWAN (1)

9 for 43 v. Warwickshire at Birmingham, 1960

A COXON (1)

8 for 31 v. Worcestershire at Leeds, 1946

A DRAKE (2)

8 for 59 v. Gloucestershire at Sheffield, 1913
10 for 35 v. Somerset at Weston-super-Mare, 1914

T EMMETT (8)

9 for 34 v. Nottinghamshire at Dewsbury, 1868
9 for 23 v. Cambridgeshire at Hunslet, 1869
8 for 31 v. Nottinghamshire at Sheffield, 1871
8 for 46 v. Gloucestershire at Clifton, 1877
8 for 16 v. MCC at Scarborough, 1877
8 for 22 v. Surrey at The Oval, 1881
8 for 52 v. MCC at Scarborough, 1882
8 for 32 v. Sussex at Huddersfield, 1884

S D FLETCHER (1)

8 for 58 v. Essex at Sheffield, 1988

T W FOSTER (1)

9 for 59 v. MCC at Lord's, 1894

G FREEMAN (2)

8 for 11 v. Lancashire at Holbeck, 1868
8 for 29 v. Surrey at Sheffield, 1869

L GREENWOOD (1)

8 for 35 v. Cambridgeshire at Dewsbury, 1867

S HAIGH (5)

8 for 78 v. Australians at Bradford, 1896
8 for 35 v. Hampshire at Harrogate, 1896
8 for 21 v. Hampshire at Southampton, 1898
8 for 33 v. Warwickshire at Scarborough, 1899
9 for 25 v. Gloucestershire at Leeds, 1912

P J HARTLEY (2)

8 for 111 v. Sussex at Hove, 1992
9 for 41 v. Derbyshire at Chesterfield, 1995

G H HIRST (8)

8 for 59 v. Warwickshire at Birmingham, 1896
8 for 48 v. Australians at Bradford, 1899
8 for 25 v. Leicestershire at Hull, 1907
9 for 45 v. Middlesex at Sheffield, 1907
9 for 23 v. Lancashire at Leeds, 1910
8 for 80 v. Somerset at Sheffield, 1910
9 for 41 v. Worcestershire at Worcester, 1911
9 for 69 v. MCC at Lord's, 1912

EIGHT WICKETS OR MORE IN AN INNINGS *(Continued)*

R ILLINGWORTH (5)

8 for 69 v. Surrey at The Oval, 1954
9 for 42 v. Worcestershire at Worcester, 1957
8 for 70 v. Glamorgan at Swansea, 1960
8 for 50 v. Lancashire at Manchester, 1961
8 for 20 v. Worcestershire at Leeds, 1965

R KILNER (2)

8 for 26 v. Glamorgan at Cardiff, 1923
8 for 40 v. Middlesex at Bradford, 1926

S P KIRBY (1)

8 for 80 v. Somerset at Taunton, 2003

E LEADBEATER (1)

8 for 83 v. Worcestershire at Worcester, 1950

M LEYLAND (1)

8 for 63 v. Hampshire at Huddersfield, 1938

G G MACAULAY (3)

8 for 43 v. Gloucestershire at Bristol, 1926
8 for 37 v. Derbyshire at Hull, 1927
8 for 21 v. Indians at Harrogate, 1932

H MYERS (1)

8 for 81 v. Gloucestershire at Dewsbury, 1904

A G NICHOLSON (2)

9 for 62 v. Sussex at Eastbourne, 1967
8 for 22 v. Kent at Canterbury, 1968

E PEATE (6)

8 for 24 v. Lancashire at Manchester, 1880
8 for 30 v. Surrey at Huddersfield, 1881
8 for 69 v. Sussex at Hove, 1881
8 for 32 v. Middlesex at Sheffield, 1882
8 for 5 v. Surrey at Holbeck, 1883
8 for 63 v. Kent at Gravesend, 1884

R PEEL (6)

8 for 12 v. Nottinghamshire at Sheffield, 1888
8 for 60 v. Surrey at Sheffield, 1890
8 for 54 v. Cambridge University at Cambridge, 1893
9 for 22 v. Somerset at Leeds, 1895
8 for 27 v. South of England XI at Scarborough, 1896
8 for 53 v. Kent at Halifax, 1897

J M PRESTON (2)

8 for 27 v. Sussex at Hove, 1888
9 for 28 v. MCC at Scarborough, 1888

EIGHT WICKETS OR MORE IN AN INNINGS *(Continued)*

W RHODES (18)

9 for 28 v. Essex at Leyton, 1899
8 for 38 v. Nottinghamshire at Nottingham, 1899
8 for 68 v. Cambridge University at Cambridge, 1900
8 for 43 v. Lancashire at Bradford, 1900
8 for 23 v. Hampshire at Hull, 1900
8 for 72 v. Gloucestershire at Bradford, 1900
8 for 28 v. Essex at Harrogate, 1900
8 for 53 v. Middlesex at Lord's, 1901
8 for 55 v. Kent at Canterbury, 1901
8 for 26 v. Kent at Catford, 1902
8 for 87 v. Worcestershire at Worcester, 1903
8 for 61 v. Lancashire at Bradford, 1903
8 for 90 v. Warwickshire at Birmingham, 1905
8 for 92 v. Northamptonshire at Northampton, 1911
8 for 44 v. Warwickshire at Bradford, 1919
8 for 39 v. Sussex at Leeds, 1920
8 for 48 v. Somerset at Huddersfield, 1926
9 for 39 v. Essex at Leyton, 1929

W RINGROSE (1)

9 for 76 v. Australians at Bradford, 1905

E ROBINSON (3)

9 for 36 v. Lancashire at Bradford, 1920
8 for 32 v. Northamptonshire at Huddersfield, 1927
8 for 13 v. Cambridge University at Cambridge, 1928

E P ROBINSON (2)

8 for 35 v. Lancashire at Leeds, 1939
8 for 76 v. Surrey at The Oval, 1946

M A ROBINSON (1)

9 for 37 v. Northamptonshire at Harrogate, 1993

A SIDEBOTTOM (1)

8 for 72 v. Leicestershire at Middlesbrough, 1986

T F SMAILES (2)

8 for 68 v. Glamorgan at Hull, 1938
10 for 47 v. Derbyshire at Sheffield, 1939

G B STEVENSON (2)

8 for 65 v. Lancashire at Leeds, 1978
8 for 57 v. Northamptonshire at Leeds, 1980

F S TRUEMAN (8)

8 for 70 v. Minor Counties at Lord's, 1949
8 for 68 v. Nottinghamshire at Sheffield, 1951
8 for 53 v. Nottinghamshire at Nottingham, 1951
8 for 28 v. Kent at Dover, 1954
8 for 84 v. Nottinghamshire at Worksop, 1962
8 for 45 v. Gloucestershire at Bradford, 1963
8 for 36 v. Sussex at Hove, 1965
8 for 37 v. Essex at Bradford, 1966

EIGHT WICKETS OR MORE IN AN INNINGS *(Continued)*

H VERITY (20)

9 for 60 v. Glamorgan at Swansea, 1930
10 for 36 v. Warwickshire at Leeds, 1931
8 for 33 v. Glamorgan at Swansea, 1931
8 for 107 v. Lancashire at Bradford, 1932
8 for 39 v. Northamptonshire at Northampton, 1932
10 for 10 v. Nottinghamshire at Leeds, 1932
8 for 47 v. Essex at Leyton, 1933
9 for 44 v. Essex at Leyton, 1933
9 for 59 v. Kent at Dover, 1933
8 for 28 v. Leicestershire at Leeds, 1935
8 for 56 v. Oxford University at Oxford, 1936
8 for 40 v. Worcestershire at Stourbridge, 1936
9 for 12 v. Kent at Sheffield, 1936
9 for 48 v. Essex at Westcliff-on-Sea, 1936
8 for 42 v. Nottinghamshire at Bradford, 1936
9 for 43 v. Warwickshire at Leeds, 1937
8 for 80 v. Sussex at Eastbourne, 1937
8 for 43 v. Middlesex at The Oval, 1937
9 for 62 v. MCC at Lord's, 1939
8 for 38 v. Leicestershire at Hull, 1939

A WADDINGTON (3)

8 for 34 v. Northamptonshire at Leeds, 1922
8 for 39 v. Kent at Leeds, 1922
8 for 35 v. Hampshire at Bradford, 1922

E WAINWRIGHT (3)

8 for 49 v. Middlesex at Sheffield, 1891
9 for 66 v. Middlesex at Sheffield, 1894
8 for 34 v. Essex at Bradford, 1896

J H WARDLE (4)

8 for 87 v. Derbyshire at Chesterfield, 1948
8 for 26 v. Middlesex at Lord's, 1950
9 for 48 v. Sussex at Hull, 1954
9 for 25 v. Lancashire at Manchester, 1954

C WHITE (1)

8 for 55 v. Gloucestershire at Gloucester, 1998

A C WILLIAMS (1)

9 for 29 v. Hampshire at Dewsbury, 1919

R WOOD (1)

8 for 45 v. Scotland at Glasgow, 1952

SIX WICKETS IN AN INNINGS AT LESS THAN FOUR RUNS EACH

A complete list of 5 wickets at less than 4 runs each up to and including 2007 is to be found in the 2008 edition

R APPLEYARD (2)

6 for 17 v. Essex at Bradford, 1951
6 for 12 v. Hampshire at Bournemouth, 1954

T ARMITAGE (1)

6 for 20 v. Surrey at Sheffield, 1876

R ASPINALL (1)

6 for 23 v. Northamptonshire at Northampton, 1947

W BATES (5)

6 for 11 v. Middlesex at Huddersfield, 1879
6 for 22 v. Kent at Bradford, 1881
6 for 17 v. Nottinghamshire at Nottingham, 1881
6 for 12 v. Kent at Sheffield, 1882
6 for 19 v. Lancashire at Dewsbury, 1886

A BOOTH (1)

6 for 21 v. Warwickshire at Birmingham, 1946

W E BOWES (4)

6 for 17 v. Middlesex at Lord's, 1934
6 for 16 v. Lancashire at Bradford, 1935
6 for 20 v. Gloucestershire at Sheffield, 1936
6 for 23 v. Warwickshire at Birmingham, 1947

J T BROWN (Darfield) (1)

6 for 19 v. Worcestershire at Worcester, 1899

R.O CLAYTON (1)

6 for 20 v. Nottinghamshire at Sheffield, 1876

A COXON (1)

6 for 17 v. Surrey at Sheffield, 1948

T EMMETT (6)

6 for 7 v. Surrey at Sheffield, 1867
6 for 13 v. Lancashire at Holbeck, 1868
6 for 21 v. Middlesex at Scarborough, 1874
6 for 12 v. Derbyshire at Sheffield, 1878
6 for 19 v. Derbyshire at Bradford, 1881
6 for 22 v. Australians at Bradford, 1882

H FISHER (1)

6 for 11 v. Leicestershire at Bradford, 1932

SIX WICKETS IN AN INNINGS AT LESS THAN FOUR RUNS EACH *(Continued)*

S HAIGH (10)

6 for 18 v. Derbyshire at Bradford, 1897
6 for 22 v. Hampshire at Southampton, 1898
6 for 21 v. Surrey at The Oval, 1900
6 for 23 v. Cambridge University at Cambridge, 1902
6 for 19 v. Somerset at Sheffield, 1902
6 for 22 v. Cambridge University at Sheffield, 1903
6 for 21 v. Hampshire at Leeds, 1904
6 for 21 v. Nottinghamshire at Sheffield, 1905
6 for 13 v. Surrey at Leeds, 1908
6 for 14 v. Australians at Bradford, 1912

A HILL (2)

6 for 9 v. United South of England XI at Bradford, 1874
6 for 18 v. MCC at Lord's, 1881

G H HIRST (7)

6 for 23 v. MCC at Lord's, 1893
6 for 20 v. Lancashire at Bradford, 1906
6 for 12 v. Northamptonshire at Northampton, 1908
6 for 7 v. Northamptonshire at Northampton, 1908
6 for 23 v. Surrey at Leeds, 1908
6 for 23 v. Lancashire at Manchester, 1909
6 for 20 v. Surrey at Sheffield, 1909

R ILLINGWORTH (2)

6 for 15 v. Scotland at Hull, 1956
6 for 13 v. Leicestershire at Leicester, 1963

F S JACKSON (1)

6 for 19 v. Hampshire at Southampton, 1897

R KILNER (5)

6 for 22 v. Essex at Harrogate, 1922
6 for 13 v. Hampshire at Bournemouth, 1922
6 for 14 v. Middlesex at Bradford, 1923
6 for 22 v. Surrey at Sheffield, 1923
6 for 15 v. Hampshire at Portsmouth, 1924

G G MACAULAY (10)

6 for 10 v. Warwickshire at Birmingham, 1921
6 for 3 v. Derbyshire at Hull, 1921
6 for 8 v. Northamptonshire at Northampton, 1922
6 for 12 v. Glamorgan at Cardiff, 1922
6 for 18 v. Northamptonshire at Bradford, 1923
6 for 19 v. Northamptonshire at Northampton, 1925
6 for 22 v. Leicestershire at Leeds, 1926
6 for 11 v. Leicestershire at Hull, 1930
6 for 22 v. Leicestershire at Bradford, 1933
6 for 22 v. Middlesex at Leeds, 1934

SIX WICKETS IN AN INNINGS AT LESS THAN FOUR RUNS EACH *(Continued)*

E PEATE (5)

6 for 14 v. Middlesex at Huddersfield, 1879
6 for 12 v. Derbyshire at Derby, 1882
6 for 13 v. Gloucestershire at Moreton-in-Marsh, 1884
6 for 16 v. Sussex at Huddersfield, 1886
6 for 16 v. Cambridge University at Sheffield, 1886

R PEEL (4)

6 for 21 v. Nottinghamshire at Sheffield, 1888
6 for 19 v. Australians at Huddersfield, 1888
6 for 22 v. Gloucestershire at Bristol, 1891
6 for 19 v. Leicestershire at Scarborough, 1896

A C RHODES (1)

6 for 19 v. Cambridge University at Cambridge, 1932

W RHODES (12)

6 for 21 v. Somerset at Bath, 1898
6 for 16 v. Gloucestershire at Bristol, 1899
6 for 4 v. Nottinghamshire at Nottingham, 1901
6 for 15 v. MCC at Lord's, 1902
6 for 16 v. Cambridge University at Cambridge, 1905
6 for 9 v. Essex at Huddersfield, 1905
6 for 22 v. Derbyshire at Glossop, 1907
6 for 17 v. Leicestershire at Leicester, 1908
6 for 13 v. Sussex at Hove, 1922
6 for 23 v. Nottinghamshire at Leeds, 1923
6 for 22 v. Cambridge University at Cambridge, 1924
6 for 20 v. Gloucestershire at Dewsbury, 1927

W RINGROSE (1)

6 for 20 v. Leicestershire at Dewsbury, 1903

R J SIDEBOTTOM (1)

6 for 16 v. Kent at Leeds, 2000

W SLINN (1)

6 for 19 v. Nottinghamshire at Nottingham, 1864

G B STEVENSON(1)

6 for 14 v. Warwickshire at Sheffield, 1979

F S TRUEMAN (4)

6 for 23 v. Oxford University at Oxford, 1955
6 for 23 v. Oxford University at Oxford, 1958
6 for 18 v. Warwickshire at Birmingham, 1963
6 for 20 v. Leicestershire at Sheffield, 1968

H VERITY (5)

6 for 11 v. Surrey at Bradford, 1931
6 for 21 v. Glamorgan at Swansea, 1931
6 for 12 v. Derbyshire at Hull, 1933
6 for 10 v. Essex at Ilford, 1937
6 for 22 v. Hampshire at Bournemouth, 1939

SIX WICKETS IN AN INNINGS AT LESS THAN FOUR RUNS EACH *(Continued)*

A WADDINGTON (2)

6 for 21 v. Northamptonshire at Harrogate, 1921
6 for 21 v. Northamptonshire at Northampton, 1923

S WADE (1)

6 for 18 v. Gloucestershire at Dewsbury, 1887

E WAINWRIGHT (4)

6 for 16 v. Sussex at Leeds, 1893
6 for 23 v. Sussex at Hove, 1893
6 for 18 v. Sussex at Dewsbury, 1894
6 for 22 v. MCC at Scarborough, 1894

J H WARDLE (8)

6 for 17 v. Sussex at Sheffield, 1948
6 for 10 v. Scotland at Edinburgh, 1950
6 for 12 v. Gloucestershire at Hull, 1950
6 for 20 v. Kent at Scarborough, 1950
6 for 23 v. Somerset at Sheffield, 1951
6 for 21 v. Glamorgan at Leeds, 1951
6 for 18 v. Gloucestershire at Bristol, 1951
6 for 6 v. Gloucestershire at Bristol, 1955

D WILSON (3)

6 for 22 v. Sussex at Bradford, 1963
6 for 15 v. Gloucestershire at Middlesbrough, 1966
6 for 22 v. Middlesex at Sheffield, 1966

FOUR WICKETS IN FOUR BALLS

A Drake v. Derbyshire at Chesterfield, 1914

FOUR WICKETS IN FIVE BALLS

F S Jackson v. Australians at Leeds, 1902
A Waddington v. Northamptonshire at Northampton, 1920
G G Macaulay v. Lancashire at Manchester, 1933
P J Hartley v. Derbyshire at Chesterfield, 1995
D Gough v. Kent at Leeds, 1995
J D Middlebrook v. Hampshire at Southampton, 2000

BEST BOWLING ANALYSES IN A MATCH FOR AND AGAINST YORKSHIRE

Best For Yorkshire:
17 for 91 (8 for 47 and 9 for 44) H Verity v Essex at Leyton, 1933

Against Yorkshire:
17 for 91 (9 for 62 and 8 for 29) H Dean for Lancashire at Liverpool, 1913 (non-championship)

County Championship
16 for 114 (8 for 48 and 8 for 66) G Burton for Middlesex at Sheffield, 1888

Yorkshire versus:

Derbyshire	*For Yorkshire:*	14 for 58 (4 for 11 and 10 for 47) T F Smailes at Sheffield, 1939
	Against:	13 for 65 (7 for 33 and 6 for 32) W Mycroft at Sheffield, 1879
Most 10 wickets	*For Yorkshire:*	P Carrick and E Peate 4 each
in a match	*Against:*	W Mycroft 3
Durham	*For Yorkshire:*	10 for 101 (6 for 57 and 4 for 44) M A Robinson at Durham, 1992
	Against:	10 for 144 (7 for 81 and 3 for 63) O D Gibson at Chester-le-Street, 2007
Most 10 wickets	*For Yorkshire:*	M A Robinson 1
in a match	*Against:*	G R Breese and O D Gibson 1 each
Essex	*For Yorkshire:*	17 for 91 (8 for 47 and 9 for 44) H Verity at Leyton, 1933
	Against:	14 for 127 (7 for 37 and 7 for 90) W Mead at Leyton, 1899
Most 10 wickets	*For Yorkshire:*	W Rhodes 7
in a match	*Against:*	J K Lever, W Mead 2 each
Glamorgan	*For Yorkshire:*	15 for 123 (8 for 70 and 7 for 53) R Illingworth at Swansea. 1960
	Against:	12 for 76 (7 for 30 and 5 for 46) D J Shepherd at Cardiff, 1957
Most 10 wickets	*For Yorkshire:*	H Verity 5
in a match	*Against:*	D J Shepherd, J S Pressdee 1 each
Gloucestershire	*For Yorkshire:*	14 for 64 (7 for 58 and 7 for 6) R Illingworth at Harrogate, 1967
	Against:	15 for 79 (8 for 33 and 7 for 46) W G Grace at Sheffield, 1872
Most 10 wickets	*For Yorkshire:*	W Rhodes 8
in a match	*Against:*	E G Dennett 5
Hampshire	*For Yorkshire:*	14 for 43 (8 for 21 and 6 for 22) S Haigh at Southampton, 1898
	Against:	12 for 145 (7 for 78 and 5 for 67) D Shackleton at Bradford, 1962
Most 10 wickets	*For Yorkshire:*	W Rhodes, E Robinson, H Verity 3 each
in a match	*Against:*	A S Kennedy 3

BEST BOWLING ANALYSES IN A MATCH FOR AND AGAINST YORKSHIRE *(continued)*

Yorkshire versus

Kent	*For Yorkshire:*	15 for 38 (6 for 26 and 9 for 12) H Verity at Sheffield, 1936
	Against:	13 for 48 (5 for 13 and 8 for 35) A Hearne at Sheffield, 1885
Most 10 wickets	*For Yorkshire:*	E Peate and J H Wardle 4 each
in a match	*Against:*	C Blythe 6
Lancashire	*For Yorkshire:*	14 for 80 (6 for 56 and 8 for 24) E Peate at Manchester, 1880
	Against:	17 for 91 (9 for 62 and 8 for 29) H Dean at Liverpool, 1913 (non-championship) 14 for 90 (6 for 47 and 8 for 43) R Tattersall at Leeds, 1956 (championship)
Most 10 wickets	*For Yorkshire:*	T Emmett 5
in a match	*Against:*	J Briggs 8
Leicestershire	*For Yorkshire:*	15 for 63 (8 for 25 and 7 for 38) G H Hirst at Hull, 1907
	Against:	12 for 139 (8 for 85 and 4 for 54) A D Pougher at Leicester, 1895
Most 10 wickets	*For Yorkshire:*	G H Hirst 5
in a match	*Against:*	A D Pougher 2
Middlesex	*For Yorkshire:*	13 for 94 (6 for 61 and 7 for 33) S Haigh at Leeds, 1900
	Against:	16 for 114 (8 for 48 and 8 for 66) G Burton at Sheffield, 1888
Most 10 wickets	*For Yorkshire:*	W Rhodes 5
in a match	*Against:*	J T Hearne 7
Northamptonshire	*For Yorkshire:*	16 for 35 (8 for 18 and 8 for 17) W E Bowes at Kettering, 1935
	Against:	15 for 31 (7 for 22 and 8 for 9) G E Tribe at Northampton, 1958
Most 10 wickets in a match	*For Yorkshire:*	W E Bowes, G G Macaulay, H Verity, A Waddington 3 each
	Against:	G E Tribe 3
Nottinghamshire	*For Yorkshire:*	14 for 33 (8 for 12 and 6 for 21) R Peel at Sheffield, 1888
	Against:	14 for 94 (8 for 38 and 6 for 56) F Morley at Nottingham, 1878
Most 10 wickets	*For Yorkshire:*	G H Hirst 5
in a match	*Against:*	F Morley, J C Shaw 4 each
Somerset	*For Yorkshire:*	15 for 50 (9 for 22 and 6 for 28) R Peel at Leeds, 1895
	Against:	15 for 71 (6 for 30 and 9 for 41) L C Braund at Sheffield, 1902
Most 10 wickets	*For Yorkshire:*	G H Hirst 7
in a match	*Against:*	L C Braund 3

BEST BOWLING ANALYSES IN A MATCH FOR AND AGAINST YORKSHIRE *(continued)*

Yorkshire versus

Surrey	*For Yorkshire:*	14 for 77 (6 for 47 and 8 for 30) E Peate at Huddersfield, 1881
	Against:	15 for 154 (7 for 55 and 8 for 99) T Richardson at Leeds, 1897
Most 10 wickets	*For Yorkshire:*	W Rhodes 7
in a match	*Against:*	G A Lohmann, T Richardson 6 each
Sussex	*For Yorkshire:*	16 for 112 (9 for 48 and 7 for 64) J H Wardle at Hull, 1954
	Against:	12 for 110 (6 for 71 and 6 for 39) G R Cox at Sheffield, 1907
Most 10 wickets	*For Yorkshire:*	R Peel, E Wainwright 3 each
in a match	*Against:*	Twelve players 1 each
Warwickshire	*For Yorkshire:*	14 for 92 (9 for 43 and 5 for 49) H Verity at Leeds, 1937
	Against:	12 for 55 (5 for 21 and 7 for 34) T W Cartwright at Bradford, 1969
Most 10 wickets	*For Yorkshire:*	S Haigh 4
in a match	*Against:*	E F Field 4
Worcestershire	*For Yorkshire:*	14 for 211 (8 for 87 and 6 for 124) W Rhodes at Worcester, 1903
	Against:	13 for 76 (4 for 38 and 9 for 38) J A Cuffe at Bradford, 1907
Most 10 wickets	*For Yorkshire:*	S Haigh, G G Macaulay 4 each
in a match	*Against:*	N Gifford 2
Australians	*For Yorkshire:*	13 for 149 (8 for 48 and 5 for 101) G H Hirst at Bradford, 1899
	Against:	13 for 170 (6 for 91 and 7 for 79) J M Gregory at Sheffield, 1919
Most 10 wickets	*For Yorkshire:*	S Haigh 2
in a match	*Against:*	C V Grimmett, F R Spofforth, C T B Turner, H Trumble 2 each

BEST BOWLING ANALYSES IN AN INNINGS FOR AND AGAINST YORKSHIRE

Best For Yorkshire:

10 for 10 H Verity v Nottinghamshire at Leeds, 1932

Against Yorkshire:

10 for 37 C V Grimmett for Australians at Sheffield, 1930
(non-championship)

County Championship

10 for 51 H Howell for Warwickshire at Birmingham, 1923

Yorkshire versus:

Derbyshire	*For Yorkshire:*	10 for 47	T F Smailes at Sheffield, 1939
	Against:	9 for 27	J J Hulme at Sheffield, 1894
Most 5 wickets	*For Yorkshire:*	S Haigh, E Peat, W Rhodes 11 each	
in an innings	*Against:*	W Mycroft 10	

BEST BOWLING ANALYSES IN AN INNINGS FOR AND AGAINST YORKSHIRE *(continued)*

Yorkshire versus			
Durham	*For Yorkshire:*	6 for 37	R D Stemp at Durham, 1994
		6 for 37	J N Gillespie at Chester-le-Street, 2006
	Against:	7 for 58	J Wood at Leeds, 1999
Most 5 wickets	*For Yorkshire:*	D Gough and M J Hoggard 2 each	
in an innings	*Against:*	G R Breese, S J E Brown, S J Harmison and G Onions 2 each	
Essex	*For Yorkshire:*	9 for 28	W Rhodes at Leyton, 1899
	Against:	8 for 44	F G Bull at Bradford, 1896
Most 5 wickets	*For Yorkshire:*	W Rhodes 18	
in an innings	*Against:*	W Mead 14	
Glamorgan	*For Yorkshire:*	9 for 60	H Verity at Swansea, 1930
	Against:	9 for 43	J S Pressdee at Swansea, 1965
Most 5 wickets	*For Yorkshire:*	H Verity 12	
in an innings	*Against:*	D J Shepherd 6	
Gloucestershire	*For Yorkshire:*	9 for 25	S Haigh at Leeds, 1912
	Against:	9 for 36	C W L Parker at Bristol, 1922
Most 5 wickets	*For Yorkshire:*	W Rhodes 22	
in an innings	*Against:*	T W J Goddard 17	
Hampshire	*For Yorkshire:*	9 for 29	A C Williams at Dewsbury, 1919
	Against:	8 for 49	O W Herman at Bournemouth, 1930
Most 5 wickets	*For Yorkshire:*	G H Hirst 10	
in an innings	*Against:*	A S Kennedy 10	
Kent	*For Yorkshire:*	9 for 12	H Verity at Sheffield, 1936
	Against:	8 for 35	A Hearne at Sheffield, 1885
Most 5 wickets	*For Yorkshire:*	W Rhodes 12	
in an innings	*Against:*	A P Freeman 14	
Lancashire	*For Yorkshire:*	9 for 23	G H Hirst at Leeds, 1910
	Against:	9 for 41	A Mold at Huddersfield, 1890
Most 5 wickets	*For Yorkshire:*	T Emmett 16	
in an innings	*Against:*	J Briggs 19	
Leicestershire	*For Yorkshire:*	8 for 25	G H Hirst at Hull, 1907
	Against:	9 for 63	C T Spencer at Huddersfield, 1954
Most 5 wickets	*For Yorkshire:*	G H Hirst 15	
in an innings	*Against:*	H A Smith 7	
Middlesex	*For Yorkshire:*	9 for 45	G H Hirst at Sheffield 1907
	Against:	9 for 57	F A Tarrant at Leeds, 1906
Most 5 wickets	*For Yorkshire:*	W Rhodes 18	
in an innings	*Against:*	J T Hearne 21	
Northamptonshire	*For Yorkshire:*	9 for 37	M A Robinson at Harrogate, 1993
	Against:	9 for 30	A E Thomas at Bradford, 1920
Most 5 wickets	*For Yorkshire:*	G G Macaulay 14	
in an innings	*Against:*	G E Tribe, W Wells 7 each	
Nottinghamshire	*For Yorkshire:*	10 for 10	H Verity at Leeds, 1932
	Against:	8 for 32	J C Shaw at Nottingham, 1865
Most 5 wickets	*For Yorkshire:*	W Rhodes 17	
in an innings	*Against:*	F Morley 17	

BEST BOWLING ANALYSES IN AN INNINGS FOR AND AGAINST YORKSHIRE *(continued)*

Yorkshire versus

Somerset	*For Yorkshire:*	10 for 35	A Drake at Weston-super-Mare, 1914
	Against:	9 for 41	L C Braund at Sheffield, 1902
Most 5 wickets	*For Yorkshire:*	G H Hirst 16	
in an innings	*Against:*	E J Tyler 8	
Surrey	*For Yorkshire:*	8 for 5	E Peate at Holbeck, 1883
	Against:	9 for 47	T Richardson at Sheffield, 1893
Most 5 wickets	*For Yorkshire:*	W Rhodes 17	
in an innings	*Against:*	W Southerton 19	
Sussex	*For Yorkshire:*	9 for 48	J H Wardle at Hull, 1954
	Against:	9 for 34	James Langridge at Sheffield, 1934
Most 5 wickets	*For Yorkshire:*	W Rhodes 14	
in an innings	*Against:*	G R Cox, J A Snow 6 each	
Warwickshire	*For Yorkshire:*	10 for 36	H Verity at Leeds, 1930
	Against:	10 for 51	H Howell at Birmingham, 1923
Most 5 wickets	*For Yorkshire:*	W Rhodes 18	
in an innings	*Against:*	E F Field, W E Hollies 7 each	
Worcestershire	*For Yorkshire:*	9 for 41	G H Hirst at Worcester, 1911
	Against:	9 for 38	J A Cuffe at Bradford, 1907
Most 5 wickets	*For Yorkshire:*	S Haigh, W Rhodes 11 each	
in an innings	*Against:*	R T D Perks 7	
Australians	*For Yorkshire:*	9 for 76	W Ringrose at Bradford, 1905
	Against:	10 for 37	C V Grimmett at Sheffield, 1930
Most 5 wickets	*For Yorkshire:*	R Peel 7	
in an innings	*Against:*	F R Spofforth 7	

HAT-TRICKS

G Freeman v. Lancashire at Holbeck, 1868
G Freeman v. Middlesex at Sheffield, 1868
A Hill v. United South of England XI at Bradford, 1874
A Hill v. Surrey at The Oval, 1880
E Peate v. Kent at Sheffield, 1882
G Ulyett v. Lancashire at Sheffield, 1883
E Peate v. Gloucestershire at Moreton-in-Marsh, 1884
W Fletcher v. MCC at Lord's, 1892
E Wainwright v. Sussex at Dewsbury, 1894
G H Hirst v. Leicestershire at Leicester, 1895
J T Brown v. Derbyshire at Derby, 1896
R Peel v. Kent at Halifax, 1897
S Haigh v. Derbyshire at Bradford, 1897
W Rhodes v. Kent at Canterbury, 1901
S Haigh v. Somerset at Sheffield, 1902
H A Sedgwick v. Worcestershire at Hull, 1906
G Deyes v. Gentlemen of Ireland at Bray, 1907
G H Hirst v. Leicestershire at Hull, 1907
J T Newstead v. Worcestershire at Bradford, 1907
S Haigh v. Lancashire at Manchester, 1909
M W Booth v. Worcestershire at Bradford, 1911
A Drake v. Essex at Huddersfield, 1912

HAT-TRICKS *(Continued)*

M W Booth v. Essex at Leyton, 1912
A Drake v. Derbyshire at Chesterfield, 1914 (4 in 4)
W Rhodes v. Derbyshire at Derby, 1920
A Waddington v. Northamptonshire at Northampton, 1920 (4 in 5)
G G Macaulay v. Warwickshire at Birmingham, 1923
E Robinson v. Sussex at Hull, 1928
G G Macaulay v. Leicestershire at Hull, 1930
E Robinson v. Kent at Gravesend, 1930
H Verity v. Nottinghamshire at Leeds, 1932
H Fisher v. Somerset at Sheffield, 1932 (all lbw)
G G Macaulay v. Glamorgan at Cardiff, 1933
G G Macaulay v. Lancashire at Manchester, 1933 (4 in 5)
M.Leyland v. Surrey at Sheffield, 1935
E Robinson v. Kent at Leeds, 1939
A Coxon v. Worcestershire at Leeds, 1946
F S Trueman v. Nottinghamshire at Nottingham, 1951
F S Trueman v. Nottinghamshire at Scarborough, 1955
R Appleyard v. Gloucestershire at Sheffield, 1956
F S.Trueman v. MCC at Lord's, 1958
D Wilson v. Nottinghamshire at Middlesbrough, 1959
F S Trueman v. Nottinghamshire at Bradford, 1963
D Wilson v. Nottinghamshire at Worksop, 1966
D Wilson v. Kent at Harrogate, 1966
G A Cope v. Essex at Colchester, 1970
A L Robinson v. Nottinghamshire at Worksop, 1974
P W Jarvis v. Derbyshire at Chesterfield, 1985
P J Hartley v. Derbyshire at Chesterfield, 1995 (4 in 5)
D Gough v. Kent at Leeds, 1995 (4 in 5)
C White v. Gloucestershire at Gloucester, 1998
M J Hoggard v. Sussex at Hove, 2009

52 Hat-Tricks: G G Macaulay and F S Trueman took four each, S Haigh and D Wilson three each. There have been seven hat-tricks versus Kent and Nottinghamshire, and six versus Derbyshire.

200 WICKETS IN A SEASON

Bowler	*Season*	*Overs*	*Maidens*	*Runs*	*Wickets*	*Average*
W Rhodes	1900	1366.4	411	3054	240	12.72
W Rhodes	1901	1455.3	474	3497	233	15.00
G H Hirst	1906	1111.1	262	3089	201	15.36
G G Macaulay	1925	1241.2	291	2986	200	14.93
R Appleyard†	1951	1323.2	394	2829	200	14.14

† First full season in First-Class cricket.

100 WICKETS IN A SEASON

Bowler		*Wickets taken*	*Wickets taken*	*Wickets taken*
R Appleyard	(3)	200 in 1951	141 in 1954	110 in 1956
A Booth	(1)	111 in 1946	—	—
M W Booth	(3)	104 in 1912	167 in 1913	155 in 1914
W E Bowes	(8)	117 in 1931	168 in 1932	130 in 1933
		109 in 1934	154 in 1935	113 in 1936
		106 in 1938	107 in 1939	—

100 WICKETS IN A SEASON *(Continued)*

Bowler		*Wickets taken*	*Wickets taken*	*Wickets taken*
D B Close	(2)	105 in 1949	114 in 1952	—
A Coxon	(2)	101 in 1949	129 in 1950	—
A Drake	(2)	115 in 1913	158 in 1914	—
T Emmett	(1)	112 in 1886	—	—
S Haigh	(10)	100 in 1898	160 in 1900	154 in 1902
		102 in 1903	118 in 1904	118 in 1905
		161 in 1906	120 in 1909	100 in 1911
		125 in 1912	—	—
G H Hirst	(12)	150 in 1895	171 in 1901	121 in 1903
		114 in 1904	100 in 1905	201 in 1906
		169 in 1907	164 in 1908	138 in 1910
		130 in 1911	113 in 1912	100 in 1913
R Illingworth	(5)	103 in 1956	120 in 1961	116 in 1962
		122 in 1964	105 in 1968	—
R Kilner	(4)	107 in 1922	143 in 1923	134 in 1924
		123 in 1925	—	—
G G Macaulay	(10)	101 in 1921	130 in 1922	163 in 1923
		184 in 1924	200 in 1925	133 in 1926
		130 in 1927	117 in 1928	102 in 1929
		141 in 1933	—	—
J T Newstead	(1)	131 in 1908	—	—
A G Nicholson	(2)	113 in 1966	101 in 1967	—
E Peate	(3)	131 in 1880	133 in 1881	165 in 1882
R Peel	(6)	118 in 1888	132 in 1890	106 in 1892
		134 in 1894	155 in 1895	108 in 1896
W Rhodes	(22)	141 in 1898	153 in 1899	240 in 1900
		233 in 1901	174 in 1902	169 in 1903
		118 in 1904	158 in 1905	113 in 1906
		164 in 1907	100 in 1908	115 in 1909
		105 in 1911	117 in 1914	155 in 1919
		156 in 1920	128 in 1921	100 in 1922
		127 in 1923	102 in 1926	111 in 1928
		100 in 1929	—	—
E Robinson	(1)	111 in 1928	—	—
E P Robinson	(4)	104 in 1938	120 in 1939	149 in 1946
		108 in 1947	—	—
T F Smailes	(4)	105 in 1934	125 in 1936	120 in 1937
		104 in 1938	—	—
F S Trueman	(8)	129 in 1954	140 in 1955	104 in 1959
		150 in 1960	124 in 1961	122 in 1962
		121 in 1965	107 in 1966	—
H Verity	(9)	169 in 1931	146 in 1932	168 in 1933
		100 in 1934	199 in 1935	185 in 1936
		185 in 1937	137 in 1938	189 in 1939
A Waddington	(5)	100 in 1919	140 in 1920	105 in 1921
		132 in 1922	105 in 1925	—
E Wainwright	(3)	114 in 1893	157 in 1894	102 in 1896
J H Wardle	(10)	148 in 1948	100 in 1949	172 in 1950
		122 in 1951	169 in 1952	126 in 1953
		122 in 1954	159 in 1955	146 in 1956
		106 in 1957	—	—
D Wilson	(3)	100 in 1966	107 in 1968	101 in 1969

BOWLERS WHO HAVE TAKEN OVER 500 WICKETS

Player	M	Runs	Wkts	Av'ge	Best
W Rhodes	883	57634	3598	16.01	9 for 28
G H Hirst	717	44716	2481	18.02	9 for 23
S Haigh	513	29289	1876	15.61	9 for 25
G G Macaulay	445	30554	1774	17.22	8 for 21
F S Trueman	459	29890	1745	17.12	8 for 28
H Verity	278	21353	1558	13.70	10 for 10
J H Wardle	330	27917	1539	18.13	9 for 25
R Illingworth	496	26806	1431	18.73	9 for 42
W E Bowes	301	21227	1351	15.71	9 for 121
R Peel	318	20638	1311	15.74	9 for 22
T Emmett	299	15465	1216	12.71	9 for 23
D Wilson	392	22626	1104	20.49	7 for 19
P Carrick	425	30530	1018	29.99	8 for 33
E Wainwright	352	17744	998	17.77	9 for 66
D B Close	536	23489	967	24.29	8 for 41
Emmott Robinson	413	19645	893	21.99	9 for 36
A G Nicholson	.282	17296	876	19.74	9 for 62
R Kilner	365	14855	857	17.33	8 for 26
A Waddington	255	16203	835	19.40	8 for 34
T F Smailes	262	16593	802	20.68	10 for 47
E Peate	154	9986	794	12.57	8 for 5
Ellis P Robinson	208	15141	735	20.60	8 for 35
C M Old	222	13409	647	20.72	7 for 20
R Appleyard	133	9903	642	15.42	8 for 76
W Bates	202	10692	637	16.78	8 for 21
G A Cope	230	15627	630	24.80	8 for 73
P J Hartley	195	17438	579	30.11	9 for 41
A Sidebottom	216	13852	558	24.82	8 for 72
M W Booth	144	11017	557	19.17	8 for 47
A Hill	140	7002	542	12.91	7 for 14
Hon F S Jackson	207	9690	506	19.15	7 for 42

BOWLERS UNCHANGED IN A MATCH

(IN WHICH THE OPPONENTS WERE DISMISSED TWICE)

There have been 31 instances. The first and most recent are listed below. A complete list is to be found in the 2008 edition.

First: L Greenwood (11 for 71) and G Freeman (8 for 73) v. Surrey at The Oval, 1867

Yorkshire won by an innings and 111 runs

Most Recent: E Robinson (8 for 65) and G G Macaulay (12 for 50) v. Worcestershire at Leeds, 1927

Yorkshire won by an innings and 106 runs

FIELDERS (IN MATCHES FOR YORKSHIRE)

MOST CATCHES IN AN INNINGS

6	E P Robinson v. Leicestershire at Bradford, 1938
5	J Tunnicliffe v. Leicestershire at Leeds, 1897
5	J Tunnicliffe v. Leicestershire at Leicester, 1900
5	J Tunnicliffe v. Leicestershire at Scarborough, 1901
5	A B Sellers v. Essex at Leyton, 1933
5	D Wilson v. Surrey at The Oval, 1969
5	R G Lumb v. Gloucestershire at Middlesbrough, 1972

MOST CATCHES IN A MATCH

7	J Tunnicliffe v. Leicestershire at Leeds, 1897
7	J Tunnicliffe v. Leicestershire at Leicester, 1900
7	A B Sellers v Essex at Leyton, 1933
7	E P Robinson v. Leicestershire at Bradford, 1938
7	D Byas v. Derbyshire at Leeds, 2000

MOST CATCHES IN A SEASON

70	J Tunnicliffe in 1901
70	P J Sharpe in 1962
61	J Tunnicliffe in 1895
60	J Tunnicliffe in 1904
59	J Tunnicliffe in 1896
57	J V Wilson in 1955
54	J V Wilson in 1961
53	J V Wilson in 1957
51	J V Wilson in 1951

MOST CATCHES IN A CAREER

665	J Tunnicliffe (1.40 per match)
586	W Rhodes (0.66 per match)
564	D B Close (1.05 per match)
525	P J Sharpe (1.27 per match)
520	J V Wilson (1.09 per match)
518	G H Hirst (0.72 per match)

WICKET-KEEPERS IN MATCHES FOR YORKSHIRE

MOST DISMISSALS IN AN INNINGS

7	(7ct)	D L Bairstow v. Derbyshire at Scarborough, 1982
6	(6ct)	J Hunter v. Gloucestershire at Gloucester, 1887
6	(5ct,1st)	D Hunter v. Surrey at Sheffield, 1891
6	(6ct)	D Hunter v. Middlesex at Leeds, 1909
6	(2ct,4st)	W R Allen v. Sussex at Hove, 1921
6	(5ct,1st)	J G Binks v. Lancashire at Leeds, 1962
6	(6ct)	D L Bairstow v. Lancashire at Manchester, 1971
6	(6ct)	D L Bairstow v. Warwickshire at Bradford, 1978
6	(5ct,1st)	D L Bairstow v. Lancashire at Leeds, 1980
6	(6ct)	D L Bairstow v. Derbyshire at Chesterfield, 1984
6	(6ct)	R J Blakey v. Sussex at Eastbourne, 1990
6	(5ct,1st)	R J Blakey v. Gloucestershire at Cheltenham, 1992
6	(5ct,1st)	R J Blakey v. Glamorgan at Cardiff, 1994
6	(6ct)	R J Blakey v. Glamorgan at Leeds, 2003
6	(6ct)	G L Brophy v. Durham at Chester-le-Street, 2009

MOST DISMISSALS IN A MATCH

11	(11ct)	D L Bairstow v. Derbyshire at Scarborough, 1982 (Equalled World Record)
9	(9ct)	J.Hunter v. Gloucestershire at Gloucester, 1887
9	(8ct,1st)	A Dolphin v. Derbyshire at Bradford, 1919
9	(9ct)	D L Bairstow v. Lancashire at Manchester, 1971
9	(9ct)	R J Blakey v. Sussex at Eastbourne, 1990
8	(2ct,6st)	G Pinder v. Lancashire at Sheffield, 1872
8	(2ct,6st)	D Hunter v. Surrey at Bradford, 1898
8	(7ct,1st)	A Bairstow v. Cambridge University at Cambridge, 1899
8	(8ct)	A Wood v. Northamptonshire at Huddersfield, 1932
8	(8ct)	D L Bairstow v. Lancashire at Leeds, 1978
8	(7ct,1st)	D L Bairstow v. Derbyshire at Chesterfield, 1984
8	(6ct,2st)	D L Bairstow v. Derbyshire at Chesterfield, 1985
8	(8ct)	R J Blakey v. Hampshire at Southampton, 1989
8	(8ct)	R J Blakey v. Northamptonshire at Harrogate, 1993
8	(8ct)	A J Hodd v. Glamorgan at Leeds, 2012

MOST DISMISSALS IN A SEASON

107	(96ct,11st)	J G Binks, 1960
94	(81ct,13st)	JG Binks, 1961
89	(75ct,14st)	A Wood, 1934
88	(80ct,8st)	J G Binks, 1963
86	(70ct,16st)	J G Binks, 1962
82	(52ct,30st)	A Dolphin, 1919
80	(57ct,23st)	A. Wood, 1935

MOST DISMISSALS IN A CAREER

1186	(863ct,323st)	D Hunter (2.29 per match)
1044	(872ct,172st)	J G Binks (2.12 per match)
1038	(907ct,131st)	D L Bairstow (2.41 per match)
855	(612ct,243st)	A Wood (2.09 per match)
829	(569ct,260st)	A Dolphin (1.94 per match)
824	(768ct, 56st)	R J Blakey (2.43 per match)

YORKSHIRE PLAYERS WHO HAVE COMPLETED THE "DOUBLE"

(all First-Class matches)

Player	*Year*	*Runs*	*Average*	*Wickets*	*Average*
M W Booth (1)	1913	1,228	27.28	181	18.46
D B Close (2)	†1949	1,098	27.45	113	27.87
	1952	1,192	33.11	114	24.08
A Drake (1)	1913	1,056	23.46	116	16.93
S Haigh (1)	1904	1,055	26.37	121	19.85
G H Hirst (14)	1896	1,122	28.20	104	21.64
	1897	1,535	35.69	101	23.22
	1901	1,950	42.39	183	16.38
	1903	1,844	47.28	128	14.94
	1904	2,501	54.36	132	21.09
	1905	2,266	53.95	110	19.94
	††1906	2,385	45.86	208	16.50
	1907	1,344	28.38	188	15.20
	1908	1,598	38.97	114	14.05
	1909	1,256	27.30	115	20.05
	1910	1,840	32.85	164	14.79
	1911	1,789	33.12	137	20.40
	1912	1,133	25.75	118	17.37
	1913	1,540	35.81	101	20.13
R Illingworth (6)	1957	1,213	28.20	106	18.40
	1959	1,726	46.64	110	21.46
	1960	1,006	25.79	109	17.55
	1961	1,153	24.53	128	17.90
	1962	1,612	34.29	117	19.45
	1964	1,301	37.17	122	17.45
F S Jackson (1)	1898	1,566	41.21	104	15.67
R Kilner (4)	1922	1,198	27.22	122	14.73
	1923	1,404	32.24	158	12.91
	1925	1,068	30.51	131	17.92
	1926	1,187	37.09	107	22.52
R Peel (1)	1896	1,206	30.15	128	17.50
W Rhodes (16)	1903	1,137	27.07	193	14.57
	1904	1,537	35.74	131	21.59
	1905	1,581	35.93	182	16.95
	1906	1,721	29.16	128	23.57
	1907	1,055	22.93	177	15.57
	1908	1,673	31.56	115	16.13
	1909	2,094	40.26	141	15.89
	1911	2,261	38.32	117	24.07
	1914	1,377	29.29	118	18.27
	1919	1,237	34.36	164	14.42
	1920	1,123	28.07	161	13.18
	1921	1,474	39.83	141	13.27
	1922	1,511	39.76	119	12.19
	1923	1.321	33.02	134	11.54
	1924	1,126	26.18	109	14.46
	1926	1,132	34.30	115	14.86
T F Smailes (1)	1938	1,002	25.05	113	20.84
E Wainwright (1)	1897	1,612	35.82	101	23.06

† First season in First-Class cricket.

†† The only instance in First-Class cricket of 2,000 runs and 200 wickets in a season.

H Sutcliffe (194) and M Leyland (45) hit 102 off six consecutive overs for Yorkshire v. Essex at Scarborough in 1932.

From 1898 to 1930 inclusive, Wilfred Rhodes took no less than 4,187 wickets, and scored 39,969 runs in First-Class cricket at home and abroad, a remarkable record. He also took 100 wickets and scored 1,000 in a season 16 times, and G H Hirst 14 times.

Of players with a qualification of not less than 50 wickets, Wilfred Rhodes was first in bowling in First-Class cricket in 1900, 1901, 1919, 1920, 1922, 1923 and 1926; Schofield Haigh in 1902, 1905, 1908 and 1909; Mr E R Wilson in 1921; G G Macaulay in 1924; H Verity in 1930, 1933, 1935, 1937 and 1939; W E Bowes in 1938; A Booth in 1946; R Appleyard in 1951 and 1955, and F S Trueman in 1952 and 1963.

The highest aggregate of runs made in one season in First-Class cricket by a Yorkshire player is 3,429 by L Hutton in 1949. This total has been exceeded three times, viz: D C S Compton 3,816 and W J Edrich 3,539 in 1947, and 3,518 by T Hayward in 1906. H Sutcliffe scored 3,336 in 1932.

Three players have taken all 10 Yorkshire wickets in an innings. G Wootton, playing for All England XI at Sheffield in 1865, took all 10 wickets for 54 runs. H Howell performed the feat for Warwickshire at Edgbaston in 1923 at a cost of 51 runs; and C V Grimmett, Australia, took all 10 wickets for 37 runs at Sheffield in 1930.

The match against Sussex at Dewsbury on June 7th and 8th, 1894, was brought to a summary conclusion by a remarkable bowling performance on the part of Edward Wainwright. In the second innings of Sussex, he took the last five wickets in seven balls, including the "hat trick". In the whole match he obtained 13 wickets for only 38 runs.

M D Moxon has the unique distinction of scoring a century in each of his first two First-Class matches in Yorkshire — 116 (2nd inns.) v. Essex at Leeds and 111 (1st inns.) v. Derbyshire at Sheffield, June 1981).

In the Yorkshire v. Norfolk match — played on the Hyde Park Ground, Sheffield, on July 14th to 18th, 1834 — 851 runs were scored in the four innings, of which no fewer than 128 were extras: 75 byes and 53 wides. At that time wides were not run out, so that every wide included in the above total represents a wide actually bowled. This particular achievement has never been surpassed in the annals of county cricket.

L Hutton reached his 1,000 runs in First-Class cricket in 1949 as early as June 9th.

W Barber reached his 1,000 runs in 1934 on June 13th. P Holmes reached his 1,000 in 1925 on June 16th, as also did H Sutcliffe in 1932. J T Brown reached his 1,000 in 1899 on June 22nd. In 1905, D Denton reached his 1,000 runs on June 26th; and in 1906 G H Hirst gained the same total on June 27th.

In 1912, D Denton scored over 1,000 runs during July, while M Leyland and H Sutcliffe both scored over 1,000 runs in August 1932.

L Hutton scored over 1,000 in June and over 1,000 runs in August in 1949.

H Verity took his 100th wicket in First-Class cricket as early as June 19th in 1936 and on June 27th in 1935. In 1900, W Rhodes obtained his 100th wicket on June 21st, and again on the same date in 1901, while G H Hirst obtained his 100th wicket on June 28th, 1906.

In 1930, Yorkshiremen (H Sutcliffe and H Verity) occupied the first places by English players in the batting and the bowling averages of First-Class cricket, which is a record without precedent. H Sutcliffe was also first in the batting averages in 1931 and 1932.

G Boycott was the first player to have achieved an average of over 100 in each of two English seasons. In 1971, he scored 2,503 runs for an average of 100.12, and in 1979 he scored 1,538 runs for an average of 102.53.

FIRST-CLASS MATCHES BEGUN AND FINISHED IN ONE DAY

Yorkshire v. Somerset, at Huddersfield, July 9th, 1894.

Yorkshire v. Hampshire, at Southampton, May 27th, 1898

Yorkshire v. Worcestershire, at Bradford, May 7th, 1900

YORKSHIRE TEST CRICKETERS 1877-2012 (Correct to December 17, 2012)

Player	*M.*	*I*	*NO*	*Runs*	*HS.*	*Av'ge.*	*100s*	*50s*	*Balls*	*R*	*W*	*Av'ge*	*Best*	*5wI*	*10wM*	*c/st*
APPLEYARD, R ...1954-56	9	9	6	51	19*	17.00	—	—	1596	554	31	17.87	5-51	1	—	4
ARMITAGE, T 1877	2	3	0	33	21	11.00	—	—	12	15	0	—	—	—	—	—
ATHEY, C W .J 1980-88	23	41	1	919	123	22.97	1	4	—	—	—	—	—	—	—	13
BAIRSTOW, D L ...1979-81	4	7	1	125	59	20.83	—	1	—	—	—	—	—	—	—	12/1
BAIRSTOW, J M .2012-12/13	5	7	1	196	95	32.66	—	2	—	—	—	—	—	—	—	5
BARBER, W 1935	2	4	0	83	44	20.75	—	—	2	0	1	0.00	1-0	—	—	1
BATES, W 1881-87	15	26	2	656	64	27.33	—	5	2364	821	50	16.42	7-28	4	1	9
BINKS, J G 1964	2	4	0	91	55	22.75	—	1	—	—	—	—	—	—	—	8/—
BLAKEY, R J 1993	2	4	0	7	6	1.75	—	—	—	—	—	—	—	—	—	2/—
BOOTH, M W 1913-14	2	2	0	46	32	23.00	—	—	312	130	7	18.57	4-49	—	—	—
BOWES, W E 1932-46	15	11	5	28	10*	4.66	—	—	3655	1519	68	22.33	6-33	6	—	2
†BOYCOTT, G 1964-82	108	193	23	8114	246*	47.72	22	42	944	382	7	54.57	3-47	—	—	33
BRENNAN, D V 1951	2	2	0	16	16	8.00	—	—	—	—	—	—	—	—	—	—/1
BRESNAN, T T ..2009-12/13	18	17	3	438	91	31.28	—	3	3753	1855	57	32.54	5-48	1	—	7
BROWN, J T 1894-99	8	16	3	470	140	36.15	1	1	35	22	0	—	—	—	—	7
†CLOSE, D B 1949-76	22	37	2	887	70	25.34	—	4	1212	532	18	29.55	4-35	—	—	24
COPE, G A 1977-78	3	3	0	40	22	13.33	—	—	864	277	8	34.62	3-102	—	—	1
COXON, A 1948	1	2	0	19	19	9.50	—	—	378	172	3	57.33	2-90	—	—	—
DAWSON, R K J ...2002-03	7	13	3	114	19*	11.40	—	—	1116	677	11	61.54	4-134	—	—	3
DENTON, D 1905-10	11	22	1	424	104	20.19	1	1	—	—	—	—	—	—	—	8
DOLPHIN, A. 1921	1	2	0	1	1	0.50	—	—	—	—	—	—	—	—	—	1/—
EMMETT, T 1877-82	7	13	1	160	48	13.33	—	—	728	284	9	31.55	7-68	1	—	9
GIBB, PA 1938-46	8	13	0	581	120	44.69	2	3	—	—	—	—	—	—	—	3/1
GOUGH, D 1994-2003	58	86	18	855	65	12.57	—	2	11821	6503	229	28.39	6-42	9	—	13
GREENWOOD, A 1877	2	4	0	77	49	19.25	—	—	—	—	—	—	—	—	—	2

For England

YORKSHIRE TEST CRICKETERS 1877-2012 (Continued)

Player	M.	I	NO	Runs	HS.	Av'ge.	100s	50s	Balls	R	W	Av'ge	Best	5wI	10wM	c/st
HAIGH, S 1899-1912	11	18	3	113	25	7.53	—	—	1294	622	24	25.91	6-11	1	—	8
HAMILTON, G.M. 1999	1	2	0	0	0	0.00	—	—	90	63	0	—	—	—	—	—
HAMPSHIRE, J H . . .1969-75	8	16	1	403	107	26.86	1	2	—	—	—	—	—	—	—	9
†HAWKE, LORD 1896-99	5	8	1	55	30	7.85	—	—	—	—	—	—	—	—	—	3
HILL, A 1877	2	4	2	101	49	50.50	—	—	340	130	7	18.57	4-27	—	—	1
HIRST, G H 1897-1909	24	38	3	790	85	22.57	—	5	3967	1770	59	30.00	5-48	3	—	18
HOGGARD, M J . .2000-2008	67	92	27	473	38	7.27	—	—	13909	7564	248	30.50	7-61	7	1	24
HOLMES, P 1921-32	7	14	1	357	88	27.46	—	4	—	—	—	—	—	—	—	3
HUNTER, J 1884-85	5	7	2	93	39*	18.60	—	—	—	—	—	—	—	—	—	8/3
†HUTTON, L 1937-55	79	138	15	6971	364	56.67	19	33	260	232	3	77.33	1-2	—	—	57
HUTTON, R A 1971	5	8	2	219	81	36.50	—	2	738	257	9	28.55	3-72	—	—	9
†ILLINGWORTH, R .1958-73	61	90	11	1836	113	23.24	2	5	11934	3807	122	31.20	6-29	3	—	45
†JACKSON, Hon F S1893-1905	20	33	4	1415	144*	48.79	5	6	1587	799	24	33.29	5-52	1	—	10
JARVIS, P W 1988-93	9	15	2	132	29*	10.15	—	—	1912	965	21	45.95	4-107	—	—	2
KILNER, R 1924-26	9	8	1	233	74	33.28	—	2	2368	734	24	30.58	4-51	—	—	6
LEADBEATER, E . . .1951-52	2	2	0	40	38	20.00	—	—	289	218	2	109.00	1-38	—	—	3
LEYLAND, M 1928-38	41	65	5	2764	187	46.06	9	10	1103	585	6	97.50	3-91	—	—	13
LOWSON, F A 1951-55	7	13	0	245	68	18.84	—	2	—	—	—	—	—	—	—	5
McGRATH, A 2003	4	5	0	201	81	40.20	—	2	102	56	4	14.00	3-16	—	—	3
MACAULAY, G G . . .1923-33	8	10	4	112	76	18.66	—	1	1701	662	24	27.58	5-64	1	—	5
MILLIGAN, F W 1899	2	4	0	58	38	14.50	—	—	45	29	0	—	—	—	—	1
MITCHELL, A 1933-36	6	10	0	298	72	29.80	—	2	6	4	0	—	—	—	—	9
*MITCHELL, F 1899	2	4	0	88	41	22.00	—	—	—	—	—	—	—	—	—	2
MOXON, M D 1986-89	10	17	1	455	99	28.43	—	3	48	30	0	—	—	—	—	10
OLD, CM 1972-81	46	66	9	845	65	14.82	—	2	8858	4020	143	28.11	7-50	4	—	22

For England

YORKSHIRE TEST CRICKETERS 1877-2012 (Continued)

Player	M.	I	NO	Runs	HS.	Av'ge.	100s	50s	Balls	R	W	Av'ge	Best	5wI	10wM	c/st
PADGETT, D E V 1960	2	4	0	51	31	12.75	—	—	12	8	0	—	—	—	—	—
PEATE, E 1881-86	9	14	8	70	13	11.66	—	—	2096	682	31	22.00	6-85	2	—	2
PEEL, R 1884-96	20	33	4	427	83	14.72	—	3	5216	1715	101	16.98	7-31	5	1	17
RHODES, W 1899-1930	58	98	21	2325	179	30.19	2	11	8231	3425	127	26.96	8-68	6	1	60
ROOT, J E 2012/13	1	2	1	93	73	93.00	—	1	6	5	0	—	—	—	—	0
SHARPE, P J 1963-69	12	21	4	786	111	46.23	1	4	—	—	—	—	—	—	—	17
SHAHZAD, A 2010	1	1	0	5	5	5.00	—	—	102	63	4	15.75	3-45	—	—	2
SIDEBOTTOM, A 1985	1	1	0	2	2	2.00	—	—	112	65	1	65.00	1-65	—	—	—
SIDEBOTTOM, R J ..2001-10	22	31	11	313	31	15.65	—	—	4812	2231	79	28.24	7-47	5	1	5
SILVERWOOD, CEW1997-2003	6	7	3	29	10	7.25	—	—	828	444	11	40.36	5-91	1	—	2
SMAILES, T F 1946	1	1	0	25	25	25.00	—	—	120	62	3	20.66	3-44	—	—	—
SMITHSON, G A 1948	2	3	0	70	35	23.33	—	—	—	—	—	—	—	—	—	—
†STANYFORTH, R T 1927-28	4	6	1	13	6*	2.60	—	—	—	—	—	—	—	—	—	7/2
STEVENSON, G B ..1980-81	2	2	1	28	27*	28.00	—	—	312	183	5	36.60	3-111	—	—	—
SUTCLIFFE, H 1924-35	54	84	9	4555	194	60.73	16	23	—	—	—	—	—	—	—	23
TAYLOR, K 1959-64	3	5	0	57	24	11.40	—	—	12	6	0	—	—	—	—	1
TRUEMAN, F S 1952-65	67	85	14	981	39*	13.81	—	—	15178	6625	307	21.57	8-31	17	3	64
ULYETT, G 1877-90	25	39	0	949	149	24.33	1	7	2627	1020	50	20.40	7-36	1	—	19
†VAUGHAN M P ..1999-2008	82	147	9	5719	197	41.44	18	18	978	561	6	93.50	2-71	—	—	44
VERITY, H 1931-39	40	44	12	669	66*	20.90	—	3	11173	3510	144	24.37	8-43	5	2	30
WADDINGTON, A ..1920-21	2	4	0	16	7	4.00	—	—	276	119	1	119.00	1-35	—	—	1
WAINWRIGHT, E ...1893-98	5	9	0	132	49	14.66	—	—	127	73	0	—	—	—	—	2
WARDLE, J H 1948-57	28	41	8	653	66	19.78	—	2	6597	2080	102	20.39	7-36	5	1	12
WATSON, W 1951-59	23	37	3	879	116	25.85	2	3	—	—	—	—	—	—	—	8
WHITE, C 1994-2002	30	50	7	1052	121	24.46	1	5	3959	2220	59	37.62	5-32	3	—	14
WILSON, C E M 1899	2	4	1	42	18	14.00	—	—	—	—	—	—	—	—	—	—

YORKSHIRE TEST CRICKETERS 1877-2012 (Continued)

For England

Player	M.	I	NO	Runs	HS.	Av'ge.	100s	50s	Balls	R	W	Av'ge	Best	5wI	10wM	c/st
WILSON, D 1964-71	6	7	1	75	42	12.50	—	—	1472	466	11	42.36	2-17	—	—	1
WILSON, E R 1921	1	2	0	10	5	5.00	—	—	123	36	3	12.00	2-28	—	—	—
WOOD, A 1938-39	4	5	1	80	53	20.00	—	1	—	—	—	—	—	—	—	10/1
†YARDLEY, N W D ...1938-50	20	34	2	812	99	25.37	—	4	1662	707	21	33.66	3-67	—	—	14
†Captained England																
*Also represented and captained South Africa																
For South Africa																
†MITCHELL, F 1912	3	6	0	28	12	4.66	—	—	—	—	—	—	—	—	—	—
†Captained South Africa																
Overseas Players																
(Qualification: 20 first-class matches for Yorkshire)																
For Australia																
BEVAN, M G 1994-98	18	30	3	785	91	29.07	—	6	1285	703	29	24.24	6-82	1	1	8
GILLESPIE, J N 1996-2006	71	93	28	1218	201*	18.73	1	2	14234	6770	259	26.13	7-37	8	—	27
JAQUES, P A 2005-2008	11	19	0	902	150	47.47	3	6	—	—	—	—	—	—	—	7
LEHMANN, D S 1999-2004	27	42	2	1798	177	44.95	5	10	974	412	15	27.46	3-42	—	—	11
For South Africa																
RUDOLPH, J A 2003-12/13	48	83	9	2622	222*	35.43	6	11	664	432	4	108.00	1-1	—	—	29
For West Indies																
RICHARDSON, R B 1983-84/95	86	146	12	5949	194	44.39	16	27	66	18	0	—	—	—	—	90

CENTURIES FOR ENGLAND

C W J ATHEY (1)

123 v Pakistan at Lord's, 1987

G BOYCOTT (22)

113 v. Australia at The Oval, 1964
117 v. South Africa at Port Elizabeth, 1965
246* v. India at Leeds, 1967
116 v. West Indies at Georgetown, 1968
128 v. West Indies at Manchester, 1969
106 v. West Indies at Lord's, 1969
142* v. Australia at Sydney, 1971
119* v. Australia at Adelaide, 1971
121* v. Pakistan at Lord's, 1971
112 v. Pakistan at Leeds, 1971
115 v. New Zealand at Leeds, 1973
112 v West Indies at Port-of-Spain, 1974
107 v. Australia at Nottingham, 1977
191 v. Australia at Leeds, 1977
100* v. Pakistan at Hyderabad, 1978
131 v. New Zealand at Nottingham, 1978
155 v. India at Birmingham, 1979
125 v. India at The Oval, 1979
128* v. Australia at Lord's, 1980
104* v. West Indies at St John's, 1981
137 v. Australia at The Oval, 1981
105 v. India at Delhi, 1981

J T BROWN (1)

140 v. Australia at Melbourne, 1895

D DENTON (1)

104 v. South Africa at Old Wanderers, Johannesburg, 1910

P A GIBB (2)

106 v. South Africa at Old Wanderers, Johannesburg, 1938
120 v. South Africa at Kingsmead, Durban, 1939

J H HAMPSHIRE (1)

107 v. West Indies at Lord's, 1969

L HUTTON (19)

100 v. New Zealand at Manchester, 1937
100 v. Australia at Nottingham, 1938
364 v. Australia at The Oval, 1938
196 v. West Indies at Lord's, 1939
165* v. West Indies at The Oval, 1939
122* v. Australia at Sydney, 1947
100 v. South Africa at Leeds, 1947
158 v. South Africa at Ellis Park, J'b'rg, 1948
123 v. South Africa at Ellis Park, J'b'rg, 1949
101 v. New Zealand at Leeds, 1949
206 v. New Zealand at The Oval, 1949
202* v. West Indies at The Oval, 1950
156* v. Australia at Adeladide, 1951
100 v. South Africa at Leeds, 1951
150 v. India at Lord's, 1952
104 v. India at Manchester, 1952
145 v. Australia at Lord's, 1953
169 v. West Indies at Georgetown, 1954
205 v. West Indies at Kingston, 1954

R ILLINGWORTH (2)

113 v. West Indies at Lord's, 1969
107 v. India at Manchester, 1971

Hon. F S JACKSON (5)

103 v. Australia at The Oval, 1893
118 v. Australia at The Oval, 1899
128 v. Australia at Manchester, 1902
144* v. Australia at Leeds, 1905
113 v. Australia at Manchester, 1905

M LEYLAND (9)

137 v. Australia at Melbourne, 1929
102 v. South Africa at Lord's, 1929
109 v. Australia at Lord's, 1934
153 v. Australia at Manchester, 1934
110 v. Australia at The Oval, 1934
161 v. South Africa at The Oval, 1935
126 v. Australia at Woolloongabba, Brisbane, 1936
111* v. Australia at Melbourne, 1937
187 v. Australia at The Oval, 1938

CENTURIES FOR ENGLAND

W RHODES (2)

179 v. Australia at Melbourne, 1912
152 v. South Africa at Old Wanderers, Johannesburg, 1913

P J SHARPE (1)

111 v. New Zealand at Nottingham, 1969

H SUTCLIFFE (16)

122 v. South Africa at Lord's, 1924
115 v. Australia at Sydney, 1924
176 v. Australia at Melbourne, 1925 (1st Inns)
127 v. Australia at Melbourne, 1925 (2nd Inns)
143 v. Australia at Melbourne, 1925
161 v. Australia at The Oval, 1926
102 v. South Africa at Old Wanderers, Jbg.1927
135 v. Australia at Melbourne, 1929
114 v. South Africa at Birmingham, 1929
100 v. South Africa at Lord's, 1929
104 v. South Africa at The Oval, 1929 (1st inns)
109* v. South Africa at The Oval, 1929 (2nd inns)
161 v. Australia at The Oval, 1930
117 v. New Zealand at The Oval, 1931
109* v. New Zealand at Manchester, 1931
194 v. Australia at Sydney, 1932

G ULYETT (1)

149 v. Australia at Melbourne, 1882

M P VAUGHAN (18)

120 v. Pakistan at Manchester, 2001
115 v. Sri Lanka at Lord's, 2002
100 v. India at Lord's, 2002
197 v. India at Nottingham, 2002
195 v. India at The Oval, 2002
177 v. Australia at Adelaide, 2002
145 v. Australia at Melbourne, 2002
183 v. Australia at Sydney, 2003
156 v. South Africa at Birmingham, 2003
105 v. Sri Lanka at Kandy, 2003
140 v. West Indies at Antigua, 2004
103 v. West Indies at Lord's (1st inns) 2004
101* v. West Indies at Lord's (2nd inns) 2004
120 v. Bangladesh at Lord's, 2005
166 v. Australia at Manchester,2005
103 v. West Indies at Leeds, 2007
124 v. India at Nottingham, 2007
106 v. New Zealand at Lord's, 2008

W WATSON (2)

109 v. Australia at Lord's, 1953
116 v. West Indies at Kingston, 1954

C WHITE (1)

121 v. India at Ahmedabad, 2001

Summary of the Centuries

versus	Total	In England	Away
Australia	40	21	19
Bangladesh	1	1	0
India	12	10	2
New Zealand	9	9	—
Pakistan	5	4	1
South Africa	18	10	8
Sri Lanka	2	1	1
West Indies	17	10	7
Totals	104	66	38

For Australia

J N GILLESPIE (1)

201* v. Bangladesh at Chittagong, 2006

P A JAQUES (3)

100 v. Sri Lanka at Brisbane, 2007
150 v. Sri Lanka at Hobart, 2007
108 v. West Indies at Bridgetown, 2008

D S LEHMANN (5)

160 v. West Indies at Port of Spain, 2003
110 v. Bangladesh at Darwin, 2003
177 v. Bangladesh at Cairns, 2003
129 v. Sri Lanka at Galle, 2004
153 v. Sri Lanka at Columbo, 2004

10 WICKETS IN A MATCH FOR ENGLAND

W BATES (1)

14 for 102 (7 for 28 and 7 for 74) v. Australia at Melbourne, 1882

M J HOGGARD (1)

12 for 205 (5 for 144 and 7 for 61) v. South Africa at Johannesburg, 2005

R PEEL (1)

11 for 68 (7 for 31 and 4 for 37) v. Australia at Mancester, 1888

Note: The scorebook for the Australia v. England Test match at Sydney in February 1888 shows that the final wicket to fall was taken by W Attewell, and not by Peel
Peel therefore took 9, and not 10 wickets, in the match
His career totals have been amended to take account of this alteration

W RHODES (1)

15 for 124 (7 for 56 and 8 for 68) v. Australia at Melbourne, 1904

R J SIDEBOTTOM (1)

10 for 139 (4 for 90 and 6 for 49) v. New Zealand at Hamilton, 2008

F S TRUEMAN (3)

11 for 88 (5 for 58 and 6 for 30) v. Australia at Leeds, 1961
11 for 152 (6 for 100 and 5 for 52) v. West Indies at Lord's, 1963*
12 for 119 (5 for 75 and 7 for 44) v. West Indies at Birmingham, 1963*
**consecutive Tests*

H VERITY (2)

11 for 153 (7 for 49 and 4 for 104) v. India at Chepauk, Madras, 1934
15 for 104 (7 for 61 and 8 for 43) v. Australia at Lord's, 1934

J H WARDLE (1)

12 for 89 (5 for 53 and 7 for 36) v. South Africa at Cape Town, 1957

Summary of Ten Wickets in a Match

versus	Total	In England	Away
Australia	5	3	2
India	1	—	1
New Zealand	1	—	1
Pakistan	—	—	—
South Africa	2	—	2
Sri Lanka	—	—	—
West Indies	2	2	—
Totals	11	5	6

For Australia

M G BEVAN (1)

10 for 113 (4 for 31and 6 for 82) v. West Indies at Adelaide, 1997

5 WICKETS IN AN INNINGS FOR ENGLAND

R APPLEYARD (1)

5 for 51 v. Pakistan at Nottingham, 1954

W BATES (4)

7 for 28 v. Australia at Melbourne, 1882
7 for 74 v. Australia at Melbourne, 1882
5 for 31 v. Australia at Adelaide, 1884
5 for 24 v. Australia at Sydney, 1885

5 WICKETS IN AN INNINGS FOR ENGLAND *(Continued)*

W E BOWES (6)

6 for 34 v. New Zealand at Auckland, 1933
6 for 142 v. Australia at Leeds, 1934*
5 for 55 v. Australia at The Oval, 1934*
5 for 100 v. South Africa at Manchester, 1935
5 for 49 v. Australia at The Oval, 1938
6 for 33 v. West Indies at Manchester, 1939

**consecutive Test matches*

T T BRESNAN (1))

5 for 48 v. India at Nottingham, 2011

T EMMETT (1)

7 for 68 v. Australia at Melbourne, 1879

D GOUGH (9)

6 for 49 v. Australia at Sydney, 1995
5 for 40 v.New Zealand at Wellington, 1997
5 for 149 v. Australia at Leeds, 1997
6 for 42 v.South Africa at Leeds, 1998
5 for 96 v. Australia at Melbourne, 1998
5 for 70 v. South Africa at Johannesburg, 1999
5 for 109 v. West Indies at Birmingham, 2000
5 for 61 v. Pakistan at Lord's, 2001
5 for 103 v. Australia at Leeds, 2001

S HAIGH (1)

6 for 11 v. South Africa at Cape Town, 1909

G H HIRST (3)

5 for 77 v. Australia at The Oval, 1902
5 for 48 v. Australia at Melbourne, 1904
5 for 58 v. Australia at Birmingham, 1909

M J HOGGARD (7)

7 for 63 v. New Zealand at Christchurch, 2002
5 for 92 v. Sri Lanka at Birmingham, 2002
5 for 144 v. South Africa at Johannesburg, 2005*
7 for 61 v. South Africa at Johannesburg, 2005*
5 for 73 v. Bangladesh at Chester-le-Street, 2005
6 for 57 v. India at Nagpur, 2006
7 for 109 v. Australia at Adelaide, 2006

**Consecutive Test innings*

R ILLINGWORTH (3)

6 for 29 v. India at Lord's, 1967
6 for 87 v. Australia at Leeds, 1968
5 for 70 v. India at The Oval, 1971

Hon F S JACKSON (1)

5 for 52 v. Australia at Nottingham, 1905

G G MACAULAY (1)

5 for 64 v. South Africa at Cape Town, 1923

C M OLD (4)

5 for 113 v. New Zealand at Lord's, 1973
5 for 21 v. India at Lord's, 1974
6 for 54 v. New Zealand at Wellington, 1978
7 for 50 v. Pakistan at Birmingham, 1978

E PEATE (2)

5 for 43 v. Australia at Sydney, 1882
6 for 85 v. Australia at Lord's, 1884

R PEEL (5)

5 for 51 v. Australia at Adelaide, 1884
5 for 18 v. Australia at Sydney, 1888
7 for 31 v. Australia at Manchester, 1888
6 for 67 v. Australia at Sydney, 1894
6 for 23 v. Australia at The Oval, 1896

W RHODES (6)

7 for 17 v. Australia at Birmingham, 1902
5 for 63 v. Australia at Sheffield, 1902
5 for 94 v. Australia at Sydney, 1903*
7 for 56 v. Australia at Melbourne, 1904*
8 for 68 v. Australia at Melbourne, 1904*
5 for 83 v. Australia at Manchester, 1909

5 WICKETS IN AN INNINGS FOR ENGLAND *(Continued)*

C E W SILVERWOOD (1)

5 for 91 v. South Africa, at Cape Town, 2000

R J SIDEBOTTOM (5)

5 for 88v. West Indies at Chester-le-Street, 2007
6 for 49 v. New Zealand at Hamilton, 2008
5 for 105 v. New Zealand at Wellington, 2008
7 for 47 v. New Zealand at Napier, 2008
6 for 47 v. New Zealand at Nottingham, 2008

F S TRUEMAN (17)

8 for 31 v. India at Manchester, 1952
5 for 48 v. India at The Oval, 1952
5 for 90 v. Australia at Lord's, 1956
5 for 63 v. West Indies at Nottingham, 1957
5 for 31 v. New Zealand at Birmingham, 1958
5 for 35 v. West Indies at Port-of-Spain, 1960
5 for 27 v. South Africa at Nottingham, 1960
5 for 58 v. Australia at Leeds, 1961*
6 for 30 v. Australia at Leeds, 1961*
6 for 31 v. Pakistan at Lord's, 1962
5 for 62 v. Australia at Melbourne, 1963
7 for 75 v. New Zealand at Christchurch, 1963
6 for 100 v. West Indies at Lord's, 1963*
5 for 52 v. West Indies at Lord's, 1963*
5 for 75 v. West Indies at Birmingham, 1963*
7 for 44 v. West Indies at Birmingham, 1963*
5 for 48 v. Australia at Lord's, 1964

G ULYETT (1)

7 for 36 v. Australia at Lord's, 1884

H VERITY (5)

5 for 33 v. Australia at Sydney, 1933
7 for 49 v. India at Chepauk, Madras, 1934
7 for 61 v. Australia at Lord's, 1934*
8 for 43 v. Australia at Lord's, 1934*
5 for 70 v. South Africa at Cape Town, 1939

J H WARDLE (5)

7 for 56 v. Pakistan at The Oval, 1954
5 for 79 v. Australia at Sydney, 1955
5 for 53 v. South Africa at Cape Town, 1957*
7 for 36 v. South Africa at Cape Town, 1957*
5 for 61 v. South Africa at Kingsmead, Durban, 1957*

C WHITE (3)

5 for 57 v. West Indies at Leeds, 2000
5 for 32 v. West Indies at The Oval, 2000
5 for 127 v. Australia at Perth, 2002

**consecutive Test innings*

Summary of Five Wickets in an Innings

versus	Total	In England	Away
Australia	42	22	20
Bangladesh	1	1	—
India	7	5	2
India	8	6	2
New Zealand	11	3	8
Pakistan	5	5	—
South Africa	13	3	10
Sri Lanka	1	1	—
West Indies	11	10	1
Totals	92	51	41

For Australia

M G BEVAN (1)

6 for 82 v. West Indies at Adelaide, 1997

5 WICKETS IN AN INNINGS

For Australia *(Continued)*

J N GILLESPIE (8)

5 for 54	v.	South Africa at Port Elizabeth, 1997
7 for 37	v.	England at Leeds, 1997
5 for 88	v.	England at Perth, 1998
5 for 89	v.	West Indies at Adelaide, 2000
6 for 40	v.	West Indies at Melbourne, 2000
5 for 53	v.	England at Lord's, 2001
5 for 39	v.	West Indies at Georgetown, 2003
5 for 56	v.	India at Nagpur, 2004

HAT-TRICKS

W Bates v. Australia at Melbourne, 1882
D Gough v. Australia at Sydney, 1998
M J Hoggard v. West Indies at Bridgetown, 2004
R J Sidebottom v. New Zealand at Hamilton, 2008

FOUR WICKETS IN FIVE BALLS

C M Old v. Pakistan at Birmingham, 1978

THREE WICKETS IN FOUR BALLS

R Appleyard v. New Zealand at Auckland, 1955
D Gough v. Pakistan at Lord's, 2001

YORKSHIRE PLAYERS WHO PLAYED ALL THEIR TEST CRICKET AFTER LEAVING YORKSHIRE

For England

Player	*M.*	*I*	*NO*	*Runs*	*HS.*	*Av'ge.*	*100s*	*50s*	*Balls*	*R*	*W*	*Av'ge*	*Best*	*5wI*	*10wM*	*c/st*
BALDERSTONE, J C 1976	2	4	0	39	35	9.75	—	—	96	80	1	80.00	1:80	—	—	1
BATTY, G J 2003	4	7	1	136	38	22.66	—	—	992	504	8	63.00	3.55	—	—	—
BIRKENSHAW, J . . .1973-74	5	7	0	148	64	21.14	—	1	1017	469	13	36.07	5:57	1	—	3
BOLUS, J B 1963-64	7	12	0	496	88	41.33	—	4	18	16	0	—	—	—	—	2
†PARKIN, C H 1920-24	10	16	3	160	36	12.30	—	—	2095	1128	32	35.25	5:38	2	—	3
RHODES, S J 1994-95	11	17	5	294	65*	24.50	—	1	—	—	—	—	—	—	—	46/3
†SUGG, F H 1888	2	2	0	55	31	27.50	—	—	—	—	—	—	—	—	—	—
WARD, A 1893-95	7	13	0	487	117	37.46	1	3	—	—	—	—	—	—	—	1
WOOD, B 1972-78	12	21	0	454	90	21.61	—	2	98	50	0	—	—	—	—	6
For South Africa																
THORNTON, P G 1902	1	1	1	1	1*	—	—	—	24	20	1	20.00	1:20	—	—	1

†Born outside Yorkshire

CENTURIES FOR ENGLAND

A WARD (1)
117 v. Australia at Sydney, 1894

5 WICKETS IN AN INNINGS FOR ENGLAND

J BIRKENSHAW (1)
5 : 57 v. Pakistan at Karachi, 1973

C H PARKIN (2)
5 : 60 v. Australia at Adelaide, 1921
5 : 38 v. Australia at Manchester, 1921

YORKSHIRE'S TEST CRICKET RECORDS

R APPLEYARD

Auckland 1954-55: took 3 wickets in 4 balls as New Zealand were dismissed for the lowest total in Test history (26).

C W J ATHEY

Perth 1986-87: shared an opening stand of 223 with B C Broad – England's highest for any wicket at the WACA Ground.

W BATES

Melbourne 1882-83 (Second Test): achieved the first hat-trick for England when he dismissed P S McDonnell, G Giffen and G J Bonnor in Australia's first innings. Later in the match, he became the first player to score a fifty (55) and take 10 or more wickets (14 for 102) in the same Test.

W E BOWES

Melbourne 1932-33: enjoyed the unique satisfaction of bowling D G Bradman first ball in a Test match (his first ball to him in Test cricket).

G BOYCOTT

Leeds 1967: scored 246 not out off 555 balls in 573 minutes to establish the record England score against India. His first 100 took 341 minutes (316 balls) and he was excluded from the next Test as a disciplinary measure; shared in hundred partnerships for three successive wickets.

Adelaide 1970-71: with J H Edrich, became the third opening pair to share hundred partnerships in both innings of a Test against Australia.

Port-of-Spain 1973-74: first to score 99 and a hundred in the same Test.

Nottingham 1977: with A P E Knott, equalled England v. Australia sixth-wicket partnership record of 215 – the only England v. Australia stand to be equalled or broken since 1938. Batted on each day of the five-day Test (second after M L Jaisimha to achieve this feat).

Leeds 1977: first to score his 100th First Class hundred in a Test; became the fourth England player to be on the field for an entire Test.

Perth: 1978-79: eighth to score 2,000 runs for England against Australia.

Birmingham 1979: emulated K F Barrington by scoring hundreds on each of England's six current home grounds.

Perth: 1979-80: fourth to carry his bat through a completed England.

innings (third v. Australia) and the first to do so without scoring 100; first to score 99 not out in a Test.

Lord's 1981: 100th Test for England – second after M C Cowdrey (1968).

The Oval, 1981: second after Hon F S Jackson to score five hundreds v. Australia in England.

Gained three Test records from M C Cowdrey: exceeded England aggregate of 7,624 runs in 11 fewer Tests (Manchester 1981); 61st fifty – world record (The Oval 1981); 189th innings – world record (Bangalore 1981-82).

Delhi, 4.23p.m. on 23 December 1981: passed G St.A Sobers's world Test record of 8,032 runs, having played 30 more innings and batted over 451 hours (cf. 15 complete five-day Tests); his 22nd hundred equalled the England record.

J T BROWN

Melbourne 1894-95: his 28-minute fifty remains the fastest in Test cricket, and his 95-minute hundred was a record until 1897-98; his third-wicket stand of 210 with A Ward set a Test record for any wicket.

YORKSHIRE'S TEST CRICKET RECORDS *(Continued)*

D B CLOSE

Manchester 1949: at 18 years 149 days he became – and remains – the youngest to represent England.

Melbourne 1950-51: became the youngest (19 years 301 days) to represent England against Australia.

T EMMETT

Melbourne 1878-79: first England bowler to take seven wickets in a Test innings.

P A GIBB

Johannesburg 1938-39: enjoyed a record England debut, scoring 93 and 106 as well as sharing second-wicket stands of 184 and 168 with E Paynter.

Durban 1938-39: shared record England v. South Africa second-wicket stand of 280 with W J Edrich, his 120 in 451 minutes including only two boundaries.

D GOUGH

Sydney 1998-99: achieved the 23rd hat-trick in Test cricket (ninth for England and first for England v. Australia since 1899).

Lord's 2001: took 3 wickets in 4 balls v. Pakistan.

S HAIGH

Cape Town 1898-99: bowled unchanged through the second innings with A E Trott, taking 6 for 11 as South Africa were dismissed for 35 in the space of 114 balls.

J H HAMPSHIRE

Lord's 1969: became the first England player to score 100 at Lord's on his debut in Tests.

A HILL

Melbourne 1876-77: took the first wicket to fall in Test cricket when he bowled N Thompson, and held the first catch when he dismissed T P Horan.

G H HIRST

The Oval: 1902: helped to score the last 15 runs in a match-winning tenth-wicket partnership with W Rhodes.

Birmingham 1909: shared all 20 Australian wickets with fellow left-arm spinner C Blythe (11 for 102).

M J HOGGARD

Bridgetown 2004: became the third Yorkshire player to take a hat-trick in Test cricket (see W Bates and D Gough). It was the 10th hat-trick for England and the third for England versus West Indies.

L HUTTON

Nottingham 1938: scored 100 in his first Test against Australia.

The Oval 1938: his score (364) and batting time (13 hours 17 minutes – the longest innings in English First-Class cricket) remain England records, and were world Test records until 1958. It remains the highest Test score at The Oval. His stand of 382 with M Leyland is the England second-wicket record in all Tests and the highest for any wicket against Australia. He also shared a record England v. Australia sixth-wicket stand of 216 with J Hardstaff Jr. – the first instance of a batsman sharing in two stands of 200 in the same Test innings. 770 runs were scored during his innings (Test record) which was England's 100th century against Australia, and contained 35 fours. England's total of 903 for 7 declared remains the Ashes Test record.

Lord's 1939: added 248 for the fourth wicket with D C S Compton in 140 minutes.

YORKSHIRE'S TEST CRICKET RECORDS *(Continued)*

L HUTTON *(Continued)*

The Oval 1939: shared (then) world-record third-wicket stand of 264 with W R Hammond, which remains the record for England v. West Indies. Hutton's last eight Tests had brought him 1,109 runs.

The Oval 1948: last out in the first innings, he was on the field for all but the final 57 minutes of the match.

Johannesburg 1948-49: shared (then) world-record first-wicket stand of 359 in 310 minutes with C Washbrook on the opening day of Test cricket at Ellis Park; it remains England's highest opening stand in all Tests.

The Oval 1950: scored England's first 200 in a home Test v. West Indies, and remains alone in carrying his bat for England against them; his 202 not out (in 470 minutes) is the highest score by an England batsman achieving this feat.

Adelaide 1950-51: only England batsman to carry his bat throughout a complete Test innings twice, and second after R Abel (1891-92) to do so for any country against Australia.

Manchester 1951: scored 98 not out, just failing to become the first to score his 100th First Class hundred in a Test match.

The Oval 1951: became the only batsman to be out 'obstructing the field' in Test cricket.

1952: first professional to be appointed captain of England in the 20th Century.

The Oval 1953: first captain to win a rubber after losing the toss in all five Tests.

Kingston 1953-54: scored the first 200 by an England captain in a Test overseas.

R ILLINGWORTH

Manchester 1971: shared record England v. India eighth-wicket stand of 168 with P. Lever.

Hon. F S JACKSON

The Oval 1893: his 100 took 135 minutes, and was the first in a Test in England to be completed with a hit over the boundary (then worth only four runs).

The Oval 1899: his stand of 185 with T W Hayward was then England's highest for any wicket in England, and the record opening partnership by either side in England v. Australia Tests.

Nottingham 1905: dismissed M A Noble, C Hill and J Darling in one over (W01W0W).

Leeds 1905: batted 268 minutes for 144 not out – the first hundred in a Headingley Test.

Manchester 1905: first to score five Test hundreds in England.

The Oval 1905: first captain to win every toss in a five-match rubber.

M LEYLAND

Melbourne 1928-29: scored 137 in his first innings against Australia.

1934: first to score three hundreds in a rubber against Australia in England.

Brisbane 1936-37: scored England's only 100 at 'The Gabba' before 1974-75.

The Oval 1938: contributed 187 in 381 minutes to the record Test total of 903 for 7 declared, sharing in England's highest stand against Australia (all wickets) and record second-wicket stand in all Tests: 382 with L Hutton. First to score hundreds in his first and last innings against Australia.

G G MACAULAY

Cape Town 1922-23: fourth bowler (third for England) to take a wicket (G A L Hearne) with his first ball in Test cricket. Made the winning hit in the fourth of only six Tests to be decided by a one-wicket margin.

Leeds 1926: shared a match-saving ninth-wicket stand of 108 with G Geary.

YORKSHIRE'S TEST CRICKET RECORDS *(Continued)*

C M OLD

Birmingham 1978: took 4 wickets in 5 balls in his 19th over (0WW no-ball WW1) to emulate the feat of M J C Allom.

R PEEL

Took his 50th wicket in his ninth Test and his 100th in his 20th Test – all against Australia.

W RHODES

Birmingham 1902: his first-innings analysis of 7 for 17 remains the record for all Tests at Edgbaston.

The Oval 1902: helped to score the last 15 runs in a match-winning tenth-wicket partnership with G H Hirst.

Sydney 1903-04: shared record England v. Australia tenth-wicket stand of 130 in 66 minutes with R E Foster.

Melbourne 1903-04: first to take 15 wickets in England v. Australia Tests; his match analysis of 15 for 124 remains the record for all Tests at Melbourne.

Melbourne 1911-12: shared record England v. Australia first-wicket stand of 323 in 268 minutes with J B Hobbs.

Johannesburg 1913-14: took his 100th wicket and completed the first 'double' for England (in 44 matches).

Sydney 1920-21: first to score 2,000 runs and take 100 wickets in Test cricket.

Adelaide 1920-21: third bowler to take 100 wickets against Australia.

The Oval 1926: set (then) record of 109 wickets against Australia.

Kingston 1929-30: ended the world's longest Test career (30 years 315 days) as the oldest Test cricketer (52 years 165 days).

H SUTCLIFFE

Birmingham 1924: shared the first of 15 three-figure partnerships with J B Hobbs at the first attempt.

Lord's 1924: shared stand of 268 with J B Hobbs, which remains the first-wicket record for all Lord's Tests, and was then the England v. South Africa record.

Sydney 1924-25: his first opening stands against Australia with J B Hobbs realised 157 and 110.

Melbourne 1924-25 (Second Test): with J B Hobbs achieved the first instance of a batting partnership enduring throughout a full day's Test match play; they remain the only England pair to achieve this feat, and their stand of 283 in 289 minutes remains the longest for the first wicket in this series. Became the first to score 100 in each innings of a Test against Australia, and the first Englishman to score three successive hundreds in Test cricket.

Melbourne 1924-25 (Fourth Test): first to score four hundreds in one rubber of Test matches; it was his third 100 in successive Test innings at Melbourne. Completed 1,000 runs in fewest Test innings (12) – since equalled.

Sydney 1924-25: his aggregate of 734 runs was the record for any rubber until 1928-29.

The Oval 1926: shared first-wicket stand of 172 with J B Hobbs on a rain-affected pitch.

The Oval 1929: first to score hundreds in each innings of a Test twice; only England batsman to score four hundreds in a rubber twice.

Sydney 1932-33: his highest England innings of 194 overtook J B Hobbs's world record of 15 Test hundreds.

F S TRUEMAN

Leeds 1952: reduced India to 0 for 4 in their second innings by taking 3 wickets in 8 balls on his debut.

Manchester 1952: achieved record England v. India innings analysis of 8 for 31.

The Oval 1952: set England v. India series record with 29 wickets.

YORKSHIRE'S TEST CRICKET RECORDS *(Continued)*

F S TRUEMAN *(Continued)*

Leeds 1961: took 5 for 0 with 24 off-cutters at a reduced pace v. Australia.

Lord's 1962: shared record England v. Pakistan ninth-wicket stand of 76 with T W Graveney.

Christchurch 1962-63: passed J B Statham's world Test record of 242 wickets; his analysis of 7 for 75 remains the record for Lancaster Park Tests and for England in New Zealand.

Birmingham 1963: returned record match analysis (12 for 119) against West Indies in England and for any Birmingham Test, ending with a 6 for 4 spell from 24 balls.

The Oval 1963: set England v. West Indies series record with 34 wickets.

The Oval 1964: first to take 300 wickets in Tests.

G ULYETT

Sydney 1881-82: with R G Barlow shared the first century opening partnership in Test cricket (122).

Melbourne 1881-82: his 149 was the first Test hundred for England in Australia, and the highest score for England on the first day of a Test in Australia until 1965-66.

M P VAUGHAN

Scored 1481 runs in 2002 – more than any other England player in a calendar year, surpassing the 1379 scored by D L Amiss in 1979. It was the fourth highest in a calendar year.

Scored 633 runs in the 2002-3 series versus Australia – surpassed for England in a five Test series versus Australia only by W R Hammond, who scored 905 runs in 1928-29, H Sutcliffe (734 in 1924-25), J B Hobbs (662 in 1911-12) and G Boycott (657 in 1970-71), when he played in five of the six Tests.

Scored six Test Match centuries in 2002 to equal the record set for England by D C S Compton in 1947.

Lord's 2004: scored a century in each innings (103 and 101*) versus West Indies and so became the third player (after G A Headley and G A Gooch) to score a century in each innings of a Test match at Lord's.

Lord's 2005: only the second player (J B Hobbs is the other) to have scored centuries in three consecutive Test match innings at Lord's. Scored the 100th century for England by a Yorkshire player.

H VERITY

Lord's 1934: took 14 for 80 on the third day (six of them in the final hour) to secure England's first win against Australia at Lord's since 1896. It remains the most wickets to fall to one bowler in a day of Test cricket in England. His match analysis of 15 for 104 was then the England v. Australia record, and has been surpassed only by J C Laker.

W WATSON

Lord's 1953: scored 109 in 346 minutes in his first Test against Australia.

N W D YARDLEY

Melbourne 1946-47: dismissed D G Bradman for the third consecutive innings without assistance from the field. Became the first to score a fifty in each innings for England and take five wickets in the same match.

Nottingham 1947: shared record England v. South Africa fifth-wicket stand of 237 with D C S Compton.

* * *

Facts adapted by Bill Frindall from his *England Test Cricketers – The Complete Record from 1877* (Collins Willow, 1989). With later additions.

TEST MATCHES AT HEADINGLEY, LEEDS 1899-2012

1899 **Australia 172** (J Worrall 76) and **224** (H Trumble 56, J T Hearne hat-trick). **England 220** (A F A Lilley 55, H Trumble 5 for 60) and **19 for 0 wkt.**
Match drawn Toss: Australia

1905 **England 301** (Hon F S Jackson 144*) and **295 for 5 wkts dec** (J T Tyldesley 100, T W Hayward 60, W W. Armstrong 5 for 122). **Australia 195** (W W Armstrong 66, A R Warren 5 for 57) and **224 for 7 wkts** (M A Noble 62).
Match drawn Toss: England

1907 **England 76** (G A Faulkner 6 for 17) and **162** (C B Fry 54). **South Africa 110** (C Blythe 8 for 59) and **75** (C Blythe 7 for 40).
England won by 53 runs Toss: England

1909 **Australia 188** and **207** (S F Barnes 6 for 63). **England 182** (J Sharp 61, J T Tyldesley 55, C G Macartney 7 for 58) and **87** (A Cotter 5 for 38).
Australia won by 126 runs Toss: Australia

1912 **England 242** (F E Woolley 57) and **238** (R H Spooner 82, J B Hobbs 55). **South Africa 147** (S F Barnes 6 for 52) and **159**.
England won by 174 runs Toss: England

1921 **Australia 407** (C G Macartney 115, W W Armstrong 77, C E Pellew 52, J M Taylor 50) and **273 for 7 wkts dec** (T J E Andrew 92). **England 259** (J W H T Douglas 75, Hon L H Tennyson 63, G Brown 57) and **202.**
Australia won by 219 runs Toss: Australia

1924 **England 396** (E H Hendren 132, H Sutcliffe 83) and **60 for 1 wkt. South Africa 132** (H W Taylor 59*, M W Tate 6 for 42) and **323** (H W Taylor 56, R H Catterall 56).
England won by 9 wickets Toss: England

1926 **Australia 494** (C G Macartney 151, W M Woodfull 141, A J Richardson 100). **England 294** (G G Macaulay 76, C V Grimmett 5 for 88) and **254 for 3 wkts** (H Sutcliffe 94, J B Hobbs 88).
Match drawn Toss: England

1929 **South Africa 236** (R H Catterall 74, C L Vincent 60, A P Freeman 7 for 115) and **275** (H G Owen-Smith 129). **England 328** (F E Woolley 83, W R Hammond 65, N A Quinn 6 for 92) and **186 for 5 wkts** (F E Woolley 95*).
England won by 5 wickets Toss: South Africa

1930 **Australia 566** (D G Bradman 334, A F Kippax 77, W M Woodfull 50, M W Tate 5 for 124). **England 391** (W R Hammond 113, C V Grimmett 5 for 135) and **95 for 3 wkts.**
Match drawn Toss: Australia

1934 **England 200** and **229 for 6 wkts. Australia 584** (D G Bradman 304, W H Ponsford 181, W E Bowes 6 for 142).
Match drawn Toss: England

1935 **England 216** (W R Hammond 63, A Mitchell 58) and **294 for 7 wkts dec** (W R Hammond 87*, A Mitchell 72, D Smith 57). **South Africa 171** (E A B Rowan 62) and **194 for 5 wkts** (B Mitchell 58).
Match drawn Toss: England

1938 **England 223** (W R Hammond 76, W .J O'Reilly 5 for 66) and **123** (.W J O'Reilly 5 for 56). **Australia 242** (D G Bradman 103, B A Barnett 57) and **107 for 5 wkts.**
Australia won by 5 wickets Toss: England

1947 **South Africa 175** (B Mitchell 53, A Nourse 51) and **184** (A D Nourse 57). **England 317 for 7 wkts dec** (L Hutton 100, C Washbrook 75) and **47 for 0 wkt.**
England won by 10 wickets Toss: South Africa

1948 **England 496** (C Washbrook 143, W .J Edrich 111, L Hutton 81, A V Bedser 79) and **365 for 8 wkts dec** (D C S. Compton 66, C Washbrook 65, L Hutton 57, W J Edrich 54). **Australia 458** (R N Harvey 112, S J E Loxton 93, R R Lindwall 77, K R Miller 58) and **404 for 3 wkts** (A R Morris 182, D G Bradman 173*).
Australia won by 7 wickets Toss: England

1949 **England 372** (D C S Compton 114, L Hutton 101, T B Burtt 5 for 97, J Cowie 5 for 127) and **267 for 4 wkts dec** (C Washbrook 103*, W J Edrich 70). **New Zealand 341** (F B Smith 96, M P Donnelly 64, T E Bailey 6 for 118) and **195 for 2 wkts** (B Sutcliffe 82, F Smith 54*).
Match drawn Toss: England

1951 **South Africa 538** (E A B Rowan 236, P N F Mansell 90, C B. van Ryneveld 83, R A McLean 67) and **87 for 0 wkt** (E A B Rowan 60*). **England 505** (P B H May 138, L Hutton 100, T E Bailey 95, F A Lowson 58, A M B Rowan 5 for 174).
Match drawn Toss: South Africa

1952 **India 293** (V L Manjrekar 133, V S Hazare 89) and 165 (D G Phadkar 64, V S Hazare 56). **England 334** (T W Graveney 71, T G Evans 66, Ghulam Ahmed 5 for 100) and **128 for 3 wkts** (R T Simpson 51).
England won by 7 wickets Toss: India

1953 **England 167** (T W Graveney 55, R R Lindwall 5 for 54) and **275** (W J Edrich 64, D C S Compton 61). **Australia 266** (R N Harvey 71, G B Hole 53, A V Bedser 6 for 95) and **147 for 4 wkts.**
Match drawn Toss: Australia

1955 **South Africa 171** and **500** (D J McGlew 133, W R Endean 116*, T L Goddard 74, H J Keith 73). **England 191** (D C S Compton 61) and **256** (P B H May 97, T L Goddard 5 for 69, H J Tayfield 5 for 94).
South Africa won by 224 runs Toss: South Africa

1956 **England 325** (P B H May 101, C Washbrook 98). **Australia 143** (J C Laker 5 for 58) and **140** (R N Harvey 69, J C Laker 6 for 55).
England won by an innings and 42 runs Toss: England

1957 **West Indies 142** (P J Loader 6 for 36, including hat-trick) and **132. England 279** (P B H May 69, M C Cowdrey 68, Rev D S Sheppard 68, F M M Worrell 7 for 70).
England won by an innings and 5 runs Toss: West Indies

1958 **New Zealand 67** (J C Laker 5 for 17) and **129** (G A R Lock 7 for 51). **England 267 for 2 wkts dec** (P B H May 113*, C A Milton 104*).
England won by an innings and 71 runs Toss: New Zealand

1959 **India 161** and **149. England 483 for 8 wkts dec** (M C Cowdrey 160, K F Barrington 80, W G A Parkhouse 78, G Pullar 75).
England won by an innings and 173 runs Toss: India

1961 **Australia 237** (R N Harvey 73, C C McDonald 54, F S Trueman 5 for 58) and **120** (R N Harvey 53, F S Trueman 6 for 30); **England 299** (M C Cowdrey 93, G Pullar 53, A K Davidson 5 for 63) and **62 for 2 wkts.**
England won by 8 wickets Toss: Australia

1962 **England 428** (P H Parfitt 119, M J Stewart 86, D A Allen 62, Munir Malik 5 for 128). **Pakistan 131** (Alimuddin 50) and **180** (Alimuddin 60, Saeed Ahmed 54).
England won by an innings and 117 runs Toss: Pakistan

1963 **West Indies 397** (G St A Sobers 102, R B Kanhai 92, J S Solomon 62) and **229** (B F Butcher 78, G St.A Sobers 52). **England 174** (G A R Lock 53, C C Griffith 6 for 36) and **231** (J M Parks 57, D B Close 56).
West Indies won by 221 runs Toss: West Indies

1964 **England 268** (J M Parks 68, E R Dexter 66, N J N Hawke 5 for 75) and 229 (K F Barrington 85). **Australia 389** (P J P Burge 160, W M Lawry 78) and **111 for 3 wkts** (I R Redpath 58*).
Australia won by 7 wickets Toss: England

1965 **England 546 for 4 wkts dec** (J H Edrich 310*, K F Barrington 163). **New Zealand 193** (J R Reid 54) and **166** (V Pollard 53, F J Titmus 5 for 19).
England won by an innings and 187 runs Toss: England

1966 **West Indies 500 for 9 wkts dec** (G.St.A Sobers 174, S M Nurse 137). **England 240** (B L D'Oliveira 88, G.St.A Sobers 5 for 41) and **205** (R W Barber 55, L R Gibbs 6 for 39).
West Indies won by an innings and 55 runs Toss: West Indies

1967 **England 550 for 4 wkts dec** (G Boycott 246*, B L D'Oliveira 109, K F Barrington 93, T W Graveney 59) and **126 for 4 wkts. India 164** (Nawab of Pataudi jnr 64) and **510** (Nawab of Pataudi jnr 148, A L Wadekar 91, F M Engineer 87, Hanumant Singh 73).
England won by 6 wickets Toss: England

1968 **Australia 315** (I R Redpath 92, I M Chappell 65) and **312** (I M Chappell 81, K D Walters 56, R Illingworth 6 for 87). **England 302** (R M Prideaux 64, J H Edrich 62, A N Connolly 5 for 72) and **230 for 4 wkts** (J H Edrich 65).
Match drawn Toss: Australia

1969 **England 223** (J H Edrich 79) and **240** (G.St A Sobers 5 for 42). **West Indies 161** and **272** (B F Butcher 91, G S Camacho 71).
England won by 30 runs Toss: England

1971 **England 316** (G Boycott 112, B L D'Oliveira 74) and **264** (B L D'Oliveira 72, D L Amiss 56) **Pakistan 350** (Zaheer Abbas 72, Wasim Bari 63, Mushtaq Mohammad 57) and **205** (Sadiq Mohammad 91).
England won by 25 runs Toss: England

1972 **Australia 146** (K R Stackpole 52) and **136** (D L Underwood 6 for 45). **England 263** (R Illingworth 57, A A Mallett 5 for 114) and **21 for 1 wkt.**
England won by 9 wickets Toss: Australia

1973 **New Zealand 276** (M G Burgess 87, V Pollard 62) and **142** (G M Turner 81, G G Arnold 5 for 27). **England 419** (G Boycott 115, K W R Fletcher 81, R Illingworth 65, RO Collinge 5 for 74).
England won by an innings and 1 run Toss: New Zealand

1974 **Pakistan 285** (Majid Khan 75, Safraz Nawaz 53) and **179**. **England 183** and **238 for 6 wkts** (J H Edrich 70, K W R Fletcher 67*).
Match drawn Toss: Pakistan

1975 **England 288** (D S Steele 73, J H Edrich 62, A W Greig 51, G J Gilmour 6 for 85) and **291** (D S Steele 92). **Australia 135** (P H Edmonds 5 for 28) and **220 for 3 wkts** (R B McCosker 95*, I M Chappell 62).
Match drawn Toss: England

1976 **West Indies 450** (C G Greenidge 115, R C Fredericks 109, I V A Richards 66, L G Rowe 50) and **196** (C L King 58, R G D Willis 5 for 42). **England 387** (A W Greig 116, A P E Knott 116) and **204** (A W Greig 76*).
West Indies won by 55 runs Toss: West Indies

1977 **England 436** (G Boycott 191, A P E Knott 57). **Australia 103** (I T Botham 5 for 21) and **248** (R W Marsh 63).
England won by an innings and 85 runs Toss: England

1978 **Pakistan 201** (Sadiq Mohammad 97). **England 119 for 7 wkts** (Safraz Nawaz 5 for 39).
Match drawn Toss: Pakistan

1979 **England 270** (I T Botham 137). **India 223 for 6 wkts** (S M Gavaskar 78, D B Vengsarkar 65*).
Match drawn Toss: England

1980 **England 143 and 227 for 6 wkts dec** (G A Gooch 55). **West Indies 245.**
Match drawn Toss: West Indies

1981 **Australia 401 for 9 wkts dec** (J Dyson 102, K J Hughes 89, G N Yallop 58, I T Botham 6 for 95) and **111** (R G D Willis 8 for 43). **England 174** (I T Botham 50) and **356** (I T Botham 149*, G R Dilley 56, T M Alderman 6 for 135).
England won by 18 runs Toss: Australia

1982 **Pakistan 275** (Imran Khan 67*, Mudassar Nazar 65, Javed Miandad 54) and **199** (Javed Miandad 52, I T Botham 5 for 74). **England 256** (D I Gower 74, I T Botham 57, Imran Khan 5 for 49) and **219 for 7 wkts** (G Fowler 86).
England won by 3 wickets Toss: Pakistan

1983 **England 225** (C J Tavaré 69, A J Lamb 58, B L Cairns 7 for 74) and **252** (D I Gower 112*, E J Chatfield 5 for 95). **New Zealand 377** (J G Wright 93, B A Edgar 84, R J Hadlee 75) and **103 for 5 wkts** (R G D Willis 5 for 35).
New Zealand won by 5 wickets Toss: New Zealand

1984 **England 270** (A J Lamb 100) and **159** (G Fowler 50, M D Marshall 7 for 53). **West Indies 302** (H A Gomes 104*, M A Holding 59, P J W Allott 6 for 61) and **131 for 2 wkts.**
West Indies won by 8 wickets Toss: England

1985 **Australia 331** (A M J Hilditch 119) and **324** (W B Phillips 91, A M J Hilditch 80, K C Wessels 64, J E Emburey 5 for 82). **England 533** (R T Robinson 175, I T Botham 60, P R Downton 54, M W Gatting 53) and **123 for 5 wkts.**
England won by 5 wickets Toss: Australia

1986 **India 272** (D B Vengsarkar 61) and **237** (D B Vengsarkar 102*). **England 102** (R M H Binny 5 for 40) and **128.**
India won by 279 runs Toss: India

1987 **England 136** (D J Capel 53) and **199** (D I Gower 55, Imran Khan 7 for 40). **Pakistan 353** (Salim Malik 99, Ijaz Ahmed 50, N A Foster 8 for 107).
Pakistan won by an innings and 18 runs Toss: England

1988 **England 201** (A J Lamb 64*) and **138** (G A Gooch 50). **West Indies 275** (R A Harper 56, D L Haynes 54, D R Pringle 5 for 95) and **67 for 0 wkt.**
West Indies won by 10 wickets Toss: West Indies

1989 **Australia 601 for 7 wkts dec** (S R Waugh 177*, M A Taylor 136, D M Jones 79, M G Hughes 71, A R Border 66) and **230 for 3 wkts dec** (M A Taylor 60, A R Border 60*). **England 430** (A J Lamb 125, K J Barnett 80, R A Smith 66, T M Alderman 5 for 107) and **191.** (G A Gooch 68, T M Alderman 5 for 44).
Australia won by 210 runs Toss: England

1991 **England 198** (R A Smith 54) and **252** (G A Gooch 154*, C E L Ambrose 6 for 52). **West Indies 173** (I V A Richards 73) and **162** (R B Richardson 68).
England won by 115 runs Toss: West Indies

1992 **Pakistan 197** (Salim Malik 82*) and **221** (Salim Malik 84*, Ramiz Raja 63, N A Mallinder 5 for 50). **England 320** (G A Gooch 135, M A Atherton 76, Waqar Younis 5 for 117) and **99 for 4 wkts.**
England won by 6 wickets Toss: Pakistan

1993 **Australia 653 for 4 wkts dec** (A R Border 200*, S R Waugh 157*, D C Boon 107, M J Slater 67, M E Waugh 52). **England 200** (G A Gooch 59, M A Atherton 55, P R Reiffel 5 for 65) and **305** (A J Stewart 78, M A Atherton 63).
Australia won by an innings and 148 runs Toss: Australia

1994 **England 477 for 9 wkts dec** (M A Atherton 99, A J Stewart 89, G P Thorpe 72, S J Rhodes 65*) and **267 for 5 wkts dec** (G A Hick 110, G P Thorpe 73). **South Africa 447** (P N Kirsten 104, B M McMillan 78, C R Matthews 62*) and **116 for 3 wkts** (G Kirsten 65).
Match drawn Toss: England

1995 **England 199** (M A Atherton 81, I R Bishop 5 for 32) and **208** (G P Thorpe 61). **West Indies 282** (S L Campbell 69, J C Adams 58, B C Lara 53) and **129 for 1 wkt** (C L Hooper 73*).
West Indies won by 9 wickets Toss: West Indies

1996 **Pakistan 448** (Ijaz Ahmed 141, Mohin Khan 105, Salim Malik 55, Asif Mujtaba 51, D G Cork 5 for 113) and **242 for 7 wkts dec** (Inzamam-ul-Haq 65, Ijaz Ahmed sen 52) **England 501** (A J Stewart 170, N V Knight 113, J P Crawley 53).
Match drawn Toss: England

1997 **England 172** (J N. Gillespie 7 for 37) and **268** (N Hussain 105, J P Crawley 72, P R Reiffel 5 for 49). **Australia 501 for 9 wkts dec** (M T G Elliott 199, R T Ponting 127, P R Reiffel 54*, D Gough 5 for 149).
Australia won by an innings and 61 runs Toss: Australia

1998 **England 230** (M A Butcher 116) and **240** (N Hussain 94, S M Pollock 5 for 53, A A Donald 5 for 71). **South Africa 252** (W J. Cronje 57, A R C Fraser 5 for 42) and **195** (J N Rhodes 85, B M McMillan 54, D Gough 6 for 42).
England won by 23 runs Toss: England

2000 **West Indies 172** (R R Sarwan 59*, C White 5 for 57) and **61** (A R Caddick 5 for 14). **England 272** (M P Vaughan 76, G A Hick 59).
England won by an innings and 39 runs Toss: West Indies

2001 **Australia 447** (R T Ponting 144, D R Martyn 118, M E Waugh 72, D Gough 5 for 103) and **176 for 4 wkts dec** (R T Ponting 72). **England 309** (A J Stewart 76*, G D McGrath 7 for 76) and **315 for 4 wkts** (M A Butcher 173*, N Hussain 55).
England won by 6 wickets Toss: Australia

2002 **India 628 for 8 wkts dec** (S R Tendulkar 193, R S Dravid 148, S C Ganguly 128, S B Bangar 68). **England 273** (A J Stewart 78*, M P Vaughan 61) and **309** (N Hussain 110.)
India won by an innings and 46 runs Toss: India

2003 **South Africa 342** (G Kirsten 130, M Zondeki 59, J A Rudolph 55) and **365** (A J Hall 99*, G Kirsten 60). **England 307** (M A Butcher 77, M E Trescothick 59, A Flintoff 55) and **209** (M A Butcher 61, A Flintoff 50, J H Kallis 6 for 54.)
South Africa won by 191 runs Toss: South Africa

2004 **New Zealand 409** (S P Fleming 97, M H W Papps 86, B B McCullum 54) and **161. England 526** (M E Trescothick 132, G O Jones 100, A Flintoff 94, A J Strauss 62) and **45 for 1 wkt**
England won by 9 wickets Toss: England

2006 **England 515** (K P Pietersen 135, I R Bell 119, Umar Gul 5 for 123) and **345** (A J Strauss 116, M E Trescothick 58, C M W Reid 55). **Pakistan 538** (Mohammad Yousuf 192, Younis Khan 173) and **155**.
England won by 167 runs Toss: England

2007 **England 570 for 7 wkts dec** (K P Pietersen 226, M P Vaughan 103, M J Prior 75). **West Indies 146** and **141** (D J Bravo 52).
England won by an innings and 283 runs Toss: England

2008 **England 203** and **327** (S C J Broad 67*, A N Cook 60). **South Africa 522** (A B de Villiers 174, A G Prince 149) and **9 for 0 wkt**.
South Africa won by 10 wickets Toss: South Africa

2009 **England 102** (P M Siddle 5 for 21) and **263** (G P Swann 62, S C J Broad 61, M G Johnson 5 for 69). **Australia 445** (M J North 110, M J Clarke 93, R T Ponting 78, S R Watson 51, S C J Broad 6 for 91).
Australia won by an innings and 80 runs Toss: England

2010 **Australia 88** and **349** (R T Ponting 66, M J Clarke 77, S P D Smith 77). **Pakistan 258** (S R Watson 6-33) and **180-7** (Imran Farhat 67, Azhar Ali 51).
Pakistan won by 3 wickets Toss: Australia
(This was a Home Test Match for Pakistan)

2012 **South Africa 419** (A N Petersen 182, G C Smith 52) and **258-9 dec** (J A Rudolph 69, GC Smith 52, S C J Broad 5-69). **England 425** (K P Pietersen 149, M J Prior 68) and **130-4.**
Match drawn Toss: England

SUMMARY OF RESULTS

ENGLAND	First played	Last played	Played	Won	Lost	Drawn
v. Australia	1899	2009	24	7	9	8
v. India	1952	2002	6	3	2	1
v. New Zealand	1949	2004	6	4	1	1
v. Pakistan	1962	2006	9	5	1	3
v. South Africa	1907	2012	13	6	3	4
v. West Indies	1957	2007	12	5	6	1
Totals	1899	2012	70	30	22	18

SIX HIGHEST AGGREGATES

Runs	*Wkts*	
1723	31	in 1948 (England 496 and 365 for 8 wkts dec; Australia 458 and 404 for 3 wkts)
1553	40	in 2006 (England 515 and 345; Pakistan 538 and 155)
1452	30	in 1989 (Australia 601 for 7 wkts dec and 230 for 3 wkts dec; England 430 and 191)
1350	28	in 1967 (England 550 for 4 wkts dec and 126 for 4 wkts; India 164 and 510)
1311	35	in 1985 (Australia 331 and 324; England 533 and 123 for 5 wkts)
1307	28	in 1994 (England 477 and 267 for 5 wkts dec; South Africa 447 and 116 for 3 wkts)

Note: The highest aggregate prior to the Second World War

1141	37	in 1921 (Australia 407 and 272 for 7 wkts dec; England 259 and 202)

SIX LOWEST AGGREGATES

Runs	*Wkts*	
423	40	in 1907 (England 76 and 162; South Africa 110 and 75)
463	22	in 1958 (New Zealand 67 and 129; England 267 for 2 wkts)
505	30	in 2000 (West Indies 172 and 61; England 272)
553	30	in 1957 (West Indies 142 and 132; England 279)
566	31	in 1972 (Australia 146 and 136; England 263 and 21 for 1 wkt)
608	30	in 1956 (England 325; Australia 143 and 140)

SIX HIGHEST TOTALS

653 for 4 wkts dec	Australia v. England, 1993
608 for 8 wkts dec	India v. England, 2002
601 for 7 wkts dec	Australia v. England, 1989
584	Australia v. England, 1934
570 for 7 wkts dec	England v. West Indies, 2007
566	Australia v. England, 1930

SIX LOWEST TOTALS

61	West Indies v. England, 2000
67	New Zealand v. England, 1958
75	South Africa v. England, 1907
76	England v. South Africa, 1907
87	England v Australia, 1909
88	Australia v. Pakistan, 2010

SIX HIGHEST INDIVIDUAL SCORES

For England

310*	J H Edrich versus New Zealand, 1965
246*	G Boycott versus India, 1967
226	K P Pietersen versusWest Indies, 2007
191	G Boycott versus Australia, 1977
175	R T Robinson versus Australia, 1985
173*	M A Butcher versus Australia, 2001

For Australia

334	D G Bradman, 1930
304	D G Bradman, 1934
200*	A R Border, 1993
199	M T G Elliott, 1997
182	A R Morris, 1948
181	W H Ponsford, 1934

For Pakistan

192	Mohammad Yousuf, 2006
173	Younis Khan, 2006
141	Ijaz Ahmed, 1996
105	Moin Khan, 1996
99	Salim Malik, 1987
97	Sadiq Mohammad, 1978

SIX HIGHEST INDIVIDUAL SCORES *(Continued)*

For India

193	S R Tendulkar, 2002
148	Nawab of Pataudi jnr, 1967
148	R S Dravid, 2002
133	V L Manjrekar, 1952
128	S C Gangulay, 2002
102*	D B Vengsarkar, 1986

For South Africa

236	E A B Rowan, 1951
182	A N Petersen, 2012
174	A B de Villiers, 2008
149	A G Prince, 2008
133	D J McGlew, 1955
130	G Kirsten, 2003

For New Zealand

97	S P Fleming, 2004
96	F B Smith, 1949
93	J G Wright, 1983
87	M G Burgess, 1973
86	M H W Papps, 2004
84	B A Edgar, 1983

For West Indies

174	G St.A Sobers, 1966
137	S M Nurse, 1966
115	C G. Greenidge, 1976
109	R C Fredericks, 1976
104*	H A Gomes, 1984
102	G St A Sobers, 1963

HUNDRED BEFORE LUNCH

First day

112*	C G Macartney for Australia, 1926
105*	D G Bradman for Australia, 1930

Third day

102	(from 27* to 129) H G Owen-Smith for South Africa, 1929

CARRYING BAT THROUGH A COMPLETED INNINGS

154* out of 252 G A Gooch, England v. West Indies, 1991

MOST CENTURIES IN AN INNINGS

3	1926	C G Macartney (151), W M Woodfull (141) and A J Richardson for Australia
3	1993	A R Border (200*), S R Waugh (157*) and D C Boon (107) for Australia
3	2002	S R Tendulkar (193), R S Dravid (148) and S C Gangulay (128) for India

MOST CENTURIES IN A MATCH

5	1948	C Washbrook (143) and W J Edrich (111) for England; R N Harvey (112), A R Morris (182) and D G Bradman (173*) for Australia
5	2006	K P Pietersen (135), I R Bell (119) and A J Strauss (116) for England: Younis Khan (173) and Mohammad Yousuf (192) for Pakistan
4	1976	C G Greenidge (115) and R C Fredericks (109) for West Indies; A W Greig (116) and A P E Knott (116) for England
4	1996	Ijaz Ahmed (141) and Moin Khan (105) for Pakistan; A J Stewart (170) and N V Knight (113) for England
4	2002	S R Tendulkar (193), R S Dravid (148) and S C Gangulay (128) for India; N Hussain (110) for England

CENTURY PARTNERSHIPS

For England

(six highest)

For the 1st wicket

168 L Hutton (81) and C Washbrook (143) v. Australia, 1948 (1st inns)
168 G A Gooch (135) and M A Atherton (76) v. Pakistan, 1992
158 M E Trescothick (58) and A J Strauss (116) v. Pakistan, 2006
156 J B Hobbs (88) and H Sutcliffe (94) v. Australia, 1926
153 M E Trescothick (132) and A J Strauss (62) v. New Zealand, 2004
146 W G A Parkhouse (78) and G Pullar (75) v. India, 1959

For all other wickets

369 (2nd wkt) J H Edrich (310*) and K F Barrington (163) v. New Zealand, 1965
252 (4th wkt) G Boycott (246*) and B L D'Oliveira (109) v. India, 1967
194* (3rd wkt) C A Milton (104*) and P B H May (113*) v. New Zealand, 1958
193 (4th wkt) M C Cowdrey (160) and K F Barrington (80) v. India, 1959
187 (4th wkt) P B H May (101) and C Washbrook (98) v. Australia, 1956
181 (3rd wkt) M A Butcher (173*) and N Hussain (55) v. Australia, 2001

For Australia

(six highest)

For the 1st wkt – none

For all other wickets

388 (4th wkt) W H Ponsford (181) and D G Bradman (304), 1934
332* (5th wkt) A R Border (200*) and S R Waugh (157*), 1993
301 (2nd wkt) A R Morris (182) and D G Bradman (173*), 1948
268 (5th wkt) M T G Elliott (199) and R T Ponting (127), 1997
235 (2nd wkt) W M Woodfull (141) and C G Macartney (151), 1926
229 (3rd wkt) D G Bradman (334) and A F Kippax (77), 1930

For other countries in total

India

249 (4th wkt) S R Tendulkar (193) and S C Gangulay (128), 2002
222 (4th wkt) V S Hazare (89) and V L Manjrekar (133), 1952
170 (2nd wkt) S B Bangar (68) and R S Dravid (148), 2002
168 (2nd wkt) F M Engineer (87) and A L Wadekar (91), 1967
150 (3rd wkt) R S Dravid (148) and S R Tendulkar (193), 2002
134 (5th wkt) Hanumant Singh (73) and Nawab of Pataudi jnr (148), 1967
105 (6th wkt) V S Hazare (56) and D G Phadkar (64), 1952

New Zealand

169 (2nd wkt) M H W Papps (86) and S P Fleming (97), 2004
120 (5th wkt) M P Donnelly (64) and F B Smith (96), 1949
116 (2nd wkt) J G Wright (93) and M D Crowe (37), 1983
112 (1st wkt) B Sutcliffe (82) and V J Scott (43), 1949
106 (5th wkt) M G Burgess (87) and V Pollard (62), 1973

Pakistan

363 (3rd wkt) Younis Khan (173) and Mohammad Yousuf (192), 2006
130 (4th wkt) Ijaz Ahmed (141) and Salim Malik (55), 1996
129 (3rd wkt) Zaheer Abbas (72) and Mushtaq Mohammed (57), 1971
112 (7th wkt) Asif Mujtaba (51) and Moin Khan (105), 1996
110 (2nd wkt) Imran Farhat (67) and Azhar Ali (51), 2010 v. Australia
100 (3rd wkt) Mudassar Nazar (65) and Javed Miandad (54), 1982
100 (4th wkt) Majid Khan (75) and Zaheer Abbas (48), 1974

CENTURY PARTNERSHIPS *(Continued)*

South Africa

212 (5th wkt) A G Prince (149) and A B de Villiers (174), 2008
198 (2nd wkt) E A B Rowan (236) C B van Ryneveld (83), 1951
176 (1st wkt) D J McGlew (133) and T L Goddard (74), 1955
150 (8th wkt) G Kirsten (130) and M Zondeki (59), 2003
120 (1st wkt) A N Petersen (182) and G C Smith (52), 2012
120 (1st wkt) J A Rudolph (69) and G C Smith (52), 2012
117 (6th wkt) J N Rhodes (85) and B M McMillan (54), 1998
115 (7th wicket) P N Kirsten (104) and B M McMillan (78), 1994
108 (5th wkt) E A B Rowan (236) and R A McLean (67), 1951
103 (10th wkt) H G Owen-Smith (129) and A J Bell (26*), 1929

West Indies

265 (5th wkt) S M Nurse (137) and G St A Sobers (174), 1966
192 (1st wkt) R C Fredericks (109) and C G Greenidge (115), 1976
118* (2nd wkt) C L Hooper (73*) and B C Lara (48*), 1995
143 (4th wkt) R B Kanhai (92) and G St A Sobers (102), 1963
108 (3rd wkt) G S Camacho (71) and B F Butcher (91), 1969
106 (1st wkt) C G Greenidge (49) and D L Haynes (43), 1984

6 BEST INNINGS ANALYSES

For England

8 for 43 R G D Willis v. Australia, 1981
8 for 59 C Blythe v. South Africa, 1907 (1st inns)
8 for 107 N A Foster v. Pakistan, 1987
7 for 40 C Blythe v. South Africa, 1907 (2nd inns)
7 for 51 G A R Lock v. New Zealand, 1958
7 for 115 A P Freeman v. South Africa, 1929

For Australia

7 for 37 J N Gilliespie, 1997
7 for 58 C G Macartney, 1909
7 for 76 G D McGrath, 2001
6 for 33 S R Watson, 2010 v. Pakistan
6 for 85 G J Gilmour, 1975
6 for 135 T M Alderman, 1981

5 WICKETS IN AN INNINGS

For India (2)

5 for 40 R M H Binny, 1986
5 for 100 Ghulam Ahmed, 1952

For New Zealand (5)

7 for 74 B L Cairns, 1983
5 for 74 R O Collinge, 1973
5 for 95 E J Chatfield, 1983
5 for 97 T B Burtt, 1949
5 for 127 J Cowie, 1949

For Pakistan (6)

7 for 40 Imran Khan, 1987
5 for 39 Sarfraz Nawaz, 1978
5 for 49 Imran Khan, 1982
5 for 117 Waqar Younis, 1992
5 for 123 Umar Gul, 2006
5 for 128 Munir Malik, 1962

For South Africa (7)

6 for 17 G A Faulkner, 1907
6 for 92 N A Quinn, 1929
6 for 54 J H Kallis, 2003
5 for 53 S M Pollock, 1998
5 for 69 T L Goddard, 1955
5 for 71 A A Donald, 1998
5 for 94 H J Tayfield, 1955
5 for 174 A M B Rowan, 1951

For West Indies (8)

7 for 53 M D Marshall, 1984
7 for 70 F M Worrell, 1957
6 for 36 C C Griffith, 1963
6 for 39 L R Gibbs, 1996
6 for 52 C E L Ambrose, 1991
5 for 32 I R Bishop, 1995
5 for 41 G.St.A Sobers, 1966
5 for 42 G.St A Sobers, 1969

10 WICKETS IN A MATCH

For England (7)

15 for 99	(8 for 59 and 7 for 40) C Blythe v. South Africa, 1907
11 for 65	(4 for 14 and 7 for 51) G A R Lock v. New Zeland, 1958
11 for 88	(5 for 58 and 6 for 30) F S Trueman v. Australia, 1961
11 for 113	(5 for 58 and 6 for 55) J C Laker v. Australia, 1956
10 for 82	(4 for 37 and 6 for 45) D L Underwood v. Australia, 1972
10 for 115	(6 for 52 and 4 for 63) S F Barnes v. South Africa, 1912
10 for 207	(7 for 115 and 3 for 92) A P Freeman v. South Africa, 1929

For Australia (3)

11 for 85	(7 for 58 and 4 for 27) C G Macartney, 1909
10 for 122	(5 for 66 and 5 for 56) W J O'Reilly, 1938
10 for 151	(5 for 107 and 5 for 44) T M Alderman, 1989

For New Zealand (1)

10 for 144	(7 for 74 and 3 for 70) B L Cairns, 1983

For Pakistan (1)

10 for 77	(3 for 37 and 7 for 40) Imran Khan, 1987

Note: Best bowling in a match for:

India:	7 for 58 (5 for 40 and 2 for 18) R M H Binney, 1986
South Africa:	9 for 75 (6 for 17 and 3 for 58) G A Faulkner, 1907
West Indies:	9 for 81 (6 for 36 and 3 for 45) C C Griffith, 1963

HAT-TRICKS

J T Hearne v. Australia, 1899
P J Loader v. West Indies, 1957

TEST MATCH AT BRAMALL LANE, SHEFFIELD 1902

1902 **Australia 194** (S F Barnes 6 for 49) and **289** (C Hill 119, V T Trumper 62, W Rhodes 5 for 63) **England 145** (J V Saunders 5 for 50, M A Noble 5 for 51) and **195** (A C MacLaren 63, G L Jessop 55, M A Noble 6 for 52).
Australia won by 143 runs Toss: Australia

For England

YORKSHIRE ONE-DAY INTERNATIONAL CRICKETERS 1971-2012/13 (Correct to January 27, 2013)

Player	M	I	NO	Runs	HS	Av'ge	100s	50s	Balls	Runs	W	Av'ge	Best	4wI	Ct/St
ATHEY, C W J 1980-88	31	30	3	848	142*	31.40	2	4	—	—	—	—	—	—	16
BAIRSTOW, D L ...1979-84	21	20	6	206	23*	14.71	—	—	—	—	—	—	—	—	17/4
BAIRSTOW, J M ...2011-12	7	6	1	119	41*	23.80	—	—	—	—	—	—	—	—	3
BLAKEY, R J 1992-93	3	2	0	25	25	12.50	—	—	—	—	—	—	—	—	2/1
BOYCOTT, G 1971-81	36	34	4	1082	105	36.06	1	9	168	105	5	21.00	2-14	—	5
BRESNAN, T T ..2006-12/13	69	49	13	719	80	19.97	—	1	3439	3099	88	35.21	5-48	4	19
COPE, G A 1977-78	2	1	1	1	1*	—	—	—	112	35	2	17.50	1-16	—	—
GOUGH, D 1994-2006	158	87	38	609	46*	12.42	—	—	8422	6154	234	26.29	5-44	10	24
HAMPSHIRE, J H ..1971-72	3	3	1	48	25*	24.00	—	—	—	—	—	—	—	—	—
HOGGARD, M J 2001-06	26	6	2	17	7	4.25	—	—	1306	1152	32	36.00	5-49	1	5
JARVIS, P W 1988-93	16	8	2	31	16*	5.16	—	—	879	672	24	28.00	5-35	2	1
LOVE, J D 1981	3	3	0	61	43	20.33	—	—	—	—	—	—	—	—	1
McGRATH, A 2003-04	14	12	2	166	52	16.60	—	1	228	175	4	43.75	1-13	—	4
MOXON, M D 1985-88	8	8	0	174	70	21.75	—	1	—	—	—	—	—	—	5
OLD, C M 1973-81	32	25	7	338	51*	18.77	—	1	1755	999	45	22.20	4- 8	2	8
RASHID, A U 2009	5	4	1	60	31*	20.00	—	—	204	191	3	63.66	1-16	—	2
ROOT, J E 2012/13	5	4	1	163	57*	54.33	—	1	126	114	0	—	—	—	3
SHAHZAD, A 2010-11	11	8	2	39	9	6.50	—	—	588	490	17	28.82	3-41	—	4
SIDEBOTTOM, R J .2001-10	25	18	8	133	24	13.30	—	—	1277	1039	29	35.82	3-19	—	6
SILVERWOOD, C E W 1996-2001	7	4	0	17	12	4.25	—	—	306	244	6	40.66	3-43	—	—
STEVENSON, G B ..1980-81	4	4	3	43	28*	43.00	—	—	192	125	7	17.85	4-33	1	2
VAUGHAN, M P ...2001-07	86	83	10	1982	90*	27.15	—	16	796	649	16	40.56	4-22	1	25
WHITE, C 1994-2003	51	41	5	568	57*	15.77	—	1	2364	1726	65	26.55	5-21	2	12
For Scotland															
BLAIN, J A R 1999-2009	33	25	6	284	41	14.94	—	—	1329	1173	41	28.60	5-22	4	8
HAMILTON, G M 1999-2010	38	38	3	1231	119	35.17	2	7	220	160	3	53.33	2-36	—	6/1

YORKSHIRE PLAYERS WHO PLAYED ALL THEIR ONE-DAY INTERNATIONAL CRICKET AFTER LEAVING YORKSHIRE

For England

Player	M	I	NO	Runs	HS	Av'ge	100s	50s	Balls	Runs	W	Av'ge	Best	4wI	Ct/St
BATTY, G J 2002-09	10	8	2	30	17	5.00	—	—	440	366	5	73.20	2-40	—	4
CLOSE, D B 1972	3	3	0	49	43	16.33	—	—	18	21	0	—	—	—	1
GRAYSON, A P 2000-01	2	2	0	6	6	3.00	—	—	90	60	3	20.00	3-40	—	1
ILLINGWORTH, R .1971-72	3	2	0	5	4	2.50	—	—	130	84	4	21.00	3-50	—	1
RHODES, S J 1989-95	9	8	2	107	56	17.83	—	1	—	—	—	—	—	—	9/2
WHARF, A G 2004-05	13	5	3	19	9	9.50	—	—	584	428	18	23.77	4-24	1	1
WOOD, B 1972-82	13	12	2	314	78*	31.40	—	2	420	224	9	24.88	2-14	—	6
Overseas Players															
(Qualification: 24 List A matches for Yorkshire)															
For Australia															
BEVAN, M G 1994-2004	232	196	67	6912	108*	53.58	6	46	1,966	1655	36	45.97	3-36	—	128
JAQUES, P A 2006-2007	6	6	0	125	94	20.83	—	1	—	—	—	—	—	—	3
LEHMANN, D S . 1996-2005	117	101	22	3078	119	38.96	4	17	1,793	1445	52	27.78	4-7	1	26
For South Africa															
RUDOLPH, J A 2003-06	43	37	6	1157	81	37.32	—	7	24	26	0	—	—	—	11
For West Indies															
RICHARDSON, R B 1983-96	224	217	30	6248	122	33.41	5	44	58	46	1	46.00	1-4	—	75

LIST OF PLAYERS AND CAREER AVERAGES IN ALL FIRST-CLASS MATCHES FOR YORKSHIRE 1863-2012

Based on research by John T Potter, Roy D Wilkinson and the late Anthony Woodhouse

The Editor and Statistics Editor welcome any information which will help in keeping this list up to date. The present compilers do not believe that we should alter the status of matches from that determined at the time they were played. Therefore, these averages include the match versus Gentlemen of Scotland in 1878, and exclude the matches versus Liverpool and District played in 1889, 1891, 1892 and 1893 in line with what appear to be the decisions of the Club at the time.

* Played as an amateur © Awarded County Cap § Born outside Yorkshire

Player	*Date of Birth*	*Date of Death (if known)*	*First Played*	*Last Played*	*M*	*Inns*	*NO*	*Runs*	*HS*	*Av'ge*	*100s*	*Runs*	*Wkts*	*Av'ge*	*Ct/St*
Ackroyd, A *	Aug. 29, 1858	Oct. 3, 1927	1879	1879	1	1	1	2	2*	—	0	7	0	—	—
Allen, S *	Dec 20, 1893	Oct 9, 1978	1924	1924	1	2	0	8	6	4.00	0	116	2	58.00	—
Allen, W R	Apr14, 1893	Oct 14, 1950	1921	1925	30	32	10	475	95*	21.59	—	—	—	—	45/21
Ambler, J	Feb 12, 1860	Feb 10 1899	1886	1886	4	7	0	68	25	9.71	—	22	0	—	2
Anderson, G	Jan 20, 1826	Nov 27, 1902	1851	1869	19	31	6	520	99*	20.80	0	—	—	—	19
Anderson, P N	Apr. 28, 1966		1988	1988	1	1	0	0	0	0.00	—	47	1	47.00	1
Anson, C E *	Oct 14, 1889	Mar 26, 1969	1924	1924	1	2	0	27	14	13.50	0	—	—	—	1
Appleton, C *	May15, 1844	Feb 26, 1925	1865	1865	3	6	1	56	18	11.20	0	—	—	—	—
Appleyard, R ©	June 27, 1924		1950	1958	133	122	43	679	63	8.59	0	9,903	642	15.42	70
Armitage, C I *	Apr 24, 1849	Apr 24, 1917	1873	1878	3	5	0	26	12	5.20	0	29	0	—	—
Armitage, T	Apr 25, 1848	Sept 21, 1922	1872	1878	52	85	8	1,053	95	13.67	0	1,614	107	15.08	20
Ash, D L	Feb 18, 1944		1965	1965	3	3	0	22	12	7.33	0	22	0	—	—
Ashman, J R	May 20, 1926		1951	1951	1	1	1	0	0*	—	0	116	4	29.00	—
Ashraf, Moin A	**Jan 5, 1992**		**2010**	**2012**	**19**	**19**	**5**	**56**	**10**	**4.00**	**0**	**1149**	**39**	**29.46**	**2**
Aspinall, R ©	Oct 26, 1918	Aug 16, 1999	1946	1950	36	48	8	763	75*	19.07	0	2,670	131	20.38	18
Aspinall, W	Mar 24, 1858	Not known	1880	1880	2	3	0	16	14	5.33	0	—	—	—	1
Asquith, F T	Feb 5, 1870	Jan 11, 1916	1903	1903	1	1	0	0	0	0.00	0	—	—	—	2
Athey, C W J ©	Sept 27, 1957		1976	1983	151	246	21	6,320	134	28.08	10	1,003	21	47.76	144/2
Atkinson, G R	Sept 21, 1830	May 3, 1906	1861	1870	27	38	8	399	44	13.30	0	1,146	54	21.22	14
Atkinson, H	Feb 1, 1881	Dec 22, 1959	1907	1907	1	2	0	0	0	0.00	0	17	0	—	—
Azeem Rafiq	**Feb 27, 1991**		**2009**	**2012**	**18**	**19**	**2**	**439**	**100**	**25.82**	**1**	**1466**	**43**	**34.09**	**8**
Backhouse, E N	May 13, 1901	Nov 1, 1936	1931	1931	1	1	0	2	2	2.00	0	4	0	—	—
Badger, H D *	Mar 7, 1900	Aug 10, 1975	1921	1922	2	4	2	6	6*	3.00	0	145	6	24.16	1

LIST OF PLAYERS AND CAREER AVERAGES IN ALL FIRST-CLASS MATCHES FOR YORKSHIRE *(Continued)*

Player	*Date of Birth*	*Date of Death (if known)*	*First Played*	*Last Played*	*M*	*Inns*	*NO*	*Runs*	*HS*	*Av'ge*	*100s*	*Runs*	*Wkts*	*Av'ge*	*Ct/St*
Bainbridge, A B	Oct 15, 1932		1961	1963	5	10	0	93	24	9.30	0	358	20	17.90	3
Baines, F E *	June 18, 1864	Nov 17, 1948	1888	1888	1	1	0	0	0	0.00	0	—	—	—	—
Bairstow, A ©	Aug 14, 1868	Dec 7, 1945	1896	1900	24	24	10	69	12	4.92	0	—	—	—	41/18
Bairstow, D L ©	Sept 1, 1951	Jan 5, 1998	1970	1990	429	601	113	12,985	145	26.60	9	192	6	32.00	907/131
Bairstow, J M ©	**Sept 26, 1989**		**2009**	**2012**	**50**	**84**	**16**	**3113**	**205**	**45.77**	**5**	—	—	—	**107/5**
Baker, G R	Apr 18, 1862	Feb 6, 1938	1884	1884	7	11	1	42	13	4.20	0	—	—	—	5
Baker, R *	July 13, 1849	June 21, 1896	1874	1875	3	5	1	45	22	11.25	0	43	0	—	3
Balderstone, J C	Nov 16, 1940	Mar 6, 2000	1961	1969	68	81	6	1,332	82	17.76	0	790	37	21.35	24
§ Ballance, G S ©	**Nov 22, 1989**		**2008**	**2012**	**33**	**50**	**11**	**1569**	**121***	**40.23**	**2**	**34**	**0**	—	**19**
Barber, A T * ©	June 17, 1905	Mar 10, 1985	1929	1930	42	54	3	1,050	100	20.58	1	0	0	—	40
Barber, W ©	Apr 18, 1901	Sept 10, 1968	1926	1947	354	495	48	15,315	255	34.26	27	404	14	28.85	169
Barraclough, E S	Mar 30, 1923	May 21, 1999	1949	1950	2	4	2	43	24*	21.50	0	136	4	34.00	—
Bates, W	Nov 19, 1855	Jan 8, 1900	1877	1887	202	331	12	6,499	136	20.37	8	10,692	637	16.78	163
Bates, W E ©	Mar 5, 1884	Jan 17, 1957	1907	1913	113	167	15	2,634	81	17.32	0	57	2	28.50	64
Batty G J	Oct 13, 1977		1997	1997	1	2	0	18	18	9.00	0	70	2	35.00	—
Batty, J D	May 15, 1971		1989	1994	64	67	20	703	51	14.95	0	5,286	140	37.75	25
Bayes, G W	Feb 27, 1884	Dec 6, 1960	1910	1921	18	24	11	165	36	12.69	0	1,534	48	31.95	7
Beaumont, H	Oct 14, 1916	Nov. 15, 2003	1946	1947	28	46	6	716	60	17.90	0	236	9	26.22	11
Beaumont, J	Sept 16, 1855	May 1, 1920	1877	1878	5	9	3	60	24	10.00	0	50	2	25.00	—
Bedford, H	July 17, 1907	July 5, 1968	1928	1928	5	5	1	57	24	14.25	0	179	8	22.37	—
Bedford, W	Feb 24, 1879	July, 28 1939	1903	1903	2	2	1	38	30*	38.00	0	117	2	58.50	1
Bell, J T	June 16, 1895	Aug 8, 1974	1921	1923	7	8	1	125	54	17.85	0	—	—	—	—
Berry, John	Jan 10, 1823	Feb 26, 1895	1849	1867	18	32	2	492	78	16.40	0	149	8	18.62	12
Berry, Joseph	Nov 29, 1829	Apr 20, 1894	1861	1874	3	4	0	68	30	17.00	0	—	—	—	1
Berry, P J	Dec 28, 1966		1986	1990	7	7	6	76	31*	76.00	0	401	7	57.28	2
§ Best T L	Aug 26, 1981		2010	2010	9	9	0	86	40	9.55	0	793	18	44.05	4
Betts, G	Sept 19, 1843	Sept 26, 1902	1873	1874	2	4	1	56	44*	18.66	0	—	—	—	—
§ Bevan, M G ©	May 8, 1970		1995	1996	32	56	8	2,823	160*	58.81	9	720	10	72.00	24
Binks, J G ©	Oct 5, 1935		1955	1969	491	587	128	6,745	95	14.69	0	66	0	—	872/172
Binns, J	Mar 31, 1870	Dec 8, 1934	1898	1898	1	1	0	4	4	4.00	0	—	—	—	0/3
Bird, H D	Apr 19, 1933		1956	1959	14	25	2	613	181*	26.65	1	—	—	—	3

LIST OF PLAYERS AND CAREER AVERAGES IN ALL FIRST-CLASS MATCHES FOR YORKSHIRE *(Continued)*

Player	Date of Birth	Date of Death (if known)	First Played	Last Played	M	Inns	NO	Runs	HS	Av'ge	100s	Runs	Wkts	Av'ge	Ct/St
Birkenshaw, J.	Nov 13, 1940		1958	1960	30	42	7	588	42	16.80	0	1,819	69	26.36	21
Birtles, T J D	Oct 26, 1886	Jan 13, 1971	1913	1924	37	57	11	876	104	19.04	1	20	0	—	19
Blackburn, J D H *	Oct 27, 1924	Feb 19, 1987	1956	1956	1	2	0	18	15	9.00	0	—	—	—	—
Blackburn, J S	Sept 24, 1852	July 8, 1922	1876	1877	6	11	1	102	28	10.20	0	173	7	24.71	4
§ Blackburn, W E *	Nov 24, 1888	June 3, 1941	1919	1920	10	13	6	26	6*	3.71	0	1,113	45	24.73	9
§ Blain J A R	Jan 4, 1979		2004	2010	15	17	7	137	28*	13.70	0	1312	38	34.52	4
Blake, W	Nov 29, 1854	Not known	1880	1880	2	3	0	44	21	14.66	0	17	1	17.00	—
Blakey, R J ©	Jan 15, 1967		1985	2003	339	541	84	14,150	223*	30.96	12	68	1	68.00	768/56
Blamires, E	July 31, 1850	Mar 22, 1886	1877	1877	1	2	0	23	17	11.50	0	82	5	16.40	—
§ Blewett, G S ©	Oct 29, 1971		1999	1999	12	23	2	655	190	31.19	1	212	5	42.40	5
Bloom, G R	Sept 13, 1941		1964	1964	1	1	0	2	2	2.00	0	—	—	—	2
Bocking, H	Dec 10, 1835	Feb 22, 1907	1865	1865	2	2	0	14	11	7.00	0	—	—	—	—
Boden, J G *	Dec 27, 1848	Jan 3, 1928	1878	1878	1	1	0	6	6	6.00	0	—	—	—	1
Bolton, B C *	Sept 23, 1862	Nov 18, 1910	1890	1891	4	6	0	25	11	4.16	0	252	13	19.38	2
Bolus, J B ©	Jan 31, 1934		1956	1962	107	179	18	4,712	146*	29.26	7	407	13	31.30	45
Booth, A ©	Nov 3, 1902	Aug 17, 1974	1931	1947	36	36	16	114	29	5.70	0	1,684	122	13.80	10
Booth, M W ©	Dec 10, 1886	July 1, 1916	1908	1914	144	218	31	4,244	210	22.69	2	11,017	557	19.17	114
Booth, P A	Sept 5, 1965		1982	1989	23	29	9	193	33*	9.65	0	1,517	35	43.34	7
Booth, R	Oct 1, 1926		1951	1955	65	76	28	730	53*	15.20	0	—	—	—	79/29
Bore, M K	June 2, 1947		1969	1977	74	78	21	481	37*	8.43	0	4,866	162	30.03	27
Borrill, P D	July 4, 1951		1971	1971	2	—	—	—	—	—	—	61	5	12.20	—
Bosomworth W E	Mar 8, 1847	June 7, 1891	1872	1880	4	7	1	20	7	3.33	0	140	9	15.55	2
Bottomley, I H *	Apr 9, 1855	Apr 23, 1922	1878	1880	9	12	0	166	32	13.83	0	75	1	75.00	1
Bottomley, T	Dec 26, 1910	Feb 19, 1977	1934	1935	6	7	0	142	51	20.28	0	188	1	188.00	5
Bower, W H	Oct 17, 1857	Jan 31, 1943	1883	1883	1	2	0	10	5	5.00	0	—	—	—	—
Bowes, W E ©	July 25, 1908	Sept 4, 1987	1929	1947	301	257	117	1,251	43*	8.93	0	21,227	1,351	15.71	118
Boycott, G ©	Oct 21, 1940		1962	1986	414	674	111	32,570	260*	57.85	103	665	28	23.75	200
Brackin, T	Jan 5, 1859	Oct 7, 1924	1882	1882	3	6	0	12	9	2.00	0	—	—	—	—
Brayshay, P B *	Oct 14, 1916	July 6, 2004	1952	1952	2	3	0	20	13	6.66	0	104	3	34.66	—
Brearley, H *	June 26, 1913	Aug 14, 2007	1937	1937	1	2	0	17	9	8.50	0	—	—	—	—
Brennan, D V * ©	Feb 10, 1920	Jan 9, 1985	1947	1953	204	221	66	1,653	47	10.66	0	—	—	—	280/100

LIST OF PLAYERS AND CAREER AVERAGES IN ALL FIRST-CLASS MATCHES FOR YORKSHIRE *(Continued)*

Player	Date of Birth	Date of Death (if known)	First Played	Last Played	M	Inns	NO	Runs	HS	Av'ge	100s	Runs	Wkts	Av'ge	Ct/St
Bresnan, T T ...©	**Feb 28, 1985**		**2003**	**2012**	**91**	**125**	**22**	**2,694**	**116**	**26.15**	**2**	**7,679**	**245**	**31.34**	**37**
Britton, G	Feb 7, 1843	Jan 3, 1910	1867	1867	1	2	0	3	3	1.50	0	—	—	—	—
Broadbent, A	June 7, 1879	July 19, 1958	1909	1910	3	5	0	66	29	13.20	0	252	5	50.40	1
Broadhead, W B	May 31, 1903	Apr 2, 1986	1929	1929	1	2	0	5	3	2.50	0	—	—	—	1
Broadhurst, M	June 20, 1974		1991	1994	5	3	0	7	6	2.33	0	231	7	33.00	—
§ Brophy, G L ......©	Nov 26, 1975		2006	2012	73	112	12	3,012	177*	30.12	3	6	0	—	176/15
Brook, J W	Feb 1, 1897	Mar.3 1989	1923	1923	1	1	0	0	0	0.00	0	—	—	—	—
Brooke, B	Mar 3, 1930		1950	1950	2	4	0	16	14	4.00	0	191	2	95.50	—
Broughton, P N	Oct 22, 1935		1956	1956	6	5	2	19	12	6.33	0	365	16	22.81	1
Brown, A	June 10, 1854	Nov 2, 1900	1872	1872	2	3	0	9	5	3.00	0	47	3	15.66	4
Brown, J T (Driffield) ©	Aug 20, 1869	Nov 4, 1904	1889	1904	345	567	41	15,694	311	29.83	23	5,183	177	29.28	188
Brown, J T (Darfield) ©	Nov 24, 1874	Apr 12, 1950	1897	1903	30	32	3	333	37*	11.48	0	2,071	97	21.35	18
Brown, W	Nov 19, 1876	July 27, 1945	1902	1908	2	2	1	2	2	2.00	0	84	4	21.00	—
Brownhill, T	Oct 10, 1838	Jan 6, 1915	1861	1871	14	20	3	185	25	10.88	0	—	—	—	7
Brumfitt, J *	Feb. 18, 1917	Mar 16, 1987	1938	1938	1	1	0	9	9	9.00	0	—	—	—	—
Buller, J S	Aug 23, 1909	Aug 7, 1970	1930	1930	1	2	0	5	3	2.50	0	—	—	—	2
Bulmer, J R L	Dec 28, 1867	Jan 20, 1917	1891	1891	1	2	0	0	0	0.00	0	79	1	79.00	—
Burgess, T	Oct 1, 1859	Feb 22, 1922	1895	1895	1	2	1	0	0*	0.00	0	—	—	—	2
Burgin, E	Jan 4, 1924		1952	1953	12	10	3	92	32	13.14	0	795	31	25.64	—
Burman, J	Oct 5, 1838	May 14, 1900	1867	1867	1	2	1	1	1*	1.00	0	—	—	—	—
Burnet, J R * ....©	Oct 11, 1918	Mar 7, 1999	1958	1959	54	75	6	889	54	12.88	0	26	1	26.00	7
§ Burrows, M	Aug 18, 1855	May 29, 1893	1880	1880	6	10	0	82	23	8.20	0	—	—	—	2
Burton, D C F * .....©	Sept 13, 1887	Sept 24, 1971	1907	1921	104	130	15	2,273	142*	19.76	2	—	—	—	44
Burton, R C *	Apr 11, 1891	Apr 30, 1971	1914	1914	2	2	0	47	47	23.50	0	73	6	12.16	2
Butterfield, E B *	Oct 22, 1848	May 6, 1899	1870	1870	1	2	0	18	10	9.00	0	—	—	—	—
Byas, D ....©	Aug 26, 1963		1986	2001	268	449	42	14,398	213	35.37	28	727	12	60.58	351
Byrom, J L *	July, 20, 1851	Aug 24, 1931	1874	1874	2	4	0	19	11	4.75	0	—	—	—	1
Cammish, J W	May 21, 1921	July 16, 1974	1954	1954	2	1	0	0	0	0.00	0	155	3	51.66	—
Carrick, P ....©	July, 16 1952	Jan 11, 2000	1970	1993	425	543	102	9,994	131*	22.66	3	30,530	1,018	29.99	183
Carter, Rev E S *	Feb 3, 1845	May 23, 1923	1876	1881	14	21	2	210	39*	11.05	0	104	8	13.00	4

LIST OF PLAYERS AND CAREER AVERAGES IN ALL FIRST-CLASS MATCHES FOR YORKSHIRE *(Continued)*

Player	Date of Birth	Date of Death (if known)	First Played	Last Played	M	Inns	NO	Runs	HS	Av'ge	100s	Runs	Wkts	Av'ge	Ct/St
Cartman, W H	June 20, 1861	Jan 16, 1935	1891	1891	3	6	0	57	49	9.50	0	—	—	—	—
Cawthray, G	Sept 28, 1913	Jan 5, 2000	1939	1952	4	6	0	114	30	19.00	0	304	4	76.00	1
Chadwick, J P G	Nov 8, 1934		1960	1965	6	9	3	106	59	17.66	0	67	2	33.50	7
Champion, A	Dec 27, 1851	June 30, 1909	1876	1879	14	23	4	148	29	7.78	0	17	1	17.00	7
Chapman, C A	June 8, 1971		1990	1998	8	13	2	238	80	21.63	0	—	—	—	13/3
Charlesworth, A P	Feb 19, 1865	May 11, 1926	1894	1895	7	12	1	241	63	21.90	0	—	—	—	2
§ Chichester-Constable, R C J *	Dec 21, 1890	May 26, 1963	1919	1919	1	1	0	0	0	0.00	0	6	0	—	—
Clarkson, A	Sept 5, 1939		1963	1963	6	8	1	80	30	11.42	0	92	5	18.40	5
Claughton, H M	Dec 24, 1891	Oct 17, 1980	1914	1919	4	6	0	39	15	6.50	0	176	3	58.66	1
§ Claydon, M E	Nov 25, 1982		2005	2006	3	2	0	38	38	19.00	0	263	3	87.66	—
§ Clayton, R O	Jan 1, 1844	Nov 26, 1901	1870	1879	70	115	23	992	62	10.78	0	2,478	153	16.19	26
§ Cleary, M F	July 19, 1980		2005	2005	2	2	0	23	12	11.50	0	250	8	31.25	—
Clegg, H	Dec 8, 1850	Dec 30, 1920	1881	1881	6	8	1	63	25*	9.00	0	—	—	—	2
Clifford, C C	July, 5, 1942		1972	1972	11	12	4	39	12*	4.87	0	666	26	25.61	5
Close, D B ©	Feb 24, 1931		1949	1970	536	811	102	22,650	198	31.94	33	23,489	967	24.29	564
Clough, G D	May 23, 1978		1998	1998	1	2	0	34	33	17.00	0	11	0	—	1
Collinson, R W *	Nov 6, 1875	Dec 26, 1963	1897	1897	2	3	0	58	34	19.33	0	—	—	—	—
Cooper, H P	Apr 17, 1949		1971	1980	98	107	29	1,159	56	14.85	0	6,327	227	27.87	60
Cooper, P E *	Feb 19, 1885	May 21, 1950	1910	1910	1	2	0	0	0	0.00	0	—	—	—	—
Cope, G A ©	Feb 23, 1947		1966	1980	230	249	89	2,241	78	14.00	0	15,627	630	24.80	64
Corbett, A M	Nov 25, 1855	Oct 7, 1934	1881	1881	1	2	0	0	0	0.00	0	—	—	—	1
Coverdale, S P	Nov 20, 1954		1973	1980	6	4	0	31	18	7.75	0	—	—	—	11/4
Coverdale, W *	July 8, 1862	Sept 23, 1934	1888	1888	2	2	0	2	1	1.00	0	—	—	—	2
Cowan, M J ©	June 10, 1933		1953	1962	91	84	48	170	19*	4.72	0	6,389	266	24.01	37
Cownley, J M	Feb 24, 1929	Nov 7, 1998	1952	1952	2	2	1	19	19	19.00	0	119	1	119.00	—
Coxon, A ©	Jan 18, 1916	Jan 22, 2006	1945	1950	142	182	33	2,747	83	18.43	0	9,528	464	20.53	124
Craven, V J	July 31, 1980		2000	2004	33	55	6	1,206	81*	24.61	0	584	15	38.93	18
Crawford, G H	Dec 15, 1890	June 28, 1975	1914	1926	9	8	0	46	21	5.75	0	541	21	25.76	3
Crawford, M G *	July 30, 1920		1951	1951	1	2	0	22	13	11.00	0	—	—	—	1
Creighton, E	July 9, 1859	Feb 17, 1931	1888	1888	4	8	2	33	10	5.50	0	181	10	18.10	—

LIST OF PLAYERS AND CAREER AVERAGES IN ALL FIRST-CLASS MATCHES FOR YORKSHIRE *(Continued)*

Player	Date of Birth	Date of Death (if known)	First Played	Last Played	M	Inns	NO	Runs	HS	Av'ge	100s	Runs	Wkts	Av'ge	Ct/St
Crick, H	Jan 29, 1910	Feb 10, 1960	1937	1947	8	10	0	88	20	8.80	0	—	—	—	18/4
Crookes, R	Oct 9, 1846	Feb 15, 1897	1879	1879	1	2	1	2	2*	2.00	0	14	0	—	—
Crossland, S M	Aug 16, 1851	April 11, 1906	1883	1886	4	6	2	32	20	8.00	0	—	—	—	3/5
Crowther, A	Aug 1, 1878	June 4, 1946	1905	1905	1	2	0	0	0	0.00	0	—	—	—	1
Cuttell, W	Jan 28, 1835	June 10, 1896	1862	1871	15	27	6	271	56	12.90	0	596	36	16.55	4
Dalton, A J	Mar 14, 1947		1969	1972	21	31	2	710	128	24.48	3	—	—	—	6
§ Darnton, T	Feb 12, 1836	Oct 25, 1874	1864	1868	13	22	1	314	81*	14.95	0	349	12	29.08	3
Davidson, K R ©	Dec 24, 1905	Dec 25, 1954	1933	1935	30	46	5	1,331	128	32.46	2	—	—	—	18
Dawes, J	Feb 14, 1836	Not known	1865	1865	5	9	2	93	28*	13.28	0	196	5	39.20	3
Dawood, I	July 23, 1976		2004	2005	20	31	7	636	75	26.50	0	—	—	—	46/3
Dawson, E	May 1, 1835	Dec 1, 1888	1863	1874	16	25	1	224	20	9.33	0	—	—	—	5
Dawson, R K J ©	Aug 4, 1980		2001	2006	72	106	9	2,179	87	22.46	0	6,444	157	41.04	39
Dawson, W A *	Dec 3, 1850	Mar 6, 1916	1870	1870	1	2	0	0	0	0.00	0	—	—	—	1
Day, A G *	Sept 20, 1865	Oct 16, 1908	1885	1888	6	10	0	78	25	7.80	0	—	—	—	3
Dennis, F ©	June 11, 1907	Nov 21, 2000	1928	1933	89	100	28	1,332	67	18.50	0	4,517	156	28.95	58
Dennis, S J ©	Oct 18, 1960		1980	1988	67	62	24	338	53*	8.89	0	5,548	173	32.06	19
Denton, D ©	July 4, 1874	Feb 16, 1950	1894	1920	676	1,058	61	33,282	221	33.38	61	957	34	28.14	360/1
Denton, J	Feb 3, 1865	July 19, 1946	1887	1888	15	24	1	222	59	9.65	0	—	—	—	6
Dewse, H	Feb 23, 1836	July 8, 1910	1873	1873	1	2	0	14	12	7.00	0	15	0	—	1
Deyes, G	Feb 11, 1879	Jan 11, 1963	1905	1907	17	24	4	44	12	2.20	0	944	41	23.02	6
Dick, R D *	Apr 16, 1889	Dec 14, 1983	1911	1911	1	1	0	2	2	2.00	0	37	2	18.50	1
Dobson, A	Feb 22, 1854	Sept 17, 1932	1879	1879	2	3	0	1	1	0.33	0	—	—	—	1
Doidge, M J	July 2, 1970		1990	1990	1	—	—	—	—	—	—	106	0	—	—
Dolphin, A ©	Dec 24, 1885	Oct 23, 1942	1905	1927	427	446	157	3,325	66	11.50	0	28	1	28.00	569/260
Douglas, J S	Apr 4, 1903	Dec 27, 1971	1925	1934	23	26	8	125	19	6.94	0	1,310	49	26.73	14
Drake, A ©	Apr 16, 1884	Feb 14, 1919	1909	1914	156	244	24	4,789	147*	21.76	3	8,623	479	18.00	93
Drake, J	Sept 1, 1893	May 22, 1967	1923	1924	3	4	1	21	10	7.00	0	117	1	117.00	2
Driver, J	May 16, 1861	Dec 10, 1946	1889	1889	2	4	1	24	8	8.00	0	—	—	—	2
Dury, T S *	June 12, 1854	Mar 20, 1932	1878	1881	13	24	1	329	46	14.30	0	21	0	—	3
Dyson, W L	Dec 11, 1857	May 1, 1936	1887	1887	2	4	0	8	6	2.00	0	—	—	—	2

Player	Date of Birth	Date of Death (if known)	First Played	Last Played	M	Inns	NO	Runs	HS	Av'ge	100s	Runs	Wkts	Av'ge	Ct/St
Earnshaw, W	Sept 20, 1867	Nov 24, 1941	1893	1896	6	7	3	44	23	11.00	0	—	—	—	6/2
Eastwood, D	Mar 30, 1848	May 17, 1903	1870	1877	29	51	2	591	68	12.06	0	349	11	31.72	16
Eckersley, R	Sept 4, 1925	May 30, 2009	1945	1945	1	1	1	9	9*	—	0	62	0	—	—
Elam, F W *	Sept 13, 1871	Mar 19, 1943	1900	1902	2	3	1	48	28	24.00	0	—	—	—	—
§ Elliott, M T G	Sept 28, 1971		2002	2002	5	10	1	487	127	54.11	1	77	1	77.00	7
Ellis, J E	Nov 10, 1864	Dec 1, 1927	1888	1892	11	15	6	14	4*	1.55	0	—	—	—	11/10
Ellis, S *	Nov 23, 1851	Oct 28, 1930	1880	1880	2	3	0	12	9	4.00	0	—	—	—	2
Elms, J E	Dec 24, 1874	Nov 1, 1951	1905	1905	1	2	0	20	20	10.00	0	28	1	28.00	1
Elstub, C J	Feb 3, 1981		2000	2002	6	7	6	28	18*	28.00	0	356	9	39.55	2
Emmett, T ...©	Sept 3, 1841	June 29, 1904	1866	1888	299	484	65	6,315	104	15.07	1	15,465	1,216	12.71	179
Farrar, A	Apr 29, 1884	Dec 25, 1954	1906	1906	1	1	0	2	2	2.00	0	—	—	—	1
Fearnley, M C	Aug 21, 1936	July 7, 1979	1962	1964	3	4	2	19	11*	9.50	0	133	6	22.16	—
Featherby, W D	Aug 18, 1888	Nov 20, 1958	1920	1920	2	—	—	—	—	—	—	12	0	—	—
Fellows, G M	July 30, 1978		1998	2003	46	71	6	1,526	109	23.47	1	1,202	32	37.56	23
Fiddling, K	Oct 13, 1917	June 19, 1992	1938	1946	18	24	6	182	25	10.11	0	—	—	—	24/13
Firth, A *	Sept 3, 1847	Jan 16, 1927	1869	1869	1	1	0	4	4	4.00	0	—	—	—	—
Firth, Rev E B *	Apr 11, 1863	July 25, 1905	1894	1894	1	1	0	1	1	1.00	0	—	—	—	—
Firth, J	June 27, 1918	Sept 7, 1981	1949	1950	8	8	5	134	67*	44.66	0	—	—	—	14/2
Fisher, H ...©	Aug 3, 1903	Apr 16, 1974	1928	1936	52	58	14	681	76*	15.47	0	2,621	93	28.18	22
Fisher, I D	Mar 31, 1976		1996	2001	24	32	9	545	68*	23.69	0	1,382	43	32.13	1
Flaxington, S	Oct 14, 1860	Mar 10, 1895	1882	1882	4	8	0	121	57	15.12	0	—	—	—	1
§ Fleming, S P	Apr 1, 1973		2003	2003	7	14	2	469	98	39.08	0	—	—	—	13
Fletcher, S D ...©	June 8, 1964		1983	1991	107	91	31	414	28*	6.90	0	7,966	234	34.04	25
Fletcher, W	Feb 16, 1866	June 1, 1935	1892	1892	5	8	1	80	31*	11.42	0	157	7	22.42	4
Foord, C W	June 11, 1924		1947	1953	51	34	16	114	35	6.33	0	3,412	126	27.07	19
Foster, E	Nov 23, 1873	April 16, 1956	1901	1901	1	1	0	2	2	2.00	0	27	0	—	—
Foster, M J	Sept 17, 1972		1993	1994	5	7	1	165	63*	27.50	0	156	6	25.00	6
§ Foster, T W	Nov 12, 1871	Jan 31, 1947	1894	1895	14	20	5	138	25	9.20	0	952	58	16.41	6
Frank, J *	Dec 17, 1857	Oct 22, 1940	1881	1881	1	2	0	10	7	5.00	0	17	1	17.00	3
Frank R W * ...©	May 29, 1864	Sept 9, 1950	1889	1903	18	28	4	298	58	12.41	0	9	0	—	8
Freeman, G	July 27, 1843	Nov 18, 1895	1865	1880	32	54	2	752	53	14.46	0	2,079	209	9.94	16

LIST OF PLAYERS AND CAREER AVERAGES IN ALL FIRST-CLASS MATCHES FOR YORKSHIRE *(Continued)*

Player	Date of Birth	Date of Death (if known)	First Played	Last Played	M	Inns	NO	Runs	HS	Av'ge	100s	Runs	Wkts	Av'ge	Ct/St
Gale, A W ©	**Nov 28, 1983**		**2004**	**2012**	**87**	**138**	**12**	**4472**	**151***	**35.49**	**11**	**144**	**1**	**144.00**	**33**
Geldart, C J	**Dec 17, 1991**		**2010**	**2011**	**2**	**2**	**0**	**51**	**34**	**25.50**	**0**	—	—	—	**1**
Gibb, P A *©	July 11, 1913	Dec 7, 1977	1935	1946	36	54	7	1,545	157*	32.87	2	82	3	27.33	25/8
Gibson, B P	**Mar 31, 1996** **		**2011**	**2011**	**1**	**1**	**1**	**1**	**1***	—	**0**	—	—	—	**6/0**
§ Gifkins, C J *	Feb 19, 1856	Jan 31, 1897	1880	1880	2	3	0	30	23	10.00	0	—	—	—	1
Gilbert, C R	Apr 16, 1984		2007	2007	1	1	0	64	64	64.00	0	11	0	—	1
Gill, F	Sept 3, 1883	Nov 1, 1917	1906	1906	2	4	0	18	11	4.50	0	—	—	—	—
§ Gillespie, J N ©	April 19, 1975		2006	2007	26	34	11	640	123*	27.82	1	2,013	59	34.11	4
Gillhouley, K	Aug 8, 1934		1961	1961	24	31	7	323	56*	13.45	0	1,702	77	22.10	16
Gough, D ©	Sept 18, 1970		1989	2008	146	188	29	2,922	121	18.37	1	12,487	453	27.56	30
Goulder, A	Aug 16, 1907	June 11, 1986	1929	1929	2	1	0	3	3	3.00	0	90	3	30.00	—
§ Gray, A K D	May 19, 1974		2001	2004	18	26	3	649	104	28.21	1	1,357	30	45.23	16
Grayson, A P	Mar 31, 1971		1990	1995	52	80	10	1,958	100	27.97	1	846	13	65.07	36
Greenwood, A	Aug 20, 1847	Feb 12, 1889	1869	1880	95	166	12	2,762	91	17.93	0	9	0	—	33
Greenwood, F E * ©	Sept 28, 1905	July 30, 1963	1929	1932	57	66	8	1,458	104*	25.13	1	36	2	18.00	37
Greenwood, L	July 13, 1834	Nov 1, 1909	1861	1874	50	84	12	885	83	12.29	0	1,615	85	19.00	24
Grimshaw, C H	May 12, 1880	Sept 25, 1947	1904	1908	54	75	7	1,219	85	17.92	0	221	7	31.57	42
Grimshaw, I	May 4, 1857	Jan 18, 1911	1880	1887	125	194	14	3,354	129*	18.63	4	—	—	—	76/3
Guy S M	Nov 17, 1978		2000	2011	37	52	6	742	52*	16.13	0	8	0	—	98/12
Haggas, S	Apr 18, 1856	Mar 14, 1926	1878	1882	31	47	3	478	43	10.86	0	—	—	—	10
Haigh S ©	Mar 19, 1871	Feb 27, 1921	1895	1913	513	687	110	10,993	159	19.05	4	29,289	1,876	15.61	276
Hall, B	Sept 16, 1929	Feb 27, 1989	1952	1952	1	2	0	14	10	7.00	0	55	1	55.00	1
Hall, C H	Apr 5, 1906	Dec 11, 1976	1928	1934	23	22	9	67	15*	5.15	0	1,226	45	27.24	11
§ Hall, J	Nov 11, 1815	Apr 17, 1888	1844	1863	1	2	0	4	3	2.00	0	—	—	—	2
Hall, L ©	Nov 1, 1852	Nov 19, 1915	1873	1894	275	477	58	9,757	160	23.28	9	781	15	52.06	173
Halliday, H ©	Feb 9, 1920	Aug 27, 1967	1938	1953	182	279	18	8,361	144	32.03	12	3,119	101	30.88	140
Halliley, C	Dec 5, 1852	Mar 23, 1929	1872	1872	3	5	0	27	17	5.40	0	—	—	—	2
Hamer, A	Dec 8, 1916	Nov 3, 1993	1938	1938	2	2	0	3	3	1.50	0	64	1	64.00	2
§ Hamilton, G M ©	Sept 16, 1974		1994	2003	73	108	18	2,228	125	24.75	1	5,479	222	24.68	25

** At 15 years and 27 days on April 27, 2011, First Day of Yorkshire's match v. Durham MCCU, he became the youngest ever English First Class cricketer.

LIST OF PLAYERS AND CAREER AVERAGES IN ALL FIRST-CLASS MATCHES FOR YORKSHIRE *(Continued)*

Player	Date of Birth	Date of Death (if known)	First Played	Last Played	M	Inns	NO	Runs	HS	Av'ge	100s	Runs	Wkts	Av'ge	Ct/St
Hampshire, A W	Oct 18, 1950		1975	1975	1	2	0	18	17	9.00	0	—	—	—	1
Hampshire, J	Oct 5, 1913	May 23, 1997	1937	1937	3	2	0	5	5	2.50	0	109	5	21.80	1
Hampshire, J H ©	Feb 10, 1941		1961	1981	456	724	89	21,979	183*	34.61	34	1,108	24	46.16	368
Hannon-Dalby O J	**Jun 20, 1989**		**2008**	**2012**	**24**	**25**	**10**	**45**	**11***	**3.00**	**0**	**1938**	**43**	**45.06**	**2**
§ Harbord, W E *	Dec 15, 1908	July 28, 1992	1929	1935	16	21	1	411	109	20.55	1	—	—	—	7
§ Harden, R J	Aug 16, 1965		1999	2000	12	22	3	439	69	23.10	0	—	—	—	2
Hardisty, C H ©	Dec 10, 1885	Mar 2, 1968	1906	1909	38	55	5	991	84	19.82	0	—	—	—	18
Hargreaves, H S	Mar 22, 1913	Sept 29, 1990	1934	1938	18	20	6	51	9	3.64	0	1,145	55	20.81	3
§ S J Harmison	Oct 23, 1978		2012	2012	3	3	0	25	23	8.33	0	195	8	24.37	1
Harris, W	Nov 21, 1861	May 23, 1923	1884	1887	4	8	2	45	25	7.50	0	18	0	—	1
Harrison, G P ©	Feb 11, 1862	Sept 14, 1940	1883	1892	59	87	26	407	28	6.67	0	3,276	226	14.49	36
Harrison, H	Jan 26, 1885	Feb 11, 1962	1907	1907	2	1	1	4	4*	—	0	39	2	19.50	1
Harrison, W H	May 27, 1863	July 15, 1939	1888	1888	3	6	1	12	7	2.40	0	—	—	—	—
Hart, H W *	Sept 21, 1859	Nov 2, 1895	1888	1888	1	2	0	6	6	3.00	0	32	2	16.00	—
Hart, P R	Jan 12, 1947		1981	1981	3	5	0	23	11	4.60	0	140	2	70.00	1
Hartington, H E	Sept 18, 1881	Feb 16, 1950	1910	1911	10	10	4	51	16	8.50	0	764	23	33.21	2
Hartley, P J ©	Apr 18, 1960		1985	1997	195	237	51	3,844	127*	20.66	2	17,438	579	30.11	60
Hartley, S N ©	Mar 18, 1956		1978	1988	133	199	27	4,193	114	24.37	4	2,052	42	48.85	47
§ Harvey, I J	Apr 10, 1972		2004	2005	20	31	2	1,045	209*	36.03	2	831	37	22.45	12
Hatton, A G	Mar 25, 1937		1960	1961	3	1	1	4	4*	—	0	202	6	33.66	1
§ Hawke, Lord * ©	Aug 16, 1860	Oct 10, 1938	1881	1911	510	739	91	13,133	166	20.26	10	16	0	—	159
Hayley, H	Feb 22, 1860	June 3, 1922	1884	1898	7	12	1	122	24	11.09	0	48	0	—	3
Haywood, W J	Feb 25, 1841	Jan 7, 1912	1878	1878	1	2	0	7	7	3.50	0	14	1	14.00	—
Hicks, J	Dec 10, 1850	June 10, 1912	1872	1876	15	25	3	313	66	14.22	0	17	0	—	12
Higgins, J	Mar 13, 1877	July 19, 1954	1901	1905	9	14	5	93	28*	10.33	0	—	—	—	10/3
Hill, A	Nov 14, 1843	Aug 29, 1910	1871	1882	140	223	25	1,705	49	8.61	0	7,002	542	12.91	91
Hill, H *	Nov 29, 1858	Aug 14, 1935	1888	1891	14	27	2	337	34	13.48	0	—	—	—	10
Hill, L G *	Nov 2, 1860	Aug 27, 1940	1882	1882	1	2	0	13	8	6.50	0	—	—	—	1
Hirst, E T *	May 6, 1857	Oct 26, 1914	1877	1888	21	33	2	328	87*	10.58	0	—	—	—	7
Hirst, E W *	Feb 27, 1855	Oct 24, 1933	1881	1881	2	3	0	33	28	11.00	0	3	0	—	—
Hirst, G H ©	Sept 7, 1871	May 10, 1954	1891	1921*	717	1,050	128	32,024	341	34.73	56	44,716	2,481	18.02	518

LIST OF PLAYERS AND CAREER AVERAGES IN ALL FIRST-CLASS MATCHES FOR YORKSHIRE *(Continued)*

Player	Date of Birth	Date of Death (if known)	First Played	Last Played	M	Inns	NO	Runs	HS	Av'ge	100s	Runs	Wkts	Av'ge	Ct/St
Hirst, T H	May 21, 1865	Apr 3, 1927	1899	1899	1	1	1	5	5*	—	0	27	0	—	—
§ A J Hodd		**Jan 12, 1984**	**2012**	**2012**	**4**	**5**	**0**	**91**	**58**	**18.20**	**0**	—	—	—	**18**
Hodgson, G	July 24, 1938		1964	1964	1	1	0	4	4	4.00	0	—	—	—	0/2
Hodgson, I	Nov 15, 1828	Nov 24, 1867	1855	1866	21	35	14	164	21*	7.80	0	1,537	88	17.46	11
Hodgson, L J	Jun 29, 1986		2009	2010	3	3	0	99	34	33.00	0	158	2	79.00	1
Hodgson, P	Sept 21, 1935		1954	1956	13	6	2	33	8*	8.25	0	648	22	29.45	6
Hoggard, M J ©	Dec 31, 1976		1996	2009	102	120	34	956	89*	11.11	0	8,956	331	27.05	23
Holdsworth, W E N	Sept 17, 1928		1952	1953	27	26	12	111	22*	7.92	0	1,598	53	30.15	7
Holgate, G	June 23, 1839	July 11, 1895	1865	1867	12	19	0	174	38	9.15	0	—	—	—	17/1
Holmes, P ©	Nov 25, 1886	Sept 3, 1971	1913	1933	485	699	74	26,220	315*	41.95	60	124	1	124.00	319
Horner, N F	May 10, 1926	Dec 24, 2003	1950	1950	2	4	0	114	43	28.50	0	—	—	—	2
Houseman I J	Oct 12, 1969		1989	1991	5	2	1	18	18	18.00	0	311	3	103.66	—
Hoyle, T H	Mar 19, 1884	June 2, 1953	1919	1919	1	2	0	7	7	3.50	0	—	—	—	0/1
Hudson, B	June 29, 1852	Nov 11, 1901	1880	1880	3	4	0	13	5	3.25	0	—	—	—	2
Hunter, D ©	Feb 23, 1860	Jan 11, 1927	1888	1909	517	681	323	4,177	58*	11.66	0	43	0	—	863/323
Hunter, J	Aug 3, 1855	Jan 4, 1891	1878	1888	143	213	61	1,183	60*	7.78	0	—	—	—	207/102
Hutchison, P M ©	June 9, 1977		1996	2001	39	39	23	187	30	11.68	0	3,244	143	22.68	8
Hutton, L ©	June 23, 1916	Sept, 6, 1990	1934	1955	341	527	62	24,807	280*	53.34	85	4,221	154	27.40	278
Hutton, R A ©	Sept 6, 1942		1962	1974	208	292	45	4,986	189	20.18	4	10,254	468	21.91	160
Iddison, R	Sept 15, 1834	Mar 19, 1890	1855	1876	72	108	15	1,916	112	20.60	1	1,540	102	15.09	70
Illingworth, R ©	June 8, 1932		1951	1983	496	668	131	14,986	162	27.90	14	26,806	1,431	18.73	286
§ Imran Tahir	Mar 27, 1979		2007	2007	1	2	0	5	5	2.50	0	141	0	—	—
Ingham, P G	Sept 28, 1956		1979	1981	8	14	0	290	64	20.71	0	—	—	—	—
Inglis, J W	Oct 19, 1979		2000	2000	1	2	0	4	2	2.00	0	—	—	—	—
§ Inzamam-ul-Haq	Mar 3, 1970		2007	2007	3	4	0	89	51	22.25	0	—	—	—	5
Jackson, Hon F S * ©	Nov 21, 1870	Mar 9, 1947	1890	1907	207	328	22	10,371	160	33.89	21	9,690	506	19.15	129
Jackson, S R *	July 15, 1859	July 19, 1941	1891	1891	1	2	0	9	9	4.50	0	—	—	—	—
Jacques, T A	Feb 19, 1905	Feb 23, 1995	1927	1936	28	20	7	162	35*	12.46	0	1,786	57	31.33	12
Jakeman, F	Jan 10, 1920	May 18, 1986	1946	1947	10	16	2	262	51	18.71	0	—	—	—	3

LIST OF PLAYERS AND CAREER AVERAGES IN ALL FIRST-CLASS MATCHES FOR YORKSHIRE *(Continued)*

Player	Date of Birth	Date of Death (if known)	First Played	Last Played	M	Inns	NO	Runs	HS	Av'ge	100s	Runs	Wkts	Av'ge	Ct/St
James, B	Apr 23, 1934		1954	1954	4	5	3	22	11*	11.00	0	228	8	28.50	—
§ Jaques P A	**May 3, 1979**		**2004**	**2012**	**39**	**61**	**3**	**3269**	**243**	**56.36**	**9**	**37**	**0**	**—**	**41**
Jarvis, P W ©	June 29, 1965		1981	1993	138	160	46	1,898	80	16.64	0	11,990	449	26.70	36
Johnson, C	Sept 5, 1947		1969	1979	100	152	14	2,960	107	21.44	2	265	4	66.25	50
Johnson, J	May 16, 1916	Jan 16, 2011	1936	1939	3	3	2	5	4*	5.00	0	27	5	5.40	1
Johnson, M	Apr 23, 1958		1981	1981	4	4	2	2	2	1.00	0	301	7	43.00	1
Joy, J	Sept 29, 1826	Sept 27, 1889	1849	1867	3	5	0	107	74	21.40	0	5	0	—	3
Judson, A	July 10, 1885	Apr 8, 1975	1920	1920	1	—	—	—	—	—	—	5	0	—	—
§ Katich, S M	Aug 21, 1975		2002	2002	1	2	0	37	21	18.50	0	25	0	—	1
Kaye, Harold S *	May 9, 1882	Nov 6, 1953	1907	1908	18	25	1	243	37	10.12	0	—	—	—	9
Kaye, Haven	June 11, 1846	Jan 24, 1892	1872	1873	8	14	0	117	33	8.35	0	—	—	—	3
Keedy, G	Nov 27, 1974		1994	1994	1	1	0	1	1	1.00	0	—	—	—	—
§ Keighley, W G * ©	Jan 10, 1925	June 14, 2005	1947	1951	35	51	5	1,227	110	26.67	1	18	0	—	12
Kellett, S A ©	Oct 16, 1967		1989	1995	86	147	10	4,204	125*	30.68	2	7	0	—	74
Kennie, G	May 17, 1904	Apr 11, 1994	1927	1927	1	2	0	6	6	3.00	0	—	—	—	1
Kettleborough, R A	Mar 15, 1973		1994	1997	13	19	2	446	108	26.23	1	153	3	51.00	9
Kilburn, S	Oct 16, 1868	Sept 25, 1940	1896	1896	1	1	0	8	8	8.00	0	—	—	—	—
Kilner, N	July 21, 1895	Apr 28, 1979	1919	1923	69	73	7	1,253	112	18.98	2	—	—	—	34
Kilner, R ©	Oct 17, 1890	Apr 5, 1928	1911	1927	365	478	46	13,018	206*	30.13	15	14,855	857	17.33	231
King, A M	Oct 8, 1932		1955	1955	1	1	0	12	12	12.00	0	—	—	—	—
Kippax, P J	Oct 15, 1940		1961	1962	4	7	2	37	9	7.40	0	279	8	34.87	—
§ Kirby, S P ©	Oct 4, 1977		2001	2004	47	61	14	342	57	7.27	0	5,143	182	28.25	11
§ Kruis, G J ©	May 9, 1974		2005	2009	54	64	31	617	50*	18.69	0	5,431	154	35.26	11
§ Lambert, G A	Jan 4, 1980		2000	2000	2	3	2	6	3*	6.00	0	133	4	33.25	1
Lancaster, W W	Feb 4, 1873	Dec 30, 1938	1895	1895	7	10	0	163	51	16.30	0	29	0	—	1
§ Landon, C W *	May 30, 1850	Mar 5, 1903	1878	1882	9	13	0	51	18	3.92	0	74	0	—	7
§ Law, W *	Apr 9, 1851	Dec 20, 1892	1871	1873	4	7	0	51	22	7.28	0	—	—	—	3
Lawson, M A K	Oct 24, 1985		2004	2007	15	21	5	197	44	12.31	0	1,699	42	40.45	7
Leadbeater, B ©	Aug 14, 1943		1966	1979	144	236	27	5,247	140*	25.10	1	5	1	5.00	80
Leadbeater, E	Aug 15, 1927	Apr 17, 2011	1949	1956	81	94	29	898	91	13.81	0	5,657	201	28.14	49

LIST OF PLAYERS AND CAREER AVERAGES IN ALL FIRST-CLASS MATCHES FOR YORKSHIRE *(Continued)*

Player	Date of Birth	Date of Death (if known)	First Played	Last Played	M	Inns	NO	Runs	HS	Av'ge	100s	Runs	Wkts	Av'ge	Ct/St
Leadbeater, H *	Dec 31, 1863	Oct 9, 1928	1884	1890	6	10	2	141	65	17.62	0	11	0	—	4
Leatham, G A B *	Apr 30, 1851	June 19, 1932	1874	1886	12	18	5	61	14	4.69	0	—	—	—	21/7
Leather, R S *	Aug 17, 1880	Jan 31, 1913	1906	1906	1	2	0	19	14	9.50	0	—	—	—	—
Lee, C	Mar 17, 1924	Sept 4, 1999	1952	1952	2	4	0	98	74	24.50	0	—	—	—	1
Lee, F ©	Nov 18, 1856	Sept 13, 1896	1882	1890	105	182	10	3,622	165	21.05	3	—	—	—	53/1
Lee, G H	Aug 24, 1854	Oct 4, 1919	1879	1879	1	2	0	13	9	6.50	0	—	—	—	—
Lee, Herbert	July 2, 1856	Feb 4, 1908	1885	1885	5	6	0	20	12	3.33	0	—	—	—	2
Lee, J E *	Mar 23, 1838	Apr 2, 1880	1867	1867	2	3	0	9	6	3.00	0	—	—	—	—
Lee, J E	Dec 23, 1988		2006	2009	2	3	1	24	21*	12.00	0	149	2	74.50	1
Lees A Z	**Apr 14, 1993**		**2010**	**2011**	**2**	**2**	**0**	**38**	**38**	**19.00**	**0**	—	—	—	—
Legard, A D *	June 19, 1878	Aug 15, 1939	1910	1910	4	5	0	50	15	10.00	0	26	0	—	1
§ Lehmann, D S ©	Feb 5, 1970		1997	2006	88	137	8	8,871	339	68.76	26	1,952	61	32.00	35
Lester, E I ©	Feb 18, 1923		1945	1956	228	339	27	10,616	186	34.02	24	160	3	53.33	106
Leyland, M ©	July 20, 1900	Jan 1, 1967	1920	1946	548	720	82	26,180	263	41.03	62	11,079	409	27.08	204
Lilley A E	**Apr 17, 1992**		**2011**	**2011**	**1**	**1**	**0**	**0**	**0**	**0.00**	**0**	**34**	**0**	—	—
Linaker, L	Apr 8, 1885	Nov 17, 1961	1909	1909	1	2	0	0	0	0.00	0	28	1	28.00	—
Lister, B	Dec 9, 1850	Dec 3, 1919	1874	1878	7	11	1	36	10	3.60	0	—	—	—	2
§ Lister-Kaye, K A *	Mar 27, 1892	Feb 28, 1955	1928	1928	2	2	1	13	7*	13.00	0	64	1	64.00	2
Lister, J *	May 14, 1930	Jan 28, 1991	1954	1954	2	4	0	35	16	8.75	0	—	—	—	2
Lockwood, E	Apr 4, 1845	Dec 19, 1921	1868	1884	214	364	29	7,789	208	23.25	6	2,265	141	16.06	164/2
Lockwood, H	Oct 20, 1855	Feb 18, 1930	1877	1882	16	27	2	408	90	16.32	0	37	0	—	8
Lodge, J T	Apr 16, 1921	July 9, 2002	1948	1948	2	3	0	48	30	16.00	0	17	0	—	—
Love, J D ©	Apr 22, 1955		1975	1989	247	388	58	10,263	170*	31.10	13	835	12	69.58	123
Lowe, G E	Jan 12, 1878	Aug 15, 1932	1902	1902	1	1	1	5	5*	—	0	—	—	—	1
Lowe J R	Oct 19,1991		2010	2010	1	1	0	5	5	5.00	0	—	—	—	—
Lowson, F A ©	July 1, 1925	Sept 8, 1984	1949	1958	252	404	31	13,897	259*	37.25	30	15	0	—	180
§ Loxley-Firth, E *	Mar 7, 1886	Jan 8, 1949	1912	1912	2	4	0	43	37	10.75	0	—	—	—	1
§ Lucas, D S	Aug 19, 1978		2005	2005	1	—	—	—	—	—	—	84	8	10.50	—
Lumb, E * ©	Sept 12, 1852	Apr 5, 1891	1872	1886	14	23	4	311	70*	16.36	0	—	—	—	5
§ Lumb, M J ©	Feb 12, 1980		2000	2006	78	135	12	4,194	144	34.09	8	199	5	39.80	43

LIST OF PLAYERS AND CAREER AVERAGES IN ALL FIRST-CLASS MATCHES FOR YORKSHIRE *(Continued)*

Player	Date of Birth	Date of Death (if known)	First Played	Last Played	M	Inns	NO	Runs	HS	Av'ge	100s	Runs	Wkts	Av'ge	Ct/St
Lumb, R G ©	Feb 27, 1950		1970	1984	239	395	30	11,525	165*	31.57	22	5	0	—	129
Lupton, A W * ©	Feb 23, 1879	Apr 14, 1944	1908	1927	104	79	15	668	43*	10.43	0	88	0	—	25
Lynas, G G	Sept 7, 1832	Dec 8, 1896	1867	1867	2	3	1	4	4*	2.00	0	—	—	—	2
Lyth, A ©	**Sept 25, 1987**		**2007**	**2012**	**60**	**97**	**2**	**3,729**	**248***	**39.25**	**5**	**297**	**3**	**99.00**	**54**
Macaulay, G G ©	Dec 7, 1897	Dec 13, 1940	1920	1935	445	430	112	5,717	125*	17.97	3	30,554	1,774	17.22	361
McGrath, A ©	**Oct 6, 1975**		**1995**	**2012**	**242**	**405**	**29**	**14,091**	**211**	**37.47**	**32**	**4,652**	**128**	**36.34**	**168**
McHugh, F P	Nov 15, 1925		1949	1949	3	1	0	0	0	0.00	0	147	4	36.75	1
Marshall, A	July 10, 1849	Aug 3, 1891	1874	1874	1	2	0	2	2	1.00	0	11	0	—	—
§ Martyn, D R	Oct 21, 1971		2003	2003	2	3	1	342	238	171.00	1	—	—	—	2
Mason, A	May 2, 1921	Mar, 2006.	1947	1950	18	19	3	105	22	6.56	0	1,473	51	28.88	6
Maude, E *	Dec 31, 1839	July 2, 1876	1866	1866	2	2	0	17	16	8.50	0	—	—	—	—
Metcalfe, A A ©	Dec 25, 1963		1983	1995	184	317	19	10,465	216*	35.11	25	344	3	114.66	72
Micklethwait, W H *	Dec 13, 1885	Oct 7, 1947	1911	1911	1	1	0	44	44	44.00	0	—	—	—	—
Middlebrook, J D	May 13, 1977		1998	2001	23	31	3	485	84	17.32	0	1,458	49	29.75	14
Middlebrook, W	May 23, 1858	Apr 26, 1919	1888	1889	17	27	7	88	19*	4.40	0	895	50	17.90	17
Midgley, C A *	Nov 11, 1877	June 24, 1942	1906	1906	4	6	2	115	59*	28.75	0	149	8	18.62	3
Milburn, S M	Sept 29, 1972		1992	1995	6	8	2	22	7	3.66	0	431	14	30.78	—
§ Milligan, F W * ©	Mar 19, 1870	Mar 31, 1900	1894	1898	81	113	10	1,879	74	18.24	0	2,736	112	24.42	40
Mitchell, A ©	Sept 13, 1902	Dec 25, 1976	1922	1945	401	550	69	18,189	189	37.81	39	291	5	58.20	406
Mitchell, F * ©	Aug 13, 1872	Oct 11, 1935	1894	1904	83	125	5	4,104	194	34.20	10	16	1	16.00	52
Monks, G D	Sept 3, 1929		1952	1952	1	1	0	3	3	3.00	0	—	—	—	1
Moorhouse, R ©	Sept 7, 1866	Jan 7, 1921	1888	1899	206	315	45	5,217	113	19.32	3	1,232	43	28.65	92
§ Morkel, M	Oct 6, 1984		2008	2008	1	2	0	8	8	4.00	0	33	1	33.00	—
Morris, A C	Oct 4, 1976		1995	1997	16	23	2	362	60	17.23	0	508	9	56.44	12
Mosley, H	Mar 8, 1852	Nov 29, 1933	1881	1881	2	4	0	1	1	0.25	0	34	3	11.33	1
Motley, A *	Feb 5, 1858	Sept 28, 1897	1879	1879	2	2	1	10	8*	10.00	0	135	7	19.28	1
Mounsey, J T ©	Aug 30, 1871	Apr 6, 1949	1891	1897	92	145	21	1,939	64	15.63	0	444	10	44.40	45
Moxon, M D ©	May 4, 1960		1981	1997	277	476	42	18,973	274*	43.71	41	1,213	22	55.13	190
Myers, H ©	Jan 2, 1875	June 12, 1944	1901	1910	201	289	46	4,450	91	18.31	0	7,095	282	25.15	106
Myers, M	Apr 12, 1847	Dec 8, 1919	1876	1878	22	40	4	537	49	14.91	0	20	0	—	11

LIST OF PLAYERS AND CAREER AVERAGES IN ALL FIRST-CLASS MATCHES FOR YORKSHIRE *(Continued)*

Player	*Date of Birth*	*Date of Death (if known)*	*First Played*	*Last Played*	*M*	*Inns*	*NO*	*Runs*	*HS*	*Av'ge*	*100s*	*Runs*	*Wkts*	*Av'ge*	*Ct/St*
§ Naved-ul-Hasan, Rana	Feb 28, 1978		2008	2009	11	16	3	207	32	15.92	0	1,018	26	39.15	3
Naylor, J E	Dec 11, 1930	June 26, 1996	1953	1953	1	—	—	—	—	—	—	88	0	—	1
Newstead, J T ©	Sept 8, 1877	Mar 25, 1952	1903	1913	96	128	17	1,791	100*	16.13	1	5,555	297	18.70	75
Nicholson, A G ©	June 25, 1938	Nov 3, 1985	1962	1975	282	267	125	1,667	50	11.73	0	17,296	876	19.74	85
Nicholson, N G	Oct 17, 1963		1988	1989	5	8	3	134	56*	26.80	0	25	0	—	5
Oates, William	Jan 1, 1852	Dec 9, 1940	1874	1875	7	13	7	34	14*	5.66	0	—	—	—	5/1
Oates, W F	June 11, 1929	May 15, 2001	1956	1956	3	3	0	20	9	6.66	0	—	—	—	—
Old, C M ©	Dec 22, 1948		1966	1982	222	262	56	4,785	116	23.22	5	13,409	647	20.72	131
Oldham, S	July 26, 1948		1974	1985	59	39	18	212	50	10.09	0	3,849	130	29.60	18
Oldroyd, E ©	Oct 1, 1888	Dec 29, 1964	1910	1931	383	509	58	15,891	194	35.23	37	1,658	42	39.47	203
Oyston, C	May 12, 1869	July 15, 1942	1900	1909	15	21	8	96	22	7.38	0	872	31	28.12	3
Padgett, D E V ©	July 20, 1934		1951	1971	487	774	63	20,306	161*	28.55	29	208	6	34.66	250
Padgett, G H	Oct 9, 1931		1952	1952	6	7	4	56	32*	18.66	0	336	4	84.00	5
Padgett, J	Nov 21, 1860	Aug 2, 1943	1882	1889	6	9	0	92	22	10.22	0	—	—	—	2
Parker, B	June 23, 1970		1992	1998	44	71	10	1,839	138*	30.14	2	3	0	—	19
§ Parkin, C H	Feb 18, 1886	June 15, 1943	1906	1906	1	1	0	0	0	0.00	0	25	2	12.50	—
Parratt, J	Mar 24, 1859	May 6, 1905	1888	1890	2	2	0	11	11	5.50	0	75	1	75.00	4
§ Parton, J W	Jan 31, 1863	Jan. 30, 1906	1889	1889	1	2	0	16	14	8.00	0	4	1	4.00	—
Patterson, S A ©	**Oct 3, 1983**		**2005**	**2012**	**56**	**64**	**20**	**660**	**53**	**15.00**	**0**	**4,272**	**141**	**30.29**	**11**
Pearson, H E	Aug 7, 1851	July 8, 1903	1878	1880	4	7	5	31	10*	15.50	0	90	5	18.00	1
Pearson, J H	May 14, 1915	May 13, 2007	1934	1936	3	3	0	54	44	18.00	0	—	—	—	—
Peate, E ©	Mar 2, 1855	Mar 11, 1900	1879	1887	154	226	61	1,793	95	10.86	0	9,986	794	12.57	97
Peel, R ©	Feb 12, 1857	Aug 12, 1941	1882	1897	318	510	42	9,322	210*	19.91	6	20,638	1,311	15.74	141
Penny, J H	Sept 29, 1856	July 29, 1902	1891	1891	1	1	1	8	8*	—	0	31	2	15.50	1
Pickles, C S	Jan 30, 1966		1985	1992	58	76	21	1,336	66	24.29	0	3,638	83	43.83	24
Pickles D	Nov 16, 1935		1957	1960	41	40	20	74	12	3.70	0	2,062	96	21.47	10
Pinder, G	July 15, 1841	Jan 15, 1903	1867	1880	125	199	44	1,639	57	10.57	0	325	19	17.10	145/102
Platt, R K ©	Dec 26, 1932		1955	1963	96	103	47	405	57*	7.23	0	6,389	282	22.65	35
Pollard, D	Aug 7, 1835	Mar 26, 1909	1865	1865	1	2	0	3	3	1.50	0	19	0	—	—
Pollitt, G	June 3, 1874	Not known	1899	1899	1	1	0	51	51	51.00	0	—	—	—	1

LIST OF PLAYERS AND CAREER AVERAGES IN ALL FIRST-CLASS MATCHES FOR YORKSHIRE *(Continued)*

Player	Date of Birth	Date of Death (if known)	First Played	Last Played	M	Inns	NO	Runs	HS	Av'ge	100s	Runs	Wkts	Av'ge	Ct/St
Prest, C H *	Dec 9, 1841	Mar 4, 1875	1864	1864	2	4	0	57	31	14.25	0	—	—	—	3
Preston, J M ©	Aug 23, 1864	Nov 26, 1890	1885	1889	79	134	11	1,935	93	15.73	0	3,232	178	18.15	36
Pride, T	July 23, 1864	Feb 16, 1919	1887	1887	1	1	0	1	1	1.00	0	—	—	—	4/3
Priestley, I M	Sept 25, 1967		1989	1989	2	4	2	25	23	12.50	0	119	4	29.75	1
Pullan, P	Mar 29, 1857	Mar 3, 1901	1884	1884	1	1	0	14	14	14.00	0	5	0	—	1
Pyrah, R M ©	**Nov 1, 1982**		**2004**	**2012**	**37**	**48**	**5**	**1,186**	**134***	**27.58**	**3**	**1,901**	**47**	**40.44**	**15**
§ Radcliffe, E J R H * ©	Jan 27, 1884	Nov 23, 1969	1909	1911	64	89	13	826	54	10.86	0	134	2	67.00	21
Ramage, A	Nov 29, 1957		1979	1983	23	22	9	219	52	16.84	0	1,649	44	37.47	1
Ramsden, G	Mar 2, 1983		2000	2000	1	1	1	0	0*	—	0	68	1	68.00	0
Randhawa G S	**Jan 25, 1992**		**2011**	**2011**	**1**	**1**	**0**	**5**	**5**	**5.00**	**0**	**62**	**2**	**31.00**	—
Raper, J R S *	Aug 9, 1909	Mar 9, 1997	1936	1947	3	4	0	24	15	6.00	0	—	—	—	—
Rashid, A U ©	**Feb 17, 1988**		**2006**	**2012**	**85**	**118**	**21**	**3,225**	**157***	**33.24**	**4**	**9,043**	**265**	**34.12**	**43**
Rawlin, E R	Oct 4, 1897	Jan 11, 1943	1927	1936	8	10	1	72	35	8.00	0	498	21	23.71	2
Rawlin, J T	Nov 10, 1856	Jan 19, 1924	1880	1885	27	36	2	274	31	8.05	0	258	11	23.45	13
Rawlinson, E B	Apr 10, 1837	Feb 17, 1892	1867	1875	37	68	5	991	55	15.73	0	62	5	12.40	16
Redfearn, J	May 13, 1862	Jan 14, 1931	1890	1890	1	1	0	5	5	5.00	0	—	—	—	—
Render, G W A	Jan 5, 1887	Sept 17, 1922	1919	1919	1	1	0	5	5	5.00	0	—	—	—	—
Rhodes, A C ©	Oct 14, 1906	May 21, 1957	1932	1934	61	70	19	917	64*	17.98	0	3,026	107	28.28	45
§ Rhodes, H E *	Jan 11, 1852	Sept 10, 1889	1878	1883	10	16	1	269	64	17.93	0	—	—	—	1
Rhodes, S J	June 17, 1964		1981	1984	3	2	1	41	35	41.00	0	—	—	—	3
Rhodes, Wilfred ©	Oct 29, 1877	July 8, 1973	1898	1930	883	1,195	162	31,075	267*	30.08	46	57,634	3,598	16.01	586
Rhodes, William	Mar 4, 1883	Aug 5, 1941	1911	1911	1	1	1	1	1*	—	0	40	0	—	—
Richardson, J A *	Aug 4, 1908	Apr 2, 1985	1936	1947	7	12	2	308	61	30.80	0	90	2	45.00	3
§ Richardson, R B ©	Jan 12, 1962		1993	1994	23	39	1	1,310	112	34.47	1	23	1	23.00	18
§ Richardson, S A	Sept 5, 1977		2000	2003	13	23	2	377	69	17.95	0	—	—	—	11
Riley, H	Aug 17, 1875	Nov 6, 1922	1895	1900	4	5	1	36	25*	9.00	0	54	1	54.00	1
Riley, M *	Apr 5, 1851	June 1, 1899	1878	1882	17	28	1	361	92	13.37	0	10	0	—	3
Ringrose, W ©	Sept 2, 1871	Sept 14, 1943	1901	1906	57	66	9	353	23	6.19	0	3,224	155	20.80	25
Robinson, A L ©	Aug 17, 1946		1971	1977	84	69	31	365	30*	9.60	0	4,927	196	25.13	48
Robinson, Edward *	Dec 27, 1862	Sept 3, 1942	1887	1887	1	2	1	23	23*	23.00	0	—	—	—	—
Robinson, Emmott ©	Nov 16, 1883	Nov 17, 1969	1919	1931	413	455	77	9,651	135*	25.53	7	19,645	893	21.99	318

LIST OF PLAYERS AND CAREER AVERAGES IN ALL FIRST-CLASS MATCHES FOR YORKSHIRE *(Continued)*

Player	Date of Birth	Date of Death (if known)	First Played	Last Played	M	Inns	NO	Runs	HS	Av'ge	100s	Runs	Wkts	Av'ge	Ct/St
Robinson, E P ©	Aug 10, 1911	Nov 10, 1998	1934	1949	208	253	46	2,596	75*	12.54	0	15,141	735	20.60	189
Robinson, H	May 12, 1858	Dec 14, 1909	1879	1879	1	2	0	5	4	2.50	0	20	1	20.00	—
Robinson, M A ©	Nov 23, 1966		1991	1995	90	93	36	240	23	4.21	0	6,866	218	31.49	17
Robinson, P E ©	Aug 3, 1963		1984	1991	132	217	31	6,668	189	35.84	7	238	1	238.00	96
Robinson, W	Nov 29, 1851	Aug 14, 1919	1876	1877	7	14	1	151	68	11.61	0	—	—	—	3
Roebuck C G	Aug 14, 1991		2010	2010	1	1	0	23	23	23.00	0	—	—	—	—
Root, J E ©	**Dec 30, 1990**		**2010**	**2012**	**32**	**54**	**7**	**1,721**	**222***	**36.61**	**3**	**476**	**8**	**59.50**	**15**
Roper, E *	Apr 8, 1851	Apr 27, 1921	1878	1880	5	7	1	85	68	14.16	0	—	—	—	2
Rothery, J W ©	Sept 5, 1877	June 2, 1919	1903	1910	150	236	18	4,614	161	21.16	3	44	2	22.00	45
Rowbotham, J	July 8, 1831	Dec 22, 1899	1861	1876	94	162	9	2,624	113	17.15	3	37	3	12.33	52
§ Rudolph J A ©	May 4, 1981		2007	2011	68	112	8	5429	228*	52.20	18	311	1	311.00	79
Rudston, H	Nov 22, 1879	April 14, 1962	1902	1907	21	30	0	609	164	20.30	1	—	—	—	3
Ryan, M ©	June 23, 1933		1954	1965	150	149	58	682	26*	7.49	0	9,466	413	22.92	59
Ryder, L	Aug 28, 1899	Jan 24, 1955	1924	1924	2	2	1	1	1	1.00	0	151	4	37.75	2
Sanderson B W	Jan 3, 1989		2008	2010	3	2	1	6	6	6.00	0	190	6	31.66	—
Savile, G *	Apr 26, 1847	Sept 4, 1904	1867	1874	5	7	0	140	65	20.00	0	—	—	—	2
Sayers, J J ©	**Nov 5, 1983**		**2004**	**2012**	**91**	**152**	**12**	**4,772**	**187**	**34.08**	**9**	**166**	**6**	**27.66**	**56**
Schofield, C J	Mar 21, 1976		1996	1996	1	1	0	25	25	25.00	0	—	—	—	—
Schofield, D	Oct 9, 1947		1970	1974	3	4	4	13	6*	—	0	112	5	22.40	—
Scott, E	July 6, 1834	Dec 3, 1898	1864	1864	1	1	0	8	8	8.00	0	27	2	13.50	1
Sedgwick, H A	Apr 8, 1883	Dec 28, 1957	1906	1906	3	5	2	53	34	17.66	0	327	16	20.43	2
Sellers, Arthur * ©	May 31, 1870	Sept 25, 1941	1890	1899	49	88	1	1,643	105	18.88	2	84	2	42.00	40
Sellers, A B * ©	Mar 5, 1907	Feb 20, 1981	1932	1948	334	437	51	8,949	204	23.18	4	653	8	81.62	264
Shackleton, W A	Mar 9, 1908	Nov 16, 1971	1928	1934	5	6	0	49	25	8.16	0	130	6	21.66	3
Shahzad, Ajmal ©	July 27, 1985		2006	2012	45	58	14	1,145	88	26.02	0	4,196	125	33.56	5
Sharp, K ©	Apr. 6, 1959		1976	1990	195	320	35	8,426	181	29.56	11	836	12	69.66	95
§ Sharpe, C M *	Sept 6, 1851	June 25, 1935	1875	1875	1	1	0	15	15	15.00	0	17	0	—	—
Sharpe, P J ©	Dec 27, 1936		1958	1974	411	666	71	17,685	203*	29.72	23	140	2	70.00	525
Shaw C	Feb 17, 1964		1984	1988	61	58	27	340	31	10.96	0	4,101	123	33.34	9
Shaw, J	Mar 12, 1865	Jan 22, 1921	1896	1897	3	3	0	8	7	2.66	0	181	7	25.85	2

LIST OF PLAYERS AND CAREER AVERAGES IN ALL FIRST-CLASS MATCHES FOR YORKSHIRE *(Continued)*

Player	Date of Birth	Date of Death (if known)	First Played	Last Played	M	Inns	NO	Runs	HS	Av'ge	100s	Runs	Wkts	Av'ge	Ct/St
Sheepshanks, E R *	Mar 22, 1910	Dec 31, 1937	1929	1929	1	1	0	26	26	26.00	0	—	—	—	—
Shepherd, D A *	Mar 10, 1916	May 29, 1998	1938	1938	1	1	0	0	0	0.00	0	—	—	—	—
Shotton, W	Dec 1, 1840	May 26, 1909	1865	1874	2	4	0	13	7	3.25	0	—	—	—	—
Sidebottom, A ©	Apr 1, 1954		1973	1991	216	249	50	4,243	124	22.33	1	13,852	558	24.82	60
Sidebottom, R J	**Jan 15, 1978**		**1997**	**2012**	**81**	**107**	**31**	**1,135**	**61**	**14.93**	**0**	**6,258**	**249**	**25.13**	**25**
Sidgwick, R *	Aug 7, 1851	1934	1882	1882	9	13	0	64	17	4.92	0	—	—	—	7
Silverwood, C E W ©	Mar 5, 1975		1993	2005	131	179	33	2,369	80	16.22	0	11,413	427	27.62	30
Silvester, S	Mar 12, 1951		1976	1977	6	7	4	30	14	10.00	0	313	12	26.08	2
Simpson, E T B *	Mar 5, 1867	Mar 20, 1944	1889	1889	1	2	0	1	1	0.50	0	—	—	—	—
§ Sims, Rev H M *	Mar 15, 1853	Oct 5, 1885	1875	1877	5	10	1	109	35*	12.11	0	—	—	—	2
Slinn, W	Dec 13, 1826	June 19, 1888	1861	1864	9	14	3	22	11	2.00	0	742	48	15.45	5
Smailes, T F ©	Mar 27, 1910	Dec 1, 1970	1932	1948	262	339	42	5,686	117	19.14	3	16,593	802	20.68	153
Smales, K	Sept 15, 1927		1948	1950	13	19	3	165	45	10.31	0	766	22	34.81	4
Smith, A F	Mar 7, 1847	Jan 6, 1915	1868	1874	28	49	4	692	89	15.37	0	—	—	—	11
Smith, E (Barnsley)	July 11, 1888	Jan 2, 1972	1914	1926	16	21	5	169	49	10.56	0	1,090	46	23.69	5
Smith, Ernest (Morley)* ©	Oct 19, 1869	Feb 9, 1945	1888	1907	154	234	18	4,453	129	20.61	2	6,278	248	25.31	112
Smith, Fred (Idle)	Dec 26, 1885	Not known	1911	1911	1	1	0	11	11	11.00	0	45	2	22.50	—
Smith, Fred (Yeadon)	Dec 18, 1879	Oct 20, 1905	1903	1903	13	19	1	292	55	16.22	0	—	—	—	3
Smith, G	Jan 13, 1876	Jan 16, 1929	1901	1906	2	1	0	7	7	7.00	0	62	0	—	3
Smith, J	Mar 23, 1833	Feb 12, 1909	1865	1865	2	3	0	28	16	9.33	0	72	6	12.00	3
Smith, N	Apr 1, 1949	Mar 4, 2003	1970	1971	8	11	5	82	20	13.66	0	—	—	—	14/3
Smith, R	Apr 6, 1944		1969	1970	5	8	3	99	37*	19.80	0	—	—	—	—
Smith, Walker	Aug 14, 1847	July 7, 1900	1874	1874	5	9	0	152	59	16.88	0	—	—	—	3
§ Smith, William	Nov 1, 1839	Apr 19, 1897	1865	1874	11	19	3	260	90	16.25	0	—	—	—	8
Smithson, G A ©	Nov 1, 1926	Sept 6, 1970	1946	1950	39	60	5	1,449	169	26.34	2	84	1	84.00	21
Smurthwaite, J	Oct 17, 1916	Oct 20, 1989	1938	1939	7	9	5	29	20*	7.25	0	237	12	19.75	4
Sowden, A	Dec 1, 1853	July 5, 1921	1878	1887	8	11	0	137	37	12.45	0	22	0	—	1
Squire, D	Dec 31, 1864	Apr 28, 1922	1893	1893	1	2	0	0	0	0.00	0	25	0	—	—
Squires, P J	Aug 4, 1951		1972	1976	49	84	8	1,271	70	16.72	0	32	0	—	14
Stanley, H C *	Feb 16, 1888	May 18, 1934	1911	1913	8	13	0	155	42	11.92	0	—	—	—	6
§ Stanyforth, R T *	May 30, 1892	Feb 20, 1964	1928	1928	3	3	0	26	10	8.66	0	—	—	—	2

LIST OF PLAYERS AND CAREER AVERAGES IN ALL FIRST-CLASS MATCHES FOR YORKSHIRE *(Continued)*

Player	Date of Birth	Date of Death (if known)	First Played	Last Played	M	Inns	NO	Runs	HS	Av'ge	100s	Runs	Wkts	Av'ge	Ct/St
§ M A Starc	**Jan 13, 1990**		**2012**	**2012**	**2**	**1**	**1**	**28**	**28***	**—**	**0**	**153**	**7**	**21.85**	—
Stead, B	June 21, 1939	Apr 15, 1980	1959	1959	2	3	0	8	8	2.66	0	115	7	16.42	—
§ Stemp, R D ©	Dec 11, 1967		1993	1998	104	135	36	1,267	65	12.79	0	8,557	241	35.50	49
Stephenson, E	June 5, 1832	July 5, 1898	1861	1873	36	61	5	803	67	14.33	0	—	—	—	30/27
Stephenson, J S *	Nov 10, 1903	Oct 7, 1975	1923	1926	16	19	2	182	60	10.70	0	65	0	—	6
Stevenson, G B ©	Dec 16, 1955		1973	1986	177	217	32	3,856	115*	20.84	2	13,254	464	28.56	73
Stott, W B ©	July 18, 1934		1952	1963	187	309	19	9,168	186	31.61	17	112	7	16.00	91
Stringer, P M	Feb 23, 1943		1967	1969	19	17	8	101	15*	11.22	0	696	32	21.75	7
Stuchbury, S	June 22, 1954		1978	1981	3	3	2	7	4*	7.00	0	236	8	29.50	—
§ Sugg, F H	Jan 11, 1862	May 29, 1933	1883	1883	8	12	4	80	13*	10.00	0	—	—	—	4/1
§ Sugg, W	May 21, 1860	May 21, 1933	1881	1881	1	1	0	9	9	9.00	0	—	—	—	—
Sullivan, J H B *	Sept 21, 1890	Feb 8, 1932	1912	1912	1	2	0	41	26	20.50	0	43	0	—	—
Sutcliffe, H ©	Nov 24, 1894	Jan 22, 1978	1919	1945	602	864	96	38,558	313	50.20	112	381	8	47.62	402
Sutcliffe, W H H * ©	Oct 10, 1926	Sept 16, 1998	1948	1957	177	273	34	6,247	181	26.13	6	152	6	25.33	80
Swallow, I G	Dec 18, 1962		1983	1989	61	82	18	1,296	114	20.25	1	3,270	64	51.09	28
§ Swanepoel, P J	Mar 30, 1977		2003	2003	2	3	0	20	17	6.66	0	129	3	43.00	1
§ Tait, T	Oct 7, 1872	Sept 6, 1954	1898	1899	2	3	1	7	3	3.50	0	—	—	—	1
Tasker, J * ©	Feb 4, 1887	Aug 24, 1975	1912	1913	31	43	4	586	67	15.02	0	—	—	—	14
Tattersall, G *	Apr 21, 1882	June 29, 1972	1905	1905	1	2	0	26	26	13.00	0	—	—	—	—
Taylor, C R	Feb 21, 1981		2001	2005	16	27	3	416	52*	17.33	0	—	—	—	8
Taylor, H	Dec 18, 1900	Oct 28, 1988	1924	1925	9	13	0	153	36	11.76	0	—	—	—	1
Taylor, H S	Dec 11, 1856	Nov 16, 1896	1879	1879	3	5	0	36	22	7.20	0	—	—	—	—
Taylor, J	Apr 2, 1850	May 27, 1924	1880	1881	9	13	1	107	44	8.91	0	—	—	—	4
Taylor, K ©	Aug 21, 1935		1953	1968	303	505	35	12,864	203*	27.37	16	3,680	129	28.52	146
Taylor, N S	June 2, 1963		1982	1983	8	6	1	10	4	2.00	0	720	22	32.72	2
Taylor, T L * ©	May 25, 1878	Mar. 16, 1960	1899	1906	82	122	10	3,933	156	35.11	8	—	—	—	47/2
§ Tendulkar, S R ©	Apr 24, 1973		1992	1992	16	25	2	1,070	100	46.52	1	195	4	48.75	10
Thewlis, H	Aug 31, 1865	Nov 30, 1920	1888	1888	2	4	1	4	2*	1.33	0	—	—	—	2
Thewlis, John Jun.	Sept 21, 1850	Aug 9, 1901	1879	1879	3	4	0	21	10	5.25	0	—	—	—	—
Thewlis, John Sen.	June 30, 1828	Dec 29, 1899	1861	1875	44	80	3	1,280	108	16.62	1	—	—	—	21/1

LIST OF PLAYERS AND CAREER AVERAGES IN ALL FIRST-CLASS MATCHES FOR YORKSHIRE *(Continued)*

Player	Date of Birth	Date of Death (if known)	First Played	Last Played	M	Inns	NO	Runs	HS	Av'ge	100s	Runs	Wkts	Av'ge	Ct/St
Thornicroft, N D	Jan 23, 1985		2002	2007	7	10	4	50	30	8.33	0	545	16	34.06	2
Thornton, A	July 20, 1854	Apr 18, 1915	1881	1881	3	4	0	21	7	5.25	0	—	—	—	2
Thornton, G *	Dec 24, 1867	Jan 31, 1939	1891	1891	3	4	0	21	16	5.25	0	74	2	37.00	—
Thorpe, G	Feb 20, 1834	Mar 2, 1899	1864	1864	1	2	1	14	9*	14.00	0	—	—	—	2
Threapleton, J W	July 20, 1857	July 30, 1918	1881	1881	1	1	1	8	8*	—	0	—	—	—	2/1
Tinsley, H J	Feb 20, 1865	Dec 10, 1938	1890	1891	9	13	0	56	15	4.30	0	57	4	14.25	1
Townsley, R A J	June 24, 1952		1974	1975	2	4	0	22	12	5.50	0	0	0	—	1
Towse, A D	Apr 22, 1968		1988	1988	1	1	0	1	1	1.00	0	50	3	16.66	1
Trueman, F S ©	Feb 6, 1931	July 1, 2006	1949	1968	459	533	81	6,852	104	15.15	2	29,890	1,745	17.12	325
Tunnicliffe, J ©	Aug 26, 1866	July 11, 1948	1891	1907	472	768	57	19,435	243	27.33	22	388	7	55.42	665
Turner, A	Sept 2, 1885	Aug 29, 1951	1910	1911	9	16	1	163	37	10.86	0	—	—	—	7
Turner, B	July 25, 1938		1960	1961	2	4	2	7	3*	3.50	0	47	4	11.75	2
Turner, C ©	Jan 11, 1902	Nov 19, 1968	1925	1946	200	266	32	6,132	130	26.20	2	5,320	173	30.75	181
Turner, F I	Sept 3, 1894	Oct 18, 1954	1924	1924	5	7	0	33	12	4.71	0	—	—	—	2
Tyson, C T	Jan 24, 1889	Apr 3, 1940	1921	1921	3	5	2	232	100*	77.33	1	—	—	—	1
Ullathorne, C E	Apr 11, 1845	May 2, 1904	1868	1875	27	46	8	283	28	7.44	0	—	—	—	19
Ulyett, G ©	Oct 21, 1851	June 18, 1898	1873	1893	355	618	31	14,157	199*	24.11	15	8,181	457	17.90	235
§ Usher, J	Feb 26, 1859	Aug 10, 1905	1888	1888	1	2	0	7	5	3.50	0	31	2	15.50	1
van Geloven, J	Jan 4, 1934	Aug 21, 2003	1955	1955	3	2	1	17	16	17.00	0	224	6	37.33	2
§ Vaughan, M P ©	Oct 29, 1974		1993	2009	151	267	14	9,160	183	36.20	20	4,268	92	46.39	55
§ Verelst, H W *	July 2, 1846	Apr 5, 1918	1868	1869	3	4	1	66	33*	22.00	0	—	—	—	1
Verity, H ©	May 18, 1905	July 31, 1943	1930	1939	278	294	77	3,898	101	17.96	1	21,353	1,558	13.70	191
Waddington, A ©	Feb 4, 1893	Oct 28, 1959	1919	1927	255	250	65	2,396	114	12.95	1	16,203	835	19.40	222
Wade, S ©	Feb 8, 1858	Nov 5, 1931	1886	1890	65	11	20	1,438	74*	15.80	0	2,498	133	18.78	31
Wainwright D J ©	Mar 21, 1985		2004	2011	29	36	11	914	104*	36.56	2	2,480	69	35.94	6
Wainwright, E ©	Apr 8, 1865	Oct 28, 1919	1888	1902	352	545	30	11,092	228	21.53	18	17,744	998	17.77	327
Wainwright, W	Jan 21, 1882	Dec 31, 1961	1903	1905	24	36	3	648	62	19.63	0	582	19	30.63	21
Wake, W R *	May 21, 1852	Mar 14, 1896	1881	1881	3	3	0	13	11	4.33	0	—	—	—	2
Walker, A *	June 22, 1844	May 26, 1927	1863	1870	9	16	1	138	26	9.20	0	74	1	74.00	3

Player	*Date of Birth*	*Date of Death (if known)*	*First Played*	*Last Played*	*M*	*Inns*	*NO*	*Runs*	*HS*	*Av'ge*	*100s*	*Runs*	*Wkts*	*Av'ge*	*Ct/St*
Walker, C	June 26, 1919	Dec 3, 1992	1947	1948	5	9	2	268	91	38.28	0	71	2	35.50	1
Walker, T	Apr 3, 1854	Aug 28, 1925	1879	1880	14	22	2	179	30	8.95	0	7	0	—	3
Waller, G	Dec 3, 1864	Dec 11, 1937	1893	1894	3	4	0	17	13	4.25	0	70	4	17.50	1
Wallgate, L *	Nov 12, 1849	May 9, 1887	1875	1878	3	3	0	9	6	3.00	0	17	1	17.00	3
Ward, A	Nov 21, 1865	Jan 6, 1939	1886	1886	4	7	1	41	22	6.83	0	1	0	—	1
Ward, F	Aug 31, 1881	Feb 28, 1948	1903	1903	1	1	0	0	0	0.00	0	16	0	—	—
Ward, H P *	Jan 20, 1899	Dec 16 1946	1920	1920	1	1	1	10	10*	—	0	—	—	—	1
Wardall, T A ©	Apr 19, 1862	Dec 20, 1932	1884	1894	43	73	2	1,003	106	14.12	2	489	23	21.26	25
Wardlaw, I	**Jun 29, 1985**		**2011**	**2012**	**4**	**3**	**2**	**31**	**17***	**31.00**	**0**	**368**	**4**	**92.00**	**2**
Wardle, J H ©	Jan 8, 1923	July 23, 1985	1946	1958	330	418	57	5,765	79	15.96	0	27,917	1,539	18.13	210
Waring, J S	Oct 1, 1942		1963	1966	28	27	15	137	26	11.41	0	1,122	53	21.16	17
Waring, S	Nov 4, 1838	Apr 17, 1919	1870	1870	1	1	0	9	9	9.00	0	—	—	—	—
Washington, W A I ©	Dec 11, 1879	Oct 20, 1927	1900	1902	44	62	6	1,290	100*	23.03	1	—	—	—	18
Watson, H	Sept 26, 1880	Nov 24, 1951	1908	1914	29	35	11	141	41	5.87	0	—	—	—	46/10
Watson, W ©	Mar 7, 1920	Apr 24, 2004	1939	1957	283	430	65	13,953	214*	38.22	26	75	0	—	170
Waud, B W *	June 4, 1837	May 30, 1889	1862	1864	6	10	1	165	42	18.33	0	—	—	—	2
Webster, C	June 9, 1838	Jan 6, 1881	1861	1868	3	5	1	30	10	7.50	0	—	—	—	1
Webster, H H	May 8, 1844	Mar 5, 1915	1868	1868	2	3	0	10	10	3.33	0	—	—	—	—
§ Weekes, L C	July 19, 1971		1994	2000	2	2	0	20	10	10.00	0	191	10	19.10	1
West, J	Oct 16, 1844	Jan 27, 1890	1868	1876	38	64	13	461	41	9.03	0	853	53	16.09	14
Wharf, A G	June 4, 1975		1994	1997	7	9	1	186	62	23.25	0	454	11	41.27	2
Whatmough, F J	Dec 4, 1856	June 3, 1904	1878	1882	7	11	1	51	20	5.10	0	111	5	22.20	4
Wheater, C H *	Mar 4, 1860	May 11, 1885	1880	1880	2	4	1	45	27	15.00	0	—	—	—	3
White, Sir A W * ©	Oct 14, 1877	Dec 16, 1945	1908	1920	97	128	28	1,457	55	14.57	0	7	0	—	50
White, C ©	Dec 16, 1969		1990	2007	221	350	45	10,376	186	34.01	19	7,649	276	27.71	140
Whitehead, J P	Sept 3, 1925	Aug 15, 2000	1946	1951	37	38	17	387	58*	18.42	0	2,610	96	27.47	11
Whitehead, Lees ©	Mar 14, 1864	Nov 22, 1913	1889	1904	119	172	38	2,073	67*	15.47	0	2,408	99	24.32	68
Whitehead, Luther	June 25, 1869	Jan 16, 1931	1893	1893	2	4	0	21	13	5.25	0	—	—	—	—
Whiteley, J P	Feb 28, 1955		1978	1982	45	38	17	231	20	11.00	0	2,410	70	34.42	21
Whiting, C P	Apr 18, 1888	Jan 14, 1959	1914	1920	6	10	2	92	26	11.50	0	416	15	27.73	2

LIST OF PLAYERS AND CAREER AVERAGES IN ALL FIRST-CLASS MATCHES FOR YORKSHIRE *(Continued)*

Player		Date of Birth	Date of Death (if known)	First Played	Last Played	M	Inns	NO	Runs	HS	Av'ge	100s	Runs	Wkts	Av'ge	Ct/St
Whitwell, J F *		Feb 22, 1869	Nov 6, 1932	1890	1890	1	2	0	8	4	4.00	0	11	1	11.00	—
§ Whitwell, W F *		Dec 12, 1867	Apr 12, 1942	1890	1890	10	14	2	67	26	5.58	0	518	25	20.72	2
Widdup, S		Nov 10, 1977		2000	2001	11	18	1	245	44	14.41	0	22	1	22.00	5
Wigley, D H		Oct 26, 1981		2002	2002	1	2	1	19	15	19.00	0	116	1	116.00	—
§ Wilkinson, A J A *		May 28, 1835	Dec 11, 1905	1865	1868	5	6	0	129	53	21.50	0	57	0	—	1
Wilkinson, F		May 23, 1914	Mar 26, 1984	1937	1939	14	14	1	73	18*	5.61	0	590	26	22.69	12
Wilkinson, H *	©	Dec 11, 1877	Apr 15, 1967	1903	1905	48	75	3	1,382	113	19.19	1	121	3	40.33	19
Wilkinson, R		Nov 11, 1977		1998	1998	1	1	0	9	9	9.00	0	35	1	35.00	—
Wilkinson, W H	©	Mar 12, 1881	June 4, 1961	1903	1910	126	192	14	3,812	103	21.41	1	971	31	31.32	93
Williams, A C		Mar 1, 1887	June 1, 1966	1911	1919	12	14	10	95	48*	23.75	0	678	30	22.60	6
Wilson, B B	©	Dec 11, 1879	Sept 14, 1957	1906	1914	185	308	12	8,053	208	27.50	15	278	2	139.00	53
Wilson, C E M *	©	May 15, 1875	Feb 8, 1944	1896	1899	8	13	3	256	91*	25.60	0	257	12	21.41	3
Wilson, D	©	Aug 7, 1937	July 21, 2012	1957	1974	392	502	85	5,788	83	13.88	0	22,626	1,104	20.49	235
Wilson, E R *	©	Mar 25, 1879	July 21, 1957	1899	1923	66	72	18	902	104*	16.70	1	3,106	197	15.76	30
Wilson, Geoffrey *	©	Aug 21, 1895	Nov 29, 1960	1919	1924	92	94	14	983	70	12.28	0	11	0	—	33
Wilson, G A *		Feb 2, 1916	Sept 24, 2002	1936	1939	15	25	5	352	55*	17.60	0	138	1	138.00	7
Wilson, John *		June 30, 1857	Nov 11, 1931	1887	1888	4	5	1	17	13*	4.25	0	165	12	13.75	3
Wilson, J P *		Apr 3, 1889	Oct 3, 1959	1911	1912	9	14	1	81	36	6.23	0	24	1	24.00	2
Wilson, J V	©	Jan 17, 1921	June 5, 2008	1946	1962	477	724	75	20,548	230	31.66	29	313	3	104.33	520
Wood, A	©	Aug 25, 1898	Apr 1, 1973	1927	1946	408	481	80	8,579	123*	21.39	1	33	1	33.00	612/243
Wood, B		Dec 26, 1942		1964	1964	5	7	2	63	35	12.60	0	—	—	—	4
Wood, C H		July 26, 1934	June 28, 2006	1959	1959	4	4	1	22	10	7.33	0	319	11	29.00	1
Wood, G W		Nov 18, 1862	Dec 4, 1948	1895	1895	2	2	0	2	2	1.00	0	—	—	—	0/1
Wood, H *		Mar 22, 1855	July 31, 1941	1879	1880	10	16	1	156	36	10.40	0	212	10	21.20	8
Wood, J H *				1881	1881	2	1	0	14	14	14.00	0	—	—	—	—
Wood, M J	©	Apr 6, 1977		1997	2007	128	222	20	6,742	207	33.37	16	27	2	13.50	113
Wood, R		June 3, 1929	May 22, 1990	1952	1956	22	18	4	60	17	4.28	0	1,346	51	26.39	5
Woodford, J D		Sept 9, 1943		1968	1972	38	61	2	1,204	101	20.40	1	185	4	46.25	12

Player	Date of Birth	Date of Death (if known)	First Played	Last Played	M	Inns	NO	Runs	HS	Av'ge	100s	Runs	Wkts	Av'ge	Ct/St
Woodhead, F E *	May 29, 1868	Aug 25, 1943	1893	1894	4	8	0	57	18	7.12	0	—	—	—	3
Woodhouse, W H *	Apr 16, 1856	Mar 4, 1938	1884	1885	9	13	0	218	63	16.76	0	—	—	—	6
Wormald, A	May 10, 1855	Feb 6, 1940	1885	1891	7	11	3	161	80	20.12	0	—	—	—	10/2
Worsley, W A * .....©	Apr 5, 1890	Dec 4, 1973	1928	1929	60	50	4	722	60	15.69	0	—	—	—	32
Wrathmell, L F	Jan 22, 1855	Sept 16, 1928	1886	1886	1	2	0	18	17	9.00	0	—	—	—	—
Wright, R	July 19, 1852	May 25, 1891	1877	1877	2	4	1	28	22	9.33	0	—	—	—	—
Wright, T J *	Mar 5, 1900	Nov 7, 1962	1919	1919	1	1	0	12	12	12.00	0	—	—	—	—
Yardley, N W D * ...©	Mar 19, 1915	Oct 4, 1989	1936	1955	302	420	56	11,632	183*	31.95	17	5, 818	195	29.83	220
Yeadon, J	Dec 10, 1861	May 30, 1914	1888	1888	3	6	2	41	22	10.25	0	—	—	—	5/3
§ Younus Khan .....©	Nov 29, 1977		2007	2007	13	19	2	824	217*	48.47	3	342	8	42.75	11
§ Yuvraj Singh	Dec 12, 1981		2003	2003	7	12	2	145	56	14.50	0	130	3	43.33	12

In the career averages it should be noted that the bowling analysis for the second Cambridgeshire innings at Ashton-under-Lyne in 1865 has not been found. G R Atkinson took 3 wickets, W Cuttell 2, G Freeman 4 and R Iddison 1.The respective bowling averages have been calculated excluding these wickets.

Matches	Player	Matches	Player	Matches	Player
883	W Rhodes (1898-1930)	496	R Illingworth (1951-1983)	429	D L Bairstow (1970-1990)
717	G H Hirst (1891-1929)	491	† J G Binks (1955-1969)	427	A Dolphin (1905-1927)
676	D Denton (1894-1920)	487	D E V Padgett (1951-1971)	425	P Carrick (1970-1993)
602	H Sutcliffe (1919-1945)	485	P Holmes (1913-1933)	414	G Boycott (1962-1986)
548	M Leyland (1920-1947)	477	J V Wilson (1946-1962)	413	E. Robinson (1919-1931)
536	D B Close (1949-1970)	472	J Tunnicliffe (1891-1907)	411	P J Sharpe (1958-1974)
517	D Hunter (1888-1909)	459	F S Trueman (1949-1968)	408	A Wood (1927-1946)
513	S Haigh (1895-1913)	456	J H Hampshire (1961-1981)	401	A Mitchell (1922-1945)
510	Lord Hawke (1881-1911)	445	G G Macaulay (1920-1935)		

MOST TOTAL APPEARANCES FOR YORKSHIRE
(First-Class, Domestic List A and t20)

Matches	*Player*
883	W Rhodes (1898-1930)
827	D L Bairstow (1970-1990)
727	P Carrick (1970-1993)
717	R J Blakey (1985-2004)
717	G H Hirst (1891-1929)
687	J H Hampshire (1961-1981)
676	D Denton (1894-1920)
674	G Boycott (1962-1986)
602	H Sutcliffe (1919-1945)
580	A McGrath (1995-2012)
577	D Byas (1986-2001)
568	D B Close (1949-1970)
548	M Leyland (1920-1947)
545	C White (1990-2007)
544	D E V Padgett (1951-1971)
536	R Illingworth (1951-1983)
521	J G Binks (1955-1969)
517	D Hunter (1888-1909)
513	S Haigh (1895-1913)

Matches	*Player*
512	M D Moxon (1980-1997)
510	Lord Hawke (1881-1911)
500	P J Sharpe (1958-1974)
485	P Holmes (1913-1933)
477	J V Wilson (1946-1962)
472	J Tunicliffe (1891-1907)
470	F S Trueman (1949-1968)
467	J D Love (1975-1989)
451	D Wilson (1957-1974)
449	A Sidebottom (1973-1991)
445	G G Macauley(1920-1935)
440	C M Old (1966-1982)
427	A Dolphin (1905-1927)
413	E Robinson (1919-1931)
411	P J Hartley (1985-1997)
408	A Wood (1927-1946)
401	A Mitchell (1922-1945)
401	A G Nicholson (1962-1975)

FRIENDS PROVIDENT TROPHY, CHELTENHAM & GLOUCESTER TROPHY, GILLETTE CUP AND NATWEST TROPHY 1963-2009

WINNERS 1965, 1969 AND 2002

SEMI-FINALISTS 1980, 1982, 1995, 1996, 1999, 2004, 2005 AND 2008

Played 137, Won 77 (in Yorkshire 36, Away 41). Lost 54 (in Yorkshire 21, Away 33).
No Result 4 (in Yorkshire 3, Away 1). Abandoned 2 (in Yorkshire 1, Away 1)

Highest Score:	By Yorkshire:	411:6 v. Devon at Exmouth, 2004
	Against Yorkshire:	339:7 by Northamptonshire at Northampton, 2006
†Lowest Score:	By Yorkshire:	76 v. Surrey at Harrogate, 1970
	Against Yorkshire:	53 by Ireland at Leeds, 1997
Highest Individual Score:	For Yorkshire:	160 M J Wood v. Devon at Exmouth, 2004
	Against Yorkshire:	177 S A Newman for Surrey at The Oval, 2009

Highest Partnerships: For Yorkshire:

1st wkt	242*	M D Moxon (107*) and A A Metcalfe (127*) v. Warwickshire at Leeds, 1990
2nd wkt	202	G Boycott (87) and C W J Athey (115) v. Kent at Leeds, 1980
3rd wkt	164	A McGrath (105*) and J A Rudolph (82) v. Scotland at Leeds, 2008
4th wkt	207	S A Kellett (107) and C White (113) v. Ireland at Leeds, 1995
5th wkt	160*	G M Fellows (80*) and C White (73*) v Surrey at Leeds, 2001
6th wkt	128*	A McGrath (72*) and G M Fellows (68*) v. Essex at Chelmsford, 2002
7th wkt	102	D L Bairstow (92) and C M Old (55*) v. Worcestershire at Leeds, 1982
8th wkt	79	P J Hartley (83) and D Gough (46) v. Ireland at Leeds, 1997
9th wkt	66	T T Bresnan (55) and A Shahzad (33) v. Durham at Chester-le-Street, 2008
10th wkt	29*	R Illingworth (32*) and A G Nicholson (15*) v. Warwickshire at Birmingham, 1968

Best Bowling:	For Yorkshire:	7 for 27 D Gough v. Ireland at Leeds, 1997
	Against Yorkshire:	7 for 33 R D Jackman for Surrey at Harrogate, 1970
Most Economical Bowling:	For Yorkshire:	12-9-4-1 D Wilson v. Norfolk at Lakenham, 1969
	Against Yorkshire:	12-6-10-0 D L Underwood for Kent at Canterbury, 1981
Most Expensive Bowling:	For Yorkshire:	10-0-82-3 T T Bresnan v. Northamptonshire at Northampton, 2006
	Against Yorkshire:	12-1-96-0 M E. Waugh for Essex at Chelmsford, 1995

†Lowest score is either the lowest all-out score or the lowest score at completion of 60 overs (65 overs in 1963. 50 overs from 1999)

Centuries (23)

C W J Athey	115	v. Kent at Leeds, 1980
G Boycott	146	v. Surrey at Lord's, 1965
M T G Elliott	128*	v. Somerset at Lord's, 2002
J H Hampshire	110	v. Durham at Middlesbrough, 1978
S A Kellett	107	v. Ireland at Leeds, 1995
D S Lehmann (2)	105	v. Glamorgan at Cardiff, 1997
	118*	v. Northamptonshire at Northampton, 2006
A McGrath (3)	135*	v. Lancashire at Manchester, 2007
	100	v. Durham at Leeds, 2007
	105*	v. Scotland at Leeds, 2008
A A Metcalfe	127*	v. Warwickshire at Leeds, 1990
M D Moxon (2)	107*	v. Warwickshire at Leeds, 1990
	137	v. Nottinghamshire at Leeds, 1996
J A Rudolph (2)	100	v. Leicestershire at Leeds, 2007
	118	v Gloucestershire at Leeds, 2009
M P Vaughan	116*	v Lancashire at Manchester, 2004
C White (4)	113	v. Ireland at Leeds, 1995
	100*	v. Surrey at Leeds, 2002
	112	v. Northamptonshire at Northampton, 2006
	101*	v. Durham at Chester-le-Street, 2006
M J Wood (2)	118*	v. Cambridgeshire at March, 2003
	160	v. Devon at Exmouth, 2004
Younus Khan	100	v. Nottinghamshire at Nottingham, 2007

FRIENDS PROVIDENT TROPHY, CHELTENHAM & GLOUCESTER TROPHY, GILLETTE CUP AND NATWEST TROPHY RECORDS 1963-2009 — *(Continued)*

5 Wickets in an Innings (8)

D Gough (2)	7 for 27 v. Ireland at Leeds, 1997
	5 for 30 v. Yorkshire CB at Harrogate, 2000
P J Hartley	5 for 46 v. Hampshire at Southampton, 1990
M J Hoggard	5 for 65 v. Somerset at Lord's, 2002
R Illingworth	5 for 29 v. Surrey at Lord's, 1965
A Sidebottom	5 for 27 v. Glamorgan at Leeds, 1987
G B Stevenson	5 for 27 v. Berkshire at Reading, 1983
F S Trueman	6 for 15 v. Somerset at Taunton, 1965

Man of the Match Awards

M D Moxon	5
J H Hampshire	4
C White	4
M P Vaughan	3
C W J Athey	2
M G Bevan	2
G Boycott	2
G L Brophy	2
D Gough	2
A McGrath	2
A A Metcalfe	2
P J Sharpe	2
C E W Silverwood	2
M J Wood	2

D L Bairstow, T T Bresnan, P Carrick, D B Close, M T G Elliott, G M Fellows, S D Fletcher, P J Hartley, P M Hutchison, R Illingworth, S A Kellett, B Leadbeater, D S Lehmann, M J Lumb, R M Pyrah, A Sidebottom, G B Stevenson, F S Trueman (1 each). (54 Awards: 32 Players).

versus Derbyshire: Played 5, Won 3 (in Yorkshire 1, Away 2), Lost 1 (in Yorkshire), No Result 1 (Away)

Highest Score:	By Yorkshire	253:4	at Derby, 2007
	By Derbyshire	251:6	at Leeds, 2006
Lowest Score:	By Yorkshire	219:8	at Lord's, 1969
	By Derbyshire	94	at Leeds, 2008
Highest Individual Score:	For Yorkshire	81	J A Rudolph at Derby, 2007
	For Derbyshire	100	C R Taylor at Leeds, 2006
Best Bowling:	For Yorkshire	3-16	A McGrath at Leeds, 2008
	For Derbyshire	3-31	A Ward at Lord's, 1969

versus Durham: Played 9, Won 5 (in Yorkshire 3, Away 2), Lost 4 (in Yorkshire 2, Away 2)

Highest Score:	By Yorkshire	268:7	at Chester-le-Street, 2009
	By Durham	266:8	at Leeds, 2007
Lowest Score:	By Yorkshire	135	at Harrogate, 1973
	By Durham	166	at Leeds, 2009
Highest Individual Score:	For Yorkshire	110	J H Hampshire at Middlesbrough, 1978
	For Durham	124*	J P Maher at Chester-le-Street, 2006
Best Bowling:	For Yorkshire	4-9	C M Old at Middlesbrough, 1978
	For Durham	5-15	B R Lander at Harrogate, 1973

versus Essex: Played 4, Won 3 (in Yorkshire 1, Away 2), Lost 1 (Away)

Highest Score:	By Yorkshire	307:3	at Chelmsford, 1995
	By Essex	285:8	at Chelmsford, 2008
Lowest Score:	By Yorkshire	198	at Chelmsford, 2008
	By Essex	132	at Leeds, 1982
Highest Individual Score:	For Yorkshire	92	S A Kellett at Chelmsford, 1995
	For Essex	95	A N Cook at Chelmsford, 2008
Best Bowling:	For Yorkshire	3-21	A Sidebottom at Leeds, 1982
	For Essex:	3-30	R N ten Doeschate at Chelmsford, 2008

FRIENDS PROVIDENT TROPHY, CHELTENHAM & GLOUCESTER TROPHY, GILLETTE CUP AND NATWEST TROPHY RECORDS 1963-2009 — *(Continued)*

versus Glamorgan: Played 2, Won 1 (in Yorkshire), Lost 1 (Away)

Highest Score:	By Yorkshire	236:8	at Cardiff, 1997
	By Glamorgan	237:9	at Cardiff, 1997
Lowest Score:	By Yorkshire	—	
	By Glamorgan	83	at Leeds, 1987
Highest Individual Score:	For Yorkshire	105	D S Lehmann at Cardiff, 1997
	For Glamorgan	62	M P Maynard at Cardiff, 1997
Best Bowling:	For Yorkshire	5-27	A Sidebottom at Leeds, 1987
	For Glamorgan	3-26	D A Cosker at Cardiff, 1997

versus Gloucestershire: Played 7, Won 2 (Away 2), Lost 5 (in Yorkshire 2, Away 3)

Highest Score:	By Yorkshire	243:6	at Bristol, 2004
		243:8	at Bristol, 1993
	By Gloucestershire	269	at Leeds, 2009
Lowest Score:	By Yorkshire	217:9	at Bristol, 2009
	By Gloucestershire	201	at Bristol, 2008
Highest Individual Score:	For Yorkshire	118	J A Rudolph at Leeds, 2009
	For Gloucestershire	143*	C M Spearman at Bristol, 2004
Best Bowling:	For Yorkshire	4-31	T T Bresnan at Bristol, 2008
	For Gloucestershire	4-21	M J Procter at Leeds, 1976

versus Hampshire: Played 5, Won 2 (in Yorkshire 1, Away 1), Lost 3 (in Yorkshire 0, Away 3)

Highest Score:	By Yorkshire	233:6	at Bradford, 1974
	By Hampshire	261	at Bournemouth, 1977
Lowest Score:	By Yorkshire	118	at Southampton, 1990
	By Hampshire	192	at Bradford, 1974
Highest Individual Score:	For Yorkshire	93*	C W J Athey at Southampton, 1980
	For Hampshire	100	S M Ervine at Southampton, 2005
Best Bowling:	For Yorkshire	5-46	P J Hartley at Southampton, 1990
	For Hampshire	5-35	J M Rice at Bournemouth, 1977

versus Kent: Played 3, Won 1 (in Yorkshire 1, Away 0), Lost 2 (in Yorkshire 0, Away 2)

Highest Score:	By Yorkshire	279:6	at Leeds, 1980
	By Kent	233	at Leeds, 1980
Lowest Score:	By Yorkshire	148	at Canterbury, 1971
	By Kent	233	at Leeds, 1980
Highest Individual Score:	For Yorkshire	115	C W J Athey at Leeds, 1980
	For Kent	118*	C J Tavaré at Canterbury, 1981
Best Bowling:	For Yorkshire	4-35	A Sidebottom at Leeds, 1980
	For Kent	5-25	B D Julien at Canterbury, 1971

versus Lancashire: Played 12, Won 5 (in Yorkshire 2, Away 3), Lost 6 (in Yorkshire 1, Away 5), No result 1 (in Yorkshire)

Highest Score:	By Yorkshire	292:4	at Leeds, 2006
	By Lancashire	293:9	at Manchester, 1996
Lowest Score:	By Yorkshire	173	at Leeds, 1974
	By Lancashire	169	at Leeds, 1995
Highest Individual Score:	For Yorkshire	135*	A McGrath at Manchester, 2007
	For Lancashire	141*	B J Hodge at Manchester, 2007
Best Bowling:	For Yorkshire	4-18	G S Blewett at Manchester, 1999
	For Lancashire	4-17	P Lever at Leeds, 1974

FRIENDS PROVIDENT TROPHY, CHELTENHAM & GLOUCESTER TROPHY, GILLETTE CUP AND NATWEST TROPHY RECORDS 1963-2009 — *(Continued)*

versus Leicestershire: Played 7, Won 3 (in Yorkshire 1, Away 2), Lost 4 (in Yorkshire 3, Away 1)

Highest Score:	By Yorkshire	310:5	at Leicester, 1997
	By Leicestershire	284:4	at Leeds, 2007
Lowest Score:	By Yorkshire	109	at Leeds, 1975
	By Leicestershire	168	at Leicester, 1965
Highest Individual Score:	For Yorkshire	100	J A Rudolph at Leeds, 2007
	For Leicestershire	90	I J Sutcliffe at Leicester, 1997
Best Bowling:	For Yorkshire	4-18	H P Cooper at Leeds, 1975
	For Leicestershire	5-34	P A J DeFreitas at Leeds, 1987

versus Middlesex: Played 5, Won 2 (in Yorkshire 2, Away 0), Lost 3 (in Yorkshire 1, Away 2)

Highest Score:	By Yorkshire	205:9	at Leeds, 1986
	By Middlesex	225:7	at Leeds, 1988
Lowest Score:	By Yorkshire	90	at Lord's, 1964
	By Middlesex	151	at Lord's, 1964
Highest Individual Score:	For Yorkshire	73*	D Byas at Leeds, 1996
	For Middlesex	104	P N Weekes at Leeds, 1996
Best Bowling:	For Yorkshire	4-29	H P Cooper at Lord's, 1979 and C Shaw at Leeds, 1988
	For Middlesex	4-24	N G Cowans at Leeds, 1986

versus Northamptonshire: Played 8, Won 4 (in Yorkshire 2, Away 2), Lost 4 (in Yorkshire 2, Away 2)

Highest Score:	By Yorkshire	341:3	at Northampton, 2006
	By Northamptonshire	339:7	at Northampton, 2006
Lowest Score:	By Yorkshire	165	at Leeds, 1983
	By Northamptonshire	211:7	at Leeds, 1983
Highest Individual Score:	For Yorkshire	118*	D S Lehmann at Northampton, 2006
	For Northamptonshire	161	D J G Sales at Northampton, 2006
Best Bowling:	For Yorkshire	4-36	D Gough at Northampton, 2000
	For Northamptonshire	5-33	B J Griffiths at Leeds, 1983

versus Nottinghamshire: Played 6, Won 5 (in Yorkshire 4, Away 1), Lost 0, Abandoned 1 (in Yorkshire)

Highest Score:	By Yorkshire	345:5	at Leeds, 1996
	By Nottinghamshire	243	at Nottingham, 2007
Lowest Score:	By Yorkshire	191	at Scarborough, 1969
	By Nottinghamshire	123	at Scarborough, 1969
Highest Individual Score:	For Yorkshire	137	M D Moxon at Leeds, 1996
	For Nottinghamshire	100*	J B Bolus at Middlesbrough, 1963
Best Bowling:	For Yorkshire	4-30	F S Trueman at Middlesbrough, 1963
	For Nottinghamshire	4-33	K Gilhouley at Middlesbrough, 1963

versus Somerset: Played 5, Won 2 (in Yorkshire 0, Away 2), Lost 3 (in Yorkshire 2, Away 1)

Highest Score:	By Yorkshire	260:4	at Lord's, 2002
	By Somerset	256:8	at Lord's, 2002
Lowest Score:	By Yorkshire	150	at Taunton, 1966
	By Somerset	63	at Taunton, 1965
Highest Individual Score:	For Yorkshire	128*	M T G Elliott at Lord's, 2002
	For Somerset	87*	I V A Richards at Leeds, 1985
Best Bowling:	For Yorkshire	6-15	F S Trueman at Taunton, 1965
	For Somerset	4-33	R Palmer at Taunton, 1966

FRIENDS PROVIDENT TROPHY, CHELTENHAM & GLOUCESTER TROPHY, GILLETTE CUP AND NATWEST TROPHY RECORDS 1963-2009 — *(Continued)*

versus Surrey: Played 9, Won 5 (in Yorkshire 2, Away 3), Lost 4 (in Yorkshire 2, Away 2)

Highest Score:	By Yorkshire	330:6	at The Oval, 2009
	By Surrey	329:8	at The Oval, 2009
Lowest Score:	By Yorkshire	76	at Harrogate, 1970
	By Surrey	134	at The Oval, 1969 and 134:8 at Harrogate, 1970
Highest Individual Score:	For Yorkshire	146	G Boycott at Lord's, 1965
	For Surrey	177	S A Newman at The Oval, 2009
Best Bowling:	For Yorkshire	5-29	R Illingworth at Lord's, 1965
	For Surrey	7-33	R D Jackman at Harrogate, 1970

versus Sussex: Played 6, Won 2, (in Yorkshire 1, Away 1), Lost 4 (in Yorkshire 2, Away 2)

Highest Score:	By Yorkshire	270	at Hove, 1963
	By Sussex	292	at Hove, 1963
Lowest Score:	By Yorkshire	125	at Leeds, 1986
	By Sussex	212:9	at Hove, 1996
Highest Individual Score:	For Yorkshire	82	M P Vaughan at Leeds, 2009
	For Sussex	90	J M Parks at Hove, 1963
Best Bowling:	For Yorkshire	4-35	T T Bresnan at Leeds, 2009
	For Sussex	4-17	G S Le Roux at Leeds, 1986

versus Warwickshire: Played 10, Won 2 (in Yorkshire 1, Away 1), Lost 6 (in Yorkshire 3, Away 3), No Result 1 (in Yorkshire), Abandoned 1 (Away)

Highest Score:	By Yorkshire	242:0	at Leeds, 1990
	By Warwickshire	245	at Leeds, 1993
Lowest Score:	By Yorkshire	123	at Birmingham, 1991
	By Warwickshire	157	at Birmingham, 1965
Highest Individual Score:	For Yorkshire	127*	A A Metcalfe at Leeds, 1990
	For Warwickshire	113	K D Smith at Birmingham, 1982
Best Bowling:	For Yorkshire	3-26	P Carrick at Leeds, 1990
	For Warwickshire	4-16	A A Donald at Birmingham, 1991

versus Worcestershire: Played 5, Won 2 (in Yorkshire), Lost 2 (Away), No Result 1 (in Yorkshire)

Highest Score:	By Yorkshire	290:7	at Leeds, 1982
	By Worcestershire	286:5	at Leeds, 1982
Lowest Score:	By Yorkshire	177	at Worcester, 2003
	By Worcestershire	215:7	at Leeds, 2007
Highest Individual Score:	For Yorkshire	92	D L Bairstow at Leeds, 1982
	For Worcestershire	105	G M Turner at Leeds, 1982
Best Bowling:	For Yorkshire	3-41	I J Harvey at Leeds, 2005
	For Worcestershire	5-49	M Hayward at Worcester, 2003

versus Ireland: Played 4, Won 4 (in Yorkshire 3, Away 1), Lost 0

Highest Score:	By Yorkshire	299:6	at Leeds, 1995
	By Ireland	228:7	at Leeds, 1995
Lowest Score:	By Yorkshire	249	at Leeds, 1997
	By Ireland	53	at Leeds, 1997
Highest Individual Score:	For Yorkshire	113	C White at Leeds, 1995
	For Ireland	82	S J S Warke at Leeds, 1995
Best Bowling:	For Yorkshire	7-27	D Gough at Leeds, 1997
	For Ireland	3-26	P McCrum at Leeds, 1997

FRIENDS PROVIDENT TROPHY, CHELTENHAM & GLOUCESTER TROPHY, GILLETTE CUP AND NATWEST TROPHY RECORDS 1963-2009 — *(Continued)*

versus Scotland: Played 5, Won 5 (in Yorkshire 3, Away 2)

Highest Score:	By Yorkshire	259:8	at Edinburgh, 2007
	By Scotland	244	at Leeds, 2008
Lowest Score:	By Yorkshire	—	
	By Scotland	193:8	at Edinburgh, 2008
Highest Individual Score:	For Yorkshire	105*	A McGrath at Leeds, 2008
	For Scotland	73	I L Philip at Leeds, 1989
Best Bowling:	For Yorkshire	3-22	T T Bresnan at Edinburgh, 2007
	For Scotland	3-62	J A R Blain at Edinburgh, 2007

versus Bedfordshire: Played 1, Won 1 (Away)

Highest Score:	By Yorkshire	212:6	at Luton, 2001
	By Bedfordshire	211:9	at Luton, 2001
Highest Individual Score:	For Yorkshire	88	D S Lehmann at Luton, 2001
	For Bedfordshire	34	O J Clayton at Luton, 2001
Best Bowling:	For Yorkshire	4-39	R J Sidebottom at Luton, 2001
	For Bedfordshire	4-54	S Rashid at Luton, 2001

versus Berkshire: Played 2, Won 2 (Away 2)

Highest Score:	By Yorkshire	131:3	at Reading, 1983
	By Berkshire	128:9	at Reading, 1983
Lowest Score:	By Yorkshire	Have not been dismissed, nor batted through entire overs	
	By Berkshire	105	at Finchampstead, 1988
Highest Individual Score:	For Yorkshire	74*	A A Metcalfe at Finchampstead, 1988
	For Berkshire	29	G R J Roope at Reading, 1983
Best Bowling:	For Yorkshire	5-27	G B Stevenson at Reading, 1983
	For Berkshire	1-15	M Lickley at Reading, 1983

versus Cambridgeshire: Played 3, Won 3 (in Yorkshire 2, Away 1)

Highest Score:	By Yorkshire	299:5	at March, 2003
	By Cambridgeshire	214:8	at March, 2003
Lowest Score:	By Cambridgeshire	176:8	at Leeds, 1986
Highest Individual Score:	For Yorkshire	118*	M J Wood March, 2003
	For Cambridgeshire	85	J D R Benson at Leeds, 1986
Best Bowling:	For Yorkshire	3-11	A G Nicholson at Castleford, 1967
	For Cambridgeshire	3-53	Ajaz Akhtar at March, 2003

versus Cheshire: Played 1, Won 1 (Away)

Highest Score:	By Yorkshire	160:0	at Oxton, 1985
	By Cheshire	159:7	at Oxton, 1985
Highest Individual Score:	For Yorkshire	82*	M D Moxon at Oxton, 1985
	For Cheshire	46	K Teesdale at Oxton, 1985
Best Bowling:	For Yorkshire	2-17	G B Stevenson at Oxton, 1985
	For Cheshire	No wicket taken	

versus Devon: Played 4, Won 4, (Away 4)

Highest Score:	By Yorkshire	411:6	at Exmouth, 2004
	By Devon	279:8	at Exmouth, 2004
Lowest Score:	By Devon	80	at Exmouth, 1998
Highest Individual Score:	For Yorkshire	160	M J Wood at Exmouth, 2004
	For Devon	83	P M Roebuck at Exmouth, 1994
Best Bowling:	For Yorkshire	4-26	D S Lehmann at Exmouth, 2002
	For Devon	2-42	A O F Le Fleming at Exmouth, 1994

FRIENDS PROVIDENT TROPHY, CHELTENHAM & GLOUCESTER TROPHY, GILLETTE CUP AND NATWEST TROPHY RECORDS 1963-2009 — *(Continued)*

versus Dorset: Played 1, Won 1, (Away)

Scores:	By Yorkshire	101:2	at Bournemouth, 2004
	By Dorset	97	at Bournemouth, 2004
Highest Individual Score:	For Yorkshire	71*	M J Wood at Bournemouth, 2004
	For Dorset	23	C L Park at Bournemouth, 2004
Best Bowling:	For Yorkshire	4-18	C E W Silverwood at Bournemouth, 2004
	For Devon	2-31	D J L Worrad at Bournemouth, 2004

versus Herefordshire: Played 1, Won 1 (Away)

Highest Score:	By Yorkshire	275:8	at Kington, 1999
	By Herefordshire	124:5	at Kington, 1999
Highest Individual Score:	For Yorkshire	77	G S Blewett at Kington, 1999
	For Herefordshire	39	R D Hughes at Kington, 1999
Best Bowling:	For Yorkshire	2-22	G M Hamilton at Kington, 1999
	For Herefordshire	2-41	C W Boroughs at Kington, 1999

versus Norfolk: Played 2, Won 2 (in Yorkshire 1, Away 1)

Highest Score:	By Yorkshire	167	at Lakenham, 1969
	By Norfolk	104	at Leeds, 1990
Lowest Score:	By Yorkshire	167	at Lakenham, 1969
	By Norfolk	78	at Lakenham, 1969
Highest Individual Score:	For Yorkshire	56*	M D Moxon at Leeds, 1990
	For Norfolk	25	R J Finney at Leeds, 1990
Best Bowling:	For Yorkshire	3-8	P Carrick at Leeds, 1990
	For Norfolk	6-48	T I Moore at Lakenham, 1969

versus Northumberland: Played 1, Won 1 (Away)

Highest Score:	By Yorkshire	138:2	(51.3 overs) at Leeds, 1992
	By Northumberland	137	at Leeds, 1992
Highest Individual Score:	For Yorkshire	38	S A Kellett at Leeds, 1992
	For Northumberland	47	G R Morris at Leeds, 1992
Best Bowling:	For Yorkshire	3-18	M A Robinson at Leeds, 1992
	For Northumberland	2-22	S Greensword at Leeds, 1992

versus Shropshire: Played 2, Won 1 (Away 1), Lost 1 (Away 1)

Highest Score:	By Yorkshire	192	at Telford, 1984
	By Shropshire	229:5	at Telford, 1984
Lowest Score:	By Yorkshire	192	at Telford, 1984
	By Shropshire	185	at Wellington, 1976
Highest Individual Score:	For Yorkshire	59	J H Hampshire at Wellington, 1976
	For Shropshire	80	Mushtaq Mohammed at Telford, 1984
Best Bowling:	For Yorkshire	3-17	A L Robinson at Wellington, 1976
	For Shropshire	3-26	Mushtaq Mohammed at Telford, 1984

versus Wiltshire: Played 1, Won 1 (Away)

Highest Score:	By Yorkshire	304:7	at Trowbridge, 1987
	By Wiltshire	175	at Trowbridge, 1987
Highest Individual Score:	For Yorkshire	85	A A Metcalfe at Trowbridge, 1987
	For Wiltshire	62	J J Newman at Trowbridge, 1987
Best Bowling:	For Yorkshire	4-40	K Sharp at Trowbridge, 1987
	For Wiltshire	2-38	R C Cooper at Trowbridge, 1987

versus Yorkshire Cricket Board: Played 1, Won 1 (Away)

Scores:	By Yorkshire	240:5	at Harrogate, 2000
	By Yorkshire CB	130	at Harrogate, 2000
Highest Individual Score:	For Yorkshire	70	M P Vaughan at Harrogate, 2000
	For Yorkshire CB	31	R A Kettleborough at Harrogate, 2000
Best Bowling:	For Yorkshire	5-30	D Gough at Harrogate, 2000
	For Yorkshire CB	1-25	A E McKenna at Harrogate, 2000

CAREER AVERAGES FOR YORKSHIRE

FRIENDS PROVIDENT TROPHY, CHELTENHAM & GLOUCESTER TROPHY, GILLETTE CUP AND NATWEST TROPHY 1963-2009

Player	*M*	*Inns*	*NO*	*Runs*	*HS*	*Av'ge*	*100s*	*50s*	*Runs*	*Wkts*	*Av'ge*	*Ct/St*
Athey, C W J . . .	15	15	2	485	115	37.30	1	2	41	1	41.00	2
Bairstow, D L . .	34	27	5	492	92	22.36	—	2	—	—	—	38/3
Balderstone, J C	5	3	0	65	34	21.66	—	—	10	1	10.00	1
Batty, J D	3	2	0	7	4	3.50	—	—	97	1	97.00	1
Bevan, M G	8	8	2	388	91*	64.66	—	4	89	3	29.66	—
Binks, J G	16	10	1	107	22	11.88	—	—	—	—	—	15/6
Blain, J A R	3	2	0	13	7	6.50	—	—	63	3	21.00	—
Blakey, R J	48	35	13	516	75	23.45	—	2	—	—	—	54/5
Blewett, G S . . .	3	3	0	83	77	27.66	—	1	57	7	8.14	1
Booth, P A	1	1	1	6	6*	—	—	—	33	0	—	—
Bore, M K	3	2	1	0	0*	0.00	—	—	98	5	19.60	—
Boycott, G	40	39	4	1378	146	39.37	1	9	238	8	29.75	9
Bresnan, T T . .	**36**	**20**	**4**	**309**	**55**	**19.31**	**—**	**1**	**1360**	**47**	**28.93**	**8**
Brophy, G L . . .	**23**	**19**	**7**	**437**	**68**	**36.41**	**—**	**4**	**—**	**—**	**—**	**29/3**
Byas, D	34	32	3	912	73*	31.45	—	8	23	1	23.00	23
Carrick, P	32	23	3	320	54	16.00	—	1	741	24	30.87	6
Chapman, C . . .	1	—	—	—	—	—	—	—	—	—	—	1
Claydon, M E . .	7	2	0	15	9	7.50	—	—	293	8	36.62	—
Close, D B	15	15	2	407	96	31.30	—	2	357	22	16.22	6
Cooper, H P . . .	11	9	4	49	17	9.80	—	—	347	15	23.13	2
Cope, G A	4	2	2	1	1*	—	—	—	130	5	26.00	3
Craven, V J	4	3	1	38	26	19.00	—	—	41	2	20.50	2
Dawson, R K J .	22	7	0	77	24	11.00	—	—	762	15	50.80	9
Dawood, I	4	3	0	26	23	8.66	—	—	—	—	—	1/1
Dennis, S J	5	2	0	14	14	7.00	—	—	202	6	33.66	—
Elliott, M T G . .	1	1	1	128	128*	—	1	—	—	—	—	—
Fellows, G M . .	12	8	3	230	80*	46.00	—	2	55	0	—	3
Fisher, I D	3	1	0	5	5	5.00	—	—	87	3	29.00	2
Fletcher, S D . . .	15	7	4	36	16*	12.00	—	—	576	15	38.40	2
Gale, A W	**26**	**22**	**4**	**567**	**69***	**35.43**	**—**	**4**	**—**	**—**	**—**	**2**
Gilbert, C R	3	2	0	9	6	4.50	—	—	134	6	22.33	—
Gillespie, J N . .	11	2	1	15	15*	15.00	—	—	363	9	40.33	3
Gough, D	44	20	3	251	46	14.76	—	—	1596	86	18.55	9
Gray, A K D . . .	3	1	0	0	0	0.00	—	—	152	5	30.40	3
Grayson, A P . . .	7	6	0	91	29	15.16	—	—	241	4	60.25	3
Guy, S M	12	7	1	45	22	7.50	—	—	—	—	—	17/3
Hamilton, G M .	9	8	3	146	39	29.20	—	—	254	15	16.93	2
Hampshire, A W	1	1	0	0	0	0.00	—	—	—	—	—	1
Hampshire, J H .	32	31	5	877	110	33.73	1	6	4	0	—	10
Harden R J	4	4	0	54	37	13.50	—	—	—	—	—	—
Hartley, P J	28	17	8	250	83	27.77	—	2	1108	45	24.62	2
Hartley, S N . . .	15	12	0	263	69	21.91	—	2	114	1	114.00	5
Harvey, I J	4	4	0	151	74	37.75	—	2	184	6	30.66	1
Hoggard, M J . .	16	4	4	8	7*	—	—	—	555	23	24.13	1
Hutchison, P M .	3	1	1	4	4*	—	—	—	62	5	12.40	—
Hutton, R A	13	10	2	136	61	17.00	—	1	341	13	26.23	3
Illingworth, R . .	15	10	7	150	45	50.00	—	—	260	8	32.50	7
Jaques, P A	**6**	**6**	**1**	**211**	**55***	**42.20**	**—**	**2**	**—**	**—**	**—**	**2**
Jarvis, P W	16	9	2	86	16	12.28	—	—	655	19	34.47	3
Johnson, C	4	4	0	62	44	15.50	—	—	—	—	—	—
Katich, S M	1	1	1	40	40*	—	—	—	—	—	—	—
Kellett, S A	9	7	0	246	107	35.14	1	1	—	—	—	6
Kirby, S P	2	1	0	0	0	0.00	—	—	74	2	37.00	—
Kruis, G J	25	9	5	42	11	10.50	—	—	774	26	29.76	3
Leadbeater, B . .	9	9	0	155	76	17.22	—	1	47	3	15.66	2

FRIENDS PROVIDENT TROPHY, CHELTENHAM & GLOUCESTER TROPHY, GILLETTE CUP AND NATWEST TROPHY 1963-2009 *(Continued)*

Player	*M*	*Inns*	*NO*	*Runs*	*HS*	*Av'ge*	*100s*	*50s*	*Runs*	*Wkts*	*Av'ge*	*Ct/St*
Lehmann, D S . .	23	19	5	853	118*	60.92	2	6	462	20	23.10	4
Lester, E I	1	1	0	0	0	0.00	—	—	—	—	—	—
Love, J D	21	18	3	266	67	17.73	—	3	39	2	19.50	5
Lumb, M J	20	18	3	628	89	41.86	—	4	—	—	—	6
Lumb, R G	12	12	0	222	56	18.50	—	1	—	—	—	—
Lyth, A	**11**	**9**	**1**	**218**	**83**	**27.25**	**—**	**1**	**—**	**—**	**—**	**4**
McGrath, A . . .	**60**	**54**	**8**	**1879**	**135***	**40.84**	**3**	**15**	**732**	**22**	**33.27**	**19**
Metcalfe, A A . .	20	20	3	714	127*	42.00	1	5	44	2	22.00	4
Middlebrook, J D	2	1	1	6	6*	—	—	—	38	0	—	3
Morris, A C	1	1	1	1	1*	—	—	—	43	1	43.00	—
Moxon, M D . . .	34	34	6	1316	137	47.00	2	10	68	4	17.00	12
Nicholson, A G .	17	12	4	42	15*	5.25	—	—	467	21	22.23	6
Old, C M	28	23	3	268	55*	13.40	—	1	799	43	18.58	7
Oldham, S	8	5	3	35	19	17.50	—	—	309	15	20.60	—
Padgett, D E V .	17	15	1	309	46	22.07	—	—	—	—	—	4
Parker, B	6	4	0	87	69	21.75	—	1	—	—	—	—
Patterson, S A .	**9**	**3**	**3**	**17**	**14***	**—**	**—**	**—**	**320**	**7**	**45.71**	**—**
Pickles, C S	3	2	0	15	12	7.50	—	—	111	4	27.75	1
Pyrah, R M . . .	**28**	**18**	**5**	**273**	**67**	**21.00**	**—**	**1**	**1015**	**40**	**25.37**	**12**
Ramage, A	4	1	0	14	14	14.00	—	—	167	4	41.75	1
Rana Naved -ul-Hasan	7	7	1	134	53*	22.33	—	1	324	10	32.40	4
Rashid, A U . . .	**18**	**11**	**2**	**105**	**41***	**11.66**	**—**	**—**	**466**	**13**	**35.84**	**5**
Richardson, R B	5	5	0	194	90	38.80	—	2	—	—	—	—
Robinson, A L . .	5	2	1	18	18*	18.00	—	—	179	9	19.88	1
Robinson, M A .	11	4	3	1	1*	1.00	—	—	390	12	32.50	—
Robinson, P E . .	8	5	0	113	66	22.60	—	1	—	—	—	3
Rudolph, J A . . .	26	25	3	873	118	39.68	2	5	8	0	—	16
Ryan, M	3	2	1	7	6*	7.00	—	—	149	5	29.80	3
Sayers, J J	**6**	**6**	**0**	**111**	**51**	**18.50**	**—**	**1**	**—**	**—**	**—**	**1**
Shahzad, A	**8**	**6**	**2**	**110**	**43***	**27.25**	**—**	**—**	**292**	**7**	**41.71**	**2**
Sharp, K	17	13	2	228	50	20.72	—	1	47	4	11.75	6
Sharpe, P J	22	20	1	331	68	17.42	—	2	—	—	—	18
Shaw, C	6	5	2	10	6*	3.33	—	—	194	11	17.63	—
Sidebottom, A . .	25	16	5	192	45	17.45	—	—	700	37	18.91	9
Sidebottom, R J .	14	2	1	13	7*	13.00	—	—	432	20	21.60	4
Silverwood,CEW	26	12	3	161	61	17.88	—	1	841	27	31.15	7
Smith, N	1	1	0	5	5	5.00	—	—	—	—	—	—
Squires, P J	2	2	0	46	42	23.00	—	—	—	—	—	1
Stemp, R D	11	3	2	1	1*	1.00	—	—	406	14	29.00	1
Stevenson, G B .	19	13	1	190	34	15.83	—	—	612	30	20.40	5
Stott, W B	2	2	0	30	30	15.00	—	—	—	—	—	—
Stringer, P M . . .	2	2	2	7	5*	—	—	—	21	4	5.25	—
Swallow, I G . . .	2	1	1	17	17*	—	—	—	16	0	—	—
Taylor, C R	1	—	—	—	—	—	—	—	—	—	—	—
Taylor, K	10	10	0	135	30	13.50	—	—	168	11	15.27	3
Tendulkar, S R .	2	2	1	53	32*	53.00	—	—	—	—	—	1
Thornicroft, N D	2	1	1	10	10*	—	—	—	97	1	97.00	1
Trueman, F S . .	11	9	1	127	28	15.87	—	—	348	21	16.57	5
Vaughan, M P . .	41	40	3	1356	116*	36.64	1	10	333	6	55.50	10
Wainwright, D J	**7**	**4**	**3**	**50**	**15***	**50.00**	**—**	**—**	**237**	**7**	**33.85**	**4**
Waring, J	1	1	1	1	1*	—	—	—	11	0	—	—
White, C	60	55	14	1809	113	44.12	4	10	1130	40	28.25	19
Whiteley, J P . . .	1	—	—	—	—	—	—	—	48	0	—	—
Wilson, D	15	13	1	72	16	6.00	—	—	391	21	18.62	10
Wood, M J	28	28	6	908	160	41.27	2	3	45	3	15.00	11
Woodford, J D . .	1	1	0	15	15	15.00	—	—	—	—	—	—
Younus Khan . . .	7	6	0	234	100	39.00	1	0	124	2	62.00	3
Yuvraj Singh . . .	1	1	0	27	27	27.00	—	—	27	0	—	—

WINNERS OF THE GILLETTE CUP, NATWEST TROPHY, CHELTENHAM & GLOUCESTER TROPHY AND FRIENDS PROVIDENT TROPHY 1963-2009

GILLETTE CUP

1963 **Sussex**, who beat Worcestershire by 14 runs
1964 **Sussex**, who beat Warwickshire by 8 wickets
1965 **Yorkshire**, who beat Surrey by 175 runs
1966 **Warwickshire**, who beat Worcestershire by 5 wickets
1967 **Kent**, who beat Somerset by 32 runs
1968 **Warwickshire**, who beat Sussex by 4 wickets
1969 **Yorkshire**, who beat Derbyshire by 69 runs
1970 **Lancashire**, who beat Sussex by 6 wickets
1971 **Lancashire**, who beat Kent by 24 runs
1972 **Lancashire**, who beat Warwickshire by 4 wickets
1973 **Gloucestershire**, who beat Sussex by 40 runs
1974 **Kent**, who beat Lancashire by 4 wickets
1975 **Lancashire**, who beat Middlesex by 7 wickets
1976 **Northamptonshire**, who beat Lancashire by 4 wickets
1977 **Middlesex**, who beat Glamorgan by 5 wickets
1978 **Sussex**, who beat Somerset by 5 wickets
1979 **Somerset**, who beat Northamptonshire by 45 runs
1980 **Middlesex**, who beat Surrey by 7 wickets

NATWEST TROPHY

1981 **Derbyshire**, who beat Northamptonshire by losing fewer wickets with the scores level.
1982 **Surrey**, who beat Warwickshire by 9 wickets
1983 **Somerset**, who beat Kent by 24 runs
1984 **Middlesex**, who beat Kent by 4 wickets
1985 **Essex**, who beat Nottinghamshire by 1 run
1986 **Sussex**, who beat Lancashire by 7 wickets
1987 **Nottinghamshire**, who beat Northamptonshire by 3 wickets
1988 **Middlesex**, who beat Worcestershire by 3 wickets
1989 **Warwickshire**, who beat Middlesex by 4 wickets
1990 **Lancashire**, who beat Northamptonshire by 7 wickets
1991 **Hampshire**, who beat Surrey by 4 wickets
1992 **Northamptonshire**, who beat Leicestershire by 8 wickets
1993 **Warwickshire**, who beat Sussex by 5 wickets
1994 **Worcestershire**, who beat Warwickshire by 8 wickets
1995 **Warwickshire**, who beat Northamptonshire by 4 wickets
1996 **Lancashire**, who beat Essex by 129 runs
1997 **Essex**, who beat Warwickshire by 9 wickets
1998 **Lancashire**, who beat Derbyshire by 9 wickets
1999 **Gloucestershire**, who beat Somerset by 50 runs
2000 **Gloucestershire,** who beat Warwickshire by 22 runs

CHELTENHAM & GLOUCESTER TROPHY

2001 **Somerset**, who beat Leicestershire by 41 runs
2002 **Yorkshire**, who beat Somerset by 6 wickets
2003 **Gloucestershire**, who beat Worcestershire by 7 wickets
2004 **Gloucestershire**, who beat Worcestershire by 8 wickets
2005 **Hampshire**, who beat Warwickshire by 18 runs
2006 **Sussex**, who beat Lancashire by 15 runs

FRIENDS PROVIDENT TROPHY

2007 **Durham**, who beat Hampshire by 125 runs
2008 **Essex,** who beat Kent by 5 wickets
2009 **Hampshire,** who beat Sussex by 6 wickets

CLYDESDALE BANK 40, PRO40, NATIONAL AND SUNDAY LEAGUES 1969-2012

JOHN PLAYER SPECIAL LEAGUE WINNERS 1983

Played 672, Won 301 (in Yorkshire 166, Away 135), Lost 310 (in Yorkshire 139, Away 171)
Ties 4 No Result 24 Abandoned 33

Highest Score:	By Yorkshire	352:6 v. Nottinghamshire at Scarborough, 2001
	Against Yorkshire	375:4 by Surrey at Scarborough, 1994
†Lowest Score:	By Yorkshire	54 v. Essex at Leeds, 2003
	Against Yorkshire	23 by Middlesex at Leeds, 1974
Highest Individual Score:	For Yorkshire	191 D S Lehmann v. Nottinghamshire at Scarborough, 2001
	Against Yorkshire	155* B A Richards for Hampshire at Hull, 1970
Most Runs in a Season:		851 J A Rudolph in 2010

†Lowest score is the lowest all-out score or the lowest score at completion of allotted overs

Highest Partnerships: For Yorkshire

1st wkt	233*	A W Gale (125*) and J A Rudolph (101*) v. Essex at Chelmsford, 2010
2nd wkt	172	D Byas (86) and D S Lehmann (99) v. Kent at Maidstone, 1998
3rd wkt	176	R J Blakey (86) and S R Tendulkar (107) v. Lancashire at Leeds, 1992
4th wkt	198*	M T G Elliott (115*) and A McGrath (85*) v. Kent at Leeds, 2002
5th wkt	190	R J Blakey (96) and M J Foster (118) v. Leicestershire at Leicester, 1993
6th wkt	110	B Leadbeater (69) and C Johnson (51*) v. Nottinghamshire at Hull, 1972
7th wkt	129*	D Byas (74*) and D Gough (72*) v. Leicestershire at Leicester, 1991
8th wkt	89	R J Blakey (60) and R K J Dawson (41) v. Leicestershire at Scarborough, 2002
9th wkt	88	S N Hartley (67) and A Ramage (32*) v. Middlesex at Lord's, 1982
10th wkt	64	R J Blakey (47) and R J Sidebottom (30*) v. Glamorgan at Leeds, 2002

Best Bowling:	For Yorkshire	7 for 15 R A Hutton v. Worcestershire at Leeds, 1969
	Against Yorkshire	6 for 15 A A Donald for Warwickshire at Birmingham, 1995
Most Economical Bowling:	For Yorkshire	8-5-3-3 A L Robinson v. Derbyshire at Scarborough, 1973
	Against Yorkshire	8-4-6-2 P J Sainsbury for Hampshire at Hull, 1970
		8-5-6-3 M J Procter for Gloucestershire at Cheltenham, 1979
Most Expensive Bowling:	For Yorkshire	9-0-87-1 T T Bresnan v. Somerset at Taunton, 2005
	Against Yorkshire	9-0-78-1 Mohammed Akram for Surrey at The Oval, 2005
Most Wickets In A Season:		37 M J Hoggard in 2000

CLYDESDALE BANK 40, PRO40, NATIONAL AND SUNDAY LEAGUES 1969-2012 *(Continued)*

Centuries (57)

C W J Athey	118	v. Leicestershire at Leicester, 1978
J M Bairstow	114	v. Middlesex at Lord's, 2011
G S Ballance	103*	v. Unicorns at Scarborough, 2012
M G Bevan (2)	103*	v. Gloucestershire at Middlesbrough, 1995
	101	v. Worcestershire at Scarborough, 1995
G Boycott (2)	104*	v. Glamorgan at Colwyn Bay, 1973
	108*	v. Northamptonshire at Huddersfield, 1974
R J Blakey (3)	100*	v. Gloucestershire at Cheltenham, 1990
	130*	v. Kent at Scarborough, 1991
	105*	v. Warwickshire at Scarborough, 1992
D Byas (3)	106*	v. Derbyshire at Chesterfield, 1993
	101*	v. Nottinghamshire at Leeds, 1994
	111*	v. Lancashire at Leeds, 1996
M T G Elliott (2)	109	v. Leicestershire at Leicester, 2002
	115*	v. Kent at Leeds, 2002
S P Fleming	139*	v. Warwickshire at Leeds, 2003
M J Foster	118	v. Leicestershire at Leicester, 1993
A W Gale (2)	125*	v Essex at Chelmsford, 2010
	112	v. Kent at Canterbury, 2011
J H Hampshire (6)	108	v. Nottinghamshire at Sheffield, 1970
	119	v. Leicestershire at Hull, 1971
	106*	v. Lancashire at Manchester, 1972
	111*	v. Sussex at Hastings, 1973
	100*	v. Warwickshire at Birmingham, 1975
	114*	v. Northamptonshire at Scarborough, 1978
P A Jaques	105	v Sussex at Leeds, 2004
S A Kellett	118*	v. Derbyshire at Leeds, 1992
D S Lehmann (3)	103	v. Leicestershire at Scarborough, 2001
	191	v. Nottinghamshire at Scarborough, 2001
	104	v. Somerset at Taunton, 2002
J D Love (3)	100*	v. Gloucestershire at Gloucester, 1985
	104*	v. Nottinghamshire at Hull, 1986
	118*	v. Surrey at Leeds, 1987
R G Lumb	101	v. Nottinghamshire at Scarborough, 1976
A Lyth	109*	v Sussex at Scarborough, 2009
A McGrath (2)	102	v. Kent at Canterbury, 2001
	148	v. Somerset at Taunton, 2006
A A Metcalfe (2)	115*	v. Gloucestershire at Scarborough, 1984
	116	v. Middlesex at Lord's, 1991
M D Moxon (3)	105	v. Somerset at Scarborough, 1990
	129*	v. Surrey at The Oval, 1991
	112	v. Sussex at Middlesbrough, 1991
R B Richardson	103	v. Nottinghamshire at Nottingham, 1993
J A Rudolph (7)	127	v. Somerset at Scarborough, 2007
	120	v. Leicestershire at Leeds, 2008
	101*	v Essex at Chelmsford, 2010
	105	v. Derbyshire at Chesterfield, 2010
	124*	v. Middlesex at Scarborough, 2010
	106	v. Warwickshire at Scarborough, 2010
	132*	v. Sussex at Scarborough 2011
K Sharp (2)	112*	v. Worcestershire at Worcester, 1985
	114	v. Essex at Chelmsford, 1985
S R Tendulkar	107	v. Lancashire at Leeds, 1992
M P Vaughan	116*	v. Kent at Leeds, 2005
C White	148	v. Leicestershire at Leicester, 1997
M J Wood (2)	105*	v. Somerset at Taunton, 2002
	111	v. Surrey at The Oval, 2005

CLYDESDALE BANK 40, PRO40, NATIONAL AND SUNDAY LEAGUES 1969-2012 *(Continued)*

5 Wickets in an Innings (31)

C W J Athey	5 for 35 v. Derbyshire at Chesterfield, 1981
M G Bevan	5 for 29 v. Sussex at Eastbourne, 1996
P Carrick (2)	5 for 22 v. Glamorgan at Leeds, 1991
	5 for 40 v. Sussex at Middlesbrough, 1991
H P Cooper (2)	6 for 14 v. Worcestershire at Worcester, 1975
	5 for 30 v. Worcestershire at Middlesbrough, 1978
D Gough (2)	5 for 13 v. Sussex at Hove, 1994
	5 for 25 v. Surrey at Leeds, 1998
G M Hamilton (2)	5 for 16 v. Hampshire at Leeds, 1998
	5 for 34 v. Sussex at Scarborough, 2000
P .J. Hartley (2)	5 for 38 v. Worcestershire at Worcester, 1990
	5 for 36 v. Sussex at Scarborough, 1993
M J Hoggard (2)	5 for 28 v. Leicestershire at Leicester, 2000
	5 for 30 v. Northamptonshire at Northampton, 2000 (consecutive matches)
R A Hutton	7 for 15 v. Worcestershire at Leeds, 1969
P W Jarvis (3)	6 for 27 v. Somerset at Taunton, 1989
	5 for 18 v. Derbyshire at Leeds, 1990
	5 for 29 v. Northamptonshire at Northampton, 1992
A G Nicholson (2)	6 for 36 v. Somerset at Sheffield, 1972
	5 for 17 v. Nottinghamshire at Hull, 1972 (Consecutive matches).
C M Old (2)	5 for 33 v. Sussex at Hove, 1971
	5 for 38 v. Northamptonshire at Sheffield, 1972
S A Patterson	6 for 32 v. Derbyshire at Leeds, 2010
C Shaw	5 for 41 v. Hampshire at Bournemouth, 1984
R J Sidebottom (2)	6 for 40 v. Glamorgan at Cardiff, 1998
	5 for 42 v. Leicestershire at Leicester, 2003
G B Stevenson	5 for 41 v. Leicestershire at Leicester, 1976
S Stuchbury	5 for 16 v. Leicestershire at Leicester, 1982
N D Thornicroft	5 for 42 v. Gloucestershire at Leeds, 2003
C White	5 for 19 v. Somerset at Scarborough, 2002
D Wilson	6 for 18 v. Kent at Canterbury, 1969

versus Derbyshire: Played 43, Won 23 (in Yorkshire 13, Away 10), Lost 16 (in Yorkshire 8, Away 8), Tied 1 (Away), No Result 1, Abandoned 2

Highest Score:	By Yorkshire	276:6 at Chesterfield, 2010
	By Derbyshire	268:6 at Chesterfield, 2010
Lowest Score:	By Yorkshire	117 at Huddersfield, 1978
	By Derbyshire	87 at Scarborough, 1973
Highest Individual Score:	For Yorkshire	118* S A Kellett at Leeds, 1992
	For Derbyshire	109* C J Adams at Derby, 1997
Best Bowling:	For Yorkshire	6-32 S A Patterson at Leeds, 2010
	For Derbyshire	4-14 A E Warner at Chesterfield, 1995

versus Durham: Played 15, Won 7 (in Yorkshire 4, Away 3) Lost 6 (in Yorkshire 3, Away 3), No Result 1, Abandoned 1

Highest Score:	By Yorkshire	269:5 at Chester-le-Street, 2002
	By Durham	256:4 at Chester-le-Street, 2005
Lowest Score:	By Yorkshire	122 at Chester-le-Street, 2007
	By Durham	121 at Scarborough, 1997
Highest Individual Score:	For Yorkshire	83 A W Gale at Scarborough, 2009
	For Durham	114 W Larkins at Leeds, 1993
Best Bowling:	For Yorkshire	4-18 C White at Scarborough, 1997
	For Durham	4-20 S J E Brown at Leeds, 1995

CLYDESDALE BANK 40, PRO40, NATIONAL AND SUNDAY LEAGUES 1969-2012 *(Continued)*

versus Essex:	Played 38, Won 16 (in Yorkshire 9, Away 7) Lost 19 (in Yorkshire 10, Away 9), Abandoned 3	
Highest Score:	By Yorkshire	264:6 at Ilford, 1997
	By Essex	262:9 at Ilford, 1997
Lowest Score:	By Yorkshire	54 at Leeds, 2003
	By Essex	108 at Leeds, 1996
Highest Individual Score:	For Yorkshire	125* A W Gale at Chelmsford, 2010
	For Essex	114 N Hussain at Leeds, 1999
Best Bowling:	For Yorkshire	4-21 C White at Leeds, 1996
	For Essex	6-18 R E East at Hull, 1969
versus Glamorgan:	Played 36, Won 16 (in Yorkshire 8, Away 8), Lost 18 (in Yorkshire 7, Away 11), Abandoned 2	
Highest Score:	By Yorkshire	253:4 at Leeds, 1991
	By Glamorgan	238:8 at Colwyn Bay, 2003
Lowest Score:	By Yorkshire	139 at Hull, 1981
	By Glamorgan	90 at Neath, 1969
Highest Individual Score:	For Yorkshire	104* G Boycott at Colwyn Bay, 1973
	For Glamorgan	97* G P Ellis at Leeds, 1976
Best Bowling:	For Yorkshire	6-40 R J Sidebottom at Cardiff, 1998
	For Glamorgan	5-16 G C Holmes at Swansea, 1985
versus Gloucestershire:	Played 42, Won 17 (in Yorkshire 11, Away 6), Lost 20 (in Yorkshire 6, Away 14), No Result 3, Abandoned 2	
Highest Score:	By Yorkshire	262:7 at Bristol, 1996
	By Gloucestershire	294:6 at Cheltenham, 2010
Lowest Score:	By Yorkshire	115 at Leeds, 1973
	By Gloucestershire	90 at Tewkesbury, 1972
Highest Individual Score:	For Yorkshire	115* A A Metcalfe at Scarborough, 1984
	For Gloucestershire	146* S Young at Leeds, 1997
Best Bowling:	For Yorkshire	5-42 N D Thornicroft at Leeds, 2003
	For Gloucestershire	5-33 M C J Ball at Leeds, 2003
versus Hampshire:	Played 34, Won 13 (in Yorkshire 7, Away 6), Lost 19 (in Yorkshire 9, Away 10), No Result 1, Abandoned 1	
Highest Score:	By Yorkshire	264:2 at Southampton, 1995
	By Hampshire	257:6 at Middlesbrough, 1985
Lowest Score:	By Yorkshire	74:9 at Hull, 1970
	By Hampshire	122 at Leeds, 1994
Highest Individual Score:	For Yorkshire	98* M G Bevan at Leeds, 1996
	For Hampshire	155* B A Richards at Hull, 1970
Best Bowling:	For Yorkshire	5-16 G M Hamilton at Leeds, 1998
	For Hampshire	5-31 D W White at Southampton, 1969
versus Kent:	Played 49, Won 19 (in Yorkshire 11, Away 8), Lost 27 (in Yorkshire 10, Away 17) No Result 1, Abandoned 2	
Highest Score:	By Yorkshire	299:3 at Leeds, 2002
	By Kent	266:5 at Maidstone, 1998
Lowest Score:	By Yorkshire	75 at Leeds, 1995
	By Kent	105 at Canterbury, 1969
Highest Individual Score:	For Yorkshire	130* R J Blakey at Scarborough, 1991
	For Kent	118* M H Denness at Scarborough, 1976
Best Bowling:	For Yorkshire	6-18 D Wilson at Canterbury, 1969
	For Kent	6-32 M T Coles at Leeds, 2012

CLYDESDALE BANK 40, PRO40, NATIONAL AND SUNDAY LEAGUES 1969-2012 *(Continued)*

versus Lancashire:	Played 34, Won 10 (in Yorkshire 4, Away 6), Lost 19 (in Yorkshire 11, Away 8), No Result 3, Abandoned 2	
Highest Score:	By Yorkshire	260:6 at Leeds, 1992
	By Lancashire	264:3 at Leeds, 1992
Lowest Score:	By Yorkshire	81 at Leeds, 1998
	By Lancashire	68 at Leeds, 2000
Highest Individual Score:	For Yorkshire	111* D Byas at Leeds, 1996
	For Lancashire	102* N J Speak at Leeds, 1992
Best Bowling:	For Yorkshire	4-14 C White at Leeds, 2000
	For Lancashire	6-25 G Chapple at Leeds, 1998
versus Leicestershire:	Played 47, Won 21 (in Yorkshire 14, Away 7), Lost 22 (in Yorkshire 11, Away 11), Tie 1, No Result 2, Abandoned 1	
Highest Score:	By Yorkshire	318:7 at Leicester, 1993
	By Leicestershire	302:7 at Leeds, 2008
Lowest Score:	By Yorkshire	89:9 at Leicester, 1989
	By Leicestershire	53 at Leicester, 2000
Highest Individual Score:	For Yorkshire	148 C White at Leicester, 1997
	For Leicestershire	108 N E Briers at Bradford, 1984
Best Bowling:	For Yorkshire	5-16 S Stuchbury at Leicester, 1982
	For Leicestershire	5-24 C W Henderson at Leeds, 2004
versus Middlesex:	Played 37, Won 19 (in Yorkshire 11, Away 8), Lost 14 (in Yorkshire 3, Away 11), No Results 4	
Highest Score:	By Yorkshire	275-4 at Lord's 2011
	By Middlesex	273:6 at Southgate, 2004
Lowest Score:	By Yorkshire	94 at Lord's, 1969
	By Middlesex	23 at Leeds, 1974
Highest Individual Score:	For Yorkshire	124* J A Rudolph at Scarborough, 2010
	For Middlesex	125* O A Shah at Southgate, 2004
Best Bowling:	For Yorkshire	4-6 R Illingworth at Hull, 1983
	For Middlesex	4-22 K P Dutch at Lord's, 1998
versus Northamptonshire:	Played 39, Won 26 (in Yorkshire 12, Away 14), Lost 9 (in Yorkshire 5, Away 4), No Result 2, Abandoned 2	
Highest Score:	By Yorkshire	262-8 at Northampton, 2012
	By Northamptonshire	282:4 at Middlesbrough, 1982
Lowest Score:	By Yorkshire	112 at Northampton, 1975
	By Northamptonshire	109 at Northampton, 2000
Highest Individual Score:	For Yorkshire	114* J H Hampshire, Scarborough, 1978
	For Northamptonshire	104* P Willey at Bradford, 1976
Best Bowling:	For Yorkshire	5-29 P W Jarvis at Northampton, 1992
	For Northamptonshire	5-15 Sarfraz Nawaz, Northampton, 1975

CLYDESDALE BANK 40, PRO40, NATIONAL AND SUNDAY LEAGUES 1969-2012 *(Continued)*

versus Nottinghamshire:	Played 37, Won 16 (in Yorkshire 11, Away 5), Lost 16 (in Yorkshire 6, Away 10), Tie 1, No Result 3, Abandoned 1	
Highest Score:	By Yorkshire	352:6 at Scarborough, 2001
	By Nottinghamshire	291:6 at Nottingham, 2004
Lowest Score:	By Yorkshire	147 at Nottingham, 1975
	By Nottinghamshire	66 at Bradford, 1969
Highest Individual Score:	For Yorkshire	191 D S Lehmann at Scarborough, 2001
	For Nottinghamshire	123 D W Randall at Nottingham, 1987
Best Bowling:	For Yorkshire	5-17 A G Nicholson at Hull, 1972
	For Nottinghamshire	5-41 C L Cairns at Scarborough, 1996

versus Somerset:	Played 43, Won 21 (in Yorkshire 13, Away 8), Lost 20 (in Yorkshire 8, Away 12), No Result 1, Abandoned 1	
Highest Score:	By Yorkshire	343:9 at Taunton, 2005
	By Somerset	345:4 at Taunton, 2005
Lowest Score:	By Yorkshire	110 at Scarborough, 1977
	By Somerset	139 at Taunton, 2004
Highest Individual Score:	For Yorkshire	148 A McGrath at Taunton, 2006
	For Somerset	131 D B Close at Bath, 1974
Best Bowling:	For Yorkshire	6-27 P W Jarvis at Taunton, 1989
	For Somerset	5-27 J Garner at Bath, 1985

versus Surrey:	Played 39, Won 15 (in Yorkshire 9, Away 6), Lost 22 (in Yorkshire 8, Away 14), Abandoned 2	
Highest Score:	By Yorkshire	334:5 at The Oval, 2005
	By Surrey	375:4 at Scarborough, 1994
Lowest Score:	By Yorkshire	91 at Scarborough, 1970
	By Surrey	90 at Leeds, 1996
Highest Individual Score:	For Yorkshire	129* M D Moxon at The Oval, 1991
	For Surrey	136 M A Lynch at Bradford, 1985
Best Bowling:	For Yorkshire	5-25 D Gough at Leeds, 1998
	For Surrey	5-22 R D Jackman at The Oval, 1978

versus Sussex:	Played 41, Won 17 (in Yorkshire 9, Away 8), Lost 19 (in Yorkshire 9, Away 10), Abandoned 5	
Highest Score:	By Yorkshire	302:4 at Scarborough, 2011
	By Sussex	272:6 at Arundel, 2000
Lowest Score:	By Yorkshire	89 at Hove, 1998
	By Sussex	108 at Hove, 1971
Highest Individual	For Yorkshire	132* J A Rudolph at Scarborough, 2011
	For Sussex	129 A W Greig at Scarborough, 1976
Best Bowling:	For Yorkshire	5-13 D Gough at Hove, 1994
	For Sussex	4-10 M H Yardy at Hove, 2011

CLYDESDALE BANK 40, PRO40, NATIONAL AND SUNDAY LEAGUES 1969-2012 *(Continued)*

versus Warwickshire: Played 44, Won 15 (in Yorkshire 8, Away 7), Lost 22 (in Yorkshire 11, Away 11), Tied 1, No Result 1, Abandoned 5

Highest Score:	By Yorkshire	274:3 at Leeds, 2003
	By Warwickshire	309:3 at Birmingham, 2005
Lowest Score:	By Yorkshire	56 at Birmingham, 1995
	By Warwickshire	59 at Leeds, 2001
Highest Individual Score:	For Yorkshire	139* S P Fleming at Leeds, 2003
	For Warwickshire	137 I R Bell at Birmingham, 2005
Best Bowling:	For Yorkshire	4-21 C E W Silverwood at Leeds, 2001
	For Warwickshire	6-15 A A Donald at Birmingham, 1995

versus Worcestershire: Played 44, Won 22 (in Yorkshire 7, Away 15), Lost 20 (in Yorkshire 13, Away 7), No Result 1, Abandoned 1

Highest Score:	By Yorkshire	231:4 at Leeds, 2011
	By Worcestershire	251:4 at Scarborough, 1995
Lowest Score:	By Yorkshire	90 at Worcester, 1987
	By Worcestershire	86 at Leeds, 1969
Highest Individual Score:	For Yorkshire	112* K Sharp at Worcester, 1985
	For Worcestershire	113* G A Hick at Scarborough, 1995
Best Bowling:	For Yorkshire	7-15 R A Hutton at Leeds, 1969
	For Worcestershire	5-30 R J Chapman at Worcester, 1998

versus Netherlands: Played 4, Won 2 (in Yorkshire 1, Away 1), Lost 2 (in Yorkshire 1, Away 1)

Highest Score:	By Yorkshire	204:6 at Leeds, 2010
	By Netherlands	200:8 at Leeds, 2010
Lowest Score:	By Yorkshire	123 at Amsterdam, 2011
	By Netherlands	154:9 at Rotterdam, 2010
Highest Individual Score:	For Yorkshire	83* J A Rudolph at Leeds, 2010
	For Netherlands	62 M G Dighton at Leeds, 2010
Best Bowling:	For Yorkshire	4-24 R M Pyrah at Rotterdam, 2010
	For Netherlands	3-26 Mudassar Bukhari at Leeds, 2011

versus Scotland: Played 4, Won 4 (in Yorkshire 2, Away 2),

Highest Score:	By Yorkshire	240:5 at Leeds, 2004
	By Scotland	203:9 at Edinburgh, 2005
Lowest Score:	By Yorkshire	199:8 at Edinburgh, 2004
	By Scotland	140 at Edinburgh, 2004
Highest Individual Score:	For Yorkshire	88* D S Lehmann at Leeds, 2004
	For Scotland	78 J A Beukes at Edinburgh, 2005
Best Bowling:	For Yorkshire	4-20 R K J Dawson at Edinburgh, 2004
	For Scotland	3-47 Asim Butt at Edinburgh, 2004

versus Unicorns: Played 2, Won 2 (in Yorkshire)

Highest Score:	By Yorkshire	186:2 at Scarborough, 2012
	By Unicorns	184 at Scarborough, 2012
Lowest Score:	By Unicorns	150-6 at Leeds 2012
Highest Individual Score:	For Yorkshire	103* G S Ballance at Scarborough, 2012
	For Unicorns	83* T J New at Scarborough, 2012
Best Bowling:	For Yorkshire	3-24 A U Rashid at Leeds, 2012
	For Unicorns	2-25 R J Woolley at Leeds, 2012

CAREER AVERAGES FOR YORKSHIRE

CLYDESDALE BANK 40, PRO40, NATIONAL AND SUNDAY LEAGUE RECORDS 1969-2012

Player	*M*	*Inns*	*NO*	*Runs*	*HS*	*Av'ge*	*100s*	*50s*	*Runs*	*Wkts*	*Av'ge*	*Ct/St*
Ashraf, M A . . .	13	3	3	3	3*	—	—	—	491	13	37.76	2
Athey, C W J . . .	94	86	8	2560	118	32.82	1	18	315	14	22.50	30
Azeem Rafiq . .	12	8	4	81	35*	20.25	—	—	417	11	37.90	4
Bairstow, D L . .	279	227	51	3677	83*	20.89	—	16	—	—	—	234/23
Bairstow, J M .	29	25	3	592	114	26.90	1	2	—	—	—	18/1
Baker, T M	1	0	0	0	0	—	—	—	22	1	22.00	1
Balderstone, J C	8	8	2	108	46	18.00	—	—	28	1	28.00	2
Ballance, G S . .	21	21	6	833	103*	55.53	1	5	—	—	—	10
Batty, J D	31	13	6	41	13*	5.86	—	—	1091	40	27.27	16
Best, T L	5	1	1	8	8*	—	—	—	166	10	16.60	1
Bevan, M G	29	27	5	1108	103*	50.36	2	7	399	23	17.34	9
Binks, J G	14	11	2	140	34	15.55	—	—	—	—	—	11/2
Blain, J A R	11	6	3	21	11*	7.00	—	—	364	11	33.08	3
Blakey, R J	249	218	52	5531	130*	33.31	3	27	—	—	—	244/48
Blewett, G S . . .	11	11	0	178	48	16.18	—	—	116	4	29.00	6
Booth, P A	2	—	—	—	—	—	—	—	67	1	67.00	1
Bore, M K	44	18	7	67	15	6.09	—	—	1300	37	35.13	14
Boycott, G	163	157	24	5051	108*	37.97	2	37	611	14	43.64	69
Bresnan, T T . .	89	66	18	827	61	17.22	—	2	3065	90	34.05	26
Broadhurst, M . .	1	—	—	—	—	—	—	—	27	0	—	—
Brophy, G L . . .	45	38	5	803	93*	24.33	—	5	—	—	—	38/11
Byas, D	217	211	27	5352	111*	29.08	3	28	463	19	24.36	88
Carrick, P	210	143	42	1481	48*	14.66	—	—	5030	170	29.58	53
Chapman, C A . .	7	6	3	89	36*	29.66	—	—	—	—	—	2
Cleary, M F	4	3	1	50	23*	25.00	—	—	159	2	79.50	—
Close, D B	17	16	0	224	50	14.00	—	1	118	1	118.00	8
Cooper, H P . . .	103	50	24	358	29*	13.76	—	—	3038	120	25.31	20
Cope, G A	28	14	7	61	16*	8.71	—	—	750	18	41.66	6
Coverdale, S P .	3	3	2	18	17*	18.00	—	—	—	—	—	3
Craven, V J	36	34	4	540	59	18.00	—	2	297	18	16.50	11
Dalton, A J	17	16	1	280	55	18.66	—	1	—	—	—	7
Dawood, I	20	16	4	212	57	17.66	—	1	—	—	—	17/7
Dawson, R K J .	65	46	9	303	41	8.18	—	—	1914	70	27.34	20
Dennis, S J	41	19	11	87	16*	10.87	—	—	1188	27	44.00	6
Elliott, M T G . .	5	5	2	266	115*	88.66	2	—	—	—	—	—
Elstub, C J	9	3	3	4	4*	—	—	—	259	11	23.55	—
Fellows, G M . .	62	52	8	893	67	20.29	—	4	589	13	45.30	21
Fisher, I D	24	11	3	63	20	7.87	—	—	595	25	23.80	3
Fleming, S P . . .	7	7	1	285	139*	47.50	1	1	—	—	—	3
Fletcher, S D . . .	86	19	11	53	11*	6.62	—	—	3136	114	27.50	26
Foster, M J	20	14	1	199	118	15.30	1	—	370	6	61.66	6
Gale, A W	73	69	5	2132	125*	33.31	2	11	—	—	—	18
Gilbert, C R	1	1	0	9	9	9.00	—	—	40	2	20.00	—
Gillespie, J N . .	7	2	0	14	11	7.00	—	—	238	9	26.44	3
Gough, D	129	80	24	845	72*	15.08	—	1	3929	159	24.71	23
Gray, A K D . . .	24	14	6	111	30*	13.87	—	—	612	17	36.00	5
Grayson, A P . . .	49	35	6	367	55	12.65	—	1	1051	31	33.90	14
Guy S M	18	14	3	188	40	17.09	—	—	—	—	—	18/8
Hamilton, G M .	74	52	12	743	57*	18.57	—	2	2033	81	25.09	12
Hampshire, A W	3	2	0	3	3	1.50	—	—	—	—	—	—

CLYDESDALE BANK 40, PRO40, NATIONAL AND SUNDAY LEAGUE 1969-2012 *(Continued)*

Player	*M*	*Inns*	*NO*	*Runs*	*HS*	*Av'ge*	*100s*	*50s*	*Runs*	*Wkts*	*Av'ge*	*Ct/St*
Hampshire, J H .	155	152	15	4505	119	32.88	6	26	22	1	22.00	47
Hannon-Dalby, O J	**5**	**1**	**1**	**21**	**21***	**—**	**—**	**—**	**202**	**5**	**40.40**	**3**
Harden, R J	12	10	2	133	42	16.62	—	—	—	—	—	1
Hartley, P J	145	102	31	1164	52	16.39	—	2	4778	174	27.45	26
Hartley, S N ...	130	119	25	2087	83*	22.20	—	9	1587	48	33.06	40
Harvey, I J	24	23	2	486	69	23.14	—	1	766	24	31.91	7
Hodgson, D M .	**4**	**3**	**1**	**19**	**9**	**9.50**	**—**	**—**	**—**	**—**	**—**	**3**
Hodgson L J ...	6	2	0	9	9	4.50	—	—	161	4	40.25	1
Hoggard, M J ..	56	21	12	23	5*	2.55	—	—	1777	82	21.67	5
Hutchison, P M .	23	8	5	8	2*	2.66	—	—	670	28	23.92	3
Hutton, R A	77	60	19	761	65	18.56	—	3	2215	94	23.56	19
Illingworth, R ..	23	4	3	12	8*	12.00	—	—	453	26	17.42	7
Ingham, P G ...	12	10	4	312	87*	52.00	—	2	—	—	—	2
Inzamam-ul-Haq	3	3	0	69	53	23.00	—	1	—	—	—	—
Jaques, P A	**30**	**29**	**1**	**1087**	**105**	**38.82**	**1**	**8**	**—**	**—**	**—**	**14**
Jarvis, P W	94	49	21	316	38*	11.28	—	—	2914	138	21.11	25
Johnson, C	100	81	17	1186	67*	18.53	—	3	5	2	2.50	24
Johnson, M	10	4	1	30	15*	10.00	—	—	317	5	63.40	2
Katich, S M	2	2	1	39	39*	39.00	—	—	—	—	—	2
Kellett, S A	30	30	2	697	118*	24.89	1	3	16	0	—	6
Kettleborough, RA	10	6	3	71	28	23.66	—	—	72	3	24.00	4
Kirby, S P	25	10	3	38	15	5.42	—	—	919	22	41.77	6
Kruis, G J	30	13	6	96	31*	13.71	—	—	1019	36	28.30	6
Lawson, M A K .	4	4	0	30	20	7.50	—	—	141	3	47.00	1
Leadbeater, B ..	73	68	14	1423	86*	26.35	—	6	38	2	19.00	18
Leaning, J A ...	**1**	**1**	**0**	**11**	**11**	**11.00**	**—**	**—**	**—**	**—**	**—**	**—**
Lee, J E	4	0	0	0	0	—	—	—	116	7	16.57	—
Lees, A Z	**2**	**2**	**1**	**35**	**23**	**35.00**	**—**	**—**	**—**	**—**	**—**	**—**
Lehmann, D S ..	77	77	11	3091	191	46.83	3	24	1222	47	26.00	24
Love, J D	157	146	18	2919	118*	22.80	3	10	83	3	27.66	32
Lucas, D S	5	2	0	40	32	20.00	—	—	187	3	62.33	1
Lumb, M J	71	69	4	1838	92	28.27	—	14	28	0	—	22
Lumb, R G	87	75	10	1588	101	24.43	1	9	—	—	—	15
Lyth, A	**50**	**46**	**3**	**1229**	**109***	**28.58**	**1**	**6**	**14**	**0**	**—**	**14**
McGrath, A ...	**179**	**165**	**29**	**4448**	**148**	**32.70**	**2**	**28**	**1772**	**55**	**32.21**	**60**
Metcalfe, A A ..	140	135	7	3529	116	27.57	2	23	—	—	—	32
Middlebrook, JD	14	9	2	52	15*	7.42	—	—	417	13	32.07	1
Milburn, S M ..	4	2	1	14	13*	14.00	—	—	118	2	59.00	1
Miller, D A	**3**	**3**	**0**	**45**	**44**	**15.00**	**—**	**—**	**—**	**—**	**—**	**3**
Morris, A C. ...	23	15	3	208	48*	17.33	—	—	362	15	24.13	4
Moxon, M D ...	151	143	8	4128	129*	30.57	3	24	868	21	41.33	46
Nicholson, A G .	83	28	14	97	13*	6.92	—	—	1998	117	17.07	8
Nicholson, N G .	2	2	1	1	1*	1.00	—	—	—	—	—	2
Old, C M	143	112	27	1711	82*	20.12	—	6	3847	192	20.03	38
Oldham, S	71	26	15	144	38*	13.09	—	—	2064	83	24.86	10
Padgett, D E V .	40	39	2	760	68	20.54	—	2	25	1	25.00	9
Parker, B	56	49	6	723	42	16.81	—	—	18	0	—	8
Patterson, S A .	**37**	**15**	**11**	**93**	**25***	**23.25**	**—**	**—**	**1339**	**50**	**26.78**	**6**
Pickles, C S	56	38	17	259	30*	12.33	—	—	1896	53	35.77	20
Pyrah, R M ...	**60**	**39**	**10**	**546**	**69**	**18.82**	**—**	**1**	**1627**	**62**	**26.24**	**18**
Ramage, A	20	12	5	90	32*	12.85	—	—	658	14	47.00	—
Ramsden, G	1	—	—	—	—	—	—	—	26	2	13.00	—

Player	*M*	*Inns*	*NO*	*Runs*	*HS*	*Av'ge*	*100s*	*50s*	*Runs*	*Wkts*	*Av'ge*	*Ct/St*
Rana Neved -ul-Hasan	10	9	0	241	74	26.77	—	2	357	16	22.31	1
Rashid, A U	**46**	**31**	**10**	**358**	**42***	**17.04**	—	—	**1562**	**58**	**26.93**	**16**
Rhodes, S J	2	1	0	6	6	6.00	—	—	—	—	—	3
Richardson, R B	21	21	6	740	103	49.33	1	5	—	—	—	5
Robinson, A L	69	28	14	94	14	6.71	—	—	1904	81	23.50	11
Robinson, M A	65	21	11	35	7	3.50	—	—	2030	63	32.22	7
Robinson, P E	104	100	12	2194	78*	24.93	—	11	—	—	—	37
Root, J E	**15**	**14**	**2**	**443**	**63**	**36.91**	—	**2**	**204**	**7**	**29.14**	**8**
Rudolph J A	39	37	7	2217	132*	73.90	7	14	29	0	—	16
Sanderson B W	10	2	1	14	12*	—	—	—	247	8	30.87	5
Sayers, J J	**21**	**21**	**2**	**388**	**62**	**20.42**	—	**3**	**79**	**1**	**79.00**	**1**
Scofield, D	3	1	0	0	0	0.00	—	—	111	2	55.50	1
Shahzad, A	21	15	4	125	59*	11.36	—	1	839	22	38.13	5
Sharp, K	141	135	13	3392	114	27.80	2	20	1	0	—	45
Sharpe, P J	52	50	0	871	81	17.42	—	4	11	0	—	22
Shaw, C	38	14	7	113	26	16.14	—	—	1142	45	25.37	8
Sidebottom, A	156	86	33	835	52*	15.75	—	1	4561	149	30.61	29
Sidebottom, R J	**77**	**41**	**19**	**260**	**30***	**11.81**	—	—	**2463**	**89**	**27.67**	**12**
Silverwood, CEW	106	64	27	555	58	15.00	—	2	3168	146	21.69	11
Smith, N	6	1	1	0	0*	—	—	—	—	—	—	2
Smith, R	3	2	0	17	17	8.50	—	—	—	—	—	1
Squires, P J	47	39	4	602	79*	17.20	—	3	4	0	—	8
Starc, M A	**4**	**2**	**2**	**5**	**4***	—	—	—	**181**	**8**	**22.62**	**1**
Stemp, R D	60	21	7	114	23*	8.14	—	—	1978	67	29.52	13
Stevenson, G B	153	116	16	1275	81*	12.75	—	2	4641	186	24.95	25
Stringer, P M	9	6	4	22	13*	11.00	—	—	235	11	21.36	—
Stuchbury, S	20	7	3	15	9*	3.75	—	—	588	26	22.61	2
Swallow, I G	2	1	0	2	2	2.00	—	—	31	0	—	—
Swanepoel, P J	3	2	2	9	8*	—	—	—	100	3	33.33	—
Taylor, C R	5	5	0	102	28	20.40	—	—	—	—	—	—
Tendulkar, S R	13	13	1	464	107	38.66	1	1	102	3	34.00	1
Thornicroft, N D	11	6	3	42	20	14.00	—	—	447	15	29.80	1
Townsley, R A J	5	4	1	81	34	27.00	—	—	62	0	—	1
Vaughan, M P	101	99	7	2344	116*	25.47	1	11	988	34	29.05	34
Wainwright D J	40	16	10	100	26	16.66	—	—	1145	29	39.48	12
Wardlaw, I	**8**	**5**	**2**	**11**	**6***	**3.66**	—	—	**326**	**8**	**40.75**	**2**
Warren, A C	1	1	0	3	3	3.00	—	—	35	1	35.00	—
Wharf, A G	4	1	1	2	2*	—	—	—	87	3	29.00	1
White, C	185	168	18	3643	148	24.28	1	13	3479	159	21.88	50
Whiteley, J P	5	4	0	19	14	4.75	—	—	147	2	73.50	1
Widdup, S	4	4	0	49	38	12.25	—	—	—	—	—	2
Wilson, D	39	32	7	352	46	14.08	—	—	958	42	22.80	11
Wood, M J	103	94	6	2053	111	23.32	2	10	26	0	—	41
Woodford, J D	60	50	12	834	69*	21.94	—	2	1401	60	23.35	20
Younus Khan	4	2	0	14	14	7.00	—	—	20	0	—	2
Yuvraj Singh	8	8	0	169	50	21.12	—	1	170	3	56.66	1

CAREER AVERAGES FOR YORKSHIRE

ALL LIMITED-OVERS COMPETITIONS (LIST A) OF 40 TO 65 OVERS 1963-2012

Player	*M*	*Inns*	*NO*	*Runs*	*HS*	*Av'ge*	*100s*	*50s*	*Runs*	*Wkts*	*Av'ge*	*Ct/St*
Ashraf, M A	**13**	**3**	**3**	**3**	**3***	**—**	**—**	**—**	**491**	**13**	**37.76**	**2**
Athey, C W J	138	127	14	3653	118	32.32	2	25	431	19	22.68	45
Azeem Rafiq	**12**	**8**	**4**	**81**	**34***	**20.25**	**—**	**—**	**417**	**11**	**37.90**	**4**
Bairstow, D L	398	313	70	5114	103*	21.04	1	19	17	0	—	389/31
Bairstow, J M	**29**	**25**	**3**	**592**	**114**	**26.90**	**1**	**2**	**—**	**—**	**—**	**18/1**
Baker, T M	4	1	0	3	3	3.00	—	—	89	4	22.25	3
Balderstone, J C	13	11	2	173	46	19.22	—	—	38	2	19.00	3
Ballance, G S	**21**	**21**	**6**	**833**	**103***	**55.53**	**1**	**5**	**—**	**—**	**—**	**10**
Batty, J D	38	16	7	50	13*	5.55	—	—	1297	42	30.88	18
Berry, P J	1	0	0	0	—	—	—	—	28	0	—	—
Best, T L	5	1	1	8	8*	—	—	—	166	10	16.60	1
Bevan, M G	47	44	11	2040	103*	61.82	2	18	513	27	19.00	10
Binks, J G	30	21	3	247	34	13.72	—	—	—	—	—	26/8
Blain, J A R	14	8	3	34	11*	6.80	—	—	427	14	30.50	3
Blakey, R J	371	317	83	7355	130*	31.43	3	35	—	—	—	369/59
Blewett, G S	17	17	0	345	77	20.29	—	2	196	11	17.81	7
Booth, P A	5	2	1	7	6*	7.00	—	—	147	3	49.00	1
Bore, M K	53	23	10	80	15	6.15	—	—	1591	50	31.82	15
Boycott, G	260	251	37	8481	146	39.63	6	62	1076	24	44.83	92
Bresnan, T T	**131**	**90**	**25**	**1159**	**61**	**17.83**	**—**	**3**	**4544**	**140**	**32.45**	**35**
Broadhurst, M	1	—	—	—	—	—	—	—	27	0	—	—
Brophy, G L	68	57	12	1240	93*	27.55	—	9	—	—	—	67/14
Byas, D	309	298	35	7691	116*	29.24	5	43	641	25	25.64	128
Carrick, P	302	204	52	2141	54	14.08	—	2	7361	236	31.19	68
Chapman, C A	8	6	3	89	36*	29.66	—	—	—	—	—	3
Claydon, M E	7	2	0	15	9	7.50	—	—	293	8	36.62	—
Cleary, M F	4	3	1	50	23*	25.00	—	—	159	2	79.50	—
Close, D B	32	31	2	631	96	21.75	—	3	475	23	20.65	14
Cooper, H P	142	74	34	483	29*	12.07	—	—	4184	177	23.63	26
Cope, G A	36	20	13	96	18*	13.71	—	—	1011	24	42.12	9
Coverdale, S P	3	3	2	18	17*	18.00	—	—	—	—	—	3
Craven, V J	41	38	5	579	59	17.54	—	2	338	20	16.90	14
Dalton, A J	17	16	1	280	55	18.66	—	1	—	—	—	7
Dawood, I	24	19	4	238	57	15.86	—	1	—	—	—	18/8
Dawson, R K J	90	56	11	396	41	8.80	—	—	2711	90	30.12	30
Dennis, S J	55	23	11	111	16*	9.25	—	—	1717	40	42.92	7
Elliott, M T G	6	6	3	394	128*	131.33	3	—	—	—	—	—
Elstub, C J	9	9	3	4	4*	—	—	—	259	11	23.54	—
Fellows, G M	94	78	15	1342	80*	21.30	—	6	836	22	38.00	27
Fisher, I D	28	12	3	68	20	7.55	—	—	708	29	24.41	6
Fleming, S P	7	7	1	285	139*	47.50	1	1	—	—	—	3
Fletcher, S D	128	32	18	109	16*	7.78	—	—	4686	164	28.57	34
Foster, M J	20	14	1	199	118	15.30	1	—	370	6	61.66	6
Gale, A W	**99**	**91**	**9**	**2699**	**125***	**32.91**	**2**	**15**	**—**	**—**	**—**	**20**
Gilbert, C R	4	3	0	18	9	6.00	—	—	174	8	21.75	—
Gillespie, J N	18	4	1	29	15*	9.66	—	—	601	18	33.38	6
Gough, D	212	119	33	1273	72*	14.80	—	1	6770	290	23.34	43
Gray, A K D	30	18	7	128	30*	11.63	—	—	814	23	35.39	8
Grayson, A P	65	48	7	575	55	14.02	—	1	1410	38	37.10	19
Guy, S M	30	21	4	233	40	13.70	—	—	—	—	—	35/11
Hamilton, G M	100	70	18	1059	57*	20.36	—	2	2761	118	23.39	15

ALL LIMITED-OVERS COMPETITIONS OF 40 TO 65 OVERS 1963-2010 *(Continued)*

Player	*M*	*Inns*	*NO*	*Runs*	*HS*	*Av'ge*	*100s*	*50s*	*Runs*	*Wkts*	*Av'ge*	*Ct/St*
Hampshire, A W	4	3	0	3	3	1.00	—	—	—	—	—	1
Hampshire, J H	231	220	24	6248	119	31.87	7	36	26	1	26.00	69
Hannon-Dalby, O J	**5**	**1**	**1**	**21**	**21***	**—**	**—**	**—**	**202**	**5**	**40.40**	**3**
Harden, R J	19	16	2	230	42	16.42	—	—	—	—	—	1
Hartley, P J	216	145	49	1609	83	16.76	—	4	7425	280	26.51	40
Hartley, S N	170	153	31	2810	83*	23.03	—	13	2122	67	31.67	52
Harvey, I J	28	27	2	637	74	25.48	—	3	950	30	31.66	8
Hodgson D M	**4**	**3**	**1**	**19**	**9**	**9.50**	**—**	**—**	**—**	**—**	**—**	**3/1**
Hodgson, L J	6	2	0	9	9	4.50	—	—	161	4	40.25	1
Hoggard, M J	83	28	19	41	7*	4.55	—	—	2682	118	22.72	7
Hutchison, P M	32	11	8	18	4*	6.00	—	—	844	43	19.62	3
Hutton, R A	105	78	24	1015	65	18.79	—	4	2990	128	23.35	27
Illingworth, R	40	15	11	171	45	42.75	—	—	764	39	19.58	14
Ingham, P G	12	10	4	312	87*	52.00	—	2	—	—	—	2
Inzamam-ul-Haq	3	3	0	69	53	23.00	—	1	—	—	—	—
Jaques, P A	**36**	**35**	**2**	**1298**	**105**	**39.33**	**1**	**10**	**—**	**—**	**—**	**16**
Jarvis, P W	142	72	27	512	42	11.37	—	—	4575	209	21.88	32
Johnson, C	127	101	22	1614	73*	20.43	—	4	28	2	14.00	33
Johnson, M	14	6	3	34	15*	11.33	—	—	455	12	37.91	2
Katich, S M	3	3	2	79	40*	79.00	—	—	—	—	—	2
Kellett, S A	53	49	3	1182	118*	25.69	2	4	16	0	—	12
Kettleborough, R A	10	6	3	71	28	23.66	—	—	72	3	24.00	4
Kirby, S P	28	12	3	38	15	4.22	—	—	1036	24	43.16	6
Kruis, G J	55	22	11	138	31*	12.54	—	—	1793	62	28.91	9
Lawson, M A K	4	4	0	30	20	7.50	—	—	141	3	47.00	1
Leadbeater, B	103	98	19	2179	90	27.58	—	11	95	5	19.00	25
Leaning, J A	**1**	**1**	**0**	**11**	**11**	**11.00**	**—**	**—**	**—**	**—**	**—**	**—**
Lee, J E	4	0	0	0	0	—	—	—	116	7	16.57	—
Lees, A Z	**2**	**2**	**1**	**35**	**23**	**35.00**	**—**	**—**	**—**	**—**	**—**	**—**
Lehmann, D S	130	126	20	5229	191	49.33	8	38	1990	79	25.18	41
Lester, E I	1	1	0	0	0	0.00	—	—	—	—	—	—
Love, J D	220	203	33	4298	118*	25.28	4	18	129	5	25.80	44
Lucas, D S	5	2	0	40	32	20.00	—	—	187	3	62.33	1
Lumb, M J	102	96	8	2592	92	29.45	—	18	28	0	—	31
Lumb, R G	135	121	13	2747	101	25.43	1	16	—	—	—	21
Lyth, A	**61**	**55**	**4**	**1447**	**109***	**28.37**	**1**	**7**	**14**	**0**	**—**	**18**
McGrath, A	**272**	**250**	**39**	**7067**	**148**	**33.49**	**6**	**44**	**2514**	**79**	**31.82**	**90**
Metcalfe, A A	191	186	14	5520	127*	32.09	4	36	44	2	22.00	44
Middlebrook, J D	18	11	3	61	15*	7.62	—	—	530	13	40.76	5
Milburn, S M	4	2	1	14	13*	14.00	—	—	118	2	59.00	1
Miller, D A	3	3	0	45	44	15.00	—	—	—	—	—	3
Morris, A C	25	16	4	209	48*	17.41	—	—	409	16	25.56	5
Moxon, M D	235	227	21	7307	141*	35.47	7	48	1178	34	34.64	77
Nicholson, A G	119	45	22	154	15*	6.69	—	—	2943	173	17.01	16
Nicholson, N G	2	2	1	1	1*	1.00	—	—	—	—	—	2
Old, C M	218	166	37	2550	82*	19.76	—	10	5817	306	19.00	56
Oldham, S	105	40	21	192	38*	10.10	—	—	3136	142	22.08	17
Padgett, D E V	57	54	3	1069	68	20.96	—	2	25	1	25.00	13
Parker, B	72	60	8	964	69	18.53	—	1	18	0	—	11
Patterson, S A	**46**	**18**	**14**	**110**	**25***	**27.50**	**—**	**—**	**1659**	**57**	**29.10**	**6**
Pickles, C S	69	47	19	370	37*	13.21	—	—	2355	62	37.98	22
Pyrah, R M	**88**	**57**	**15**	**819**	**69**	**19.50**	**—**	**2**	**2642**	**102**	**25.90**	**30**
Ramage, A	34	17	8	134	32*	14.88	—	—	1178	30	39.26	3

Player	*M*	*Inns*	*NO*	*Runs*	*HS*	*Av'ge*	*100s*	*50s*	*Runs*	*Wkts*	*Av'ge*	*Ct/St*
Ramsden, G	1	—	—	—	—	—	—	—	26	2	13.00	—
Rana Naved -ul-Hasan	17	16	1	375	74	25.00	—	3	681	26	26.19	5
Rashid, A U	**64**	**42**	**12**	**463**	**43**	**15.43**	**—**	**—**	**2028**	**71**	**28.56**	**21**
Rhodes, S J	2	1	0	6	6	6.00	—	—	—	—	—	3
Richardson, R B ...	28	28	6	993	103	45.13	1	8	—	—	—	5
Robinson, A L	92	36	19	127	18*	7.47	—	—	2588	105	24.64	14
Robinson, M A	86	30	16	41	7	2.92	—	—	2725	89	30.61	7
Robinson, P E	134	123	15	2738	78*	25.35	—	14	—	—	—	47
Root, J E	**15**	**14**	**2**	**443**	**63**	**36.91**	**—**	**2**	**204**	**7**	**29.14**	**8**
Rudolph, J A	65	62	10	3090	132*	59.42	9	19	37	0	—	32
Ryan, M	3	2	1	7	6*	7.00	—	—	149	5	29.80	3
Sanderson, B W	10	2	1	14	12*	14.00	—	—	247	8	30.87	5
Sayers, J J	**27**	**27**	**2**	**499**	**62**	**19.96**	**—**	**4**	**79**	**1**	**79.00**	**2**
Scofield, D	3	1	0	0	0	0.00	—	—	111	2	55.50	1
Shahzad, A	29	21	6	235	59*	15.66	—	1	1131	29	39.00	7
Sharp, K	203	188	18	4693	114	27.60	3	27	48	4	12.00	66
Sharpe, P J	89	84	4	1499	89*	18.73	—	8	11	0	16.50	52
Shaw, C	48	20	10	127	26	12.70	—	—	1396	58	24.06	8
Sidebottom, A	233	129	47	1273	52*	15.52	—	1	6841	258	26.51	51
Sidebottom, R J ...	**111**	**50**	**22**	**293**	**30***	**10.46**	**—**	**—**	**3517**	**121**	**29.06**	**24**
Silverwood,C E W ..	164	93	32	866	61	14.19	—	4	5145	223	23.07	25
Smith, N	7	2	1	5	5	5.00	—	—	—	—	—	2
Smith, R	3	2	0	17	17	8.50	—	—	—	—	—	1
Squires, P J	56	48	5	708	79*	16.46	—	3	4	0	—	10
Starc, M A	4	2	2	5	4*	—	—	—	181	8	22.62	1
Stemp, R D	88	28	10	118	23*	6.55	—	—	2996	100	29.96	14
Stevenson, G B	216	157	23	1699	81*	12.67	—	2	6820	290	23.51	38
Stott, W B	2	2	0	30	30	15.00	—	—	—	—	—	—
Stringer, P M	11	8	6	29	13*	14.50	—	—	256	15	17.06	—
Stuchbury, S	22	8	4	21	9*	5.25	—	—	677	29	23.34	2
Swallow, I G	8	5	3	37	17*	18.50	—	—	198	2	99.00	5
Swanepoel, P G	3	2	2	9	8*	—	—	—	100	3	33,33	—
Taylor, C R	6	5	0	102	28	20.40	—	—	—	—	—	—
Taylor, K	10	10	0	135	30	13.50	—	—	168	11	15.27	3
Tendulkar, S R	17	17	2	540	107	36.00	1	1	167	6	27.83	3
Thornicroft, N D ...	13	7	4	52	20	17.33	—	—	544	16	34.00	2
Townsley, R A J	5	4	1	81	34	27.00	—	—	62	0	—	1
Trueman, F S	11	9	1	127	28	15.87	—	—	348	21	16.57	5
Vaughan, M P	182	177	13	4890	125*	29.81	3	28	1836	59	31.11	56
Wainwright, D J	47	20	13	150	26	21.42	—	—	1382	36	38.38	16
Wardlaw, I	**8**	**5**	**2**	**11**	**6***	**3.66**	**—**	**—**	**326**	**8**	**40.75**	**2**
Waring, J	1	1	1	1	1*	—	—	—	11	0	—	—
Warren, A C	1	1	0	3	3	3.00	—	—	35	1	35.00	—
Wharf, A G	6	1	1	2	2*	—	—	—	176	8	22.00	1
White, C	291	265	39	6376	148	28.21	5	28	6088	246	24.74	84
Whiteley, J P	6	4	0	19	14	4.75	—	—	195	2	97.50	1
Widdup, S	4	4	0	49	38	12.25	—	—	—	—	—	2
Wilson, D	59	45	8	424	46	11.45	—	—	1502	74	20.29	22
Wood, M J	143	132	14	3209	160	27.19	5	14	71	3	23.66	56
Woodford, J D	72	57	14	890	69*	20.69	—	2	1627	77	21.12	25
Younus Khan	11	8	0	248	100	31.00	1	—	144	2	72.00	5
Yuvraj Singh	9	9	0	196	50	21.77	—	1	197	3	65.66	1

YORKSHIRE T20i CRICKETERS 2003-2012/13 (Correct to February 16, 2013)

For England

Player	M	I	NO	Runs	HS	Av'ge	100s	50s	Balls	Runs	W	Av'ge	Best	4wI	Ct/St
BAIRSTOW, J M .2011-12/13	18	14	4	194	60*	19.40	—	1	—	—	—	—	—	—	21
BRESNAN, T T . .2006-12/13	25	14	6	80	23*	10.00	—	—	490	610	19	32.10	3-10	—	6
RASHID, A U 2009	5	2	1	10	9*	10.00	—	—	84	120	3	40.00	1-11	—	—
ROOT, J E 2012/13	2	0	0	0	—	—	—	—	12	15	1	15.00	1-15	—	3
SHAHZAD, A 2010-11	3	1	1	0	0*	—	—	—	66	97	3	32.33	2-38	—	1
VAUGHAN, M P 2005-7	2	2	0	27	27	13.50	—	—	—	—	—	—	—	—	—
For Scotland															
BLAIN, J A R 2007-8	6	3	1	4	3*	2.00	—	—	120	108	6	18.00	2-23	—	1
HAMILTON, G M . .2007-10	12	8	0	90	32	11.25	—	—	—	—	—	—	—	—	3

YORKSHIRE PLAYERS WHO PLAYED ALL THEIR T20i CRICKET AFTER LEAVING YORKSHIRE

For England

Player	M	I	NO	Runs	HS	Av'ge	100s	50s	Balls	Runs	W	Av'ge	Best	4wI	Ct/St
BATTY, G J 2009	1	1	0	4	4	4.00	—	—	18	17	0	—	—	—	—
GOUGH, D 2005-06	2	0	0	0	—	—	—	—	41	49	3	16.33	3-16	—	—
LUMB, M J 2010-12/13	14	14	1	287	53*	22.07	—	2	—	—	—	—	—	—	5
SIDEBOTTOM, R J .2007-10	18	1	1	5	5*	—	—	—	367	437	23	19.00	3-16	—	5

Overseas Players

(Qualification: 24 t20 matches for Yorkshire)

For South Africa

Player	M	I	NO	Runs	HS	Av'ge	100s	50s	Balls	Runs	W	Av'ge	Best	4wI	Ct/St
RUDOLPH, J A 2006	1	1	1	6	6*	—	—	—	—	—	—	—	—	—	—

TWENTY20 CUP 2003-2012

BEST SEASON — LOSING FINALIST 2012

Played 101, Won 46 (in Yorkshire 25, Away 20, Neutral 1)
Lost 45 (in Yorkshire 19, Away 25, Neutral 1)
Tied 2 (in Yorkshire 1, Away 1), No Result 4 (in Yorkshire 1, Away 3)
Abandoned 4 (in Yorkshire 3, Away 1)

Highest Score:	By Yorkshire	213:7 v. Worcestershire at Leeds, 2010
	Against Yorkshire	222:5 by Derbyshire at Leeds, 2010
†Lowest Score:	By Yorkshire	90:9 v. Durham at Chester-le-Street, 2009
	Against Yorkshire	98 by Durham at Chester-le-Street, 2006
Highest Individual Score:	For Yorkshire	109 I J Harvey v. Derbyshire at Leeds, 2005
	Against Yorkshire	111 D L Maddy for Leicestershire at Leeds, 2004

†Lowest score is the lowest all-out score or the lowest score at completion of 20 overs

Highest Partnerships: For Yorkshire

1st wkt	131	A Lyth (78) and P A Jaques (64) v. Derbyshire at Leeds, 2012
2nd wkt	137*	A W Gale (60*) and H H Gibbs (76*) v. Durham at Leeds, 2010
3rd wkt	121	J A Rudolph (56) and A McGrath (59) v. Leicestershire at Leicester, 2008
4th wkt	93	P A Jaques (92) and T T Bresnan (42) v. Leicestershire at Leeds, 2004
5th wkt	91	D A Miller (54) and G S Ballance (42) v. Lancashire at Leeds, 2012
6th wkt	65	A McGrath (39) and A U Rashid (34) v. Worcestershire at Worcester, 2010
7th wkt	56	V J Craven (44) and R J Blakey (18) v. Durham at Chester-le-Street, 2004
8th wkt	43*	R M Pyrah (22*) and C J McKay (21*) v. Worcestershire at Worcester, 2010
9th wkt	33*	A U Rashid (5*) and D Gough (20*) v. Lancashire at Leeds, 2008
10th wkt	28*	A U Rashid (28*) and G J Kruis (12*) v. Durham at Chester-le-Street, 2009

Best Bowling:	For Yorkshire:	5 for 16 R M Pyrah v. Durham at Scarborough, 2011
	Against Yorkshire	4 for 9 C K Langerveldt for Derbyshire at Leeds, 2008
Most Economical Bowling (4 overs):		
	For Yorkshire	4-0-12-2 T T Bresnan v. Lancashire at Manchester, 2008
	Against Yorkshire	4-0-9-4 C K Langeveldt for Derbyshire at Leeds, 2008
Most Expensive Bowling:		
	For Yorkshire	4-0-65-2 M J Hoggard v. Lancashire at Leeds, 2005
	Against Yorkshire	4-0-58-0 G Welch for Derbyshire at Leeds, 2003

versus Derbyshire: Played 15, Won 10 (in Yorkshire 4, Away 6), Lost 4 (in Yorkshire 4)
No Result 1 (Away)

Highest Score:	By Yorkshire	210:3 at Derby, 2006
	By Derbyshire	222:5 at Leeds, 2010
Lowest Score:	By Yorkshire	109 at Derby, 2012
	By Derbyshire	119:7 at Leeds, 2007
Highest Individual Score:		
	For Yorkshire	109 I J Harvey at Leeds, 2005
	For Derbyshire	100* G M Smith at Leeds, 2008
Best Bowling:	For Yorkshire	4 for 21 B W Sanderson at Derby, 2011
	For Derbyshire	4 for 9 C K Langeveldt at Leeds, 2008

TWENTY20 CUP RECORDS 2003-2012 *(Continued)*

versus Durham:	Played 18, Won 10 (in Yorkshire 6, Away 4), Lost 6 (in Yorkshire 2, Away 4), Tied 1 (in Yorkshire), No Result 1 (Away)	
Highest Score:	By Yorkshire	198:4 at Leeds, 2003
	By Durham	159:7 at Leeds, 2008, and
		159 at Chester-le-Street, 2012
Lowest Score:	By Yorkshire	90:9 at Chester-le-Street, 2009
	By Durham	98 at Chester-le-Street, 2006
Highest Individual Score:		
	For Yorkshire	76* H H Gibbs at Leeds, 2010
	For Durham	76 H H Gibbs at Chester-le-Street, 2012
Best Bowling:	For Yorkshire	5 for 16 R M Pyrah at Scarborough, 2011
	For Durham	4 for 38 S J Harmison at Leeds, 2008
versus Essex:	Played 1, Lost 1 (Away)	
Scores:	By Yorkshire	143:7 at Chelmsford, 2006
	By Essex	149:5 at Chelmsford, 2006
Highest Individual Score:		
	For Yorkshire	43 G L Brophy at Chelmsford, 2006
	For Essex	48* J S Foster at Chelmsford, 2006
Best Bowling:	For Yorkshire	2 for 22 A Shahzad at Chelmsford, 2006
	For Essex	2 for 11 T J Phillips at Chelmsford, 2006
versus Hampshire:	Played 1, Lost 1 (Neutral)	
Scores:	By Yorkshire	140-6 at Cardiff, 2012
	By Hampshire	150-6 at Cardiff, 2012
Highest Individual Score:		
	For Yorkshire	72* D A Miller at Cardiff, 2012
	For Hampshire	43 J H K Adams at Cardiff, 2012
Best Bowling:	For Yorkshire	2 for 20 R J Sidebottom at Cardiff, 2012
	For Hampshire	3 for 26 C P Wood at Cardiff, 2012
versus Lancashire:	Played 18, Won 9 (in Yorkshire 6, Away 3), Lost 7 (in Yorkshire 2, Away 5), Abandoned 2 (in Yorkshire 1, Away 1)	
Highest Score:	By Yorkshire	180:6 at Leeds, 2012
	By Lancashire	207 at Manchester, 2005
Lowest Score:	By Yorkshire	97 at Manchester, 2005
	By Lancashire	104:3 at Manchester, 2003
Highest Individual Score:	For Yorkshire	108* I J Harvey at Leeds, 2004
	For Lancashire	101 S G Law at Manchester, 2005
Best Bowling	For Yorkshire	4 for 26 A U Rashid at Leeds, 2011
	For Lancashire	3 for 10 D G Cork at Manchester, 2005
versus Leicestershire:	Played 15, Won 5 (in Yorkshire 2, Away 3), Lost 9 (in Yorkshire 4, Away 5), Abandoned 1 (in Yorkshire)	
Highest Score:	By Yorkshire	211:6 at Leeds, 2004
	By Leicestershire	221:3 at Leeds, 2004
Lowest Score:	By Yorkshire	134 at Leeds, 2006
	By Leicestershire	147:9 at Leicester, 2012
Highest Individual Score:	For Yorkshire	92 P A Jaques at Leeds, 2004
	For Leicestershire	111 D L Maddy at Leeds, 2004
Best Bowling:	For Yorkshire	4 for 20 A U Rashid at Leeds, 2010
	For Leicestershire	3 for 3 J K H Naik at Leeds, 2011

TWENTY20 CUP RECORDS 2003-2012 *(Continued)*

versus Northamptonshire:	Played 4, Won 1 (Away), Lost 1 (in Yorkshire), Tied 1 (Away), Abandoned 1 (in Yorkshire)
Highest Score:	By Yorkshire 180:3 at Northampton, 2010
	By Northamptonshire 180:5 at Northampton, 2010
Lowest Score:	By Yorkshire 144 at Northampton, 2011
	By Northamptonshire 132-7 at Northampton, 2011
Highest Individual Score:	For Yorkshire 101* H H Gibbs at Northampton, 2010
	For Northamptonshire 53 W P U J C Vaas at Northampton, 2010
Best Bowling:	For Yorkshire 3 for 23 A U Rashid at Leeds, 2010
	For Northamptonshire 4 for 23 A J Hall at Northampton 2011

versus Nottinghamshire:	Played 18, Won 7 (in Yorkshire 4, Away 3), Lost 10 (in Yorkshire 4, Away 6), No Result 1 (In Yorkshire)
Highest Score:	By Yorkshire 207:7 at Nottingham, 2004
	By Nottinghamshire 215:6 at Nottingham, 2011
Lowest Score:	By Yorkshire 112:7 at Nottingham, 2010
	By Nottinghamshire 136:8 at Nottingham, 2008
Highest Individual Score:	For Yorkshire 96* M J Wood at Nottingham, 2004
	For Nottinghamshire 91 M A Ealham at Nottingham, 2004
Best Bowling:	For Yorkshire 4 for 23 Rana Naved-ul-Hasan at Leeds, 2009
	For Nottinghamshire 3 for 42 S C G MacGill at Leeds, 2003

versus Sussex:	Played 2, Won 1 (Neutral), Lost 1 (Away)
Highest Score:	By Yorkshire 172:6 at Cardiff, 2012
	By Sussex 193:5 at Hove, 2007
Lowest Score:	By Yorkshire 155 at Hove, 2007
	By Sussex 136:8 at Cardiff, 2012
Highest Individual Score:	For Yorkshire 68* J M Bairstow at Cardiff, 2012
	For Sussex 80* C D Nash at Cardiff, 2012
Best Bowling:	For Yorkshire 2 for 22 T T Bresnan at Cardiff, 2012
	For Sussex 3 for 22 S B Styris at Cardiff, 2012

versus Warwickshire:	Played 4, Lost 3 (in Yorkshire 2, Away 1), No Result 1 (Away)
Highest Score:	By Yorkshire 161:8 at Leeds, 2011
	By Warwickshire 164:5 at Leeds, 2011
Lowest Score:	By Yorkshire 121:9 at Leeds, 2010
	By Warwickshire 145:8 at Birmingham, 2010
Highest Individual Score:	For Yorkshire 54 A W Gale at Leeds, 2011
	For Warwickshire 64 W T S Porterfield at Leeds, 2011
Best Bowling:	For Yorkshire 3 for 22 R M Pyrah at Leeds, 2010
	For Warwickshire 4 for 19 K H D Barker at Birmingham, 2010

versus Worcestershire:	Played 5, Won 3 (in Yorkshire), Lost 2 (Away)
Highest Score:	By Yorkshire 213:7 at Leeds, 2010
	By Worcestershire 208:7 at Worcester, 2010
Lowest Score:	By Yorkshire 142 at Worcester 2011
	By Worcestershire 109 at Leeds, 2010
Highest Individual Score:	For Yorkshire 65 J E Root at Leeds, 2012
	For Worcestershire 80* P J Hughes at Leeds, 2012
Best Bowling:	For Yorkshire 4 for 21 R M Pyrah at Leeds, 2011
	For Worcestershire 4 for 31 Shakib al Hasan at Worcester, 2011

CAREER AVERAGES FOR YORKSHIRE

TWENTY20 CUP 2003-2012

Player	*M*	*Inns*	*NO*	*Runs*	*HS*	*Av'ge*	*100s*	*50s*	*Runs*	*Wkts*	*Av'ge*	*Ct/St*
Ashraf, M A	**12**	**0**	**0**	**0**	**—**	**—**	**—**	**—**	**359**	**15**	**23.93**	**1**
Azeem Rafiq	**35**	**15**	**9**	**67**	**21***	**11.16**	**—**	**—**	**925**	**30**	**30.83**	**14**
Bairstow, J M	**37**	**32**	**5**	**520**	**68***	**19.25**	**—**	**1**	**—**	**—**	**—**	**8/2**
Ballance, G S	**28**	**24**	**5**	**484**	**48***	**25.47**	**—**	**—**	**—**	**—**	**—**	**17**
Best, T L	8	3	2	10	10*	10.00	—	—	243	7	34.71	4
Blakey, R J	7	5	1	119	32	29.75	—	—	—	—	—	5/1
Bresnan T T	**50**	**35**	**12**	**412**	**42**	**17.91**	**—**	**—**	**1228**	**51**	**24.07**	**15**
Brophy, G L	54	46	9	717	57*	19.37	—	2	—	—	—	25/7
Claydon, M E	7	2	2	14	12*	—	—	—	188	5	37.60	2
Craven, V J	6	6	4	76	44*	38.00	—	—	67	0	—	3
Dawood, I	11	8	3	44	15	8.80	—	—	—	—	—	5/2
Dawson, R K J	22	8	3	71	22	14.20	—	—	558	24	23.25	7
Fleming, S P	4	4	0	62	58	15.50	—	1	—	—	—	1
Gale, A W	**73**	**67**	**7**	**1713**	**91**	**28.55**	**—**	**14**	**—**	**—**	**—**	**25**
Gibbs, H H	15	15	3	443	101*	36.91	1	2	—	—	—	8
Gilbert, C R	13	9	2	107	36*	15.28	—	—	—	—	—	7
Gillespie, J N	17	4	2	14	8*	7.00	—	—	422	17	24.82	5
Gough, D	17	7	3	42	20*	10.50	—	—	416	16	26.00	2
Gray, A K D	8	3	0	17	13	5.66	—	—	211	9	23.44	4
Guy, S M	10	6	1	44	13	8.80	—	—	—	—	—	2
Hamilton, G M	3	3	1	41	41*	20.50	—	—	—	—	—	1
Harvey, I J	10	10	1	438	109	48.66	2	2	258	10	25.80	4
Hodgson, L J	2	1	1	39	39*	—	—	—	59	2	29.50	1
Hoggard, M J	15	2	1	19	18	19.00	—	—	472	13	36.30	4
Jaques, P A	**25**	**24**	**2**	**718**	**92**	**32.63**	**—**	**5**	**15**	**0**	**—**	**4**
Kirby, S P	3	—	—	—	—	—	—	—	119	4	29.75	1
Kruis, G J	20	5	3	41	22	20.50	—	—	486	19	25.57	6
Lawson, M A K	2	1	1	4	4*	—	—	—	87	3	29.00	1
Lehmann, D S	9	9	3	252	48	42.00	—	—	180	8	22.50	4
Lumb, M J	26	26	3	442	84*	19.21	—	4	65	3	21.66	8
Lyth, A	**40**	**35**	**1**	**704**	**78**	**20.70**	**—**	**2**	**—**	**—**	**—**	**14**
McGrath, A	**66**	**61**	**12**	**1403**	**73***	**28.63**	**—**	**8**	**698**	**23**	**30.34**	**26**
McKay, C J	8	6	3	54	21*	18.00	—	—	258	10	25.80	1
Miller, D A	**12**	**11**	**3**	**390**	**74***	**48.75**	**—**	**4**	**—**	**—**	**—**	**4**
Patterson, S A	**20**	**4**	**3**	**3**	**3***	**3.00**	**—**	**—**	**653**	**17**	**38.41**	**3**
Pyrah, R M	**74**	**50**	**15**	**406**	**35**	**11.60**	**—**	**—**	**1620**	**79**	**20.50**	**26**
Rana Naved-ul-Hasan	8	8	2	63	20*	10.50	—	—	159	11	14.45	2
Rashid, A U	**45**	**29**	**6**	**242**	**34**	**10.52**	**—**	**—**	**1189**	**52**	**22.86**	**15**
Root, J E	**21**	**18**	**4**	**347**	**65**	**24.78**	**—**	**1**	**148**	**2**	**74.00**	**8**
Rudolph, J A	39	35	5	710	61	23.66	—	3	145	6	24.16	7
Sanderson, B W	4	—	—	—	—	—	—	—	74	6	12.33	—
Sayers, J J	**12**	**9**	**0**	**172**	**44**	**19.11**	**—**	**—**	**—**	**—**	**—**	**2**
Shahzad, A	22	16	4	129	20	10.75	—	—	576	17	33.88	5
Sidebottom, R J	**20**	**9**	**5**	**68**	**16***	**17.00**	**—**	**—**	**531**	**23**	**23.08**	**7**
Silverwood, C E W	9	5	2	32	13*	10.66	—	—	264	7	37.71	4
Swanepoel, P	2	1	1	2	2*	—	—	—	60	3	20.00	1
Starc, M A	**10**	**2**	**1**	**0**	**0***	**0.00**	**—**	**—**	**218**	**21**	**10.38**	**1**
Taylor, C R	2	2	1	10	10*	10.00	—	—	—	—	—	—
Vaughan, M P	16	16	1	292	41*	19.46	—	—	81	1	81.00	2
Wainwright, D J	26	9	6	23	6*	7.66	—	—	551	21	26.23	9
Wardlaw, I	**5**	**0**	**0**	**0**	**—**	**—**	**—**	**—**	**87**	**2**	**43.50**	**—**
Warren, A C	2	—	—	—	—	—	—	—	70	4	17.50	—
White, C	33	31	0	570	55	18.38	—	2	132	2	66.00	8
Wood, M J	15	15	3	328	96*	27.33	—	2	32	2	16.00	11
Younus Khan	2	2	0	55	40	27.50	—	—	32	2	16.00	0
Yuvraj Singh	5	5	0	154	71	30.80	—	1	51	5	10.20	0

SECOND ELEVEN RECORDS

in the

SECOND ELEVEN CHAMPIONSHIP 1959-1961 AND 1975-2012

SUMMARY OF RESULTS BY SEASON

Season	*Played*	*Won*	*Lost*	*Drawn*	*Tied*	*Abandoned*	*Position in Championship*
1959	10	4	1	5	0	0	7
1960	10	1	3	6	0	0	14
1961	9	2	2	5	0	1	11
1975	14	4	0	10	0	0	4
1976	14	5	5	4	0	0	5
1977	**16**	**9**	**0**	**7**	**0**	**1**	**1**
1978	15	5	2	8	0	0	4
1979	16	5	0	11	0	0	3
1980	14	5	2	7	0	1	5
1981	16	2	3	11	0	0	11
1982	16	2	3	11	0	0	14 =
1983	11	5	1	5	0	3	2
1984	**15**	**9**	**3**	**3**	**0**	**0**	**1**
1985	14	3	3	8	0	1	12
1986	16	5	1	10	0	0	5
1987	**15**	**5**	**2**	**8**	**0**	**1**	**1 =**
1988	16	4	1	11	0	0	9
1989	17	2	3	12	0	0	9 =
1990	16	1	6	9	0	0	17
1991	**16**	**8**	**1**	**7**	**0**	**0**	**1**
1992	17	5	2	10	0	0	5
1993	17	6	1	10	0	0	3
1994	17	6	2	9	0	0	2
1995	17	7	1	9	0	0	5
1996	17	6	3	8	0	0	4
1997	16	8	5	3	0	1	2
1998	15	4	2	9	0	0	9
1999	16	3	8	5	0	1	14
2000	14	5	2	7	0	1	5
2001	12	8	2	2	0	1	2
2002	12	5	1	6	0	0	3
2003	**10**	**7**	**1**	**2**	**0**	**0**	**1**
2004	7	2	0	5	0	1	8
2005	12	2	4	6	0	0	10
2006	14	6	4	4	0	0	3
2007	12	4	5	3	0	0	10
2008	12	4	4	4	0	2	5
2009	9	5	0	4	0	0	(Group A) 2
2010	9	2	4	3	0	0	(Group A) 8
2011	9	0	4	4	1	0	(Group A) 10
2012	9	1	2	4	0	2	(North) 9
Totals	550	181	97	271	1	15	

Matches abandoned without a ball being bowled are not counted as a match played. The Championship was divided into two groups from 2009, each team playng each other once. The two group winners played for the Championship

ANALYSIS OF RESULTS AGAINST EACH OPPONENT

County	*Played*	*Won*	*Lost*	*Drawn*	*Tied*	*Abandoned*	*First Played*
Derbyshire	52	12	8	32	0	3	1959
Durham	28	9	6	13	0	2	1992
Essex	13	9	2	2	0	0	1990
Glamorgan	38	10	3	25	0	2	1975
Gloucestershire	10	3	3	4	0	0	1990
Hampshire	12	4	1	7	0	0	1990
Kent	26	5	4	17	0	1	1981
Lancashire	64	14	17	33	0	3	1959
Leicestershire	26	10	5	10	1	1	1975
MCC Young Cricketers .	3	3	0	0	0	0	2005
MCC Universities	2	1	0	1	0	0	2011
Middlesex	18	7	2	9	0	0	1977
Northamptonshire	46	13	6	27	0	1	1959
Nottinghamshire	55	17	10	28	0	2	1959
Scotland	2	1	0	1	0	0	2007
Somerset	18	9	3	6	0	0	1988
Surrey	36	9	9	18	0	2	1976
Sussex	16	6	5	5	0	0	1990
Warwickshire	57	21	12	24	0	0	1959
Worcestershire	36	19	4	13	0	0	1961
Totals	558	182	100	275	1	17	

Note: Matches abandoned are not included in the total played.

Highest Total

By Yorkshire: 538 for 9 wkts dec v. Worcestershire at Stamford Bridge, 2007
Against Yorkshire: 567 for 7 wkts dec by Middlesex at RAF Vine Lane, Uxbridge, 2000

Lowest Total

By Yorkshire: 69 v. Lancashire at Heywood, 1983
Against Yorkshire: 36 by Lancashire at Elland, 1979

Highest Individual Score

For Yorkshire: 273* by R J Blakey v. Northamptonshire at Northampton, 1986
Against Yorkshire: 235 by O A Shah for Middlesex at Leeds, 1999

Century in Each Innings

For Yorkshire:	C White	209* and 115*	v. Worcestershire at Worcester, 1990
	K Sharp	150* and 127	v. Essex at Elland, 1991
	A A Metcalfe	109 and 136*	v. Somerset at North Perrott, 1994
	R A Kettleborough	123 and 192*	v. Nottinghamshire at Todmorden, 1996
	C R Taylor	201* and 129	v. Sussex at Hove, 2005
	A W Gale	131 and 123	v. Somerset at Taunton, 2006
	J J Sayers	157 and 105	v. Lancashire at Leeds, 2007
Against Yorkshire:	N Nannan	100 and 102*	for Nottinghamshire at Harrogate, 1979
	G D Lloyd	134 and 103	for Lancashire at Scarborough, 1989
	A J Swann	131 and 100	for Northamptonshire at York, 1998
	G J Kennis	114 and 114	for Somerset at Taunton, 1999

Best Bowling in an Innings

For Yorkshire: 9 for 27 by G A Cope v. Northamptonshire at Northampton, 1979
Against Yorkshire: 8 for 15 by I Folley for Lancashire at Heywood, 1983

Best Bowling in a Match

For Yorkshire: 13 for 92 (6 for 48 and 7 for 44) by M K Bore v. Lancashire at Harrogate, 1976
Against Yorkshire: 13 for 100 (7 for 45 and 6 for 55) by N J Perry for Glamorgan at Cardiff, 1978

Totals of 450 and over

By Yorkshire (26)

Score	Versus	Ground	Season
538 for 9 wkts dec	Worcestershire	Stamford Bridge	2007
534 for 5 wkts dec	Lancashire	Stamford Bridge	2003
530 for 8 wkts dec	Nottinghamshire	Middlesbrough	2000
514 for 3 wkts dec	Somerset	Taunton	1988
509 for 4 wkts dec	Northamptonshire	Northampton	1986
502	Derbyshire	Chesterfield	2003
501 for 5 wkts dec	MCC Young Cricketers	Stamford Bridge	2009
497	Derbyshire	Chesterfield	2005
495 for 5 wkts dec	Somerset	Taunton	2006
488 for 8 wkts dec	Warwickshire	Harrogate	1984
486 for 6 wkts dec	Glamorgan	Leeds	1986
476 for 3 wkts dec	Glamorgan	Gorseinon	1984
475 for 9 wkts dec	Nottinghamshire	Nottingham	1995
474 for 3 wkts dec	Glamorgan	Todmorden	2003
474	Durham	Stamford Bridge	2003
470	Lancashire	Leeds	2006
469	Warwickshire	Castleford	1999
462	Scotland	Stamford Bridge	2007
461 for 8 wkts dec	Essex	Stamford Bridge	2006
459 for 3 wkts dec	Leicestershire	Oakham	1997
459 for 6 wkts dec	Glamorgan	Bradford	1992
457 for 9 wkts dec	Kent	Canterbury	1983
456 for 6 wkts dec	Nottinghamshire	York	1986
456 for 5 wkts dec	Gloucestershire	Todmorden	1990
454 for 9 wkts dec	Derbyshire	Chesterfield	1959
452 for 9 wkts dec	Glamorgan	Cardiff	2005

Against Yorkshire (12)

Score	For	Ground	Season
567 for 7 wkts dec	Middlesex	RAF Vine Lane, Uxbridge	2000
555 for 7 wkts dec	Derbyshire	Stamford Bridge	2002
525 for 7 wkts dec	Sussex	Hove	2005
493 for 8 wkts dec	Nottinghamshire	Lady Bay, Nottingham	2002
488 for 8 wkts dec	Warwickshire	Castleford	1999
486	Essex	Chelmsford	2000
485	Gloucestershire	North Park, Cheltenham	2001
477	Lancashire	Headingley	2006
471	Warwickshire	Clifton Park, York	2010
458	Lancashire	Bradford	1997
454 for 7 wkts dec	Lancashire	Todmorden	1993
450 for 7 wkts (inns closed)	Derbyshire	Bradford	1980

Completed Innings under 75

By Yorkshire (3)

Score	Versus	Ground	Season
69	Lancashire	Heywood	1983
74	Derbyshire	Chesterfield	1960
74	Nottinghamshire	Bradford	1998

Against Yorkshire (10)

Score	By	Ground	Season
36	Lancashire	Elland	1979
49	Leicestershire	Leicester	2008
50	Lancashire	Liverpool	1984
60	Derbyshire	Bradford	1977
60	Surrey	Sunbury-on-Thames	1977
62	MCC YC	High Wycombe	2005
64	Nottinghamshire	Brodsworth	1959
66	Leicestershire	Lutterworth	1977
72	Sussex	Horsham	2003
74	Worcestershire	Barnsley	1978

Individual Scores of 150 and over (60)

Score	Player	Versus	Ground	Season
273*	R J Blakey	Northamptonshire	Northampton	1986
238*	K Sharp	Somerset	Taunton	1988
233	P E Robinson	Kent	Canterbury	1983
221*	K Sharp	Gloucestershire	Todmorden	1990
219	G M Hamilton	Derbyshire	Chesterfield	2003
218*	A McGrath	Surrey	Elland	1994
212	G S Ballance	MCC Young Cricketers	Stamford Bridge	2009
209*	C White	Worcestershire	Worcester	1990
205	C R Taylor	Glamorgan	Todmorden	2003
204	B Parker	Gloucestershire	Bristol	1993
203	A McGrath	Durham	Headingley	2005
202*	J M Bairstow	Leicestershire	Oakham	2009
202	M J Wood	Essex	Stamford Bridge	2006
201*	C R Taylor	Sussex	Hove	2005
200*	D Byas	Worcestershire	Worcester	1992
200*	A McGrath	Northamptonshire	Northampton	2012
192*	R A Kettleborough	Nottinghamshire	Todmorden	1996
191	P E Robinson	Warwickshire	Harrogate	1984
191	M J Wood	Derbyshire	Rotherham	2000
191	M J Lumb	Nottinghamshire	Middlesbrough	2000
189*	C S Pickles	Gloucestershire	Bristol	1991
186	A McGrath	MCC Universities	York	2011
184	J D Love	Worcestershire	Headingley	1976
183	A W Gale	Durham	Stamford Bridge	2006
174	G L Brophy	Worcestershire	Stamford Bridge	2007
173	S N Hartley	Warwickshire	Edgbaston	1980
173	A A Metcalfe	Glamorgan	Gorseinon	1984
173	B Parker	Sussex	Hove	1996
173	R A Kettleborough	Leicestershire	Oakham School	1997

Individual Scores of 150 and over *(Continued)*

Score	*Player*	*Versus*	*Ground*	*Season*
172	A C Morris	Lancashire	York	1995
170*	R A J Townsley	Glamorgan	Harrogate	1975
169	J E Root	Warwickshire	York	2010
168	M J Wood	Leicestershire	Oakham School	1997
166	A A Metcalfe	Lancashire	York	1984
166	C A Chapman	Northamptonshire	York	1998
165*	A Lyth	Durham	Stamford Bridge	2006
165	J J Sayers	Sussex	Hove	2006
164*	A W Gale	Leicestershire	Harrogate	2002
164	J C Balderstone	Nottinghamshire	Harrogate	1960
163*	J E Root	Leicestershire	Oakham	2009
163	A A Metcalfe	Derbyshire	Chesterfield	1992
162*	D Byas	Surrey	Scarborough	1987
160	A A Metcalfe	Somerset	Bradford	1993
157	J J Sayers	Lancashire	Headingley	2007
155	S M Guy	Derbyshire	Chesterfield	2005
154*	C R Taylor	Surrey	Whitgift School	2005
153*	A A Metcalfe	Warwickshire	Bingley	1995
153	C White	Worcestershire	Marske-by-the-Sea	1991
153	R A Stead	Surrey	Todmorden	2002
152	A A Metcalfe	Gloucestershire	Bristol	1993
151*	P E Robinson	Nottinghamshire	York	1986
151*	S J Foster	Kent	Elland	1992
151*	J J Sayers	Durham	Stamford Bridge	2004
151	P J Hartley	Somerset	Clevedon	1989
151	A McGrath	Somerset	Elland	1995
151	V J Craven	Glamorgan	Todmorden	2003
150*	K Sharp	Essex	Elland	1991
150*	G M Fellows	Hampshire	Todmorden	1998
150*	S M Guy	Nottinghamshire	Headingley	2005
150*	J A Leaning	Worcestershire	Worcester	2011
150	K Sharp	Glamorgan	Ebbw Vale	1983
150	S N Hartley	Nottinghamshire	Worksop	1988
150	C R Taylor	Derbyshire	Chesterfield	2003

7 Wickets in an Innings (30)

Analysis	*Player*	*Versus*	*Ground*	*Season*
9 for 27	G A Cope	Northamptonshire	Northampton	1977
9 for 62	M K Bore	Warwicshire	Scarborough	1976
8 for 53	S J Dennis	Nottinghamshire	Nottingham	1983
8 for 57	M K Bore	Lancashire	Manchester	1977
8 for 79	P J Berry	Derbyshire	Harrogate	1991
7 for 13	P Carrick	Northamptonshire	Marske-by-the-Sea	1977
7 for 21	S Silvester	Surrey	Sunbury-on-Thames	1977
7 for 22	J A R Blain	Surrey	Purley	2004
7 for 32	P W Jarvis	Surrey	The Oval	1984
7 for 34	P Carrick	Glamorgan	Leeds	1986
7 for 37	P M Hutchison	Warwickshire	Coventry	2001

7 Wickets in an Innings *(Continued)*

Analysis	*Player*	*Versus*	*Ground*	*Season*
7 for 39	G M Hamilton	Sussex	Leeds	1995
7 for 40	M K Bore	Worcestershire	Old Hill	1976
7 for 44	M K Bore	Lancashire	Harrogate	1976
7 for 44	J P Whiteley	Worcestershire	Leeds	1979
7 for 51	J D Middlebrook	Derbyshire	Rotherham	2000
7 for 53	J P Whiteley	Warwickshire	Birmingham	1980
7 for 55	C White	Leicestershire	Bradford	1990
7 for 58	K Gillhouley	Derbyshire	Chesterfield	1960
7 for 58	P J Hartley	Lancashire	Leeds	1985
7 for 63	M J Hoggard	Worcestershire	Harrogate	1998
7 for 65	M K Bore	Nottinghamshire	Steetley	1976
7 for 70	J D Batty	Leicestershire	Bradford	1992
7 for 71	J D Batty	Hampshire	Harrogate	1994
7 for 81	K Gillhouley	Lancashire	Scarborough	1960
7 for 84	I J Houseman	Kent	Canterbury	1989
7 for 88	I G Swallow	Nottinghamshire	Nottingham	1983
7 for 90	A P Grayson	Kent	Folkestone	1991
7 for 93	D Pickles	Nottinghamshire	Nottingham	1960
7 for 94	K Gillhouley	Northamptonshire	Redcar	1960

12 Wickets in a Match (6)

Analysis		*Player*	*Versus*	*Ground*	*Season*
13 for 92	(6-48 and 7-44)	M K Bore	Lancashire	Harrogate	1976
13 for 110	(7-70 and 6-40)	J D Batty	Leicestershire	Bradford	1992
13 for 111	(4-49 and 9-62)	M K Bore	Warwickshire	Scarborough	1976
12 for 69	(5-32 and 7-37)	P M Hutchison	Warwickshire	Coventry	2001
12 for 120	(5-39 and 7-81)	K Gillhouley	Lancashire	Scarborough	1960
12 for 163	(5-78 and 7-84)	I J Houseman	Kent	Canterbury	1989

Hat-tricks (4)

Player	*Versus*	*Ground*	*Season*
I G Swallow	Warwickshire	Harrogate	1984
S D Fletcher	Nottinghamshire	Marske-by-the-Sea	1987
I G Swallow	Derbyshire	Chesterfield	1988
M Broadhurst	Essex	Southend-on-Sea	1992

ANNUAL REPORT
and
Statement of Account
for the year ended
December 31, 2012

CHAIRMAN'S REPORT

COLIN GRAVES

The entire squad were magnificent throughout the season, and I am sure that at times when the weather was conspiring against us as we tried to complete matches they must have thought it was going to be a year of disappointment.

To get back into the elite level of English cricket was always the main objective. The catalyst for me was the effort the players showed to record three successive victories in our last three County Championship matches. To play the entire season and not lose a match in the Championship has not been achieved since 1928, so this team has something to be proud about. In Martyn Moxon's report you will read in detail his appraisal of the season. It is not for me to pick out individual performances to highlight apart from complimenting the Captain, Andrew Gale, on his endeavours and achievements with a very young and exciting team supporting him.

The one thing I constantly did notice, as the season progressed, was the fantastic team spirit which developed in the squad as everybody wanted to be part of a successful team. I was proud of every player who represented the Club throughout the season, and I look forward to our 150th year with great optimism and excitement. The new campaign will be a great challenge for us all. We have strengthened the squad with the recruitment of two frontline bowlers in England Lion Jack Brooks, from Northamptonshire, and England international Liam Plunkett, from Durham. With the investment we have made in our recruitment drive I believe we now have a bowling attack that will be the envy of county cricket and give us every chance of winning the First Division.

In one-day cricket, I felt we came of age in 2012. The game plans, and our aggressive and effective way of playing *T20 cricket* were mastered by the coaching team, and executed brilliantly by the players. To reach the *T20* Finals Day at the end of August was momentous — an honour we have never achieved since the inception of *T20* cricket. We eventually lost the final to Hampshire, but ultimately we secured our place in the lucrative *T20* Champions League tournament.

It was a memorable day and the support we experienced was unbelievable. I applaud everyone who came along to support our players. The whole experience of finals cricket, whether it be in Cardiff or in the sunshine of South Africa, gave everyone connected to the Club great experiences. We can only build on this for 2013, and make a real effort to repeat the rewards that 2012 delivered.

David Miller and Mitchell Starc were inspired overseas signings for our *T20* campaign, and without doubt the rising star of this competition was Gary Ballance, who played some crucial innings throughout the campaign. The success in reaching the final of the *T20* competition gave us a platform and opportunity to play in the Champions League in South Africa, competing against high-quality teams from around the world, who included many international players. The young squad certainly were not overawed by the occasion, and against all odds progressed to the group stages after two fantastic wins against Trinidad and Tobago and Uva Next from Sri Lanka. The experience alone was invaluable to our squad, who represented the *White Rose* with style and passion.

Overall, on the playing field in 2012 we had a superb season to remember and be proud of. Now we have tasted success I firmly believe that everyone in the Club wants to see more of it — so let's all get behind the players and give them our full support in all forms of cricket in our 150th year.

The coaching structure at the Club changed radically in 2012. The new structure, I believe, was the major catalyst in our performances throughout the season. Without doubt Jason Gillespie and Paul Farbrace have been instrumental in bringing a new positive approach to the Club, and this has been infectious to everyone around them. I wish to offer my sincere thanks to them and Martyn Moxon, who has established a new ethos in playing cricket for The Yorkshire County Cricket Club.

For those who did not attend the Test Match in August, you missed a fantastic game with a superb atmosphere. Five full days of Test cricket played by the two best sides in the world resulted in a game to be remembered for many reasons. International cricket at Headingley is the life blood of sustaining a superb arena with fantastic facilities which allow all players to perform to the highest levels.

For the Club to prosper and grow it is imperative that you all continue to support our international matches at Headingley, so that we retain these superb fixtures in the future, when competition from other venues around the country is on the increase. Headingley is unique in many ways, but I personally believe the beauty of the venue is the atmosphere that makes it one of the best venues in world cricket.

Finally, may I take this opportunity to personally thank the entire staff and Board of Directors who have supported me over the past 12 months in achieving our objectives. Our aim is to achieve financial stability by repaying debt as quickly as we can.

The year ahead will be an exciting period for the Club. We hope to continue our progression on the field and to maintain our efforts in developing a top-class side. We will also develop new income streams which will help to make the Club more commercially viable.

COLIN GRAVES
Executive Chairman
The Yorkshire
County Cricket Club

FINANCE DIRECTOR'S REPORT

CHARLES HARTWELL

2012 was a very frustrating year from a financial perspective, with the rain gods doing everything they could to ensure that life was as challenging as possible.

The effect of rain was the underlying reason why the Club is reporting a pre-tax deficit of £153k for the year. Even though this is significantly better than 2011's pre-tax deficit (£1.2m) it is still disappointing that a surplus is not being reported.

Included within this deficit is exceptional expenditure of £110k, which reflects the costs incurred during the year, predominantly relating to the restructuring of the coaching department. Without these costs the Club would have made a notional deficit before taxation of £43k.

Income for the year was £7.8m, an increase of £2.3m over 2011. On a very basic level this variance can be accounted for by the additional ticket-and-hospitality income generated from the return of Test cricket to Headingley, thus underlying income remained flat in 2012. Looking at the financial performance of the Test Match, ticket income achieved budget, but the continuing difficult economic times, coupled with the impact of the Olympics, resulted in hospitality income falling short of expectation. All five days were rain-affected, resulting in each day going past 7pm, which had a knock-on impact on steward and police costs. Matchday expenditure was, therefore, higher than expected.

The ODI was abandoned without a ball bowled, due to the horrendous weather, and this was a major factor in ticket revenues falling short of expectation, but the impact was mitigated to an extent by a reduction in stewarding costs. Domestic ticket revenues and attendances for regular season games were obviously below the levels of 2011. Only two home Championship matches were completed, due to the weather, which also impacted on the fixtures played at Scarborough.

Thankfully, the additional income generated from the home quarter-final within the *FLt20* competition, the additional income from reaching Finals Day, and the bonus money generated from the *CLT20* competition in South Africa brought overall ticket revenues back in line with expectation, and exceeded 2011 levels.

Membership-subscription income (probably influenced by playing in the Second Division) fell by 16 per cent to £492k. During 2012 the Club revisited the membership and affiliation offerings, simplifying the membership categories and also introducing Club Yorkshire in an attempt to convert some of the huge passive following (including 21k Twitter followers) into a more formal affiliation with the Club. Club Yorkshire is positioned as an entry-level link to the Club, and the start of the journey which will cumulate with a conversion to Membership. Coupled with promotion, and our 150th anniversary celebrations, I am confident that the Club will increase the current number of members and supporters.

ECB income in 2011 included a one-off £200k payment for the ground to meet material compliance as an international venue — more covered seating and permanent floodlights were all that held us back from full compliance. With this one-off income stream stripped out, like-with-like income increased by £103k, which reflects the success of the Club in producing top-class players and a successful Championship squad. Commercial income increased by £394k to £1.8m, primarily reflecting the fact that Test cricket generates significant additional perimeter advertising income for the Club.

Total Club expenditure in 2012 was £7.9m, an increase of £1.3m on 2011. The cost of staging the Test match was £1.1m, leaving like-with-like costs £200k higher than 2011. Cricket expenses have increased by £174k, driven by increased cost of player salaries and performance bonuses. Overhead increased by £327k to £2.0m. This reflects an increased investment in headcount, now that regular Test matches have returned to Headingley. In addition, the costs of operations and infrastructure have increased, due to an increase in utility costs and additional maintenance around the ground.

Looking to 2013, I am expecting to generate a small surplus before taxation. The Club has very recently secured the required permissions that will enable outdoor concerts to be held at the ground, and this is certainly something that we are looking at for the summer. In addition, the introduction of Club Yorkshire, the return to Division 1 in the Championship and the sesquicentennial events should ensure that a surplus is generated. However, the budget assumes that the weather stays fine and dry, and some glorious sunshine from May 24 to 28 would be very much appreciated.

I would like to take this opportunity to thank Leeds City Council, HSBC, and our Chairman, Colin Graves for their continued and invaluable financial support for the Club. I would also like to thank the numerous members who volunteer on various committees and associations, and who promote the Club around the country and beyond. Once again, the Yorkshire Cricket Taverners have been very generous in their support to the Club, and this is greatly appreciated.

On a separate note, the Yorkshire Cricket Foundation (YCF) continues to grow and develop its reach. From January 1, 2013, the YCF will assume responsibility for the stewardship of the Club's archives and memorabilia, and the Archives Committee, chaired by David Allan, will come under the auspices of the YCF.

Because it is a registered charity, people can donate, loan, or bequeath their items of Yorkshire's cricket heritage in a tax-efficient manner, safe in the knowledge that the items will be protected for future generations to enjoy. The YCF will also have a bespoke website (www. yorkshire-cricketfoundation.org), ready for the start of the cricket season, with pages dedicated to the history and heritage of cricket within Yorkshire The YCF has also recently been granted Heritage Lottery Funding, which has allowed for the production of a mobile museum to build on the success of the Headingley Museum. The mobile museum will be taken to schools, cricket grounds, and events throughout Yorkshire.

I would like to end my report on a very positive note. In October Andy Dawson and I were fortunate enough to accompany the team to South Africa for the *CLT20* competition. We were overwhelmed by the way we were welcomed into the fold and were immediately treated as part of the team. It is clear that we have a very special group of players and coaches, who love what they do, have immense pride in playing for Yorkshire, and have 100 per cent trust in each other.

Witnessing firsthand how our team works both on and off the field, I have high hopes for 2013.

CHARLES HARTWELL ACA
Director of Finance
Yorkshire County Cricket Club

DIRECTOR OF PROFESSIONAL CRICKET'S REPORT

MARTYN MOXON

At last year's AGM it was clearly stated that gaining promotion from the Second Division of the LV County Championship was our priority. Obviously, this was achieved, and I would like to take this opportunity of congratulating the players and staff for their outstanding efforts throughout 2012.

There was a determination throughout the Club to bounce back from last year, and we admirably overcame a difficult summer weatherwise to achieve our goal. Statistically, it has been proven that we lost more time in LV=CC matches than any other county. The players handled this frustration very well, and maintained a philosophical attitude, so that when the rain relented they were focused and got the job done.

The performances in the last three games of the season were excellent. We were under pressure to win them all, and duly did. The manner of the victories was the most pleasing aspect for me, as they were by no means straightforward. We found ourselves in tricky positions at both Scarborough and Chelmsford, but the character and skill of individuals and the team shone through, and we eventually prevailed. Experiencing that final afternoon in Chelmsford is what it is all about — there is no better feeling in sport.

Of course, the success of last season was not limited to four-day cricket. Reaching Finals Day of the *FLt20* competition for the first time in the Club's history was an outstanding achievement. We lost the first group game, albeit in controversial circumstances, but then remained unbeaten until the final. To achieve this in the *T20* format is an exceptional performance, and it was an exciting journey which culminated in the Champions League in South Africa. Finals Day in Cardiff was a great experience for all the players and staff, and was very enjoyable, although it was, of course, disappointing to lose the final.

It did, however, give the players a taste of the big stage, and they loved it and want more of it. Our qualification for the *CLT20* meant that this was achieved again very quickly. It was a fantastic experience, and again the lads performed admirably in qualifying for the main competition. A number of players from the squad were unavailable, but it gave others who would not normally have been there the chance to rub shoulders with some of the best players in the world. Although we did not manage to qualify for the semi-final, apart from the game against Sydney Sixers the team were competitive, and again it was pleasing to see the players enjoy the big stage rather than freeze on it. This stands us in good stead for the future.

Our challenge now is to build on the success of last season. Everyone is working hard during the winter to ensure that we give ourselves the best chance of success in all forms of the game. Having said that, our main priority is the LV=CC, and to win this in the Club's 150th Anniversary year would be special.

In order to try and compete in both four-day and one-day cricket we need a strong squad. We recruited Liam Plunkett and Jack Brooks, who both are excellent cricketers, and are highly motivated. They will provide added quality to our seam-bowling resources, and ensure that we can manage the group effectively. I would like to welcome them to the Club, and wish them every success. I feel we now have an exciting squad that has potential to achieve the sustained success we all want. The Club is working hard to ensure that we keep this group of players together, and contract negotiations are on-going with a number of players. I hope that these are successful, and we can move forward together.

It is obviously fantastic when our players are selected for England, and Joe Root's selection and performances so far this winter have given us a lot of pride and pleasure. It now means that we have Tim Bresnan, Jonathan Bairstow and Joe involved with the full England squad. and Gary Ballance has been selected for the Lions' tour of Australia in February/March. We also had Azeem Rafiq join Gary on the England Performance programme in India during November/December.

All good news, although it does make planning for the 2013 season a challenge, as we do not know at this stage who might or might not be available to us. We therefore have to have a big enough and strong enough squad to cater for all eventualities. I am sure you can understand that this in turn provides us with financial challenges, and again everyone at the Club is working hard to overcome them.

I would also like to thank our support staff — Jason Gillespie, Paul Farbrace, Ian Dews, Richard Damms, Tom Summers, Scot McAllister, James Clegg and Tony Pickersgill — who have been outstanding this year. It has been a pleasure working with them, and they have all contributed to the success of last season. I feel we now have an environment in which the players can flourish.

Finally, thank you once again for your continued support. Let us hope that the summer of 2013 is a lot drier than 2012!

MARTYN MOXON
Director of Professional Cricket
Yorkshire County Cricket Club

MEMBERS' COMMITTEE CHAIRMAN'S REPORT

The following served on the Members' Committee during the year.

Chairman:	**Mr S J Mann**
Elected Members:	**Mrs C Evers** **Mr R Levin** **Mr S J Mann** **Mr E Stephens**
Appointed Members:	**Mr G Clark** **Mr A Kilburn** **Mr R W Stott**
In Attendance:	**Mr R Smith,** Board Director **Mr A Dawson,** Commercial Director

There were eight full committee meetings during the year. A full minute of each meeting is presented to the Board of the Club, and a summary of the issues debated appears on the Club website. In addition to these meetings the Committee hosted three Member Forums in the Long Room through the season.

Communications with Members continues to be the focus of the Committee. The use of the forum concept has proved to be a productive and welcome platform for the exchange of views and information, with attendance levels of approximately 80 members at each gathering. The Committee decided to reduce the number of forums from four in 2011 to three in 2012 in an attempt to avoid some of the repetition of questions and questioners. At the November Committee meeting a decision was taken to retain three forums in 2013, and to supplement them with surgeries for members to seek a more personal discussion of membership issues. The Committee have asked, and the Club have agreed, that members of the management team with responsibilities for operations and membership should attend all forums.

The major and most frequent topic of debate in 2012 was the future structure of the first-class game. The Committee constantly sought the views of the membership, and communicated such to the Club. With only one or two exceptions, there was a strong view that the County Championship should remain unchanged: the two-division structure was working well, and producing competitive cricket right up until the final round of matches. There was some indifference as to whether the one-day game should be of 40 overs or 50. Generally, 50 was chosen, but only on the basis that it was the format at international level. The reduced *T20* format used for 2012 was held to be sufficient.

Another topic of frequent discussion and, indeed, frustration was the fixture schedule experienced in 2012. Frankly, it was a shambles, and hardly conducive to attracting spectators. It is difficult to determine the logic of there being no first-class fixture at Headingley for over two months in midseason or why the team had to play four Championship matches in succession away from home.

STEPHEN MANN

Members can be assured that the Club are aware of the widely held views that such a situation should not recur.

The Committee devoted considerable time to examining the Membership Options Scheme with a view to potential adjustments for 2013. Since inception the scheme has been widely accepted, particularly for the choice it gave to suit individual watchers and their personal circumstances. The decision by the Club to provide for an early-payment discount is something the Committee have sought for some years.

Other changes were not so welcome, as they appear to be change for change's sake. Discussions are continuing to ameliorate the impact of the decisions on junior members and those whose work commitments restrict the frequency of attendance. Concern has also been expressed to the Club at the 2013 Test and ODI pricing, which is higher for members than non-members in some areas of the ground.

Members will be aware that 2013 sees the Club celebrate 150 years since inception. Under the chairmanship of my Members' Committee colleague Bob Stott an excellent programme of celebratory events has been developed. It is hoped that all members will attend a number of the events, and enjoy celebrating a major anniversary of this great Club.

As this is the final annual report of my term of office I would like to record my appreciation to all my Committee colleagues for their support and endeavour over the last few years. Also to the many members I have met since I first joined the Committee in 2005. It has been a pleasure to represent and meet you.

STEPHEN MANN,
Chairman,
Members' Committee
Yorkshire County Cricket Club

INDEPENDENT AUDITORS' REPORT

TO THE MEMBERS OF THE YORKSHIRE COUNTY CRICKET CLUB

We have audited the financial statements of The Yorkshire County Cricket Club for the year ended 31 December, 2012, set out on Pages 439 to 448. The financial reporting framework that has been applied in their preparation is applicable in law and UK Accounting Standards (UK Generally Accepted Accounting Practice).

This report is made solely to the Club's members, as a body, in accordance with Section 9 of the Friendly and Industrial and Provident Societies Act 1968. Our audit work has been undertaken so that we might state to the Club's members those matters we are required to state to them in an auditor's report and for no other purpose. To the fullest extent permitted by law, we do not accept or assume responsibility to anyone other than the Club and the Club's members, as a body, for our audit work, for this report, or for the opinions we have formed.

Respective responsibilities of directors and auditor

As more fully explained in the Statement of Directors' Responsibilities set out on Page 438 the Club's directors are responsible for the preparation of financial statements which give a true and fair view. Our responsibility is to audit, and express an opinion on, the financial statements in accordance with applicable law and International Standards on Auditing (UK and Ireland). Those standards require us to comply with the Auditing Practices Board's (APB's) Ethical Standards for Auditors.

Scope of the audit of the financial statements

A description of the scope of an audit of financial statements is provided on the APB's website at www.frc.org.uk/auditscopeukprivate

Opinion on financial statements

In our opinion the financial statements:

- give a true and fair view, in accordance with UK Generally Accepted Accounting Practice, of the state of the Club's affairs as at 31 December, 2012, and of its deficit for the year then ended; and
- have been properly prepared in accordance with the Industrial and Provident Societies Acts 1965 to 2003.

Matters on which we are required to report by exception

We have nothing to report in respect of the following.

Under the Industrial and Provident Societies Acts 1965 to 2003 we are required to report to you if, in our opinion:

- a satisfactory system of control over transactions has not been maintained; or
- the association has not kept proper accounting records; or
- the financial statements are not in agreement with the books of account; or
- we have not received all the information and explanations we need for our audit.

A J SILLS (Senior Statutory Auditor) for and on behalf of KPMG LLP, Statutory Auditor
Chartered Accountants,
Leeds FEBRUARY 7, 2013

CORPORATE GOVERNANCE

The Board is accountable to the Club's members for good corporate governance, and this statement describes how the principles of governance are applied.

THE BOARD

The Board is responsible for approving Club policy and strategy. It meets monthly, or more frequently if business needs require, and has a schedule of matters specifically reserved to it for decision, including all significant commercial issues and all capital expenditure.

The Executive Management Team supply the Board with appropriate and timely information, and the Board Members are free to seek any further information they consider necessary.

NOMINATIONS COMMITTEE

The Nominations Committee is formally constituted with written terms of reference, which are defined in the Club Rules and reviewed regularly. It consists of the President, Secretary and two other Board members, currently C J Graves and R A Smith.

RELATIONS WITH MEMBERS

The Club encourages effective communication with its members, and a specific Committee, as defined in the Club Rules, is appointed for that purpose.

INTERNAL CONTROL

The Board acknowledges its responsibility to maintain a sound system of internal control relating to operational, financial and compliance controls and risk management to safeguard the members' interests and the Club's assets, and will regularly review its effectiveness. Such a system, however, is designed to manage and meet the Club's particular needs and mitigate the risks to which it is exposed, rather than eliminate the risk of failure to achieve business objectives, and can provide only reasonable and not absolute assurance against material mis-statement or loss.

The Club considers its key components to provide effective internal control and improve business efficiency are:

- Regular meetings with senior management to review and assess progress made against objectives and deal with any problems which arise from such reviews.
- A financial reporting system of annual budgets, periodic forecasts and detailed monthly reporting which includes cash-flow forecasts. Budgets and forecasts are reviewed and approved by the Board.
- A defined management and organisation structure with defined responsibilities and appropriate authorisation limits and short lines of communication to the Executive Chairman.

ACCOUNTABILITY AND AUDIT

The Board's responsibilities

The following statement, which should be read in conjunction with the Report of the Independent Auditors, is made with a view to distinguishing for members the respective responsibilities of the Board and of the auditors in relation to the accounts:

The Board is required by UK law to prepare accounts which give a true and fair view of the state of affairs of the Club at the end of the financial year and of the surplus or deficiency of the Club for the financial year then ended.

The Board is also responsible for maintaining adequate accounting records and for taking reasonable steps to safeguard the assets of the Club and detect irregularities and fraud.

The Board confirms that in preparing the Club's accounts appropriate policies have been consistently applied and applicable accounting standards complied with. Further, in all material respects the accounts are supported by prudent judgments and estimates made by reference to information available at the time of their preparation.

All Board members bring independent judgment to bear on their deliberations concerning strategy and performance. The Board is satisfied that it has had access to sufficient information to enable it to make proper decisions in a timely manner, and the Chairman has ensured that Board Members were kept properly briefed.

INCOME AND EXPENDITURE ACCOUNT

for the year ended 31st December, 2012

	Note	2012 £	2011 £
Income			
International ticket and hospitality revenue		**3,135,963**	936,582
Domestic ticket and hospitality revenue		**451,669**	508,559
Subscriptions		**491,558**	583,405
England and Wales Cricket Board		**1,874,697**	1,971,717
Commercial income		**1,783,957**	1,389,695
Other income		**37,816**	41,923
		7,775,660	5,431,881
Cost of sales			
International match and hospitality expenditure		**1,461,424**	429,997
Domestic match and hospitality costs (home fixtures)		**214,907**	279,979
Retail		**113,924**	92,027
Catering		**39,557**	30,560
		(1,829,812)	(832,563)
Cricket expenses			
Staff remuneration and employment expenses *1		**2,144,045**	2,038,804
Match expenses (away fixtures)		**258,845**	245,618
Development expenses		**279,845**	254,505
Other cricket expenses		**61,297**	30,932
		(2,744,032)	(2,569,859)
Overhead			
Infrastructure and ground operations		**717,462**	585,681
Commercial		**608,648**	530,581
Administration *1		**500,956**	394,720
Ticket and membership office		**136,116**	125,063
		(1,963,182)	(1,636,045)
Earnings before interest, tax, depreciation and amortisation		**1,238,634**	393,414
Below the line expenditure:			
Loan Interest		**(1,010,811)**	(1,026,764)
Depreciation		**(540,057)**	(732,208)
Release of Capital Grants		**159,496**	181,960
		(1,391,372)	(1,577,012)
(Deficit) before taxation and exceptional items		**(43,201)**	(1,183,598)
Exceptional items *1		**(109,537)**	—
Deficit before taxation		**(152,738)**	(1,183,598)
Taxation	4	**35,091**	723,495
(Deficit) for the year after taxation		**(117,647)**	(460,103)

*1 During the year, exceptional costs of £109,537 were incurred in relation to redundancy and related restructuring costs in respect of the Club's coaching and administrative staff, of which £59,281 is included within Cricket Staff remuneration and employment expenses and £50,256 within Administration. The costs included within Adminsitration predomantly relate to associated legal costs.

BALANCE SHEET

as at 31st December, 2012

	Note	2012 £	2012 £	2011 £	2011 £
Assets employed:					
Fixed Assets	5		**28,650,114**		28,957,564
Current assets:					
Stocks		**64,198**		40,044	
Debtors	6	**1,176,541**		982,623	
Cash at bank and in hand		—		—	
		1,240,739		1,022,667	
Creditors: amounts falling due within one year	7	**(5,333,632)**		(5,967,888)	
Net current liabilities			**(4,092,893)**		(4,945,221)
Total assets less current liabilities			**24,557,221**		24,012,343
Funded by:					
Creditors: amounts falling due after more than one year	8		**22,043,243**		21,221,274
Deferred income — capital grants	9		**4,844,128**		5,003,623
			26,887,371		26,224,897
Capital and Reserves					
Called up share capital	11		**264**		275
Capital redemption reserve	12		**626**		564
Income and expenditure account	12		**(2,331,040)**		(2,213,393)
			(2,330,150)		(2,212,554)
			24,557,221		24,012,343

These accounts were approved by the Board on 7th February 2013

C J GRAVES, Chairman

R A SMITH, Director

The accompanying notes form an integral part to these accounts. There were no other gains and losses in the current or preceding year other than those stated above.

CASH FLOW STATEMENT

for the year ended 31st December, 2012

	Note	2012 £	2011 £
Cash inflow from operating activities	13	**285,671**	14,857
Returns on investments and servicing of finance	14	**(1,010,811)**	(1,026,764)
Capital expenditure and financial investment	14	**(209,709)**	(232,427)
Cash (outflow) / inflow before financing		**(934,849)**	(1,244,334)
Financing	14	**964,899**	(481,516)
(Decrease) / increase in cash in the period		**30,050**	(1,725,850)

Reconciliation of net cash flow to movement in net debt

	2012 £	2011 £
Increase / (decrease) in cash in period	**30,050**	(1,725,850)
HSBC loan repayment	**700,000**	—
Leeds City Council loan repayment	**200,000**	—
Additional C J Graves loan	**(2,100,000)**	—
Additional debentures	**(2,000)**	(32,633)
Other loans - ECB net repayment	**40,000**	305,000
New finance leases	**(23,011)**	—
Capital element of finance lease repayments	**197,050**	209,150
	(957,911)	(1,244,333)

ANALYSIS OF NET DEBT

	At 1 Jan 2012 £	Cash flow 2012 £	Other changes 2012 £	At 31 Dec 2012 £
Cash at bank and in hand	—	—	—	—
Overdraft - current	(1,310,357)	30,050	—	(1,280,307)
	(1,310,357)	**30,050**	—	**(1,280,307)**
Debt due within one year:				
HSBC loan	(568,502)	200,000	168,502	(200,000)
Leeds City Council loan	(743,000)	200,000	(254,000)	(797,000)
Other loans ECB	(150,000)	40,000	—	(110,000)
Finance leases less than one year	(209,533)	197,050	(204,720)	(217,203)
Debt due after one year:				
HSBC loan	(3,600,512)	500,000	(168,502)	(3,269,014)
Leeds City Council loan	(7,764,000)	—	254,000	(7,510,000)
Pride Appeal loan	(1,005,000)	—	1,000,000	(5,000)
Graves Family Trusts loans	(3,600,000)	—	—	(3,600,000)
C J Graves loan	(400,000)	(2,100,000)	(1,000,000)	(3,500,000)
Debentures	(323,896)	(2,000)	—	(325,896)
Finance leases more than one year	(1,610,576)	—	181,709	(1,428,867)
	(19,975,019)	**(964,950)**	**(23,011)**	**(20,962,980)**
Total	**(21,285,375)**	**(934,900)**	**(23,011)**	**(22,243,287)**

NOTES TO THE ACCOUNTS

for the year ended 31st December, 2012

1. Accounting policies

The accounts have been prepared in accordance with applicable accounting standards and under the historical cost convention. The principal accounting policies of the Club have remained unchanged from the previous year.

The format of the Income and Expenditure Account has been changed in the year to provide more meaningful analysis of the Club's financial performance. Comparatives have been adjusted accordingly.

(a) Income

All income is accounted for on an accruals basis, except for donations which are accounted for in the year of receipt.

Income represents amounts receivable from the Club's principal activities. Income is analysed between international-ticket and hospitality revenue, domestic-ticket and hospitality revenue, subscriptions, England and Wales Cricket Board, commercial and other income.

Subscriptions

Subscription income comprises amounts receivable from members in respect of the current season. Subscriptions received in respect of future seasons are treated as deferred income.

Domestic-ticket and hospitality revenue

Relate to amounts received from gate charges, ticket sales, hospitality and guarantees directly attributable to staging domestic-cricket matches in Yorkshire.

International-ticket and hospitality revenue

Relate to amounts received from gate charges, ticket sales, hospitality and guarantees directly attributable to staging international cricket matches in Yorkshire.

England and Wales Cricket Board (ECB)

ECB income relates to fees receivable, including performance-related elements, in the current season distributed from central funds in accordance with the First Class Memorandum of Understanding. ECB fees received in respect of future seasons are treated as deferred income. ECB distributions receivable to fund capital projects are treated as deferred income and are released to the Income and Expenditure Account by equal instalments over the expected useful lives of the relevant assets in accordance with accounting policy (b) Fixed assets and depreciation, as set out below.

Commercial and other income

Commercial income relates to amounts received, net of related expenditure, from ground advertising, catering guarantees, box lettings, facility hire, dinners and other events.

Advertising income received in respect of future seasons is treated as deferred income.

Other income relates to amounts received, net of related expenditure, from retail, Cricket Centre bar, Taverners' Club, fund-raising activities and other sundry items.

(b) Fixed assets and depreciation

All expenditure in connection with the development of Headingley Carnegie Cricket Ground and the related facilities has been capitalised. Finance costs relating to and incurred during the period of construction were also capitalised. Depreciation is only charged once a discrete phase of the development is completed.

Depreciation is calculated to write down the cost of fixed assets by equal annual instalments over their expected useful lives.

The periods generally applicable are:

Headingley Carnegie Cricket Ground and Cricket Centre

Buildings	Carnegie Pavilion	125 years
	Other buildings	50 years
Fixtures		4 years
Plant & Equipment		Between 4 and 10 years
Office equipment		
— telephone system		4 years
Computer equipment		2 years

Freehold land is not depreciated.

All other expenditure on repairs to Headingley Carnegie Cricket Ground and other grounds is written off as and when incurred.

(c) Carnegie Pavilion

The Club's contribution towards the design and build cost of the Carnegie Pavilion is £3m, of which £1.5m is payable over 20 years under a 125-year lease agreement. The £3m, together with the associated legal, professional and capital fit-out costs of the areas within the Pavilion that the Club occupies, have been capitalised and depreciated over the 125-year lease term. The £1.5m payable under the lease agreement has been treated as a finance lease within the financial statements with the capital element reported within Creditors (Finance leases), and the interest element charged to the Income and Expenditure Account on a straight -line basis over the 20-year term.

(d) Stocks

Stocks represent goods for resale, and are stated at the lower of cost and net realisable value.

(e) Grants

Capital grants relating to the development of Headingley Carnegie Cricket Ground (including the Yorkshire Cricket Museum) and Cricket Centre are included within the Balance Sheet as deferred income, and are released to the Income and Expenditure Account by equal instalments over the expected useful lives of the relevant assets in accordance with accounting policy (b) Fixed asets and depreciation, as set out above.

Grants of a revenue nature are credited to the Income and Expenditure Account in the same period as their related expenditure.

(f) Disclosure of information to Auditor

The members of the Board who held office at the date of approval of the Annual Report and Accounts confirm that, so far as they are aware, there is no relevant information of which the Club's auditor is unaware; or each member has taken all the steps that he ought to have taken as a member to make himself aware of any relevant audit information or to establish that the Club's auditor is aware of that information.

2. Financial Position

The Club is in a net current liability position of £4.1m (2011: £4.9m). This includes deferred income of £1.6m (2010: £2.0m). Details of the loan and overdraft-maturity analysis which impact on the financial position can be found in Note 8.

The Board expected the Club to return to consistent annual profitability from 2012. However, due to terrible weather during the 2012 cricket season and the larger-than-expected impact of the Olympics upon corporate-hospitality demand at the Test Match the Club may not generate a surplus until 2013. However, Mr C J Graves has agreed to provide such cash-flow support as the Club requires during 2013. During 2012 the Club restructured its term debt with HSBC, and is in the final stages of restructuring its term debt with Leeds City Council. This will help to alleviate cash-flow pressure. It is expected that the Leeds City Council loan restructure will be finalised by March 31, 2013.

The Board therefore considers it appropriate to prepare the financial statements on a going-concern basis.

3. Directors' remuneration

	2012	2011
	£	£
Wages and salaries	**40,000**	—
Social security costs	**5,089**	—
Pension costs	—	—
	45,089	—

	2012 £	2011 £
4. Taxation		
UK corporation tax	—	—
Total current tax	—	—
Deferred tax (see Note 10)	**(35,091)**	(723,495)
Tax on (deficit) on ordinary activities	**(35,091)**	(723,495)
(Deficit) on ordinary activities before taxation	**(152,738)**	(1,183,598)
Current tax at 26.5% (2010: 27.0%)	**(37,421)**	(313,654)
Effects of:		
Expenses not deductable for taxation purposes	**34,797**	—
Non taxable income	**(77,332)**	(96,324)
Depreciation for the period in excess of capital allowances	**56,882**	148,063
Losses not utilised	**23,074**	261,915
Total current tax (see above)	**£ —**	£ —

5. Fixed assets (See next page)

	2012 £	2011 £
6. Debtors		
Trade debtors	**185,838**	126,382
Deferred tax asset (see Note 10)	**758,586**	723,495
Other debtors	**232,117**	132,746
	1,176,541	982,623
7. Creditors: amounts falling due within one year		
Leeds City Council loan	**797,000**	743,000
Bank Loan	**200,000**	568,502
Bank overdraft (secured)	**1,280,306**	1,310,356
ECB loans	**110,000**	150,000
Trade creditors	**557,266**	291,319
Finance leases	**217,203**	209,533
Social security and other taxes	**262,067**	239,441
Other creditors	**318,166**	329,563
Accruals	**18,627**	172,925
Deferred income	**1,572,997**	1,953,249
	5,333,632	5,967,888

	Cricket Centre		Headingley Carnegie Cricket Ground				
	Freehold Land and Buildings £	Plant & Equipment £	Freehold Land and Buildings £	Plant and Equipment £	Improvements to Leasehold Property £	Office Equipment £	Total £
Cost							
At January 1, 2012	535,837	758,603	25,293,079	4,567,525	4,507,653	367,387	36,030,084
Additions	65,287	14,573	—	71,387	77,009	4,350	232,606
At December 31, 2012	601,124	773,176	25,293,079	4,638,912	4,584,662	371,737	36,262,690
Depreciation							
At January 1, 2012	92,041	734,464	1,885,172	3,945,600	72,802	342,440	7,072,519
Provided in the year	14,372	24,865	245,481	203,576	41,522	10,241	540,057
At December 31, 2012	106,413	759,329	2,130,653	4,149,177	114,324	352,681	7,612,576
Net book value							
At 31 December 31, 2011	443,796	24,139	23,407,907	621,924	4,434,851	24,947	28,957,564
At 31 December 31, 2012	**494,711**	**13,847**	**23,162,426**	**489,736**	**4,470,338**	**19,056**	**28,650,114**

Improvements to Leasehold Property consist of the Club's share of the costs associated with the design and build of the Carnegie Pavilion. This cost includes a £3m base-capital contribution (£1.5m of which has been treated as a finance lease, with the outstanding capital balance shown within creditors). The remaining £1.5m represents costs associated with fit-out, structural amendments, legal and consultancy fees. The total cost is depreciated over 125 years, which represents the useful economic life of the building.

	2012	2011
	£	£
8. Creditors: amounts falling due after more than one year		
Leeds City Council Loan	**7,510,000**	7,764,000
Bank Loan	**3,269,014**	3,600,512
Pride Appeal Loans	**5,000**	1,005,000
CJ and J Graves Accumulation and Maintenance Trusts Loans	**3,600,000**	3,600,000
C J Graves Loan	**3,500,000**	400,000
Debentures	**325,691**	323,896
Finance Leases	**1,428,868**	1,610,577
Deferred income	**2,404,670**	2,917,290
	22,043,243	21,221,275
Loan and overdraft maturity analysis:		
In one year or less or on demand	**2,604,510**	2,981,391
In more than one year but not more than two years	**4,925,721**	1,575,034
In more than two years but not more than five years	**4,353,690**	8,888,000
In more than five years	**10,359,161**	7,840,950
	22,243,082	21,285,375

The Leeds City Council loan is repayable by April 30, 2020, at an interest rate of 4.5 per cent per annum. The Club has given a First Legal Charge over the freehold property known as Headingley Carnegie Cricket Ground, St Michaels Lane, Leeds, to Leeds City Council in respect of this loan. The Club are in the final stages of renegotiating the repayment profile of this loan, and also extending the term so the loan will be cleared down by December 15, 2025. These negotiations will be concluded in early 2013. Mr C J Graves has provided a shortfall guarantee in respect of this loan. The Club has also given a First Legal Charge to HSBC Bank plc over the Cricket Centre known as 41/43 St Michael's Lane, Headingley, Leeds, and a Second Legal Charge over the property known as Headingley Carnegie Cricket Ground, St Michael's Lane, Leeds, in respect of the bank loan and overdrafts. HSBC Bank plc also has a fixed and floating charge over all the assets of the Club, subject to the Legal Charges referred to above. This loan is repayable by April 30, 2020, and bears an interest rate of 4.00 per cent over the Bank's base rate. Mr C J Graves has also provided a £6m guarantee in respect of the indebtedness to HSBC Bank plc.

All loans from Mr C J Graves (including the £1m Pride Appeal loan) have been consolidated, with interest payable at the rate of 4.00 per cent plus the Bank of England Base Rate. The loan is repayable on demand with 12 months' notice. The C J Graves Accumulation and Maintenance Trust and J Graves Accumulation and Maintenance Trust each bear interest at the rate of 5.5 per cent per annum and are repayable in April 2014.

	2012	2011
9. Deferred income -capital grants		
At January 1, 2012	**5,003,624**	5,180,160
Received in year	—	5,423
Released to Income and Expenditure Account	**(159,496)**	(181,960)
At December 31, 2012	**4,844,128**	5,003,623
10. Provision for Liabilities		
— Deferred Taxation Asset / (Liability)		
At January 1, 2012	**(723,495)**	—
(Credit) to Income and Expenditure Account for the year	**(35,091)**	(723,495)
At December 31, 2012	**(758,586)**	(723,495)
The elements of deferred taxation are as follows:		
Difference between accumulated depreciation and capital allowances	**162,925**	(240,111)
Tax losses	**(921,511)**	963,606
	(758,586)	(723,495)

	2012	2011
	£	£
11. Share capital		
Allotted, called up and fully paid Ordinary shares of 5p each	**264**	275

During the year there was a net reduction in qualifying members of 227. This has been recorded as 1,016 new qualifying members and 1,243 retiring qualifying nmembers, each with one ordinary share. However, included in these figures will be a large number of members who have changed their membership option, and have not necessarily retired or taken out a new membership. Each member of the Club owns one Ordinary share, and the rights attached thereto are contained within the Club's rules.

12. Reserves.

	Income and Expenditure Account	Capital Redemption Reserve
At January 1, 2012	**(2,213,393)**	564
Deficit for the year	**(117,647)**	—
Shares in respect of retiring members	—	62
At December 31, 2012	**(2,331,040)**	626

13. Reconciliation of operating profit to cash flow		
(Deficit) for the year before taxation	**(152,738)**	(1,183,598)
Loan interest and similar amounts payable	**1,010,811**	1,026,764
Operating (Deficit)	**858,073**	(156,834)
Depreciation of tangible assets	**540,057**	753,078
Capital grants received	—	5,423
Release of capital grants	**(159,496)**	(181,960)
(Increase) / decrease in stock	**(24,155)**	2,306
(Increase) / decrease in debtors	**(158,825)**	5,602
Increase / (decrease) in creditors	**122,889**	(931,167)
(Decrease) / increase in deferred income	**(892,872)**	518,409
Cash inflow from operating activities	**285,671**	14,857

14. Analysis of cash flows		
Returns on investment and servicing of finance		
Loan interest and facility fees	**(1,010,811)**	(1,026,764)
	(1,010,811)	(1,026,764)
Capital expenditure and financial investment		
Purchase of tangible fixed assets	**(209,709)**	(232,427)
	(209,709)	(232,427)
Financing		
Other loans received in year:		
ECB	**192,500**	182,500
Debentures	**2,000**	32,633
C J Graves	**2,100,000**	—
ECB loan repayment	**(232,500)**	(487,500)
HSBC loan repayment	**(700,000)**	—
LCC Loan repayment	**(200,000)**	—
Capital element of finance lease rental payments	**(197,050)**	(209,150)
Issue of ordinary share capital	**11**	1
Repurchase of ordinary share capital	**(62)**	—
	964,899	(481,516)

15. Leasing commitments

Operating lease payments amounting to £43,273 (2011: £41,569) are due within one year. The leases to which these amounts relate exipre as follows:

	2012 Land and buildings £	**2012 Other £**	2011 Land and buildings £	2011 Other £
In one year or less	—	**3,360**	—	861
Between two and five years	—	**9,913**	—	10,708
In five years or more	**30,000**	—	30,000	—
	£30,000	**£13,273**	£30,000	£11,569

16. Related party transactions

Mr C J Graves was the Chairman of Costcutter Supermarkets Group Limited during part of the year. The Club has purchased printing and software maintenance and a new till system from Costcutter Supermarkets Group Limited. The turnover for the year is £8,860 (2011: £1,200) of which £nil remains outstanding at December 31, 2011 (2011: £600). Costcutter are also sponsors of the Club and boxholders at Headingley Carnegie Cricket Ground under the Club's normal commercial terms.

During the year Mr R A Smith was a Board Member and Trustee of the Yorkshire Cricket Foundation (YCF). During 2012 the YCF awarded capital grants of £nil (2011: £5,424) and non-capital grants of £14,283 (2011: £8,850).

17. Pensions

The Club operates defined contribution pension schemes for the benefit of certain employees. The amounts paid during the year were £174,763 (2011: £191,781). The assets of these schemes are administered in funds independent from those of the Club.

18. Audit Fee

The Club paid its auditors £16,500 (2011: £16,000) in respect of the audit of its Financial Statements.